The "Who's Who" of the Canadian Jewish Establishment of the 1920s

*The classic work,
originally published 1926
& long out of print*

*Newly republished
in a handy, abridged &
affordable volume*

*Brimming with capsule biographies,
synagogue and organizational histories,
photographs and illustrations*

*A treasure trove
for genealogists
& historians*

The JEW in CANADA

Toronto   2010

AARON HART
Born London, Eng., 1724. Died Three Rivers, Que., 1800
The First Jew to Settle in Canada

THE JEW IN CANADA

A COMPLETE RECORD OF CANADIAN JEWRY
FROM THE DAYS OF THE FRENCH
RÉGIME TO THE PRESENT
TIME

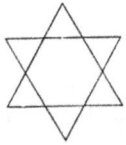

COMPILED AND EDITED BY
ARTHUR DANIEL HART

JEWISH PUBLICATIONS LIMITED
PUBLISHERS
TORONTO AND MONTREAL - CANADA

Copyright Canada, 1926
BY
JEWISH PUBLICATIONS, LIMITED

Abridged Facsimile Edition
Copyright © 2010
BY
Now & Then Books
Toronto Canada

Library and Archives Canada Cataloguing in Publication

Hart, Arthur Daniel
    The Jew in Canada / compiled and edited by Arthur Daniel Hart. -- Abridged facsimile ed.

Abridged reprint of ed. published: Toronto ; Montreal : Jewish Publications, 1926 ; includes original t.p.
ISBN 978-0-9784435-4-2

    1. Jews--Canada--History. 2. Jews--Canada--Biography. I. Title.

FC106.J5H37 2010   971'.004924   C2010-903706-5

PRINTED IN CANADA

Printed and Bound by
The Hunter-Rose Co., Limited
Toronto

A Note About This Edition (2010)

In order to keep this volume to a reasonable size and price, the opening section on the "History of the Jews in Canada" (by B. G. Sack) was omitted as it is readily available elsewhere. That and several other smaller omissions are marked with gray bars on the Table of Contents pages. This edition is 466 pages long but follows the pagination of the 576-page original. A Biographical Index follows the Table of Contents.

This book is dedicated to the pioneers who unfurled the banner of Judaism in Canada, commemorating their protracted struggle for civil, political and religious rights, today the inalienable heritage of all citizens of the British Empire.

Honourary Board of Advisory Editors

THE HONOURABLE WILLIAM RENWICK RIDDELL, LL.D., L.H.D., F.R.S.C., etc.
    Justice of the Supreme Court of Ontario.

SAMUEL WILLIAM JACOBS, ESQ., K.C.,
    Member of the House of Commons,
    Vice-President, Jewish Publication Society of America.

EDMUND SCHEUER, ESQ., J.P.,
    President, Toronto Branch, Anglo-Jewish Association,
    Honourary President, Federation of Jewish Philanthropies, Toronto.

LYON COHEN, Esq.,
    Chairman, Canadian Committee, Jewish Colonization Association,
    Honourary Vice-President, Zionist Organization of Canada,
    President, Canadian Jewish Congress.

NATHAN GORDON, Esq. M.A., B.C.L.,
    President, and formerly Rabbi, Temple Emanu-El, Montreal,
    Formerly Professor of Oriental Languages, McGill University.

REV. DR. BARNETT ROBERT BRICKNER, PH.D.,
    Formerly Rabbi, Holy Blossom Toronto Hebrew Congregation,
    President, Ontario Branch, Jewish Immigrant Aid Society,
    Chaplain, Palestine Lodge, A.F. & A.M.

REV. HERBERT J. SAMUEL, B.A.,
    Rabbi, Temple Emanu-El, Montreal,
    Chaplain, 1924, Canadian Club, Winnipeg,
    Ex-Member of Committee, Winnipeg Ministerial Association.

Assistant Editor, SARAH JOLOFSKY GARFIELD

PREFACE

IN undertaking the publication of THE JEW IN CANADA, we have been influenced by a desire to give to the world the glorious record that belongs to the Jews of Canada; to hold up before the young the inspiring example of worthy men and women of the Jewish faith in Canada; and to perpetuate the names of those who, by their sterling character and untiring zeal, have helped to build up our country. In commerce, in educational and professional life, in the arts, and in communal endeavour, our people have played a noble part in the history of Canada.

In writing the history of the Jews of Canada, many years have been spent searching archives in Canada, Europe, and the United States. Old diaries have been delved into, old portraits resurrected where possible, and all information thereby acquired, thoroughly sifted as to its authenticity and accuracy. Unfortunately, many of the congregations have not kept records, others have been destroyed, and in such cases it has not been possible to furnish any details. The acquirement of the needed information has meant an expenditure of time and labour, in many cases covering a tremendous amount of effort and much expense and it was necessary that all sections of Canada be visited and hundreds of persons interviewed.

Any man or woman who has in any conspicuous way contributed to the moral, intellectual, industrial or political growth of the country, or to philanthropic endeavour therein, has been deemed worthy of inclusion in these pages. The biographies gathered embrace more than a history of individuals, for in the life and record of these is written the growth of a great people in the land of their adoption. In the selection of subjects we have acted upon information furnished us by leading citizens of each community. We have tried to do our part thoroughly and well, and have spared neither pains nor expense in our efforts to make this a book of which the Jewish people of Canada shall be justly proud; in fact a book in which all Canadians shall take pride, for it is a record of achievements benefiting the whole community.

Its compilation has been an arduous task of long duration, but if it preserves the names of worthy men and women whose deeds deserve to be remembered, it will surely have well repaid the time and anxiety that have been expended upon it. Prejudices, indifference and imperfect records are among the obstacles which have retarded the progress of the work. In the preparation of the manuscript, our hands have often been tied by requests that sketches should appear just as written, and that incidents which to us have not seemed important, should be retained. This problem has been satisfactorily solved. Dates and facts have all been verified, either by reference to the best published authorities or to the persons themselves.

Our contributors are acknowledged to be the best posted sources of information on the various subjects on which they have written, and we offer them our sincere thanks and appreciation for the splendid manner in which they have treated their subjects, and for the help and assistance they have given us. We wish to thank those gentlemen who have acted as our Honorary Board of Advisory Editors, for the whole-hearted support we have received from them, and our thanks are also due to all those who have so liberally subscribed towards the production of this volume. We fully believe that our work will meet a much needed want, and will be of great value not only to the Jews of Canada, but also to members of the race and others in all parts of the world.

CONTENTS

HISTORY OF THE JEWS IN CANADA PAGE

The Jews under the French Régime.
- Chapter I. The First Contact with the Land 1
- Chapter II. Jews in Early Canadian Commerce 5
- Chapter III. The Seven Years' War 9

In the English Colonial Period.
- Chapter IV. The Beginning of Jewish Settlement 13
- Chapter V. The First Jewish Community Founded 16
- Chapter VI. The Jew in Canada during the American War of Independence ... 20

The Formative or Sephardic Period.
- Chapter VII. The Question of Jewish Disabilities first raised 24
- Chapter VIII. The Stormy Debates in the House, and Ezekiel Hart's second expulsion .. 28
- Chapter IX. Jews Attaining a Status of Political Equality 32
- Chapter X. During the Time of Transition 36

The Period of Greater Jewish Activity.
- Chapter XI. Beginning of German-Polish Immigration 41
- Chapter XII. A Glimpse of Social Relations 46
- Chapter XIII. New Communities Founded 50
- Chapter XIV. Communal Activity and the Settlement on the Pacific Coast .. 54
- Chapter XV. Before the Immigration Tide of the Eighties 58

The Russian Period of Immigration.
- Chapter XVI. After the Pogroms of 1881 62
- Chapter XVII. An Interesting Agricultural Plan 66
- Chapter XVIII. Practical Efforts and New Activities 70
- Chapter XIX. The Broader Aspect of Jewish Life 74
- Chapter XX. At the End of the Century 78

(omitted from the abridged edition)

SYNAGOGUES IN CANADA 81
- Corporation of Spanish and Portuguese Jews, Montreal 83
- Shaar Hashomayim Congregation, Montreal 93
- Holy Blossom Toronto Hebrew Congregation 105
- Congregation Emanu-El, Victoria 117
- Temple Emanu-El, Montreal 121
- Shaary Zedek Congregation, Winnipeg 127
- Goel Tzedec Congregation, Toronto 131
- Chestnut Street Synagogue, Toronto 139
- McCaul Street Synagogue, Toronto 140
- Hebrew Men of England Congregation, Toronto 141
- Edmonton Hebrew Congregation 143
- Calgary Congregation 147
- Saskatoon Congregation 147
- House of Jacob Congregation, Winnipeg 149
- Beth Jacob Congregation, Hamilton 149
- B'ne Israel Congregation, London 149
- House of Jacob Congregation, Regina 155
- Congregation Emanu-El, Vancouver 155
- Shaarey Zedeck Congregation, Vancouver 155
- Beth Jacob Congregation, Toronto 156
- Bay Street Synagogue, Toronto 159
- Adath Israel Congregation, Toronto 159
- Rosh Pina Synagogue, Winnipeg 159
- Ben Judah Congregation, London 159
- Beth Israel Congregation, Kingston 159
- Anshe Sholom Congregation, Hamilton 161
- Additional List of Synagogues 166

HEBREW EDUCATION 170
- Winnipeg Talmud Torahs 175
- Regina Talmud Torah 179
- Saskatoon Talmud Torah 180
- Edmonton Talmud Torah 181
- Toronto Hebrew Free School 182
- Simcoe Street Talmud Torah, Toronto 183
- Jewish Folks' School, Toronto 183
- Euclid Avenue Talmud Torah, Toronto 184

	PAGE
Vancouver Hebrew School	184
Quebec Talmud Torah	185
Calgary Talmud Torah	185
United Talmud Torahs of Montreal	187
Jewish People's Schools of Montreal	189

CHARITABLE AND WELFARE WORK ... 193

Federation of Jewish Philanthropies of Montreal	195
Baron de Hirsch Institute	201
Montreal Hebrew Orphans' Home	209
Mount Sinai Sanatorium	211
Herzl Dispensary	212
Hebrew Maternity Hospital	212
Hebrew Free Loan Association, Montreal	215
Federation of The Jewish Philanthropies of Toronto	218
Hebrew National Association, Toronto	220
Toronto G'milath Chasodim Association	221
Jewish Children's Home, Toronto	222
Mount Sinai Hospital, Toronto	223
Hebrew Consumptive Aid Association, Montreal	223
Toronto Jewish Old Folks' Home	224
Hebrew Burial Society, Toronto	224
United Hebrew Relief, Winnipeg	226
Jewish Orphanage and Children's Aid of Western Canada	227
Jewish Old Folks' Home of Western Canada	232
Vancouver Hebrew Free Loan Association	234
Winnipeg Free Loan Societies	234
Hebrew Aid Society, Vancouver	236
Ottawa Charitable Organizations	238
Hamilton Charitable Organizations	238

ACTIVITIES OF CANADIAN JEWISH WOMEN ... 240

Ladies' Hebrew Benevolent Society, Montreal	244
Ladies' Montefiore Benevolent Society, Toronto	244
General Activities of Montreal Jewish Women	247
Jewish Chapters, Imperial Order Daughters of the Empire	250
Montreal Council of Jewish Women	252
Council of Jewish Women, Calgary Section	253
Council of Jewish Women, Edmonton Section	253
Council of Jewish Women, Toronto Section	255
Council of Jewish Women, Vancouver Section	255
Ottawa Ladies' Hebrew Benevolent Society	258
Other Ottawa Institutions	258
Hebrew Young Ladies' Boot and Shoe Society, Toronto	261
Ezras Noshem Society, Toronto	261
Toronto Hebrew Ladies' Aid Society	262
Hebrew Ladies' Maternity Aid Society, Toronto	264
Daughters of Israel, St. John	266
Halifax Women's Activities	266
Calgary Ladies' Aid Society	267
Saskatoon Ladies' Aid Society	267
Auxiliary of Temple Emanu-El, Vancouver	267
Jewish Endeavour Sewing School, Montreal	268
Women's Organizations in Hamilton	268
Jewish Girls' Club, Toronto	269
Hebrew Ladies' Sewing Society, Montreal	269
Auxiliary of the Maternity Hospital, Montreal	270
Sisterhood of the Holy Blossom Congregation, Toronto	271
Sisterhood of the Shaary Zedek Congregation, Winnipeg	273
Auxiliary of the Goel Tzedec Congregation, Toronto	273
The Hadassah Organization	277
Activities of Hadassah	282

FEDERATION OF YOUNG JUDAEA OF CANADA ... 289

ZIONIST ORGANIZATION OF CANADA ... 291

THE JEW IN THE COMMERCIAL LIFE OF CANADA ... 321

THE JEW IN PUBLIC AND POLITICAL LIFE OF CANADA ... 369-546

THE JEW IN THE LEGAL LIFE OF CANADA ... 374

CANADIAN JEWS IN THE MEDICAL AND OTHER PROFESSIONS ... 410

	PAGE
THE SOCIAL LIFE OF THE JEWS IN CANADA	431
The B'nai B'rith in Canada	433
Mount Sinai Lodge, A.F. & A.M.	439
Palestine Lodge, A.F.& A.M.	440
Mount Sinai Chapter, R.A.M.	441
Jewish Interests in Masonry in British Columbia	441
Young Men's Hebrew Association, Montreal	442
Young Women's Hebrew Association, Montreal	444
Young Men's and Young Women's Hebrew Association, Toronto	447
Big Brother Movement, Toronto	450
Concordia Club, Vancouver	451
Baron de Hirsch Book Club, Montreal	451
Montefiore Club, Montreal	453
Montefiore Club, Winnipeg	454
Primrose Club, Toronto	454
Hebrew Friends' Lodge, Winnipeg	455
Grand Order of Israel, Hamilton	455
THE JEWISH PRESS IN CANADA	457
THE JEWISH LABOR MOVEMENT IN CANADA	460
LEGISLATION IN CANADA AFFECTING JEWS	461
THE CANADIAN JEWISH CONGRESS	465
JEWISH COLONIZATION IN CANADA	483
The Federated Jewish Farmers of Ontario	489
The Jewish Immigrant Aid Society of Canada	490
POPULATION OF THE JEWS OF CANADA	496
THE JEWISH QUESTION IN THE SCHOOLS OF QUEBEC	497
DESECRATION OF THE JEWISH CEMETERIES AT THREE RIVERS	499
ATTEMPTS AT PROSELYTISM	501
THE JEW IN THE MILITARY LIFE OF CANADA	503
MENORAH SOCIETIES IN CANADA	512
WAR ORPHANS' RELIEF WORK	513
ASSOCIATED WAR RELIEF WORK	524
THE JEW IN THE CULTURAL ARTS	529
CHRONOLOGICAL TABLE	534
CALENDAR	544
ADDENDA	547
APPRECIATION	576

Omitted from the abridged edition

BIOGRAPHICAL INDEX

Name	PAGE
Abramowitz, Rabbi H.	92
Adaskin, H.	528
Aiken, M.	403
Albert, M.	452
Ansell, D. A.	200
Baltzan, Dr. D. M.	414
Benjamin, A. D.	110
Benjamin, Chas.	366
Benjamin, F. D.	111
Bercovitch, P., K.C., M.P.P.	381
Berger, Rabbi J.	167
Berner, Rev. M.	146
Bernfeld, M.	401
Bilsky, M.	151
Bilsky, Mrs. M.	548
Birnbaum, S. J.	573
Blackstone, M.	528
Blumenthal, A.	363
Blumenthal, R. H.	360
Brainin, R.	456
Breslin, Dr. L. J.	417
Brickner, Rabbi B. R.	104
Brodey, Dr. A.	419
Brodey, I.	568
Brody, M.	138
Bronfman, E.	169
Brookstone, A.	438
Caplan, C.	153
Caplan, L.	569
Cherniack, J. A.	407
Cohen, Abraham	394
Cohen, A. C.	346
Cohen, Harry	401
Cohen, Rabbi H.	186
Cohen, I.	567
Cohen, Jacob	101
Cohen, Jos.	400
Cohen, Magistrate J.	372
Cohen, Lazarus	99
Cohen, Lyon	339
Cohen, Mrs. Lyon	246
Cohen, M.	553
Cohen, M. M.	559
Cohen, S. W.	429
Corcos, Rabbi J.	82
Darwin, R. A.	558
Davies, J. P.	561
Davis, Harry E.	352
Davis, Henry	114
Davis, Sir Mortimer B.	337
Davis, Mrs. S.	243
Davis, Samuel	123
De la Penha, Rev. I.	89
Denberg, D. S.	405
DeSola, Rev. Dr. A.	86
DeSola, A. C. M.	385
DeSola, Clarence I.	314
DeSola, Mrs. C. I.	245
DeSola, Rev. Meldola	87
Diamond, Wm.	142
Dobrofsky, J. A.	357
Donalda, Madame Pauline	531
Dover, Dr. H.	418
Dover, J.	561
Draimin, C.	565
Dunkelman, D.	162
Dunkelman, Mrs. D.	288
Edelstein, H.	532
Eisen, S.	409
Endleman, H. M.	358
Enzer, J.	367
Enzer, Miss J.	528
Factor, S.	404
Finberg, I.	573
Fineberg, N. S.	217
Fineberg, Z.	214
Finkle, H. M.	402
Finkelstein, C. E.	408
Finkelstein, M. J.	382
Finkelstein, M.	128
Finkelstein, Mrs. M.	272
Finkelstein, Dr. M.	422
Fox, B.	404
Frankel, L.	354
Franklin, A.	113
Freedman, I.	349
Freiman, A. J.	290
Freiman, Mrs. A. J.	276
Friedman, D. S.	103
Friedman, H. A.	386
Friedman, N.	96
Frumharz, P.	557
Gardner, A.	109
Garfield, Dr. B. D.	425
Garfunkel, Chas.	157
Gelber, L.	133
Gelber, M.	319
Gintzburger, S.	237
Gintzburger, Mrs. S.	254
Gittleson, A. L.	199
Glanz, J. A.	158
Glass, J. J.	404
Goldberg, A. H.	145
Goldberg, A. M. P.	556
Goldenstein, I. S.	90
Goldfield, B.	399
Goldman, L.	320
Goldstein, A.	124
Goldstein, J.	171
Goldstein, Maxwell, K.C.	378
Goldstick, I.	148
Goldstine, S. L.	407
Goldston, S. A.	178
Gordon, H.	365
Gordon, Rabbi J.	130
Gordon, J. M.	403
Gordon, Nathan	125
Green, N.	552
Green, S. Hart	387
Green, Mrs. S. Hart	274
Greenberg, J. H.	403
Greenfield, S. M.	365
Greisman, H.	347
Grossman, M. M.	391
Gurofsky, A. M.	572
Harris, J.	446
Harris, Dr. Wm.	422
Hart, A. J.	348
Hart, Dr. D. A.	411
Hart, G. E.	530
Hart, L. A.	376
Hart, S.	550
Herlick, C. M.	102
Hermant, P.	345
Hirsch, J.	97
Hirsch, Michael	194
Hyams, Dr. B. L.	426
Hyman, M.	395
Hyman, W.	333
Illievitz, Dr. A. B.	416
Isaacs, Dr. H. D.	560a
Isaacs, J. M.	560a
Isaacs, M. J.	365
Isserman, Rabbi F.	555
Jacobs, A.	98
Jacobs, J. A.	341
Jacobs, L. W., K.C.	393
Jacobs, N. W.	400
Jacobs, S. W., K.C., M.P.	379
Jacobs, Rabbi S.	108
Jacobs, Mrs. (Rabbi)	256
Joseph, A.	332
Joseph, A. P.	430
Joseph, J. H.	330
Joseph, Jesse	331
Joseph, K. de S.	430
Joseph, Montefiore	340
Joseph, Mrs. M.	251
Kahanovitch, Rabbi I. I.	154
Kamins, A. A.	406
Kaplan, H. S.	430
Kaplansky, A. L.	91
Kaufman, S.	571
Kellert, H.	102
Kert, I., N.P.	385
Kert, L.	573
Keyfetz, M. L.	405
Keyfitz, N.	136
Kirschberg, A.	88
Kirschberg, I.	91
King, C.	335
Kliman, D. B.	409
Kronick, S.	225
Landsberg, Mrs. A.	263
Landsberg, F.	116
Landsberg, Dr. H. A.	425
Lavine, Dr. J. J.	425
Lehrer, H. M.	572
Leiser, S.	119
Leo, J. S.	315
Lepofsky, S.	406
Lesser, Al.	210
Levin, A.	316
Levin, N. C.	408
Levinsky, I.	135
Levinson, S.	100
Levy, G. H., K.C.	380

	PAGE
Levy, H.	361
Levy, Mrs. Camilla	257
Lieberman, M. I.	398
Luxenberg, B.	403
Maldaver, L. A.	572
Margolick, M.	350
Marks, J. J.	560
Markus, M.	522
Merritt, Rabbi M. J.	120
Meyerovitch, P.	401
Michaels, J.	551
Miller, H.	336
Mintz, Rabbi M. J.	150
Mohr, S.	427
Mond, Rt. Hon. Sir A., M.P.	344
Montefiore, W. Sebag	511
Morris, M. L.	206
Moss, Dr. S. I.	425
Nathan, Henry	371
Nathanson, Dr. J. N.	421
Nathanson, N. L.	368
Nordheimer, A.	334
Palter, E.	362
Papernick, H.	405
Pearson, Dr. H. H.	426
Pearlstein, J. D.	402
Perlman, Dr. S. I.	426
Phillips, L.	401
Phillips, N.	397
Phillips, P.	406
Pivnick, Dr. M.	424
Pullan, E.	134
Rabinovitch, G.	364
Rhinewine, A.	458
Rittenberg, M.	208
Roback, Dr. A. A.	533
Robinson, Rev. N.	112
Robinson, R. S.	231

	PAGE
Rosenbaum, Dr. J.	574
Rosenthal, Aaron	239
Rosenthal, Mrs. A.	259
Rosenthal, H.	449
Rotenberg, Harry	353
Rothbart, I.	365
Rubenstein, I.	152
Rubenstein, Dr. J.	422
Rubenstein, L.	373
Rubin, Dr. J.	423
Rubinovich, J. B.	560b
Rudolph, A.	213
Rusen, I. D.	407
Sabbath, J. L.	359
Samuel, Rabbi H. J.	126
Samuel, L.	109
Samuel, S.	355
Saxe, M.	570
Scheuer, E.	115
Schott, M.	406
Schwartz, Mrs. L. M.	521
Schwartz, Rabbi J.	554
Schwob, M.	207
Seiden, Miss R.	528
Selick, Mrs. A.	275
Shaffer, N. W.	408
Ship, Dr. A.	574
Ship, F.	563
Shultz, Justice S.	377
Siderski, H.	566
Siegel, Mrs. I. H.	265
Siegel, Dr. M.	560a
Silverman, F. A.	404
Silverman, Lyon	206
Singer, A.	402
Singer, Dr. B.	422
Singer, E. F.	392
Singer, Jacob	163
Singer, Joseph	390
Singer, L. M.	384
Slobinsky, A.	233
Smith, N.	173

	PAGE
Smith, Mrs. N.	549
Solway, Dr. L. J.	415
Sommer, A.	343
Soskin, M.	408
Sperber, M., K.C.	388
Sperber, Dr. S. S.	413
Sprachman, A.	430
Steinkopf, M.	389
Sugarman, E. R.	396
Sugarman, I.	153
Sukloff, L. N.	405
Sweet, D.	160
Sylvester, F.	118
Tobias, W. V., M.C.	407
Vineberg, A. M.	523
Vineberg, Harris	342
Vineberg, M. A.	562
Waisman, M.	235
Weber, S.	137
Weidman, H. L.	174
Weidman, M. S.	129
Weidman, N. J.	560
Weinfield, H.	383
Wener, S.	351
Wershof, Dr. E.	420
Wilder, H. E.	318
Wilder, Mrs. H. E.	274
Williams, M. E.	560
Willinsky, Dr. A. I.	412
Willinsky, Mrs. M. L.	260
Wolfe, L.	356
Wolff, M.	428
Wolff, Mrs. M.	249
Wolofsky, H.	459
Wood, P.	564
Workman, M.	338
Zimmerman, B.	177
Zlotnik, Rabbi J. L.	317

SYNAGOGUES IN CANADA

IN preparing the histories of the numerous synagogues throughout Canada, we have met with almost insurmountable difficulties, and it has been impossible to complete them as we would like to. In many cases incomplete records, often absolute lack of records, have rendered the task beyond the power of anyone to accomplish. It is regrettable that such is a fact, particularly when such an undertaking should be so easy.

The older established synagogues have, in every case, kept very clear and authentic records, from which the influences they have had on the different communities can easily be gathered, and in this same manner the names of those who have taken active part in their upkeep and work have been preserved. It is with the congregations that have been established in only recent years that no data are available and yet these congregations have large memberships and are influential in all communal undertakings. We trust that the absence of details of such institutions in these pages may cause the officials of these congregations to realize the need of keeping proper records of their proceedings, as in future years, when the Jewish population of Canada will be very much larger than it is at the present time, such records will be very valuable from more than one view-point.

The oldest established synagogue in Canada, the Congregation of Spanish and Portuguese Jews "Shearith Israel" of Montreal, was established almost one hundred and sixty years ago, and for the greater part of a century was the only Jewish place of worship in Canada. It was formed by the first Jews known to have set foot in this country, and during the entire period of its existence has had men at the helm who have taken great pride in the perpetuation of the beauties of the traditional Hebrew services. They strictly followed, as they do today, the ancient ritual of the Sephardic Jews. On the arrival of the German Jews, who were accustomed to the Ashkenazic ritual, congregations were established where this ritual would be followed, among them being;—the congregation of German and Polish Jews (now the Shaar Hashomoyim) of Montreal; the Toronto Hebrew Congregation (the Holy Blossom); and the Anshe Sholom Congregation of Hamilton, which were all formed within a few years of each other, between seventy-five and eighty years ago, and soon after the Congregation Emanuel of Victoria, B.C., was organized. These are the pioneer places of worship of the Jews of Canada and since then, and particularly during the two decades between 1880 and 1900 numerous congregations have come into being. Today there are 125 synagogues in Canada, and in addition a number of societies and organizations where the members meet to worship on the Holy days.

The majority of the congregations are strictly orthodox at the present time, but three of them being known as Reform, these being in chronological order, the Temple Emanu-El, Montreal; the Anshe Sholom Congregation, Hamilton; and the Holy Blossom Congregation, Toronto. The Anshe Sholom Congregation and the Holy Blossom Congregation have both made a complete evolution from strictly Orthodox to Liberal, Progressive and Reform Judaism.

The congregation with the largest membership is the Shaar Hashomoyim, Montreal, where over two thousand worshippers have assembled at one service. Numbers of the synagogues in Montreal, Toronto and Winnipeg can accommodate from seven to eight hundred worshippers. Perhaps the most outstanding feature are the beautiful synagogues built in small communities where it has meant much to the members to construct such places of worship. In all communities the congregation has been the means of bringing the members together, and all charitable and philanthropic work has originated there. It is to the credit of the Jew that just as soon as a "minyan" can be gathered together in some small community, it is practically sure that in a short time a synagogue will be built.

RABBI JOSEPH CORCOS, MONTREAL

AN author, historian, and poet, Rabbi Joseph Corcos of the Spanish and Portuguese Synagogue (Shearith Israel) was born at Mogador, Morocco, December 21st, 1872, the son of Moses and Julia Rodriques Brandon Corcos. He is a grandson of the late Dr. Abraham Corcos, who was for many years Dayan of the Spanish and Portuguese Jews of England. Joseph Corcos received his Hebrew and Talmudical education in Mogador, Morocco, where he studied under the famous chief Rabbis, Judah ben Muyab, Joseph ben Attar and Rabbi M. Cohen, from whom he received his rabbinical degree, and he is also a graduate of the Royal College of Salamanca, Spain. In 1893 he received his rabbinical diploma in England from the Rev. Dr. Moses Gaster, Chief Rabbi of the Spanish and Portuguese Jews of England. In the same year he was elected Minister of the Spanish and Portuguese Congregation of Kingston, Jamaica, where he remained until 1903. He then became Rabbi of the Jewish Community of Curacao, D. W. I. From 1918 to 1922 he was connected with the Spanish and Portuguese Synagogue (Shearith Israel) New York, and in 1922 he was unanimously elected Rabbi of his present congregation in Montreal. Rabbi Corcos has been recognized as one of the greatest living Chazans of the Spanish and Portuguese Jews. As a writer, he is best known by his works, "The Spanish Inquisition," "The Jews of Curacao," and "Auto-da-Fe in Mexico". He translated the Dinim of Shechitah and Bedikah into English, and included among his poems is "Kol Yosef" (The Voice of Joseph). His "Bendigamos" has been introduced into almost every Spanish and Portuguese congregation in the world. He is the author of the film story "The Birth of America" in which he shows the part played by the Jews in the development of the nation. Rabbi Corcos is married to Angelita, daughter of Sydney Cohen Henriques, of Kingston, Jamaica, B. W. I. He has three sons, and four daughters.

CORPORATION OF SPANISH AND PORTUGUESE JEWS
(*SHEARITH ISRAEL*) MONTREAL
שארית ישראל

ALMOST one hundred and sixty years have passed since the founding in Montreal of the Spanish and Portuguese Jewish Congregation "Shearith Israel," the first Jewish body of any kind established in Canada.

It counts amongst its founders the first Jews known to have put foot in Canada, and for almost a century after its organization, it was the sole Jewish congregation in the Dominion.

In 1768 the early Jewish settlers met together in Montreal and organized themselves into a congregation and prepared to build a synagogue, where they and their children could worship the God of Israel, as their fore-fathers had done since hoary antiquity. "Shearith Israel" (Remnant of Israel) was the name they adopted and in this way was founded the second oldest Jewish place of worship in America, the Spanish and Portuguese Synagogue of New York being the oldest. As nearly all were descended from exiles of Spain and Portugal, they strictly followed the historic customs and impressive ritual of the Sephardic Jews, and their descendants have ever since remained tenaciously loyal to the same venerable and imposing rites.

They first met for worship in a hall in St. James Street, and in 1777 they built the first Canadian synagogue upon a lot of land belonging to David David, and upon which he had given them the privilege of placing their sanctuary. The building stood on Notre Dame Street, at the junction of St. James Street, and was a low-walled edifice of stone, with a high red roof. A tablet erected by the Numismatic and Antiquarian Society now marks the site. In the corner-stone of the building were deposited some coins, brought from Spain and Portugal, and also some thin brass plates perforated with the names of some of the founders. These were, many years later, removed to the corner-stone of the Chenneville Street building, and when, a few years ago the contents of the latter were removed in turn to the corner-stone of the Stanley Street Synagogue, it was found that several of the relics deposited in the first building in 1777 were in a good state of preservation, notably some of the brass or copper plates dated 1777. An inscription on vellum stated that these mementoes had been placed in the corner-stone of the first synagogue in 1777. Shortly before the erection of their first building the congregation bought a lot of land on St. Janvier Street, near the present Dominion Square, for a burial-ground. The deed of purchase was dated 1775, and the first one interred was Lazarus David, who was an extensive owner of real estate in Montreal and its vicinity as far back as 1767. He took an active part in public affairs and was a prominent man in civic matters in those days. He died on the 22nd October, 1776, and his remains, together with the original headstone bearing that date, were subsequently removed to the present cemetery of the congregation, when the first one was closed. It still stands there and is the oldest Jewish grave in Canada.

STANLEY STREET SYNAGOGUE

Amongst the first members of the congregation were Abraham Franks, Levy Solomons, Aaron Hart, Lazarus David, Uriel Moresco, Andrew Hays, Isaac and Uriah Judah, Manuel Gomez, Simon Levy, Fernandez da Fonseca, Emanuel de Cordova, Isaac Miranda, Jacob de Maurera and Joseph Bindona. These were the first Jews to set foot in Canada, arriving at the time of the British Conquest in the year 1760. Several of them were connected with the army, and others were merchants and traders, and judging from their undertakings, men of considerable means.

In 1778 they drew up their first set of by-laws, which are still preserved in the old minutes of the congregation. The executive consisted of a Parnas (President), Gabay (Treasurer), and three others who were styled the "Junto." All who had once been members of the Junto became "Gentlemen of the Mahamad" or Elders. They were very proud of their traditions and were vested with rather autocratic powers. Members could be summoned before them and reprimanded, and even heavily fined, for any misdemeanor. The minutes of 25th Elul, 5538, or September 1778, record that on that date Ezekiel Solomons and Levy Michaels were elected respectively "Hatan Torah" and "Hatan Bereshith" for that year, after Isaac Judah, Myer Michaels and Andrew Hays had each been fined two pounds ten shillings for refusing these offices; while Samuel Judah was fined three pounds for refusing to serve as Parnas. The original founders of the congregation were accorded a double vote at all meetings, and this privilege extended to their eldest sons on attaining their majority. The by-laws exacted fines for the violation of certain articles, and particularly heavy fines against any member who should do aught to impair the harmony of the community. One clause imposes a fine and other penalties on "any person absenting himself from the House of God on any frivolous pretence." These by-laws, long since rescinded, bear the signatures of Levy Solomons, Parnas; Uriah Judah, Gabay; David David, Abraham Franks, Andrew Hays, and a number of others, and are dated "3rd day of the month Tebeth, 5539, or 1778."

The congregation always maintained correspondence with the Portuguese Jews of London, and the latter presented them, in 1768, with two costly manuscripts of the law, already then very old. They are still occasionally used at services. Questions of ecclesiastical law were generally referred, in the early beginnings of "Shearith Israel" to the Chief Rabbi of England, Dr. Raphael Meldola, for decision.

As the land on which the first synagogue stood became the property of David David's heirs, after his death in 1824, the congregation decided to remove to another site. The old building was demolished and funds subscribed for a new one. Some time however, passed before anything definite was accomplished, and meanwhile the congregation met for worship in a place off the residence of Mr. Benjamin Hart, at the southwest corner of St. Helens and Recollet Streets. In 1832 the land was purchased and in 1835 the congregation erected the Synagogue on Chenneville Street. The corner-stone was laid by M. E. David, a grandson of Lazarus David, and the building was dedicated in 1838. The financing of this building was largely due to the efforts of Benjamin Hart and among the subscribers was Moses Montefiore of London England. The munificent gift of a large sum from Mrs. Francis Michaels, sister of David David, also assisted the undertaking. The planning and erecting of the building was supervised and greatly furthered by Moses Judah Hays, who was a trustee and later attained the position of president. For over half a century the congregation worshipped in this shrine, and many a man and woman, destined afterwards to play his or her part in influencing the course of Jewish history in Canada, received training and inspiration in this modest fane.

In 1846 the congregation secured a new Act of Incorporation, this step having become essential, as a second Jewish congregation was formed here that year. A number of arrivals at that time were unused to the Sephardic Ritual, and decided to start a synagogue where they would follow the Ashkenazic Ritual, but it was not until 1858 that the "Shaar Hashomayim" congregation was permanently established. The trustees of Shearith Israel presented them with a Sefer Torah, to enable them to conduct their first service.

In 1883, the Chenneville Street Synagogue being no longer adequate to the requirements of the congregation, it was resolved to build a more commodious place of worship, and in 1887 the corner-stone of the present Stanley Street Synagogue was laid, by Mr. Gershom Joseph, then President of the congregation. The building was completed and dedicated on August 31st, 1890, with characteristic ceremonies. The synagogue is of Judeo-Egyptian style and is of most attractive design, presenting an imposing interior with colonnades of Egyptian pillars, between which are suspended oriental lamps. At the east end is an ark of mahogany and white marble, the centre portion of which previously stood in the Chenneville Street building. The general design was due to Mr. C. I. de Sola, who acted as Secretary of the building committee, and who supervised its erection.

The first regularly ordained minister of the Congregation was the Rev. J. Cohen, who came from London in 1778, and after some years with the congregation, went to the Sephardic synagogue in Philadelphia. He was succeeded by Hazan R. de Lara who retained the position until 1810, when Mr. M. Levy, and after him Mr. Isaac Valentine, temporarily occupied the ministerial position. In 1840, the Rev. David Piza was elected Minister, and remained until 1846, when he was appointed one of the ministers at the Sephardic congregation of Bevis Marks, London.

THE ARK OF THE STANLEY STREET SYNAGOGUE

On the retirement of Rev. David Piza, the congregation elected the Rev. Abraham de Sola, LL.D., as their Rabbi, and for thirty-six years he acted as spiritual head of the congregation. His reputation as a scholar and upholder of traditional Judaism was worldwide, and no man did more to reflect lustre on the Jewish community in Canada than Dr. de Sola. On his death in 1882, he was succeeded by his eldest son, the late Rev. Meldola de Sola, who occupied the pulpit until his death in April, 1918. The Rev. Meldola de Sola followed the teachings of his father, and was known as one of the staunchest upholders of traditional Judaism in America and one of the most vigorous and relentless opponents of the Reform Movement. The exceptionally excellent choir maintained during his term of office was due to his indefatigable work.

During the pastorate of Dr. de Sola and Rev. Meldola de Sola many familiar names are noticeable among the officers of the congregation. Dr. Aaron Hart David frequently held the presidency and served as an honorary officer in many capacities. Jacob Henry Joseph was treasurer of the congregation soon after the erection of the Chenneville Street building and filled different offices on the Board during the early and middle Victorian period. Jesse Joseph took a very prominent part in the affairs of the congregation during his entire lifetime. He was for a long period treasurer and was one of the largest contributors towards its support. At the time of his death in 1904, he was president of the congregation. Samuel, Goodman and William Benjamin, three brothers, were all staunch members of "Shearith Israel" and occupied in turn the highest lay offices of the synagogue. Lawrence and Charles Levey were both active members of the Board. Edwin Morris was an active member of the Board of Trustees. Simon Hart was Parnas of the congregation in 1865, and held the office for several years. Alexander Levy was one of the most zealous and capable workers who ever held office on the Board of Trustees. He was in office between

1850 and 1860. G. I. Ascher held the office of Parnas for some time. Lewis Alexander Hart was President of the congregation for a number of years and acted as treasurer for a very long period.

In 1890, the congregation received a new Act of Incorporation from the Provincial Parliament. The Act was drawn up by Mr. Gershom Joseph and Mr. Lewis A. Hart, both prominent members of the legal profession.

Mr. Louis Davis was President of the congregation when the Stanley Street edifice was consecrated and Mr. Jacob H. Blumenthal was a member of the Board at that date. Alexander Saunders, Edward Cohen, Maurice Jacobs, and Moses Gutman were all Trustees of the synagogue during the second half of the past century, and the names of Abraham Brahadi and Samuel Brahadi, M. Fonseca, M. Blackman, J. Garcia, S. De Lara and J. Miranda appear among the substantial supporters of that period. Jacob L. Samuel labored for the welfare of the congregation in a loyal and indefatigable manner for over fifty years. He was honorary secretary of the congregation for the greater part of this period and in the latter years of his life was elected President. He had the advantage of being gifted with an exceptionally beautiful tenor voice, which was heard, ever leading, in the choir and congregational singing. Congregational singing in "Shearith Israel" has been whole-souled and inspiring and there have been several members who were particularly distinguished by their musical rendering of the chants and traditional music, notably Gershom de Sola, the youngest son of Dr. de Sola, whose deep rich basso voice was heard both in the choir and in the chanting of the service in which he occasionally assisted until his death in 1902. Mr. Isaac Kirschberg is another member who has been notable for his assistance in the musical portions of the service. Clarence I. de Sola, a son of Dr. de Sola, was Parnas of the congregation from 1906 until his death in 1920, and he was a member of the Board of Trustees since 1891. He devoted much time and work to all branches of the synagogue activities, and like other members of his family took great interest in perpetuating the traditional beauties of the synagogue service and upholding its time-honored traditions and customs.

In 1908, the Rev. I. de la Penha was elected assistant Minister of the Congregation, a position that he still occupies. In October, 1918, Dr. Raphael Melamed was elected Minister of the Congregation and after a short period was succeeded by the Rev. M. Haddad, who in turn was succeeded by the Rev. Dr. Joseph Corcos, the present Rabbi of the congregation.

The congregation has always maintained a school for instruction in Judaism and Hebrew and at several periods during its existence it also maintained a day school for instruction in Hebrew and other subjects, and the teaching was always given with much efficiency. The congregation also occupied itself with philanthropic work and with branches of activity, which in the present day are undertaken by separate institutions; but during the first hundred years of the existence of the congregation there were scarcely any outside bodies to undertake benevolent work. Hence it was that the congregation itself had to create organizations for this purpose, and in 1848, the congregation established the Hebrew Philanthropic Society; with Moses Judah Hays and Dr. Abraham de Sola as its Executive heads. The Ladies' Auxiliary has become an important feature in the life of the congregation and they are taking a prominent part in many of the synagogue activities and in many branches of congregational work.

Space does not permit the mention of all those who took an active part in the work and welfare of the congregation, but no record would be complete without the mention of David Salesby Franks, who was Parnas in 1775, Henry and Abraham Joseph, Ezekiel Hart, David and Samuel David, who took active parts during the first fifty years of the Congregation, and among those who came later may be mentioned, D. A. Ansell, Jacob G. Ascher, David, Edward and Lawrence Moss, S. Silverman, Z. Auerbach, and A. Kirschberg, who was assistant minister for almost twenty years, and who held the love and esteem of the entire community. Z. Fineberg was a trustee for many years, and also later served as Parnas. Among the elder living members of the Congregation may be mentioned Dr. D. A. Hart, I. S. Goldenstein, who was President for a long period and who is the present Parnas, Israel Rubenstein, who was Parnas for almost thirty years, J. S. Leo, who was a trustee for over twenty-five years, Louis Rubenstein, Harris Vineberg, and many others.

J. L. SAMUEL

During the great war 1914-1918, amongst the members of the congregation who enlisted and saw service at the Front were Captains Wm. Montefiore, M.C., Hyman H. Lightstone, D.S.O., M.C., and Albert Freedman, and Ira and Gordon Lightstone, Abraham S. Michelson, Hugh Joseph, Arthur Hart, Philip Blumenthal, David and Samuel Ruttenberg, Maitland Leo, Ralph Groner, Irwin Rubinovitch, Alex Solomon (who was killed in action) and many others.

In 1893, the Congregation held an imposing service to commemorate the one hundred and twenty-fifth Anniversary of its foundation. It also held a notable service on the fiftieth Anniversary of Queen Victoria's reign and a similar celebration in 1897, in honor of the "Diamond Jubilee," or sixty years of the Queen's reign. In 1918, the congregation celebrated the one hundred and fiftieth Anniversary of its foundation and on the occasion published a handsome booklet containing the history of "Shearith Israel".

The present officers of the Congregation are: President, Captain Wm. Sebag Montefiore; Hon. Parnas, Mr. Israel Rubenstein; Parnas, Mr. I. S. Goldenstein; Treasurer, Mr. A. L. Kaplansky; Hon. Secretary, Mr. P. B. Hart; Board of Trustees, Marcus M. Sperber, K.C., Michael A. Michael, Joseph A. Dobrofsky, Isaac Kirschberg, Charles L. Samuel, Michael Lightstone.

THE LATE DR. ABRAHAM DE SOLA

THE LATE DR. ABRAHAM DE SOLA was appointed Rabbi of the Spanish and Portuguese Synagogue Montreal in 1847, and acted as spiritual head of Shearith Israel Congregation until his death in 1882. A profound scholar and an eloquent preacher, he ranked among the foremost savants of his day and acquired a reputation that was well-nigh world-wide. In 1848 he was appointed professor of Hebrew and Oriental literature at McGill University and held that position with marked ability during the remainder of his life. In 1858 he had conferred on him by the university the degree of LL.D., he being the first Jew to receive this honor. Among the many works of which he was author, some of the most important are:—"The Cosmography of Peritsol," "Scripture Zoology," "The Mosaic Cosmogony," "Shabethai Tsevi," "History of the Jews of Poland," "The Jews of France." His address on the study of Natural Science delivered before Prince Arthur, afterwards Duke of Connaught, called forth a personal letter of commendation from Queen Victoria. In 1872, Dr. de Sola was invited by the then President of the United States, General Grant, to open the United States Congress with prayer, and the scene was then witnessed of one who was a British subject, performing (with covered head, according to Jewish custom) the opening ceremonies at the assembling of Congress at Washington. In 1868, Dr. de Sola was unanimously elected to the pulpit of the Mickve Israel Synagogue in Philadelphia, but he declined this and many similar offers. His whole life was one of self-sacrifice and devotion to the intellectual and moral advancement of his race. He was a prominent figure in many learned bodies and was for many years President of the Natural History Society. Dr. de Sola was the son of Dr. David Aaron de Sola, the senior minister of Bevis Marks, London, and his maternal grandfather was Dr. Raphael Meldola, chief Rabbi of the Sephardic Jews of Britain. His wife was Esther, youngest daughter of Henry Joseph of Berthier, and the Rev. Meldola, Clarence I., and Gershom de Sola were his sons.

THE LATE REV. MELDOLA DE SOLA

Photo by Notman

THE late Rev. Meldola de Sola was the eldest son of the late Dr. Abraham de Sola. He was born in Montreal, May 22, 1853, and was educated under his father's direction. For some years he followed a commercial life, but during his father's failing health, turned to the work of the ministry and from 1876 to 1882 officiated regularly as voluntary lay reader at the Spanish and Portuguese Synagogue, Montreal, where his father had ministered for a long period. On the latter's death in 1882 he was elected to succeed him and thus became the first Jewish minister of Canadian birth. He became the recognized leader of the Orthodox majority of the community and was one of the ablest and most uncompromising opponents of the reform movement. It was through his efforts that the first conference of the representatives of Orthodox Judaism was held, and he was elected vice-president and was one of the three Rabbis who drew up the Declaration of Principles governing the convention. During one of his visits to England he was invited by Dr. Adler, chief rabbi of the United Congregations of the British Empire, to occupy his pulpit and at another time he received what he considered the greatest honor of his career, when he was invited by Dr. Gaster, chief Rabbi of the Saphordic Jews, to preach at the Bevis Marks Synagogue, on the occasion of the installation of a new minister. He officiated at the laying of the corner stone and offered the prayer of dedication at the consecration of the Spanish & Portuguese Synagogue, New York. His sermons have frequently been published in pamphlet form. He was a generous contributor to the press on various subjects on which he was an authority and his work always received the greatest attention. He was an accomplished musician, and under his guidance, the choir of the Shearith Israel Synagogue was one of its most impressive institutions. In 1887 Mr. de Sola was married to Kate, daughter of Rev. I. Samuel, Senior Minister of Bayswater Synagogue, London, England, and he had one son, Bram C. de Sola and one daughter, Miss Louise de Sola. Mr. de Sola's death took place 29th April, 1918.

THE LATE ABRAHAM KIRSCHBERG

ABRAHAM KIRSCHBERG, Talmudist and scholar, was born in Wistinetz, Poland in 1844 and died in Montreal in August, 1902. He first came to America at the age of twelve, but returned to Poland and settled in Wilkowiski, where he continued his religious studies and became eminent for his learning. He was the leading spirit in the religious and charitable institutions of that city. His wife was Cirla Washutzky of Wilkowitz, niece of the famous Cathologist of the nineteenth century, of that name, and of Samson Ransuk, Hebrew Poet Laureate of England (1848-1877). On returning to Canada, Mr. Kirschberg settled in Montreal, where he became assistant minister at the Spanish and Portuguese Synagogue, remaining as such for nineteen years, until his death. Mr. Kirschberg devoted his life in labour for the congregation and endeared himself to the entire Jewish community of Montreal. His truly pious nature, and love of peace, his learned counsel, his love and consideration for the poor, his broad tolerance, made him an outstanding figure, and truly loved in the community. Mr. Kirschberg was one of the founders of the Talmud Torah and the Chevra Shass. He was Chief Gabbai for the collection of funds for Palestine, and Honorary Mohel of the Baron de Hirsch Institute. He often travelled to the primitive parts of the country to perform the sacred office of Brith-millah, and at all times gladly rendered his services gratuitously to the poor. His sons and daughters taught in the Sunday School, and his sons Joseph and Isaac continue their activities in the Spanish & Portuguese Synagogue. Mr. Isaac Kirschberg besides being a Trustee of the Synagogue, is the leader of the choir, and often renders the Haftorah readings, being gifted with a very fine voice. The oldest son-in-law of Mr. Kirschberg, the late Zigmond Fineberg, was founder and President of the Hebrew Free Loan Association, now carried on by his second son, Nathaniel S. Fineberg, M.A., B.C.L. One of Mr. Kirschberg's younger daughters, Miriam, married Dr. Israel Schapiro of Washington, D.C., eminent Orientalist and Hebrew Scholar and writer.

REVEREND I. DE LA PENHA, MONTREAL

THE REVEREND ISAAC DE LA PENHA was born in Amsterdam, Holland, on June 9th, 1869. His parents were the late Abraham and Sara (da Silva Abenator) de la Penha, who were members of one of the first families of Spanish and Portuguese Jews to settle in Holland. In the 17th century the de la Penhas were prominent merchants of Amsterdam and Rotterdam and a member of the family was created a Count by William of Orange (William III of England). They subscribed largely to his campaign funds and were granted large tracts of land in Labrador. One of the members of this family was instrumental in the building of the Spanish and Portuguese Synagogue, which is the oldest synagogue in Rotterdam. Isaac de la Penha received his education at the Abe Jetomim in Amsterdam, and graduated from there as Chazan in 1886. For many years he was assistant Minister to Dr. H. Pereira Mendes of the Shearith Israel Congregation of New York, and in 1908 was appointed assistant Minister to the late Reverend Meldola de Sola at the Spanish and Portuguese Synagogue (Shearith Israel) Montreal. Rev. de la Penha still occupies the position of Chazan at this synagogue, and he holds the regard and esteem of the entire Congregation. He is untiring in his work in the Synagogue Sunday School, and teaches Hebrew and gives religious instruction to a large number of the Jewish young. He takes a very prominent part in all the social and welfare work of the Congregation, in which he is ably assisted by Mrs. de la Penha. Mr de la Penha was married in Amsterdam to Clara, daughter of Philip and Yehudith (Lars) Barber, and they have two sons, Abraham and Philip de la Penha. In June 1912 they suffered the loss of their only daughter, Sarah. He is a member of the Royal Arcanum. Mr. de la Penha also took up the art of diamond cutting in his youthful days, and is recognized as one of the best judges of precious stones in Canada, although he does not now take an active interest in this pursuit.

ISRAEL S. GOLDENSTEIN, MONTREAL

ISRAEL S. GOLDENSTEIN is the son of the late Solomon Goldenstein who was very prominent in religious and educational matters in his life-time and was born at Tatarbunar, Bessarabia, a Province of South-Eastern Russia, about sixty years ago. He is also the grandson of Mr. Hesel Silberman, one of the most prominent commercial, religious and financial men in his time in that part of the country. He received a very thorough commercial and religious education through private tuition in his home community, and came to Canada in 1886, settling in Montreal. Commencing his business career here as a commercial traveller, handling various lines, in 1896 he became a member of the firm of I. L. Michalson & Sons, wholesale jewellers, remaining with them until 1902 when he established business under his own name as a wholesale jeweller and diamond merchant. Shortly after arriving in Montreal he became a member of the Spanish and Portuguese Synagogue (Shearith Israel) and for many years served on its Board, first as Trustee, and later as President. At the present time he holds the office of Parnas. It was during his term as President that this congregation, the second oldest in America, celebrated its 150th anniversary, and suffered the great loss of its minister, the late Rev. Meldola de Sola. Much improvement was made to the cemetery and buildings, and the financial condition of the congregation was much stronger during his term. Mr. Goldenstein is a life Governor of the following institutions:— The Western Hospital, Montreal; the Protestant Hospital for the Insane; the Baron de Hirsch Institute; the Mount Sinai Sanatorium; and the Hebrew Free Loan Association. He is a member of the Montefiore Club, Montreal; Dominion Commercial Travellers' Association, Montreal; Mount Royal Lodge, Independent Order B'nai Brith, No. 729; St. George's Lodge, No. 10, A. F. & A. M., G. R. Q; and is a Royal Arch Mason. On April 17th, 1893, he was married to Rose Michalson, daughter of Mr. and Mrs. I. L. Michalson, and he has one son, Daniel Edward Goldenstein, born 1st February, 1898.

ISAAC KIRSCHBERG is a member of a family, who for generations, have been eminent for their Jewish learning. He is the youngest son of the late Rev. Abraham and Cirla (Washutzky) Kirschberg of Montreal. He has, since his boyhood, been actively connected with the Shearith Israel Synagogue, in which his father was for many years assistant minister. Isaac Kirschberg has for years been a leader of the choir, and his rendering of the musical portions of the prayers has always been a feature of the services. He is a Trustee of the congregation, and also was very active in connection with the congregational Sunday School, in which he was for years an instructor of Hebrew. He is a strong exponent of traditional Judaism. He is active in communal work, and is a supporter of the various Montreal Jewish charities. Mr. Kirschberg is married to a daughter of Hiram Levy of Montreal.

A. L. KAPLANSKY, J.P., MONTREAL

ISAAC KIRSCHBERG, MONTREAL

ABRAHAM L. KAPLANSKY was born in Bialostock, Poland, May 1st, 1860. He was married on the 7th of March, 1891, to Elka, daughter of Hirsch Rabinovitch, Sokolka, Poland. In 1889, he arrived in New York, where he was in the steamship ticket business until 1893 when he moved to Montreal, and where he has since resided. He established the first Jewish printing business in Canada, and continued in this until 1907, when he retired and took up the study of Law. In 1910, he was appointed Superintendent of the Legal Aid Department of the Baron de Hirsch Institute, which position he has since occupied. Since 1915, he has been Treasurer of the Spanish and Portuguese Synagogue, Shearith Israel. In 1907, he was appointed Justice of the Peace, and Acting Magistrate for the District of Montreal. Both in New York and Montreal, Mr. Kaplansky was keenly interested in all charitable institutions and fraternal societies. He was District Deputy Grand Master for the Province of Quebec, of the Independent Order of the Sons of Benjamin, while they were in existence.

REVEREND DR. H. ABRAMOWITZ, MONTREAL.
Photo by Notman

RABBI HERMAN ABRAMOWITZ, was born in Russia in 1880, and came to America in 1890. He was educated at the public schools, the College of the City of New York (from which he graduated in 1900 with the B.A. degree) and at the Jewish Theological Seminary. From 1900 to 1903, he took a post-graduate course in Philosophy at Columbia University. In 1907, he received the degree of Doctor of Hebrew Literature from the Seminary, being the first graduate to receive this honour. In 1903, he accepted a call from the Shaar Hashomayim Congregation, Montreal. Dr. Abramowitz developed the congregational Sunday School, and Hebrew Day School; the Women's Auxiliary; the Young Peoples' Society, and other activities. He is active in all communal enterprises of a philanthropic and educational character, and in 1910 personally raised from subscriptions the entire cost of the building of the Mount Sinai Sanatorium for tubercular patients, and was in charge of the organization which raised annual subscriptions for the maintenance of this institution. His part in the Plamondon libel case will be found on another page. In 1909, Dr. Abramowitz visited the Jewish agricultural colonies in the Western Provinces of Canada to establish religious schools and other institutions and accomplished this work in so favorable a manner that he was invited to become a member of the Canadian Committee and in 1913, he was sent to Paris to confer with the Jewish Colonization Association heads. He also represented Canada at the Congress held that year in Vienna. Shortly after the outbreak of war, Dr. Abramowitz was appointed Jewish Chaplain in the Canadian Army with the rank of Captain. He was also active on the speakers' team in all the Victory Loan campaigns and relief drives held during the war. He is Vice-President of the United Synagogue of America; Director, Federation of Jewish Philanthropies of Montreal; Director, Montreal United Talmud Torahs; and a life Governor of the Montreal General Hospital. Dr. Abramowitz was married in 1911 to Theresa Bockar, and has one son, David Lester, and one daughter, Miss Judith Abramowitz.

THE SHAAR HASHOMAYIM SYNAGOGUE, MONTREAL
Congregation of English, German and Polish Jews
שער השמים

IT is now over seventy-five years since this congregation came into existence, and its history is one that its members justly pride themselves in. The second oldest in the Dominion, it is the largest numerically, and its finances are second to none in this country.

Since its inception it has at all times had on its board of management, men of sound business principles and intellect; it can, therefore, not be wondered at that to-day it is looked upon by those interested in synagogual affairs as a model congregation and one to be copied by younger formations.

Previous to the German and Polish Congregation taking shape and form the only place of worship in Montreal was the Spanish and Portuguese synagogue, "Shearith Israel". The Jewish population had by this time risen to fair proportions, amongst whom were many Germans, Poles, English, and Russians. Besides the fact that the Shearith Israel synagogue had become too small to accommodate all those of Jewish faith in Montreal it was also felt amongst a number of these, that the form of prayer (Sephardic Ritual) was one that they were not acquainted with, and consequently the necessity of a separate formation became more and more apparent, one which would use the Ashkenazic Ritual.

By 1846, this feeling became so intense that a charter incorporating this congregation was obtained. For some time the members worshipped in different places until the year 1858, when a movement was started for the establishment of a permanent synagogue. The Jewish population in Montreal, seventy-five years ago, was not in the affluent position it is in to-day, and consequently the undertaking was fraught with many difficulties. Nothing daunted, and with the courage and enterprise that is characteristic of this congregation, the members met on September 12th in that year, in the rooms on Great St. James Street, when it was decided to build a synagogue. A list of those present included Louis Ollendorf, Solomon Silverman, C. Blankensen, Meyer Kortosk, James M. Anthony, Jacob Samson, Lewis Levy, I. Cochenthaler, Jacob Samuels, Wolf Sternberg, Marcus Ollendorf, Marcus Levine, Samuel Hoffnung, Bernard Kortosk, Simon Silverman Jr., B. W. Warner, I. Blankensen, Abraham Hoffnung, Louis Anthony, M. Rubenstein, S. Michael, M. Runkel, Edward Himes, M. Miller, Jacob Hirsch, G. G. Wolfe, and Samuel Littauer. At this meeting these gentlemen subscribed $2,856.00 or an average of $82.00 each, which, under the circumstances, must be admitted as an excellent performance. This sum, however, was quite inadequate to justify the erection of a building, and the matter thus remained in abeyance for ten years. Neither was the congregation in a position to engage the services of a minister; but they had in their midst self-sacrificing men, and Messrs Samuel Hoffnung and Wolf Sternberg volunteered their services gratuitously until such time as the congregation's finances would justify the engagement of a permanent minister. Mr. Hoffnung also volunteered to teach a class of Jewish youths.

In October, 1858, a meeting was called to organize and elect officers to work under the charter granted in 1846, and the first officers of the congregation were; M. A. Ollendorf, President; Edward Himes, Treasurer; A. Hoffnung, Honorary Secretary; and Lewis Anthony, Parnas. It was also decided at this meeting to build a synagogue without delay; for this purpose it was decided to purchase a certain lot of land on St. Constant Street for the sum of $1,375.00 and the building thereon erected was "to be used for no other form of worship than that of the German and Polish Jews, and such building or lot of land shall never be sold except for the purpose of applying the proceeds for a precisely similar purpose". During the past ten years the progress of the congregation had steadily become most satisfactory. The membership roll had increased to a great extent, and consequently its finances were now in such a position as to justify a permanent minister being engaged. The choice of the congregation fell upon the Rev. S. Hoffnung, of Cheltenham, England. During that year and the following two years until the completion of their new building, the congregation met in rooms on St. Gabriel Street. The corner stone of the new synagogue was laid on the 12th of July, 1859, by David Moss, assisted by Dr. Raphael of New York, who delivered an address on the occasion in the presence of a large and representative gathering, including the Mayor and Aldermen of the City.

THE SHAAR HASHOMAYIM SYNAGOGUE, MONTREAL

The Moss family, David, Lawrence, and Edward, had during the past few years, by their indefatigable labours and generous donations, rendered inestimable assistance, and as a mark of appreciation free seats for life were conferred upon these three gentlemen, together with their wives. The completion of the synagogue was celebrated by a dinner, and it was consecrated on May 22nd, 1860, the Rev. S. M. Isaacs, of New York, officiating. In the same year the Rev. Mr. Fasheimer was appointed chazan at a salary of $400 per annum. Meanwhile the Rev. Mr. Foss had succeeded the Rev. Mr. Hoffnung as minister to the Congregation. In February, 1869, the congregation mourned the loss of one who, since the formation of this congregation, had rendered self-sacrificing and valuable services, Mr. W. Sternberg.

It was this gentleman who, when the congregation was not in a position to pay a minister, acted as one gratuitously. At his death the congregation, at its own expense, ordered that a suitable tombstone be placed over his grave as a mark of esteem. It was in July of the same year that Mr. Edward Moss resigned the office of Parnas on leaving for England, and presented the congregation with $1,000 for the building of a school. Mr. Moss died in 1872, and in his will he left $400 to be invested in a bank at Montreal for the purpose of giving prizes to the two best scholars in the Sunday School.

SAMUEL LITTAUER

For the next half decade the population of Montreal had increased rapidly, and the Jewish immigrants kept pace with the general influx. It was therefore natural that the Shaar Hashomayim felt the increase, and during the years 1875-77 discussions took place regarding the erection of larger and more commodious premises. Nothing was done of a tangible character, and in 1884, the Rev. E. Friedlander was elected to the position of first minister. In 1885 matters had progressed so far that a lot of land was purchased on McGill College Avenue, and the building of that handsome synagogue was commenced. The corner-stone was laid by John E. Moss, the President, and the invited guests consisted of the mayor and corporation and the principal citizens. On September 15th, 1886, the synagogue was consecrated with impressive ceremonies in the presence of an audience that completely filled the edifice. Rabbi Friedlander officiated and delivered an appropriate sermon on the occasion. The members who held office at the time were John E. Moss, President; Hyam D. Moss, Parnas; Jacob Hirsch, Treasurer; Harris Vineberg, Secretary; and L. Cohen, J. Cohen and S. Roman, Trustees. In 1890, Messrs John & Hyam Moss left Montreal to reside in England and the congregation thereby lost two of its most important members. In consideration of their work they were elected honorary life members. On the resignation of the Rev. E. Friedlander in 1896, the Rev. Isidore Myers was appointed minister, and this Rabbi receiving and accepting a call to San Francisco in the following year, he was succeeded by the Rev. Bernard M. Kaplan. In 1902, the Rev. Dr. Herman Abramowitz, the present Rabbi of the congregation, was appointed to the pulpit, and during the long time he has officiated he has retained the esteem, honour, and friendship, not only of his own congregation, but of Montreal Jewry in general. Never a year passes but the President in his annual report dwells at length upon the high esteem Dr. Abramowitz is held in, and of him it may truly be said that he is considered as much a friend of each and every member as their spiritual adviser.

Again the question of larger premises came up and property was purchased at the corner of Kensington Avenue and Cote St. Antoine Road, in the finest residential district of Westmount and on November 10th, 1921, the corner-stone of the present handsome synagogue was laid by Mr. Lyon Cohen. This new synagogue is an achievement which they could hardly have thought possible. A structure, cathedral-like in its imposing proportions, and dominating its immediate surroundings, it breathes the very life of stateliness and permanence. Built in a grey vitrified brick and sandstone, it is capped by a series of small Moorish cupolas that lend a touch of mystic orientalism to the whole. Fifteen hundred worshippers can be housed in its vast and lofty auditorium, unique in being furnished with two pulpits on either side of the Ark, one of which is reserved for the Rabbi only, and the other a separate reading desk for the Reader. There are no side galleries nor pillars to mar the interior. Two large loges raised about two feet from the floor, flanking the sides, are reserved for the ladies, and replace the oldfashioned galleries. In addition to this auditorium, which is the Synagogue proper, the building has many of the features of a modern Community Centre. There is a large lecture hall, capable of accommodating 600 auditors; a dozen school rooms—for its Hebrew and Religious Classes; a dome-capped salon for the Ladies' Auxiliary, that is, under their resourceful hands, palatial in its appointments. The dedication of the new Synagogue took place on September 17, 1922—(Ellul 24, 5682) with appropriate ceremonies. The entire cost of land and building amounted to over one half a million dollars.

The congregational cemetery on Mount Royal is noted for its beauty, and it has always been the endeavor of the congregation to attend to this part of their duties with the same care and attention that is given to other branches. The success they have attained is not a little due to Mr. David S. Friedman, who has been chairman of the cemetery committee for the past twenty-five years.

The congregation maintains for the children of its members a Hebrew day school, in which Hebrew, Jewish history, and the Jewish religion are taught. Besides this there are classes every Sunday. The congregation has a Women's Auxiliary; a Young People's Society; the Ladies Chevra Kedisha; the Choral Society; the Junior Circle, and supports a Boy Scout and Girl Guide organization

MARCUS LEVINE

The following is a list of the presidents of the congregation from 1860 to the present time: M. Ollendorf 1860, 1862-3; David Moss 1861; Edward Moss, 1864; S. Silverman, 1867-71; H. D. Moss, 1871, 1881-4 H. Davis, 1872-75; Lyon Silverman, 1876-79; L. Abrahams 1888; J. E. Moss, 1885-90; M. A. Vineberg, 1890-92, 1894-6, 1901-04; D. A. Ansell, 1892-94; Lazarus Cohen, 1896-1901, 1907-14; Lyon Cohen, 1904-1907, 1914 to the present time.

Amongst the names that stand out prominently for zealous and conscientious workers for the congregation are the Cohens, Vinebergs, Hirschs, Kellerts, Jacobs, Friedmans, Romans, Ships, Levinsons, Glickmans, M.

Markus, J. Sherman, and Moses Glickman. Few of these, among the older generation, are left, but their descendants are worthily upholding their ideals. Mr. Moses Vineberg, who died last year, was for over thirty years a member of the Board in one capacity or another and his labors and generous donations have always been of great assistance. Mr. Lazarus Cohen was for years looked upon as one of the pillars of the congregation and his zeal, energy and generosity were at all times at the service of the congregation. Seldom was there any opposition when Mr. Cohen was willing to take the management of any movement, for all felt that no better chief could be desired, and his level-headed judgment was largely responsible for the erection of the new synagogue. Mr. Lyon Cohen, the present President, has occupied this position since the death of his father, and is the youngest man ever chosen to fill this high office. The worthy son of a worthy sire, he has made his presence felt in every communal affair in Montreal, and throughout Canada, when it was a national question. He has held almost every executive position in the congregation and has at all times fulfilled his arduous duties to the entire satisfaction of its members. Although a man of wide business interests, Mr. Cohen devotes practically his entire time to the welfare of the Jewish people, and Canadian Jewry is fortunate to possess a man of his type.

During the great war many of the younger members of the congregation enlisted for service and they all acquitted themselves in the same worthy manner as did the rest of the co-religionists in the army. Three of the members of the congregation lost their lives whilst serving in the King's uniform,—Flight-Lieut. Benjamin Cohen, and Cadets Samuel Rosenthal and Louis Sessenwein; and amongst those who enlisted may be mentioned, Major Doc. M. Lauterman, Captains Horace Cohen, Jos. Levy, Leo. Livingstone; Lieutenants Philip Abinovitch, N. B. Cohen, William Cowan, Charles Lesser, Sol Rubin, Herbert Vineberg, Noel Friedman, Henry Matts, Lazarus Phillips, Lawrence Glickman and M. Gittleson. Rabbi Abramowitz was early during the war appointed Jewish Chaplain to the Canadian forces.

MARCUS OLLENDORF
First President

The present officers of the congregation are: President, Lyon Cohen; Vice-President, J. Levinson, Sr.; Hon. Treasurer, J. Kellert; Hon. Secretary, A. M. Vineberg; Trustees, M. A. Vineberg, A. Rudolph, N. Silver, Samuel Wener, A. Lesser, A. Levin, M. J. Heillig, Samuel Hart; Ministers, Rabbi, Rev. Dr. H. Abramowitz; Cantors, Rev. M. A. Siegel, Rev. I Cohen.

THE LATE NOAH FRIEDMAN

THE late Mr. Noah Friedman was born at Sareah, Poland, in 1831, and died in Montreal in 1881. He received his education in Poland and arrived in Canada in 1857 and settled in North Lancaster, Ontario, where he remained until 1869. In that year he moved to Montreal and entered into the wholesale dry goods business in partnership with his brother-in-law, the late Louis Kellert, remaining in that business until his death in 1881. At the time of his arrival in Montreal the Jewish population was very small and Mr. Friedman was widely known and respected for his upright character, his learning and his charity. During his long residence in North Lancaster and Montreal, his home was always open to his co-religionists who arrived in Canada from persecution in European countries. His great ambition was to make them feel that they had friends here and a wonderful future in this country. He was indefatigable in his efforts to instruct his co-religionists in the rights and duties of Canadian citizenship. Of ordinary means, he found many ways to do works of charity and his numerous and helpful intercessions on behalf of Jewish immigrants are remembered by many. Numbers of those who received the hospitality of Mr. Friedman, can today be counted amongst the most successful Jewish citizens of Canada. For many years Mr. Friedman was an active member of the Young Men's Hebrew Benevolent Society, the first Jewish charitable organization in Canada (now the Baron de Hirsch Institute) and he was for several years the president of this society. Originally a member of the Spanish and Portuguese Synagogue, he took a very active part in the early days of the English, German and Polish Congregation (now the Shaar Hashomayim Synagogue) and he was the Parnas of this congregation at the time of his death. Mr. Friedman was married to Sarah, daughter of the late Juda Kellert, and Mrs. Friedman survived her husband for many years. They had seven sons, Charles L., David S., Isaac, Jacob, Raphael, Hirsch N., and the late Abraham L. Friedman, and two daughters, Rachel (Mrs. Lyon Cohen), and Rebecca (Mrs. Nathan J. Fraid).

THE LATE JACOB HIRSCH

THE LATE MR. JACOB HIRSCH, in his lifetime one of the best known citizens of Montreal, was born at Dobrezca, P.P. Germany, January 30th, 1833, the son of the late Joseph Leiser Hirsch. He was educated in London, England, and came to Canada from England in 1857, settling in Montreal. He was married in 1863, to Lizzie, daughter of Marcus and Rika Levine, members of one of the oldest Jewish families of Montreal. After his marriage, Mr. Hirsch moved to Richmond, Que., where he entered into business and where he remained until 1875, when he returned to Montreal, and where he resided until his death which took place on March 19th, 1916. Mr. Hirsch was survived by his widow, three sons, Michael, Robert, and Marcus Joseph, and three daughters, Rebecca (Mrs. Archie Jacobs), and the Misses Sophia and Essie Hirsch, all of Montreal. Mr. Hirsch was the founder of the firm of J. Hirsch & Sons, Montreal, one of the best known firms of cigar manufacturers in Canada. He took a most active part in communal undertakings, and was associated with all the Jewish charities in Montreal. His connection with the congregation of the German and Polish Jews dated back to the days of his first arrival in Canada, and he always took a keen interest in this institution, and this connection has been ably maintained by his sons. His father-in-law, Mr. Marcus Levine, was one of the most active founders of this congregation. Mr. Hirsch was always regarded as one of the most representative members of the Jewish community, and the recollection of his charity and piety will remain in the memory of those who were privileged to have known him. His charity knew no creed, and any deserving undertaking was enriched by his assistance and advice. He was very modest and retiring and seldom took office, but believed that the best results could be done in an unostentatious manner. In his welfare work he at all times had the invaluable assistance of Mrs. Hirsch, and his sons and daughters, long previous to his death, had shown the same public spirit. Their activities on behalf of the Jewish community are in keeping with the ideals bequeathed them by Mr. Jacob Hirsch.

THE LATE ABRAHAM JACOBS

THE LATE MR. ABRAHAM JACOBS was born in Poland in 1842. He came to Canada as a young man, prior to the first influx of Russian Jews to this country, and settled in Lancaster, Ont., where a number of his coreligionists had established themselves when the Indian lands there were opened up. After a few years' residence there he removed to Montreal, where he resided until his death, which took place in 1914. During his long residence in Montreal, Mr. Jacobs took a leading part in the communal life of his fellow-Jews, and he was a supporter of all worthy causes, both with his time and money. On his arrival in Canada he became connected with the congregation of German and Polish Jews (now the Shaar Hashomayim) and he was an active member of this congregation until his death, for a long time being a member of the Board of Trustees. He was one of the early members of the Baron de Hirsch Institute, and always took a great interest in this institution, being at different times on the Board of Management. Mr. Jacobs was particularly prominent in assisting newly arrived immigrants to become settled, and his services on behalf of the Roumanian immigrants who arrived in Canada in 1885 are especially remembered. He was one of the first woollen merchants in Canada in a large way, and for a long time was interested in the wholesale men's furnishing business. In an unassuming manner he assisted many of his coreligionists in their businesses, very often without any remuneration to himself, and in this way Mr. Jacobs was a forerunner of the Free Loan Society, which was an institution he always favored. He was recognized as one of the representative citizens of Montreal, and at all times took an interest in any question for the public good. Mr. Jacobs had a family of four sons, Joseph H., Israel R., Jacob H., and Saul A., and two daughters, Miriam, the late Mrs. David S. Friedman, and Sarah, Mrs. Alex Bilsky. His interest in communal affairs has been ably maintained by his children, who have been at all times ready to take their place in supporting the philanthropic institutions of Montreal.

THE LATE MR. LAZARUS COHEN

From a painting by Miss Seiden

THE LATE MR. LAZARUS COHEN was born in Budwitch near Wilkovishk, Poland, in 1844, the son of Hyam and Sarah Cohen, known and respected for their Hebrew learning and piety. He graduated with honours from Weloshin Yeshiva and at the age of 21 he married, and in 1869 emigrated to Canada, being followed two years later by his wife and child. They settled in the village of Maberly, Ontario, where Mr. Cohen established a general store. He moved to Montreal in 1883. Here Mr. Cohen became associated with Mr. Wales L. Lee, under the name of Lee & Cohen, coal merchants, with whom he continued in business until 1890, when he admitted his son, Lyon Cohen, into partnership, under the name of L. Cohen & Son. Mr. Cohen also became head of W. R. Cuthbert & Co., brass founders. He also established the Canada Improvement Company, and some very important dredging works have been successfully performed by this company under his personal supervision. His was the first Jewish firm in Canada to engage in the dredging business. Shortly after Mr. Cohen came to Montreal, he became interested in communal work and was elected a trustee of the McGill College Avenue Synagogue, and for many years occupied the position of President, holding that office at the time of his death. He was an officer of the Baron de Hirsch Institute, and visited its colonies in the North West, where many of the colonists still remember him. He was chosen by the Montreal Chovevei Zion Society in 1893 to visit Palestine and reported favorably on the possibility of colonization work there. During his visit to Paris, he interviewed Baron de Rothschild and Baron de Hirsch on colonization matters. Mr. Cohen was for some years President of Montreal Lodge of the B'nai B'rith. He was Treasurer of the Baron de Hirsch Institute. He was chiefly responsible for the building of the Hebrew Free School on St. Urbain St., and many who are to-day interested in the Talmud Torahs owe their devotion to his inspiration. Mr. Cohen died on November 29th, 1914, and was survived by his wife and two sons, Mr. Lyon Cohen and Mr. A. Z. Cohen.

S. LEVINSON, MONTREAL

Notman

SOLOMON LEVINSON, President of the firm of S. Levinson, Son & Company, was born at Maryampol, Lithuania, on July 15th, 1851, the son of the late Judah Loeb Levinson. He received his early education at the schools of his native city. Mr. Levinson was married in New York City, in September 1874, to Jochabed, daughter of Aaron and Bluma Klishinsky, who died in Montreal in 1923, and he has two sons, Joseph Jr. and Zave, and four daughters, Bessie L. (Mrs. H. Saxe), May (Mrs. Samuel Wener), Sarah (Mrs. David Kirsch), and Lillian H. (Mrs. Maxwell Sloves). He came to Canada early in the year of 1869, at the age of 17, settling near Lancaster, Ont. In 1873, he removed to New York, and in 1874, he returned to Montreal, where he has resided ever since. He was one of the early Jewish settlers of that community, whose number at that time did not exceed three hundred families, the total population of the City of Montreal being about eighty thousand souls. Soon after his return, Mr. Levinson started in the clothing business, and met with moderate success in the retail trade. By dint of hard work and good business judgment, and by practising strict economy, Mr. Levinson succeeded in enlarging his connections and branching out to wholesale manufacturing in 1894, when his eldest son, Joseph Jr., joined him. In 1900 his brother, Mr. Joseph Levinson was admitted, at which time the present firm of S. Levinson, Son & Co. was organized. Mr. Levinson is known in commercial circles for his integrity and honesty of purpose. He is unassuming by nature, but takes a lively interest in all communal affairs, and he is a large supporter of every worthy undertaking in the community, being a member of the many charitable institutions of Montreal. He is one of the oldest members of the Congregation Shaar Hashomayim, and has served on the Board of Trustees of that body. He is a strong supporter of the Zionist Movement, and a lover of the Holy Land. Many of the institutions in Palestine, as well as a number of the individuals there, receive from him yearly subscriptions in munificent sums.

JACOB COHEN, MONTREAL

JACOB AARON COHEN, one of the oldest and most highly respected residents of the City of Montreal, was born at Gudlevi, Russian Poland, December 25th, 1850, the son of the late Israel Cohen. He was educated in the Yeshiva of Slabodky, and received his English education through intensive reading and study. He was married at Lancaster, Ont., by the late Dr. Abraham de Sola, in May 1874, to Fanny, daughter of the late Isaac Yorayach Livingstone, and he has four sons, Isaac, Herman and Clarence of Montreal, and Harris of Detroit; and five daughters, Mrs. B. J. Baettle, Mrs. A. W. Muhlstock, and Miss Naomi Cohen of Montreal, Mrs. A. H. Jackson of Detroit, and Mrs. Jack Maurice of Rio de Janeiro, Brazil. Mr. Cohen came to Canada in 1869, settling first in Lancaster, Ontario, where he joined the Jewish colony there. In 1874, he removed to Montreal, where he has since resided, and where he became engaged in the retail clothing business subsequently entering the manufacturing of men's clothing. At one time Mr. Cohen was the leading clothing manufacturer of Canada. Jacob Cohen took a keen and active interest in all the various communal institutions in the early days of Montreal, and was particularly interested in the Shaar Hashomayim Congregation, of which he is one of the oldest members. He served in this congregation at various times as Parnass, Treasurer and Trustee. The pre-eminent position occupied by this congregation in Canadian and American Orthodox Jewry is undoubtedly due to the influence exerted by such staunch adherents to traditional Judaism as Mr. Cohen and his contemporaries. Mr. Cohen was one of the early members of the Young Men's Hebrew Benevolent Society, (now the Baron de Hirsch Institute), and he was Vice-President of the first Zionist Society in Canada. He has at all times retained his interest in this Movement, and is one of its earliest supporters. He is a charter member of the Independent Order B'nai B'rith, Montreal Lodge, and also a charter member of the Royal Guardians' Lodge, Montreal. He held office as Treasurer in St. Lawrence Lodge, A. F. & A. M.

THE LATE HARRIS KELLERT

HARRIS KELLERT, one of Montreal's oldest and most respected Jewish citizens, was born in Goleve, province of Kovno, Russia, on July 12th, 1844. He came to Canada in 1867, and settled in Lancaster, Ont., where he operated a general store. He remained in Lancaster until 1883, when he removed to Montreal and started the manufacturing of men's clothing, in partnership with his brother-in-law, the late Mr. Noah Friedman. He later organized the business which is still carried on under the name of H. Kellert & Sons. Mr. Kellert was one of the pioneers of this industry, and with his two sons, Jacob and Solomon, he built up one of the largest wholesale clothing firms in Canada. He always took a prominent part in all welfare and religious activities in the Jewish community, and was one of the earliest supporters of the charitable associations in Montreal. When he first settled in that city, the Jewish population was very small and there was not much need for philanthropic work at that time. Mr. Kellert was particularly interested in assisting the new arrivals in the country, and many who are today in good circumstances can trace their first advancement to the assistance furnished so willingly by him. He was for many years one of the outstanding members of the Shaar Hashomayim synagogue, and frequently held office in this congregation. He was a member of the Federation of Jewish Philanthropies, and a life governor of the Montreal General Hospital. At the time of his death he was the oldest member of the Montefiore Club. His death took place in Montreal on June 3rd, 1925. Mr. Kellert was married in 1867, to Esther Matts, and they had two sons, Jacob and Solomon, both of whom are very active in communal work, and four daughters, Mrs. Louis Fraid, Mrs. Moe Heillig, Miss Hattie Kellert and Miss Rebecca Kellert. In 1917, Mr. and Mrs. Kellert had the good fortune to celebrate their golden wedding. A lasting example of the constructive work done in this country by Mr. Kellert, is the Kellert Building, one of the handsomest and largest business structures in Montreal.

D. S. FRIEDMAN, MONTREAL

ONE of the foremost citizens of Montreal, David Solomon Friedman was born at North Lancaster, Ont., on March 15th, 1863. His parents were Noah and Sarah (Kellert) Friedman, for many years residents of Montreal. David Friedman was educated at the Belmont Street School, Montreal, and in the year 1881 he founded the wholesale clothing firm of Friedman Brothers, which concern was, at the time he and his brothers retired from business in 1913, one of the largest firms of clothing manufacturers in Canada. Mr. Friedman is one of the most active welfare workers in Montreal, and he is associated with most of the charitable organizations. For over forty years he has been Chairman of the Cemetery Committee of the Shaar Hashomayim Congregation, and he was the first secretary of that congregational school. At different times he held office as both secretary and treasurer of the Baron de Hirsch Institute and he was treasurer of the fund for the Sunday Working Bill, and of the fund for the Quebec School Bill of 1903. His connection with the work of the various immigration committees has entailed an immense amount of time and labor, all of which is cheerfully given. Mr. Friedman was a Judge on the Exemption Court during the war, and was on the General Committee of the Patriotic Fund and on different relief committees. He was the second vice-president of the Federation of Jewish Philanthropies, and was treasurer of the Canadian Jewish War Relief Committee, and also treasurer of the Canadian Jewish War Orphans' Committee. He was the first treasurer of the Jewish Colonization Association. Mr. Friedman is one of the leading members of the Conservative party in Montreal. He is a member of the Shaar Hashomayim Synagogue, Montreal. In 1897 Mr. Friedman was married to Miriam, daughter of the late Abraham Jacobs, of Montreal, and he has one son, Norman H. Friedman. Mrs. Friedman died some years ago and during her lifetime she actively assisted her husband in his communal work. She held office in many charitable organizations and was regarded as one of the most active Jewish lady workers in Montreal.

RABBI B. R. BRICKNER, TORONTO

REVEREND DR. BARNETT ROBERT BRICKNER was born in New York City, Sept. 14, 1891, the son of Joseph and Bessie (Furman) Brickner. He received his education at the New York schools and Columbia College (B.Sc. 1913), Columbia University (M.A. 1914) and Teachers' College, Columbia (M.A. in Education). In 1915, he continued his graduate studies at the University of Cincinnati, majoring in Social Sciences, Education and Philosophy, where in 1920 he submitted a thesis on "Jewish Community Organization" in partial fulfilment of the Ph. D. degree. His Jewish education was received in the graduate department of the Teachers' Institute of the Jewish Theological Seminary and the Hebrew Union College, from which he graduated with the degree of Rabbi in 1919. While still a young student, Rabbi Brickner was one of the organizers of the National Young Judaea Movement in the United States. From 1910-1915, Rabbi Brickner joined the Bureau of Jewish Education, New York City, and held the position of Director of Extension of Jewish Education. During the Great War he went to New York to assume the position of Director of the Training School and Personnel Division of the Jewish Welfare Board of the U.S.A. Army and Navy. In December, 1920, Rabbi Brickner accepted a call to the pulpit of the "Holy Blossom" Toronto Hebrew Congregation, which under his leadership changed its ritual from conservatism to moderate reform. Rabbi Brickner has taken a foremost position in the ranks of Canadian Jewry, having won a reputation as a sturdy champion of Judaism and of liberal thought. He was President of the Toronto Federation of the Jewish Philanthropies and the Ontario Jewish Immigrant Aid Society, and also served on the boards of numerous Jewish and non-Jewish institutions. He is a member of the General Ministerial Association of Toronto, and the Chaplain of Palestine Masonic Lodge. In August, 1919, Rabbi Brickner was married to Rebecca Ena, daughter of Mr. and Mrs. Max Aronson of Baltimore, Md. They have one daughter, Joy Miriam Brickner.

THE HOLY BLOSSOM TORONTO HEBREW CONGREGATION

THE first authentic evidence of Jewish communal life in the City of Toronto, is a deed entered in the abstract book in the registry office, wherein under date of September 1st, 1849, the Hon. John Beverley Robinson conveyed to Judah G. Joseph and Abraham Nordheimer of Toronto, Merchants, Trustees of the Hebrew Congregation of Toronto, in trust for a burial ground for the use of the Hebrew Congregation, the land on Pape Avenue, which is still used as the cemetery of the Congregation. The consideration paid for the land was twenty pounds currency. The earliest tombstones in the cemetery mark the graves of Simeon Alfred Joseph, who died on September 17th, 1850; Lewis, son of Joseph Lyons, Feb. 1st, 1851; J. G. Joseph, May 12th, 1852; and Charlotte Nordheimer, daughter of Abraham and Fanny Nordheimer aged nine years, who died on February 27th, 1855.

A book, bearing on its title page the inscription: MINUTE BOOK OF THE SONS OF ISRAEL OF THE CITY OF TORONTO—1856—5617, shows on its first page the record of a meeting held on September 7th, 1856. The following: Joseph Lyons, L. Levine, I. Anthony, Sam Berhends, Mr. Marcoso, Lewis Samuel, H. Altman, I. Davis, Mr. Rosenberg, Mr. Coan, A. S. Aarons, Joseph Koplick, A. Bellem, S. Shengoot, I. Fisher, Reuben Abrahams, Wolf Shengoot, resolved "that from the increase of the persons of the Jewish creed becoming inhabitants of the City of Toronto it was most proper that a Congregation be now formed." Thirty-one annual subscriptions varying from £1.5.0 to £10 then follow with a total of £127.5.0. Joseph Lyons was elected Chairman and A. S. Aarons Honorary Secretary.

The minutes throughout the book show a decided effort to follow parliamentary rules in the conduct of the business on hand. Notwithstanding the protracted discussions over matters that may seem trifling to us, the procedure at the meetings which were held weekly, was invariably courteous, the decisions showing a marked spirit of fairness.

The monetary sacrifices by these early settlers though small must have loomed large in the sight of people, most of whom possessed scanty means only. At a meeting held on September 21st, 1856, a committee, appointed at the previous meeting, reported that they had secured a room over Coombs' drug store at the corner of Yonge and Richmond Streets at a rental of £40 currency per annum, and they were having the same fitted up as a place of worship. Rev. Dr. de Sola of Montreal granted the loan of a Sepher Torah, which was used at the services held for the first time on Rosh Hashonoh 1856. The distribution of the Mitzvos was left to the discretion of the President. The room over Coombs' drug store served as a "Shool" for twenty years. The name of "the Sons of Israel" used until October 5th, 1856, was discontinued after that date, and that of "the Congregation" substituted, which term was used until 1869 when the present name was adopted. "The Holy Blossom Toronto Hebrew Congregation" was chartered in 1894 under the provincial act regarding religious institutions.

The officers elected for the first year were Joseph Lyons, President; S. Berhends, Treasurer; A. S. Aarons, Secretary; L. Levine and Moses Levy, Trustees. A. Mr. Joseph was engaged as Shamus, Collector, etc. for one year at a salary of £12.10.0 and five per cent. commission on all moneys he collected.

The engagement of Mr. Solom Sharmant as reader, Shochet, Mohel, etc., at a salary of £75 per year was made subject to his going to New York to be examined as to his capability to act as Shochet, and to obtain a certificate to that effect, the congregation to defray his expenses.

BOND STREET SYNAGOGUE

Mr. Sharmant however refused to be submitted to the ordeal, and his engagement was cancelled. Steps were taken immediately to replace Mr. Sharmant, and Mr. Goldberg, a then resident of Buffalo, who presented credentials from the New York officials as to his competency as a Shochet, was engaged at a salary of £75 for one year, as Reader, Shochet, Mohel, etc. and thus became the first Chazan of the congregation. The affairs of the congregation were conducted in the then prevailing autocratic style in England. Thus we find a member fined 2/6 for smoking in the hall of the "shool" during divine worship. The treasurer and secretary had to pay a fine of 5/- each for non-attendance at divine service, without sending an apology for their absence. Five other members paid 2/6 each for being absent at a general meeting of the congregation.

Mr. and Mrs. G. I. Asher presented the congregation with a beautiful Sepher Torah, Yod etc., and in appreciation of their gift were made Honorary life members of the congregation.

At the election of officers on October 4th, 1857, Lewis Samuel, who for thirty years, till the time of his death, was the leader and foremost worker of the congregation, was elected a trustee.

Balloting for applicants to membership was introduced in April, 1858. The following month Abraham Nordheimer and Mark Samuel became members of the congregation. Commencing at that date accounts were calculated in Dollar Currency. Mr. Nordheimer paid $20 as his entrance fee and Mr. Mark Samuel $10 as his. The minimum admission fee was fixed at $10.

One of the privileges of the members consisted in being supplied with Kosher meat at a stated price, which was to be regulated by the trustees or by the congregation. The non-Jewish butcher worked under a written agreement with the congregation, and his actions were dictated and supervised by the trustees. Three members were expelled from the congregation at that time, for having publicly insulted the Rev. Mr. Goldberg. It was the custom in almost every small congregation, that the Shochet who at the same time officiated at divine services, styled himself a "Reverend." If able to sign his name in English, he would invariably prefix the abridged Rev. to his signature. The butcher, by the name of Hutty, was instructed not to serve meat to the three expelled members before ten o'clock, and to charge them one penny above the fixed price for every pound of meat they purchased.

DR. B. A. ELZAS

The further pages in the minute book deal mostly with the question of finance, Kosher meat, and the securing of suitable men for the position of Shochet and reader. The salary of the latter did not exceed at any time $420 per year. There seems to have been a continual struggle to raise the necessary funds for the upkeep of the congregation. No records are available from the fall of 1871 until the year 1890.

In the Spring of 1875, mainly due to the efforts of Lewis Samuel and his wife Kate, an acre of land, located one block east of Yonge Street was purchased, and the Synagogue known as the Richmond Street Synagogue erected thereon. The price paid for the land was six thousand dollars. The trustees mentioned in the deed of conveyance of the land to the congregation, were elected life trustees on the third day of Sivan, 1875. Their names are inscribed on a marble tablet which was removed from the Richmond Street building to the present Bond Street Synagogue, and read: Lewis Samuel, Marcus Green, Alexander Miller, Marx Kassel, Isaac Davis, Mark Solomon, Lipman Walters.

The Richmond Street Synagogue served as the place of worship of the congregation until September 15th, 1897, when the present Bond Street Synagogue was dedicated. The cost of the edifice was $40,000. The greater part of this money was collected by Alfred D. Benjamin. He and his brother Frank started the building fund by donating ten thousand dollars towards it.

The first trained Cantor of the Congregation, whose memory is still revered by all who knew him, was Mr. Gluck. Under his ministry, 1873 to 1882, the Synagogue service was greatly improved. He was ably assisted in his efforts by Mrs. Rebeccah Lyon Morris, mother of Mrs. Mattie Miller, who for years, too, was a singer in the choir, and is still a respected member of the congregation. The very type of a fine Jewish woman, and a gifted singer herself, Mrs. Morris in 1873 formed the first synagogue choir. The services of the ladies who composed the same were voluntary. In the teeth of a strong opposition by the ultra orthodox wing of the congregation, Mrs. Morris succeeded in introducing instrumental music in the synagogue. She was the soul of the choir and remained its voluntary unselfish leader for twenty years.

Mr. Gluck was succeeded by Cantor Herman Phillips, a pupil of the world renowned music teacher Levandoski. He was elected Cantor and minister to the congregation in 1883 and held the position for eight years. Gifted with a very fine voice, he was instrumental in improving the synagogue service. He resigned in 1891, returning to New York where he became principal of the school of the Hebrew Sheltering Guardian Orphan Asylum, a position he retained unto his death in 1898.

Changes in the old fashioned methods in which the services in the synagogue were conducted were first made in 1890 under the guidance of Dr. Barnett A. Elzas, a graduate of Jews' College, London, the first ordained Rabbi ministering to the spiritual wants of the congregation. Dr. Elzas had to bear the brunt of making these reforms which insignificant as they were, could only be introduced by the consent of a majority vote of the members of the congregation. This consent was only obtained after protracted and acrimonious discussions at numerous congregational meetings. The abolition of the long chain of offerings during and after the reading of the Law, the use of instrumental music at the high holy days, the reading of the Haftorah in the vernacular by the Rabbi, the closing of all services with a prayer in English and the priestly benediction, the doing away with the sale of the Mitzvos on holy days to the highest bidder—these and similar matters trifling in themselves were nevertheless the cause of much friction among the members of the congregation. Rabbi Elzas, discouraged by the continued unpleasant task resigned the position in 1893, and accepted the call to the congregation of Sacramento where he officiated for one year. Leaving Sacramento in 1894, he occupied the pulpit of the historic Beth Elohim Congregation of Charleston S.C. for 16 years. He has been residing in New York since, and is minister of the Beth Miriam Congregation of Long Branch, N.J. He is a prominent author of articles and books treating of Jewish matters. During his stay in Toronto, Dr. Elzas did excellent work in the pulpit, in the Jewish Sabbath School, and in the field of charity and communal welfare. He was held in high esteem, alike by Jew and non-Jew.

The incumbent of the pulpit succeeding Dr. Elzas was Abraham Lazarus, B.A., graduate of Jews' College, London. A native of Liverpool, he came to Toronto at the age of 24. He remained the spiritual head of the congregation for five years. He was a very gifted young man, studious and painstaking, devoted heart and soul to his sacred calling. An excellent teacher, the Sabbath School flourished under his direction and reached a high state of efficiency. He introduced the late Friday evening services to which crowds of non Jews flocked, attracted by his scholarly and impressive lectures, at which men and women sat together, an innovation which later on was extended to all services in the syna-

RABBI A. LAZARUS, B.A.

gogue. He held the office of Chaplain of Zetland Lodge A.F. & A.M. A masterly address on the religion of masonry he delivered in 1898 was ordered to be printed, and copies thereof were widely distributed in masonic circles. In December 1898, he answered the call to the

Houston (Texas) reform congregation, where one year later he succumbed to an attack of malarial fever, cut off at the threshold of a very promising career.

The successor of Rabbi Lazarus—Rabbi David H. Wittenberg of New York—held the position from February 1899 to August 1900.

He was succeeded by Rabbi Solomon Jacobs who occupied the pulpit of the Congregation until the time of his death, August 1920. A true pastor of his flock whose joys and sorrows he shared, his services were at all times at the beck and call of all members of the community, regardless of nationality, race or creed. He still lives in the memory of all those who had the good fortune of his acquaintance.

Dr. Barnett R. Brickner, for the last five years the spiritual head of the Congregation, has proved a valuable asset, not only to the Jewish community but to Canada as well. Under his able leadership, the congregation has grown in number and importance and has made progress in every branch of its work. His lectures draw large audiences which at many a time exceed the seating capacity of the Synagogue.

The Congregation from the day of its inception has always taken a deep interest in the religious training of the young.

The early "Cheder", started in 1859 with less than ten pupils, has long since grown into an orderly, well regulated Sabbath School which now numbers over three hundred pupils. The Congregation conducts also a High School Department in the Community Building, attended by one hundred and fifty students. This department is under the direction of Rabbi Brickner. A third school, for girls only, under the auspices of the Holy Blossom Temple Sisterhood is carried on in the Hebrew men of England Synagogue, and has an average attendance of two hundred and seventy pupils. Up to recently when salaried teachers were engaged, the schools were manned by voluntary teachers, to whose unselfish labor much of their success is to be attributed. The schools, from the commencement, were open to children of members and non-members alike, and no charge for tuition was ever made. With the exception of Rabbi Jacobs, the Superintendents of the school were members of the congregation who volunteered their services. Thus, Mr. Edmund Scheuer acted as honorary superintendent from 1886 to 1906; the late Rabbi Jacobs, from 1907 to 1909; Johanna (Mrs. Maurice) Frankel, from 1910 to 1915; the late Lena (Mrs. Leo) Frankel, from 1916 to 1919; and Mr. E. F. Singer from 1919 to date.

The state of efficiency of the synagogue choir at the time of the retirement of Mrs. Morris in 1893 was further enhanced by the advent of Cantor S. Solomon, for many years first Chazan of the Notre Dame de Nazaret Synagogue of Paris, France. He held the office from 1894 to 1901, when he accepted the position of cantor of the San Francisco Reform Congregation, which he occupied until the time of his death in 1914. Valuable services too were rendered by Mrs. Edward Youngheart, now Mrs. Berthold Hirschbergg of Berlin, who, a gifted singer herself, occupied the position of honorary leader of the choir from 1893 to 1899. Mr. Benno Scheuer succeeded her and remained the voluntary leader of the volunteer members from 1900 until the time of his demise, in February, 1921. His enthusiasm for the embellishment of the services, his conscientious and indefatigable efforts were an inspiration to his loyal band of singers, and under his able direction, the synagogue choir earned the reputation of being one of the best in the city.

The congregation also occupied itself with charity work. In the early years of its existence, the minutes record the distribution of matzoth to the few needy families in the city, and some instances of monetary grants for relief. The Congregation originated most of the benevolent institutions, which had for their object the betterment of conditions of the indigent. These institutions were taken over by the Federation of the Jewish Philanthropies of Toronto, established in 1917. Many of the members of the Congregation are among the founders of the latter organization, and prominent today in all branches of its activities.

The two hundred and twenty-five members of the Temple Sisterhood have done excellent work by taking a prominent part in the synagogue activities. Two of their number are now members of the Board of Trustees.

The congregation from its small beginning, with an annual budget of less than one thousand dollars, has developed into one of the leading congregations of the Dominion. The synagogue services, moderate reform, are most inspiring and might serve as a pattern for true devotion. The membership has reached the number of three hundred and fifty. The annual revenue is $25,000.

CANTOR H. PHILLIPS

One of the outstanding personalities of the congregation is Mr. M. Geldzaeler, the assistant Chazan since March 1892.

The presidents of the Congregation have been Joseph Lyons, who held the office from 1856 to 1859; M. Lumley from 1860 to 1862; Lewis Samuel 1863, 1864, 1867, and from 1870 to the time of his death in 1887; Max Kassel, 1865 to 1867; Alexander Miller, 1868 and 1869; B. S. Rosenthal, 1887 to 1891; Mark Cohen, 1892; Alfred D. Benjamin, 1892 to 1900, (Parnas from 1887 to 1891), all deceased. Mr. Frank D. Benjamin held the office from 1901 to 1908, when he moved to London, England, where he has since resided. Mr. Leo Frankel, the present incumbent, has been president for the last seventeen years.

Marked services were also rendered by the Honorary Secretaries, A. S. Aarons, who held office from 1856 to 1860; Geo. J. Joseph, S. M. Solomon, the late Mark Marks, (whose sons, Harry and Elly are members of the congregation), the late J. L. Levy, Sol Michael, 1888 to 1902, the year of his death, and the late Henry Davis, 1902 to 1907.

Among the early workers who held the office of treasurer mention should be made of the names of M. Finetuch, A. J. Mintz, and the late A. Franklin, who for over forty years was a member of the board of trustee, and vice-president for a number of years.

The present officers of the congregation are; Leo. Frankel, President; Edmund Scheuer, Vice-President; Harry Samuel, Treasurer; E. F. Singer, Honorary Secretary; Trustees, Arthur Cohen, Mark G. Cohen, Julius Eisman, Isidor Fineberg, Egmont L. Frankel, Percy Hermant, S. Lubelsky, N. L. Nathanson, Ralph Raphael, Harry Rotenberg, Louis M. Singer; Representatives of the Temple Sisterhood, Mrs. Arthur Cohen and Mrs. Harry Marks.

THE LATE RABBI S. JACOBS

RABBI SOLOMON JACOBS (born 1861, died 1920), was born at Sheffield, England, the son of Michael Joseph and Rachel Miriam Jacobs. He was educated at the People's College, Sheffield, and at Aria College, Portsmouth, and was the first minister to be trained at this institution. He was ordained in 1883 and received his Rabbinical degree in 1886. For some years he was master of the Manchester Jews' School and afterwards was elected minister of the Newcastle-on-Tyne Congregation. At the recommendation of the Chief Rabbi, in 1886 he was appointed minister of the United Congregation of Kingston, Jamaica, and he held this position till 1899. During this time he was on many important public committees and was Director of the Kingston City Dispensary and other public works. In 1901 he was called to the pulpit of the Holy Blossom Synagogue, Toronto, and for 19 years he endeared himself to the hearts of his congregation as pastor and as a leader in all movements for the benefit of his people. He was not only interested in the affairs of his own race, but took an active part in anything tending to the benefit of mankind, irrespective of race or religion. Very charitable, no needy person left him empty-handed. Rabbi Jacobs was an eloquent preacher, modern in thought and style, and his motto ever was "Have we not all one Father, has not one God created us all?" He was intensely proud of his British birth and during the Great War was constant in his attention to the Jew in khaki. He acted as chaplain in various camps and was always a comforter to the wounded and sick in the hospitals. On many occasions he preached from Christian pulpits and took part in public services. He was Vice-President of the Associated Charities of Toronto and was a member of the first charity Commission appointed by the City Council. Rabbi Jacobs was married in Birmingham, England, to Edith, daughter of the late Philip Cohen and left one son, Arthur, and two daughters, Mrs. Marcus Sperber of Montreal, and Miss Ray Jacobs of Toronto.

THE LATE LEWIS SAMUEL

THE LATE MR. LEWIS SAMUEL, a prominent citizen of Toronto for thirty-two years, was born in Hull, Yorkshire, England, in 1827. He left England in 1848 and made Syracuse in New York State his first home. British born, he desired to live under the British flag, and in 1851 moved to Montreal, where he resided for three years. He came to Toronto in 1854, and with his brother, Mark, established the wholesale hardware business of M. & L. Samuel. This business, after a most successful and honorable career of over seventy years, is now under the direction of his son, Mr. Sigmund Samuel. Widely known by the firm name of Samuel & Benjamin, Limited, it still remains one of the leading wholesale metal concerns in the Dominion. Mr. Samuel, a gentleman of simple habits, was held in high regard by all classes of the community on account of his kindness of heart, and sterling integrity. Very few Jewish families lived in Toronto at the time of Mr. Samuel's arrival in the then small city. Ably assisted by his wife, he did pioneer work in the upbuilding of the Jewish community. One of the founders of the Holy Blossom Congregation, of which he was a most active member from the time of its inception, he occupied the position of president almost continuously from 1862 to 1885. He was instrumental in the purchase of the land and in the erection of the Richmond Street Synagogue, which was dedicated in 1876. Mr. Samuel's activities were by no means confined to the members of his own faith. He was a supporter of all the charitable institutions of the city, and lent his aid to everything pertaining to the betterment of conditions in the community. He died in April, 1887, his widow following him in 1894. Mr. Samuel was married in 1851 to Kate, daughter of Jacob and Carolin Seckleman of Sulzbach, Bavaria. Besides a son, Sigmund, residing in Toronto, they are survived by three daughters, Amelia, widow of Joseph Rosenbaum of New York, Miss Matilda, artist painter of Toronto, and Rosetta, wife of George Joseph of London, England.

THE LATE A. D. BENJAMIN

ALFRED D. BENJAMIN was born in Melbourne in 1848. He was educated by private tuition and followed in the paths of his father David Benjamin, a retired Melbourne (Victoria) merchant, prominent philanthropist and communal worker, who helped to found a Jewish Congregation in Launceston (Tasmania), and laid the foundation stone of the Bourke Street Synagogue in Melbourne. On his return to London, in 1854, he devoted all his time to the service of the community. He died in London in 1893 at the age of 78. Mr. Alfred Benjamin came to Canada in 1875, and after residing in Montreal for a few years, entered the wholesale hardware firm of M. & L. Samuel, the firm name then becoming M. & L. Samuel, Benjamin & Co. He was president of The Holy Blossom Congregation from 1886 to the time of his death. The erection of the Bond Street Synagogue was entirely due to his initiative, and he contributed, jointly with his brother Frank, the sum of ten thousand dollars to create a building fund, which was largely augmented by subscriptions he personally solicited. The members of the congregation, in appreciation of the immeasurable services, cheerfully and unselfishly rendered at all times, presented him with his own portrait in oil, a replica of which still adorns the walls of the synagogue assembly room. In the building of the synagogue, Mr. Benjamin has erected to his memory a monument of brick and mortar, but a still greater and more lasting monument has he reared to himself in the hearts of the people by his loving kindness, his ever ready untiring personal service, and his unbounded charity. Mr. Benjamin died in January, 1900. He married in 1886, Rosetta Benjamin of London, England, who still survives him. They were the parents of three children all born and raised in Toronto; two daughters, Esther, wife of Frank Samuel of London, and Miss Louise residing with her mother in London. Their son John, born in 1892, enlisted at the beginning of the war in the Duke of Wellington's West Riding Regiment, rose to the rank of Captain, and lost his life in action at Contalmaison, France, July 5th, 1916.

FRANK D. BENJAMIN

FRANK D. BENJAMIN was born in London, England in 1866, and was educated by private tuition and at University College School. He is the youngest son of the late David Benjamin, a retired Australian merchant, who lived in London until his death in 1893, and who was a widely known Jewish philanthropist and communal worker. Frank Benjamin went to Toronto in 1888 and resided there until 1908. He was a partner in the wholesale metal firm of M. & L. Samuel, Benjamin & Company. He was married in 1897, to Rachael Levy of London, England. In 1895, Mr. Benjamin received a commission in the Queen's Own Rifles of Canada, retiring with the rank of Captain on his return to London in 1908. He was for many years treasurer of the regiment. He was appointed a Justice of the Peace for the County of York, in 1902, and during his stay in Toronto was a very active member of the National Club, in which he still retains membership. At all times interested in the welfare of the Jewish community in Toronto, he was the Secretary of the Building Committee of the Holy Blossom Synagogue, and President of the congregation from 1901 to 1908. He was also treasurer of the Toronto branch of the Anglo-Jewish Association. Mr. Benjamin is at the present time a prominent communal worker in London, England. He is treasurer of the United Synagogue, and is a member of the various committees connected therewith. He is treasurer of the Union of Hebrew and Religious Classes, and member of the Council of Jews' College; Jewish Board of Guardians; Anglo-Jewish Association; Jewish War Memorial; Central Committee for Jewish Education; and Board of Management of the new West-end Synagogue. He is a director and vice-chairman of the committee of the London Metal Exchange. His son, Ernest F. Benjamin, was born in Toronto in 1900 and was educated at Clifton College, England. He received his military training at the Royal Military Academy, Woolwich, and at Chatham. At the present time he is a Lieutenant in the Royal Engineers, attached to the 42nd Field Company stationed in Egypt.

THE LATE REV. NATHAN ROBINSON

THE LATE REV. NATHAN ROBINSON was born in the town of Kalwarya, Russian Poland, in 1840, and died in Toronto, June 30th, 1899 (22nd Tamuz, 5660). He was the son of Reuben and Pesha Sarah (Baas Abraham Zev) Reubenson. His father was, until his death, Dayan of his native town. His mother lived to the ripe old age of ninety years. Nathan Robinson was educated by his father and also in the Yeshiva in Kalwarya. In addition to his Talmudic education he studied German in Eastern Prussia, where for some years he officiated as minister in the City of Insterburgh. He later studied English in the United States and Canada. In May 1877, he arrived in Toronto, on receiving a call to the pulpit of the Bnei Shalom Congregation. This was a small community that had their place of worship in a hall on Richmond Street and after a brief existence, they amalgamated with the Holy Blossom Synagogue. The President of the Bnei Shalom Congregation was the late Abraham Franklin, and the Vice-President, the late Harris Rosenthal, both well-known former residents of Toronto. The total population of Toronto at that time was quite small, and the Jewish community did not number more than one hundred souls. As in all small, partially settled Jewish communities, there were no special Rabbis and Mr. Robinson, during his first years in Toronto, acted as Shochat, Chazan and Mohel. He was sufficiently versed in Hebrew Law to "Pasken Shaiyless," and was also "Baalkorak," or "Reader of the Law." Mr. Robinson filled the positions described until the time when the community became larger, when they added a special Chazan and English lecturer. During his entire residence in Toronto (about twenty-two years), Mr. Robinson devoted himself to his congregation and endeared himself to the members as their pastor and spiritual leader. Mr. Robinson married in 1862, the late Esther Gittel Ludwinowsky of Wizan, Russian Poland, who died in New York at the age of seventy. He left three sons, R. S. Robinson of Winnipeg, and Samuel A. and Elias Robinson of New York; and three daughters, Mrs. P. Schlansky, Mrs. S. P. Schlansky and Mrs. Jacob Cohen.

THE LATE ABRAHAM FRANKLIN

THE LATE MR. ABRAHAM FRANKLIN, in his life-time a well-known Jewish resident of Toronto, was born in Russia, and was married there to the late Fanny Nocinsky of Suvalsky Gubarna, Russian Poland. He was the son of the late Mr. Jacob Lidwinoski Franklin. He came to Canada as a young man and settled in Toronto, where he became engaged in the jewelry business, in which he continued until his death, which took place on September 11th, 1905. Mr. Franklin took an active part in all Jewish communal undertakings, and was particularly identified with the Congregation B'nai Shalom on Richmond Street. This congregation was first located in a hall at the corner of Richmond and Yonge Streets, but afterwards occupied quarters on the corner of Richmond and Victoria Streets, which they made into a synagogue. Mr. Franklin was one of the organizers of this congregation, and was actively connected with it during its existence. At various times he occupied the positions of President, Vice-President and Treasurer. When this congregation was absorbed by the Holy Blossom Synagogue, Mr. Franklin joined the latter congregation and was one of its most active members, retaining his connection with it, until his death. He was a generous supporter of all Jewish charities, and in a quiet, unassuming manner, did a great amount of good in the community, being assisted in his communal work by his son, the late Jacob Franklin, who died on December 18th, 1902. Mr. Franklin was prosperous in his business, and he early showed his confidence in the future of his adopted city, and became a large holder of real estate. He took a great interest in public questions, and was a staunch supporter of the Conservative party. He was a member of the Masonic Order, and of all the Jewish communal societies. Mr. Franklin left a family of three sons; Harry, Hyman and Simon Franklin of Toronto, and three daughters; Mrs. Elias Robinson of New York, and the Misses Dora and Kate Franklin of Toronto. Mrs. Franklin who also took a keen interest in all Jewish matters died on November 7th, 1908.

THE LATE N. H. DAVIS

THE LATE MR. NATHANIEL HENRY DAVIS was born at Buffalo, N.Y., on May 1st, 1854, the son of the late Isaac Davis of Toronto. He came to Canada when a child with his parents, settling in Toronto, where he resided until his death, which took place in 1914. He received his education at the Louisa Street School and Jarvis Street Collegiate Institute, Toronto. He was married to Emilie, daughter of Philip Nathan Casper of London, England, and had three sons, Lionel, Arthur and Bertram, and one daughter, Miss Violet Davis. Mr. Davis established the woollen manufacturing industry which is now being conducted by his youngest son. For some years he lived in London, England, where he was identified with many communal undertakings for the betterment of his co-religionists. On his return to Toronto he continued to take a keen and active interest in all philanthropic work and charitable movements in the Jewish community. He was one of the earliest members of the Toronto Men's Benevolent Society, of which he was the Honorary Secretary. Mr. Davis was one of the first to propose a Federation of Jewish Charities in Toronto, but he did not live to see this an accomplished fact, the Federation of Jewish Philanthropies of Toronto not being established until 1916. In his communal activities Mr. Davis had the earnest co-operation of his wife and family, who have continued to maintain a spirited interest in all that takes place in charitable and congregational work. His son Arthur served throughout the war with the Imperial troops holding a commission as Lieutenant. He took part in the fighting in Mesopotamia, and was later stationed for a long time with the forces in India. Mr. Davis was a life-long member of the Holy Blossom Congregation of Toronto, and was Honorary Secretary during the Presidency of Mr. Frank D. Benjamin. He was strictly orthodox in his religious views, but he was very broadminded, and during his lifetime numbered many friends among the non-Jewish people. Mr. Davis was a keen naturalist, his hobby being the study and culture of flowers.

EDMUND SCHEUER, TORONTO

After a portrait by Joshua Smith, R.B.A.

A PUBLIC-SPIRITED citizen, and the oldest established wholesale diamond importer in Canada, Edmund Scheuer has been for over fifty years active in general welfare work and in the religious and educational field among the Jews of Canada. Born in Berncastel on the Moselle, October 30th, 1847, the son of Isaac and Johanna Scheuer, he received his education in the public and high schools of his home community, and at the École Supérieure, Metz, Lorraine. In 1865, he went to Paris, France and joined the firm of Bernard S. Merzbach remaining with them until he established a commission house under his own name. The Franco-Prussian war having stopped all export business, Mr. Scheuer accepted an invitation from Levy Bros. of Hamilton, Ontario, already a well-known wholesale jewellery firm, whose purchasing agent he had been in Paris, and in 1871 became a partner in this firm, the firm name becoming Levy Bros., & Scheuer. In 1886 he moved to Toronto. Mr. Scheuer was president of the Anshe Sholom congregation in Hamilton from 1873 to 1885. In 1882 through his efforts, was erected the quaint Hughson Street Synagogue, the first Reform Temple in Canada. In 1872 he established a Jewish Sabbath School, the first one in the province of Ontario, and for fifty-two years has continued to instruct Jewish children in the tenets of their faith. In 1886, he joined the Holy Blossom Congregation in Toronto and was treasurer of the fund for the building of the Bond Street Synagogue, of which he is Vice-president. In 1892, he founded the first Jewish Benevolent Society in Toronto, and was for the first four years of its existence, president of the Federation of The Jewish Philanthropies of Toronto. He is still a member of its executive Board. He is president of the Toronto branch of the Anglo-Jewish Association of London, England. Mr. Scheuer married on July 2nd, 1873, at Forbach, Lorraine, Oda Strauss, who died November 16th, 1913. He is an esteemed member of the Canadian Club, and has been a member of the Toronto Board of Trade since 1886, and a Justice of the Peace since 1902.

F. LANDSBERG, VICTORIA, B.C.

FRED LANDSBERG is an outstanding figure of the City of Victoria. He was born in Berditchen, Russia, December 12th, 1861, the son of Marcus Landsberg. He was educated by private tuition in Russia, and on May 1st, 1884, located in Victoria, where he has since resided. For the past eighteen years, Mr. Landsberg has been established in the real estate business and has earned an enviable reputation for clean and honest dealings. He has extensively developed realty in the business section of Victoria. For years Mr. Landsberg has been the moving spirit in drives for funds for the relief of Russian, Jewish, Armenian, Belgian and Chinese famine sufferers, and also for the local Y.M.C.A. In most relief drives he has acted as campaign manager. In 1922, the School Trustees of British Columbia decided that Bible reading should be introduced in the public schools of the province, and passed a resolution urging the Government to include same in their curriculum. Mr. Landsberg convinced the Minister of Education that Bible reading would create religious and racial prejudice, and obtained a promise from him that all the schools of the province would be conducted on strictly non-sectarian lines. His philanthropy is universal, and he is the first one called upon when help is required to raise funds for any charitable object. There are few men in British Columbia with such a record for kindliness, although much of his work is done anonymously. He is on the executive of the Red Cross Society, and he was mainly responsible for the financial success of their "Superfluities" section, which raised many thousands of dollars for the organization, during the Great War. Mr. Landsberg is Chairman, Social Service League; Chairman of Committees, Chamber of Commerce; Director, Real Estate Board of Victoria; Vice-Pres., North West Real Estate Board; and a member of the Independent Order of Foresters; A.O.F.; K. of M., and Ancient Order of United Workmen. On May 31st, 1895, Mr. Landsberg was married to Erna, daughter of Marcus Marymont, and has one daughter, Miss Beatrice Landsberg.

CONGREGATION EMANU-EL, VICTORIA, B. C.

THE CONGREGATION EMANU-EL is one of the oldest in Canada, and was the first incorporated religious place of worship on the Pacific Coast. It was formed by a number of Jews who arrived in Victoria in the years between 1855 and 1860. Most of these men came from the gold rush in California, and were on their way to the newly discovered goldfields at Cariboo.

The original membership consisted of thirty-five, Mr. D. Shirpser being the first President, and Mr. S. Hoffman, Vice-President.

On Tuesday, 3rd of June, 1863, the laying of the corner-stone was performed. The participants of the ceremony were not confined to the Jewish portion of the City of Victoria, but representatives of every creed and nationality were present.

Mr. A. Hoffman acted as Grand Marshal. The members of the congregation assembled in the rooms where they had formerly worshipped, in the upper portion of a building on Government Street. At two o'clock the procession was formed, headed by the band of H.M.S. Topaz followed by the Germania Singing Club, St. Andrew's Society, the Hebrew Benevolent Society, the French Benevolent Society, two Masonic Lodges in full regalia, Victoria Lodge (No. 1085, Robt. Burnaby, Esq. W. Master), and Vancouver Lodge (No. 461, I. W. Powell, M.D., W. Master), and started for the grounds on which the synagogue stands.

The then Chief Justice of British Columbia, David Cameron, walked in the procession, as well as the Mayor, Thomas Harris.

Arriving at the grounds, the various societies took the positions assigned them, the Masonic Order surrounding the corner-stone.

SYNAGOGUE, VICTORIA, B.C.

The proceedings were opened with an invocation by Mr. M. Malowanski, followed by a psalm chanted by the Germania Sing Verein. Addresses were then given by the President, the Vice-President, Mr. J. P. Davies, and Mr. J. H. Boscowitz. After these addresses, Mr. Vaenberg offered a prayer in Hebrew, and the stone was laid with full Masonic honors. An oblation of the corn of plenty, the wine of refreshment, and the oil of joy was poured upon it.

Beneath the stone was placed the constitution of the Hebrew Benefit Society, deposited by Mr. Malowanski; list of officers and members of the Germania Singing Club by Pres. N. Koshland; the same of St. Andrew's Society by Capt. Reid; the French Benevolent Society by P. Corbiniere; a list of subscribers and a copy of the deed of ground on which the synagogue was erected by A. Simpson; a list of the officers and members of the congregation Emanu-El by A. H. Vaenberg; a list of subscriptions to the synagogue by David Hart; constitution of the congregation by the President, D. Shirpser; newspapers of the day, coins, etc. by A. Hoffman.

The stone was then lowered into position and the Grand Master of Masons, Mr. Robt. Burnaby declared it to be well and truly laid. Benediction and prayer was read by Chief Justice Cameron, and the Masonic ceremony was then closed.

On Sept. 13, 1863, the Temple was completed and the consecration took place. On this occasion the sermon was given in English by the Rev. Dr. Cohen, who was the first Rabbi.

An interesting feature about this congregation is a clause in the deed of property whereby it states that, should at any time the Jewish population of Victoria be unable to raise a "Minyan", the building is to become the property of the city, to be used as a public institution.

Shortly after the erection of the synagogue, the Rev. Dr. Cohen resigned as Minister, and for many years the congregation was without a spiritual head. An order-in-council was put through the Legislature, whereby any officer of the congregation who was properly authorized by the congregation, could legally perform the marriage ceremony.

Much credit is due to Mrs. Frank Sylvester for her assistance in raising funds for the building of the synagogue, and this lady up to the present time, has shown an unfailing interest and devotion to it.

Mr. Fred Landsberg has held almost every office in the gift of the congregation, and for many years officiated during the Holidays.

The present Rabbi is the Rev. E. Friedlander.

Among those who were prominent in the early days of the congregation, may be mentioned the following:— A. Blackman, Jacob Cohen, A. Belasco (father of David Belasco, the famous playwright), I. Braverman, H. M. Cohen, J. Cohen, Michael Cohen, J. P. Davies, Joshua Davies, Lewis Davies, Mark Goldsmith, A. Kayser, K. Gambitz, David Green, W. F. Herre, David Hart, I. Lash, A. Myers, Lewis Lewis, Harris Lichtenstein, Morris Moss, John Malowanski, Eli Marks, E. C. Neufelder, Henry Nathan (whose son took such a prominent part in the early political life of British Columbia), Alex Phillips, Martin Prag, J. Rueff, A. Simpson, Frank Sylvester, Herman Shultz (father of Judge Shultz), A. Vaenberg, L. Wolfe, A. Zilner, S. Zinn, Cerf Freeman, the Greenbaum, Hoffman, Levy, Martin, Schwabacher, Oppenheimer, Franklin, Lenz, Leiser and Shirpser families.

The Oppenheimer Brothers, David, Godfrey, and Isaac were associated with many of the greatest ventures in British Columbia, David being Mayor of Vancouver for four terms, and the first President of the Vancouver Board of Trade.

Although Victoria does not hold a large Jewish population, the congregation has always flourished and has been the center of all Jewish activities.

The present officers of the congregation are as follows;—President, H. I. Nallik; Vice-President, H. Greenfelder; Treasurer, A. Lanonsky; and Secretary, E. Fromson. Trustees, I. M. Nodeck, I. Winstock, and E. P. Nathan.

THE LATE FRANK SYLVESTER

THE LATE MR. FRANK SYLVESTER, a member of an old Sephardic family, and who in his lifetime was one of the best known citizens of the city of Victoria, was born in New York City in 1837, and received his education in the schools of that city. As a youth he crossed the continent overland in 1857, arriving in Victoria in 1858, at the time of the first Cariboo gold rush. Mr. Sylvester was one of the first Jews to arrive in Victoria, and took a leading part in the early life of that city. After spending some years in the gold fields, he went back to Victoria in 1863, where he joined the firm of J. P. Davies & Company, Auctioneers. He was one of the founders of the Jewish congregation established in Victoria at that time, and was active in all public affairs and undertakings, taking an interest in all matters for the advancement of the community. Mr. Sylvester was married to the youngest daughter of Mr. J. P. Davies, a lady who was one of the most active workers for the establishment of the synagogue. He remained in partnership with his father-in-law for fifteen years, when he entered the business of Accountant, in which he remained engaged until his retirement many years later. Although one of the most public-spirited citizens of Victoria, Mr. Sylvester refused all municipal offices. He assisted in every project for the advancement of the city with money, influence and time. He was particularly interested in all Jewish undertakings, and served as an officer of the Synagogue for many years. Mr. Sylvester was an enthusiastic naturalist, and was a member of the Natural History Society from its first start. He contributed many valuable articles on this subject, on which he was regarded as an outstanding authority. Mr. Sylvester died on the 28th of December, 1908, and was survived by his widow, three sons, W., C. B. and Jesse, and five daughters, Mrs. Manckus, Mrs. A. B. Ellis, Mrs. Campbell, Mrs. McCrae, and Miss Louise Sylvester. He was a member of the Ancient Order of Workmen.

THE LATE SIMON LEISER

SIMON LEISER Ex. President of the Victoria Board of Trade, and who died on May 12th, 1917, was looked upon as one of British Columbia's foremost citizens. He came to Victoria in 1880 and set up in business as a grocer on Johnson Street, the business prospering rapidly. He soon launched into the wholesale trade and shortly afterwards built the Leiser Block on Yates Street, and in 1890 he conducted the largest wholesale business in British Columbia. Mr. Leiser was always ready to take a venture in the field of commerce and was one of the leading figures in Victoria's great sealing industry, then the chief characteristic of the port. He personally operated the "Wanderer" in the northern waters, and was prominent in the protracted negotiations, which eventually led to the cessation of pelagic sealing by Canadian ships. In the nineties, during the Klondike rush, Mr. Leiser formed the limited liability company which, until quite recently, bore the name of Simon Leiser and Company, Limited, and the directorate included some of the most influential residents of Victoria. The interests of this firm on Vancouver Island employed over one hundred people. His chief public work was done as a member of the Council of the Board of Trade, and he served on this body for fifteen years. He was Vice-President in 1907, and was elected President in the following year, serving two terms in the chair. Mr. Leiser was for some time a director of the Royal Jubilee Hospital, and a member of the Executive of the Vancouver Island Publicity Bureau. He was also actively identified with the fortunes of the Victoria Opera House Company, and took a leading part in the building of the Royal Victoria Theatre, making the inaugural address when the building was opened on December 29th, 1913. On that occasion he was presented by the shareholders with a loving cup, and later a bust was placed in the lobby of the theatre in memory of his services. He took an active interest in all questions affecting the Jewish community of Victoria; and was a member of the Congregation Emanu-El.

RABBI M. J. MERRITT, MONTREAL.

RABBI MAX JOHN MERRITT, son of John Merritt and Caroline (Rosenthal) Merritt, was born in Omaha, Nebraska, U.S.A. February 23rd, 1879. He received a common school education in Omaha, at the age of fifteen he went to enter the preparatory department of the Hebrew Union College. He graduated from Hughes High School in 1898, winning the Hughes High School Oratorical medal. In 1902, he graduated from the University of Cincinnati with the degree of B.A., winning the Phi Beta Kappa Key for scholarship. In 1903, he graduated from the Hebrew Union College with the title of Rabbi, and went directly to Germany to continue his post graduate work at the Rabbinical Seminary in Berlin, and at the University of Berlin, under Gunkel, Delitsch, Meyer and Harnack. Returning to the United States in 1904, he was elected Rabbi of Congregation B'nai Israel of Evansville, Indiana, serving there for fourteen years. During the world war, he took an active part in mobilising the civilian resources, having been appointed by the Government, Chairman of the Speakers' Bureau of Vanderburg County, and of the Four Minute Speakers of Evansville, Indiana. He also served with the Jewish Welfare Board, being assigned for active service to the Camp Custer Cantonment, with the Michigan Division, at Battle Creek, Michigan. In 1919, he was elected Rabbi of the B'nai Abraham-Zion Congregation of Chicago, leaving that congregation in 1920 to accept a unanimous call to Temple Emanu-El of Montreal, Quebec. In Montreal he has continued his civic and community welfare work, taking active part in all such movements. He is a member of the Non-Catholic Juvenile Court Committee; member of the Executive Board of the Montreal Big Brothers' Association; member of the Executive Board of The Child Welfare Association, Chaplain of the Montreal Post No. 1 of the American Legion; Grand Chaplain of the Grand Lodge of the Province of Quebec, A.F. and A.M., and member of the Kiwanis and Montefiore Clubs. In 1914 he married Ruth Davida Wolffe of London, England, daughter of the late David Wolffe of London and Nairobi, British East Africa, and they have two sons, John Fara and Roger Henry Merritt.

TEMPLE EMANU-EL, MONTREAL

AMONGST all the organizations in this city none has had so precarious and unique an existence as Temple Emanu-El. Its career has been throughout characterized by typical Jewish stiff-neckedness and a righteous obstinacy for a great cause. Its history is the history of a handful of men who, for a quarter of a century, fought and strove and struggled to ensure the permanency of a great movement in this community. For over forty years it has been the only reform congregation in the Province of Quebec. The records of the congregation form one graphic tale of the opposition it has been forced to encounter in a city so pre-eminently orthodox as Montreal, of the dire predictions of speedy failure and extinction which it was compelled to live down, of the excessive frequency with which its nourishers and supporters were called upon to contribute their last mite in order that it might preserve its equipoise. It has taken all of these struggles within and without to establish Temple Emanu-El on a strong and solid foundation, and its phenomenal growth within recent years has not only given the lie to the quondam prognostications of utter downfall, but has given its constituents sanguine assurances of its future noble work.

In the year 1882 two congregations existed in Montreal that were wholly orthodox. There was, at that time, a small minority upon whom the aim of American Reform Judaism had made an indelible impression, and who, thinking of the great advantage that would accrue to them if it were permitted to strike root in Canada, decided to take steps to launch upon an uncertain sea the bark of reform. Accordingly on August 24, 1882, seven gentlemen met at the old Lindsay Hall, on St. Catherine Street, as a committee to consider the following document: "We, the undersigned Israelites of this city, recognizing the necessity of preserving Judaism in all its pristine glory, and making it clear and comprehensible to the rising generation, are in favor of organizing a progressive congregation and to discuss the best means to reach this desirable object, at a meeting called for this purpose." This was signed by about thirty-six gentlemen, among whom were: B. A. Boas, B. Goldstein, E. Lichtenheim, S. Abrahams, J. Goldstein, G. Fischel, A. Goldstein, H. Lazarus, B. Kortosk, M. Goldstein, L. Lewis, S. Fischel, Wm. Raphael, A. Blumenthal, Mark Workman. The committee considered this document, as well as the details requisite for the formation of such a congregation. Officers, pro tem, were chosen, namely; B. A. Boas, chairman; Wm. Goldstein, secretary; A. Goldstein, treasurer; and it was decided, first, to start a subscription list to defray the preliminary expenses; second, to call a meeting of all who had designated their intention of becoming members of the contemplated progressive congregation.

This meeting took place on August 29, 1882. All who had signed the document were present, and the following results are recorded. Committees were appointed:
(a) To apply for a charter.
(b) To lease Albert Hall for three years and eight months.
(c) To adopt "Minhag America" as the prayer book.
(d) To engage a Rabbi.
(e) To engage an organist and choir.
(f) To consider the name of the organization.
(g) To draft by-laws and constitution.
(h) To procure land for a cemetery.

These affairs having been transacted, the meeting was adjourned, but was again convoked on September 4, when it was shown that a choir had been engaged and the first rabbi appointed, the Rev. Samuel Marks. The following officers were then elected: President, B. A. Boas; vice-president, B. Kortosk; secretary, L. Abrahams; treasurer, S. Fischel; directors, L. Robinson, A. Goldstein, L. Isaacs, A. Silverstein, E. Lichtenheim.

TEMPLE EMANU-EL, MONTREAL

The subscription committee reported that it had in hand $440 from individual subscriptions, and with this small sum in the treasury the new congregation, for which the name of "Temple Emanu-El" had been chosen, nothing daunted, held its first services during the high holidays in the fall of 1882.

The first duty that confronted the congregation after the holidays was that of obtaining funds to carry on its work properly. With this aim in view a fair was held in December, 1882, and the first large sum was realized—$3,343.69. The financial condition of the organization being now fairly sound, the committee that had been appointed at the first meeting began their work. On March 30, 1883, an act of incorporation was granted and was adopted by the congregation on April 11. At the end of June, 1883, land was purchased on Back River road for a cemetery, and just one year after that, June 23, 1884, the Jastrow Prayer Book was adopted unanimously. Thus the congregation began to forge ahead slowly but surely. As the membership increased the need for greater accommodation made itself felt, and so on April 12, 1889, a larger and roomier hall was leased for three years at the corner of Drummond and St. Catherine Streets.

For some time the congregation had been dissatisfied with its cemetery on Back River road, because of its distance from town and its damp and watery condition, and thus, after long and weary negotiations, it obtained in 1890, through the efficient ministrations of its (at that time) secretary, Mr. Maxwell Goldstein, a very excellent plot for a burying ground in Mount Royal

Cemetery. The old plot was subsequently subdivided and partly donated and sold to smaller congregations and societies.

Meantime the want of a proper place of worship was making itself keenly felt. Already on May 24, 1885, at a meeting of the board, a motion had been carried that steps be taken toward building a new synagogue, and a committee appointed to devise ways and means. This committee must have evidently encountered many difficulties in carrying out its instructions, for the matter was left in abeyance. The opportune moment, however, came during the presidency of Samuel Davis and the ministry of Hartog Veld. Strenuous efforts were put forth and on Tuesday, May 24, 1892, the cornerstone of the temple on Stanley Street was laid by Mr. Davis in the presence of the members and many invited guests. The dedication of the new building took place on September 16, 1892, at 7.30 p.m., and the Rev Dr. A. S. Isaacs, of New York, preached the dedicatory sermon.

The dedication of the synagogue was supplemented by another noteworthy event, viz., the appointment of Rabbi H. Veld, by the Dominion and Provincial Governments, as the Jewish chaplain to the penitentiary and jail, this being the first time in the history of this country that such an appointment had ever been conferred.

On November 30, 1895, the members of the temple were greatly shocked by the death, at 61 years of age, of Samuel Davis, who had been president of the congregation for nine consecutive years, and who had, since his affiliation with it, been one of its most active and zealous supporters. Resolutions were immediately drafted and dispatched to the bereaved family. The congregation attended the funeral en masse, and as a sign of esteem and regret for the loss of this noble man, the office of president was left vacant for six months.

On May 17, 1896, the congregation took another step towards a greater modernization of its service by adopting the Union Prayer Book. Thus when the Central Conference of American Rabbis, under the leadership of the Reverend Isaac M. Wise, met here in July, 1897, by the invitation of the congregation, it found a well-organized, though small body following the behests of reform earnestly and conscientiously.

Since then the congregation has been growing steadily. Its adherents have increased, and their belief in the principles of reform is being strengthened more and more. On October 15, 1907, the congregation experienced severe regret at the resignation of the late Mr. B. A. Boas from the presidency. Every one expressed genuine sorrow at the loss of so zealous a worker, and had it not been for the illness which impaired his energies and forced him to retire, Mr. Boas would have been well-nigh coerced to retain his position as president. For fourteen years he was president of Temple Emanu-El, and ever, during his period of office, was he conscious of his responsibility and worked enthusiastically to perform the duties which his position entailed. No one has ever given so much of his time, means and energy to the affairs and welfare of the congregation as has Mr. Boas, and the bestowal of the honorary presidency upon him, as well as the presentation that was made to him upon his retirement, were but a modest tribute to, and an appreciative recognition of, his zeal and activity in the cause of reform in Canada.

The resignation of Mr. Boas was followed by the accession to the presidential chair on October 16, 1907, of Mr. Maxwell Goldstein, K.C., one of the most noteworthy members of our community. Mr. Goldstein is the scion of a large and prominent family which has been, since its inception, the mainstay and prop of the temple. He is the youngest law graduate from McGill University and one of the most prominent Jewish lawyers in this city. He had been the secretary for eight consecutive years of Temple Emanu-El, and his election to the presidency of the congregation was an unanimous tribute on the part of the members to his mature judgment, his immaculate qualities and his great interest in reform.

On November 6 and 7, 1907, the congregation celebrated its twenty-fifth anniversary. The special feature of this event was the presence of Dr. D. Phillipson, of Cincinnati, O., who delivered the celebration address on November 6 at a service in the temple. His words had such effect that not only on November 7, at a congregational banquet, did the members subscribe a large sum of money to the funds, but all pledged themselves to work even more zealously in the future, and the pledge has materialized.

The activities and membership of the Congregation continued to grow and a feeling began to develop that the Temple building on Stanley Street no longer could accommodate its requirements. In the fall of 1910, a large plot of ground, situated on Sherbrooke Street, between Wood and Elm Avenues, in Westmount, was acquired and building operations on a new Temple were commenced at once. The new building was formally dedicated on September 17th 1911. The dedication program opened with a solemn procession headed by Mr. B. Kortosk and Mr. A. Goldstein (now both deceased) each carrying a Torah. Messrs. Kortosk and Goldstein had been among the original founders of the Congregation and had been present at the dedication of the old building. The procession proceeded to the pulpit where the Chairman of the Building Committee, Mr. Mark Workman, delivered the key of the edifice to the President, Mr. Maxwell Goldstein, K.C. Rabbi Nathan Gordon gave the dedicatory sermon.

The building is built in the Byzantine style and is valued at nearly $200.000. It has seating accommodation for about 700 and is thoroughly equipped to meet the needs of a modern congregation.

In anticipation of further increased activities and of greater demands upon its capacity, the Temple acquired, during the summer of 1922, the adjoining property situated at the south-east corner of Elm Ave. and Sherbrooke Street. It is the intention of the Congregation to construct, in the near future, a large community centre, containing in addition to school-rooms, a large assembly hall, library and gymnasium.

The following are the names of the presidents of the temple:—B. A. Boas—1882 to 1887; B. Kortosk—1887 to 1888; S. Davis—1888 to 1895; B. A. Boas—1895 to 1898; E. Lichtenheim—1898 to 1900; S. Fischel—1900 to 1901; B. A. Boas—1901 to 1907; M. Goldstein—1907 to 1923; N. Gordon—1923.

The following are the names of the rabbis of the temple:—Samuel Marks—1882 to 1889; S. Eisenberg—1889 to 1890; A. M. Bloch—1890 to 1891; H. Veld—1891 to 1899; E. Friedlander—1899 to 1901; Isaac Landman—1901 to 1904; Jos. Kornfeld—1904 to 1906; Nathan Gordon—1906 to 1916; Samuel Schwartz—1916 to 1919; M. J. Merritt—1920.

The present officers of the congregation are:—Maxwell Goldstein, K.C., Honorary President; Sir Mortimer B. Davis, Mark Workman, Honorary Trustees; Nathan Gordon, President; Peter Bercovitch, K.C., Vice-President; A. Sommer, Honorary Treasurer; Harry Shaer, Honorary Secretary.

Trustees:—Herman Frankel, H. E. Davis, Morris Ginsberg, Martin Simon, J. N. Neumann.

Advisory Trustees:—Messrs. B. Goldstein, Meyer C. Ginsberg, S. W. Cohen, Max Jacobs, A. H. Jassby Louis Wolfe, Sol S. Vineberg, Jr.

Representing the Temple Sisterhood:—Mrs. G. Fischel and Mrs. J. Lewinson.

Representing the Temple Brotherhood:—Clarence Michaels and Joseph Horwitz.

THE LATE SAMUEL DAVIS

THE LATE MR. SAMUEL DAVIS was born in London, England, July 4th, 1834, and died in Montreal, November 30th, 1895. He arrived in Canada in 1861, and on reaching this country made Montreal his home. He started business in a small way as a cigar manufacturer, and gradually extended until an immense business was built up, and the firm name of S. Davis & Sons became known all over the American continent. He also became the head of the tobacco firm of D. Ritchie & Co., Montreal, which later became the American Tobacco Co. of Canada, Ltd. Acquiring wealth in abundance, Mr. Davis did not keep it to himself, but was ever ready to contribute to charitable objects and worthy institutions, his generosity being limited to neither creed nor race. He subscribed to all the city charities, and was a life governor of many hospitals. He took a lively interest in the Baron de Hirsch Institute, and was amongst those who worked hardest in obtaining a grant for the founding of that colony in the West, to which so many Jewish immigrants, who have since landed on our shores, have been sent. For seventeen years, Mr. Davis was President of the Spanish and Portuguese Congregation, Montreal. In 1882, he became interested in the Reform Movement, and he was one of the founders of the Temple Emanu-El, the first reform congregation in Montreal. Mr. Davis was President of this congregation for almost ten years, and held this office at the time of his death, when it was left vacant for a period of six months as a mark of respect. He was one of the most prominent citizens of Montreal, and no man has shed more lustre on the name of Jew than did Mr. Samuel Davis. He was married to Minnie Falk, daughter of the late James Falk, and he was the father of five sons, Eugene H., Maurice E., Sir Mortimer B., Melvin H., and David T., and of two daughters.

THE LATE MR. ADOLPHE GOLDSTEIN

A TRUE patriarch in Israel, a faithful servant of the community, the late Mr. Adolphe Goldstein for over sixty years labored for the welfare of the Jews of Canada, and he left an unblemished name and a memory that will remain indelibly in the annals of Canadian Jewry. He was born in Russian Poland in 1834, and at an early age went to England, where he remained a couple of years, and then came to Canada and settled in Quebec. On the 12th of October, 1854, he was married to Rebecca Stein, of New York, and they had a family of eight children, raised in Quebec, where Mr. Goldstein was a worthy citizen and a recognized representative of the Jewish community dwelling there. In 1878, with his wife and family he removed to Montreal, where he resided continuously until his death, which took place on January 9th, 1917. Mr. Goldstein was for many years engaged in the manufacture of tobaccos and cigarettes, but he retired from business in 1894, afterwards devoting the whole of his energies to charitable work, in which he had at all times been deeply interested. The Baron de Hirsch Institute claimed the greatest part of his attention, and until his last illness he was there daily, assisting in looking after the needs of the poor. So greatly were his services appreciated by his fellow members, that he was elected to the highest offices in the Institution and was unanimously named its first Honorary President. He was a charter member of the Temple Emanu-El Congregation, the first and only Reform Jewish Congregation in Montreal, founded in 1882, and through his active co-operation saw it emerge from its early trials and develop into a strong spiritual and elevating cause. He held high office in this congregation, and was one of its Honorary Life Trustees. Mrs. Goldstein died on October 3rd 1915, but they had the good fortune to celebrate both their golden and diamond wedding anniversaries, surrounded by a family of eight children, thirty-one grandchildren, and six great grandchildren. Their greatest legacy to the community was a family of sons and daughters, whose high standard in the religious, social, professional, communal and commercial life of the country is acknowledged

NATHAN GORDON, M.A., B.C.L., MONTREAL.

NATHAN GORDON was born at New Orleans, La., U.S.A. on the 8th of December, 1882. He is the son of the Reverend S. and Mrs. Gordon of New Orleans, and was educated in the Public Schools of his home city and at the Hughes High School of Cincinnati. He graduated from the Cincinnati University in 1906 with the degree of B.A., (winning the Phi Beta Kappa Key for Scholarship), and as Rabbi from the Hebrew Union College. In September 1906 Rabbi Gordon was called to the pulpit of the Temple Emanu-El, Montreal, and he occupied this position until September 1916, when he resigned, to take up the practice of Law. During his term as Rabbi he took a leading part in the Jewish life of Montreal, and was active in all communal and welfare movements. In 1908, Rabbi Gordon was appointed instructor of Oriental Languages at McGill University, Montreal, and in 1909 he received the degree of M.A. from McGill University. Becoming interested in Law, he took the legal course at the Laval University (now University of Montreal) and he received his degree of B.C.L. in May 1916. Commencing his legal practice, Mr Gordon was first associated with Mr. Peter Bercovitch, K.C., M.P.P., but in 1919 he accepted the appointment as Prosecuting Attorney for the City of Montreal, which he held until 1921, when he resigned, to again take up private practice. Mr. Gordon was one of the speakers for the various Victory Loans, and has always, since his arrival in Montreal, been regarded as one of the foremost members of the community. He was one of those responsible for the raising of the funds for the building of the Mount Sinai Sanatorium and for the annual upkeep of that institution. He is a member of the Non-Catholic Juvenile Court Committee and is the President of the Temple Emanu-El, being elected to this high position to succeed Mr. Maxwell Goldstein. Mr. Gordon is a member of the Montefiore Club, the Montreal Reform Club, and of the Independent Order of B'nai Brith. He is married to Gertrude, daughter of Mr. and Mrs. Mark Workman, of Montreal, and has one son, Edmund Gordon.

RABBI H. J. SAMUELS, B.A., WINNIPEG

HERBERT J. SAMUEL, B.A., spiritual head of the Congregation Shaarey Zedek of Winnipeg, Manitoba, since March 1914, was born in Glasgow, Scotland, October 13th, 1882. He comes of an old Sephardic and rabbinical family who have given the Jews many famous rabbis and scholars. His great-grandfather Isaac Davidson, was the Rabbi of the Dublin Hebrew Congregation, and he was succeeded in that office by his son-in-law, Rabbi Julius Sandheim, a relative of the renowned Rabbi Akiba Eger. Another great-grandfather of Rabbi Samuel was Moses Samuel, of Liverpool, who was editor of the Anglo-Jewish periodical "The Cup of Salvation", and who translated into English a number of the writings of Moses Mendelssohn. An ancestress of Rabbi Samuel in the seventh generation was Mrs. Sarah Lyon, who was born at Ipswich in 1704. Herbert Samuel was educated at Jews' College, London, and at University College, London, where he was Hollier Hebrew Scholar in 1903. His first charge was as minister to the Hebrew Congregation at Swansea, Wales, where he officiated from 1906 to 1914, when he resigned to accept a call of the Shaarey Zedek Congregation. Since his arrival in Winnipeg, he has been very active in all branches of communal work and has identified himself with many public movements. He is held in the highest esteem by all sections of the community, and is a member of the committee of the Winnipeg Ministerial Association. In 1924, Rabbi Samuel was elected Chaplain of the Canadian Club, and in 1925 he was elected Literary Secretary of the same institution. He is prominently identified with all the communal undertakings in Winnipeg and has been at the head of the B'nai Brith Lodge for some time. Rabbi Samuel has been a staunch upholder of traditional Judaism, and in his congregation he has maintained dignity and decorum in the services. In 1909, he was married to Ida, daughter of the late Israel Neft, formerly of Kovna, Russia, and he has two daughters.

SHAARY ZEDEK CONGREGATION, WINNIPEG

THE first Jew to arrive in Winnipeg was one Reuben Goldstein in the year 1879, who brought his family here in 1880, which year also saw the advent of Philip Brown, George Frankfurter, Max Goldstine, Louis Wertheim, A. Bieber, D. Ripstein and S. A. Ripstein, men whose names later became synonymous with Jewish activities. No wonder then, that this handful, with a few others, should start a place of worship which became the progenitor of the Shaarey Zedek Congregation but which, as such, did not come into existence until a later period. Then in the year 1882, arrived those who became joint leaders in the community, T. Finkelstein, H. L. and M. Weidman, A. Lechtzier, D. Balcovske, I. Goldbloom, I. Rosen, B. Zimmerman and many others. These with their predecessors formed a congregation known as the Children of Israel, and as time rolled on were joined by new arrivals. New congregations arose, the chief of which was the Bethel in 1885, with George Frankfurter, Philip Brown and Rev. A. Benjamin as the prime movers. In 1890, the principal members of Bethel with their supporters, left the others to themselves and founded the congregation Shaarey Zedek, which became and has maintained the proud position of the premier Jewish organization west of Toronto, strong in numbers, sound financially, leader in communal activities and the recognized head of Winnipeg Jewry.

The Shaarey Zedek cemetery, situated one mile and a half north of the city limits on the main road, was acquired by the congregation twenty years ago and covers an area of ten acres, with a frontage of two hundred and sixty-five feet and a depth of sixteen hundred and fifty feet. Some years prior to this the community had used a site for cemetery purposes some six miles east of the city, but it was found, as time passed, that it became too difficult of access and the roads then had not become what they are to-day, so the Shaarey Zedek Congregation determined to purchase the present property for its own use.

The first burial which took place in the year 1896, was that of Mrs. Rae Goldsmith, a niece of the late Philip Brown, one of the Jewish pioneers.

In 1903, dissatisfaction at the existing conditions was expressed by several members, who requested what they considered ameliorations in the conduct of the services, such as an English-speaking minister, English interpolations, weekly sermons and proper decorum. These were denied and a number of the members who were amongst the founders started, with the assistance of others, the formation of a congregation which would fill their requirements and which was named the Holy Blossom, with Rev. A. Bonheim of Las Vegas, as its first minister.

In 1906 a new congregation obtained a charter similar to that of the Shaarey Zedek, under the name of "Shaarey Shomayim," and by this action gained in strength. A site (on which the present building stands) was purchased and plans prepared for the erection of a synagogue to seat 520. During that winter the contract was let and the foundation stone was laid on May 7, 1907, by G. Frankfurter, president, and the building consecrated in time for the new year by Rev. J. K. Levin,

SHAARY ZEDEK, WINNIPEG

of London, England, who had been appointed minister. Amongst the most prominent workers were the president, A. J. Bloomfield, M. H. Saunders, M. Haid, R. S. Robinson, I. Ripstein, B. Levinson, N. Goldstine, A. H. Aronovitch and H. A. Isaacs, who acted as honorary secretary from the inception. This congregation grew in numbers but gradually found the financial burden too great, and attempts were made to amalgamate with the parent congregation, but proved futile until early in 1913, at which time the Shaarey Zedek sold their property and purchased a site on which to erect a new structure. It happened that at an informal gathering of a few members from both sides, certain suggestions were made, which, when put to the two executives, brought about action causing a stay of building operations, and a series of meetings were held by representatives of both congregations, which culminated in the final amalgamation which received the approval of all the members. The name of "Shaarey Zedek" was adopted, and it was decided to use the present Synagogue (the Shaarey Shomayim), subject to enlargement. A provisional Board of Management was elected, with six members of each congregation, until a new charter could be obtained. These were H. A. Isaacs, chairman, S. Bere, parnas, with Messrs. D. Ripstein, H. L. Weidman, G. Frankfurter, I. Ripstein, M. Haid, L. Booke, M. Goldstine, M. Wodlinger, M. Steinkopf and A. W. Myers. The year prior to this, Rev. J. K. Levin, after occupying the pulpit for five years, received a call to Helena, Mont. Thus had been brought about a union which was considered by many as being altogether improbable, and tends to show what can be achieved when a few earnest men work together for the betterment of existing conditions. As soon as the amalgamation was ratified, communication was opened with the chief Rabbi (in England) for the purpose of obtaining a minister, and during the winter of that year a contract was entered into with Rev. H. J. Samuel, who was then acting as spiritual head of the congregation in Swansea, Wales, and who arrived here in March, 1914, in time to be inducted into office before Passover. By his untiring efforts to elevate the dignity of Jewry, he has secured the utmost respect of all and is held in high esteem by our Gentile friends. His activities in every phase of Jewish life are unlimited, be it congregational or educational, anything or everything for the betterment of the community.

The activities of Shaarey Zedek extend beyond its own portals. A service of intercession was held in January of each year during the war; a farewell service for Jewish volunteers under military auspices; a memorial service and unveiling of the tablets to those who fell, attended by the Lieutenant-Governor, General Ketchen, with the headquarters staff and full regimental band; and a service of thanksgiving on the termination of the war. For some years it has been the custom to hold service every Friday evening, from the fall until Passover at 8 o'clock (this being separate from the regular service), chiefly for the benefit of those who cannot attend earlier, which is limited to one hour, and at which a sermon is delivered and a goodly number are always present.

MOSES FINKELSTEIN, WINNIPEG

MOSES FINKELSTEIN, ex-alderman of the City of Winnipeg, and one of the most representative Jews in Western Canada, was born in the province of Wohlenia, Russia in 1873, the son of Tevel Finkelstein. He came to Canada with his parents and settled in Winnipeg in 1882. Mr. Finkelstein was educated in the public schools of Winnipeg and upon completing his education went into the mercantile business with his father for a number of years, and in 1900 he started out for himself in the fur business under the name of the Northwest Hide and Fur Company, which concern he still successfully operates. Mr. Finkelstein from his boyhood days has taken a keen and active interest in all undertakings pertaining to the welfare and educational movements of the Jewish community. At the age of sixteen he was elected the first President of the Jewish Literary Society. He was also elected Secretary of the Zionist Society and held this office for many years. Mr. Finkelstein was President of the Congregation Shaarey Tzedek and was Chairman of the building committee of the Winnipeg Talmud Torah and officiated in this capacity both at its completion and opening. He was the first Jew to be elected to public office in Western Canada, and in 1905, was elected alderman of the City of Winnipeg. After the end of two years he retired, and during his term was one of the most progressive members of the council. For over ten years he has been a Justice of the Peace. He has always been known as a peacemaker and can be depended on to bring harmony and amity to the community, and it was through his efforts that the two opposing factions of the Talmud Torah were brought together. He was one of the founders of the Winnipeg Lodge, I.O.B.B., and is an active member of it. In 1890 he was married to Sarah Rosen, eldest daughter of Mr. and Mrs. Isaac Rosen of Winnipeg, and he has three sons and two daughters. His eldest son, Dr. Manly Finkelstein has a distinguished medical record and is the City Pathologist.

M. S. WEIDMAN, WINNIPEG

MORDECAI S. WEIDMAN, Vice-President of Weidman Brothers, Limited, was born in Orli, Grodno, Russian Poland, on November 15th, 1865, the son of Benjamin and Rachel (Kirshner) Weidman. He received his education at the Yeshiva of Bialystock, Poland. He arrived in Winnipeg in May, 1882, with his parents and brothers, being amongst the Jewish pioneers of that district. From 1884 to 1887, he farmed near Moosomin, Saskatchewan. He returned to Winnipeg, and with his brother organized a wholesale grocery firm, under the name of Weidman Brothers, Limited, of which concern he is Vice-President, and which is one of the largest wholesale concerns of its kind in Western Canada. Mr. Weidman has always been very active in all campaigns to raise funds for Jewish communal work and philanthropic undertakings in the City of Winnipeg, and he devotes much time to the various institutions. He takes a keen interest in the welfare of the Jewish youth, and was prominently identified in the building up of the local Young Men's Hebrew Association, being the first President of this institution, which he was instrumental in organizing in 1892. Mr. Weidman has been the National Director of the Jewish Consumptive Relief of Denver, Col., for the past twenty years. He is an ardent Zionist and is a member of the Winnipeg Zionist Council. In 1923, Mr. Weidman accompanied by his brother, Mr. H. L. Weidman, visited Palestine. They made an exhaustive study of conditions there, an account of which on their return to Canada they published in book form at the request of their many friends. Mr. Weidman was instrumental in organizing the Shaarey Zedec Congregation of Winnipeg, and has been a member since its inception. He was Parnass of the Congregation for two years. On November 4th, 1885, Mr. Weidman was married at Winnipeg, to Bessie, daughter of Mr. and Mrs. Abraham Shragge, and they have three sons, Abraham E., John P., and Sydney H., and four daughters Anne, Sara M., Etta G., and Isobel.

RABBI JACOB GORDON, TORONTO

RABBI JACOB GORDON, of the Beth Medrash Hagodel, Goel Zedek, Zemak Zedek, Shearith Israel, Kneseth Israel, Yavna Zionist, and other smaller synagogues, was born in Danilovitz, Russia, in September 1877, the son of Leib and Yita Braina (Chodosh) Gordon. He was educated at the Rabbinical Schools of Volozhin, Minsk, and Kovno, and received his Rabbinical degrees in 1896. In 1904 he came to Toronto, where he has since remained, taking a leading part in the Jewish community. He was the organizer of the Hebrew Free School, for which he raised $90,000.00 and of the Simcoe St. Talmud Torah, and was the first in America to teach the Talmud in Hebrew (which has proven very successful). He is a life-long Zionist and one of the leaders of the Mizrachi Zionist Society. In 1905-06 when Jewish refugees were coming into Canada in large numbers from European Countries, many of these people were found daily eating at Rabbi Gordon's table, and he was untiring in his efforts to place them in positions where they could help themselves. Rabbi Gordon is so highly regarded, that among a large number of the Toronto community, it is a common thing for him to act as judge or arbitrator, and even in outside communities he is regarded as the authority on religious questions. In 1919, before the Canadian Jewish Congress in Montreal, he delivered an address advocating a five-day working week, which attracted large and favorable notice from the Press. His reputation as a great Hebrew orator is such that whenever he delivers an address, either in Canada or the United States, the synagogue is filled to capacity. He is the author of "Minchas Jacob" (printed in Safad, Palestine); "Dovev Safsae Yeshanim" (The Lips of the Dead are Speaking), which is a valuable tribute to Spiritualism; and "Neziruth min Habosor," (On Vegetarianism). He also contributed largely to the "Hebrew Encyclopædia" (Azar Israel). In March 1900, Rabbi Gordon married Lifshe Sobel, daughter of Abraham S. Sobel, and he has two sons, Wilfred and Daniel, and two daughters, Mrs. (Rabbi) M. A. Mandelbaum and Miss Fannie Gordon.

CONGREGATION GOEL TZEDEC, TORONTO

IN 1883, a number of Jews of Russian extraction wishing to start a congregation where the ritual to which they were accustomed would be followed, held a meeting and organized the Goel Tzedec Congregation. Amongst the founders of this congregation were:—the late Abraham Cohen, the late David Gurofsky, the late S. Danielson, the late Mr. Robinson, the late Mr. Wood, the late Jacob Draimin, the late H. Albert, the late L. Levine, Mr. L. Levinsky, the late Mr. Garfunkel, Mr. N. Smith, and others. At a meeting held on October 21st, 1883, the following were elected the first officers:— Pres., Jacob Draimin; Parnass, Abraham Cohen; Gabbai, H. Albert; Secretary, Isaac Mintz; and Trustees, J. Rosen, Wolf Cohen and L. Levine.

The congregation first met for worship in a rented room on Richmond Street, where they remained for two years. Services on the holy days, however, were held at Temperance Hall, when tickets were sold for seats, and preference was always given to members, allowing them to have the seats in the front of the hall.

In 1884, the congregation purchased an old church on the corner of University Avenue and Elm Street, for the sum of $4,100.00. The building was remodelled and altered to fulfil the requirements of the congregation, and when completed was dedicated by the Rev. Dr. Marks, of Montreal. For over twenty years they worshipped in this building and some of the presiding officers during that period were; the late J. Draimin, the late Abraham Cohen, the late B. Yanover, the late W. Simon, the late L. Taube, Mr. J. Bachrack (president for four years), Mr. H. Albert, and Mr. L. Levinsky, who was president for six years.

On Feb. 17th, 1884, the Rev. B. Leibowitz was appointed the first minister of the congregation, but he resigned on 20th of July of the same year. The Rev. S. L. Kantor was then elected for a year, and the congregation allowed him in addition to his salary, a ton and a half of coal, providing he would teach the members' children at his house. He was succeeded by the Rev. Mr. Cohen,

In 1892, Rabbi Lasker was appointed minister and acted as spiritual head for some time.

The Rev. Mr. Eidelman, was elected Chazan in 1893, and he was succeeded by the Rev. Mr. Levingson who was followed by the Rev. Mr. Adelman.

On June 27th, 1886, as a reward for valuable services rendered to the congregation, Messrs. W. Simon, D. Gurofsky, H. Albert, H. Danielson, and A. Cohen were appointed life trustees.

The congregation had their own butcher who looked after their needs and provided them with Kosher meat. In 1884, a resolution was passed that all members who did not buy their meat from this butcher would be expelled from the congregation, and this rule was later changed, the members being made to pay $6.00 per annum extra for their dues, if they did not buy from the designated butcher.

In 1896, Mr. L. Levinsky and Mr. P. Levy brought up the suggestion of organizing a Talmud Torah for the children, but this was not carried out, owing to lack of support.

The congregation flourished and grew very rapidly. The quarters they occupied became inadequate for their needs, and in 1905, during the Presidency of Mr. A. Andrews, the site of the present synagogue was purchased for the sum of $6,000.00. The total funds of the congregation at that time were only $1,800.00 Many donations were received by the members and the erection of the building was immediately begun. Elections for the Building Committee were held, resulting as follows:— A. Andrews, Chairman; I Cooper, Secty.; Paul Levi, Treasurer and L. Levinsky, G. Solway, H. Stein, I. Brodey, J. Yanover, the late J. Draimin, N. Brenner, M. Antipitsky, J. Cadesky, M. Lavine, P. James, M. Cohen, S. Schwartz, L. Gurofsky, M. Levinsky, S. Weber, and M. L. Willinsky.

UNIVERSITY AVENUE SYNAGOGUE

The building was erected by Symons & Rae, the architectural design being carried out in a combination of the Norman and Renaissance period. The facade of the interior is similar to that of the Westminster Roman Catholic Cathedral, of London, Eng. Above the ark, directly over the everlasting light, there is a beautiful stained glass, which was donated at the time of the erection by one of the members. The building has a seating capacity of twelve hundred, and is the largest synagogue in Toronto. In the basement of the building are situated the vestry chambers, with movable partitions which are divided into class rooms for Sunday School purposes. The rooms are also used for banquets, weddings, dances, etc. There is also a Beth Medrosh in the basement, which is fitted out as a Shool, and where young High School boys have formed a Junior synagogue, conducting their own services on Saturday mornings.

The corner stone of the synagogue was laid by Mr. Isaac Brodey, on April 29th, 1906, with all the accompanying formalitites.

The late Mr. Gordon officiated as minister for a number of years, and in 1917 the congregation called Rabbi Price to the pulpit. He acted as spiritual head for about three years, being the first English-speaking Rabbi of the congregation. On his departure, he was succeeded by Rabbi Julius Siegel. Rabbi Jacob Gordon was engaged by the congregation as Senior Rabbi, and has been connected with it ever since his arrival in Toronto in 1904.

The present membership of the congregation is about three hundred.

The congregation first bought land at Agincourt to be used as a cemetery, and in 1922, also bought land on

Jones Avenue. The officers of the Hevrah Kedishah are:—Pres., I. Brodey; Vice-Pres., S. Weber; Treasurer, M. H. Keyfitz; and Sec., H. Rosenthal. Mr. I. Brodey was the organizer of this body, and has been President of it for over twenty-five years. The only other President was the late Mr. J. Draimin. The late Mr. J. Stein was Vice-President for many years.

The following gentlemen have been President of this congregation since the erection of the present synagogue; the late Mr. Levy, Mr. D. Lavine, Mr. M. Gelber, Mr. E. Pullan, Mr. L. Gelber, Mr. I. Cooper, Mr. A. Andrews, and Mr. P. James.

The present officers of the congregation are:—Pres. I. Brodey; Vice-Pres., Harry Pullan; Treas., J. Samuels; Rec. Sec., J. Oelbaum; Parnass, M. Cohen; Gabbai, L. Levinsky; Board of Governors, S. Hollinger, J. Samuels, M. Stein, Harry Rosenthal, M. Barrett, D. Lavine, Dr. M. Pivnick, I. Markus, M. Weinstock, J. Harris, J. Becker, H. Herman, E. Pullan, M. Gelber, L. Gelber, G. Solway, N. Smith, H. M. Smith, D. Levinne, S. Weber, L. Fink.

Through the efforts of Rabbi Julius Siegel, the Junior League of the Goel Tzedec Congregation was formed in March, 1924. The aims of the League as outlined in its Constitution are to bring the youth in closer contact with the synagogue, and to promote literary, social and communal work. During its first year of existence, the Junior League's program included several outstanding speakers, debates, dances, musicales and open discussions. The officers for the term 1924-1925 are;—President, Herbert J. Weiss; 1st Vice-President, Miss Gittel Siegal; 2nd Vice-President Louis H. James; Rec. Sec'y, George Cooper; Corresp. Sec'y, Miss Ruth Schwartz; Treasurer, Samuel Keyfetz; Exec., Miss Charlotte Andrews and Herman C. Bennett.

In the fall of 1921, the activities of Goel Tzedec Congregation were supplemented by the formation of a Young People's League, largely at the instigation of Rabbi Siegel, who was at that time the spiritual head of the Synagogue. Associated with Rabbi Siegel were:— H. M. Smith, J. M. Gordon, B.A., Miss Rivka Levy, Miss Mary Lavine, and Miss Bella Sher. Mr. J. M. Gordon was elected the first president of the League, and in addition to the holding of general meetings bi-weekly, there were formed dramatic, literary, religious training, debating, social and athletic circles, which met regularly at the call of their respective chairmen. Since its formation, the Young People's League has attained, admirably, its object of making a forum where the young people of the Congregation could meet and discuss literary, ethical, and religious subjects of importance. To assist in this work the Board of Trustees of the Synagogue completely re-modelled the Vestry Hall and installed an adequate stage platform for the presentation of amateur plays. Since its inception the Young People's League has been addressed on timely subjects by such well known leaders of the community as Judge Mott, Prof. A. T. DeLury, Alderman Mrs. Sidney Small, Prof. C. A. Chant, and Prof. W. A. Irwin. The past presidents of the League are;—J. M. Gordon, B.A., Murray Keyfetz, Dr. J. H. Griss, and J. D. Pearlstein, B.A.

L. GELBER, TORONTO

LOUIS GELBER, a prominent resident and active communal worker of Toronto, was born in Brzezany Galicia, November 8th, 1878, the son of Nathan Gelber of that city. He was educated in the schools of his native city, and came to Canada when a young man, in 1896. He started his commercial career in the clothing trade, and with his brother, Mr. Moses Gelber, established a clothing business in Toronto, which they operated for about twenty-five years. Some years ago, in partnership with his brother, he entered into the woollen business, under the name of Gelber Bros., with which he is still actively engaged. This business has greatly developed, and is today one of the largest firms of woollen wholesalers in Canada. Always interested in the welfare of his co-religionists, Mr. Gelber devotes much time and energy to communal undertakings and charitable work in Toronto, and is a member of the Board of the Federation of Jewish Philanthropies of Toronto. One of his greatest communal interests is the Toronto Hebrew Free Loan Association, Gamilath Chasodim, of which he is a very active member, at present being a director. His great ambition in this is to help lessen the hardships of the poor and needy, in giving them the opportunity of helping themselves. He is also deeply interested in the religious education of the Jewish young, and is an active worker for the new Talmud Torah and Jewish centre of Toronto. Mr. Gelber is an ardent supporter of the Zionist movement. He is one of the founders, and was instrumental in the building of the Chestnut Street and Bay Street Synagogues, Toronto, and is a member of the University Avenue Synagogue, of which he was President for two years. He is at present a member of the Board of Governors of that congregation. Mr. Gelber is a member of the Canadian Manufacturers' Association; Toronto Board of Trade; Mt. Sinai Lodge, A.F. & A.M.; I.O.F.; I.O.B.B.; Empire Club; and Primrose Club. He is married to Sarah Leah Morris, daughter of M. L. Morris of Montreal, and has four sons, Lionel, Marvin, Arthur and Sholom, and one daughter, Miss Sylvia Gelber.

E. PULLAN, TORONTO

ELIAS PULLAN, one of the most prominent Jewish citizens of Toronto, was born at Telz, province of Kovno, Lithuania, on July 3rd, 1865, the son of Bernard and the late Molly Pullan of Ottawa. He received his education in his home community, and in 1885 came to Canada, settling first in Toronto, where he established the waste paper and scrap business, which he still conducts, and which is the largest business of its kind in Canada. He is President, Capital Paper Stock Co., Ottawa, and President, Capital Investments Ltd., Toronto. In 1898, he removed to Ottawa, where he remained until 1904, in which year he returned to Toronto, where he has since resided. In 1890, Mr. Pullan was married to Bertha, daughter of Abraham Helner, and he has four sons, Harry, Joel, Emanuel and Gordon, and six daughters, Martha (Mrs. A. Brown), Dorothy (Mrs. M. Brenner), Bessie (Mrs. J. Rashkofsky), Rita (Mrs. J. Wecksler), and the Misses Jennie and Helen Pullan. Mr. Pullan has always been one of the most active communal workers in Canada. He organized and was first President of the Rideau Street Synagogue, Ottawa, and was the organizer and first President of the first Zionist Society of Ottawa. He joined the Goel Tzedek Congregation in 1886, before the University Avenue Synagogue was erected, and he has held, at various times, the positions of President, Treasurer and Parnass. He has always maintained a very active interest in connection with this congregation, and he is a life trustee. He was one of the founders and first President of the Simcoe Street Talmud Torah, and was Treasurer of the Building Committee of the new Hebrew Free School, and during the absence of Mr. Gelber, acted as Chairman of the Committee. He succeeded Mr. Edmund Scheuer as President of the Federation of Jewish Philanthropies, and after holding this office for two years, was appointed Vice-President. He was one of the first members of the B'nai Zion Society, and started the Toronto Zionist Society Limited, which he organized for the purpose of securing a home in Toronto for the Zionist Organization. Mr. Pullan is a member of the I.O.B.B.

LOUIS LEVINSKY, TORONTO

LOUIS LEVINSKY was born in Poland in 1862, the son of the late Alexander and Gertrude Levinsky.
He came to Canada in 1882, and settled in Toronto at the time when the city had a population of about thirty-five Jewish families. In conjunction with five others Mr. Levinsky attended a place of worship, and largely through his indefatigable efforts and zeal, developed this into the present Goel Tzedec Synagogue on University Avenue. In appreciation of his services as President and as one of the Elders, he has upon various occasions been presented with certificates of appreciation and a Loving Cup. His efforts have largely been concentrated upon the fulfilment of the Zionist Movement ideal, "Palestine as a Homeland for the Jews," and he is one of the first members of the Canadian Zionist Movement. Mr. Levinsky was one of the most active workers in the establishment of a Talmud Torah as a centre of Jewish education and ideals. The physical upbuilding of Jewish youth and their recreation is part of Mr. Levinsky's plan, and the new Talmud Torah building with its gymnasium, recreation rooms, library, as well as its classrooms and assembly hall, has been made a reality through his untiring and ceaseless efforts in making appeals and securing the co-operation of Jewish men and women as enthusiastic and high-spirited as himself. Mr. Levinsky is a successful and self-made business man. Starting his business career on such small capital as he was able to earn, he developed to his present position as one of the senior partners of the Cooper Cap Company, a manufacturing concern well known and highly respected throughout the Dominion of Canada. In 1881 he was married to Dora Gurofsky, whose gentleness and understanding has helped him materially and spiritually to establish a record for "Honesty in business" and "Service to Mankind." He is the father of four sons and one daughter. In 1888, Mr. Levinsky joined the Masonic Order. Many years ago he was selected with two other representative Jewish citizens, Mr. Edmund Scheuer and Mr. J. Cohen to officiate in the capacity of Justice of the Peace, which office he has since faithfully filled in the City of Toronto.

THE LATE MR. NATHAN KEYFITZ

NATHAN KEYFITZ, resident of Toronto for many years, was born in Moghileff, Russia in 1835, and died in 1912. He was for many years Crown Rabbi in the cities of Rogatchev and Moghileff. He was at one time in charge of a Government school in Russia, and at another time he was in charge of charitable institutions in St. Petersburg, founded by the late Baron David Gintzburg. At the cost of much diligence and determination Mr. Keyfitz attained a high degree of scholarship, being graduate of a College of Land Surveyors, but gave up this profession and was appointed by the government to the principalship of a large school in his native city. He remained at the head of this and other schools for a number of years and was the official representative of the Jewish community in the government of that province. His appointment included the Registership of births, marriages, etc., and was only given to the most honorable Jew of the district. He came to Canada as a man of middle age and in Toronto lived a life of retirement, honored and respected by all. Of ordinary means, he found many ways to do work of charity and his numerous and helpful intercessions on behalf of Jewish immigrants in their relation to the Russian Consul in Canada, are remembered by many who, immigrants then, are today well-to-do Jewish citizens of Canada. A lover of truth and of justice, a courteous, kindly unaffected doer of good in a way which only his intimates knew; with a profundity of thought that was at once refreshing and invigorating; an omniverous reader on worldly and Jewish subjects; an orthodox Jew in the best sense of the word, yet a gentleman who regarded with tolerance all who were not in agreement with his views as long as they were honest, such a man was Nathan Keyfitz. Mr. Keyfitz's death occurred shortly after the celebration of his golden wedding and he left four sons, Dr. Moses Keyfitz, Russia; Mark Keyfitz, Toronto; Arthur Keyfitz, Montreal; Samuel Keyfitz, Port McNicholl; and four daughters, Mrs. E. Wolfsohn, Winnipeg; Mrs. J. Andrews, Toronto; Mrs. D. Levinne, Toronto; and Mrs. (Dr.) Pivnick, Toronto.

S. WEBER, TORONTO

SAMUEL WEBER was born in Vilna, Russia, on April 2nd, 1875, the son the the late Pinchus Weber.

He received a very thorough Hebrew education in Russia and this was supplemented at public schools on his arrival in America. He arrived in New York when thirteen years of age and remained there in business for eleven years. On September 15th, 1891, he was married in New York, and he has six sons, David, Ben, Abe, Henry, Hirsch and Ralph Weber, and two daughters, Annie (Mrs. J. Peikes of New York), and Bessie (Mrs. Tugenhaught). In 1899, Mr. Weber moved to Toronto, where he has since resided. He joined the Goel Tzedec Synagogue on his arrival, and has been an active member of this congregation ever since; at the present time being a member of the Board of Governors. In 1906, at the time the synagogue on University Avenue was built, Mr. Weber was a member of the Building Committee. He has taken a very keen interest and prominent part in communal undertakings and welfare work in Toronto. He has organized and been President ever since its inception, of the Toronto Hebrew Burial Society (Chesed Shel Emes). Mr. Weber gave the Burial Society the property used as a cemetery, and both he and his wife have taken such an interest in and devoted so much time to this Society, that they have come to look upon it as their own special care, naturally much to its benefit. The purpose of the Society is to provide proper Jewish burial to those who cannot afford to pay the usual cost of interring their dead. Mr. Weber was also prominently identified with the Simcoe Street Talmud Torah, which was the first Talmud Torah to be established in Toronto, and which owes its inception largely to his indefatigable efforts in its behalf. He was on the Building Committee of the Toronto Hebrew Free School on Brunswick Avenue. The religious education of the Jewish youth has always been one of his most active undertakings. He is an active Zionist and is particularly interested in charitable institutions in Palestine. Since his arrival in Toronto Mr. Weber has been engaged in the woollen industry, in which business he is assisted by his sons.

Photo by Milne

M. BRODY, TORONTO

MOSES BRODY was born in Galicia, March 25th, 1857, the son of the late Benjamin and Tillie (Rosenblitt) Brody. He received his education in Galicia, where he also acquired a thorough knowlege of Jewish history and religion. He came to Canada in 1891, and settled in Toronto, where he became prominently identified with the congregation, "Shomrai Shabbas". Mr. Brody entered into the real estate business in this city, and continued in this for a number of years. From the time of his arrival in Toronto up to the present, he has officiated as Chazan at the Shomrai Shabbas synagogue, and he has at all times rendered his services free of charge. He has done this for thirty-three years, and much of the growth of the congregation can be ascribed to his untiring efforts in its behalf. For eight years, Mr. Brody was president of this congregation, and it was during his term as such that the synagogue on Chestnut Street was erected. He is active in all communal work, and has been a member of the Federation of Jewish Philanthropies since its inception. He is an ardent Zionist, and is an active supporter of the Old Folks' Home, and of the new Talmud Torah. Mr. Brody devotes much of his time to charitable and philanthropic work, and his support has always proven a tower of strength where offered. He was married in 1880, in Galicia, to Esther Sarah, daughter of Jacob David Greisman, who died in Toronto in 1902, and he later married a sister of his former wife, Miss Hannah Greisman. He has six sons, Harry, Louis Judah, William and Jacob David of Toronto, and Benjamin and Herzl (Nelson) of Windsor, Ontario; and six daughters, Tillie (Mrs. S. Baum of Windsor), Rosie (Mrs. Alter), Annie (Mrs. Stone), and the Misses Sarah, Bessie and Pearl Brody, all of Toronto. Mr. Brody's son-in-law and sons are amongst the most highly respected residents of Windsor, Ont. His son-in-law, Mr. Samuel Baum, served for some years as alderman in Windsor. Although they are non-residents, they have never dropped their support to the various Toronto Jewish charities.

CHESTNUT STREET SYNAGOGUE, TORONTO

IN 1888, a number of gentlemen of Austrian origin, who wished to attend a synagogue where the ritual of the Austrian Jews would be followed, decided to form a congregation. Among those gentlemen were;- the late Selig Greisman, the late Rev. I. Halpern, the late Louis Shumer, the late Benjamin Tugenthaft, Mr. Henry Greisman, Mr. Samuel Korn, Mr. Jacob Spring, Mr. David Zipper, Mr. Joseph Greisman, Mr. Zigmond Brody, and Mr. Napthali Tugenthaft. A charter was applied for, and the congregation "Shomrai Shabbas" was thus formed.

They first held services in a small room at No. 61 Chestnut Street, and after a few months, as the membership increased, they rented larger quarters at 127 Queen Street West. The congregation prospered, and the membership increased in a satisfactory manner, and in 1898, the congregation purchased property at 109-111 Chestnut Street. Under the supervision, and largely through the efforts of Mr. Henry Greisman, this property was remodelled and enlarged to meet their requirements and to give sufficient seating capacity to the increasing number of Jews of Austrian birth, who were arriving in Toronto at that time.

The building was dedicated in 1900. Mr. Moses Brody was President at the time of the dedication, and the trustees at that time were;- the late Mr. Leo Gelber, the late B. Tugenthaft, the late Wm. Fox, Chas. Scher, Jacob Spring, Henry Greisman, Joseph Greisman, Hyman Greisman, Benjamin Kurtz, and L. Birenbaum. The secretary at this time was Mr. Joel Gelber. The corner-stone was laid by the late Mr. Leo Gelber, who was one of the most active members of the congregation.

The first minister of the congregation was the late Rev. Mr. Halpern, who officiated for a short time. He was succeeded as Chazan by Mr. Moses Brody, who for over thirty-three years donated his services gratuitously to the congregation. Mr. Brody still officiates as Chazan. In 1900, the congregation appointed Rabbi Weinreb as minister, and brought him from Galicia for this purpose. Rabbi Weinreb remained with the congregation for six years, when he left to become Rabbi of the Terauley Street Synagogue.

CHESTNUT STREET SYNAGOGUE

In 1897, ground was purchased for a cemetery. An interesting feature about this congregation is the fact that for the first time in America, the seats were sold outright to the members. This plan has since been adopted by many large congregations.

The first President of the congregation was the late Mr. Selig Greisman, and he was succeeded in this office by Mr. Moses Brody, who was President for eight years. Mr. Henry Greisman was also President for eight years, and was succeeded by the late Mr. Samuel Shapiro. He, in turn, was succeeded by Joseph Rumm, who was followed by Louis Birenbaum and later by Joseph Spring. The present President is Mr. Hyman Schwartz. The late Mr. Leo Gelber was Treasurer, and the late Mr. Wm. Lunenfeld was Vice-President during the Presidency of Mr. Brody, and Mr. Michael Stone was Vice-President during the term of Mr. Henry Greisman. Mr. Simon Rabinovitch was Treasurer of the congregation for over fifteen years, and rendered invaluable service.

In 1906, a faction arose, who decided to sever their connection and form a new congregation. As the members who wished to leave the parent body were seat owners, it was necessary for the congregation to buy back their seats, and this was done through the generosity and efforts of the other members of the congregation led by Mr. Henry Greisman. The seceding members organized the Terauley Street synagogue.

Largely through the devoted interests of the Greisman family, the "Shomrai Shabbas" congregation has always been in a flourishing financial condition, and in 1923, over $4,000.00 was spent in decorating and renovating the interior. The membership of the congregation at the present time is in the neighborhood of one hundred, and the loyalty and enthusiasm which has always been shown by the members, is to-day as marked as ever.

The present officers of the congregation are;- Hyman Schwartz, President; Joseph Lunenfeld, Vice-President; Jacob Halpern, Treasurer; Joel Wunch, Fin. Secretary; Joseph Greisman, Recording Secretary; Michael Greisman, Isaac Stone, B. Stone, D. Harnick, S. Heller, Isaac Krugel, Harry Krugel, Trustees.

McCAUL STREET SYNAGOGUE, TORONTO

Beth Medrosh Hagodel Chevra Thillum

IN the year 1887, the above synagogue was established under the name of "Chevra Thillum", by the late Charles Moishe Barash and Chaim Wilder and others on a site at the corner of Richmond and York Streets. These were the organizers and the first officials of the congregation which started with a very small membership.

In 1892, on account of increased membership, the organization moved to larger premises a few doors east, where they changed their name to "Beth Shmoole". The congregation retained this name for one year, and then resumed its old name of "Chevra Thillum". The officials for the first three years were S. Levinter, President; Isaac Cohen, Parnas and Gabay.

In 1895, the late Yankel Mehr became President; Chaim Wilder, Parnas; and the late Israel Gebirtig, Gabay. These officials remained in office for three years. In 1903, Samuel Singer became President; the late Yankel Mehr, Parnas; Chaim Wilder, Gabay; and the late K. L. Shapiro, Treasurer. In 1904, the late Harris Cohen became President; the late Yehuda Laib Gordon, Parnas; Moishe Clyman, Gabay; and S. Levinter, Treasurer.

In 1905, Samuel Singer became President, and the incorporation under the new name of "Beth Medrosh Hagodel Chevra Thillum" was secured. Their present home on McCaul Street was purchased, and after all the necessary alterations had been made, as the building had originally been a church, possession was taken of same and services were carried on in the new synagogue. The other officers at that time were:—Chaim Wilder, Parnas; Abraham Broudy, Gabay; Isaac Taylor, Treasurer; and Isaac Granatstein, Secretary.

The first Board of Trustees of the Beth Medrosh Hagodel Chevra Thillum Congregation were:—M. Gebirtig, H. Clavir, J. Pullan, J. Pearlman, M. Simon, M. Spiegal, J. Brozofsky, D. Brozofsky, K. Jacobowitz. It was through the efforts of Mr. M. Gebirtig, Mr. I. Taylor, the late Mr. Harris Cohen, the late Mr. Yankel Mehr and the late Mr. K. L. Shapiro, that the beautiful edifice on McCaul Street was purchased and finally opened.

In 1906, the officers of the year were:—Samuel Singer, President; M. D. Pullan, Parnas; the late Yankov Bachrack, Gabay; and the late Mr. Goodman, Treasurer. In 1907, the late Harris Cohen was President; Mr. M. D. Pullan, Parnas; the late Mr. Bachrack, Gabay; and Mr. S. Levinter, Treasurer. In 1908, Mr. L. Singer became President; Mr. M. D. Pullan, Parnas; Mr. Yankel Besvinick, Gabay; and Mr. I. Taylor, Treasurer. These officers remained in office for three years.

In 1911, Mr. M. Gebirtig became President; Mr. D. Finkelstein, Parnas; Mr. Brownstein, Gabay; and Yankel Mehr, Treasurer. In 1912, Mr. M. Gebirtig remained as President; Mr. D. Finkelstein, Parnas; Mr. Brownstein, Gabay; and the late Mr. Isaac Greisman, Treasurer. In 1913, Mr. M. Gebirtig was again elected President; Mr. D. Finkelstein, Parnas; Mr. Yankel Besvinick, Gabay; and the late Mr. Isaac Greisman, Treasurer. In 1914, Mr. M. Gebirtig was elected for his fourth term as President; Mr. D. Finkelstein, Parnas; Mr. Yankel Besvinick, Gabay; and the late Mr. Isaac Greisman, Treasurer.

For the years 1915 and 1916, the late Mr. K. L. Shapiro was President; the late Mr. Gordon was Parnas; Mr. Isaac Cohen, Gabay; and the late Mr. Isaac Greisman, Treasurer. During 1917 and 1918, Mr. Morris Simon was the President; Mr. Wurtzel, Parnas; Mr. B. Brownstein, Gabay; and Mr. S. Levinter, Treasurer.

McCAUL STREET SYNAGOGUE

In the years 1919 and 1920, Mr. J. M. Pullan was President; Mr. D. Finkelstein, Parnas; Mr. Yankel Besvinick, Gabay; and Mr. S. Levinter, Treasurer. In 1921, Mr. S. Singer became President; Mr. H. Clayman, Vice-President; Mr. D. Finkelstein, Parnas; Mr. E. Lipshitz, Gabay; and Mr. S. Levinter, Treasurer. In 1922, Mr. J. M. Pullan was elected President; Mr. H. Clayman, Vice-President; Mr. D. Finkelstein, Parnas; Mr. E. Lipshitz, Gabay; and Mr. S. Levinter, Treasurer. In 1923, Mr. M. Simon became President; Mr. Isadore Levinter, Vice-President; Mr. D. Finkelstein, Parnas; Mr. E. Lipshitz, Gabay; and Mr. S. Levinter, Treasurer.

In 1923, a Board of Finance was established, with Mr. Max Clavir as Chairman.

In 1924, Mr. Max Clavir was elected President; Mr. Isadore Levinter, Vice-President; Mr. Sossinsky, Parnas; Mr. J. Siegel, Gabay; and Mr. M. Alter, Treasurer. Mr. Harry Clayman was Chairman of the Board of Finance.

In 1925, Mr. Max Clavir was re-elected as President; Mr. M. B. Palter, Vice-President; Mr. L. Sossinsky, Parnas; Mr. J. Siegel, Gabay; Mr. S. Levinter, Treasurer; and Mr. M. Axler was elected Chairman of the Board of Finance.

In 1913, largely through the efforts of Mr. M. B. Clavir, as Gabay of the Chevra Kedisha, a chapel was established on the present cemetery of the McCaul Street Synagogue, and in 1916 an addition to the cemetery was purchased.

HEBREW MEN OF ENGLAND CONGREGATION
SPADINA AVENUE, TORONTO

IN the fall of the year 1909, a group of Jewish young men who had either been born or had lived for some time in England and who were desirous of worshipping in the manner prevailing in England, came together and organized themselves as a Congregation with the main purpose of having a synagogue where the form of prayer and manner of worship would be in the manner adopted by Orthodox Jewry in England. The Congregation was first organized on September 1st in that year, and among the names of the founders are the following:— A. Charvinsky, R. Greenberg, L. Abramovitz, M. Chait, M. Leon, H. Brand, F. Pinkovich, I. Jacobson, S. Naimen and J. Fine.

The Congregation first occupied a large house on Simcoe Street, and in 1921 they purchased a property on Spadina Avenue, which had formerly been a church. After making all the necessary renovations and decorations, this building was opened as a synagogue with the accustomed ceremony and the Congregation has since worshipped in it.

In 1916 a Ladies' Auxiliary composed of the wives of the members of the Congregation was formed with the object in view of dispensing charity wherever necessary and of doing beneficial work in the Congregation as needed from time to time. The Auxiliary is also supposed to look after the decorations of the synagogue and other matters of a similar nature.

Under the Ladies' Auxiliary the Congregation has also organized a religious school which is operated under the auspices and in conjunction with the Sisterhood of the Holy Blossom Synagogue. The purpose of this school is to teach Biblical History, Post-Biblical History and other Jewish subjects, and it is open to the children of all Jewish people in the City of Toronto. Mr. Edmund Scheuer is the Principal.

SPADINA AVENUE SYNAGOGUE

The first President of the Men of England Congregation was Mr. A. Charvinsky, who occupied the chair from 1909 to 1910. The succeeding Presidents have been:—L. Abromovitz, 1911; S. Goldenberg, 1912-1913; R. Greenberg and L. Paul, 1914; L. Abromovitz, 1915-1922; and S. M. Ross, 1923-4-5.

The cemetery of the congregation is situated at North Yonge Street, Toronto, and Mr. M. Bloomstein is the present Gabay of the Chevra Kedishah.

The synagogue has a seating capacity of about one thousand, with a Beth Medrosh at the back of the main building; also business office, check room and large dance hall and dining room, which are used for weddings, banquets, and dances. The dance hall can accommodate approximately one thousand people.

The membership at the present time is about three hundred.

The present officers, who by their energy have relieved the Congregation from a serious financial crisis and to whom great credit is due for the present sound financial and moral condition of the Congregation, are: S. M. Ross, President; N. Muscovitch, Vice-President; L. Back, Treasurer; I. Hornick, Financial Secretary; J. Fine, Recording Secretary; J. Rose & D. Gollom, Wardens; and N. Sivitz, S. Clapham and C. H. Taube, Trustees.

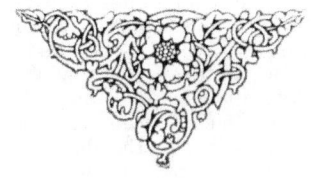

WM. DIAMOND, EDMONTON

WILLIAM DIAMOND, one of the first Jews to settle in the Prairie Provinces, and one of the most highly respected citizens of Edmonton, was born in Wilna, Russian Poland, on January 1st, 1863, the son of the late Isaac Diamond. He received his education in Poland, and went to New York in 1888. In 1892, he moved to Calgary, where his brother Jacob, the first Jewish settler in Alberta, was located. Calgary had, at that time, a population of less than three thousand souls. He started a clothing business on a small scale, and conducted this until 1906 when he moved to Edmonton, where a branch of his business had been opened some years previously under the management of Mr. Charles Benjamin. Mr. Diamond has since resided in Edmonton, but retains his interest in the Calgary store, which today is the largest clothing business in the Prairie Provinces, and which for the past eighteen years, has been under the management of Mr. Charles Benjamin. Mr. Diamond is justly regarded as the outstanding Jew of Alberta. He is the leader of all communal undertakings in his locality, irrespective of race or creed. Mr. Diamond donated the site and supervised the building of the synagogue in Edmonton, and he has been President of the congregation ever since its formation. He is a past officer of the Edmonton Lodge, Independent Order B'nai Brith, and his assistance and advice is sought in all undertakings tendering to the betterment of the community. He is an ardent Zionist, and takes a deep and active interest in this movement. Edmonton is held up as an example of what a united community can do in the way of raising funds for all worth-while causes, and no one is more responsible for the results they have accomplished, than William Diamond. He has the faculty of selecting the right assistants in his philanthropic work, and he himself sets an example that is an inspiration to leaders in other communities. In March 1892, he was married to Miss Liza Margolis of Minsk, Russia, and he has one daughter, Miss Ruth Diamond.

THE EDMONTON HEBREW CONGREGATION

A HISTORY of the Hebrew Association or for that matter the Jewish Community of Edmonton might well answer as a biography of its venerable founder, leader and president, William Diamond, a man loved and respected by all who know him—Jew or Gentile.

Nearly forty years ago, William Diamond first set foot in Alberta and after a successful business career in Calgary where he founded and still controls one of the leading establishments of its kind in the West, The Wm. Diamond Clothing Company, he came to Edmonton in 1916 to take over a branch of his business that he had established here some years before. Prior to Mr. Diamond's arrival, there were several Jewish residents in Edmonton but nothing had been attempted in a Jewish way. There was no place of worship, no facilities for giving the few children a Jewish education, no shochat, no Jewish burial ground—in fact everything was missing that is indispensable to a Jewish community. Things soon began to change, however, and the changes were rapid. They came in quick succession and each one was a step forward. Mr. Diamond's influence in the community was soon felt and we find it recorded that on the evening of Sunday the 12th of August, 1906, the following ten Jewish citizens of Edmonton assembled together for the purpose of organizing The Edmonton Hebrew Association—A. Cristall, Wm. Diamond, J. S. Berkman, L. Frankenburg, C. N. Sugarman, H. Goldstick, N. Silas, A. Spiers, D. Boyaner, Harris Iny.

Mr. A. Cristall, the oldest Jewish resident, was elected President; Mr. Wm. Diamond, Vice-President; and Mr. J. S. Berkman, Secretary. It is rather a curious coincidence that of the ten gentlemen there assembled, the only ones who now reside in Edmonton are the three officers who were first elected. One of the interesting items that appears in the minutes of this meeting is a motion "That the Secretary was authorized to purchase a butcher knife, saw and meat chopper and all necessary articles to keep the meat perfectly kosher."

Mr. H. Goldstick was appointed at a salary of $600 per annum to administer to the needs of the community and immediately afterwards left for New York to take a post graduate course in those arts in which he was deficient, in order to better qualify himself for the discharge of his duties. He soon returned and entered upon his duties which he faithfully discharged for a number of years, and included, in addition to administering to the spiritual needs of his little congregation the training of the younger generation to whom a daily course of instruction in Hebrew was given. Thus the foundation was laid for a Hebrew school, which was at a later date, for the purposes of convenience, separated from the Association but which always received its fullest support, financial and otherwise.

The Jewish population began to gradually increase and the need for a burial ground was soon manifest and in April, 1907, a beautiful plot containing three acres, adjacent to the city was purchased and still serves the needs of the community.

HOUSE OF ISRAEL, EDMONTON

In 1908, Mr. A. Cristall, owing to pressure of personal business, retired from the presidency and Mr. Wm. Diamond took the office which he has held continuously ever since. For seventeen consecutive years he has been unanimously re-elected to the office he so capably fills and it is a safe prediction and generally accepted that it is a life office, so far as Mr. Diamond is concerned. The many personal sacrifices he has made to the congregation has served a double purpose, it has endeared the congregation to him so that its needs and its welfare are always paramount and the community with full appreciation of his unselfish devotion to its welfare has supported him generously in every laudable undertaking.

In this same year, 1908, another event occurred which deserves to be chronicled. It was the arrival in Edmonton of Mr. A. H. Goldberg, than a young man in his early twenties. He soon afterwards took over the secretaryship of the Association and in a short time the effect of his magnetic personality and dynamic energy was felt. Mr. Goldberg soon began to advocate the erection of a House of Worship. Considerable opposition was encountered. It was thought that the community was as yet too small and much too poor for such an undertaking. At first even Mr. Diamond's conservative nature hesitated to fall in with what seemed like a hare-brained scheme but he soon melted under the warmth of his secretary's enthusiasm and with two such advocates it was merely a matter of time to work up the interest of the entire community. Mr. Diamond offered to donate two centrally located lots, if the necessary monies to erect the building could be secured. Twelve thousand dollars was required for the desired building, a huge sum for so small a congregation, but encouraged by a subscription of $500 from Mr. A. Cristall, the first president of the Association, Mr. Goldberg and his committee commenced their work full of hope and with but a slight realization of the difficulties they were to encounter. It was soon discovered that the task was as difficult as many had prophesied and time and time again he was urged to drop the project for the time being and wait until such time as the community had attained greater numerical and financial strength. Such pessimistic counsel was unheeded and Mr. Goldberg went on with his work, refusing to become disheartened or discouraged because the goal seemed a long way off. Long before the required amount was in sight the contract was let and on the 17th day of August 1911, the corner stone was laid by Mr. Diamond in the presence of Lieut. Governor Bulyea, Hon. Frank Oliver and the entire Jewish community. After the laying of the corner stone, moneys flowed in more freely and the building, one of the finest of its kind in Western Canada, was soon completed. With the population increasing steadily, it was found less of a burden than even the most optimistic had anticipated to keep up the Synagogue and to pay off the balance unpaid on the building.

In 1912, Mr. Goldstick resigned to engage in business and was succeeded by the Rev. A. Pinsky, who still serves the congregation, with the maximum of satisfaction. It is of some significance, and illustrative of the complete harmony that has at all times prevailed, that during the 19 years of its existence the Edmonton Hebrew Association has had but two presidents, one of whom has been in office for 17 years and two Ministers, the present incumbent now entering into his fourteenth year of service.

During the war and in the terrible years that followed, the work of The Edmonton Hebrew Association was particularly outstanding. As soon as the first call came it responded with open hearted generosity and its members donated approximately $40,000 during the several campaigns that were made. In every drive, we find Mr. Diamond and his able confrère, A. H. Goldberg, not only leading their forces with energy and devotion but also showing an example to their co-religionists, by heading the subscription lists with substantial donations.

The Talmud Torah, the Zionist Organization and every other worthy endeavour have been not only supported by the Association but have been founded, recruited and kept in existence from the ranks of the Association's membership. The example of its leaders has not been in vain, and the result of the personal sacrifices they made both in time and energy as well as money has had a result far beyond their expectations. A united and harmonious community, ready to respond to every worthy cause and prepared to make up in generosity what they lack in numbers, has been and still is the record of Edmonton's Jewish community who with few exceptions comprise The Edmonton Hebrew Association.

A. H. GOLDBERG, CALGARY

ABRAHAM HENRY GOLDBERG, one of the most prominent Jewish citizens of Alberta, was born in Russia, on December 30th, 1885, the son of the late Simon Goldberg of St. Paul, Minn., U.S.A. He went to the United States with his parents in 1894, and was educated in St. Paul. In 1907, he went to Edmonton, Alta., where he resided until 1921, when he removed to Calgary, where he has since lived. In 1911, in association with Mr. J. M. Sternberg, he organized the Northern Grain Company, and he is still actively connected with this concern. Mr. Goldberg was married on August 20th, 1920, to Marcia, daughter of the late Moses Calmenson, and he has two daughters, the Misses Mozah and Muriel Goldberg. During his residence in Edmonton, Mr. Goldberg was one of the leading members of the Jewish community, and he was actively identified with Mr. Wm. Diamond in the formation of the synagogue and Talmud Torah. He was also prominently identified with the various drives organized in Edmonton for the relief of war sufferers, and in all communal undertakings. For some time he was President of the Edmonton Lodge, Independent Order B'nai B'rith, and he was Secretary of both the synagogue and Talmud Torah. On his arrival in Calgary, he at once entered into the communal life of that city, and he has taken the same active interest there that he did in Edmonton, at the same time keeping up his support to all Edmonton institutions. Mr. Goldberg is an enthusiastic Zionist, and this organization and the B'nai B'rith are both institutions that he actively supports with time and financial assistance. His help and advice are always at the service of any worthy cause, and he is regarded as one of the representative members of the Jewish community in the Prairie Provinces. Both in Edmonton and in Calgary, Mr. Goldberg has won the respect of the entire community for his integrity and philanthropy, and his support is as freely given to non-Jewish institutions as to Jewish.

REV. MARCUS BERNER, HIRSCH, SASK.

THE REV. MARCUS BERNER, pioneer farmer, and Minister of the Jewish community of Hirsch, Sask., is the son of Baruch Berner, and was born in the Province of Grodno, Russian Poland, April 15th, 1869. He received a very thorough religious education in Russia, but at the age of twenty, owing to persecution, was forced to leave his native town and country, and first went to London, England, where he was immediately engaged to the first Talmud Torah classes, as one of the tutors. He was appointed special Hebrew teacher to the Jewish Free School, and later, with the approval of the late Chief Rabbi, Dr. H. Adler, he received his appointment as a Jewish minister. He occupied several positions as minister both in London and country towns, and then emigrated to Canada, taking along with him a group of relatives, a Sefer Torah, and all the sacred articles required for the maintenance of a Jewish congregation. On April 27th, 1899, in charge of this little band of pioneers, consisting of twelve married families, he left London and went direct to Yorkton, Sask., with the purpose of pursuing farming. After a suitable place was located and homesteads were taken up, they were induced by a representative of the Jewish Colonization Association to leave their settlements and move with all their effects to Hirsch, Sask., as a Jewish colony was being founded there. Being promised all kinds of assistance, the group was induced to move to Hirsch, where they have since remained. It appears to have been an unfortunate move, although the present administration of the Jewish Colonization Association is doing its duty towards them in a far better way than the former administration did. Rev. Mr. Berner officiates at the congregation established on their arrival, and he is the leader of the community. He is secretary of the local Zionist organization and has held public office as Municipal Councillor. During the great war, three members of Mr. Berner's family saw service, out of a total of five from that locality. He has four sons, Barnet, Isaac, Meyer and Henry, and one daughter, Miss Jane Sophia Berner.

CONGREGATION BETH JACOB, CALGARY, ALTA.

THE first religious services held by the Jews of Calgary took place on the Holy Days in 1894. They were held in the old Masonic Hall, and Mr. Jacob Diamond officiated as reader. The gathering was composed of two residents of Calgary, two from Edmonton, five commercial travellers, and a farmer from near Lacombe.

Jacob Diamond was the first Jew to settle in Calgary. He arrived there in 1889, when the population of the town was but 1500. For a number of years a "minyan" was all that could be managed, even in 1904 there being but four Jewish families residing in the town. In that year the question was forcibly brought to them of having their own cemetery, the death taking place of one of the children of the community; a daughter of Mr. N. Bell. A lot was purchased and consecrated, but it was not until 1906 that the congregation and Chevra Kedisha were organized.

The population began to increase, chiefly due to immigration, and the congregation engaged Mr. H. Sissinsky as Schochet and Cantor. Mr. Jacob Diamond had been elected the first president, and he also for a long period acted as Chazan. At this time the membership was about twenty-five, and the services were held in a public hall, on one occasion a room in a private house being utilized.

In 1911, the population having made considerable strides, and at the time numbering about seventy-five families, land was purchased and the erection of a synagogue was commenced. The building was completed in 1912, and was opened with the usual ceremony. The name "Beth Jacob" was selected as a compliment to Mr. Jacob Diamond.

As in all other communities, the synagogue has been the means of bringing the Jewish people together, and all communal activities have had their origin there.

In 1914, attempts were made to start another congregation, but these did not materialize, and today there is but the one synagogue, although the Jewish population of Calgary is now about 1250.

There is a ladies' auxiliary in connection with the synagogue, and much assistance has also been rendered by the Ladies' Aid Society, the B'nai B'rith Lodge, and the Council of Jewish Women. Mr. Morris Groberman is President of the congregation and the Rev. S. Slonemsky is the spiritual leader of the community.

SASKATOON HEBREW CONGREGATION

THE history of the Jewish community of Saskatoon reads much the same as that of any other city in the Canadian West. It was in March, 1908, that the first Jew to settle in Saskatoon, Mr. H. Sklar, took up his residence there. He had come from Kiev and shortly afterwards in the same year was joined by Messrs. W. Landa, M. Volansky, J. Mallin, M. Rose, S. Henerofsky, and S. Goodman.

As was always the case in conformity with true Jewish spirit, the first "minyan" for the Holy Days was held the very same year at the home of Mr. Sklar, the "minyan" being composed of the above named and some commercial travellers and a few of the Jewish settlers from the neighboring towns. As there was no Chazan within reach at that time, the members of the "minyan" took turns in performing the services.

In 1909, the religious activity of Saskatoon was still centered at the home of Mr. Sklar. Mr. Birnbaum who had recently arrived, officiated during the Holy Days.

With the arrival of several other Jewish families, it was found necessary in the year 1910 to rent a small hall and to engage the first Shochet, Rev. Mr. Selchenko. The small hall later gave way to a larger one in the Cahill Block, where the services during the year 1911 were held, and finally in 1912, an attempt was made to build a synagogue. Thanks to the conscientious efforts of the whole Jewish community, a synagogue was erected the same year. Although the Jewish population at that time was very small, it is worthy to note that they took upon themselves the responsibility of erecting a synagogue at a cost of $4,500. Mr. Koukoy was President; Mr. Goldstein, Vice-President; and Mr. Abromovitch was Trustee at that time.

During the next seven years the Jewish population of Saskatoon increased from twenty to one hundred families, and the erection of a more suitable and larger synagogue became the important problem.

On April 13th, 1919, work was definitely commenced in the construction of a new building and it was completed at a cost of $17,000. The official opening, which was a day of general rejoicing for the Jewish community of Saskatoon, took place in September 1919. Chief Rabbi Kahanovitch of Winnipeg officiated. The officers of the synagogue at that time were;—President, H. Lazaresco; Vice-President, S. Sklar; Secretary, L. Feinstein; and Executive, J. Claman, A. Wolochow, S. Panar and W. Landa.

In keeping with the rapid rise of the congregation, a Chevra Kedisha was inaugurated in 1911, and several acres of land were purchased for a cemetery. From the original membership of about fourteen, of which Mr. A. Volansky was President and Mr. H. Lazeresco, Secretary, there has been an increase to over fifty members at the present day. For the year 1925, the following have been elected to hold office in the Chevra Kedisha;—President, J. Claman; Vice-President, W. Adilman; Treasurer, D. Ellis; Secretary, M. Rose; and Trustees, S. Davies and W. Landa.

The present officers of the congregation are;—President, W. Adilman; Vice-President, J. Claman; Honorary Recording Secretary, M. Shertzer; Financial Secretary, B. Viner; Secretary, J. Goldenberg; Treasurer, M. Rose; and Trustees, J. Gordon, N. Adilman and M. Feiler.

I. GOLDSTICK, M.A., LONDON

ISIDORE GOLDSTICK, M.A., was born in the city of Windau, Courland, Russia, November 13th, 1890, the son of William and Sarah Goldstick. He was educated in the Chedar in Windau; at the Toronto Public Schools; and at the University of Toronto, from which he graduated in 1913, with first class honors in modern languages. In 1914, he took his M.A. degree with honors, and did post-graduate work in Pedagogy at Queen's University, Kingston, and at the University of Toronto, in 1915 graduating from the Faculty of Education. Mr. Goldstick is the first Jewish Secondary school teacher in Ontario, (possibly in Canada). He was senior master of French and German at Upper Canada College, Toronto, 1915-17. Since 1917, he has been on the staff of the London Collegiate Institute, where he is the head of the department of Modern Languages. Mr. Goldstick is one of the founders of the Young Judaea Movement in Ontario, and was a member of the Executive Committee of the Canadian Jewish Congress. He is intimately identified with the Zionist Movement, and since 1919, has been a member of the National Executive of the Zionist Organization of Canada. He has been active in Jewish communal work in London, and was a Director in London of the Restoration Fund, 1918 and 1920, and the Keren Hayesod, 1921, 1923, and 1924 campaigns. Mr. Goldstick is the author of "Shakespeare's Influence on Schiller's Dramas" and "Standardized Tests for Modern Languages" (pamphlets), and is an occasional contributor to newspapers and periodicals. He is a member of the Lovers of Zion Society; L'Alliance Francaise; Drama League; Secondary School Teachers' Federation; Immigrant Aid Society; and E.C.P. Association. Mr. Goldstick is married to Miss Anna Nathanson, daughter of Ben Zion Nathanson of Toronto, and has one daughter, Reva Emma Goldstick. He is President of London Lodge, No. 1012, I.O.B.B., and Vice-President of the Secondary School Teachers' Institute of London.

HOUSE OF JACOB CONGREGATION, WINNIPEG

THE oldest and largest Synagogue in North Winnipeg, Congregation Beth Jacob, was erected in the year 1903. The congregation was organized in that year, and among the founders were:—P. Lechtzier, who became President; L. Berger, Vice-President; and N. Kasler, Treasurer. This synagogue has exerted a powerful influence upon Winnipeg Jewry, and under its auspices, the first plans for the building of many prominent institutions such as the Talmud Torah and the Jewish Old Folks' Home, were made. Rabbi Kahanovitch, Chief Rabbi of the orthodox congregations in Winnipeg, is the minister at this synagogue. It has a membership of one hundred and fifty, a Chazan and a choir. The present officers are:—H. Sinisky, President; P. Steingarten, Vice-President; and S. Choslovsky, Treasurer.

CONGREGATION BETH JACOB, HAMILTON, ONT.

THE Congregation Beth Jacob of Hamilton was organized on December 1st, 1887, and on December 6th, 1887, the charter was received from the Provincial Government. They first held a "minyan" at a hall on King Street West, at which place, at the present time, stands the Royal Theatre (moving picture house). Two years later, in 1889, the present premises were bought from a church, which was renovated and remodelled into a synagogue. This was before the present T. H. B. Tunnel was built. On the charter appears the following list of names;—Messrs. Elias Siderski, Julius Levy, William Goldberg, Woolf Cohen, Isaac Raphael, Louis Rubens, Isaac Levy, Harris Siderski, Max Steinberg, Kalman Camman, Soloman Frank, Jacob Lewis, Max Morris, Adolph Shafer, Moritz Mittenbrown, Archibald Epstein, Barnett Frank, Isaac Diamond, Meyer Lamberg, and Samuel Moskowitz.

There is no record of the first officers. The first Board of Trustees of the congregation were;—Messrs. Abraham Levy, Max Steinberg, Kalman Camman, William Goldberg, Woolf Cohen, Elias Siderski, Julius Levy, Louis Lipschitz, and Solomon Frank.

Many of the charter members have left the city, some are deceased, others are still residents but not members of the congregation. Those of the charter members who are still members of the congregation are;—Max Steinberg, Harris Siderski, Archibald Epstein, and Meyer Lamberg.

The congregation is at present without a spiritual head, but is in the field for a modern orthodox Rabbi, and the Chazan is the Rev. Jacob Levinson. The congregation consists of about one hundred and forty members, the minimum dues being $24.00 per annum. The fees of the non-resident members and widows of members are half that amount.

In connection with the congregation, there is a ladies' auxiliary, The Jewish Ladies' Aid Society, which looks after all charitable work.

The present officers of the Society are;—Mrs. H. Freiman, President; Mrs. S. Needle, Vice-President; Mrs. M. Epstein, Secretary; and Mrs. Rose Levy, Treasurer.

There is also the Beth Jacob Social Circle, which is composed of the children of the members, who meet in the vestry chambers of the synagogue, a Junior Congregation, and a Sunday Religious School.

The congregation has large burial grounds, which are situated at Waterdown, and the Cemetery Board consists of;—J. Goldblatt, President; S. Shachnove, Vice-President; M. Levy, Deputy Gabbay; M. Grinblatt, Treasurer; and J. Freedman, Secretary.

The present officers of the congregation are;—D. S. Kauffman, President; R. Levy, Vice-President; J. Freedman, Secretary (since July 1, 1919); J. Alter, Treasurer; Trustees, A. Epstein, M. Epstein, S. Quiril, S. Lipschitz; Gabbaim, Jacob N. Goldblatt and Max Steinberg; House Committee, S. Davidovitz, S. Hershman, and A. Berg; and Life Trustees, Jacob N. Goldblatt, Harris Siderski, and Samuel Shachnove.

CONGREGATION B'NE ISRAEL, LONDON, ONT.

THIRTY-SIX years ago, (September, 1888), a handful of Jews banded themselves together for the purpose of organizing the first Jewish congregation in London.

The prospect of acquiring a synagogue seemed at first remote. There were only twelve members. They were new-comers, who had brought anything but wealth from the old land. "B'ne Israel" was the name given to the congregation, and I. Levin was chosen as its first President. For many years services on the Sabbath and on Holy Days were held in private homes.

In 1896, however, a synagogue was erected, the first Jewish synagogue to be built in London. It was situated on Richmond Street. J. Harris was President at that time. Some time before this, a cemetery had been purchased by the congregation.

In the course of a quarter of a century, with the steady, though slow growth of the Jewish population of London, the original synagogue became inadequate, despite the fact that a second congregation had meanwhile sprung up.

In 1917, B'ne Israel moved into larger quarters, when they purchased their present synagogue on the corner of Grey and Wellington Streets, originally a German church.

At the present time the congregation is in a flourishing condition; it has more than fifty members. The officers include D. Wydenbaum, President; J. Schure, Vice-President; L. Slobasky, Treasurer; Mr. Rosenfeld, Secretary; and M. Fishbein, First Trustee.

WELLINGTON STREET SYNAGOGUE, LONDON, ONT.

RABBI M. J. MINTZ, OTTAWA
Castonguay Studio

RABBI MAX JACOB MINTZ, of the Adath Jeshuran Synagogue, Ottawa, was born in Boston, Mass., U.S.A., on May 22nd, 1898, the son of Philip Mintz, of that city. He received his early education at the High School of Scranton, Pa., from which he matriculated to the New York University, and then later attended Columbia University, New York. He received his rabbinical degree after a course at the Rabbi Isaac Elchanan Theological Seminary, New York, and was the first American-born student to receive the rabbinical degree at this seminary. He was president, (1921-22) of the Students' Organization at the seminary, and after receiving his degree received the appointment as Rabbi and superintendent of the Hebrew National Orphans' Home, the largest orthodox orphanage in America, where he remained until early in 1924, when he received an unanimous call to the pulpit of the Adath Jeshuran Synagogue, King Edward Avenue, Ottawa, Ont., which appointment he holds at the present time. Rabbi Mintz has developed the various societies and activities in connection with the synagogue, and he is meeting with great success in his congregational work. Since his arrival in Ottawa, he has taken a leading position in the Jewish community and has become prominently identified with all welfare and communal movements, and is held in the highest esteem by all members of the community. An earnest student of all Jewish problems, an omnivorous reader, and a forceful speaker, a brilliant future is prophesied for Rabbi Mintz. His discourses are not confined to the pulpit and always attract deep attention. He is a member of the Alumni Society of the Rabbi Isaac Elchanan Theological Seminary, and is an active member of the Independent Order B'nai B'rith. He is an ardent Zionist and one of the leaders in the local organization. Rabbi Mintz has the distinction of being the youngest Rabbi to ever hold office in the synagogue where he officiates, which is the oldest congregation in Ottawa.

THE LATE MOSES BILSKY

THE LATE MOSES BILSKY, the first Jew to settle in Ottawa, and founder of the firm of Bilsky, Ltd., was born in Russia in 1829 and died in Ottawa on January 4th, 1923. He arrived in Canada with his father when 14 years old and first lived in Montreal, but went to Ottawa in 1857, when his father returned to Palestine. In 1861 he went to the newly-discovered Caribou gold fields of the West, in those days having to make the trip by rail to New York, thence by boat to the Isthmus of Panama and then by boat to Victoria, the trip taking several weeks. Things at the gold camps not being to his liking, he started the return trip, over land, on foot and by horse. He enlisted in the American Army in 1863 and fought during the Civil War, and was a trooper stationed in San Francisco at the time Abraham Lincoln was assassinated. In 1867, he returned to Ottawa and opened up his first jewelry store. Mr. Bilsky for over half a century was a leading figure in the Jewish life of Ottawa and during all that time took great interest in all charitable and social movements in the community. He was instrumental in starting the first synagogue there in 1895, the Adath Jeshuran on King Edward Avenue. He was also one of the leaders of the local Zionist movement and was known for his kindness and charity, never refusing worthy requests. He had a large family, leaving five sons; Alex of Montreal; Samuel, Jack and David of Ottawa; and Nathan of Chatham; and six daughters, Mrs. A. J. Freiman and Misses Eva and Tilly Bilsky of Ottawa; Mrs. A. W. Jacobs of Montreal; and Mrs. A. J. Schragge and Mrs. A. Bronfman of Winnipeg. Mr. Bilsky's funeral was one of the largest ever held in Ottawa, and during his long residence there, he shared the universal respect of the entire community, both Jewish and Christian. His children have taken a prominent part in communal undertakings and particularly in Zionistic work, one of his daughters, Mrs. Freiman, being President of the Hadassah Organization of Canada.

ISAAC RUBENSTEIN, SAULT STE. MARIE.

ISAAC RUBENSTEIN, for twenty-five years a prominent citizen of Sault Ste. Marie, Ontario, was born in Kishinev, Russia, October 25th, 1862, the son of the late William Rubenstein of that city. He received a very thorough education in his native city and came to Canada at the age of 20 years, arriving here June 5th, 1882. He followed a commercial career, and on arriving in this country resided in Winnipeg for two years, moving from there to Montreal, where he lived for five years. In 1889 he took up his residence in Ottawa, where he remained for ten years. During his residence there, Mr. Rubenstein took an active part in communal affairs, and was one of the first members of the Ottawa Hebrew Benevolent Society. He was also an officer of the first synagogue established in Ottawa. In 1899 he removed to Sault Ste. Marie, Ontario, opening up the business there that he still conducts under his own name. Mr. Rubenstein is regarded as the foremost member of the Jewish community in Northern Ontario and is a leader in all movements made for the welfare of his people. His activities are not confined to his own creed and he occupies a prominent and most respected part in the life of his city. He is very fond of athletic sports and is an enthusiastic curler, fisherman and hunter. He is a member of the Canadian Order of Foresters. On April 20, 1887, Mr. Rubenstein was married to Miss Lena Cook, daughter of the late Israel Cook of Detroit, Michigan, and he has five sons; William, who is associated with him in business, Dr. Obbie, (Detroit), Dr. Jacob, (Ottawa), David and Israel Rubenstein, and four daughters; Hattye, (Mrs. J. Bolle of Buenos Aires, Argentine), Molcha, (Mrs. A. D. Hart of Toronto), Esther, a graduate nurse of Los Angeles, California, and Miss Dorothy Rubenstein, a pupil in Mt. Sinai Hospital, New York. His sons, Obbie and Jacob, were both in the Canadian Army during the World War, the former being on active service, overseas, for over three years, and the latter on home service (being under age), and his daughter Esther also served in France for over two years as a Red Cross nurse with the American Expeditionary Force.

CASPAR CAPLAN was born in Shawville, Kovno, in September 1871, the son of Jacob Hirsch Caplan of that city. He emigrated to the United States when a young man and later went to Ottawa, where he established the firm of C. Caplan Limited, which is one of the leading Jewish stores of the Capital. Mr. Caplan has always taken a keen interest in the Jewish life of Ottawa, and he has occupied many important positions in that connection. He was Vice-President of the Ottawa Hebrew Benevolent Society, and for a number of years has been a Trustee of the Adath Jeshuran Congregation. He was President of the United Talmud Torahs of Ottawa, and is a charter member of the Independent Order B'nai B'rith, Ottawa Lodge. Mr. Caplan has been associated with almost every communal undertaking in Ottawa, and has taken a prominent part in all philanthropic work. In 1897, Mr. Caplan was married to Dora, daughter of Isaac Loeb Roston, and he has three sons, Sam, Gordon and David, and three daughters, Leslie, Miriam and Lillian.

I. SUGARMAN, OTTAWA

C. CAPLAN, OTTAWA

ISRAEL SUGARMAN was born in Wilna, Russia, July 17th, 1877, the son of Hirsch Sugarman. He received his education at the Hebrew School of his native city. On his arrival in Canada, he made his home in Ottawa, where he has since resided, and where he takes an active part in all communal undertakings. He is a member of the Ottawa Hebrew Benevolent Society; The Zionist Organization; and President of the Independent Order B'nai B'rith, Ottawa Lodge No. 885. Mr. Sugarman is one of the founders of the Rideau Street Synagogue, and was Chairman of the Building Committee when the synagogue was erected in 1912. In 1916-17, he was President of this congregation. He has always taken a keen interest in the Hebrew education of the Jewish children of Ottawa, and he is one of the founders of the Ottawa Talmud Torah. He was instrumental in securing the present site for the school, on George Street. He was formerly director of the Young Men's Hebrew Association. Mr. Sugarman is married to Leah, daughter of Abraham Joseph Sugarman, and has one daughter, Miss Florence Sugarman.

RABBI I. I. KAHANOVITCH, WINNIPEG

RABBI ISRAEL ISAAC KAHANOVITCH was born in Grodno, Poland, October 8th, 1872, the son of Joshua Falk Kahanovitch. His Hebrew training was received up to the age of sixteen years in the famous theological seminaries at Grodno and Slabodka, under the well-known scholar Rabbi I. Rabinowitch. He was ordained as Rabbi in his twentieth year by Rabbi I. Epstein, the author of "Oruch Hashulchan". In 1896, he was married to Rachel, daughter of Kappel Kleiman, of Sinee, and has three sons and five daughters. He continued his studies up until 1905, at the same time partaking in communal affairs, particularly active for the Zionist cause. In the beginning of 1906, soon after the pogrom in Keshinev, he came to America, and became Rabbi in Scranton, Pa. After being there about a year, he was invited by the Jewish community of Winnipeg to go there as Chief Rabbi of Western Canada, having jurisdiction from Winnipeg to the coast. In Winnipeg he has taken a very active part in the religious and communal life of the city. He founded the first Talmudical Study Circles in the Shaarey Zedeck Synagogue, and in the House of Jacob Congregation. He was prominent in the organization of the Winnipeg Hebrew Free School, and has always been a strong agitator for Hebrew education. He continued his activities in Zionist work, and through his influence, the community strengthened its efforts towards this movement. He attends all Zionist Conferences, and is a member of the National Executive of Canada. Rabbi Kahanovitch visited the new communities that were formed throughout the West, and helped them to arrange their spiritual and social life, and was instrumental in organizing congregations and Hebrew schools. He encouraged farming in the new districts and was instrumental in founding the colonies at Camper, Man. and Sovenfeld, Sask. During the War, he was deeply interested in relief work and helped to form the Jewish Legion. He is a member of the Organization of Orthodox Rabbis of United States and Canada. He was prominent at the Canadian Jewish Congress.

THE HOUSE OF JACOB SYNAGOGUE, REGINA

REGINA does not seem to have any record of Jewish families residing there, until about 1909. It was not until 1913, that a congregation was formed. Prior to that date, services were held irregularly and a farmer by the name of Wasserman, who farmed in the immediate vicinity, acted as mohel and schochet. Services were held on the high holidays in one of the halls, though great difficulties were experienced in getting any accommodation.

In 1911, a schochet was engaged and services were held in his home. In 1913, a move was made to build a regular place of worship. The first officers were:—President, S. Pearlman, and Secretary, B. Zurif, with S. Prosterman, J. Kliman, I. Hamer and J. Schwartzfeld as the committee. Lots were purchased on Ottawa Street and the present building was erected and opened in September, 1913, as a cost of $12,000, free of debt. Much money was raised by the permanent sale of seats which belong to the purchaser and their heirs for all time to come.

The opening ceremony marked a distinct era in the history of Judaism in the Province of Saskatchewan. The Lieutenant-Governor, Geo. Brown, and the Mayor of the city took part in the ceremony and laid two of the corner stones, the third being laid by the President, S. Pearlman. There is seating accommodation for about four hundred ladies and gentlemen, but owing to the increase in the population since the opening date, it has been found impossible to accommodate the large number desirous of taking part in the services during the high holidays. During the past three years a hall had to be engaged, with additional readers, to accommodate the local public and the many visitors from outside districts. It is more than probable that in the near future a new synagogue will be built.

The present officers are:—President, Harry Kahn; Honorary President, Jake Kliman; Vice-President, I. Shein; Treasurer, I. Hamer; Secretary, H. Kahn; first Gabbay, D. Fages; Second Gabbay, Z. Shragge; Trustees, I. Friedgut, N. Wolfman, B. Finkelstein, S. Finkelstein, W. Pechet, B. Redman and A. Basen.

CONGREGATION SHAAREY ZEDECK, VANCOUVER, B.C.

ABOUT the year 1905, with the Jewish population of Vancouver steadily growing, it was felt that the time had arrived when an orthodox synagogue should be established. Out of this sprang the synagogue known as "Congregation Sons of Israel." This congregation immediately took steps to erect a small house of worship, and arranged for the necessary services.

After a number of years of more or less constant difficulties, the congregation was broken up, and in its place the present "Congregation Shaarey Zedeck" was formed.

The synagogue building was soon found to be too small, and a campaign was then launched for funds, with which to erect a proper building. This culminated in the year 1918, when the new synagogue was completed at a cost of $50,000. The outstanding feature in this campaign, was the joining together of all the Jewish elements of the city, both for their work in the campaign, and for the moneys donated. The Building Committee consisted of Max M. Grossman as chairman, Charles Goldberg, David Marks, Nace Swartz and M. Stochinsky. During the transition period connected with the building of the new synagogue, the whole of the activities were carried on by the Building Committee, and they were able to eventually turn over a properly working organization.

Mr. I. L. Kostman was then induced to take the presidency of the synagogue, in order that it might be established along proper business lines and function to the best advantage, and during the following two years, Mr. Kostman proved himself to be worthy of the trust imposed in him, and succeeded in making the synagogue a very strong factor in the community life.

A word as to the Rabbi, M. Pastinsky. He has been with the synagogue for the past six years, and his devotion not only to the working of the synagogue itself, but to all problems that affect Jewish life, have called forth unstinted praise.

For his services as chairman of the Building Committee, an honorary life membership has been given to Max M. Grossman.

The officers of the synagogue are: President, Mr. P. Brotman; Vice-Presidents, Mr. L. Halperin and Mr. D. Davis; Treasurer, W. Zimmerman; Recording Secretary, K. Katznelson; Financial Secretary, W. J. Levin; Trustees, W. Genser, A. G. Hirschberg, A. H. Fleishman, H. Kahn and S. Rothstein.

CONGREGATION TEMPLE EMANU-EL, VANCOUVER, B.C.

THIS is the oldest congregation in Vancouver. It was initiated in the early history of the city. Vancouver was incorporated in the year 1886, and the congregation was functioning in the year 1887. At that time, the services held were strictly orthodox, and were conducted by the members themselves. But in 1890, steps were taken for its incorporation as a semi-reform congregation, and this has been continued until the present.

The first Rabbi was Rabbi R. Rosenstein. He was in turn succeeded by Dr. R. Farber, Dr. I. Friedlander and Dr. S. Rosengard.

Prior to the Great War, the congregation purchased a valuable site upon which to erect a modern synagogue, and although plans were prepared for this building, the War (1914-18) held up the project for the time being.

For the past two or three years, services were suspended, so that the Jewish population could all assist in the erection of the building now occupied by Congregation Shaarey Zedeck. Now, however, the members are directing their attention to the continuation of its services, and arrangements are being made to alter the original plans, and erect a combined synagogue and community building. It is hoped, that a start will be made before the next New Year's holidays.

A very active Sunday School is maintained, under the auspices of the Temple's Auxiliary.

The president of the congregation is Mr. Samuel Gintzburger, who is probably the earliest of the pioneers, and who occupies an enviable position in the Province.

BETH JACOB CONGREGATION, TORONTO

THE CONGREGATION BETH JACOB was organized in 1899 by a number of Polish Jews who were desirous of having a place of worship where the ritual to which they were accustomed would be carried on. Among the first members of the congregation were;—Messrs. M. Granatstein, L. Rotenberg, S. Garfinkle, G. Pesachovitch, Z. Wagman, I. Wagman, S. Lederman, J. Sugar, C. Garfunkel, H. Rotenberg, and M. Rotenberg, and the first President was Mr. Samson Garfinkle.

Their first place of worship was a small cottage at the rear of a house on Chestnut Street, and after worshipping at this place for a few years, they removed to a small place on Centre Avenue.

In 1904, finding that their quarters were far too small for their requirements, the congregation decided to move to a new site. They purchased the Baptist Church at 17-19 Elm Street, which for sixteen years they used as a place of worship. The congregation flourished, and as the membership increased rapidly, the building on Elm Street was no longer adequate. It was decided to sell these premises and to build a more commodious and modern place of worship.

In 1921, the congregation purchased two houses on Henry Street (opposite Cecil Street). These were immediately demolished, and the construction of the present synagogue was begun. The old building on Elm Street was sold at a profit of nearly $7,000.00.

The cornerstones of the new synagogue were laid on May 4th, 1921; the two in front by Mr. M. Granatstein and Mr. and Mrs. M. Goldmintz, and the two on the sides of the building, by Mr. G. Arbus and Mr. H. Sherman, with all the accompanying ceremonies.

The synagogue is a handsome structure with a seating capacity of five hundred and fifty for men, and three hundred and fifty for women.

The building is designed in the Romanesque manner, of red brick trimmed with limestone. Three arches compose the main entrance which is surmounted by a large stained glass rose window. On either side are tall flanking towers with minor entrances in them. These towers are capped with small domes, which seem to stand guard over the large central dome, covering the main auditorium. This auditorium is square and is the full height of the building with the ceiling dome supported on tall classical columns. A gallery runs around three sides with smaller domes at each of the corners. Facing the entrance as one enters the auditorium, is the Ark, forty-five feet high, of wood, a rich walnut colour. The tablets on the top are supported by twisted columns and the whole is elaborately carved, giving an exceedingly rich effect in keeping with the general character of the building.

In the basement of the building there is a Beth Medrosh, where many of the men pray and study the teachings of the Torah. This is large enough to seat two hundred people. A large dance hall and banquet hall are also situated in the basement and are used for weddings, banquets, etc. This hall can hold about one thousand people comfortably. The living quarters of the shamos are also situated in this part of the building. The architect in charge of the construction of this building was Mr. Benjamin Brown.

The money raised for the building was in the form of donations from the members of the congregation, and from the sale of seats. The total cost of the structure amounts to $115,000.00, and the congregation is today in a flourishing condition.

HENRY STREET SYNAGOGUE

Among those who have been Presidents in this congregation are;—L. Rotenberg, M. Goldhar, B. Goldhar, L. Rotstein, and others. Mr. S. Garfinkle was the President, B. Goldhar, Vice-President, B. Paskowitch, Parnass, and L. Rotstein, Gabbay, at the time of the erection of the present synagogue, and the Building Committee was composed of the following gentlemen;—M. Goldhar, S. Gotfried, L. Grossman, D. Rotstein, B. Caplan, H. Schwartz, A. Schwartz, P. Kamin, S. Brenzel, M. Brenzel, M. Priemer, B. Tator, K. Silverstein, and C. Wagman.

The congregation at the present time has a membership of about one hundred and seventy. There is also a Ladies' Auxiliary that takes a prominent part in all the activities of the congregation. The President of the Auxiliary is Mrs. M. Goldhar. The congregation at the present time has no official Rabbi. Rabbi Graubart, however, has acted as spiritual head of the congregation on different occasions, as has also Rabbi Silverstein, who is a recent arrival from Poland.

In the early days of the congregation, the members bought land in North Yonge Street, which they used as a cemetery for a number of years. They found, however, that the ground there was very swampy, and in 1924, the congregation purchased a large tract very nicely situated in Lambton, which they now use as the cemetery. The cemetery committee, or Chevra Kedisha are;—Gabbai, M. Goldhar; Treasurer, S. Gotfried, and Secretary, Meyer Goldhar.

The present officers of the congregation are;—President, M. Granatstein; Vice-President, K. Silverstein; Treasurer, C. Teishman; Rec. Sec., M. Priemer; Fin. Sec., P. Greenbaum; Parnass, S. Gotfried; Gabbay, G. Pesachovitch; and Trustees, Messrs. M. Goldhar, I. Gold, D. Wagman, M. Wagman, M. Goldmintz and L. Cutler.

CHARLES GARFUNKEL, TORONTO

CHARLES GARFUNKEL, the son of Rev. Samson Garfunkel, was born in Poland, September 19, 1884.

He came to Canada in 1895, to join his parents, who had come to Toronto a short time previously. He received his education in the public schools of Toronto. In 1904 Mr. Garfunkel was married to Gertrude, daughter of the late Benjamin Tugendhaft of Toronto, and he has one son, and two daughters. In 1917 Mrs. Garfunkel passed away, after a long illness. Mr. Garfunkel established the first steamship ticket agency in Toronto, in 1900, and he remained in this business for many years. In 1912 he went into the building and real estate business and he continued in this until 1921, when he became associated as Secretary-Treasurer and Manager of the United Press, Limited. Mr. Garfunkel has always been intensely interested in communal activities and for some time was president of the Henry Street Synagogue, Toronto. He is a director of the Toronto Hebrew Free Loan Association and also of the Federation of Jewish Philanthropies, Toronto, and is a member of the Zionist Council of Canada. He takes an active part in the political life of Toronto and for fifteen years has been a member of Ward 4 Conservative Association. He was for some years treasurer and later third vice-president, and was the first Jew to hold office in this association. Mr. Garfunkel is a member of the Palestine Lodge, A.F. & A.M., and of the I.O.B.B. Since his connection with the United Press, Limited, he has been associated with Ephraim Palter, the President and Paul Frumharz, the Vice-President of this company, and they have developed this concern from a small printing establishment into the largest Jewish publishing house in Canada. They are contractors to His Majesty's Government, and handle all the printing, binding and publishing for the Government of Ontario. They also print large numbers of school books. Much of the success of the concern is due to the untiring energy and ability of Mr. Garfunkel.

J. A. GLANZ, WINDSOR

JERRY A. GLANZ, one of the prominent Jewish citizens and the leader in communal work in Windsor, was born in Vilna, Russia, in 1888, the son of Albert Glanz. He received his education in the town of Riga, and upon coming to Canada, this was supplemented by private tuition. He arrived in Canada in 1914 and settled in Windsor, Ontario, where for four years he was engaged in the wholesale produce business. In later years, he adopted the furniture line, and is today, with his partner, conducting one of the foremost furniture stores in the border cities, under the name of the Windsor Home Furniture Company. Mr. Glanz married Miss Dora Rubin, daughter of Samuel Rubin, and he has two sons, Albert and Abraham, and one daughter, Miss Rose Glanz. When he arrived in Windsor, he found approximately fifty Jewish families there with no organization of any kind. With a progressive mind he set to work to introduce educational facilities for the Jewish residents, and the result of his activities is the Windsor Hebrew School, which today occupies its own building and accommodates from one hundred and fifty to two hundred scholars, who are receiving a proper and thorough education. Mr. Glanz was the first organizer of the Zionist movement in Windsor. Charities of every conceivable deserving character have always found in him a hearty supporter and warm friend. It is only a statement of fact to say that Mr. Glanz is an energetic and enthusiastic leader in all campaigns of local societies and national relief funds in the border cities. He is the President of the Primrose Club, Windsor; Treasurer of the Agudath B'nai Zion; Treasurer of the Windsor Hebrew School; Treasurer of the Literary Society; Treasurer, Keren Hayesod and National Fund; active member of the Shaarey Zedeck Congregation; member, Border Cities Chamber of Commerce; Border Cities Retail Merchants' Association; the Denver Sheltering Home for Jewish Children; Jewish Consumptive Relief Society of Los Angeles; I.O.B.B.; Hebrew Sheltering Immigration Aid Society of America; Local Relief Fund, and many other societies.

BAY STREET SYNAGOGUE, TORONTO "MACHZIKE HADASS"

IN 1906, a number of the members of Chestnut Street Synagogue (Shomrai Shabbas), who became dissatisfied with certain conditions that were in existence, decided to organize a new congregation and formed the Bay Street Synagogue (Machzike Hadass).

Among those who were active in the formation of this congregation were:—Samuel Fralick, Charles Scher, M. Gelber, the late L. Shumer, Charles Pasternack, and M. Sheffer.

For their rights in the Chestnut Street Synagogue, the seceding members received the sum of $10,000, for which they purchased the property on Bay Street, and on which they built their synagogue.

The first President was Mr. Samuel Fralick.

Rabbi J. Weinraub, who formerly had been connected with the Chestnut Street Synagogue, joined the Machzike Hadass, and has been connected with that congregation ever since.

The present membership consists of about one hundred and twenty, and Mr. Myer Shapiro is the President.

ROUMANIAN HEBREW CONGREGATION "ADATH ISRAEL", TORONTO

THE Roumanian Hebrew Congregation "Adath Israel" of Toronto, was organized in 1902, with a membership of twenty made up of men who had come from different parts of Roumania and who wished to have their services conducted in the manner to which they had been accustomed. They at first worshipped in different homes and halls and in 1910, built the present building at 48-50 Centre Avenue. On completion of the building, the corner stone was laid by Mr. and Mrs. B. Hashmall, with all necessary ceremony. The membership at the present time is two hundred, and the seating capacity of the synagogue is five hundred.

In 1924, a Ladies' Auxiliary of the congregation was formed, under the presidency of Mrs. H. Signer. Mrs. Leo Hertzman is Secretary of the Auxiliary. Through the efforts of its members, a Sunday School was formed on February 1st, 1925, with an attendance of seventy-five children.

The present officers of the congregation are:—Pres., Mr. Isaac Lieberman; Vice-Pres., Mr. J. Pascal; Treas., Mr. A. Joseph; and Secty., Mr. Wm. Goodman.

The cemetery of the Adath Israel Congregation is situated at Rosemount Avenue, and the officers of the Chevra Kedisha are:—Gabbay, M. Pezim, and Assistant Gabbay, J. Tishler.

ROSH PINA SYNAGOGUE, WINNIPEG

THE Rosh Pina Synagogue was organized in August 1893. The founders of the congregation were:— M. Black, W. Moscovich, P. Minuk, I. Rosen, T. Finkelstein, N. Rosenblat, H. Gartil, B. Peveles, and S. Milstein. The present officers are:—T. Portigal, President; J. Shimban, Vice-President; A. Swartz, Treasurer; and M. W. Shiffman, Secretary, and the Trustees are:— N. Rosenblat, D. Gufine, I. Brownstein, and W. Black.

CONGREGATION BEN JUDAH, LONDON, ONT.

SOME eighteen years ago (1907), a small group of Jews of London, Ont., under the leadership of the late Moses Leff and M. Pollock, now of Saskatchewan, banded themselves together to form a congregation. They purchased an old church at the corner of Colborne and Horton Streets. Owing to the lack of funds, the late Moses Leff and the late Israel Leff advanced the required amount. After remodelling and making all the necessary renovations, the synagogue was formally opened on September 12th, 1907. They held services in this building for thirteen years. The original membership of the congregation consisted of fourteen men, but slowly the number increased, until today there is a total membership of seventy.

At a meeting held on Sunday, May 15th, 1920, it was resolved that the old synagogue be demolished and a new and up-to-date building be erected. For four years the Building Committee, consisting of Messrs. H. Sigel, M. Siskind, B. Lewis, S. Hershorn, M. Jack, M. Apple, S. Sigel and H. Grace, laboured zealously and faithfully to raise the necessary funds.

The cornerstone was laid on July 2nd, 1923, by Mr. and Mrs. B. Lewis, Rabbi Jacob Gordon of Toronto officiating. On July 15th, 1924, which was a day of great rejoicing to the Jews of London, the new edifice was formally opened. The total cost of the new building is $18,000.

The present spiritual head of the congregation is Rabbi A. Ruthberg, formerly of Auburn, N.Y.

The Life Trustees are;—B. Lewis, M. Siskind and the late Moses Leff, and the present officers are;— H. Sigel, President; J. Lipowich, Vice-President; S. Sigel, Secretary; J. Siskind, Treasurer; and Trustees, M. Gootson, S. Boom and S. Hershorn.

BETH ISRAEL SYNAGOGUE, KINGSTON, ONT.

THE Hebrew Congregation of Kingston dates back many years, among the founders being Simon Obendorffer, Louis Abramson, K. Zacks, I. Zacks, S. Bennet, and M. Susman. Prior to this there were Jewish residents of the city, but never sufficient number to form a "minyan".

After the formation of the congregation the members worshipped in halls and other public places, and in the course of time a second congregation was organized, by newer arrivals and through a dispute between members of the original institution. Finally, in 1908, largely through the instrumentality of Mr. Isaac Cohen, the two organizations combined, on the assurance that Mr. Cohen would be responsible for the erection of a synagogue. This became an accomplished fact in 1910. It is a noteworthy illustration of the high esteem in which members of the Jewish community are held when the Christian population of the city subscribed largely to the erection of the synagogue.

The first president was Mr. Obendorffer, and he was succeeded in office by Mr. Joseph Abramson. The Jewish community is approximately 200 souls and practically all are members of the congregation.

The present officers of the congregation are:— Isaac Cohen, President; K. Zacks, Vice-President; A. Shaer, Treasurer, and Moses Abramsky, Secretary.

DAVID SWEET, HAMILTON

DAVID SWEET was born at Kishenev, Bessarabia, Feb. 3rd 1865, the son of the late Josef Zvi Sweet of that city. He came to Canada as a young man, in 1886, and settled in Hamilton, where he has since resided, and where he has built up a large cigar business. Mr. Sweet is a self-educated man, who ever since his arrival in this country has taken a great interest in the welfare of his less fortunate fellow-man, and in Jewish activities. Although not a rich man, he never refuses assistance to the deserving, irrespective of creed, and he occupies a leading part in the communal life of Hamilton. He was the founder (1888) and first president of the Hamilton Y.M.H.A.; secretary, Hamilton Israelite Benevolent Society, (1890); organizer and secretary, (1913) United Hebrew Association of Hamilton; one of the founders and first president, Viceroy Reading Chapter, I.O.B.B.; first president of the Young People's Society of the Anshe Sholom Congregation; present president, Jewish Immigrant Aid Society of Hamilton; and a director in many other charitable institutions. In 1915, Mr. Sweet was a vice-president of the Zionist Federation of Canada. His activities are not limited to Jewish welfare and he is a life member of the Red Cross Society. During and after the war, he was secretary of the Jewish War Funds and other similar societies. He is a prominent member of the Hamilton Health Association, Society for the Prevention of Cruelty to Animals, Children's Aid, Jewish Consumptive Relief, Chamber of Commerce, and Canadian and Commercial Clubs. In his religious beliefs, Mr. Sweet is a follower of the Reform movement, which he both advocates and practises, and he believes that as a Jew, it is his duty to be of use to his fellow-man. He is a member of the Anshe Sholom Synagogue. On April 26th, 1896, Mr. Sweet was married to a daughter of Mr. & Mrs. Joseph Blumenstiel, and in all his communal work, he has the active support of his wife. He has one son, Joseph, who is a barrister, practising in Hamilton, and one daughter, Miss Theresa Sweet.

ANSHE SHOLOM CONGREGATION, HAMILTON

THE oldest Jewish Congregation in Hamilton and one of the pioneer religious bodies of Canada, was incorporated by Parliament of Canada on May 5th, 1863, under the name of the Anshe Sholom Congregation. Among the signatories to the application for incorporation were Jacob Frey, Isaac Levy, Henry Zinshimer, Samuel Desbecker, Leopold Rosenband, Daniel Shire, Simon Shire, Leopold Loeb, Isaac Shire, William Loeb, Mendel Levy, Abraham Levy, Herman Levy, Jonas Draenger, Solomon Ungar, H. Wolf, Bernhard Weinberg, Abraham Simon, and Louis Daniels.

Under the Act of Incorporation the congregation had the power to hold property not exceeding five thousand pounds in value, to be used for the purposes of a cemetery and synagogue.

The earliest available Hamilton directory (1851-2) gives the names of three Jews, J. Samuel, David Rose, and G. J. Lazarus. This was prior to the incorporation of Hamilton as a city. In the directory of 1856 the number had increased to thirteen, and in the following year ground was purchased for a cemetery. The deed to the ground is dated that year and is signed, on behalf of the Hamilton Jews, by four members of the community, who purchased it in the name of a Hebrew Benevolent Society, which was the first Jewish communal institution in the City, and which had been formed some time previously.

HUGHSON STREET SYNAGOGUE, HAMILTON

For a number of years after the congregation was incorporated services were held in a hall on King Street West, in fact, it was not until 1882 that a synagogue was erected. There was very little wealth among the charter members, many of whom were in business in surrounding settlements, and in 1882, led by Edmund Scheuer, who had arrived in Hamilton in 1871, and by the late Mark Cohen, funds were raised for the building of the synagogue on Hughson Street, which is still used by the congregation.

Originally starting as a strictly orthodox congregation, at the time that the synagogue was erected an innovation was made by the men and women worshippers sitting together. This was the first attempt at Reform Judaism made by the Jews of Canada, and Edmund Scheuer was again instrumental in this movement.

The first confirmant in the synagogue was Adolph Levy, a son of one of the charter members, and today a leading citizen of Hamilton, who has held the office of president of the congregation, a position that has also been held by his brother, Gabriel Levy.

The first minister to the congregation was the Rev. Wolf Landau, who officiated for many years. The regularly ordained rabbis of the congregation have been Dr. Berkenthal, and Rabbis Joseph Friedlander, Jacob Minkin, Julius Berger, and the present incumbent, Iser Freund. The Rev. Mr. Wohlberg succeeded Rabbi Berkenthal, and he was succeeded by the Rev. Mr. Philo.

Foremost among those who should be mentioned for signal services rendered the congregation is the late Mrs. Herman (Camilla) Levy, who in 1875, organized the Deborah Ladies' Aid Society, as an auxiliary society. Mrs. Levy was elected the first president of this society, (of which an account is given elsewhere in this volume) and retained this office until her death in 1916. A woman who practically devoted her life to the welfare of the congregation and of her coreligionists, she set an inspiration that on various occasions was perhaps the only means of keeping the congregation alive, and Hamilton Jewry may well be said to owe everything to her. Edmund Scheuer was the president of the congregation for many years, resigning in 1886 on taking up his residence in Toronto. The late Mark Cohen was also a very active member, and for the past forty years David Sweet has been one of the leading members of the congregation, for much of this long period holding executive office.

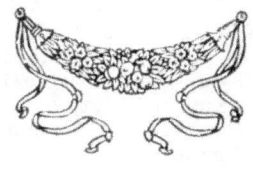

DAVID DUNKELMAN, TORONTO

Simpson Bros.

DAVID DUNKELMAN, President and proprietor of the Berger Tailoring Company, Limited, Toronto, was born in Poland on July 4th, 1883, the son of Eli and Leah (Titon) Dunkelman. As a young child he accompanied his parents when they took up their residence in the United States. He received his education at the public schools of Brooklyn, N.Y. In 1902 he came to Canada, settling in Toronto, where he has since resided. On his arrival in Toronto he took up a commercial career, and in 1910 commenced his present business as a wholesale clothing manufacturer, organizing a retail chain store clothing system. Mr. Dunkelman has developed this business into the largest firm of one price tailors in Canada, with twenty eight branches in all the leading centres from coast to coast, and employing over five hundred persons. Although his business interests are large and take up a great deal of his time, Mr. Dunkelman has not forgotten his less fortunate co-religionists, and he is one of the outstanding communal workers in the City of Toronto. His activities are not confined to any one creed, but he is particularly interested in the Zionist Movement, with which organization he has been prominently identified. He is a member of the Council of the Zionist Organization of Canada. He is a Trustee of the Federation of the Jewish Philanthropies of Toronto, a Director of both the Toronto Hebrew Free School and Toronto Hebrew Free Loan Association, and a member of all the charitable institutions of Toronto. On January 19th, 1910, Mr. Dunkelman was married to Rose, daughter of Mr. and Mrs. H. Miller, of Toronto. They have three sons, Joseph, Benjamin and Ernest, and two daughters, the Misses Zelda and Bernice Dunkelman. Mr. Dunkelman is a member of the Toronto Board of Trade; Canadian Manufacturers' Association; Empire Club; Canadian Club; and Primrose Club. He is a member of Mount Sinai Lodge, A.F. & A.M.

THE LATE JACOB SINGER *From a Painting*

THE LATE JACOB SINGER, in his lifetime one of the best-known citizens of Toronto, was born at Jawarow, Galicia, in 1844, the son of Moses Singer, of that place. He was educated in his home community and as a young man went into the business of watch manufacturing. In connection with his business he travelled over all parts of Europe. He was married in Cracow, Poland, to Annie, daughter of the late Louis and Rifka Fogler. In 1866, when twenty-two years of age, he came to Canada, settling in Toronto, where he resided continuously until his death, which took place on November 23rd, 1911. On his arrival in Toronto, he again entered the watch-making and jewellery business, and almost from the start became interested in real estate. He devoted much interest in this, and became one of the largest property holders in the city. At the time of his arrival in Toronto, the Jewish population was very small, and there was not much demand for communal activity, but Mr. Singer was associated in all the enterprises at the time. As the Jewish immigration increased, he took a very prominent part in assisting the new arrivals to become worthy, self-supporting citizens of Canada, and on innumerable occasions he assisted them by giving them lodgings in his own houses. In those days it seemed a natural thing for the needy to call on Jacob Singer, and they never called in vain. He was one of the earliest members of the Holy Blossom Synagogue, and always took a great interest in this congregation, an interest which has been maintained by his children, one of his sons, E. F. Singer, being the present Secretary. Several of his sons are prominent in the professional life of Toronto. He was survived by his widow, nine sons, Moses, the late Dr. Solomon, Max, Israel, Alex, Abraham, Isidore, E. Fred and Arthur, and three daughters, Jennie, (Mrs. Dr. G. R. Miller, Brooklyn, N.Y.) Fanny, (Mrs. Sig. Lyons) and Miss Helen Singer of Toronto.

AHAVATH ACHIM SYNAGOGUE, ST. JOHN, N.B.

A HISTORY of the Jews in the Maritime Provinces could be written around the lives of the first Jewish settlers in St. John, N.B. Arriving in that city in the early sixties, these pioneers were able to adapt themselves to existing conditions and the roots planted by them took a firm hold in the soil of the young country.

The first Jews to settle in St. John were three brothers-in-law, Nathan Green, Solomon Hart, and Henry Levy, who arrived there in 1858 from England. They were the only members of their faith there for many years and when Louis Green, a son of Nathan Green, married his cousin, a daughter of Solomon Hart, it was necessary to bring a Rabbi from Boston to perform the ceremony. This was in the year 1882, and the small community had then been enlarged by the arrival of Abraham and Israel Isaacs who had arrived from England in 1878. The two Isaacs also married daughters of Solomon Hart. These were the first weddings performed in the Maritime Provinces by members of the Jewish faith. In social and communal undertaking the small Jewish colony mingled with their neighbors and an instance of the respect in which they were held may be gathered from the fact that Nathan Green was the last man to receive the freedom of the City of St. John, prior to Confederation.

Mrs. Solomon Hart, in 1900, organized the Daughters of Israel, which undertook all the charitable and philanthropic work in St. John up to recent years, when the North End Ladies' Society was formed. A daughter of Mrs. Hart's, Rebecca, (Mrs. M. Wyzanski) was also very active in the Daughters of Israel.

It was not until 1898 that the population increased sufficiently to form a congregation, but this was done in that year.

The happiest day in the annals of the Jewish citizens of St. John was on January 11th, 1899, when the first synagogue in that city was consecrated by the Rev. Dr. A. H. Nieto, of the Shearith Israel Synagogue of New York City. The ceremony took place in the presence of all the members of the Jewish community, the Mayor of the City, and many of the most prominent residents, including several clergymen. The synagogue was handsomely decorated with cut flowers and palms.

The ceremony, which was most imposing, was opened by Master S. Hart Green, a grandson of the first settler in the city, Solomon Hart, who advanced to the reading desk and recited three verses of Genesis. When coming to the text "Let there be Light and there was Light," the building became immediately illuminated. Then came the demand for entrance, accompanied by three loud taps on the door, the Reverend Doctor Nieto exclaiming! "Open for me the gates of the righteous that

SOLOMON HART
1825-1901
Settled in St. John 1858

I may enter through them to praise the Lord." The door was then opened and the Rabbi entered, bearing a Sephar Torah and followed by Rabbis Garrovitch and Tobkin, and Messrs. J. Komiensky, J. Meyers, G. Jacobson, Max Wener and M. Odle. Three circuits of the synagogue were made, the choir chanting during the first circuit the 30th Psalm, "Dedication to the House of David" whilst the 122nd and 126th Psalms were sung during the second and third circuits. The three Sepharim were then deposited in the Ark, the first by A. Isaacs, and the other two by I. and D. Komiensky. The perpetual lamp was lighted by the President.

Doctor Nieto then gave an address, hoping that the congregation would continue to live in the honour of God and in its own self-respect. He then gave the Blessing, and declared the synagogue open for worship. The Rabbi then offered a most earnest prayer for Her Gracious Majesty Queen Victoria, the Royal Family and the Governor-General, the officials of the congregation, and all those present.

The congregation established a religious school, under the supervision of Mrs. S. D. Lewis, and Mrs. Louis Green, where the children of the members were instructed in the tenets of their faith.

LOUIS GREEN
Born London, Eng., 1854; Died St. John, N.B., 1921

ABRAHAM ISAACS
Born London, Eng., 1845; Died St. John, N.B., 1909

ISRAEL ISAACS
Born London, Eng., 1849; Died St. John, N.B., 1924

LIST OF SYNAGOGUES

Although we have made every endeavor to get full information, and have repeatedly written to the officials, it has not been possible to obtain any further details from the following congregations.

CHEVRA THILLUM CONGREGATION,
H. B. Rockitt, President,
Montreal

CHEVRA MISHNAYOTH CONGREGATION,
S. Zittrer, President,
Montreal

SHAARE TEFILLA CONGREGATION,
A. Klein, President,
Montreal

NUSACH AARI CONGREGATION,
J. Albert, President,
Montreal

PINSKER SHUL CONGREGATION,
I. Figler, Secretary,
Montreal

TIFERETH ISRAEL CONGREGATION,
Mr. Capelowich, President,
Montreal

AVATH SHOLEM CONGREGATION,
N. Miller, President,
Montreal

BETH ABRAM CONGREGATION,
N. Rohr, President,
Montreal

BETH HAMEDROSH HAGODEL CONGREGATION,
J. B. Miller, President,
Montreal

KHAL JESHURUN CONGREGATION,
I. Kugelman, President,
Montreal

TEMPLE SOLOMON CONGREGATION,
Mr. Farowich, President,
Montreal

TIFERETH JERUSALEM CONGREGATION,
S. Selbst, President,
Montreal

ISRAEL BAL SHEM TOV CONGREGATION,
Mr. Magdof, President,
Montreal

BETH ITZCHOK CONGREGATION,
M. Strudensky, President,
Montreal

ETZ CHAIM CONGREGATION,
M. Mallek, President,
Montreal

YAVNA CONGREGATION,
Montreal

BETH ISRAEL CONGREGATION,
S. Bordo, President,
Montreal

KEREM ISRAEL CONGREGATION,
P. Parnass, President,
Montreal

ANSHE MARMAROSH CONGREGATION,
B. Nathanson, President,
Montreal

NEW ADATH JESHURUN CONGREGATION,
Rabbi, Julius Berger,
Montreal

BETH ISRAEL and SAMUEL CONGREGATION,
Montreal

SHOLEM BETH ZION CONGREGATION,
Montreal

CHAVERIM KOL ISRAEL CONGREGATION,
Montreal

BETH DAVID CONGREGATION,
Montreal

SHEVETH ACHIM CONGREGATION,
Montreal

METZUDATH DAVID CONGREGATION,
Montreal

ANSHE OZEROFF CONGREGATION,
Montreal

POALE TZEDEK CONGREGATION,
Montreal

BETH JOSEPH CONGREGATION,
Montreal

CHEVRA SHASS CONGREGATION,
Montreal

BETH JEHUDA CONGREGATION,
Montreal

HADRAS KOIDESH CONGREGATION,
S. Amsel, President,
Montreal

SHROMRIN LABOKER CONGREGATION,
S. Greenberg, President,
Montreal

ADATH ISRAEL CONGREGATION,
(ROUMANIAN)
48-50 Centre Avenue,
Toronto
I. Goodman, President

BEACH HEBREW SYNAGOGUE,
109 Kenilworth Ave.,
Toronto

BETH ISRAEL ANSHE MINSK CONGREGATION,
10 St. Andrew Street,
Toronto
B. Gurman, President

Continued on page 168

RABBI JULIUS BERGER, MONTREAL

THE REVEREND JULIUS BERGER was born at Shaville in Lithuania on December 28, 1892, the son of Rabbi Joseph David Berger. Coming to Canada as a child, he received his early education at the Public School and at the Collegiate Institute, Ottawa, Ontario, and then entered Columbia University, New York. He received his degree of B.A. from Columbia and Western University, and his M.A. degree from McGill University, Montreal. His early Hebrew training he received from his grandfather Rabbi Chaim J. Baron. After a course at the Jewish Theological Seminary of America, he was given his Rabbinical degree. In 1917, he was called to the pulpit of Anshe Sholom Congregation, Hamilton, Ontario, which he ably held for six years. He was very active in immigration, civic and philanthropic work. He was one of the organizers of the Viceroy Reading Lodge No. 886, I.O.B.B., Hamilton. During the war he was appointed chaplain for the Jewish soldiers in the Hamilton area. He took a keen interest in the problem of the under-privileged child and was on the Executive of the Juvenile Court. He is a member of Barton Lodge No. 6, A. F. & A. M., and was given the honor of delivering the dedicatory address at the occasion of the unveiling of the Service Flag. He is a member of the Scottish Rite, and so far is the only Rabbi in Canada to have conferred upon him the 32nd degree. He was on the Speakers' Committee of every Victory Loan Campaign, and is a member of the Canadian Club. In August, 1923, Rabbi Berger was called to the pulpit of the New Adath Jeshurun Synagogue, Montreal, where he has become a conspicuous force in every communal endeavor. He is President of the Zionist Order, Habonim. Despite his many activities, he finds time to do considerable writing and has ready for publication; "The Status of Minhag in Jewish Law;" "The History of the Hagada Shel Pesach;" "The Education of the Jewish Child in the Light of Mishnaic and Talmudic Law." On June 19th, 1917, Rabbi Berger was married to Rebecca, daughter of Osias and Shlime Fitch of Quebec City, and has one son, Montague Berger.

LIST OF SYNAGOGUES—*Continued*

K'NESSETH ISRAEL CONGREGATION,
350 Maria Street,
Toronto
M. Greenblatt, President

SHAAREY TZEDEK CONGREGATION,
29 Centre Avenue,
Toronto
S. Dvoretskey, Secretary

SHEARITH ISRAEL ANSHE LIDA CONGREGATION,
239 Augusta Ave.,
Toronto
J. Weiner, President

B'NAI ISRAEL CONGREGATION,
257 Shaw Street,
Toronto
M. Ellenberg, Secretary

STRATENER CONGREGATION,
32 Cecil Street,
Toronto
C. Pasternack, President

TZEMACH TZEDEK CONGREGATION,
Denison and Grange Avenues,
Toronto
B. Sacken, President

BELLEVUE SYNAGOGUE,
21 Bellevue Ave.
Toronto

B'NAI ISRAEL HAMIZIACHIM CONGREGATION,
177 Berkley St.
Toronto
M. Brown, Secretary

ADATH JESHURAN CONGREGATION,
S. B. Levin, President,
Winnipeg

ATERES ISRAEL CONGREGATION,
V. Rubin, President,
Winnipeg

KENESES ISRAEL CONGREGATION,
H. Labovitch, President,
Winnipeg

BETH ABRAHAM CONGREGATION,
M. W. Triller, President,
Winnipeg

OHEL JACOB CONGREGATION,
M. Herman, President,
Winnipeg

ASHKENAZIE CONGREGATION,
M. Dorfman, President,
Winnipeg

TEFERAS ISRAEL CONGREGATION,
J. Gershfield, President,
Winnipeg

THE TEMPLE SONS OF ISRAEL CONGREGATION,
J. Sadofsky, President,
Sydney, N.S.

THE HEBREW CONGREGATION OF SYDNEY,
A. Nathanson, President,
Sydney, N.S.

COBALT HEBREW CONGREGATION,
I. Jacobson, President,
Cobalt, Ont.

ENGLEHART HEBREW CONGREGATION,
I. Kert, President,
Englehart, Ont.

HESS STREET CONGREGATION,
Rabbi, S. Levin,
Hamilton, Ont.

HIRSCH HEBREW CONGREGATION,
Reader, M. Berner,
Hirsch, Sask.

KITCHENER HEBREW CONGREGATION,
Rabbi, A. Garfinkle,
Kitchener, Ont.

LACHINE CONGREGATION,
Rabbi, Hirsch Cohen,
Lachine, Que.

OXBOW HEBREW CONGREGATION,
Reader, J. Wasserman,
Oxbow, Sask.

QUEBEC HEBREW CONGREGATION,
Rabbi, M. Eliasoph,
Quebec, Que.

ST. CATHARINES HEBREW CONGREGATION,
R. Nadell, President,
St. Catharines, Ont.

WAPELLA HEBREW CONGREGATION,
S. Barish, President,
Wapella, Sask.

YARMOUTH HEBREW CONGREGATION,
Rabbi, P. Levin,
Yarmouth, N.S.

THE LATE E. BRONFMAN

EKIEL BRONFMAN, one of the earlier Jewish pioneers in the Canadian West, was born in Bessarabia, Russia, in 1851 and married Minnie Gelman in 1880. He came to Canada in 1889 and settled at Wapella, Saskatchewan, being one of the first members of the Jewish Farm Colony established there. After farming for several years he moved to Brandon, Manitoba, where he engaged in business until 1906. From 1906 until his death on December 24th, 1919, he lived in Winnipeg. While in Brandon he was instrumental in organizing the small Jewish community, and in building the B'Nai Israel Synagogue of which he was President for many years. He and his wife were life-long adherents to Orthodoxy. True to their belief in Jewish education, they had brought with them from Russia a Hebrew teacher and his family so that their children might be sure of a Hebrew education in the new land. In Winnipeg, Ekiel Bronfman was one of the most active supporters of the Rosh Pinah Synagogue and held almost continuous office alternately as President and Parnass. He and his wife were known in the Community for the laudable example they set in their home life, where by precept and example they upheld the old traditions of Judaism, particularly in regard to Hebrew education and loyalty to the family bond. They were always envied for the delight they had in the unity that existed among their large family, all grown up and married. Mr. Bronfman was a philanthropist in the true sense of *Gemilus Chesed*, in which he heartily believed and for which he never refused an opportunity. He was a contributor to all Jewish institutions. Almost his last act in life was the laying of the corner stone in memory of his wife, Minnie, who predeceased him on November 11th, 1918, in the new building of the Jewish Orphanage of Western Canada, the premier Jewish institution in the West, of which his son Allan later became President. Surviving him are four sons, Abe, Harry, Sam, Allan all of Montreal and four daughters Laura Aaron, Montreal; Jean Groper, Los Angeles, Cal; Bee Druxerman, Montreal; and Rose Rady, Winnipeg.

HEBREW AND RELIGIOUS INSTRUCTION

AS with Jews in other countries, religious instruction has always been considered of the utmost importance, and it was only a few years after the first members of the faith had settled in this country, that the question of the religious training of the young became a serious problem. It was settled by the arrival in Canada, in 1778, of the Rev. Mr. Jacob Cohen, who was brought out by the pioneer settlers to act as the spiritual head of the community, and to give religious instruction to the children. Mr. Cohen had come from London, and after a number of years spent with the Spanish and Portuguese Congregation in Montreal, he removed to Philadelphia, where he became minister of the "Mickve Israel" Sephardic Congregation of that city.

Chazan R. de Lara, Mr. Meyer Levy and Mr. Isaac Valentine, in turn, then assumed the ministerial duties in connection with the Montreal synagogue and also gave instruction in religion and Hebrew to the younger members of the community, and during the incumbency of Mr. Valentine a Mr. Bernstein, who had arrived as an immigrant, was given the position of teacher. He was succeeded by a Mr. Mendels, who held the position for a long time, and worked in conjunction with the Reverend David Piza, who had been appointed minister to the congregation.

In 1846, the Reverend Doctor Abraham de Sola was elected Rabbi, and he acted as the spiritual head of the community until his death in 1882. It was shortly after his arrival that he established a religious school in connection with the congregation. Prior to this the only subjects taught were Judaism and Hebrew, but Doctor de Sola opened a day school where other subjects were also taught, and the teaching was given with much efficiency.

Up to this time the only community where there were sufficient members to organize a congregation was in Montreal, and in the other cities and towns where there were scattered individuals, religious instruction was given in the homes by the head of the family. But in the period between 1850 and 1860, the communities in Toronto and Hamilton had grown to such an extent that congregations were formed and just prior to this a second congregation had been organized in Montreal. From the very first, religious instruction took the leading part of their activities and in all cases the different synagogues were fortunate in the teachers they employed, as they proved themselves exceptionally capable.

In July, 1869, Mr. Edward Moss, who had been Parnas of the German and Polish Congregation, Montreal, presented the Congregation with $1,000 for the building of a school. In 1872, Mr. Moss died and he left the sum of $400 to be invested in a bank in Montreal for the purpose of giving prizes to the two leading scholars in the Sabbath School.

As the Jewish population increased, largely through immigration, other congregations were started and other communities established. In 1863 there was a considerable Jewish community in Victoria, British Columbia, and a religious school was started there in connection with the synagogue; Mrs. F. Sylvester giving invaluable work as instructress for over half a century. In Hamilton, Mr. Edmund Scheuer started his career of religious instructor, founding the first Sabbath School in Ontario, and although he was the head of an important business, he has maintained an active interest in the instruction of the young up to the present time. In 1886, Mr. Scheuer moved to Toronto and at once took charge of the congregational school of the Holy Blossom Congregation. He also acted as principal of the religious school at the Zionist Building, and at the present time has charge of the religious school of the Spadina Avenue Congregation, which is under the auspices of the Sisterhood of the Holy Blossom Congregation. Mr. Scheuer is the outstanding figure in religious instruction in Canada, and for over fifty years he has devoted much of his time to this subject.

The Baron de Hirsch Institute, Montreal, conducted a day school for many years, in addition to a Sabbath School and a night school. Up to 1893, the Protestant Board of School Commissioners had made a grant to the school, but as additional schools were built by the Board, they considered it more satisfactory to have the Jewish pupils attend the regular schools, and withdrew the grant. The Baron de Hirsch day school was then operated in three grades only, the pupils, as soon as they acquired a sufficient knowledge of English, being sent to the regular schools. Hebrew and religious instruction were, however, continued both in the day and night schools, but as the attendance kept increasing the need for special schools of religious instruction was felt, and in 1898, the first Talmud Torah was established in Montreal. Another reason for the establishment of the Talmud Torah was the fact that the first generation of immigrants had become established in the country and their children were growing up. The parents had the memory of the European "Yeshivas" fresh in their minds, and were desirous that their children should obtain as complete a religious and Hebrew education as was furnished by the old country schools, and this they considered could only be done in a purely Jewish atmosphere, such as is embraced by a Talmud Torah. Another reason for the establishment of the Talmud Torah, was the dissatisfaction felt through the teachers calling at the homes of the pupils where the latter often had the idea that their recreation hours were being taken away from them. Other children, after school hours, had this time for play, but the Jewish child had to remain at home and study with the religious instructor. Going to a religious school with their fellow pupils for a short time did not appear the same to the children, and the results proved much more satisfactory.

Largely through the efforts of Mr. Lazarus Cohen, a brilliant Hebrew scholar and the one man who had the spirit of both the old country "Yeshiva" and the Canadian system of education, a number of Montrealers became interested and gave their support to the Talmud Torah. Mr. Cohen may well be termed the father of the Talmud Torahs in this country and his portrait, in oil, hanging in the Montreal institution, is a slight acknowledgment of his public-spirited efforts in its behalf. The prominent members of the community who have given their support to this institution all owe their inspiration to Mr. Cohen.

In 1900, a meeting was held in Foresters' Hall, Toronto, which was attended by over 300 heads of families, and it was decided to establish a Talmud Torah, where pure Hebrew would be taught the children. Mr. A. D Benjamin, who was chairman of the meeting, was elected the President.

Once started, Talmud Torahs were organized in different sections, some under the auspices of certain congregations and many as private institutions. It was in Winnipeg, in 1908, that the first United Talmud Torahs came into existence, with the election of a representative Board of Education who established a uniform plan of teaching in all the city Talmud Torahs.

Continued on page 172

J. GOLDSTEIN, MONTREAL

Jacoby Studio

JACOB GOLDSTEIN was born in Quebec City, on December 11th, 1861, the son of the late Mr. Adolph Goldstein of Montreal. He was educated in the Quebec High School, from which he graduated, and in 1877 he moved to Montreal, where he joined his eldest brother, Bernard, in the tobacco manufacturing industry. Mr. Goldstein has since resided in Montreal where he has taken a most prominent part in the communal, as well as the commercial life of that city. Shortly after he took up his residence in Montreal, he became a member of the Young Men's Hebrew Benevolent Society, and was later elected Secretary. He was one of the three originators and was the Secretary of the Montefiore Club of Montreal, and for two years occupied the position of President of the Club. He took much interest in immigration work and for a time gave instruction in the night schools established for immigrants. Mr. Goldstein was one of the founders, and for many years was President, of the Young Men's Hebrew Association, and on his retirement from this office was appointed Honorary President. During his connection with this organization, he formed the Young Men's Hebrew Association Boy Scout Troop. He was one of the original members of the Reform Movement in Montreal and at one time held office in the Temple Emanu-El. Mr. Goldstein has always been much interested in fraternal work. He was twice Vice-Regent and later became Regent of Prince Albert Council, Royal Arcanum. He is a member of the Federation of Jewish Philanthropies; Young Men's Hebrew Association; Hebrew Free Loan Association of Montreal; Hebrew Maternity Aid Society; Natural History Society; Montefiore Club; and Royal Arcanum. On January 20th, 1892, Mr. Goldstein was married to Ida, daughter of Mr. & Mrs. Julius Hyman of Newark, N.J., and he has two daughters, Mrs. M. M. Grossman of Vancouver and Miss Marjorie Goldstein of Montreal. His only son, Edgar Hyman Goldstein, was killed in action at the battle of Loos (Hill 70), in the Great War, at the age of twenty years. (See page 502).

This has not yet been accomplished in the other large cities, although in Montreal there is what is called the United Talmud Torahs, but it does not embrace all places of learning as in Winnipeg. In the smaller cities the one plan of education is carried out.

In both Montreal and Toronto the Talmud Torahs are housed in fine large buildings, the property of the community, but it is in Winnipeg that the example has been set, where there are several handsome buildings under the auspices of the Talmud Torah. Arrangements have also been made with the Public School Board for the use of certain of their schools, at stated hours, for religious instruction. In the smaller communities also exceptionally fine buildings have been erected as Talmud Torahs, which show the value placed upon religious instruction by the members of the communities. In most communities, the Talmud Torah is used also as a centre of all religious and social activities and it has been of inestimable value in uniting all sections of the people. It is only to be hoped that the other large centres will follow the examples set by Winnipeg in dealing with the study of Judaism and Hebrew by the Jewish youth.

In addition to the Talmud Torahs, religious classes are held by most of the synagogues, where the instruction on religious subjects is given in English, and many thousands of boys and girls receive their knowledge of Judaism in this manner. The classes are generally under the supervision of the Rabbi, with volunteer teachers, recruited from the graduating classes. In late years a number of schools have been established by labor organizations, called Peretz Shules and Folk Shules, and although the subjects taught cover Hebrew, Yiddish and Jewish history, emphasis is placed on certain viewpoints that differ from the teachings of the regular Talmud Torahs.

NATHAN SMITH, TORONTO

NATHAN SMITH, one of the "Fathers of the Talmud Torah" in Toronto, was born at Haradock, Province of Wilna, Lithuania, in December, 1858, the son of the late Henry and Etkah Smith. His mother died in Toronto, in 1913, at the age of 99 years. Nathan Smith received a thorough education in the schools of his native province and by private tuition, and was married there to Sarah, daughter of Selig Lossinger (renowned as a Talmudist and educationist), by whom he had four sons, the late Abraham Isaac and Julius, and Dr. I. R. Smith and Hyman M. of Toronto, and four daughters, Minnie (Mrs. A. Rapp of Montreal), Rosalind (Mrs. H. Pullan), and the Misses Lillian C. and Anna Smith, all of Toronto. In 1884, Mr. Smith settled in Toronto, and in 1886 he started the leather and belting business in which he is still engaged, with his son, Hyman M. Shortly after his arrival in Toronto, Mr. Smith joined the Goel Tzedec Congregation, of which he is still a member, and he has held various offices in this institution. Always interested in communal undertakings, he is a member and supporter of all the Jewish organizations in Toronto, but it is in connection with the establishment of the Talmud Torahs that he did outstanding work. He was one of the most active founders of the Simcoe Street Talmud Torah, the oldest Jewish religious school in Toronto, and at the present time is the president of this institution, having held this office for many years. He is a life governor of the new Hebrew Free School and Community Centre on Brunswick Avenue. Some years ago he was presented with a gold-headed walking cane as a recognition of his great work for the cause of Jewish education. He is also a director of the Toronto Hebrew Free Loan Association (G'milath Chasodim). Mrs. Smith, who passed away in 1917, also took a very active interest in all philanthropic undertakings, and their sons and daughters are ably maintaining their parents' interest, being prominent in many of the local charities and communal institutions. Mr. Smith is a member of the Toronto Board of Trade.

H. L. WEIDMAN, WINNIPEG

HIRAM L. WEIDMAN, President of Weidman Brothers, Limited, was born in Orli, Grodno, Russian Poland, the son of Benjamin and Rachel (Kirshner) Weidman. He received his education at, and graduated from the Yeshiva at Bialystock, Poland. Mr. Weidman was married at Billsk, Poland, to Miss Fanny, daughter of Laima Dalin, and has three sons, Nieman J., Bert H., and John J., and six daughters, Sara (Mrs. Udow), Dorothy (Mrs. Green), Bessie (Mrs. Meyers), Lillian (Mrs. Maza), and the Misses Anne and Sybil Weidman. Mr. Weidman arrived in Winnipeg in May, 1882, with his parents and brothers, and was one of the Jewish pioneers of Western Canada. He farmed in the district of Moosemin, Sask., from 1884 to 1887, and together with his father and brothers worked on the construction of the Canadian Pacific Railway in Western Canada. In the early nineties, he assisted in the work of the Baron de Hirsch Colonization Society in the West. In 1889, he returned to Winnipeg and organized the firm of Weidman Brothers, Limited, Wholesale Grocers and Importers, of which concern he is President. This firm is one of the largest wholesale grocery concerns in Western Canada, and the sons of both Messrs. H. L. and M. S. Weidman are the active heads. He has always taken an active part in all charitable undertakings and educational matters pertaining to the welfare of the Jewish community of Winnipeg. Mr. Weidman is one of the founders of the Winnipeg Talmud Torah, and has been Chairman of the Educational Committee since its inception. He took a very active part in the building of the Hebrew Schools in Winnipeg, of which he has been a mainstay ever since. He is one of the founders of the Shaarey Zedeck Congregation of which he is a member, and is a leader in the religious life of his people in his community. Mr. Weidman has always been a keen and enthusiastic Zionist and was the organizer of the first Zionist Society of Winnipeg. He is a member of the Independent Order B'nai B'rith, Winnipeg Lodge.

WINNIPEG HEBREW FREE SCHOOLS

תלמוד תורות דער וויניפעג

SOME of the finest institutions in Canada, and of which the Jewish citizens of Winnipeg justly feel proud, are their Talmud Torahs, known as "The Winnipeg Hebrew Free Schools".

These imposing edifices standing in the very heart of the Jewish section, impress the visitors to Winnipeg with accomplishments that are possible, when communal work is undertaken by an inspired and strongly united Jewish community. These institutions are indeed a noble monument to the men and women who have had to give so unstintingly of their time and energy to accomplish a result which will live long after them, and which has done its share towards strengthening and propagating the Hebrew language and Hebrew culture.

The history of the Winnipeg Talmud Torahs really dates back to 1905, when a number of early Jewish settlers got together to solve the problem of Hebrew education for the Jewish youths of the city. The Jewish population of Winnipeg was growing rapidly, and the children were growing up without the knowledge that a Jewish child should have of the history of his nation, of its culture, language and traditions.

The demand for some organized teaching centre was felt keenly, and in 1905 the nucleus of what later developed as the present Talmud Torah was formed. This small "Cheder" was founded in a small one-room building known as the "Edwards Hall." Some fifty children registered and the classes were handled by three teachers. But within one year the "Cheder" outgrew itself. The number of pupils grew at an immense rate. More space and a more elaborate and systematic organization was required to adequately control the matter of education, so in 1906, the B'nai Zion Society, an orthodox Zionist organization of the city, took matters in hand and secured space in a building on the corner of Charles St. and Dufferin Ave., more commodious and more suitable to satisfy the requirements of a school at that time. No sooner were they comfortably settled in their new quarters, when they discovered that their foresight had not been sufficiently distant. Only two years later they found themselves unable to accommodate the rapidly growing demand for Hebrew learning, and furthermore, the organization thought it advisable to hand the reins of administration over to a special Board, whose business would be to supervise this branch of communal activity.

In 1908, the first Board of Directors of the Talmud Torah was elected with the late Mr. Abraham Berg as President, and Mr. J. Pierce as Vice-President, and an executive consisting of Messrs. A. Milmet and E. Cherniack. This Board secured a building on the corner of Dufferin Ave. and Aikins St., and there inaugurated an improved Talmud Torah with one hundred and fifty children attending, and a teaching staff of four. Thus the Talmud Torah lived until 1911. In that year the number of pupils grew to about two hundred and fifty, crowding the new school so that many had to be turned away for lack of space. The condition grew serious. The building in use was not sufficiently large nor equipped for a "regular" school. A meeting of all the Jewry in Winnipeg was called and held at the Beth Jacob (House of Jacob) Synagogue. The matter was laid there before the meeting, and the seriousness of the situation explained. A suggestion was made, that a "real" building be erected by the Jewish people, which could and would answer the present and future requirements of the community. The meeting was very enthusiastic, and a new Board was elected with Mr. R. S. Robinson as President, and Mr. A. Berg, Vice-President. These, together with the directors, planned and accomplished a successful campaign from the Great Lakes to the Pacific Coast.

The cornerstone of this new building was laid in 1912, with great ceremony by Mr. A. Milmet, and work was rushed to complete the much needed school. In 1913, it was ready for occupancy. It cost approximately $65,000.00, and each man who worked for or contributed to this cause, felt proud of the result, when looking at the splendid structure. It was indeed a splendid building fully equipped with necessary classrooms, offices, desks and blackboards. The upper floor was occupied by a large auditorium that could be, and later was used as a community centre for the Winnipeg Jews, making this building the living heart of the community. The Talmud Torah and its auditorium became the Mecca of all Jewish affairs. Meetings, conferences, weddings, dances, lectures, all were held at the Talmud Torah, and during High Holidays it was used as a place of worship. There was room for everything. The lower two floors were used for classrooms. Only on Sundays, in non-teaching hours, the rooms were allowed to be used for meetings of the various Jewish communal organizations. Thus the Winnipeg Jews are now proud of possessing a splendid Jewish educational institution, an institution where Jewish history, religion, customs, laws and rites, in other words, Judaism, is being inculcated into the hearts of the children.

TALMUD TORAH BUILDING, WINNIPEG
MAIN BUILDING

The Talmud Torah teaches its pupils the significance of our Jewish Holidays, and how and why they should observe them. It teaches them the great history of our forefathers, and how they lived, developing in the children's hearts a pride in their national history. The children are also taught national songs, and all this is taught in Hebrew. The method of teaching in the Talmud Torah is "Ivris Beivris", meaning that all teaching conversation between the teacher and pupil is carried on in our old holy Hebrew language. The result of it is, that practically every child, except the "freshies," speak Hebrew fluently. Indeed when one enters the Talmud Torah, one finds oneself in a new atmosphere, where everything is said and spoken in Hebrew, where the children talk, play and even quarrel in Hebrew. The old Hebrew tongue is seen and heard to actually live, and one goes away with the impression that were there more Talmud Torahs of this kind, the Jewish problem would perhaps be solved sooner and Palestine regained and rebuilt.

The system instituted by the then Board of Education, was commended and copied by Eastern Talmud Torahs both in Canada and the United States. As a matter of fact, in 1915, "The Yiddish Folk," a New York Publication, in an editorial mentioned that there were only three Talmud Torahs at that time that occupied a commanding position amongst the educational institutions upon the American continent; one in New York, one in Boston, and the third was the Talmud Torah in Winnipeg.

It was not long however before even this large building was filled to capacity, with a teaching staff consisting of fourteen well-learned and trained teachers. The institution, although being centrally located in the Jewish section of the city, was unable to satisfactorily take care of all or even the majority of the Jewish children.

About the year 1913, a delegation presented itself to the Board of Directors of the Talmud Torah, on behalf of a Jewish teaching centre which was conducted in the Adath Jeshurin Synagogue, with the request that this Board take under its wing this weak institution, and inaugurate there, a system similar to the one in operation at the new Talmud Torah. The Board of Directors gladly accepted this offer, and annexed these classes under the name of the McGregor St. Branch.

The Talmud Torah was and is recognized in this city, as the only systematic and successful Jewish teaching medium, and numerous requests were being received daily for information as to the method of teaching used in the Talmud Torah and system of handling the matter of communal Jewish education.

The Talmud Torah in 1919, had to further extend its activities to the southern section of the city, and under its auspices, classrooms were organized in the Shaarey Zedek Synagogue, thus forming a second Dagmar branch.

The McGregor Street branch, as said before, was located in the Adath Jeshurin Synagogue. This was an old frame building, erected years ago by a small Jewish body to be used as a synagogue. About the year 1920, this building became very shabby, frail and entirely unsuitable for the purpose it was used for. The sanitary condition of the building was also very unsatisfactory, and repairs had to be constantly made to satisfy the complaints of the City Health Department. Furthermore, the space in that building was not sufficient to hold the number of pupils registered in that branch. Classes were conducted with dim lights and the ventilation was unsatisfactory. So in the year 1921, the Board of Directors of the Talmud Torah, decided to erect a new building in the vicinity of this branch, which would provide modern, sanitary and well-lighted school rooms for the children who were compelled to attend this branch because they lived too far to be able to register in the main Talmud Torah Building. Action was immediately commenced to raise funds, and with remarkable rapidity a building was erected on the corner of Andrews St. and Magnus Ave., costing some $40,000.00, with five large school rooms and a spacious hall on the ground floor.

The number of children now being taught in the Talmud Torah branches is about 800:—the main school teaches about 400, the Magnus St. branch about 350 and the Dagmar branch about 50.

During the period of 1912-1922, the Jews of Winnipeg had considerably increased in number and scattered throughout the city, with the result that it was impossible for many who lived at a distance from any of the above Jewish schools, to send their children for Hebrew education, and compelled them to employ private tutors, who naturally did not follow the system of the Talmud Torah, to the disadvantage of the children. It was naturally impossible and not feasible for the Board of Directors of the Talmud Torah, to undertake or enter into new building enterprises, but something had to be done to take care of these children, who were handicapped by reason of their residence being far from the city Jewish schools.

An interview was arranged with the secretary of the City School Board, controlling some 70 school buildings in the city, for the purpose of ascertaining whether the School Board would permit the Winnipeg Hebrew Free School to carry on classes under its auspices in any of the city schools. The request of the Winnipeg Hebrew Free School Delegation was favorably received, and arrangements are now under way to open Talmud Torah classes in one or two schools.

The Talmud Torah takes an active interest in all things pertaining to the welfare of their pupils even outside of their studies; for example, very active groups of Boy Scouts and Girl Guides have been formed, who showed themselves to great advantage very shortly after they were organized at the annual picnic of the Talmud Torah, being already well versed in the love of Scoutism.

The Directorate is now composed as follows: Mr. S. A. Berg, President; Dr. M. Rady, Vice-President; Mr. H. Fainstein, Treasurer; Mr. S. F. Katz, Hon. Secretary; Mr. H. L. Weidman, Chairman of the Board of Education, and Mr. A. Stein, Mr. A. Skaletar, Mr. D. Rusen, Mr. S. Bookhalter, Mr. N. Korman, Mr. S. Goldin, Mr. S. Miller, Mr. N. Kushnir, Mr. N. Boxer, Mr. S. B. Levine, Mr. A. Cohen, Mr. L. Booke, Dr. C. J. Bermack, Mr. C. Tadman, Mr. S. Shore, Mr. M. Cohen, Mr. M. H. Levinson, Mr. F. M. Sures, Mr. M. Finkelstein, Mr. J. A. Chmelnitsky.

Delegations representing the Jewish community of Elmwood and Fort Rouge called on the Board, and requested that the Board take over complete supervision over their Talmud Torah branches. Their request was granted, and to-day the Board of Directors have under their jurisdiction and management, six branches scattered in all parts of Winnipeg.

During these twelve years of existence as a modern Hebrew School, the various Boards of Directors have always been greatly assisted by the Ladies' Auxiliary, who have not only worked to add a great sum of money to the maintenance fund of the institution, but also took a close interest in the home condition of the children attending the Talmud Torahs, and, where necessary, have given their moral and other assistance to improve the environment and the home atmosphere.

The Talmud Torahs certainly deserve the appreciation of the Winnipeg Jews for what they have accomplished. Hundreds of children have passed through their classrooms, and emerged with a knowledge of Hebrew and a spirit of Judaism that will redound to the benefit of Jewry at large. They have helped lay the foundation of our national language, just at a time when we Jews are preparing to become a nation and need our language. There are Jewish boys and girls in Winnipeg to-day, who speak Hebrew with no more difficulty than they do Yiddish. The Talmud Torahs have taught this to hundreds of poor children, whose parents would not have been able to give them this knowledge, if they had to pay for tuition. They have inculcated in the hearts of the Jewish children of this city a feeling of self consciousness, a feeling of patriotism, a feeling that will make them in their older years *Jewish* Jews. They have accomplished much and will accomplish much more. They have been intrusted with an important duty, and they have taken care of their trust. These institutions therefore deserve and expect the continued confidence of the Jews of Winnipeg and of Western Canada.

THE LATE BENJAMIN ZIMMERMAN

THE LATE MR. BENJAMIN ZIMMERMAN, in his lifetime a prominent member of the Jewish community of Winnipeg, was born in Kiev, Russia, in 1863. He went to Winnipeg in 1882 with the first influx of Russian Jews into the Canadian West, shortly after the construction of the Canadian Pacific Railway. Mr. Zimmerman entered into the jewellery business and remained in this until his death which took place on September 12th, 1923. He took a prominent part in every Jewish movement in Winnipeg and in the Prairie Provinces, and was one of the active founders of the first synagogue established in Winnipeg. He was the first President of the United Hebrew Relief of Winnipeg, and held this office for a number of years. He was one of the organizers of the Jewish Immigrant Aid Society of Winnipeg, and was very active in this connection. Mr. Zimmerman was one of the founders of the Winnipeg Talmud Torah, and was a staunch supporter of all movements tendering to the betterment of his co-religionists. He was particularly interested in looking after new arrivals, and in seeing that they had their requirements and the opportunities necessary to make themselves self-supporting, and becoming worthy members of the community. In the days of Major T. Mayne Daly, before Sir Hugh John McDonald was Police Magistrate, Mr. Zimmerman frequently sat on the bench as Justice of the Peace, and his impartial and judicial decisions earned him the highest respect of all classes of the community. When the Rosh Pina Synagogue was formed, Mr. Zimmerman was elected the first President. He was a member of the Oddfellows and Ancient Order of United Workmen, and was one of the earliest members of the Winnipeg Lodge, Independent Order B'nai B'rith. Mr. Zimmerman did not confine his philanthropic activities to the Jewish people, but was of assistance in any undertaking affecting the general good of the community. Mr. Zimmerman was survived by his widow and seven sons, Samuel, Joseph, Harry and Abraham of Winnipeg, and William, David and Percy Zimmerman of Vancouver, B.C.

S. A. GOLDSTON, REGINA

SIM ALFRED GOLDSTON, Accountant and Auditor, was born in London, England, April 4th, 1873, the son of the late Rev. Abraham Goldston of that city. He received a very thorough Jewish, as well as general education, by private tuition and at King's College, London. He came to Canada in 1892 to take charge of the Jewish schools in the Hirsch Colony, Sask. Mr. Goldston held this appointment for some years, during which time he did much to improve the educational conditions in the colony, and he also took a leading part in the communal life of the colonists. After resigning this position, he entered the grain business in South Eastern Assiniboine. He remained until 1917, when he moved to Regina, where he has since resided and where he is regarded as one of the representative members of the Jewish community. He entered into the business of accountant and auditor, and has gained an enviable reputation for his integrity, and sound business judgment. Mr. Goldston is Secretary of practically every Jewish organization in the City of Regina. He is particularly interested in the new Talmud Torah, and was indefatigable in his efforts towards the building of this institution, which would be a creditable work for a city many times the population of that of Regina. He has been a member of the executive committee since its inception, and devotes much time to its supervision. He is an enthusiastic Zionist, and takes a leading part in the Regina branch of the Zionist Organization, and in all other communal undertakings. He was very active in relief work during the war, and was on the general committee for the relief of Jewish sufferers in the war-stricken areas of Europe. On September 6th, 1917, Mr. Goldston was married to Adelina, daughter of Wm. Riddick, and he has two daughters, the Misses Gladys and Dorothy Goldston. Mrs. Goldston died on November 29th, 1922. Mr. Goldston's activities are not confined to any one creed, and he is highly regarded by all sections of the community.

REGINA HEBREW FREE SCHOOL

LIKE institutions of a similar nature throughout the whole of this Dominion the history of the Talmud Torah or Hebrew School is virtually the history of the congregation. It shows its increase in numbers and its prosperity. Very few Jews settled in Regina till 1909 and from that date they gradually increased till today they number two hundred families. No apparent effort was made for the tuition of the children except through the medium of various private "melamadim" who occasionally came through the city, and the result was far from satisfactory. With the advent of Zionism into Regina in 1914 the question of training the children in the language, history and traditions of Judaism became very apparent and a public meeting was called to consider the question. A committee consisting of J. Schwartzfeld as President; Z. Natanson, Vice-President; B. Zurif, Treasurer; and H. Causman, Secretary, was selected to start the work. A room was rented in a store and a teacher engaged. The school started with thirty children, but as the numbers increased it was found that the room was too small and other arrangements must be made immediately.

Another meeting was called in 1917 at which H. Isman was elected President, and M. Hechter, Vice-President, supported by a strong committee and they at once got to work and rented two lots from the city authorities next to the synagogue on Ottawa Street, and erected a building which it was thought would fulfil the requirements for some years to come. But the anticipations of the committee were doomed to disappointment for notwithstanding several additions to the building, it was found as time went on, that it was too small and unfit for scholastic purposes. In 1922, the Jewish population of Regina had increased to 150 families, and it became apparent that new arrangements must be made without further delay. Regina, which was now the capital city of the province, was the seat of education and normal schools, collegiates and colleges to which Jews from other parts of the province came without any provision being made for their religious welfare, and it was considered absolutely necessary that this phase of the work must also receive immediate attention.

The initiative in the matter was taken by the local lodge of the B'nai B'rith, Louis Brandeis Lodge, No. 833, in September, 1922, which purchased five lots in the centre of the city—Broad Street—and presented same to the Jewish community to be used only for school purposes.

On the receipt of this generous gift a meeting of the various Jewish organizations of the city was immediately called, and the question of building a modern school was discussed at great length. A committee was appointed to consider if the location of the lots was suitable and it was decided that they were too far from the Jewish centre. However, an exchange of property was arranged with the authorities of the city for the present site consisting of five lots on Halifax Street valued at $6,000. A committee representing the various organizations was selected, which was known as the Regina Talmud Torah Building Fund Committee and this committee was given full power and authority to collect moneys and proceed at once to erect a suitable building. The following comprised the original committee:—President, Z. Natanson; Hon. President, H. Bronfman; Treasurer, H. Rabinovitch; Hon. Secretary, B. Zurif; General Secretary, H. Kahn. Executive committee:—Joseph Gordon, A. Abrams, H. A. Bercovich, B. Dechter, I. Friedgut, H. Isman, M. Hechter, M. F. Kovsky, D. B. Kliman, P. Lesk, J. Gherman, S. Lexier, B. Margolius, C. Naimark, W. Natanson, S. Pearlman, S. Sandormirsky and W. Schachter.

This committee got to work immediately and advertised for plans and specifications for the building. Several plans were submitted and finally the plans submitted by Messrs. Storey & Van Egmond, architects, of Regina, were accepted. The question of finance arose and donations were solicited from the Jewish residents of the city. An appeal was made in the synagogue on the first day of Rosh Hashonah, 1923-5684, and the response being of such a generous nature the committee decided to commence at once on the building of the foundation.

REGINA HEBREW FREE SCHOOL

It was then decided that a drive be made through the province with the object of getting funds. Without making invidious distinctions, special mention must be made of the trip made by Messrs. Z. Natanson, S. Sandomirsky and Joseph Gordon, who travelled 2,200 miles by auto, visited twenty-two towns and villages at their own expense and collected over $3,000. Another committee consisting of Messrs. Schwartzfeld, Isman and Schiller went east and succeeded in raising a fair amount. Early in the spring of 1924, tenders were called for and the tender of Messrs. Wilson & Wilson, Limited, for the erection of a building consisting of four class-rooms, assembly hall, banquet hall, kitchen and play-rooms for the sum of $32,485 was accepted, and the work started at once.

The foundation was completed and on May 11, 1924, the foundation stone was laid with great ceremony. Invitations were sent out to every donor and visitors poured in from all parts of the province. Spirited addresses were given by the Rev. Rabbi Kahanovitch and M. J. Finkelstein, of Winnipeg, and the day was considered a Jewish holiday. The school children suitably attired and decorated with the Zionist colours, and members of every Jewish organization, old and young, formed into a long parade, headed by the Scouts' Band, and marched from the old building to the new site, where prayers were offered by Rev. Kalif. The honour of laying the foundation stone was sold by auction to Mrs. Z. Natanson for $1,500, who delegated the honour of laying the stone to her husband, the president. In the stone was placed a list of the donors to the Building Fund, copies of the minute book, the history of the Talmud Torah, a copy of the "Canadian Jewish Review" and copies of the London, England, "Jewish Chronicle" and "Jewish World", as well as the last edition of the Regina papers the "Leader" and "Post". After the stone was declared well and truly laid, the first layer of bricks was sold and the honour of laying the first brick went to H. M. Schiller for $300. Over three hundred bricks were sold and about $1,500 realized. Work proceeded on the building, which was finally completed early in September.

The consecration and formal opening took place on Sunday, September 7, 1924, which was a red-letter day in the history of Judaism not only in Regina, but throughout the whole Province of Saskatchewan. Visitors were present from all parts of the province, many travelling considerable distances to be present. Prior to the opening of the building the honour of raising the flag over the building was sold to Mrs. Z. Natanson for $200, and amidst great cheers, the Union Jack and the Palestine flag were raised and the National Anthem and the Hatikvah sung. The key of the front door was purchased by W. Natanson in the name of his mother, Mrs. Faiga Natanson, for $500. The religious ceremony was then recited by the Rev. Kalif, of the House of Jacob Synagogue, and the building declared open. The company then proceeded to the Assembly Hall where D. B. Kliman acted as chairman and introduced the various speakers. On the platform were seated His Honour Sir F. W. G. Haultain, the Chief Justice and acting Lieutenant-Governor, who was accompanied by his Aide-de-Camp, Major Allard; the Hon. J. A. Cross, Attorney-General of the Province; the Hon. S. J. Latta, Minister of Education of the Province; His Worship S. J. Burton, the Mayor of Regina; Rabbi Kahanovitch, Chief Rabbi of Winnipeg; M. J. Finkelstein, Barrister, of Winnipeg; and H. E. Wilder, representing the Zionist Organization of Canada, all of whom gave addresses.

After the addresses, the keys and contents of the various rooms were auctioned by H. Isman and brought large prices. Each purchaser of a key was presented with a golden key suitably inscribed. Subscriptions were also taken for the Golden Book which was purchased by A. Silver for $100 and presented to the institution. Considerable money was raised this way.

The first election of officers took place on September 24th, 1924. The following were elected:—President, Z. Natanson; Vice-President, Joseph Gordon; Treasurer, S. Sandomirsky; Trustees for two years, D. B. Kliman, Dr. Kraminsky, M.D., A. D. Chmelinsky, A. H. Friedgut, LL.B., B.A., M. F. Kovsky; Trustees for year, Dr. Gitterman, M. Hecter, H. M. Schiller, H. A. Bercovitch, A. Abrams.

At the first meeting of the new board, various committees were appointed in addition to S. A. Goldston, Secretary; D. B. Kliman, Hon. Solicitor; Dr. Gitterman, Hon. Dental Officer; and Dr. Kraminsky, Hon. Medical Officer. The school is now incorporated under a public act of the Legislature of Saskatchewan, but an application for a Private Act of Incorporation has been made and is now pending. The bill among other matters provides for the exemption of the school from taxation pursuant to a resolution to that effect obtained from the council of the city of Regina.

The opening of the school for tuition took place October 22, and there are now 165 pupils enrolled, which it is anticipated will increase to two hundred in the near future. Great difficulty was experienced in getting suitable teachers, but finally the staff was completed and consists of S. Magid, principal, L. Greenberg and L. Lederman. Mrs. A. H. Friedgut acts as singing mistress, and is training the children in Hebrew folk-song. The system of education adopted is that laid down at a conference of western educationalists held at Saskatoon in 1923 which provides for the practical needs and idealism of Judaism. It also provides for a uniformity of teaching throughout all western Hebrew schools.

The building is modern in every respect, being fully equipped with all the latest appliances as to heating and ventilation, and is claimed to be the best of its kind in the Dominion of Canada. The cost of the same is about $55,000.

In the hall-way of the building a marble tablet has been erected containing the names of all donors of $100 or more, and the names of the building committee.

The building is being used as a communal centre and all Jewish meetings and social gatherings are held there. The kitchen is fully equipped and will fill a long-felt want in the community.

In addition to money subscribed, several donations of furniture and fittings were made by friends of the institution. It is the intention of the committee in the near future to make provision for any Jewish students attending the various colleges in the city, to have a proper Jewish home and tuition in the school. It is hoped that as time rolls on, the original idea of making the Talmud Torah a communal home will be realized.

SASKATOON TALMUD TORAH

SASKATOON is no exception to the rule that a Talmud Torah demands the respect of the Jewish people more than any other institution. Even before the community of this town could boast a synagogue, rooms were rented for the purpose of teaching the children of the Jewish residents Hebrew and religious instruction. These classes were continued despite many obstacles and difficulties, and the hope of having a suitable building was always in the minds of the members and supporters. It was however, not until 1915 that the building which is at present used as a Talmud Torah was purchased on Avenue 1.

This building was purchased for an outlay of $3,000 and it was done at the time when Mr. M. Rose was President of the Talmud Torah.

Since then the work of this institution has gone ahead in a very satisfactory manner and it is supported, like most other communal institutions throughout the West, by the undivided co-operation of the whole Jewish community.

The Jewish women of Saskatoon in furthering Jewish religious and home life have ably maintained the standard set in other larger communities. They were very active in their campaign for the support of the Talmud Torah, and without their assistance the things that have taken place would never have been accomplished.

The present officers of the Talmud Torah are as follows;—President, Max Gropper; Vice-President, J. Mallin; Treasurer, J. Weinstein; Secretary, D. Wolochow; Recording Secretary, M. Trugman; and Trustees, M. Adilman and B. Zukerman.

THE EDMONTON TALMUD TORAH

THE problem of Jewish education is the one that all small Jewish communities find most difficult to solve and Edmonton's experience has been no different from the rest. Notwithstanding the difficulties, however, financial and others, we find earnest and sincere men, devoted to national traditions, willing to make the sacrifice of time, effort and money that is required to overcome these difficulties, at least to the extent that it is possible to do so. And Edmonton has never wanted for men of this type. Thus we find that for nearly twenty years, facilities have been provided for the education of the Jewish youth, comparable, at least in recent years, to those afforded in even the larger centres, and within the next few months the only thing now lacking—a new Talmud Torah building—will be completed.

At present rooms in the synagogue are used for school purposes and while these were adequate in former years, it is felt that the time has come when a change is imperative and plans for a new building are now in progress.

In 1906, according to the records of the Edmonton Hebrew Association, the pioneer Jewish institution of Edmonton, it was found necessary to provide facilities so that the children of two of its members, Mr. A. Cristall and Mr. H. B. Kline, could secure a Jewish education and this was one of the duties assigned to Mr. H. Goldstick, who had been engaged by the congregation to administer to its needs.

This was the beginning of the Edmonton Talmud Torah and laid the foundation for that institution, which was not incorporated into a separate corporate body until some years later—1912 to be exact. About a year previous to this Mr. H. Malkin had been brought from New York to take over the duties that had formerly been performed by Mr. Goldstick and such assistants as he was able to procure. It was felt however that the community had now attained a degree of numerical importance where a man specially trained for the work, and who would be able to devote his entire time to it, was essential. Shortly after Mr. Malkin's arrival, arrangements were made with the Edmonton Hebrew Asssociation for the use of suitable rooms in the synagogue and these, with necessary changes and alterations, are still in use.

With the incorporation of the Talmud Torah as a separate entity an assistant to Mr. Malkin, Mr. B. Green, was found necessary, particularly as the community was increasing rapidly in population. Due, perhaps to inexperience more than anything else, the new organization soon ran into financial difficulties from which it was unable to extricate itself and the school closed its doors, Mr. Malkin and Mr. Green departing for fields where the prospects for steady employment appeared more certain.

This state of affairs was not permitted to exist for any length of time. The Edmonton branch of the B'nai B'rith was appealed to, to take charge of affairs and a committee mostly of young men under the chairmanship of Mr. A. H. Goldberg commenced the work of re-organization and in a comparatively short time the school was once more in a flourishing condition with Mr. A. Wershof, a man of high qualifications and considerable experience, in charge.

The financial difficulties were solved by obtaining monthly contributions from the various Jewish organizations, the principal contributors being the B'nai B'rith and the Jewish Council of Women each of whom undertook and has continued to pay $25 per month; also by incorporating into the membership of the Talmud Torah and securing voluntary monthly contributions from practically every responsible citizen, young or old, regardless of whether or not he sent children to the school. In this way the financial problem was solved but there were many others which arose from time to time, the chief of which were the method of teaching to be employed and in later years the erection of a Talmud Torah building.

As to the question of method or system, after various experiments, the younger element in the community finally succeeded in having the Ivrith b'Ivrith system adopted and it is now generally conceded that it was the wisest move that could have been made.

After four years of excellent service, Mr. Wershof resigned and was succeeded by Mr. J. Yompolsky, who after a short time was replaced by Mr. E. Gurelik, under whose splendid direction the school made remarkable progress. After Mr. Gurelik's departure for Montreal, to complete his medical course, the Talmud Torah was fortunate in securing Mr. Pekarsky who is now in charge and whose services have proved highly satisfactory to the community.

A campaign to erect a building at a cost of $20,000 is now in progress with success assured, thanks to the generous assistance of the Council of Jewish Women, who not only presented the Talmud Torah with the lot, at a cost of $3,000 upon which the building is to be erected, but have also raised over $5,000 in cash by various bazaars and functions of a similar nature. Such a record achievement will stand to the credit of this worthy institution for all time.

With the entire community solidly behind the institution and with men true to the highest aims of Jewry interested in its welfare, the future of the Talmud Torah need cause no concern and the Jewish youth is assured of facilities for acquiring an education of the language, history and traditions of his forefathers, equal to the best that can be obtained in any part of Canada.

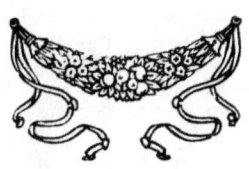

TORONTO HEBREW FREE SCHOOL

AT the present time, the Talmud Torahs of the City of Toronto have not united as in most other centres, and there are a number of different schools located in various parts of the city. The larger and more important of these are:- the Toronto Hebrew Free School on Brunswick Ave., the Simcoe St. Talmud Torah, the D'Arcy St. Talmud Torah, the Euclid Ave. Talmud Torah, the Augusta Ave. Talmud Torah, the Berkeley St. Talmud Torah, and the Maria Street Talmud Torah. Each of these conduct their courses of education independently of the others, but it is to be hoped that they will soon unite under one management. In all, many hundreds of pupils are attending these schools, where they are receiving a thorough training in the Hebrew language and Jewish religion and history.

In addition to the different Talmud Torahs mentioned above, and a number of smaller ones, the Jewish youth are taught their religion, and the Hebrew language in the various Sunday Schools attached to the different synagogues, and there are many hundreds of pupils who attend these classes every week. The largest attended of these Sunday Schools is that of the Holy Blossom Synagogue on Bond Street.

The oldest of the Talmud Torahs is that located on Simcoe Street, which was organized about twenty years ago. Among the founders were:- Messrs. L. Levinsky, M. Gelber, S. Weber, N. Smith, E. Pullan, A. Lieberman, S. Wortzel, M. Clavir and others. The first President was Mr. E. Pullan. The building was remodelled from an old house, and consisted of eight rooms, and for many years this Talmud Torah was the chief source of Hebrew education in Toronto. Mr. B. Nathanson was appointed principal, and has been in charge of the institution ever since. When the attendance of this Talmud Torah reached two hundred and fifty pupils, it was decided that the quarters were no longer adequate, and that a new building which would be modern and up-to-date in every respect, was required. It was decided that this new Talmud Torah would be equal to anything on the continent, and this optimism has been materialized.

In 1918, the idea of building a Talmud Torah with a community centre was discussed. Mr. L. Levinsky was the President of the institution at that time and in company with Rabbi Gordon, he began to solicit funds among the Jewish people for the new building. They devoted practically their entire time and the utmost energy to their mission and inside of a year were successful in raising promises for almost $90,000.00. These subscriptions were to be payable in instalments, and with the first instalment collected, land was bought on Brunswick Ave. for the building. It was not, however, until the end of 1922, that the construction of the new Talmud Torah was commenced.

A very active Building Committee, headed by Mr. M. Gelber as Chairman, and consisting of:- D. Lavine, S. Wurtzel, J. Bochneck, B. M. Speyer, A. Lieberman, N. & H. Smith, L. Levinsky, P. Levi, W. Leibel, P. James, E. Pullan, J. Becker, G. Kling, Rabbi Siegel, J. Samuels, S. Harris, L. Abramowitz, B. Weiss, D. Dunkelman, H. Pullan, M. Sigal, M. Shapiro, L. Gelber, H. Mendelson, Dr. M. Pivnick, G. Solway, N. Muscovitz, N. Margulies, B. Brown, J. S. Granatstein, Rabbi Gordon, M. Cohen, H. Greisman, D. Goldberg and M. L. Willinsky was appointed. The work on the building was started, and today is practically finished. On the 21st March, 1924, the cornerstone was sold to seven members at a meeting held for this purpose in the new building, and on September 21st, 1924, the official laying of the cornerstone took place. This ceremony was performed by the purchasers of the cornerstone.

The size of the building is sixty-six by one hundred and forty feet, and it is four and one-half storeys high. The entire cost, including land, will be about $200,000.00 and the Jewish community of Toronto can take pride in the fact that they have the finest and most complete Talmud Torah in Canada. There are seventeen rooms, with accommodation for seven hundred and fifty children at one time. There is also an Assembly Hall that can seat twelve hundred people, and which will be utilized for meetings and Divine Services for the Holy Days. The ground floor also contains a small Shool, which has been completely equipped, and which will be used by the boys who will conduct their own services. There is also a library for the boys and a separate library for the adults. Among the innovations in this building are a gymnasium and a swimming pool, which will be for the use of the children who attend the school, or for any members of the Talmud Torah. The architect in charge of this building was Mr. Benjamin Brown, a graduate of the University of Toronto. In 1925 a Ladies' Auxiliary was formed, that has undertaken to look after the expense of some of the interior furnishings of the new school and other activities connected with it.

THE SIMCOE STREET TALMUD TORAH, TORONTO

THE OLDEST TALMUD TORAH, and for years the only source of Hebrew education in Toronto, is located at 242 Simcoe Street, and was organized about eighteen years ago, in 1907. This was brought about by the members of the then existing synagogues, realizing the necessity of such an institution, uniting and making a drive for membership for a Talmud Torah, which should be situated in the centre of the Jewish community of Toronto. The drive proved very successful, and about four hundred members joined the Talmud Torah. Membership fees were paid from $3.00 to $25.00 a year, and many donations were received, resulting in the buying of the present house.

The house that was purchased contained eight rooms, and being in a rather dilapidated condition, it was remodelled and re-decorated. It was then fitted up with the necessary black boards, desks, books, etc. for a school of Hebrew learning. Four classes were immediately begun for about one hundred children (both boys and girls), and lessons were given in the teachings of the Bible, Hebrew Grammar, Hebrew Language, Religion, Jewish History and Talmudic teachings, taking in every phase of Jewish and Hebrew study.

The school was officially opened by Mrs. N. Brenner, on June 9th, 1907.

The services of Mr. B. Nathanson were secured, he having previously taught in the Hebrew schools of Rochester, and he was installed as principal of the Talmud Torah, in which capacity he has acted ever since. Several other teachers were also engaged.

The number of pupils increased very rapidly, at one time reaching about four hundred, the staff then consisting of five teachers. The Jewish population however, moving further West, other Talmud Torahs were organized; and the classes of the Simcoe Street Talmud Torah decreased to the present number of about one hundred and sixty pupils, with three teachers, Rabbi J. Gordon, Mr. L. Madorskie, and Mr. H. Bentch.

About two years ago, a kindergarten system of teaching for the little children was tried, but this however, did not prove successful.

There is a special High School class that is composed entirely of boys attending High School, which is under the supervision of Rabbi J. Gordon, where advanced Talmudic lessons are given. The students of this class organized a Junior Synagogue, services being conducted in the Beth Medrosh of the Goel Tzedeck synagogue, by one of their own class.

Among the organizers of this Talmud Torah are;— Messrs. L. Levinsky, M. Gelber, S. Weber, N. Smith, E. Pullan, M. Clavir, S. Wortzel, and A. Lieberman. The first President was Mr. E. Pullan, and succeeding him were Mr. P. Levi and Mr. N. Smith.

The present officers of the Board of Directors are;— President, N. Smith; Vice-President, M. Pullan; Treasurer, L. Pollock; Secretary, M. Alter; and the members of the Board are;—Rabbi J. Gordon, A. Lieberman, S. Mazin, J. Bochneck, P. Levi and L. Abramowitz.

The Simcoe Street Talmud Torah, however, will soon be extinct, as it will in the very near future, become affiliated with the Toronto Hebrew Free School on Brunswick Avenue.

THE JEWISH FOLKS' SCHOOL, TORONTO

THE JEWISH FOLKS' SCHOOL, 30 Bellevue Avenue, Toronto, was founded by Mr. H. A. Shubin, in 1914. It belongs to those institutions that have helped in the last ten years, to spread the national orthodox thought amongst the Toronto Jewish children.

When the Jewish Folks' School was first founded, at No. 17 Bellevue Place, not more than 20 children attended its classes. It took but a small time, however, before the name of the School spread to the different parts of the district, and at the end of the year, it was necessary for the present principal, Mr. A. Shubin, to seek larger quarters. He obtained the present house on 30 Bellevue Avenue, which contains 10 large rooms. The classes then numbered 300 pupils, with six teachers, and the hours of instruction were from three o'clock in the afternoon, until eight o'clock in the evening.

In the last few years, the classes of The Jewish Folks' School have become smaller, for various reasons. In the past ten years, about eight hundred pupils have graduated from the School, and a large number of these were well versed in T'nach, Hebrew Literature, and Jewish History, and they acquired a modern, orthodox, national outlook on Judaism.

The Principal, Mr. A. Shubin, has always endeavored to instill in his pupils the Jewish national spirit, and he has taught them to be proud of their nationality.

The Jewish Folks' School is considered one of the most important institutions for the upbringing of the Jewish child, and many of its former students may now be found in Toronto colleges and University.

EUCLID AVENUE TALMUD TORAH, TORONTO

IN 1915, a number of people who lived too far away for their children to conveniently attend the only existing Talmud Torah at that time in Toronto, located on Simcoe Street, met together and decided that to meet their requirements, a Hebrew School should be established in a part of the city west of Bathurst Street.

Mr. Chaim Lubetzky, at that time the Manager of the Simcoe Street Talmud Torah, and Mr. A. H. Farber who was also connected with that institution, became interested in this venture, and obtaining support from the people of the West end of the city, the present Talmud Torah on Euclid Avenue was inaugurated.

Among those who were early interested in the movement were;—H. Weintraub, the late S. Cohen, Mr. Rubin, Mrs. Miller and Mr. Isaac Starkman.

The first officers elected were;—Mr. H. Weintraub, Pres., Mr. Rubin, Treasurer, and Mr. Lubetzky, pro-tem Secretary. A few weeks later Mr. D. Solomansky was elected Secretary, and he held this office until May 20th, 1917.

The number of children increased daily, and soon the services of both a second and third teacher were secured.

On May 21st, 1916, (L'Ag B'Omar), the official opening of the Talmud Torah was celebrated, and as some time previously in that year the Gaon Isaac Jacob Raynes had died, Mr. Lubetzky, in order to perpetuate his memory, decided to name the Talmud Torah after him.

An attempt was made, some time later, by the officials of this Talmud Torah to organize a general Board of Education, where a common program of teaching for all the Talmud Torahs in the city would be installed. Owing to lack of support, this plan did not materialize.

On May 20th, 1917, at a general meeting, new elections were held, and Mr. Isaac Starkman became President, Max Cohen, Secretary, and Mr. Feld, Treasurer.

Realizing the fact that a rented house was not very satisfactory, it was decided to buy a house, and a committee was appointed to look after the details. In August 1918, at the suggestion of Mr. Lubetzky, the premises at 175 Euclid Avenue were purchased. An appeal was made to the entire community for financial assistance. The necessary amount was realized, and the building was properly equipped. Mr. M. Soren was Treasurer of this campaign.

Since that time the Talmud Torah has flourished, and the attendance has increased largely. Mr. Chaim Lubetzky is still the principal, and of the original members Mr. H. Weintraub and Mr. Starkman are still taking the most active interest.

VANCOUVER HEBREW SCHOOL

VANCOUVER is very proud of its Talmud Torah. With an attendance of 112 children, and a staff of three teachers, it has earned a great deal of praise from all who have visited this institution.

For a great many years there was an agitation for such a school, these agitators being led by the late Jacob Fleishman.

In 1918, a concrete program was devised by Mr. P. Tobin, an ardent worker in Judaism. This led to the formation and incorporation of the school, with Max M. Grossman as its first president.

It was soon found that teaching could not be carried on with the limited facilities at their disposal, especially as regards class rooms. Arrangements were then made with Congregation Shaarey Zedeck for the erection of a combined synagogue and school.

The finances of the school are covered by a set tuition fee to the parents of children attending, and by the annual subscriptions of the population at large.

In view of the fact that the Jewish population is scattered over a wide area, the school maintains a branch in the west end of the city, for those children who cannot, by reason of distance, attend the main school.

The school is maintained on the principle that the best method of teaching children the Hebrew language is by the elimination of all other tongues, and for this reason no language but Hebrew is allowed in the class rooms.

Mr. Grossman retained office until 1921, and on retiring, was presented with the honorary presidency for life. He was succeeded by Mr. Nace Swartz, who had been one of those whose time had been unselfishly devoted to Jewish affairs for years.

The next two years saw great strides made under the able presidency of Mr. A. Rothstein and Mr. J. W. Herman.

The present officers are: President, A. Robins; Vice-President, B. Margolius; Treasurer, L. Ripstein; Financial Secretary, M. Fouks; Recording Secretary, J. Stochinsky; Trustees, N. Swartz, A. Tanzman, J. Reed S. Levi, J. Hazan, S. Rothstein and R. Horowitz.

THE QUEBEC TALMUD TORAH

PRIOR to 1921, the Jewish children in Quebec City received their religious instruction from teachers who visited them at their homes. There were no organized classes for this purpose, and the system was very unsatisfactory. As Mr. Surchin, the Superintendent of the present Talmud Torah states, in the early days when the teacher called at the home he was looked upon with annoyance by the pupil who considered that he had come to take away time from his recreation hours.

In 1921, the death took place of Mr. Ben Zion Ortenburg, one of the leading Jewish citizens of Quebec. In his will he left his house located at St. Dominique Street to be used by the community as a school of religious instruction. The representatives of the community could not see that the house in question was suitable for their purposes, and after negotiations, Mrs. C. Ortenburg, the mother of the deceased sold the house for $3,500 and both she and her husband added $1,500 to this amount which was placed as a foundation for the construction of the Talmud Torah. On the 2nd of December, 1923, a committee was appointed to take action in the organizing of a Hebrew school. The members of the committee were;—M. H. Gardener, D. Millshtuk, David Goodman, T. Lux, A. Voloshun, D. Goodman, J. Schwartzboard and I. Ertzberg.

The committee became convinced that the amount on hand was not sufficient to erect a building such as they would like and they decided to make an appeal to all the members of the community. Mr. M. Gardener and Mr. D. Goodman volunteered to collect the necessary sum. All members of the community were approached and they contributed liberally, some doing considerably more than their share. Finally in 1924, a house was purchased on Margeuretta Street and the committee immediately started to renovate it and put it in such shape that it would be perfectly suitable for their requirements.

In September, 1924, the building was completed and instruction of the children was commenced. Mr. H. Surchin was appointed principal, with Mr. Osher Kupsky and Mr. Samuel Lerner as assistants.

Although the Talmud Torah has not been long in operation great success has already been achieved. The entire course of instruction is in Hebrew, and in this way the children learn to speak the language. The chief subject is naturally instruction in religion. The pupils have shown much devotion to their studies and the attendance is increasing rapidly.

A congregation for the children was organized in the Talmud Torah, where they are taught the form of prayers. The building has become a community centre and much progress is being made in every way.

The first Board of Education was re-organized on April 21st, 1924, and is as follows;—Mr. Olasoff, Honorary Chairman; M. Pollock, Chairman; M. Gardener, Treasurer. The committee consists of D. Goodman, A. Voloshun, T. Lux, J. Schwartzboard, David Goodman, I. Lux, and J. Ertzberg, with Moses Surchin as representative of the teachers.

On the wall fronting the street is a memorial stone on which is engraved "Talmud Torah House of the Son of Zion". The picture of the late Mr. Ortenburg, through whose generosity the Talmud Torah has come into existence, is to perpetually hang in the office of the principal.

The Talmud Torah received much assistance from the ladies of Quebec, among whom may be mentioned Mrs. D. Gardener, who supplied the benches and slates. Particular credit must be given to Messrs. M. Gardener, A. Voloshun and D. Goodman, who acted as arbitrators for the estate, and who have devoted much time and money to the organization and completion of the Talmud Torah.

THE CALGARY TALMUD TORAH

IN 1912, the Jewish residents of Calgary elected a Council to take over the management of its different institutions, and one of the first things they accomplished was the formation of a Talmud Torah. Mr. H. Cooper was the chief organizer, and Mr. M. Rubin was appointed the principal. Two recent arrivals from Europe were engaged as assistants, but their method of teaching did not seem to give satisfaction, and later a determined attempt was made to obtain experienced instructors.

The classes were held in the synagogue for some time, but were then removed to a private house, where however, they did not last, and for some time were altogether discontinued. The chief difficulty seemed to be to get teachers who would meet with the approval of every element of the community, which was somewhat difficult. The community at the time was disorganized and in factions, and it was not until 1918 that they became united and realized the urgent need of proper training for the young, in religious matters.

In 1919, the members of the Zionist society united with the members of the congregation and formed a committee to consist of six members of each organization, and to elect officers and start a campaign for funds for the Talmud Torah. Mr. Z. Goldberg was appointed chairman. The main difficulty was to secure proper teachers, and the delegates sent from Calgary to the Canadian Jewish Congress held in Montreal in that year, were authorized to obtain them. In July of that year Mr. H. Romer, an experienced instructor was put in charge, and the City Board of Education put the Central School at their disposal. Mrs. Berg, an arrival from Palestine, was appointed a teacher, and two classes were removed to the synagogue, and two classes to the Zionist building

RABBI HIRSCH COHEN, MONTREAL

RABBI HIRSCH COHEN, Chairman of the Montreal Council of Orthodox Rabbis; Chairman of the Board of Education of the United Talmud Torahs and Yeshivas, Montreal; Chairman of the Mizrachi Zionist Society; and Jewish chaplain to the prisoners at the penitentiaries, was born in 1862 (5622) in Budvitz, Poland. He studied in the Yeshivas of Vilna and Volozhin, and received his Rabbinical degree from the Presidents of these Yeshivas, and from the famous Goyen Jacob David "R.J.D.B.Z." In 1889 he arrived in Montreal where he has since occupied a foremost place in the Jewish community. He took a prominent part in the Kosher question and was the organizer of Talmud Torahs in all parts of the city, and was an active founder and is a supporter of all charitable institutions. He is a member of the executive of the Federation of Jewish Philanthropies, Montreal. During the war, 1914-1918, Rabbi Cohen organized the Central War Sufferers Relief Society of Canada that raised hundreds of thousands of dollars for relief of Jews in devastated sections of Europe and Palestine. He was founder and chairman of the Ezras Torah fund for the suffering Rabbis in Europe and Palestine. He was one of the founders and first treasurer of the Immigrant Aid Society of Canada, and also of the Ukranian War Orphans' Relief Society that brought many Jewish orphans to Canada. Rabbi Cohen is the most active propagandist in the Province of Quebec for separate Jewish Schools and his lectures and articles in the Press on this subject are given the utmost attention by Jews not only in the Province of Quebec, but elsewhere. Rabbi Cohen is recognized as one of the highest authorities on religious questions and he is in correspondence with the leading Rabbis in all countries, on Jewish problems and questions affecting the Jewish race. He is a member of the executive of the Association of Orthodox Rabbis of the United States and Canada. Rabbi Cohen is married to Leah Nachumowsky, and he has two sons, Louis Judah and Lazarus Eliazer, and three daughters, Mrs. Joseph Presner, Mrs. Harry Fierst, and Mrs. Meyer Bloch.

THE HISTORY OF THE UNITED TALMUD TORAHS OF MONTREAL

By A. J. Livinson, M.A.

IT is romantic and characteristic, this story of the United Talmud Torahs of Montreal. It bespeaks the old undying, unquenchable love for sacred learning perpetuated in the face no light obstacles, and of lack of facilities and financial means. All credit, therefore, is due to the pioneers and to their valiant successors.

In the Annual Report for 1898, of the Protestant Board of School Commissioners of Montreal, which we shall use here for lack of accurate Jewish statistics, we learn that out of a total attendance of 8,998 pupils, 1,107 were of Jewish faith. The Hebrew instruction of these children was provided for by "Chedarim" (room schools) "Melamdim"—"itinerant teachers", the Hebrew classes of the Baron de Hirsch Institute and the customary Sunday Schools. The total Jewish population in Montreal is then given as 7,000. It was natural, therefore, for the communal workers to realize the necessity of a modern Hebrew system of schools and in 1906, through the initiative of Rabbi Aaron M. Ashinsky and of Mr. Moses Coviensky, then president of B'nai Jacob Congregation, the foundation was laid for the first Talmud Torah in Montreal. The organization meeting was held in the B'nai Jacob Synagogue now bearing civic number 131 Cadieux St. It was in this holy edifice that Rabbi Ashinsky had also founded the "Agudath Zion" which was the first Zionist conference to take place in Canada.

For a time the Talmud Torah was located in Shapiro's Minyon, in a building now bearing number 130 Cadieux Street, just opposite the old B'nai Jacob Synagogue. Thence the classes through the advice of Rabbi Ashinsky, removed to 401 (now 245 East Lagauchètiere Street). This was a commodious two storey solid stone building, and had a fine large yard in the rear where both in summer and in winter playground facilities were amply provided. This in itself was a remarkably modern departure and innovation keenly remembered with pleasure by the alumni of this school.

It was in 1903, that the school followed the trend of population and removed to a newly purchased brick building at 143 St. Urbain Street. This structure was remodelled and fire-escapes added. The school became known as the Montreal Hebrew Free School and was chartered under that name. Amongst its foremost patrons was Mr. Lazarus Cohen, a highly respected citizen of the community. This school had and still has a congregation for daily worship, which is well attended, despite the fact that once again the district is fast becoming depopulated by a northward and westward movement of Jewish population.

In the meanwhile, in 1901, Rabbi Ashinsky received a call to Pittsburg, Pa., and the spiritual direction of the school fell to the lot of Rabbi Hirsch Cohen, who was then and is now Chairman of the Board of Education.

We have to wait until 1917 to reach the great milestone in Jewish sacred education. In this year, through the Herculean efforts of Messrs. Samuel Wener, Abraham Z. Cohen, Lionel Coviensky, Hyman L. Lavut, Moses Simon and Myer Block, the five existing independent Talmud Torahs having a total attendance of 800 pupils were combined for financial and educational purposes under the name of United Talmud Torahs of Montreal. The Annual Budget then was $16,000. By Act of Legislature of the Province of Quebec, the United Talmud Torahs of Montreal became finally incorporated in the year 1922.

In 1924, the number of constituent schools had increased to eight and there were 1,250 pupils in the Talmud Torahs and 57 pupils in the Yeshiva (Talmudic Academy). This Yeshiva was the first to be founded in Canada. Its sponsors were Rabbi H. Cohen, Samuel Kahn, Isaac Gold and Lionel Coviensky, the year of its creation being 1922. The Yeshiva Building is located at 412 Henri Julien Avenue, in a commodious building, pleasantly placed in an exclusive residential section of the city. Attached to the Yeshiva is a delightful chapel for daily religious services. The Annual Budget for the year 1924 was $50,000 made up from receipts from paying pupils and from contributions from 2,229 subscribers. The schools now under this arrangement are:—

Amherst Park Hebrew School	1783 de la Roche St.
Anshe Sfard Talmud Torah	11-13 Milton St.
Beth Hamedresh Hagodol School	945 Notre Dame St. W.
Bialik Hebrew School	2138 Mance St.
Montreal Hebrew Free School	143 St. Urbain St.
Poali Zedek Talmud Torah	3301 St. Urbain St.
Shaarey Zion Institute	1525 Marquette St.
The Yeshiva (Hebrew Academy)	412 Henri Julien Ave.

The presidents of the Talmud Torahs from its inception are as follows:—

Mr. Moses Coviensky	1894 to 1895
Mr. Moses Denenberg	1895 to 1897
Mr. Louis Holstein	1897 to 1898
Mr. Moses Denenberg	1898 to 1917
Mr. Samuel Wener	1917 to 1923
Mr. Louis Salomon	1923 to 1925

Of the above gentlemen, Mr. Moses Coviensky and Mr. Moses Denenberg have passed to their eternal rest, deeply mourned, sincerely respected and perpetually remembered.

To state the names of loyal friends who stood by the Talmud Torahs through good times and bad, would be in itself a lengthy catalogue. It suffices therefore to say it is thanks to these men and women that the advancement of Jewish science, religion and culture in Montreal has been so consistently progressive and that other parts of our vast Dominion of Canada have been both directly and indirectly influenced in the organization of Jewish education.

Of the schools, the Very Rev. Joseph H. Hertz, Ph.D., Chief Rabbi of the United Synagogues of Great Britain, during his pastoral visit in Montreal, spoke in most eulogistic terms. On May 6th, 1924, the Very Rev. Abraham Isaac Kook, O.B.E., Chief Rabbi of Palestine, officially visited the schools. His remarks on this occasion were highly complimentary to the instruction given in these schools. On that same occasion, Rabbi Max J. Mintz, of the Congregation Adath Jeshurun, Ottawa, Ont., who was one of the touring party, wrote the following: "It was my gratifying pleasure to visit in person the Yeshiva of Montreal, when in the presence of the eminent Rabbinic Delegation comprising Chief Rabbi R. Kook, Rabbi P. Shapiro, and Rabbi R. Epstein, a thorough test in Talmud was exercised and the boys responded to the fullest satisfaction of those present. The ceremony was one unique in the history of the Yeshiva." On March 22nd, 1925, Rabbi Margolis of Palestine and Rabbi Murriminsky of Akron, Ohio, both eminent Rabbis, visited the schools and congratulated them upon their splendid educational work.

These tributes are all well-earned and speak volumes for the sincerity of purpose on the part of teacher, pupil, parents and officers to make the schools leaders in their respective spheres.

On October 29th, 1924, there was organized in the new B'nai Jacob Synagogue, Fairmount Avenue, the first Ladies' Auxiliary of the United Talmud Torahs of Montreal. This unique society promises to do much good in supporting the endeavors of the United Talmud Torahs. The honorary organizer of the Auxiliary is Mr. J. Merson, and the officers are:—President, Mrs. F. Harris; Vice-President, Mrs. A. Kanigsberg; Treasurer, Mrs. J. L. Zlotnik; Honorary Recording Secretary, Mrs. H. Presner; Financial Secretary, Mrs. H. Singer; Convenor of Membership, Mrs. J. Merson. Another group organized to support the Talmud Torahs is Young Israel, whose president is Mr. Isidore Charnes, B.C.L. This body affiliated itself with the Talmud Torahs in April, 1925.

The officers of the United Talmud Torahs of Montreal for 1924 are:—Honorary President, Mr. Samuel Wener; President, Mr. Louis Salomon; Vice-Presidents Mr. Morris Tannenbaum, Mr. Hiram Levy, Mr. Lionel Coviensky; Treasurer, Mr. Jacob Latt; Honorary Secretary, Mr. A. J. Livinson, M.A.

Board of Directors:—B. D. Adelman, A. I. Cohen, H. Cohen, A. Z. Cohen, R. A. Darwin, I. Davine, S. Farovitch, Adolph Gardner, I. Goodman, S. Greenspon, A. Guttman, A. Harris, A. Klein, Morris Kahn, H. Lehrer, S. Leopold, H. Lande, D. Myerson, S. L. Nathanson, H. B. Rokit, M. Rabinovitch, I. Rivenovitch, N. Silver, M. Simon, M. M. Sperber, K.C., D. Sperber, S. Silverstone, N. Sloves, J. Salomon, M. Tritt, L. Ticktin, B. M. Weiner, B. Wilanski.

Board of Education:—Rabbi H. Cohen, Chairman; Rabbi A. Salmanovitch, Rabbi S. A. Garber, Rabbi J. L. Zlotnik, Rabbi Wochtfogel, Rabbi H. Abramowitz, Rabbi J. Berger, Rabbi S. Dubitzky, E. Cohen, J. Chananie, I. Cohen, O. Cohen, L. Efros, R. Epstein, Levi Kert, J. Kivenko, B. Levitt, B. Machlovitch, A. H. Rabin, A. Rabinovitch, B. Steinhouse, L. Yelin, I. Gold, Honorary Secretary.

With a school population of 12,000 Jewish children in Montreal, the United Talmud Torahs are on the threshold of an era of expansion in which a program for the erection of modern school buildings will be the essential point to be concentrated upon. Montreal now has some 60,000 Jews and the recognition of Talmud Torah instruction in the past has always met with a ready response and the writer of this history is of the opinion that this encouragement will be no less enthusiastic in the near and distant future.

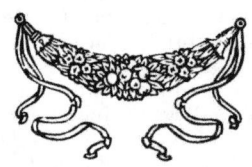

THE HISTORY OF THE JEWISH PEOPLE'S SCHOOLS OF MONTREAL

By S. Wiseman, M.A., Principal

THE movement of the Jewish People's Schools, which stands for progressive and modern Jewish education is only eleven years old.

In order to understand the principles underlying the modern system of the Jewish People's Schools and its achievements, we must dwell briefly upon the Jewish educational system found in the City of Montreal at the time when the new educational movement was started. Led by opposition to, and criticism of the old system, the founders of the Jewish People's Schools developed their positive attitude to Jewish educational problems, and constructed according to it their own system.

The Jewish settlement in Montreal is quite young, and the serious attempts made to establish a proper Jewish educational system is still younger. Some twelve years ago there were in Montreal a few Talmud Torahs, a great number of very old-fashioned private "chedars", and a still greater number of ambulatory "melamdim", who provided the Jewish children with a smattering of nothing.

The founders of the Jewish People's School movement felt a very keen dissatisfaction with this condition of Jewish education in Montreal. They clearly saw that the methods and principles applied even by the most efficient of these institutions were not taking cognizance of the necessities created by prevalent conditions in the new world, and were dwindling down the concept of Jewish culture almost to a nonentity.

The Hebrew language was being taught in a very primitive and unpedagogic manner, with the result that the pupils of the schools knew very little of it while attending them, and approximately nothing after leaving them. The Yiddish language was not taught at all in these schools. An attitude of disrespect to it was inculcated in the maturing minds of the children by the teachers, who used a very corrupt, ungrammatical and unliterary Yiddish language. The study of the modern Hebrew and Yiddish literatures, which is a very efficient and powerful pedagogic means for the inculcating of the greatest ideals of our people, and for the development of the aesthetic nature of the child, was utterly neglected. The study of Jewish history, which is all-important, and which should rank foremost in any system of Jewish education, was undertaken in a very scanty and unsystematic manner, and at that in a backward, unmodern spirit, which conflicted greatly with the methods and principles applied in similar studies pursued by the children in the public and High Schools. The study of Yiddish and Hebrew folk songs was left altogether untouched by these schools. The greatest stress was laid upon the teaching of Jewish religious ceremonies and dogmas, without any regard to the question whether these were in accord with the home atmosphere of the children attending these schools.

The founders of the Jewish People's Schools felt that the main reason for the low state of Jewish culture, the lack of earnest interest in and attachment to Jewish national ideals and aspirations, prevalent in the city at that time, was the backward and altogether inappropriate manner and spirit in which the youth had been brought up. Enthused by a very urgent desire to ameliorate and do away with this educational system and to establish one that would be adapted to the requirements of our time, the needs of our people and the nature of the Jewish child, the founders of the Jewish People's Schools approached their Herculean labour.

With due justice to historical facts it should be said at the outset that the Jewish People's School, known as "Folks' Shule", was not the first progressive Jewish national school in Montreal. At the time of its founding, June, 1914, a Jewish "National-Radical School", known at present by the name of "Peretz Shule", had already been in existence for a period of about two years. But this school, which was at first dear and near to the hearts of the founders of the Folks' Shulen, did not satisfy the standard set by them.

The main reason for this dissatisfaction was due to the fact that, both theoretically and practically, this Peretz Shule was in the main Yiddishistic, recognizing the Hebrew language as a sort of advanced study to be pursued by the senior pupils of the school. There seemed to have been, too, a slight, though at times exaggerated, difference of opinion between the founders of the Folks' Shulen and those who stood at the helm of the Peretz Shule, regarding the extent to which the spirit of the school was to be nationalistic.

The writer of this article notes with great satisfaction that the edges of these two extremes in the field of Jewish education have worn off. In fact the movement of the Folks' Shulen has caused the orthodox educational institutions to modernize somewhat, both in their theory and practice, and has likewise influenced the leaders of the Peretz Shule to a more positive attitude toward Jewish nationalism and the Hebrew language.

The first Jewish People's School, known as the Folks' Shule, was founded in June, 1914, on the initiative of a group of the Montreal Poale-Zion party, under the leadership of Dr. Jehudah Kaufman and others. The principles underlying the new system of education were then enunciated by the committee, and they have, with but few slight changes, remained to this day. They embody the national and social outlook of the founders, as well as the progressive pedagogic principles and theories that are in keeping with their general outlook.

Briefly summarized these principles are: (1) The recognition of the Hebrew and Yiddish languages as the national languages of the Jewish people, and the equal importance of both languages in Jewish life and for the education of the Jewish children; (2) The paramount importance of the study of Jewish History of all ages and of all countries; (3) The great educational importance of all forms of art, particularly Hebrew and Yiddish folk songs and dances; (4) Jewish nationalism, and particularly the rebuilding of the ancient Jewish homeland—Palestine. (5) A progressive outlook on life, and a broad progressive interpretation of all historical and present phenomena in social and other spheres in life; (6) A positive and sympathetic attitude towards the ideals of freedom, in its broadest sense, including political, economic, social and national freedom; (7) The importance of freedom, spontaneity, self-activity in the development of the child's soul and the realization of his personality; (8) The necessity of co-operation of the school and the home, thus necessitating the education of the adults; (9) The recognition that the ethical teachings of the Jewish religion embodied in the Bible and ancient Hebrew literature, are its most essential elements; (10) The importance of adapting the educational system to the needs of the times and of the country in which we live, so that the new generation should be suitable to carry on the struggle for the Jewish national existence, for the further development of the Jewish culture in all its modern aspects, and for progressive human ideals.

The registration of pupils for this school began in

September, 1914, and the first enrolment was very small. There were only about thirty parents in Montreal who realized the importance of this new trend of Jewish education and who could, in a word, be persuaded to entrust their children to this new experiment. The school fees paid by these parents were very small, in most cases not exceeding one dollar a month per child.

It was equally as difficult to find teachers who could live up to the ideals of the founders of the school. One of the chief reasons for this difficulty was the lack of the necessary funds to keep the school going. It is only the limited space allotted to me that keeps me from telling the interesting tale, a most human record, of great idealism, and superhuman efforts, connected with this new educational experiment.

The school was, at first, carried on in a few rooms, under the direction of some of the founders of the school, who were also its first principals, teachers, caretakers, collectors, propagandists, etc. But, in spite of all these difficulties, the school flourished greatly, due mainly to Dr. Jehudah Kaufman, and the teachers, who are too many to enumerate.

It may be interesting to note that many of the teachers teaching at that time in our school were young men and women who gained their livelihood by teaching in the old-established Jewish schools or by private tuition, and who gave their leisure hours, their full-hearted enthusiasm and constructive, educational idealism for the cause of the new experiment.

Meanwhile the program and the curriculum of the school was in the process of crystallization. Vast propaganda was being carried on in the city for the new experiment, which met with great and bitter opposition from all sides. It may be very curious and interesting to note that the leaders of the school found themselves against two strong extreme walls of opposition, based mainly on prejudice and ignorance. On the one side was the official orthodoxy, which denounced, in the synagogues, the school as a centre of Christian mission, of ungodliness and of lax morality. And on the other side, there was the semi-official Yiddishistic radical wing that looked upon the Folks' Shule as a modernized bourgeois Talmud Torah, certainly not fit to educate the children of Jewish workers. Fortunately, both extreme wings have now greatly modified their opinion regarding the work of the Folks' Shule.

Thus the school struggled on for a few years, changing its abode very frequently, yet increasing the number of its pupils and its classes, and gaining slow but sure recognition from the intelligent classes, and from the masses of the Jewish population of Montreal.

Dr. Jehudah Kaufman, graduate of McGill University, renowned Jewish scholar and the present director of the Jewish Teachers' Seminary of New York, was the first principal of the Shule. He was succeeded in 1916 by one of the first and ablest teachers of the school Mr. A. S. Zacher, a graduate of the Grovner Jewish Teachers' Seminary. Mr. Zacher held this responsible position up till 1920.

By 1917 the school numbered about two hundred and fifty pupils. The leaders of the school felt that unless they succeeded in obtaining a permanent abode for the school, the success of their educational work would be but partial. Still, all their efforts to raise sufficient funds to buy a school building were in vain.

In autumn, 1918, the leaders and the teachers of the school launched upon a new activity, which was destined to play a very important role in the development of the school, and in the realization of the educational ideals of the founders. That is the Hebrew kindergarten which was then opened.

It became clear at that time, that if the recognition of the equal importance of Hebrew and Yiddish in the school curriculum was to take on material forms, something must be done to obviate the difficulty attending the study of the Hebrew language, and to put this study upon a natural and modern basis as that of a living tongue. It was therefore resolved to open a two-year kindergarten course, in which youngsters of the ages from four to six years should get a modern kindergarten training in the Hebrew language. The children thus have a fair grounding in the Hebrew language at the time when they enter the elementary classes. The difficulties attending such an undertaking were quite evident. There was no means of securing a trained kindergarten teacher. The school did not have the proper accommodation for such work, and no financial means for the equipment of such a room. These difficulties were, to a certain extent, surmounted again, thanks to the idealism of the teachers. One of the women teachers and first founders of the school, Miss Z. Ackerman, undertook to prepare herself for this work. She did everything possible to adapt herself as a kindergarten teacher.

The number of the kindergarten pupils increased but gradually, due to the novelty of the experiment. It was not until the year 1920 that the kindergarten came to realize the plan that was laid out for it, and the hopes that were based on it.

By the time of the founding of the kindergarten, (Autumn, 1918), the work of the school was beginning to show its results. Children were beginning to grow up under the influence of the school, and were showing that the work was being crowned with success. The ten-year old children brought to their homes and into the homes of their friends a great deal of Jewish enthusiasm and idealism. The frequent concerts held by the school on the occasion of Jewish holidays and of great important Jewish cultural events, which were attended by many hundreds of people, were a great means of propaganda for the cause, and proved, even to the bitter opponents the great possibilities underlying the new educational experiment. The circle of friends of the new system widened extensively, and it was only due to the encouragement given to the first founders and leaders, that the school was able to go through its first years of development.

Then came the most memorable year in the history of the new movement, the year 1920. In that year, the school entered on a new era in its development. It came to stay. This was mainly due to the fact that the leaders at last succeeded in buying a school building in the very heart of the city, in which the school is at present situated, (953 St. Urbain St.). The Building Fund Campaign began in May, 1920, and lasted for several months. It was carried on under the able guidance of Mr. M. Dickstein, one of the founders of the school, and at present chairman of the Board of Directors. It was a great success, as it enlisted many enthusiastic supporters from the rank and file of the Jewish population of Montreal. The Board was then very fortunate in enlisting among its supporters a very warm-hearted, intelligent and congenial man, Mr. N. Nobleman, who then became President of the School, keeping this position uninterruptedly until the present. The school owes much of its success to the services of this man, who has worked tirelessly to put it on a solid financial basis.

The school then came under the principalship of one of its teachers, the writer of this article, who had then obtained his first academic degree from McGill University, to be followed a few years later by a Master's Degree.

The new school house opened new possibilities for the development of the school. The number of pupils increased rapidly. It reached the maximum which the school could physically hold. The number of pupils, by the year ending 1920 was close to four hundred.

The financial condition of the school was gradually improving. Due to the very energetic activity of the School Board the amount of school fees paid by the parents increased: Jewish parents of the middle and largely of the working classes were being gradually trained to pay for the Jewish education of their children. In 1920, the school fees covered two-thirds of the budget of the school, the same proportion holding up to the present time.

The Hebrew kindergarten reached a very high stage of development. A kindergarten room, equipped with all the necessary supplies was opened, and the most modern kindergarten methods (Revised Froebelian Methods) have been adopted and are practised. The school was very fortunate in securing the services of a well-trained, graduate kindergarten teacher from Palestine. Several teachers have since been in charge of the work, and they have all lived up to the standard of a modern well-regulated kindergarten.

The course of instruction in the kindergarten extends for two years. The pupils are about six years old when they graduate from the kindergarten. They then enter the elementary classes with a very fair knowledge of Hebrew as a living language, and they are thus well prepared to follow the Hebrew instruction given in the six years' elementary course of the school according to the best modern method of language-teaching, known as the Natural Method.

It was in 1920 that the teachers and the principal of the school launched upon a new activity, and that is the issuing from time to time of school magazines. The first hectographed magazine appeared in July, 1920, and was received very warmly by the parents and friends of the school. The purpose of these magazines, which have since been issued periodically, and which now appear annually in printed form, under the name of "Blienende Zweiglech", is to cultivate and develop the latent literary talents of the pupils; to develop in them the responsibility for the written and printed word, and to acquaint the numerous friends of the schools, in a very vivid and demonstrative manner, with the achievements of the pupils.

The magazine appears in Hebrew and Yiddish and contains the works of the children of all grades, from the most elementary classes to the higher courses. The material consists of stories, poems, essays on historical, literary and social problems, biographies, illustrations, pictures of the classes, etc. The last two numbers, printed in greater volume on the occasions of the graduations and the Tenth Anniversary of the School, have been very favourably received by the Yiddish and English-Yiddish Press, both in Canada and the United States, and have been very sympathetically reviewed by well-known critics and reviewers. Some of the pupils have shown distinct literary talent in these magazines, which is maturing from number to number.

It is quite important to add, in passing, that the school magazines are issued by the Sholem Aleichem Clubs of the Jewish People's Schools. I find it worth while dwelling upon this point because it illustrates one of the principles underlying the activity of our school, namely, the friendly relationship between teachers and pupils, and the importance laid by the school upon the development of the social life of the children.

The schools have about five Clubs to which most of the pupils belong, according to their ages, their attainments in general and Jewish education. The program of the Clubs is varied, ranging from light pastime to such serious occupation as debates, issuing of club magazines, and assisting the school from time to time in its different activities. The teachers are members of the Clubs and are, together with the executive chosen from the children themselves, the leaders of the Clubs. The different Clubs have, on frequent occasions, outings, picnics, sleigh drives, visits to museums, to art galleries, and to theatres.

The most important event of 1920 was the graduation of the first pupils of the school, who had completed their six-year course. The first graduation class consisted of but two pupils, while the number of graduates in succeeding classes has been as high as sixteen. The small number of the first graduates was due to the very abnormal conditions under which the school was operating during the first years of its existence. The first two graduates were Beile Epstein and Malka Urtick.

The graduation ceremony took place in the presence of a great number of appreciative friends of modern Jewish education. Reuben Brainin, the well-known Hebrew author and publicist, who helped the movement during his sojourn in Montreal, delivered a very eloquent and inspiring address to the graduates, to the leaders and to the Jewish community at large.

This graduation taught the leaders of the school a great deal. It was the fact that after so many years of such strenuous work the school succeeded in keeping only two pupils till the graduation. This made the principal and the teachers look for the most efficient means of attaching the pupils to the school, of attracting them in such a manner that would keep them to the school up till the graduation and further. New increased efforts were made by the teachers of the senior classes to keep them intact and these efforts were very successful, as will be evident from the following account.

The two graduates kept up their studies in the school for quite a long period of time. They asked the teachers and the directors of the school that a course should be given to them in most of the subjects of the school curriculum. This request was granted, and it was with great regret that they terminated their studies about two years after their graduation.

The next to graduate was the class of 1922 which ceremony took place on May 17, 1922, in the presence of many hundreds of parents and friends of the school, and the guest of the event, Dr. Jehudah Kaufman, former principal of the school.

This graduating class showed the great degree of progress which the school and the curriculum have attained. The number of graduates was fourteen. The intellectual level of the pupils was admirable. Their knowledge of the Hebrew language, Bible and Literature was high, as was also their knowledge of all the phases of Jewish history. Their ability to express critical views on many matters was quite astonishing. They had a very deep sympathetic understanding for all social problems, and for the cause of liberty from all manner of oppression; national, economic, and political. This great educational achievement was due to the untiring efforts of the teachers and the devotion of the pupils, which made it possible, in spite of all obstacles, to devote a great deal of time for the studies and for the discussions of all important questions.

The most memorable aspect of this achievement is the creation of the Mittel-Shule (High School Course) for these graduates. The pupils have learned to love Jewish culture, Jewish studies, and the school in which they pursued these studies, and they insisted that such a course be opened for them, in which they should follow up, in a more advanced manner the lessons which they so assiduously studied in the elementary course.

It is a matter of great joy and pride to the writer of this article, as to his comrades, that the Folks' Shule was the *first on the American Continent to institute a Mittel-Shule Course*. It gives them great pleasure to find that this important experiment aroused "scholarly jealousy" in the leaders of other schools, and that similar courses have been opened in a few schools on the continent.

The Mittel-Shule was opened on June 1st, 1922, and not one of the pupils abandoned these studies during the two years of the course. The average age of the Mittel-Shule pupils was close to 14 years.

The Course was a very systematic one, and it comprised the following subjects: Hebrew language and grammar; a very great and important portion of the Hebrew Bible, which was studied very thoroughly and seriously; a thorough course of the Jewish Haggadah; a systematic course in Hebrew literature; a very thorough course in Yiddish literature, and a systematic scholarly study of a number of very important Yiddish literary texts; a general course in literature with special reference to English literature, which the pupils studied in the High Schools; a course in the History of the Jewish People in the Nineteenth Century, and the History of the Jews in Russia and Poland from very early times till the present. The course included the history of all the important movements of Jewish life in the past, that would lead to a thorough understanding of the life of the Jews in the present; an elementary course on Political Economy, and social problems; talks on current events and Jewish and Hebrew Folk music.

The number of pupils of the High School Course was increased by a number of graduates of the succeeding class, in 1922. The guests of that graduation were again Reuben Brainin and Alexander Harkavy, the famous Jewish scholar, philologist and historian. The new graduates were of such a high intellectual and scholarly standard that the principal found it possible to join them with the former graduates into one big Mittel-Shule.

The work of the school went on very smoothly and successfully for the next two years. The school gained many adherents and its financial condition was comparatively solid.

Meanwhile, great events were preparing. The Tenth Anniversary of the school was nearing. A fourth six-year class was to graduate, and the greatest of them all, the Mittel-Shule (High School), founded two years ago had completed its course, and was ready for graduation. The celebration of the three events took place the week beginning May 18th, 1924, the week of "Lag Boimer", which was proclaimed as the "Folk Shulen Woch."

Dr. Jehudah Kaufman came from New York to participate in the celebration. The double graduation took place on May 18th, 1924, and it was very joyful to see about thirty children graduating the elementary and high school classes of the Schule, fully equipped with a sound and thorough knowledge of Jewish culture, and full of enthusiasm to meet Jewish life and take an active part in it.

The graduation created a very warm and appreciative atmosphere among the friends of the modern Jewish education, and this feeling of joy was given a very adequate expression at a large banquet which took place on May 26th, at which the professional and intellectual elements of our city were assembled. The very important material outcome of this celebration was the unanimous decision on the part of all present to extend the work of the school by opening a branch school in the north end of the city, and a fund was started for the purpose.

It seems that it is the destiny of the Folks' Shule to take on higher and higher forms, ever higher goals of education, as it develops. The new Board of Directors had to cope with another very interesting development. The graduate pupils of the Mittel-Shule sent a committee to the meeting of the Board to state in very emphatic terms, that they were unwilling to terminate their Jewish studies, and that the Board must, in some manner or other, provide for their further education along the lines which they had followed heretofore.

Though the Board saw the great financial and administrative difficulties that lay in the way of instituting a higher course of instruction for the Mittel-Shule graduates, it took up the request in full earnestness and with deep-felt joy at the most evident sign of the great success of its labours. For, certainly, it is something to be wondered at: boys and girls, now of the ages from sixteen and upwards, have stayed on in an educational institution for a period of time extending from five to eight years, and are still anxious to pursue their studies, at a time when their friends of the High Schools and offices "enjoy life" in an altogether different manner, and on quite a different intellectual level.

The Board had to yield to the demand of the graduates, and a higher course, known as the "Hechere Kursen", for two years, was then established. The aim of this Course, which now enters on its second year, is to prepare those that so choose to the profession of teaching in this and similar schools, and in general to give the students such a thorough training in Jewish culture, in all its phases and forms, as will enable them to be of great service in the social spheres of Jewish life.

Meanwhile, a new school house was bought at 2001 Waverley St., corner of Fairmount Ave., in the north end of the city. The opening celebration of the new school took place on September 21st, 1924, and the registration of new pupils began. Only half a year has elapsed since the opening of the school, and it already shows evident signs of a normal and successful development. The number of the pupils exceeds one hundred, and is increasing from week to week, its financial basis being quite secure.

In March, 1925, the Board of Directors of the schools launched a $10,000 campaign under the able leadership of the Chairman, Mr. M. Dickstein, for the purpose of clearing the deficit which had accumulated, and for assuring the budget for the coming year. The campaign was quite successful.

On May 17th, the sixth graduation of the elementary classes of the school will take place and a new Mittel-Shule (High School) will be instituted.

These regular and systematic graduations, the normal transitions from the elementary to the higher planes of education, the solid financial basis of the schools and the number of the idealistic supporters make the leaders of the schools feel that the schools have come to stay, that the success of the new educational movement is not an accidental phenomenon, but a sure indicator of its promising future.

There are in both schools over five hundred pupils that are divided into twenty-six classes and three kindergarten classes under the direction of a principal and twelve teachers. A detailed, supervised curriculum is being followed in each class, with a very definite transition from grade to grade.

Due to the freedom and the comradely relationship between the teachers and the pupils, there is no problem of discipline, which is found in very aggravating forms in other Jewish educational institutions. It may also be of interest to add that there is an equal proportion of boys and girls in the schools.

The work of the Jewish People's Schools has gained recognition among all the elements of our Jewish population. The movement is an intellectual force in the city, and is being seriously reckoned with by those who have a serious attitude to things Jewish, and particularly by those who are earnestly interested in general educational problems as well as in peculiarly Jewish educational problems.

CHARITABLE AND WELFARE WORK

For the poor shall never cease out of the land: therefore I command thee, saying, thou shalt open thine hand wide unto thy brother, to thy poor, and to thy needy in thy land.

If thou lend money to any of my people that is poor by thee, thou shalt not be to him as a taker of use, neither shalt thou lay usury upon him.

PERHAPS in no part of Jewish life is so much devotion shown as is displayed in rendering assistance to those in need. Charity is a fundamental part of the Jewish faith, and in philanthropic endeavor and welfare work the Jews of Canada take just pride in the fact that they have upheld and are upholding the best traditions of their race.

For many years after they settled in Canada, their numbers were not large, and the early settlers were all persons of means when they came to this country. Consequently, there was little or no demand made on them for assistance for their co-religionists, but they subscribed, what was in those days considered munificently, to the existing calls for relief. In old diaries we read where they have, in 1795, subscribed to the fund raised for the indigent of Montreal, in 1801 to the building of the English Church, and in 1813 and 1814 to the Patriotic Fund for the relief of the war sufferers in Upper Canada.

Not until 1848, when there was a considerable influx of Jewish immigration into Canada, was there need for a purely Jewish organization, but in that year the Hebrew Philanthropic Society was started in Montreal, with the Reverend Doctor Abraham de Sola and Moses Judah Hays as its executive heads. This society carried on for several years and was finally reorganized in 1873 and became the Young Men's Hebrew Benevolent Society with Laurence Levey, Jacob G. Ascher, Sullivan David, Jacob L. Samuel, Moise Schwob and Lewis A. Hart as its charter members. Later on it again was reorganized, and became the Baron de Hirsch Institute. For many years this was the sole Jewish charitable organization in Canada. It handled all philanthropic work, including immigrant aid, colonization and education, and had at its head at all times, men who showed an unselfish devotion to its cause. The Baron de Hirsch Institute owes much of the great work it has accomplished to the endowment given to it by the Baron and Baroness de Hirsch, who both, during their life-times, took the keenest interest in its undertakings.

The Russian, Roumanian and Polish immigrants who arrived in Canada between 1880-1890, taxed to the utmost the resources of the Society and assistance was also furnished by the Mansion House Russian Committee and the Jewish Colonization Association of Paris, but it was only a very short time before these immigrants had become established to such an extent that they were organizing relief for those who followed them. In all communities where the Jewish population was sufficiently large, charitable organizations were established, among the earliest being societies in Hamilton, Toronto, Winnipeg, and Ottawa. In Hamilton, Mrs. Herman Levy organized the Deborah Society which looked after the few calls for assistance that were received, and in Toronto, where the Ladies' Montefiore Society had for some years been in existence, Mr. Edmund Scheuer, shortly after he took up his residence in that city, organized and became president of the first men's philanthropic society. In Ottawa, Mr. Moses Bilsky and Mr. Aaron Rosenthal were the founders of philanthropic work, and in Winnipeg the founders were Mr. G. Frankfurter and Mr. Hyman Miller.

As the years passed and the need for charity reached a much greater scale, more societies came into existence, and the result was naturally much overlapping of work. This condition led to the formation of central organizations, or Federations, which had proved successful in the larger cities in the United States. It was in 1914 that a committee was formed in Montreal to take up the matter of Federation, under the chairmanship of Mr. Lyon Cohen. The result was the Federation of Jewish Philanthropies in Montreal, which last year, 1924, spent the sum of $188,125.06 in charitable work. Toronto followed Federation in 1916, Mr. Edmund Scheuer being the chairman of the organization committee. But in Winnipeg Federation had been born as far back as 1914 when the United Hebrew Relief was formed with Mr. S. Hart Green as chairman. This organization some years later became part of the Federation for Community Service, preparing their own budget, and in 1924, Vancouver Jews had their first drive for a "Community Chest." Hamilton was one of the first cities to take up Federation, under Messers. Adolph Levy and David Sweet.

The Jewish institutions throughout Canada are indeed a source of pride to the members of the different communities, and outstanding among them are the Western Canada Orphanage at Winnipeg, the Orphans' Home in Montreal, and the Children's Home in Toronto. The Old Folks' Homes in these three cities, and the Mount Sinai Sanitarium, at St. Agathe, Que., the Hebrew Maternity Hospital, Montreal, and the Mount Sinai Hospital in Toronto are really models of such institutions. The Herzl Dispensary in Montreal has likewise done a great amount of good work and it is only a matter of time before it becomes the nucleus of a Jewish General Hospital. In the pages that follow we have given as completely as has been possible, a record of the leading charitable organizations of the Dominion, all of which have done work that the members may well be proud of.

"Gemilath Chasodim" or Free Loan Societies, have been established in every important centre in Canada, and their work has indeed been most valuable, in maintaining self-respect among the borrowers. The total sum advanced in these Free Loans has reached an enormous figure, and the amount of losses or unpaid debts (past due) has been negligible. The first Free Loan Society in Canada was the one started in Montreal in 1911, due largely to the untiring efforts of the late Zigmond Fineberg. Toronto, Winnipeg, Regina, Calgary, Ottawa, Hamilton and Vancouver have Free Loan Societies. In many of the cities they owe their foundation to the B'nai B'rith Lodges.

The Jewish citizens of Canada have been, and are yet being taught the pleasure of giving, right up to the limit of their capacity. The example is being set by the leaders in each community, and the more one delves into facts and figures, the prouder one becomes of his fellow-Jews of Canada. An interesting example to illustrate the foregoing is the Jewish community of Edmonton, at present comprising about 150 families. In the past 6 years this small community, not yet 20 years old, has subscribed to various Jewish funds the staggering amount of over $100,000. This is an instance of what a united community can do in relief work. "He gives thrice who gives with a cheerful heart."

MICHAEL HIRSCH, MONTREAL

MICHAEL HIRSCH was born in Richmond, Quebec, February 7th, 1864, the son of the late Jacob and Lizzie (Levine) Hirsch. In 1875 he moved to Montreal, where he has resided ever since. Entering the cigar business in 1883, Mr. Hirsch occupied a prominent position in that industry, until his retirement in 1921. Mr. Hirsch has always been interested in communal matters. Thirty-five years ago he was the Secretary of the then English, German and Polish Congregation, now the Shaar Hashomayim, of which he is still a member. He has also been a member of the Temple Emanu-El for the last quarter century. For over twenty-five years he has been President of the Montefiore Club, Montreal, and he is a founder and past President of the Federation of Jewish Philanthropies. He is a life governor of the Montreal General Hospital, and member, Montreal Board of Trade, C.M.A.; Canadian Club; Elmridge Golf and Country Club; Y.M.H.A.; and Primrose Club, Toronto. Mr. Hirsch is past Master of St. George's Lodge, No. 10 since 1896, and holds the rank of V.W. in the Grand Lodge of Quebec. As a past President of the Mount Sinai Sanitarium, he was selected to represent the Federation on the newly organized Anti-Tuberculosis and Health League, of which he is a Director. Mr. Hirsch's latest contribution to communal work is in connection with the Royal Commission appointed by the Provincial Government, to examine into and report on the educational problems of the City and Island of Montreal, with special reference to those affecting the Jewish population. This task entailed five months of intensive study and investigation, and the report was submitted to the Premier and his Cabinet on December 31st, 1924— as called for in the proclamation creating the Royal Commission. In this work Mr. Hirsch was associated with two other Jewish representatives (Mr. Samuel W. Cohen, E. M., and Alderman Joseph Shubert), and three representatives each of the Catholic and Protestant citizens. In 1885, Mr. Hirsch was married to Miss Estelle Jacobs, and he has two sons, Messrs. J. Arthur of New York, and T. Percy of Montreal.

HISTORY OF THE FEDERATION OF JEWISH PHILANTHROPIES OF MONTREAL

THE story of charitable endeavour in the Jewish community of Montreal is, in its beginning, very much like that in other Jewish communities on this continent.

When the community was very small, individual efforts sufficed to alleviate the occasional cases of distress that presented themselves. As the community increased in size, the need for systematic relief brought into existence the association of individuals under the official name of the "Hebrew Benevolent Society of Montreal and the Baron de Hirsch Institute," popularly known by the latter name only. For a considerable number of years, during the formative stages of the community, practically all the charitable and philanthropic work was carried on by this Society.

As the community grew in size, and as the flow of immigration increased in volume, various activities were initiated by the Society to take care of not only the poor and needy of the community, but of the indigent arrivals, and of the education of the children who did not have the command of the English language.

As time progressed and the tide of immigration increased, the Jewish community not only increased greatly in numbers, but became more and more heterogeneous. Thus, various groups arose, either according to the country of origin abroad, or according to the locality occupied in the city.

The formation of 'Shools' and 'Chevras' along these lines brought with it the formation of allied benevolent and charitable organizations.

Although the Baron de Hirsch Institute kept on increasing and broadening its activities, and was still pre-eminent in general relief work, a number of institutions were organized to cater to particular types of necessity and misfortune, and in the founding of the most important of these, e.g., "The Mount Sinai Sanatorium" and "The Hebrew Orphans' and Sheltering Home", the leading members of the Baron de Hirsch Institute played the principal roles.

The organization and growth of a large number of charitable societies and institutions naturally led to a very considerable overlapping and duplication of work, and it therefore became apparent to those interested in the field of communal endeavour that any plan which would remedy, or even alleviate this duplication and waste of effort, would be of great benefit to the community at large, both to those who give and to those who are forced to seek aid.

The first official reference to the desirability of this co-ordination of effort is found in the Forty-ninth Annual Report of the Baron de Hirsch Institute and Hebrew Benevolent Society of Montreal for 1912 where Mr. Lyon Cohen, in his Presidential Address, included the following:—

"I wish once more to lay before you the question as to how we can best co-ordinate the various charitable bodies, with a view to obtaining the greatest efficiency with the least possible expense and labour. There are several plans of co-operation followed in other cities. There is Federation, the Union, the Board of Deputies, or other such representative bodies, any of which would be a vast improvement over this present disorganized and disunited condition. The necessity of a working union is self-evident. I . . . would suggest that a Committee be named to work out the most suitable scheme for our particular situation . . . "

In the minutes of the meeting of the Board of Directors of the Baron de Hirsch Institute of January 29th, 1913, there is a reference to a committee on the question of Federation, but nothing further is found, until we come to the minutes of January 12th, 1914, when the first official act toward Federation of the Jewish Charities of Montreal is recorded as follows:—

"The following committee was appointed to study the question of United Hebrew Charities of Montreal, with a request that they report back to the Board not later than February 15th: Messrs. Lyon Cohen, Chairman; Rev. Dr. H. Abramovitz, Rabbi N. Gordon, Maxwell Goldstein, K.C., Michael Hirsch and Messrs. Horsfall and Dainow as Secretaries."

S. W. Jacobs, K.C., (then the President of the Baron de Hirsch Institute) was a member ex-officio.

This Committee held its first meeting on February 18th, 1914, at the residence of the Chairman, 25 Rosemount Ave.

The Chairman, with the approval of the Committee, invited Solomon Vineberg, Ph.D., who had been connected with social and philanthropic work in other cities, to join the Committee and give them the benefit of his experience. After a thorough discussion of the subject, the meeting decided that a report be prepared by Dr. Vineberg, of the work of the various Federated or United Hebrew Charities in other cities, from which a plan might be selected suitable to the conditions existing in Montreal.

An outline of a plan for Federation of Jewish Philanthropies in Montreal, in which it was proposed to include all Jewish charitable and educational institutions was placed before the Committee by Dr. Vineberg at its next meeting. The Committee discussed the plan in detail and made some changes and additions. The Committee also compiled statistics bearing on the charitable contributions of the Jews of Montreal, which were to serve as a basis for the contributions to the proposed Federation.

After holding several meetings, at which the subject was carefully considered from every angle, the Committee decided that the object sought could be more easily attained if the Committee was not attached to any particular organization. Accordingly, on March 10th, 1914, the following report was sent to the Board of Directors of the Baron de Hirsch Institute by the Chairman:

March 10th, 1914.
"To the Board of Directors,
Baron de Hirsch Institute.
Gentlemen:

The Committee appointed by you on January 12th, 1914, to consider the question of a United Hebrew Charities in this City, and which is composed of.................., begs to report that a number of meetings have been held and a large amount of literature and statistics on Federation has been submitted and discussed.

The Committee has been fortunate in enlisting the valuable co-operation of Dr. S. Vineberg, who has had a great deal of experience in social work in New York and who has secured most of the data under consideration.

A plan of Federation is now being formulated, and it is hoped will meet with the approval of the societies interested.

The question has been raised as to whether the Committee, as at present constituted, is in the best position to bring about the end desired.

The Committee realizes the importance and magnitude of the undertaking, and while giving your Board credit for the initiative in trying to bring about a better relationship between the various societies, feels that this important matter should not be jeopardized through factional jealousies which might arise from the fact that the idea emanates from a particular society.

The Committee, therefore, is of the opinion that it is inadvisable to proceed further with its deliberations in its present form, and would ask your Board for an expression upon the matter.

The members suggest that, if agreeable to you, they form themselves into a Citizens' Committee and invite representatives of the various Jewish Societies, with whom plans for Federation may be further discussed."

The following reply was received from the Baron de Hirsch Institute.

March 11th, 1914.

"Lyon Cohen, Esq.,
Chairman, United Hebrew Charities' Committee.
Dear Sir:—

The Report of your Committee dated March 10th, which embodied the suggestion that its further deliberations be held as a body separate from the Institute, was discussed at a meeting of the Board of Directors held last evening. The Board was unanimously of the opinion that the view taken was the correct one, and they have therefore placed on record the discharge of your Committee, and in thanking you for the attention and earnestness you have given to the matter under discussion, they desire to add the hope that you will be entirely successful in your aims.

(Signed) D. DAINOW,
Clerk to the Board."

Thereupon, on March 26th, 1914, the Committee declared itself an independent citizens' committee under the title of "The Provisional Committee to Consider the Organization of United Jewish Charities in Montreal."

The Committee, enlarged by the addition of individuals prominently connected with or known to be interested in the various philanthropic activities of the community, continued to hold meetings at which the subject of Federation was discussed. Representatives of the various societies were invited to attend the meetings, until gradually the thought of the desirability of effecting Federation was spread among the leaders in philanthropic endeavours.

Finally, at a meeting held on November 11th, 1915, it was decided that application for a charter be made to the Quebec Legislature at its next session and that the following names be included on the said petition as the incorporators:

Mortimer B. Davis	Mark Workman
Lyon Cohen	Maxwell Goldstein, K.C.
Michael Hirsch	D. S. Friedman
S. W. Jacobs, K.C.	Clarence I. de Sola
M. A. Vineberg	J. Levinson
J. A. Jacobs	A. M. Vineberg
Louis Lewis	B. Goldstein
S. Kellert	Harris Vineberg
H. M. Levine	Rabbi Nathan Gordon
Rabbi H. Abramowitz	Dr. S. Vineberg

At this meeting, Dr. S. Vineberg was appointed Hon. Sec'y of the Committee and M. Goldstein, K.C., and S. W. Jacobs, K.C., were delegated to look after all proceedings in connection with the legal and legislative end of the work.

On March 16th, 1916, the Act of Incorporation of "Federation of Jewish Philanthropies of Montreal," and which constitutes Chapter 101 of the Quebec Statutes of 1916, was passed by the Quebec Legislature.

At a meeting of the incorporators held on April 27th, 1916, the Act of Incorporation was accepted, and a draft of a set of by-laws for the government of Federation was presented by Mr. Maxwell Goldstein, K.C.

When the election of provisional officers of Federation was arrived at, Mr. Lyon Cohen, the Chairman of the Committee, nominated Mr. Maxwell Goldstein for the office of Chairman, as he felt that the combination of Mr. Goldstein's extensive legal knowledge and his great prestige in all sections of the community would prove particularly valuable to Federation during its formative period.

Mr. Goldstein was thereupon unanimously elected as Chairman, with Mr. Lyon Cohen as Vice-Chairman, Mr. Joseph Levinson, Sr., as Treasurer and Dr. S. Vineberg as Secretary, to hold office until the first general meeting of Federation.

At this stage, it was decided to secure the services of a professional social worker, who would direct the work of organizing, and take executive charge upon actual completion of the Federation.

A fund sufficient to defray the expenses of incorporation and organization was subscribed by the incorporators and a number of other citizens who favoured the Federation idea.

On June 1st, 1916, Mr. Garfield A. Berlinsky, associated with the Federation in Denver and prominently identified with Jewish charitable organizations throughout the United States, addressed a meeting of the incorporators and others interested in the subject on the principles of Federation and of its success in various American cities.

On June 14th, 1916, Mr. Berlinsky was appointed to take charge of the executive work of Federation and on September 7th, 1916, he entered on his duties as Executive Director of Federation.

On Sept. 25th, 1916, a meeting was held, at which Mr. Berlinsky presented a brief survey of conditions in Montreal and submitted his views as to the most desirable form for Federation in Montreal. He strongly urged that the functions be made broader than those of a mere financial Federation. To obtain this end, he recommended that the plan include central purchasing and accounting and a central social service department. His views were concurred in by all present.

At this meeting, a general subscription list for membership in Federation was opened, and the following provisional executive committee of Federation was formed;—Messrs. Maxwell Goldstein, K.C., Chairman; Lyon Cohen, Vice-Chairman; J. Levinson, Sr., Dr. S. Vineberg, A. Sommer, J. Kellert, E. M. Berliner and A. Pierce.

The Provisional Executive Committee now entered on an active campaign to enroll the various charitable societies as members of Federation, and to accomplish this held a series of meetings with the individual societies at which the benefits of Federation were expounded and thoroughly discussed. In addition, a series of folders on the Federation idea were distributed to the individual contributors of the various societies.

Thus, the committee disseminated throughout the community full information concerning the plans and purposes of the Federation, and at the same time formulated plans for a whirlwind subscription campaign, which would take place at the inauguration of its activities.

Federation commenced its operations on January

1st, 1917, with the following societies as constituent members:—

    Baron de Hirsch Institute
    Mount Sinai Sanatorium
    Ladies' Hebrew Benevolent Society
    Herzl Dispensary and Hospital
    Montreal Hebrew Orphans' Home
    Montreal Hebrew Sheltering Home
    Ladies' Jewish Endeavour Sewing School
    Hebrew Young Ladies' Sewing Society
    Young Women's Hebrew Association
    Beth Israel Day Nursery and Infants' Home
    Hebrew Ladies' Aid Society
    Friendly League of Jewish Women

The campaign for general membership of Federation was held from January 2nd to 5th, 1917, and resulted in bringing in pledged subscriptions to the amount of $127,000.

The committee continued the work of completing the organization and formulated the proposed by-laws for its government.

On March 18th, 1917, the first general meeting of the membership at large of Federation was held at the Baron de Hirsch Institute for the purpose of passing the by-laws and the election of trustees-at-large.

At this meeting, the reports of the incorporators and the Provisional Executive Committees were adopted and the acts of the incorporators and Provisional Executive Committee were ratified. After a thorough discussion, which resulted in several amendments, the draft set of by-laws was adopted.

Twenty-four trustees-at-large were elected by the meeting, and these, with twenty-four trustees representing the twelve constituent societies of Federation (two from each society) constituted the first board of trustees of Federation.

The meeting also elected Sir Mortimer B. Davis and Mr. Mark Workman as the first Honorary Presidents of Federation.

At the first meeting of the Board of Trustees the following officers were elected:—

Mr. Maxwell Goldstein, K.C.,	President
Mr. Lyon Cohen,	1st Vice-President
Mr. D. S. Friedman,	2nd Vice-President
Mr. J. Levinson, Sr.,	Hon. Treasurer
Dr. Solomon Vineberg,	Hon. Secretary

An Executive Committee consisting of 25 members was appointed with Mr. Michael Hirsch as Chairman and Mr. Edgar M. Berliner as Vice-Chairman. Federation's organization was now complete, and at this stage was briefly as follows:—

Federation consisted of the twelve constituent societies mentioned above, and each person who contributed at least ten dollars per annum to Federation became not only a member of Federation-at-large, but also of each constituent society.

The powers, business and property of Federation were exercised, conducted and controlled by the Board of Trustees, then consisting of forty-eight members, half of whom were elected by the membership-at-large at the annual general meeting of Federation, under the designation of Trustees-at-large, whilst the other half were appointed by the boards of the constituent societies under the designation of Representative Trustees.

The named officers of Federation were elected by the Board of Trustees from their own number and consisted of a President, First Vice-President, Second Vice-President, Secretary and Treasurer.

The President, with the approval of the Board of Trustees, appointed an Executive Committee with a chairman and vice-chairman and the Executive Committee appointed all the other committees required by the by-laws and directed their work. It also, subject to approval by the Board of Trustees, appointed the Executive Director, and this official and his staff were under its direct control.

Two main divisions of work of the Federation were established—the Division of Finance, comprising the Departments of Accounting, Purchasing, Subscription, &c., and the Division of Social Service, comprising the Departments of Relief, Child Welfare, Correction, Health and Sanitation, &c.

One of the first acts of the Board of Trustees was to authorize the Executive Director to proceed with a survey of social conditions in the community, so as to ascertain and acquaint the Board with all pertinent facts concerning the social and economic problems of the various constituent societies of the Federation, and the extent to which these agencies were meeting the needs as they were found to exist.

As a direct result of a preliminary report concerning this survey, the Board of Trustees adopted the recommendation to close the Beth Israel Infants' Home and Day Nursery and decided to concentrate in the relief department of Federation, the work up to that time conducted by the various relief-giving constituent societies.

The principal changes inaugurated by Federation in its central relief department were as follows:—

1—Relief was given to the poor in their homes, instead of having the needy come to Relief Headquarters.

2—The actual work in connection with relief giving was done by the professional workers, who determined what relief was required.

In addition, the cases were reviewed by the Relief Committee at weekly meetings, when exceptions, criticisms or suggestions were noted for the guidance of the staff.

As the work of Federation progressed, the benefits of co-ordination became more and more apparent, and continuous efforts were made to harmonize the work of the various departments and to elaborate ways and means of improving the organization. As in the case of all experiments in social service work, it was inevitable that some features of Federation, as outlined in the preliminary survey and in the by-laws, should be found too cumbersome for efficiency or unsuited to local conditions. When it became apparent during the early part of 1919, that some of these factors led to friction and to criticism of some of Federation's activities, the Board of Trustees appointed a Ways and Means Committee, under the chairmanship of Mr. Edgar M. Berliner, which was to "submit a plan for re-organization of Federation upon lines which may enlist the greater sympathy and co-operation of all sections of the Jewish community in Montreal." The Committee was also entrusted with the conduct of a campaign to raise funds to carry on the work of Federation, and this effort resulted in pledged subscriptions amounting to almost a quarter million dollars.

The report of the Ways and Means Committee was presented to the third annual meeting of Federation, on March 30th, 1920, and in view of the many recommendations and suggestions it contained, it was decided to appoint a committee of thirty members of Federation to study the various recommendations and suggestions in conjunction with the Board of Trustees, and to report their conclusions to a general meeting of Federation.

On March 6, 1921, the "Joint Report of the Committee of Thirty and Board of Trustees, upon the Re-Organization of the Policy, Work and Administration of Federation" was presented to a special general meeting of Federation. The report was unanimously adopted, and the proposed amendments to the by-laws contained therein were accepted.

The salient features of the recommendations in the report were:

1. A more democratic method of election of the Board of Trustees.
2. A more efficient form of executive administration.
3. A more complete internal autonomy for constituent societies.
4. A more efficient budget system.

The actual work of Federation was delegated to an Executive Committee composed of seven members, and these could be appointed not only from the members of the Board of Trustees, but from the members of Federation at large. The Executive Committee was the Budget Committee, whose duty was to estimate the revenue of Federation for the whole year, and to apportion, subject to the approval of the Board of Trustees, to each society and department of Federation such amount as it considered proper, in view of the work to be carried on and the estimated revenue. At the commencement of each year, the Board of Directors of each constituent society and each department of Federation were to prepare a statement of the funds required for its administration for the ensuing year, and to transmit this statement to the Executive Committee.

With these changes, Federation has been able to carry on its activities in a manner that has proved the undoubted superiority of union in philanthropic endeavour.

On the material side, both the contributions to charity and the disbursements for the alleviation of distress have increased greatly since the very inception of Federation. In its first fiscal year, Federation's income from all sources amounted to $123,413.32, whilst the aggregate receipts from all sources by the constituent societies in the year preceding Federation amounted to $74,950.45. The contributions to Federation during its first year of existence, therefore, showed an increase of 65% over those obtained by the constituent societies in the previous year. The expenditures during the first fiscal year were $121,234.95, and the steady growth of the Federation idea can probably best be illustrated by a glance at the figures of Federation's expenditures for the last five years:

1920	$ 193,189.77
1921	213,622.81
1922	192,522.42
1923	177,504.60
1924	188,125.06

Federation, however, has increased not only the amounts contributed to charity, but also has greatly increased the numbers of subscribers to charity. By means of various campaigns and educational propaganda as to what Federation aims to accomplish, it has created a greater interest by members of the Jewish community in all activities for social betterment, and has brought the community to a realization of its responsibility to those in need of aid. In brief, one of the outstanding results achieved by Federation has been the crystallization of a COMMUNITY CONSCIENCE.

It has also, by means of its various departments and particularly by is budget system, created a COMMUNITY INDEX—an index of the distress prevalent in the community and an index of the measure in which this distress is met. These two—the creation of a COMMUNITY CONSCIENCE and a COMMUNITY INDEX, are the outstanding achievements of Federation.

In the evolution of these, the modus operandi of Federation has gradually changed to suit particular conditions in the community, but the changes have always been toward a greater cohesion and unity.

In the raising of funds, great reliance was at first placed on the sporadic campaign, but gradually, the idea of a steady, persistent effort for the collection of funds was evolved. This led to the formation, late in 1923, of the Business Men's Council, under the chairmanship of Mr. Harry Rother, whose duty was to give year-around attention to the problems of collecting outstanding accounts, and to build up a machinery for the raising of funds for philanthropic purposes along trade lines. The Council also assumed the duty of acquainting the general public, by means of propaganda and publicity, with the problems and methods of the social agencies comprising Federation, serving the Jewish community. The Business Men's Council thus took over the money-raising function of the Executive Committee, and during the short time it has been in existence, has proven a valuable aid in Federation's work. One of the outstanding achievements of Federation, on the material side, was the purchase, in the Fall of 1920, of the splendid building now occupied by the Hebrew Orphans' Home. The funds were obtained by a private campaign, authorized by Federation, and the premises were officially opened and occupied by the children in the Fall of 1921.

Federation, during its eight years of service to the community, has amply fulfilled the expectations of its advocates, and is steadily increasing its influence for good. It has indeed co-ordinated the various branches of community activities, and has greatly bettered the administration of relief. It has prevented the competition for funds between the various constituent societies, and has eliminated the overlapping of activities. It has conserved the energies of the community for constructive work, and, as far as the constituent members of Federation are concerned, has abolished the objectionable means of raising funds. It has been successful in its efforts to raise the standard of giving, as well as its standard of affording relief. Its success can not be more aptly illustrated than by the following quotation from the report of the Chairman of the Executive Committee for the year 1924:

"No needy person was turned away. No homeless child was deprived of the home that it was our duty to provide. No tubercular fighting the white plague was refused aid . . . Throughout the whole organization we are better equipped for our work than ever before."

The following have held office in Federation: Honorary Presidents—Sir Mortimer B. Davis, 1917-1924; Mark Workman, 1917-1924; Maxwell Goldstein, K.C., 1922-1924; Michael Hirsch, 1923-1924; Lyon Cohen, 1924: Presidents—Maxwell Goldstein, K.C., 1917-1920; Michael Hirsch, 1921-1922; Lyon Cohen, 1923; J. Levinson, Sr., 1924: 1st Vice-Presidents—Lyon Cohen, 1917-1922; Joseph Levinson, Sr., 1923; Al. Lesser, 1924: 2nd Vice-Presidents—D. S. Friedman, 1917; Isaac Friedman, 1918; Michael Hirsch, 1919-1920; J. Levinson, Sr., 1921-1922; Al. Lesser, 1923; Treasurers—J. Levinson, Sr., 1917-1920; Al. Lesser, 1921-1922; A. L. Gittleson, 1923-1924: Chairmen Executive Committee—Michael Hirsch, 1917; A. M. Vineberg, 1918; J. Kellert, 1919; Michael Hirsch, 1920; M. C. Ginsberg, 1921-1922; A. H. Jassby, 1923; David Kirsch, 1924: Chairman of Ways & Means Committee and of Committee of Thirty—Edgar M. Berliner, 1919-1920: Chairmen of Business Men's Council—Harry Rother, 1924; Leon H. Fischel, 1925: Honorary Secretaries—Solomon Vineberg, 1917-1918; H. E. Herschorn, 1919; Simon Kirsch, 1920-1924.

The following have had executive charge of Federation:—
Garfield A. Berlinsky, Executive Director, 1917-1918; Solomon Vineberg, Executive Secretary, 1919; Jess Perlman, Executive Director, 1920-1921; Dr. Jacob Segal, General Manager, 1922; E. G. F. Vaz, Comptroller, 1923 to date.

A. L. GITTLESON, MONTREAL

ABRAHAM L. GITTLESON, one of the leading business men of Montreal, was born in Tilsit, Prussia, on November 11th, 1872, the son of Louis and Sophie (Cohen) Gittleson. He received his early education in the Hebrew school of his native town. He is married to Rachel, eldest daughter of Hyman Bercovitch of Montreal, and has six daughters; Mrs. S. E. Mendelsohn, Mrs. Isaac Kert, Mrs. (Dr.) Louis Gross of New York, and the Misses Sophie, Sybil and Laura Gittleson. Mr. Gittleson came to Canada when nine years of age. He was educated at the Aberdeen School, later attending business college. He then entered the employ of the late firm of B. A. Boas and Company, where he remained as bookkeeper for fifteen years. In 1900, in partnership with Mr. A. Kellnor, he organized the National Garment Manufacturing Company, with which concern he is still actively associated. In 1905, he became president of the Montreal Underskirt Manufacturing Company. He was formerly vice-president of the Ladies' Garment Manufacturers' Association of Canada, an association of all the leading manufacturers of the Dominion, organized to protect their interests. He is well known throughout Canada in a commercial way, and has a very fine reputation for business integrity. Although a man of such large business interests, Mr. Gittleson has always been an active communal worker in Montreal and devotes much time to philanthropic movements in his community. For six years, he was chairman of the Accounting Committee of the Federation of Jewish Philanthropies, and he has been identified with the Federation from its very inception, being one of its first members, and at present is the treasurer. He is a life governor of both the Montreal General and Western Hospitals, and of the Mount Sinai Sanatorium. He is a member of the United Talmud Torahs; Hebrew Free Loan Association; Y.M.H.A.; the Montefiore Club; and the Montreal Board of Trade. For over ten years Mr. Gittleson was treasurer of the Shaar Hashomayim Congregation, of which he has always been a member, and he was actively connected with the construction of the new synagogue, which is the largest Jewish house of worship in Canada.

THE LATE D. A. ANSELL.

THE LATE DAVID ABRAHAM ANSELL was born in London, England, and was educated there and at Frankfurt-on-the-Main and arrived in Canada in 1866, and located in Montreal. He became engaged in mercantile business and was an early promoter of trade relations between Canada and Mexico. In 1886 he was appointed Consul-General for Mexico in Canada, which appointment he retained until his death in 1913. Mr. Ansell did much in the upbuilding of the Jewish race in Canada and was one of the founders of the Jewish Free Schools in Montreal. He was the first chairman of the Jewish Colonization Society in Canada and for many years was President of the Baron de Hirsch Institute, of which he was a charter member. It was during his term as President that the present building of this institution was erected on Bleury Street. He took a prominent part in the Legislation passed by the Quebec Government giving equal rights to Jewish children in public schools. He did much writing and was the author of "Welding the Links of Union" (in which he unfolded a scheme of preference for the Empire, which was in all essential details the plan afterwards advocated by the late Hon. Mr. Joseph Chamberlain); "Retrospective and Prospective Conservatism"; "Politics as viewed from the Fence;" and many other works. Mr. Ansell was a man of many tastes who travelled much and observed much. He held strong views and was not slow in advocating them. He held a prominent position in the social life of Montreal and was always regarded as one of the outstanding members of his race in Canada. He had several interviews in Paris with the late Baron and Baroness de Hirsch in reference to their colonization work in Canada, and was in the front of any movement tending to the advancement of the educational life of the Jews. Originally a member of the Spanish and Portuguese Congregation, Mr. Ansell joined the Shaar Hashomayim Synagogue shortly after its formation and remained a member of it until his death, and for some years served as President of the Congregation.

BARON DE HIRSCH INSTITUTE, MONTREAL

THE first body to occupy itself with philanthropic work in the Dominion of Canada was the "Hebrew Philanthropic Society" founded in Montreal in the year 1848, with Moses Judah Hays and the Rev. Dr. Abraham de Sola as its executive heads.

On July 23rd, 1863, the Young Men's Hebrew Benevolent Society was founded, which later became the Baron de Hirsch Institute and this has for many years been the centre of philanthropic endeavour of the Jewish citizens of Montreal. The Young Men's Hebrew Benevolent Society was formed by several young men including Lawrence Levey, Charles Levey, Tucker David, Isidor Ascher, Jacob L. Samuel and a number of others. A notice was issued by order of L. L. Levey calling upon the whole of the members of the Jewish persuasion of the city of Montreal to meet at a room over Mr. Wright's store on Great St. James Street on Thursday evening, July 23rd, 1863, "to consider the desirability of forming some Association to assist their needy or unfortunate co-religionists." Such are the exact words of the original document in the possession of the Society, which further says "that it was the opinion of the originators that the Society should be under the entire supervision and control of the young unmarried men of the City." It was also considered that the Society would be the means of making the Jewish young men of Montreal better known to each other.

On the motion of Messrs L. L. Levy and J. L. Samuel it was thereupon resolved that a Society based upon these principles be formed. The name suggested by these gentlemen was "Montreal Jewish Benevolent Society", but this was amended on the suggestion of Mr. Samuel and the name "Young Men's Hebrew Benevolent Society" was adopted. The first officers were: President, L. L. Levey; Vice-President, L. B. Davis; Treasurer, G. G. Levey; Secretary, H. Moss; Committee, G. Littauer, I. Ascher, S. Silverman, Lawrence Cohen, M. Gutman, H. L. Levey, S. Ollendorf, J. L. Samuel, B. Kortosk.

The Society continued to progress but it passed through some severe trials for it is recorded at the Annual Meeting July 14th, 1867, that the balance in the hands of the Treasurer was 29 cents while in 1869, it was in debt to the Treasurer to the extent of $52.

In July 1869, during the Presidency of Mr. J. L. Samuel the sphere of the Society was enlarged "whereby married co-religionists became eligible as members"! On July 10th of that year Mr. Lewis A. Hart was admitted as a member and at the same meeting a Committee consisting of Rev. Dr. A. de Sola and Messrs. Gershom Joseph, L. A. Hart and I. Levy was appointed to consider the question of the incorporation of the Society. Letters of incorporation were obtained on the 16th day of November, 1870, the following gentlemen being signatories to the Act:—Jacob G. Ascher, M. Schwob, A. E. Cohen, Sullivan David, and L. A. Hart, N.P. On the 20th November, a special meeting of the Society was held at which a vote of thanks was accorded to Messrs. Gershom Joseph and Lewis A. Hart for their services in obtaining the charter "without any expense to the Society."

For the next decade the Society was able to take care of any Jewish relief work needed in the City of Montreal, but, after the distressing massacres in Russia in 1882, a wave of immigrants arrived at the port of Montreal with which the Society could not cope, as all these unfortunate people were destitute and had no means of support. A mass meeting of all the citizens of Montreal was held, at which Bishop Bond presided, to consider ways and means of taking care of these unfortunate refugees, and too much credit cannot be given to the men who worked and organized the means of sheltering these unfortunates. Three warehouses were taken over on St. Peter Street which were turned into dormitories and dining rooms. These formed a temporary shelter where the immigrants were housed, fed and clothed until such time as they were absorbed into the community. It is a noteworthy fact that the enormous amount of work entailed in this undertaking was performed by voluntary workers. A period of tranquillity ensued during which the Society continued its work without any outside financial aid apart from the five dollar subcription of its members.

BARON DE HIRSCH INSTITUTE, MONTREAL

Persecutions broke out again in Russia in the year 1888, and another influx of refugees found their way to these shores, taxing the resources of the Society to the utmost. A critical period ensued in which at one time the advisability of disbanding the Society was discussed. At this critical juncture, during a Committee meeting at the home of one of the members, Mr. L. Aronson dramatically made first mention of the name which was to mean so much to the Jews of Canada, telling of Baron de Hirsch's generous provision for the refugees in New York. An animated discussion followed as a result of which Mr. Jacob Goldstein, then Secretary of the Society, was instructed to communicate with Baron de Hirsch and to set forth the situation in Montreal.

This letter explained that funds were urgently

needed for a sheltering home for the new arrivals, and also to set them up so that they might become self supporting, and to educate the children. Montreal laid claim to the Baron's benevolence for the reason that a larger flow of immigrants was coming to Canada than to New York due to the stringency of the American immigration restrictions, and the Montreal Jewish population was a community of old settlers with few wealthy men among them. The letter was signed by Mr. Harris Vineberg, President; Mr. J. Sherman, Vice-President; Mr. David S. Friedman, Treasurer; and Mr. A. D. Moss, Secretary; and to avoid any misconception on the part of the Baron as to the bona fide nature of the appeal the following gentlemen agreed to append their signatures in endorsation: The Hon. James McShane, Mayor of Montreal; Mr. D. A. Ansell, Consul-General for Mexico; as well as the Consuls for Austria, Germany and France. Within three weeks a reply was received stating that the Baron was in complete sympathy with the endeavours of the Young Men's Hebrew Benevolent Society and enclosing a cheque for $20,000, stating also that when more money was needed they should not fail to ask for it.

Dating from this donation in 1890, many Baron de Hirsch millions of dollars have come to Canada for charitable purposes. The arrival of this windfall roused new interest in the community and many who had been hanging back now rallied to the cause and came forward to help. Feeling the responsibility of the administration of so large a fund the young men asked some of the elders of the community to act as a special Advisory Committee and the following gentlemen consented to act as such:— Messrs. Möise Schwob, David A. Ansell, Samuel Davis, Louis Davis, B. A. Boas, Bernard Kortosk, Lewis A. Hart, Adolph Goldstein, Maxwell Goldstein, Moses Vineberg, Jacob L. Samuel and Lyon Silverman. This Committee acting with the officers of the Society decided to purchase a building as a "Home" for the temporary residence for the immigrants, suitable also for the school for the children. A big store at 7 St. Elizabeth Street was obtained at a reasonable cost and together with necessary alterations, repairs and furniture, cost about $10,000.

The official opening of this building took place June 17th, 1891, when His Worship the Mayor of Montreal, the Hon. James McShane, formally declared the building open as "The Baron de Hirsch Institute" dedicated to the purpose of "A Free School for the poor children of the Jewish faith and a home for sheltering distressed immigrants and orphans."

The school was first opened on December 1st, 1890 with 77 pupils, and this number increased during the first year to 227. Year by year the school increased both in numbers and efficiency, and has passed through its doors many thousands who to-day form a very fine type of Canadian citizen. Night schools were also started for the older people, primarily with the object of teaching them the English language, but the sphere of this school has been very much enlarged to cover a variety of subjects. The first teaching staff comprised Mr. W. H. Baker as Principal, Mr. E. N. Gordon, Hebrew teacher; Mrs. Baker, Miss Beatrice Baker, Miss Gertrude Boon, Miss Bertha Valinsky and Miss Pauline Lightstone, (who is today known the world over as Madame Donalda). Mr. Jacob Goldstein was chairman of the educational committee, a post which he ably filled for many years.

The then Governor-General, accompanied by the Countess of Aberdeen, and a distinguished suite, officially visited the Institute on December 1st, 1893, whilst the Lieut.-Governor of the Province, Sir Adolphe Chapleau performed a like ceremony on June 19th, 1895, and made a second visit accompanied by Lady Chapleau on November 6th, of the same year, on which occasion the wife of the Lieut.-Governor presented the Institute with a silk banner.

In the spring of 1892, in consequence of the large influx during the previous few years of immigrants principally from Russia, Baron de Hirsch, as President of the Jewish Colonization Association, decided to form a colony in the North West. A committee was formed with Mr. D. A. Ansell as chairman and land was obtained from the Federal Government in the district now known as Hirsch, and large sums of money have been expended on this undertaking, which for various reasons was not at first successful, but the difficulties were surmounted, and today this colony as well as others is firmly established.

Unfortunately in the year 1896, the Society lost the personal touch and interest of the Baron de Hirsch, who died in Hungary on April 21st. However, his good work was carried on by his widow, who, in April 1897, gave £2,000 or $8,733.33 towards providing a proper building in which to carry on the work of the education of the young, the existing building by this time being quite inadequate for the increased needs of the population. This donation was supplemented in February, 1898, by £1,000 sent specially to the Chairman of the School Committee for the same purpose.

In June of this year, Mr. D. A. Ansell, the president of the Society, was invited to attend a meeting of the Jewish Colonization Association in Paris, and whilst there the Baroness, who had been for some time in Austria, made a special journey in order personally to hear from the representative of the Society in Montreal what progress the children, in whom she took so great an interest, were making, and how the farmers who had been established in the North West were succeeding. Mr. Ansell never forgot the interview, nor the manner in which the world's benefactress listened even to matters of detail as to the result of the works initiated by her late husband and carried on by herself. The satisfactory nature of the information imparted induced her to promise an additional donation towards providing new school buildings.

This year also saw the formation of a cadet corps in connection with the Institute, forming the Montreal company of the Jewish Lads' Brigade, the Headquarters of which are in London, and of which Col. Goldschmidt was the commanding officer.

Nearly three years after the death of Baron de Hirsch the Baroness died in Paris on April 1st, 1899, leaving by her will a bequest to the Baron de Hirsch Institute of 600,000 francs. By the acquisition of this sum the Society was enabled to enlarge its sphere and it was decided to obtain a new charter of incorporation to change the name of the Society to "Baron de Hirsch Institute and Hebrew Benevolent Society of Montreal" and to extend its powers. This Act duly received the assent of the Lieut-Governor-in-Council on March 23rd, 1900, and enacts as follows:—

> "The said corporation is empowered to grant relief to sick and indigent persons of the Hebrew faith, to establish a home or refuge for the distressed, aged and orphans of the said faith, to provide a burial ground for the interment of their dead poor, to conduct schools for general instruction and manual training of the needy of said faith, to found a cadet corps in conjunction with said schools, to assist immigrants and settlers of the said faith to establish themselves in any of the provinces or territories of the Dominion of Canada, and to maintain all works of a charitable, patriotic or philanthropic nature for the amelioration of the condition of the Jewish poor; and for the better performing of any of the said objects the said corporation is authorized to enter into contracts

or agreements and to co-operate with any person, society or corporation. All acts done or works undertaken by the Young Men's Hebrew Benevolent Society of Montreal, which would come within the above provisions, are hereby ratified."

Having obtained these increased powers the officers of the Institute deemed it advisable to obtain larger quarters without any further loss of time. They had on hand the donation given by the late Baroness de Hirsch during her lifetime for this purpose, and from her bequest which yielded $88,771.08, $88,000.00 was kept as an endowment fund for the support of the institution and the balance placed to the building fund. The Jewish Colonization Association of Paris donated $10,000.00 and these amounts together with the donations and bequests collected in Montreal enabled the officers to purchase a piece of land on Bleury street at a cost of 65 cents a foot or a total cost of $14,800.00 and to build thereon a new school and Institute.

On Monday June 3rd, 1901, the ceremony of laying the cornerstone of this new building was performed in the presence of a large gathering of citizens of all creeds and nationalities. His Worship Mayor Prefontaine presided; Mr. D. A. Ansell, the president of the Institute, was master of ceremonies, and there were present Revs. Meldola de Sola, B. M. Kaplan, E. Friedlander and A. M. Ashinsky; Messrs. A. Goldstein, vice-president; I. Rubenstein, treasurer; and the trustees, Messrs. L. Holstein, L. Cohen, Z. Fineberg, S. Fischel, M. Coviensky and M. Markus. Among other distinguished people present were Messrs. Robert Bickerdike, M.P., James Cochrane, M.P.P., Lt.-Col. A. A. Stevenson, Rev. Principal McVicar, Rev. J. McCarter, Major Bittenger, U.S.A. Consul, and a letter of regret was received from Sir William Hingston. A guard of honour was provided by the Hirsch and Zion Cadets of the Jewish Lads' Brigade, the former commanded by Capt. Harris, the latter by Capt. Kaplan, while Capt. Levinson was in command of the parade. They marched up, headed by the bugle band of the 65th French Canadian Regiment and formed up in rear of the platform, where the girls of the Institute with their banner also took up their position.

The proceedings were opened with a prayer by Rabbi B. M. Kaplan, and Rev. Meldola de Sola delivered an address. He said that the event was historical, as for the first time the Jews laid the corner stone of an institution, which concerned not a section, but the whole community. While thanking the Heavenly Author of all blessings, they might remember His instruments, the Baron and Baroness de Hirsch, who had dispensed their charity so bountifully and with such wise discrimination. He saw in the Institute a threefold claim upon the community's support. It helped the helpless, hapless and forlorn; it educated the immigrants from Europe in the language and customs of the country, and it fostered loyalty to the British flag, under which their oppressed co-religionists could ever find the fullest liberty. After a prayer for the Royal Family had been offered by Rabbi E. Friedlander, the cadets presented arms and the stone was formally laid by Mr. D. A. Ansell, the president of the Institute.

The stone laid in the north east corner of the building bears the inscription:

THIS CORNER STONE WAS LAID BY
D. A. ANSELL ESQ., PRESIDENT
JUNE 3, 1901

and in Hebrew characters the Jewish date SIVAN 16, 5661. Beneath it was placed a box containing letters from Mr. B. Levine, president of the Jewish Colonization Association of Paris and Mr. Alfred Cohen of the Anglo-Jewish Association of London, England; lists of the officers of the Baron de Hirsch Institute and Hebrew Benevolent Society, and the Young Men's Hebrew Benevolent Society, records of the Institute, coins of the Dominion, and copies of the current Montreal daily papers, as well as a copy of the special number of the Jewish Times with supplement engraving of the building.

In laying the stone Mr. Ansell said: "As you are aware, we all feel a deep sense of gratitude to the most estimable woman, the late Baroness Hirsch de Gereuth, for her generosity in aiding in the accomplishment of such a worthy undertaking, and we are therefore relieved of much anxiety in being able, with the assistance of the Protestant Board of School Commissioners, to provide education for the children who are brought under our care."

Tapping on the cornerstone with a trowel, he said "I now declare this stone well and truly laid, and may God bless our good work."

LAWRENCE LEVEY
1st President, Young Men's Hebrew Benevolent Society

The children then sang, "O God, our help in ages past" and a silver trowel with an ebony handle was presented by Mr. I. Rubenstein to Mr. Ansell. The trowel bore the following inscription:—

Front: 5661 Foundation Stone Baron de Hirsch Institute, Montreal laid by D. A. Ansell, Esq., President.

Back: Presented by the Board of Directors to their President D. A. Ansell, Esq.

Mr. Goldstein moved a vote of thanks to Mr. Ansell, and then the Mayor came forward and in a few well chosen words congratulated the community on the success of the undertaking and paid a tribute to the memory of the Baron and Baroness de Hirsch. The Rev. Dr. MacVicar, as chairman of the Protestant Board of School Commissioners was glad to express their sympathy with the good work of the Institute, and agreed with the Mayor in his tribute to the unity of all religions and races in the city, and stated that he would rejoice at a uniform system of education for boys and girls of all nations and creeds. Mr. R. Bickerdike, M.P. followed with a few words eulogizing the Jews, and then Mr. James Cochrane, M.P.P., in the course of his remarks said that the school law ought to be amended so as to give a representative of the Jews a seat at the Board of Commissioners. Lt.-Col. A. A. Stevenson also gave a brief but eloquent address, after which Rabbi A. M. Ashinsky offered up the closing prayer in Hebrew.

In September of the same year, Their Royal Highnesses the Duke and Duchess of Cornwall and York visited Montreal on their tour through the Empire and on Wednesday the 18th, the Board of Directors of the Institute joined in a civic welcome to the heir to the throne and his consort. The address presented by the Institute was engrossed and illuminated on vellum, was 20" long and 18" broad, and consisted of the words: "The Lord preserve thy going out and thy coming in," written in English and in Hebrew. In the centre of the top was a drawing of the new building of which the corner stone had been laid in the spring, and on either side were drawings of the Shield of David in purple and gold. The address was drawn and illuminated by Mr. W. H. Baker, the principal of the school and was tied with red, white and blue ribbon.

The presentation to His Royal Highness was made

by Mr. D. A. Ansell, the President of the Board, who was accompanied by Messrs. A. Goldstein, I. Rubenstein, E. L. Rosenthal and Lyon Cohen, immediately after the Mayor had presented the citizens' address. Mr. Ansell received a copy of the reply of His Royal Highness, with the compliments of Sir Arthur Bigge and signed by the Duke of Cornwall and York, "George". In alluding to the special address of the Institute, the Duke in his reply to the various addresses said:—"The kind affectionate and in one instance sacred words of your addresses have indeed touched our hearts and the Duchess joins me in offering you and the people of Montreal our sincere gratitude for the warmth and loyalty of your greeting." The one address with sacred words was that of the Baron de Hirsch Institute. The old building on St. Elizabeth Street was decorated with coloured bunting in honour of the Royal visitors and illuminated in the evening with Chinese lanterns. A good muster of cadets attended the ceremony of the royal welcome and were appointed to line Sherbrooke St. between St. Lawrence and St. Hypolite Streets. The upper classes of the school to the number of 100 were gathered on the stand erected in front of the High School during the civic welcome and sang "The Maple Leaf" and "God Save the King."

The year 1902 stands out in the annals of the Institute as the one in which the building on Bleury Street was completed and dedicated to the objects intended. The ceremonial of the formal opening was performed by his Excellency, Lord Minto, the Governor General of the Dominion, on May 28th, 1902, and he was supported by representatives of the Federal and Provincial Cabinets, Senators, and members of Parliament, the Consular Body, the Mayor of Montreal, and a large number of influential citizens—both clerical and lay of all denominations, who were pleased to assist at the inauguration of the building which forms a fitting monument to the memory of those great and good philanthropists, the late Baron and Baroness de Hirsch.

His Excellency was received at the Institute early in the afternoon by the Board of Directors and the Mayor of Montreal, and the Guard of Honor was provided by No. 1 Company of the Jewish Lads' Brigade, under the command of Capt. Levinson, and by No. 3 Company under Lieut. Albert. An opening prayer was delivered by Rabbi Landman, and a prayer for the Royal Family by Rev. S. Goldstein. Addresses of welcome were presented to His Excellency by the President and Board of Directors of the Institute, and the children of the school. After the building was formally declared open by the Governor-General, addresses were delivered by Hon. S. N. Parent, Premier of the Province of Quebec, the Rev. Dr. McVicar, (Chairman of the Protestant Board of School Commissioners,) His Worship the Mayor of Montreal, the Rev. Dr. Shaw, (Chairman of the Protestant Committee of Public Instruction for the Province of Quebec), Sir William Hingston, and the Hon. George Washington Stephens.

The building occupies a frontage of 80 feet, and a depth of 97 feet. The design of the cut stone frontage is Egyptian in character and has six massive and ornamental pillars, the building being approached by a flight of stone steps leading to the main entrance on Bleury Street, while there are separate entrances for boys and girls from the north and south sides respectively.

BERNARD KORTOSK
A Founder of the Y.M.H.B.S.

The basement of the building comprises the usual store rooms etc., and separate playgrounds for boys and girls for use during the winter months. The ground floor contains administrative offices and a room capable of holding 100 people, a library and reading room. In the rear are two class rooms with accommodation for fifty pupils each. The second floor comprises six class rooms for 50 pupils each with cloak room attached to each class. The third floor consists of a large assembly hall capable of seating 800 people, that may be divided off by moveable partitions and has a stage at the western end.

The entire work was carried out at a cost of $45,000 under the direction of the Building Committee which consisted of Messrs. D. A. Ansell, A. Goldstein, I. Rubenstein, Lyon Cohen, and E. L. Rosenthal. The officers of the Institute at this time were;—Mr. D. A. Ansell, President and Chairman of the School Committee; Mr. A. Goldstein, Vice-President and Chairman of the Burial Committee; I. Rubenstein, Treasurer; and Mr. J. A. Jacobs, Hon. Secretary. Trustees;—Messrs. L. Holstein, M. Coviensky, Z. Fineberg, S. Fischel, Lyon Cohen and M. Markus. Hon. Officers;— Mr. Maxwell Goldstein, Hon. Counsel; Mr. Lewis A. Hart, Hon. Notary; Mr. S. W. Jacobs, Hon. Solicitor; Dr. J. B. McConnell, Hon. Consulting Physician, Dr. Hyman Lightstone, Hon. Physician; Mr. A. Kirschberg, Hon. Mohel. Mr. Kirschberg died during the year after acting in this capacity for some years, and his loss was very much regretted. The work of this department then fell upon the Rev. S. Goldstein.

With the opening of the new building the Institute was enabled to carry on its splendid work, and even to enlarge its scope. Until 1904, this School of the Baron de Hirsch Institute was the only free day school in the city of Montreal. However, during the Session of 1903-04 the Quebec Legislature passed an Act increasing the school taxes incorporating the Jews with the Protestant panel and creating free education in the Elementary Schools under its control. This necessitated the making of a new agreement between the Institute and the Protestant Board, who had, for the previous 8 years, given an annual subsidy of $2,000 towards the support of the school. By the new arrangement the subsidy was withdrawn and instead thereof the Protestant Board of School Commissioners appointed the English teachers, paid them their salaries in accordance with the scale of the Protestant Board, provided the necessary school apparatus, and paid that portion of the janitor's salary which might be fairly charged to the school. The Institute on its part had to supply the building with heating, lighting, water and maintenance generally, as well as the books necessary for free distribution, the salaries of the teacher of Hebrew, and all expenses connected with the teaching of that subject. By this agreement also, the school was reduced to a school with only three grades (it originally had 5 grades) and was bound to receive all foreign speaking Jewish children in whatever part of the city they might reside, and then transfer them to the Protestant Public School after having passed 3rd grade. Great stress was laid upon the inculcation of loyalty and patriotism to King and Country.

At the Annual Closing Exercises for 1905, Major G. W. Stephens presented the school with a handsome flag which helped a great deal in this branch of the training. This flag was carried into the Assembly Hall at the first Session of each week, when the whole school immediately after opening prayers was called to attention and saluted the flag, at the same time singing the first verse of the National Anthem. On other days the flag was placed in the Entrance Hall and saluted by every child on entering the building. In 1906, Mr. J. W. McQuat, Inspector of the Protestant Schools of the Province, stated in his report that the school was doing "excellent work amongst foreign born children, who soon gained a fair knowledge of English in its classes. In this school I saw children from nearly every part of Europe who were all learning English, and who all declared themselves to be Canadians."

As the object of the school was to fit the foreign children to take their place amongst those of Canadian birth the work was limited to third year only, and as a child was considered proficient enough in the English language to be transferred to the public schools, that transfer took place. This arrangement continued until 1908, when the erection of several new buildings by the Protestant Board provided them with ample accommodation for all Jewish as well as Protestant children in the regular schools, and the school in the Baron de Hirsch Institute was continued as a daily Hebrew and religious school, hygiene and calisthenics being later introduced as part of the curriculum. This school, as well as a Sunday School instituted in 1906, has continued to the present day; and the Night School which has done invaluable service to the adult portion of the new population in teaching them the language and customs of the country, has been found a real boon through all these years.

Until June, 1903, the school at Hirsch was under the control of the Board in Montreal, but at that time the Council of Administration of the Jewish Colonization Association was of the opinion that the time had arrived when the colonists should support their own schools, and in this decision the colonists heartily concurred.

In 1909, the Library and Reading Room were opened to the public, with about 1200 Hebrew and English volumes on the shelves, and a number of magazines and newspapers. This branch of the Institute's work has been much appreciated by students and the reading Jewish public generally, and has increased its usefulness by considerable additions to its material as the years have gone by. Until 1924, the Jewish Colonization Association gave an annual grant towards the library, considering it to be a part of the Canadianising work of the Institute, but when times became really so bad that all money was needed for relief work the grant had to be withdrawn. The Baron de Hirsch Book Club was organized in 1914 to promote the love of learning amongst the younger members of the community, and the proceeds of lectures held under its auspices are being used to buy the Library.

The Baron de Hirsch Institute continuously and consistently pursued its career of usefulness in the community, working for the poor, and particularly the immigrant poor, in every way by schools, family welfare, legal aid, and so on through life, and when needed, provided free burial as well. The Institute was the pioneer charitable and philanthropic organization in Montreal, and in its turn fostered and instituted many of the leading charitable organizations which are to-day separate entities. In 1914, it was felt that more efficient work could be done in the charitable and philanthropic field by an amalgamation of all work along these lines, as there was already a good deal of overlapping, and accordingly the Federation of Jewish Philanthropies was formed, with Headquarters in the Baron de Hirsch Institute Building, and the Baron de Hirsch Institute itself became one of the constituent societies, still continuing to conduct the religious school, library, cemetery at Sault au Recollet, family welfare, legal aid and Hebrew Court of Arbitration, all of which are known as Baron de Hirsch activities.

The following are the Board of Directors for 1924:— Hon. President, H. M. Levine; President, A. Z. Cohen; Vice-President, M. M. Sperber; Hon. Secretary, Mr. Max Bernfeld; Treasurer, Lionel Coviensky. L. Blumer, Horace Cohen, H. E. Herschorn, Jacob Kellert, A. Kellnor, Louis Salomon, Samuel Wener. The following is the list of Presidents since the foundation of the Young Men's Hebrew Benevolent Society;—1863, L. L. Levey; 1866, Chas. L. Levy; 1867, Samuel E. Moss; 1869, J. L. Samuel; 1870, Jacob G. Ascher; 1875, Lyon Silverman; 1881, Noah Friedman; 1882, Henry Jacobs; 1883, B. Kortosk; 1884, L. Robinson; 1885, A. Goldstein; 1886, M. Vineberg; 1888, Harris Vineberg; 1892, L. A. Hart; 1893, D. A. Ansell; 1908, Sir Mortimer Davis; 1909, Lyon Cohen; 1913, Sir Mortimer Davis; 1914, S. W. Jacobs; (1915 Federation formed); 1915, Louis Lewis; 1917, H. M. Levine; 1919, Jacob Kellert; 1924, A. Z. Cohen.

MORRIS LAZARUS MORRIS was born in Russian Poland in February 1858, the son of the late Barnard Morris. He came to America in 1879, and after a few years spent in New York, moved to Montreal, where he has since resided, and where he has taken a prominent part in Jewish communal affairs. He is an active supporter of all the philanthropic institutions in that city, both Jewish and Christian. Mr. Morris is a life governor of the Baron de Hirsch Institute and of the Montreal General Hospital, and is one of the founders of the Hebrew Orphans' Home. He is married to Annie, daughter of Mr. and Mrs. Max Bernstein, and has six daughters, Mrs. M. Glauberson, Mrs. L. Gelber, Mrs. A. J. Alexander, Mrs. P. Hermant, Mrs. A. Alexandor and Mrs. E. Kert, and one son, Mr. A. Morris. Mr. Morris is a member of the Masonic Order, and of the Independent Order of Oddfellows. Since his arrival in Montreal, he has been a member of the Shaar Hashomayim Congregation.

THE LATE LYON SILVERMAN

M. L. MORRIS, MONTREAL

THE LATE MR. LYON SILVERMAN was born in Benton, Miss., January 2nd, 1846, the son of the late Solomon and Rose Silverman, and died in Montreal on February 29th, 1908. He received his education in Montreal, and was engaged there in business until his death. Mr. Silverman took a very active part in all Jewish communal undertakings, and he was one of the earliest members of the German and Polish Congregation (now the Shaar Hashomayim). He was President of this congregation from 1876-1879, an office also held by his father. Mr. Silverman was a member of the Montefiore Club, and belonged to the I.O.O.F. He was married to Sarah, daughter of the late George and Dora Lazarus, of Montreal, who still survives him, with one son, Edward, and five daughters, Mrs. S. Jacobs, Mrs. D. Davis, Mrs. M. Silver, and the Misses Hattie and Louise Silverman. His communal activities have been ably carried on by his children, who have taken a deep interest in the different charitable institutions in Montreal.

MOISE SCHWOB, MONTREAL

MOISE SCHWOB, a prominent Montreal merchant, was born at Hegenheim, Alsace, on December 3rd, 1841, the son of Isaac Schwob. He received his education at Hegenheim. He came to Canada in the early part of the year 1866 and settled in Montreal, where, associated with his brother Alfred, he founded the firm of Schwob Bros. importers of Swiss watches. This business is still carried on under the original name by two of his sons and after sixty years of its existence remains the leading firm in the wholesale watch trade of the Dominion. Mr. Schwob is married to Blanche Woog, daughter of Aaron Woog. He has three sons, Julien, Fred and Alexander, all born in Montreal. Julien and Fred residing in Montreal and Alexander in New York. For a period of ten years Mr. Schwob held the post of Vice-Consul of France. From the time of his arrival in Montreal Mr. Schwob took an active part in the affairs of the Jewish community. One of the charter members of the Young Men's Hebrew Benevolent Society (the first Jewish charitable organization established in Canada) in which he held office for a number of years, Mr. Schwob has the distinction of being the only survivor of the original members. Largely through the personal influence of Mr. Schwob, the late Baron de Hirsch decided to contribute to the relief of the Jewish immigrants in Canada, and later endowed the Baron de Hirsch Institute in Montreal. Mr. Schwob did not limit his activities to the Jewish section of the community, but took a prominent part in all movements concerning the welfare of the City of Montreal and of the country. A public-spirited citizen, a man of vision, gentle, kind, broad minded, he at all times commanded the highest esteem of all classes of the community. In recent years, Mr. Schwob has spent much of his time abroad but still claims Canada as his home. Mr. Schwob maintains his membership in the St. James Club, Montreal.

M. RITTENBERG, MONTREAL

MOSES RITTENBERG was born in Russia, February 21st, 1871, the son of the late Mr. Saul Rittenberg, at one time Cantor in the Shaar Hashomayim Synagogue, Montreal. Mr. Rittenberg came to Canada as a child with his parents and he received his education in the schools of Montreal. For many years he was engaged in business in Toronto, where his mother still resides. Some twenty years ago he moved to Montreal, and in partnership with Mr. Michael Margolick, organized the Crown Pants Company, which through untiring energy and hard work they have developed into one of the large clothing manufacturing industries of Canada with a very high reputation that is recognized from one end of the country to the other. Mr. Rittenberg has always taken a great interest in all philanthropic work affecting the Jewish community. His untiring zeal and labor on behalf of the Hebrew Orphanage in Montreal has done much to place this institution in the high position it occupies among Montreal's public institutions. At the present time, Mr. Rittenberg is the President of the Orphanage, and he has spent much time in visiting similar institutions and getting further ideas for the improvement of the Montreal Home. He is a Director of the Federation of Jewish Philanthropies of Montreal, and is one of the most active workers for the Federation. Mr. Rittenberg is always willing to assist the needy and help his less fortunate co-religionist, yet his activities are by no means confined to any one section of the community, and he is a generous supporter of all charitable and philanthropic institutions. He takes a keen interest in public affairs and holds a high position in the communal life of Montreal. Mr. Rittenberg is married to Miss Minnie Kramer, and has four sons, Alfred, Abraham, Stanley and Harold Rittenberg. He is a member of the Montefiore Club, Montreal, and of Ionic Lodge, A.F. & A.M. He is one of the oldest members of the Shaar Hashomayim Congregation, Montreal.

MONTREAL HEBREW ORPHANS' HOME

THE Montreal Hebrew Orphans' Home is an outgrowth of the Montreal Hebrew Sheltering and Orphans' Home which was established in 1909 for the purpose of providing a temporary home and shelter for orphaned children, the indigent aged and transients. The quarters were at 18 Evans Street. By 1914, the population of the Home had grown to 35 children, and 6 aged folks. In the immigration department 255 men, women and children were cared for. It was realized that the quarters were inadequate, especially for children under a scientific child-care policy, and the discussion of ways and means of procuring a new Home started about this time.

The following year the immigration work was discontinued but the congestion was not relieved owing to the growing population of children, which reached the high figure of 50. In 1917, a number of the leading social service agencies of the Jewish community joined together to form the Federation of Jewish Philanthropies, the Montreal Hebrew Orphans' Home being one of this number. In joining this organization the directors of the Home felt that through a federation more time could be devoted to actual social work, whereas much time had previously been devoted to various means of raising funds. Authorization was received from Federation for a private campaign for funds in case such were required. A number of locations were considered for a new home and it was finally decided to buy the building of the Hervey Institute at 500 Claremont Avenue for the sum of $100,000. In October, 1921, the children were removed to their new Home and there was a big public reception; thousands of members of the Jewish community inspected the building and were well pleased with the new development.

The new Home has ample room for the care of 100 children; there are twelve dormitories, class rooms, locker rooms, a gymnasium, a music room, an isolation floor forming a complete unit in itself, two infirmaries, a dental room fully equipped and other necessary facilities. The isolation floor was fully equipped as a hospital in the fall of 1924.

MONTREAL HEBREW ORPHANS' HOME

The institution is fortunate in having a summer home at Shawbridge, P.Q. which however was destroyed by fire at midnight August 14th-15th, 1922, with fatal results, but a new building was erected in 1924, and the children recommenced to spend their vacations there in that year. The Shawbridge summer Home is situated on a tract of 30 acres owned by the Home in the village proper and affords all facilities for summer outings, such as ample playing fields, bathing facilities, hiking, berrying, fishing. The new building is a commodious structure with wide balconies upon which all the children sleep in the open.

The policy of the Montreal Hebrew Orphans' Home is to normalize the experience of the children under its care and to send them forth only when they are ready to face the problems of life. The life of the Home is marked by privacy, individual treatment, informality except where discipline is endangered. Discipline is based on the need of developing self reliance. On the negative side there is no group discipline, no numbering. These features are all bound up with the policy of subjecting the children as little as possible to public appearance as orphans. In the persuance of this policy, the fact that the Home is a constituent of Federation has been beneficial. There is no need to exhibit the children at any time for the direct purpose of appealing to the public for sympathy, and this helps the moral of the children.

The Home has been fortunate in the character of the men who have served on the Board since its organization. The presidents have been:—1912, M. B. Steine; 1913-16, A. M. Vineberg; 1917-18, S. Kellert; 1919-20, Albert Lesser; 1921-22, Ascher Pierce; 1923, Jacob A. Jacobs; 1924, Moses Rittenberg.

The Board of Directors for 1925 are:—Advisory Committee: Messrs. A. M. Vineberg, S. Kellert, A. Lesser, A. Pierce, and J. A. Jacobs. President, Mr. M. Rittenberg; Vice-President, Mr. H. M. Levine; Hon. Treasurer, Mr. S. Hart; Hon. Secretary, Mr. P. Meyerovitch, Messrs. M. Albert, A. J. Alexander, F. Bramson, C. Fisher, A. Kellnor, I. Kert, Norman Friedman, H. M. Ripstein, J. H. Wener, F. Leopold, and Dr. A. P. Ship; Superintendent, Mr. Irving Gerdy.

AL. LESSER, MONTREAL

ALBERT LESSER, one of the most active welfare workers in Montreal, was born in Montreal on the 23rd of September, 1870, the son of Moses Lesser, of that city. He was educated in the public schools of Montreal and was married in 1908 to Miss Jeannette Wohl, daughter of Louis Wohl of Cleveland, Ohio. At an early age Mr. Lesser entered the retail clothing business in Montreal, and has continued in this trade, building up one of the largest clothing businesses in that city, with a very fine record for business integrity as well as a name for being very charitable. He is one of the most prominent communal workers in Montreal and is a supporter of almost every charitable and philanthropic organization. Mr. Lesser is an example of the finest type of young Jewish manhood, ever looking out for the interests of those less fortunately situated than himself. He is in every sense of the word a public-spirited citizen, and he takes an active interest in all public questions. His time, money and energy are always at the disposal of the Jew in need, and his assistance is cheerfully given to every worthy cause. He never allows his personal interests to interfere with what he considers his public duty. Mr. Lesser is a vice-president of the Federation of Jewish Philanthropies, Montreal, and is honorary president of the Montreal Hebrew Orphans' Home. He is a life governor of the Montreal General Hospital, and of the Western Hospital, Montreal. He is a member, and takes much interest in the work of the Hebrew Maternity Hospital; the Hebrew Free Loan Association; the United Talmud Torahs; and the Young Men's Hebrew Association. Mr. Lesser has always been connected with the Shaar Hashomayim synagogue, and he is chairman of the House Committee. He is a director of the Montefiore Club, and a member of the Montreal Reform Club and the Elm Ridge Country Club. Mr. Lesser has always been a follower of the Liberal party, and is keenly interested in all matters for the betterment of municipal and provincial affairs.

MOUNT SINAI SANATORIUM

SITUATED on one of the loftiest and most beautiful spots in Ste. Agathe, in the Laurentian Mountains north of Montreal, stands the Mount Sinai Sanatorium, a magnificent structure, not so much in the architectural sense, though it is adequately designed for its purpose, but in the work it is doing. This building, erected through the generosity of its founders, Sir Mortimer Davis and Messrs. Jacob A. Jacobs, M. A. Vineberg, Mark Workman, Ascher Pierce, and the estate of S. Wolsey, and built on ground donated by the Jewish Colonization Association, was instituted for the free treatment of consumptives. Since it was opened to patients in August, 1912, (the official opening was on June 29th, 1913) many hundred patients have been treated by the Sanatorium, and the number of lives thus saved can never be computed; for not only are incipient cases checked, and in many instances cured, but tuberculosis being a disease that insinuates its dread bacilli so quickly and quietly, the number of those who might, and probably would have been infected had not the Sanatorium taken care of the cases by isolation and nourishment, as well as the necessary medical care, can never be known.

The building has been constructed along the latest approved lines for institutions of this nature. It comprises four light, airy wards and accommodates 48 patients. All windows are level with the floor so that all the beds may be rolled out on to a large verandah surrounding the building, where patients may get the air and sunshine so essential to recovery. There is also a bright dining room, recreation room, doctors' and nurses' rooms, marble bathrooms, warm dressing rooms, hot and cold water, with all the latest improvements, making the institution a model of its kind, and one of which the Jewish community of Montreal has had reason to be proud of ever since its foundation, for it has refused admission to no deserving and needy case, irrespective of religion or nationality. Though the original intention was to admit only incipient cases it was soon found that to fulfil the true philanthropic aim of the institution, cases of advanced tuberculosis could not be refused, and these are admitted. No paying case has ever been allowed in the Sanatorium, which was instituted solely for those of the poor who could not afford any payment whatever, and in this way the real service to the community has been performed; as these unfortunate people have not only been removed from the city where they were a menace to those with whom they spent their daily lives, but they have been in so many cases fitted to take once more their places among their fellows, armed with a new lease of life.

As the ground on which the Sanatorium is situated comprises 160 acres, it was thought expedient to cultivate a portion of the land, invest in livestock and run a farm in connection with the hospital. This continued for some years, and the farm produce for the patients was thus obtained right on the premises. However, during the war years the cost of maintenance mounted so greatly that it was decided in 1917 to sell the stock and rent the farm. In 1915, a number of friends of the institution donated a sufficient sum to instal a cold storage plant, which has enabled the purchase of supplies on a large scale, thus saving considerable expense. From the year 1916 onwards a grant has been received annually from the Provincial Government.

In August 1924, the Hon. Athanase David, Provincial Secretary, paid a visit of inspection to the Sanatorium, and was surprised to find that the first two patients to whom he spoke were French Canadians. Mr. David professed himself delighted with all the arrangements at the Sanatorium. It is the aim of the institution not only to cure tuberculosis, but even more to prevent it. A feature of this preventative work is the publication of a monthly Bulletin in English and Yiddish, "The Tablets", containing articles on tuberculosis, the prevention of the same, and on the hygienic life in general. This is printed at the Sanatorium on a press donated by kind friends, and is distributed to the patients and to persons in Montreal as well. Another preventative phase is the follow-up work, to see that cases discharged as cured or arrested have the proper occupations and surroundings in order to prevent a recurrence of the dread disease. In 1917, the Mount Sinai Sanatorium followed the example of the organization which had fostered its infancy—The Baron de Hirsch Institute—and became a constituent society of Federation. The present Board of Directors are;— President, Mr. S. Salomon; Vice-President, Mr. H. M. Ripstein; Secretary, Mr. A. W. Muhlstock; Rev. Dr. Corcos, Dr. S. Kirsch, Mr. J. B. Miller, Mr. Harry Jacoby, Mr. L. Meltzer, Mr. H. Weinfield.

Medical Board—Chairman, Dr. S. Ortenberg; Dr. J. R. Byers, Dr. L. S. Hirschberg, Dr. J. Kolber, Dr. P. L. Phelps, Dr. S. F. Stein, Dr. Garber, Dr. A. B. Illievitz, Dr. J. Lande, Dr. J. Rosenbaum, Dr. Scherzer, Dr. D. Tannenbaum.

Staff—Managing Director, Dr. David Mendel; Resident Physician, Dr. S. Gold; Steward, Mr. J. L. Fox.

MOUNT SINAI SANATORIUM, ST. AGATHE, P.Q.

THE HERZL DISPENSARY, MONTREAL

THE history of the Herzl Dispensary is very much like that of many other Jewish institutions in this country. Their founders are about a handful of energetic and devoted men and women.

In the case of the Jewish Dispensary of Montreal, a group of Jewish doctors, prominent amongst whom were Doctors Sperber, Tannenbaum, Schacher, Ortenberg, and a few others, who co-operated with several ladies, at the head of whom were Mrs. Taube Kaplan, Mrs. Adler, Mrs. Rost and Mrs. Bloomberg, and several prominent gentlemen, amongst whom the most active were Messrs. I. Goldberg, B. Steinhouse and Goldman, and a few other public-spirited Jewish men and women, who in co-operation with the Ladies' Auxiliary of the King Edward Benefit Association finally laid the foundation of this much-needed institution in the Canadian Metropolis.

At the beginning, the Dispensary did not have very smooth sailing. Many were the obstacles it had to encounter in its way, and particularly the apathy and lack of self-reliance which existed at that time among the Jewish public.

At first, its home was humble, a little building situated at 832 St. Dominique Street, with little comfort,

HERZL DISPENSARY

accompanied by many inconveniences, but time levelled the path, and now the Dispensary is rendering the aid and service expected of such institutions, and is functioning as satisfactorily as is possible. It has had its own home, a handsome little edifice at 632 St. Urbain Street, since 1914, and is at present the pride of the Jewish population. Its progress has been encouraging, and it now covers every department incumbent upon a modern well-equipped dispensary. These departments are:—Medicine (in all its branches), Eye, Ear and Nose, Nervous Diseases, Skin Diseases, and an X-Ray Department. It also handles all cases of Tuberculosis before they are admitted to the Mount Sinai Sanatorium, and upon the patient's discharge from the latter institution, they are cared for by the Herzl Dispensary.

The average number of patients has been one thousand (1,000) per month. The Medical Staff of the institution consists of twenty Jewish physicians, who devote their ability and time to render the service as efficiently as possible.

The present time bids fair that this institution will accomplish a maximum of service, and that it will form in the near future the nucleus for a large and needed Jewish General Hospital.

THE HEBREW MATERNITY HOSPITAL OF MONTREAL

THE birth of the Hebrew Maternity Hospital like all other things connected with maternity, was most romantic, but the course of love at first did not run smoothly.

There were many difficulties placed in its way by members of its own family. However, love eventually triumphed and the following is an account of the birth and growth of the institution.

It was in the eventful year of 1914 when Mrs. Taube Kaplan (The Greene Rebitzin) first conceived a vision for the necessity of a Jewish Maternity Hospital, where the poor and expectant Jewish mothers, and their newborn children would be cared for during their greatest time of helplessness and need.

It was through the sole effort of Mrs. Kaplan, who devoted a number of years of her life tramping about day and night in the cold of the winter, and heat of the summer, from door to door to collect from people equally as poor as herself in material comforts, small amounts, varying from five cents to twenty-five cents, an amount sufficient to make the first payment on a house which subsequently was bought and transformed into the Jewish Maternity Hospital. Later on, Mrs. Kaplan, through her devotedness, self-sacrifice and persevering toil attracted to her sympathetic cause, a number of men and women who gave generously of their time and money, to make her dream a reality. The important co-operators in this laudable cause were Mrs. M. Goldberg, Mrs. M. Meltzer, Mrs. R. Kositsky, and Dr. Sperber, who together with Mrs. Kaplan, devoted a great deal of their time and helped the materialization of the Hospital.

Mr. L. Meltzer was the first President, and Mr. D. H. Routtenberg, who upon Mr. Meltzer's departure from Montreal took up the difficult task of presiding over the early destiny of the institution, was the second President.

The Hebrew Maternity Hospital was incorporated on March 5th, 1916. It has a very able Medical Staff, and a Medical Board consisting of seven members, all capable physicians. The Chairman of the Medical Board is Dr. J. R. Goodall, and the members are Doctors Eidlow, Hirschberg, Wiseman, Schacher and Tannenbaum. The Hospitals has eight nurses in constant attendance. The President for the present term is Mr. J. B. Miller, who deserves a great deal of credit for having brought the institution to its present state of recognition in the Jewish community. Mr. Miller worked wholeheartedly for the welfare of the institution from its very origin.

The institution has had an average of four hundred (400) patients annually in recent years. The Board and Officers of this institution are progressive and very enterprising, and will make in the very near future, the Jewish Maternity Hospital, a model hospital in the city.

A. RUDOLPH, MONTREAL

Notman

ABRAHAM RUDOLPH, the proprietor of the Yorkshire Importing Company, was born in Bobrysk, Russia, on July 17th, 1869, the son of Mr. and Mrs. Louis Rudolph of that town. He was educated in Russia and came to Canada in 1888, when he was but eighteen years of age. Mr. Rudolph entered into the woollen business, and he has remained continuously in this trade ever since. He was one of the first Jews in Montreal to enter into this business in a large way, and his success has been due to his integrity and energy. Some years ago, Mr. Rudolph organized the Yorkshire Importing Company, of which concern he is still the active head. In 1890, he was married to Miss Goldie Singer, daughter of the Rev. Isaac Singer, and he has five daughters; Mrs. S. M. Eisenstadt, Mrs. Benjamin Levinson, Mrs. Paul Silverstone, and the Misses Lillian and Evelyn Rudolph; and one son, Mr. Arthur Rudolph. Ever since his arrival in Montreal, Mr. Rudolph has been keenly interested in welfare work, and has devoted much time and energy to communal affairs. His assistance and advice are looked to for any charitable work, and his help is never asked for in vain. He is a life governor of the Baron de Hirsch Institute, and was Treasurer of the Hebrew Maternity Hospital for five years. He was a Vice-President of the Hebrew Free Loan Association for eight years, and was associated with its founder, the late Zigmond Fineberg, in the organization of this institution. He is a trustee of the Federation of Jewish Philanthropies; member of the Board of the Mount Sinai Sanatorium; life governor of both the Montreal General and Western Hospitals; and is a director of the Hospital for Crippled Children. Mr. Rudolph was one of the most active workers for the relief of Jews who suffered during the Great War, and was on many committees for war relief work. He is a trustee of the Shaar Hashomayim Synagogue, the largest Jewish congregation in Canada, of which he has been a member since his arrival in Montreal; and a member of the Montefiore Club, Montreal.

THE LATE ZIGMOND FINEBERG

ZIGMOND FINEBERG was born in Pren, Suwalki, Poland, in March 1863. He married in Valkovishka, Poland, Jennie Kirschberg, eldest daughter of the late Rev. Abraham and Cirla (Rose) Kirschberg, of Montreal. He came to Canada in 1887 and settled in Montreal. For a number of years he was engaged in commercial business, and in 1905, he founded the real estate firm of Z. Fineberg & Sons, and remained its head until his death in 1917. He was at all times connected with the local charitable and educational organizations, having for a number of years been a Trustee of the Baron de Hirsch Institute, and the Talmud Torah. He was a member of the Board of Trade; Governor of the Montreal General Hospital; member of Ionic Lodge, A.F. & A.M.; Mount Horeb Chapter, R.A.M.; I.O.O.F.; I.O.F.; and C.O.F. Mr. Fineberg was for a number of years Trustee and Parnass of the Shearith Israel Congregation, as well as member of the Shaar Hashomayim Synagogue. He was made a Justice of the Peace in 1897. He was an active supporter of the Zionist Movement, having for a number of years been Treasurer of the Agudath Zion Society of Montreal. Mr. Fineberg's greatest claim to the respect and remembrance of the Jews of Canada is the Hebrew Free Loan Association of Montreal, his personal creation. For years he had privately carried on Gemilath Chasodim work, as a personal pleasure. It was his life-long ambition to diminish pauperism as much as possible, and with this end in view, he founded the Hebrew Free Loan Association in 1911 when he became its first President, a position he held until the time of his death. To-day this organization is one of the most successful communal institutions of Montreal, having loaned out in 1923, about $100,000, free of all interest and any other charges whatever. The work so magnificently conceived and ably begun by the father, is very loyally carried on by his two sons, Joseph and N. S. Fineberg. Mr. Fineberg died in Montreal on November 22nd, 1917. He left a widow, Jennie Fineberg, one daughter, Agnes (Mrs. Irwin Rubinovich), and five sons, Joseph, Nathaniel S., Aaron H., Dr. Moe N., and Dr. Maxwell Fineberg.

HEBREW FREE LOAN ASSOCIATION, MONTREAL

"עַל שְׁלֹשָׁה דְבָרִים הָעוֹלָם עוֹמֵד:

עַל הַתּוֹרָה וְעַל הָעֲבוֹדָה וְעַל גְמִילוּת חֲסָדִים"

THE Hebrew Free Loan Association of Montreal was founded and organized through the untiring efforts and unflinching zeal of the late Zigmond Fineberg, on May 28, 1911.

The late Mr. Fineberg was for many years fired by a life-long ambition to organize and establish in Montreal a "Gemilath Chasodim" Association. In his own unostentatious manner, he had been for years lending money privately, free of all interest, and any other charges, to people in need. His great ideal was to help people to help themselves, so that they should not become paupers, or charity receivers, but, on the contrary, rather to endeavour to encourage people to retain their self-respect in time of need, and so become self-supporting citizens.

Whilst being in full sympathy with all charity organizations, which he at all times generously supported, his main view was to diminish pauperism. For a number of years, he was intimately connected with the various charitable and philanthropic institutions of Montreal, and he felt, that at best, charity afforded only momentary relief. The recipient was sure to return for more charity, and such benevolence did not seem to have any elevating effect on the poor, as nothing lasting was being accomplished. The thing to save in a person, in a moment of distress or need, was his self-respect. This could only be done by attempting to infuse a spirit of confidence in people so unfortunately placed. There was nothing that brought courage and a new spirit to such people, as a free loan of a few hundred dollars, offered at the right moment. Instead of remaining public liabilities, such people would be lifted out of the charity rut, and, in time, become producers and assets in the community.

In 1909, Mr. Fineberg went to Europe to investigate the various Free Loan Associations there, in order to learn their type of organization. Upon his return, he immediately set out unaided and single-handed, and raised over $5,000.00 capital from various members of the community, with which to officially organize the Hebrew Free Loan Association in Montreal, the only one of its kind in Canada. The object of Mr. Fineberg then, was to obtain as many contributors as possible, so that the organization should become property of the community.

Accordingly, application was made for official incorporation from the Quebec Government, and on May 28, 1911, the Hebrew Free Loan Association of Montreal officially came into existence.

Among the applicants for incorporation, were the following prominent citizens of Montreal:—Zigmond Fineberg, the founder and organizer himself, Moses Albert, Tobias Glickman, N. H. Godine, J. A. Jacobs, Eli W. Jacobs, A. H. Jackson, Sol. Kellert, Hiram Levy, A. A. Levin.

In the act of incorporation the purpose is given as follows:—"The object of this Society is to loan money to those in need instead of giving alms, and thus assist respectable people whose character and self-respect will not permit them to receive alms, but who will accept a loan which they can repay and thus overcome the difficulties in their struggle for means of livelihood.

Money is loaned in sums of $5.00 to $150.00, to applicants, irrespective of race or creed, on notes endorsed by responsible people, absolutely free of any interest or charges whatsoever, the borrower repaying the loans in weekly payments."

The maximum loan to any one person was raised in 1923 to $200.00.

Since the inception of this Association in 1911, till May 1, 1924, 12,067 loans were issued, in all, amounting to $677,579.73, absolutely free of all interest or any other charges whatsoever.

The capital in 1911 was $5,996.00, and at May 1st, 1924, it stood at $29,110.43.

The total losses of this Association from the first day to May 1st, 1924, a period of thirteen years, was less than $700.00, or about 1/10 of 1% on the total amount of loans issued. This fact speaks volumes for the inherent honesty of people. The revenue from Membership Dues has grown to about $10,000.00 per annum, which is used to defray the running expenses of administration, and every year there is a surplus from annual revenue carried forward to capital account, which helps to automatically increase the available funds from which loans are granted.

The founder, the late Zigmond Fineberg, became the first President of the Hebrew Free Loan Association, when it was organized in 1911, and continued in office as President till the date of his death, on November 22nd, 1917, the office remaining unfilled for the remainder of the term, till May 1918, as a mark of respect to the late founder.

After his death, two of his sons, Joseph Fineberg and Nathaniel S. Fineberg, M.A., B.C.L., joined the Board of Directors, and ever since they have both shown the same interest and unflagging zeal in Gemilath Chasodim work, as their late father did. The example set by the father is being very ably followed by his two sons.

In 1918, Mr. Moses Albert became President, after having been continuously in office and intimately connected with the affairs of the Association from the very beginning, firstly, as Honorary Secretary, and later as Treasurer. Mr. Albert retained the Presidency until 1920, and discharged his duties with ability and dignity, when one of the founder's sons, Mr. N. S. Fineberg, M.A., B.C.L., became President, and has been directing the affairs of the Association, ever since.

Mr. Albert remained on the Board of Directors, and again became the Treasurer, which office he has held ever since he left the chair. Starting out as one of the founder's loyal lieutenants, in 1911, Mr. Albert has held practically every office on the Board of Directors, and much of the success of the Association is clearly traceable to his sound judgment and untiring energy.

A narrative of the Hebrew Free Loan Association would not be complete without adequate reference being made to Messrs. Joseph S. Leo, Nathan H. Godine, and Menassah Lavut, three other officers to whose sincerity and devotion much of the good administration and success of the Association is largely due. Messrs. J. S. Leo and N. H. Godine were co-directors with the late founder and organizer, from the time of the foundation, till the present time, whilst Mr. Lavut, a veteran communal worker, joined the Board in 1915, and, from that time on has been a tower of strength in his capacity of Chairman of the Investigation Committee. In this very important position, Mr. Lavut was at all times ably assisted by Mr. J. S. Leo, a prominent Jewish citizen, who has held the position of Chairman of the Loan Committee for ten years.

Mr. N. H. Godine, who has held various offices on the Board since the beginning, has at all times been faithful to the ideals of the Association, and ever ready to devote himself to its welfare.

The Association's headquarters were first located in one of the private offices of the founder's place of business, when shortly after, they removed to 52 Ontario Street, West, where they remained till 1921. From that time on the offices have been in the Molsons Bank Building, St. Lawrence Blvd., Corner Ontario Street, in the heart of the Jewish business centre.

The Association now has five Memorial Funds, contributed by the families of those in whose memory the Funds were created.

Z. Fineberg Fund	$3,000.00
The Solomon Fund	1,000.00
M. Rapp Fund	1,000.00
S. Wigdor Fund	1,000.00
Rena Raginsky Fund	1,000.00

The Jews of Montreal, in fact of Canada, now possess one of the most constructive communal organizations, thanks to the vision and devotion of the late Zigmond Fineberg. The basis of "Gemilath Chasodim" work is scientific and lofty, inasmuch as a "Free Loan," offered at the propitious moment to a person in distress, or dire need, is the agency which tends to save that person from becoming a public burden, and to encourage him to hold his head erect, because the borrower, being obliged to repay the loan, is kept away from taking charity, which at best is degrading to the recipient. "To lend to the poor and needy, is to lend to the Lord." This divine philosophy is the underlying conception of a "Gemilath Chesed."

It is written that, "Si quaeris monumentum circumspice."

The hundreds, nay thousands, that have been helped by the Hebrew Free Loan Association, are indeed, living tributes to the noble work, the foundations of which were so magnificently conceived, and so ably reared by the late Zigmond Fineberg.

Yet, to adequately commemorate this form of scientific and constructive communal work, begun by the late founder, the Board of Directors and friends, have erected in the Association's premises, as a fitting tribute and everlasting memorial, a bronze tablet, which will always remain as a monument to the founder's great contribution to the welfare of his people.

Fac-simile of Bronze Tablet erected in memory of the late Zigmond Fineberg, Founder and Organizer.

NATHANIEL S. FINEBERG, M.A., B.C.L., MONTREAL

NATHANIEL SAMUEL FINEBERG, one of Montreal's most public-spirited among the younger citizens, was born in Montreal, on January 16th, 1889, the son of the late Zigmond and Jennie (Kirschberg) Fineberg. His early education was had in the Aberdeen and High Schools, Montreal. In 1904, he entered the Arts Faculty of McGill University, and graduated with first rank honors in 1908, with the B.A. degree. Upon obtaining a University Scholarship, he engaged in post-graduate work at Yale University, where, in 1909, he was awarded his M.A. degree, with high honors. Shortly after, he joined the firm of Z. Fineberg & Sons, real estate dealers, founded by his father. While still retaining his business connections, he began the study of law in 1910 at McGill, where he won several distinctions, including the Roman Law prizes, and graduated with the B.C.L. degree in 1913, with first rank honors. He became a member of the Bar of Quebec in the same year. While a student in Arts, he was one of the prime movers and founders of the Maccabean Circle, in 1905, for the Jewish students at McGill, and was for three years its President. In 1913, he was instrumental in introducing the Zeta Beta Tau Fraternity into Canadian Jewish Student life, having been one of the charter members of Upsilon Chapter established at McGill. In 1915, he became Honorary Secretary of the National Supreme Council of Z.B.T. Fraternity. In 1920, he was one of the organizers of the Graduate Menorah Society at Montreal and is still the Treasurer. He became President of the Y.M.H.A. in 1915. In 1917, upon the death of his father, who had organized and founded the Hebrew Free Loan Association, he became a Director, later becoming Treasurer, and since 1920, he has been the President. Much of the later success of this Association is due to his able direction of the administration. He is a life Governor of the Montreal Reform Club; Trustee of the Hebrew Maternity Hospital; member of the Canadian Bar Association. Mr. Fineberg has been a frequent contributor to various magazines and periodicals.

THE FEDERATION OF THE JEWISH PHILANTHROPIES OF TORONTO

SIMILAR to the present acute situation from the standpoint of distress it will be remembered by many of the members of the Toronto Jewish Community, was the one in the fall of 1916, when all and every one of the then existing Jewish Benevolent Societies in the city were without any funds whatsoever. Some of them had even incurred debts they were unable to pay. These were the main facts that gave birth to the Federation of the Jewish Philanthropies of Toronto.

The real father and founder of the Federation is Mr. Abraham Cohen, who since its inception has so efficiently held and still holds the office of Honorary Secretary. Mr. Cohen, a very young man then, had vision and enthusiasm. After long and continued efforts he succeeded in converting Mr. Edmund Scheuer to his views, and persuaded him to call a provisory meeting. The meeting was held at Mr. Scheuer's house on October 23rd, 1916. Messrs. J. J. Allen, Jule Allen, A. Bennett, S. Factor, Leo Frankel, Moses Gelber, J. S. Granatstein, David Lavine, Louis Levinsky, Elly Marks, Barnet Stone, Edmund Scheuer, and Abraham Cohen, and Mesdames J. S. Cohen, S. Lewis, H. N. Loeser, and I. Siegel were present at the meeting and formed themselves into a temporary organization committee and passed the following resolution, which was despatched broadcast throughout the city:—

"That a Federation of Jewish Charities after the model of the Pittsburgh Federation, be formed in Toronto without delay.

The Organization Committee consists of men and women well known in the community, who are fully alive to the urgent need of a Federation and who are determined that Toronto should not lag behind other cities in this respect. The Committee believe in the maxim, ' Do not leave for to-morrow what you can do to-day '; hence the resolution to proceed with the work immediately.

The objects of the Federation are threefold;
1. To systematize the collection of charitable funds.
2. To systematize the distribution of charity.
3. To adjust the community's charities to the community's needs.

Will you not admit that a great deal of chaos prevails at present in the raising of funds for Jewish charitable institutions? Have you not often had good reason to criticize the means and methods employed in obtaining moneys for charitable purposes? Have you not often thought of the waste of financial resources caused by the unorganized and confused mode of getting funds?

Have you not pondered many times over the fact that the help doled out to the needy would be much more effective and helpful if it were distributed more systematically and methodically?

And has it not occurred to you that in a growing city new needs arise constantly—very important and urgent ones—which require attention. Who does at present keep his eye on the charity barometer to render the community's charities adequate to the changing weather conditions, so to speak?

Think of what Federation could accomplish along these lines!

The plan of Federation contemplated here is one of centralization which at the same time will preserve the autonomy of the existing organizations, thereby getting the benefit of both.

Such Federations exist in other cities. The idea is not a dream, not an Utopia. If Pittsburgh and Philadelphia and Cleveland and New York and Montreal and Hamilton can have Federation, why not Toronto?

If you are willing to help bring about Federation in Toronto, then kindly attend a very important meeting, Saturday evening, the 28th day of October, 1916, at 8 p.m., at the Zionist Institute Assembly Hall, 206 Beverley Street, Toronto.

Business of the meeting; Election of a Board of Trustees with full power to bring about Federation.

Yours faithfully,
TEMPORARY ORGANIZATION COMMITTEE"

At the meeting held on the 28th day of October, 1916, a Provisional Board of Trustees was elected, as follows:—E. Scheuer, Chairman; Abraham Cohen, Hon. Secretary; J. J. Allen, Chas. Draimin, H. S. Dworkin, Leo Frankel, Chas. Garfunkel, C. Pasternack, E. Pullan, A. Rhinewine, B. Stone, and Jos. Singer.

Then followed the preparatory work leading up to the first campaign in this city for annual subscriptions to a fund for general charitable purposes—an appeal to all Jews regardless of their differences of opinion. The Provisional Board of Trustees met frequently during November and December, 1916, and January and February 1917. The members of the Board subscribed $1,000.00 to a fund for campaign purposes, that is, for publicity and all the other incidentals to "put over" a campaign. This fund was hurriedly spent—not wasted. Bulletins in English and Yiddish, ably edited by Mr. Archie Bennett, were mailed to every known prospective subscriber. The Yiddish press, by editorials and advertisements, gave the campaign splendid support. The coming "Campaign—$30,000.00—February 18th to 23rd, 1917", was widely advertised.

The public was being educated to meet campaigners "smilingly and enthusiastically".

During the period of preparation, Miss Birdie Friedman gave her services as Assistant Secretary gratuitously, and many other young ladies and gentlemen co-operated very energetically in preparing lists and mailing bulletins and notices.

But it was not all sunshine! Some of the influential members of the Provisional Board, a week or so before the campaign, intimated that they would not care to act on the teams, whether as captains or otherwise. The truth of the matter was that there was a feeling of pessimism, and one heard remarks as follows;

"$30,000.00 is too much money for the purpose. We will never get that objective—no more than half. You cannot get the Jews of Toronto to join hands on any movement. There are too many factions", etc.

At 5.00 p.m. on the 14th day of February, 1917, the day before the meeting of campaigners, the cabinet of three, the Secretary, the Assistant Secretary and the Chairman of the Publicity Committee, decided that inasmuch as those forming the Provisional Board were somewhat downhearted and were fearful of the results of the campaign, that it would be a failure unless the Board were enlarged to include others who were somewhat envious of the honour conferred upon the members of the Provisional Board; and thirty-three "special delivery" letters to citizens requesting them to act on the Provisional Board were mailed.

That was the turning point.

* * *

On the 15th day of February, 1917, a very splendid gathering of the Provisional Board, including those who were invited by "special delivery", met one hour after the meeting of "campaigners", and right there and then over $7,500.00 was subscribed by about 50 citizens; that is, 25 per cent. of the objective was subscribed three days before the campaign commenced!

Later that evening 250 campaigners received instructions, with maps of their districts, and lists. The campaigners were ready!

During three wintry days the campaigners covered the entire city, with the following results;

1717 subscribers, totalling $25,078.00.

In the following week other subscriptions came in. At the first meeting of the Provisional Board, held one week after the campaign, several organizations applied for grants; and a few days later grants totalling $1,025 were made for the month of March, 1917, to organizations requiring immediate assistance. The Federation also paid arrears of taxes and interest which had accumulated on the Orphanage and Morgue belonging to the then defunct Associated Charities.

The following organizations submitted data concerning their past activities and requirements, and were admitted to membership as beneficiary organizations; The Ladies' Co-operative Board; The Jewish Orphans' Home; The Jewish Girls' Club; Junior Council of Jewish Women; The Hebrew Ladies' Maternity Aid and Sewing Circle (Child Welfare); The Hebrew Young Ladies' Boot and Shoe Society; The Big Brotherhood Movement, Jewish Branch; The Hebrew Free Loan Society; Sewing School; The Jewish Dispensary; The Hebrew Burial Society.

Letters Patent incorporating Federation were then obtained from the Provincial Government.

The following is a comparative table of moneys distributed by the Federation for purely charitable purposes, that is, not including moneys distributed for preventative purposes, namely, boys' and girls' activities, medical treatment, and so forth.

During April, 1917	$1,568.00
During April, 1918	2,034.00
During April, 1919	2,951.00
During April, 1920	3,442.00
During April, 1921	4,339.00
During April, 1922	4,392.00
During April, 1923	3,970.00
During April, 1924	3,691.00
During Oct., 1924	6,262.00
During Nov., 1924	4,830.00
During Dec., 1924	6,322.00

FEDERATION BUILDING, TORONTO

Since its inception Federation has collected and expended for all its activities which may be grouped under the heading of "philanthropies" $385,000 ranging from 1917—$30,000, to 1924—over $70,000.

Many campaigns since the Federation was organized have been conducted. From an income of $25,000.00—$30,000.00, the amount was increased to $45,000.00—$50,000.00. $50,000.00 was the objective of the campaign held on December 8th, 9th, 10th, 1918, under the chairmanship of Mr. Julius Eisman, who, by his dynamic methods, accomplished what was then considered impossible. Another campaign for capital for a new orphanage brought in subscriptions for that purpose in the neighborhood of $38,000. This campaign for the orphanage and Federation generally had for its objective $100,000, under the chairmanship of Mr. Sigmund Samuel. The total result of the campaign was subscriptions amounting to $94,000. To assist the Federation in this campaign, Messrs. Samuel A. Goldsmith and Benjamin D. Kaplan, of the Bureau of Jewish Social Research of New York, directed operations.

Last year, 1924, a campaign was organized by Mr. Louis D. Brenner under the Chairmanship of Mr. Charles Draimin, and notwithstanding the financial depression in the community, pledges were received to the extent of about $75,000 from about 1,600 subscribers. Since the campaign there has been a quiet drive to increase the number of subscribers, which is proving successful.

The ship of Federation for the first four years of its journey was ably guided by Mr. Edmund Scheuer. As the President of Federaton he set an example which his successors have thus far and will in the future endeavour to aspire to; without a doubt he was an ideal President of Federation—he gave his undivided attention to Federation affairs.

During the next two years Mr. Eli Pullan was at the helm and Federation was very fortunate in having a leader during those years who could and did unite all elements of the community.

In the spring of 1922, Rabbi B. R. Brickner became President of Federation and again Federation was very fortunate. As a Social Service expert Rabbi Brickner stood on a pedestal, and he brought to Federation that which was very necessary, namely, the standardizing of the methods of distributing funds and giving personal service. Whenever an emergency arose Rabbi Brickner was able to present a clear statement of the case and the necessary treatment of the same. At the present time he has just finished his second term of office as President and has served notice upon the public that he is leaving Toronto. A distinct loss is being sustained not only by the Jewish community, but by the City of Toronto and Canada as well. It is to be hoped that Rabbi Brickner will not altogether forget the organization he has so ably directed for two years.

The present President of Federation is Mr. Harry

Rotenberg, and once more Federation has indeed been fortunate in securing the right man for the position. A young man, Mr. Rotenberg has both the energy and the experience necessary to be the leader of such an institution.

During the first few years of Federation it was felt that the organization could not, because of its revenue, engage an expert Social Service Director at a salary which the services expected commanded, but it can be said that the Executive Secretaries who were in charge gave their best to the organization. The following acted as Executive Secretaries in the order given;— Herschel Alt, Morris Spector, Mrs. Mabel Morris, Mrs. L. B. Levetus.

The Federation developed to that degree that in 1921 an Executive Director, Mr. Samuel B. Kaufman, was appointed. The outstanding feature of Mr. Kaufman's activities was his zeal for giving personal service— that alone justified the appointment of Mr. Kaufman. At present Mr. Joseph A. Woolf is the Executive Director and under his supervision the organization is developing.

The affiliated organizations today are as follows:— Family Welfare Bureau, Jewish Children's Home, Jewish Boys' Club, Jewish Big Brothers, Jewish Boys' Camp, Jewish Girls' Club, Jewish Big Sisters, Fresh Air Home at Whitby, Hebrew Ladies' Maternity Aid, Mount Sinai Hospital, Hebrew Free Burial Society, Medical Service Bureau.

The Hebrew Free Loan Association has been reorganized; it was deemed advisable in the minds of the founders, that inasmuch as its applicants are not in the category of beneficiaries of charity, that the organization should not be affiliated with Federation. It is now independent in the sense that it has its own provincial charter and has its own membership.

Officers for 1925;—Edmund Scheuer, Hon. President; Harry Rotenberg, President; Elias Pullan, 1st Vice-President; Moses Gelber, 2nd Vice-President; Joseph Schwartz, 3rd Vice-President; Frank S. Hutner, 4th Vice-President; Chas. Draimin, Treasurer; Abraham C. Cohen, Hon. Secretary.

THE HEBREW NATIONAL ASSOCIATION (VOLK'S VEREIN), TORONTO

FOUNDED August 1st, 1914, by:- Chono Mozoff, A. Stern, M. Strossberg, K. Reiser, M. Kirshenbaum L. Levin, A. Gewirtsman, M. Shnittman, A. Stein, and B. Shtrikman.

The economic depression in 1914, the lack of employment for the newly arrived immigrants and the general poverty prevailing at that time necessitated the formation of some organization to come to the assistance of those who mostly needed it. The officers and members of the executive of the newly founded Hebrew National Association looked for employment for those in distress, while the Association was supporting them till work of some kind was found.

Without waiting for the poverty stricken to apply for aid, the Association looked for them and in a brotherly spirit the officers did all they could to ameliorate their distressed condition. The poor sick were taken care of, and the newly arrived immigrants were taught English, etc., etc.

The first President of the Association was Mr. J. Graner, and the first Secretary, Mr. H. M. Kirshenbaum. The present officers are:- A. Scher, President (for the last 6 years); M. Handelman, Vice-President (for the last 2 years); S. Lent, Treasurer (for the last 9 years), also Hospital Chairman; M. Kirshenbaum, Fin. Sec. (for the last 4 years); J. Rose, General Representative, (has been working for the Association for 7 years). The present membership:- 1800. The present activities of the Association are:- The General Hospital is visited by its representative daily; as well as the Western,

St. Michael's and Grace Hospitals. The Weston Hospital for Consumptives is being visited twice weekly. The Muskoka Sanatorium, bi-monthly, 999 Queen Street West, weekly, Hamilton Hospital, yearly, as are also the hospitals at Whitby, Cobourg, Orillia and Barrie, Ontario.

The Association supplies the sick poor with doctor and medicine, operations, X-rays and clothes. All the hospitals have been supplied with Jewish libraries, and are being supplied with Kosher food on Passover. The Association gives yearly donations to all the mentioned hospitals.

Under the auspices of Mr. S. Lent, the Hospital Chairman, monthly concerts are arranged at the Weston Hospital for Consumptives, where the Association has also installed a radio concert machine.

The Association daily supplies the General Hospital with an interpreter.

The Association has taken out on probation from various asylums 24 men and women, who are now well and working for their living.

The Association is also getting city orders for relief for the poor.

The Executive of the Association and especially, the Chairman, Mr. A. Scher, are doing their best to assist the poor in the community in every way possible in a spirit of brotherly love. Hence the respect and support given by the community to their beloved institution, the Hebrew National Association, and its President and officers in particular.

JEWISH CHILDREN'S HOME, TORONTO

ON SEPTEMBER 15th, 1909, a meeting of the Toronto Ladies' Aid Society was held to consider the case of a Jewish widow unable to support herself and two children. Prior to this time, any Jewish children in such circumstances, had to be taken care of at Christian institutions. At the meeting referred to, amongst others, the following ladies were present: Mrs. Norman Helpert, Mrs. Rafelman, Mrs. I. Cooper, Mrs. B. Cooper, Mrs. M. Cohen, the late Mrs. N. Smith, the late Mrs. A. Landsberg, and Mrs. M. Kaplan, also the Rev. Mr. Kaplan. It was decided to rent a house on the corner of Elizabeth and Dundas Streets. The widow already mentioned was appointed the first superintendent, and the children of poor working mothers, who had no one to look after them during the day, were taken care of here during their parents' absence at work. The house was equipped as a nursery, with a dispensary on the lower floor, and a soup kitchen was also operated. Different ladies came in to supervise, and the late Mrs. A. Landsberg, who in her lifetime was one of the most zealous workers, was in charge of the investigation. Thus was started the first Jewish Orphanage in Toronto, with Mrs. I. Cooper as its first President.

The premises on Elizabeth Street were occupied for about a year, and not being equal to the requirements, the Orphanage was moved to the building on Simcoe Street, which was at that time purchased by the United Charities. At first only the top floor of this building was needed to fill the requirements of the Orphange, but later the demands for space increased to such an extent, that the whole building was occupied, and the Orphanage remained in these premises for fourteen years.

In 1921, Miss Rose Levy assumed the superintendency, and one of the first changes she made was in changing the name to the Jewish Children's Home, and the institution has been called this ever since.

A notable day in the history of the Home was reached in 1922, when the old stand in Simcoe Street was exchanged for a beautiful residence on Annette Street, where there may be found a happy family of over twenty children. Although the building may accommodate thirty-five, there are seldom that many in residence. The Home, after all, is mainly a clearing house, for the management strongly believes in re-establishing families or in securing foster-homes for the children, when that is impossible.

The structure on Annette Street contains twenty rooms, which have been converted into dormitories for the children, and pleasant reception, writing, study and dining rooms, kitchen, laundry, sewing room, etc. There is also a dispensary in which are closets that contain all kinds of medicine and other requirements for first aid for the children.

Children of school age pursue their education at the nearby schools, and care is taken to have all present at a Jewish Sunday School every week, when they are instructed in the religion of their fathers. The Sisterhood of Bond Street Synagogue has undertaken to see that the children attend Sunday School all year and supply the price of transportation to and from the synagogue. The boys attend Chedar every day. Several of the children are taught music by voluntary teachers, and those who wish are instructed in sewing and dancing. The girls have also formed a Brownie pack. The children are taught to make their own beds, help with the dusting and dishes, and with the sorting of linens. The older boys help in the grounds and some of them during the summer holidays, spend most of their time in gardening.

Much credit is due to Mr. Edmund Scheuer for the religious instruction that he gives the children once a week, and they also look for their Saturday afternoon treat of fruit, from the same gentleman. The children also await the Friday night dish of ice cream, which is always furnished them by Mrs. D. Dunkelman.

The Superintendent, Miss Rose Levy, is a graduate nurse and another of her first moves was to have every child call her "Aunt Rose." Like all wise disciplinarians, Miss Levy imposes very few rules. She emphasizes the fact that the house belongs to the young people, and sees to it that they feel at home in every part. Blessed with an inborn love of little folk, she resents anything that would draw attention to the misfortunes of her charges, and is determined to so order her home that sunshine, and not shadow, should envelop their lives. In her own private room Miss Levy has placed an extra bed for the convenience of any sick boy or girl, and is thus able to bring many a child through a light illness. The staff also consists of a nurse, maid, cook, janitor, gardener and laundress.

The expenses of the Home are borne by the Federation of Jewish Philanthropies, and the Home is also in receipt of a municipal grant. Most of the furniture has been donated, and some of the rooms have been entirely equipped, among the donors being the following:— Eastern Star, Lions' Club, Boot and Shoe Society, Mr. Silverman (stocking darner), Mr. and Mrs. M. Kohan (Blue Room), Mrs. I. Helpert (entire room), Senior Council of Jewish Women (entire room), Mrs. M. L. Willinsky, Mrs. B. Wise, Mrs. Norman Helpert, Mrs. M. Mehr, Mrs. A. Landsberg, and others.

Mrs. S. Greenfarb was President of the Home for six years, from 1918 to 1924, when she resigned, and much credit is due her for her indefatigable work. The following are the present officers:—Rev. Mr. Kaplan, Hon. Pres.; Mrs. M. Mehr, Pres.; Mrs. M. Kaplan, 1st Vice-Pres.; Mrs. L. Bert, 2nd Vice-Pres.; Mrs. I. Cohen, 3rd Vice-Pres.; Miss Meta Rotenberg, Sec.-Treas.; Mrs. L. Adelberg, Treasurer; Mrs. H. James, Recording Secretary; Mrs. F. Hutner, Corresponding Secretary. The following are the convenors, Mrs. M. L. Willinsky, House Committee; Mrs. D. Stein, Sewing Committee; Mrs. N. Rosenberg, Ways & Means Committee; and Mrs. D. Vise, Investigating Committee.

Many friends contribute to the happiness of the children, and the Sunnyside Lodge, I.O.O.F., the I.O.B.B., The Shriners, and the Patriotic Association have given them delightful days in the country. Whenever any kind of transportation is required to move the children to any place, Mr. Harry Rosenthal has always been ready and willing to furnish it, and he is regarded as one of the staunchest friends of the institution.

At least once a month, and generally more frequently, Dr. David Perlman and Dr. I. R. Smith visit the Home to inspect the children, and at any time these physicians willingly respond to a call for professional advice. Each child must be examined by Dr. Perlman and granted a certificate, before admission to the Home.

Much of the success of the Home is due to the splendid and complete co-operation between the Superintendent and the Board of Management, and the support of the Federation of Jewish Philanthropies.

An addition to the present building is in course of construction, and when completed, the Jewish Children's Home will be one of the most attractive and perfectly equipped establishments of Toronto.

JEWISH CHILDREN'S HOME, TORONTO

ON SEPTEMBER 15th, 1909, a meeting of the Toronto Ladies' Aid Society was held to consider the case of a Jewish widow unable to support herself and two children. Prior to this time, any Jewish children in such circumstances, had to be taken care of at Christian institutions. At the meeting referred to, amongst others, the following ladies were present: Mrs. Norman Helpert, Mrs. Rafelman, Mrs. I. Cooper, Mrs. B. Cooper, Mrs. M. Cohen, the late Mrs. N. Smith, the late Mrs. A. Landsberg, and Mrs. M. Kaplan, also the Rev. Mr. Kaplan. It was decided to rent a house on the corner of Elizabeth and Dundas Streets. The widow already mentioned was appointed the first superintendent, and the children of poor working mothers, who had no one to look after them during the day, were taken care of here during their parents' absence at work. The house was equipped as a nursery, with a dispensary on the lower floor, and a soup kitchen was also operated. Different ladies came in to supervise, and the late Mrs. A. Landsberg, who in her lifetime was one of the most zealous workers, was in charge of the investigation. Thus was started the first Jewish Orphanage in Toronto, with Mrs. I. Cooper as its first President.

The premises on Elizabeth Street were occupied for about a year, and not being equal to the requirements, the Orphanage was moved to the building on Simcoe Street, which was at that time purchased by the United Charities. At first only the top floor of this building was needed to fill the requirements of the Orphanage, but later the demands for space increased to such an extent, that the whole building was occupied, and the Orphanage remained in these premises for fourteen years.

In 1921, Miss Rose Levy assumed the superintendency, and one of the first changes she made was in changing the name to the Jewish Children's Home, and the institution has been called this ever since.

A notable day in the history of the Home was reached in 1922, when the old stand in Simcoe Street was exchanged for a beautiful residence on Annette Street, where there may be found a happy family of over twenty children. Although the building may accommodate thirty-five, there are seldom that many in residence. The Home, after all, is mainly a clearing house, for the management strongly believes in re-establishing families or in securing foster-homes for the children, when that is impossible.

The structure on Annette Street contains twenty rooms, which have been converted into dormitories for the children, and pleasant reception, writing, study and dining rooms, kitchen, laundry, sewing room, etc. There is also a dispensary in which are closets that contain all kinds of medicine and other requirements for first aid for the children.

Children of school age pursue their education at the nearby schools, and care is taken to have all present at a Jewish Sunday School every week, when they are instructed in the religion of their fathers. The Sisterhood of Bond Street Synagogue has undertaken to see that the children attend Sunday School all year and supply the price of transportation to and from the synagogue. The boys attend Chedar every day. Several of the children are taught music by voluntary teachers, and those who wish are instructed in sewing and dancing. The girls have also formed a Brownie pack. The children are taught to make their own beds, help with the dusting and dishes, and with the sorting of linens. The older boys help in the grounds and some of them during the summer holidays, spend most of their time in gardening.

Much credit is due to Mr. Edmund Scheuer for the religious instruction that he gives the children once a week, and they also look for their Saturday afternoon treat of fruit, from the same gentleman. The children also await the Friday night dish of ice cream, which is always furnished them by Mrs. D. Dunkelman.

The Superintendent, Miss Rose Levy, is a graduate nurse and another of her first moves was to have every child call her "Aunt Rose." Like all wise disciplinarians, Miss Levy imposes very few rules. She emphasizes the fact that the house belongs to the young people, and sees to it that they feel at home in every part. Blessed with an inborn love of little folk, she resents anything that would draw attention to the misfortunes of her charges, and is determined to so order her home that sunshine, and not shadow, should envelop their lives. In her own private room Miss Levy has placed an extra bed for the convenience of any sick boy or girl, and is thus able to bring many a child through a light illness. The staff also consists of a nurse, maid, cook, janitor, gardener and laundress.

The expenses of the Home are borne by the Federation of Jewish Philanthropies, and the Home is also in receipt of a municipal grant. Most of the furniture has been donated, and some of the rooms have been entirely equipped, among the donors being the following:— Eastern Star, Lions' Club, Boot and Shoe Society, Mr. Silverman (stocking darner), Mr. and Mrs. M. Kohan (Blue Room), Mrs. I. Helpert (entire room), Senior Council of Jewish Women (entire room), Mrs. M. L. Willinsky, Mrs. B. Wise, Mrs. Norman Helpert, Mrs. M. Mehr, Mrs. A. Landsberg, and others.

Mrs. S. Greenfarb was President of the Home for six years, from 1918 to 1924, when she resigned, and much credit is due her for her indefatigable work. The following are the present officers:—Rev. Mr. Kaplan, Hon. Pres.; Mrs. M. Mehr, Pres.; Mrs. M. Kaplan, 1st Vice-Pres.; Mrs. L. Bert, 2nd Vice-Pres.; Mrs. I. Cohen, 3rd Vice-Pres.; Miss Meta Rotenberg, Sec.-Treas.; Mrs. L. Adelberg, Treasurer; Mrs. H. James, Recording Secretary; Mrs. F. Hutner, Corresponding Secretary. The following are the convenors, Mrs. M. L. Willinsky, House Committee; Mrs. D. Stein, Sewing Committee; Mrs. N. Rosenberg, Ways & Means Committee; and Mrs. D. Vise, Investigating Committee.

Many friends contribute to the happiness of the children, and the Sunnyside Lodge, I.O.O.F., the I.O.B.B., The Shriners, and the Patriotic Association have given them delightful days in the country. Whenever any kind of transportation is required to move the children to any place, Mr. Harry Rosenthal has always been ready and willing to furnish it, and he is regarded as one of the staunchest friends of the institution.

At least once a month, and generally more frequently, Dr. David Perlman and Dr. I. R. Smith visit the Home to inspect the children, and at any time these physicians willingly respond to a call for professional advice. Each child must be examined by Dr. Perlman and granted a certificate, before admission to the Home.

Much of the success of the Home is due to the splendid and complete co-operation between the Superintendent and the Board of Management, and the support of the Federation of Jewish Philanthropies.

An addition to the present building is in course of construction, and when completed, the Jewish Children's Home will be one of the most attractive and perfectly equipped establishments of Toronto.

THE MOUNT SINAI HOSPITAL, TORONTO

THOUGH the youngest of the Jewish institutions of Toronto, the Mount Sinai Hospital occupies a place of honour amongst them, and one of increasing importance. A Jewish hospital had been the dream of communal workers for a decade. Several attempts at founding such an institution had, for various reasons, miscarried. These repeated attempts served, however, to stress the need for a Jewish hospital, and gradually paved the way for its eventual foundation.

The building for the hospital was acquired by the Ezras Noshem Society in 1922, at an initial investment of $20,000. In 1923, the management of the hospital passed over to the Mount Sinai Hospital Board, consisting of 15 men selected by the Ezras Noshem, and 4 members of the latter organization. Subsequent boards were to be elected by and from among the subscribers to the Hospital.

The Mount Sinai Hospital is housed in a three-storey brick building with commodious verandas and attractive grounds, and is situated in a fine, quiet residential section of the city. The hospital has at present accommodation for 30 patients. There are 5 public wards, 3 semi-private rooms, 1 private room, and a sun parlour. The equipment used is of the most modern type. The operating room is particularly well-equipped and the sterilizer is said to be one of the best in the city.

The visitor to the Hospital is favourably impressed with the cleanliness and tidiness of the place, from the basement up. The procedure employed throughout is in accord with the most approved scientific hospital methods. The punctilious cleanliness and scientific precision of method is combined with a homelike atmosphere that pervades the institution. There is an absence of that cold "institutionalism" so commonly associated with hospitals.

The permanent staff consists of a superintendent, 9 trained nurses, 2 cooks, a laundress, a maid, and a janitor. It should be noted that the nurses in attendance are trained and not students, as is the case in the large Christian hospitals. The superintendent of the institution, Miss B. Pickles, is a person of wide experience and reputation in hospital work, whose competence and energy are evident in every department.

The Mount Sinai Hospital receives both paying and free patients. The leading Jewish physicians of the city are constantly in attendance, and to their unselfish efforts much of the success of the hospital is due.

The results obtained in the treatment of patients have been signally satisfactory. Much successful work is being done in the treatment of diabetes through the administration of insulin; and the surgical and general medical work is of a high order. The obstetrical cases are numerous in the hospital, and the nursery is one of the especially busy spots in the institution.

The hospital derives its maintenance from three sources; contributions by members, a yearly subsidy from the Federation of Jewish Philanthropies and the proceeds of occasional benefit functions.

The present officers of the institution are; President, E. F. Singer; Vice-President, L. Fineberg; Secretaries, Mrs. H. Dworkin and Isidore Levinter; Treasurer, Rubin Shapiro.

Much of the detailed work of the hospital is being looked after by a Ladies' Auxiliary committee. There are in addition a number of sub-committees with prescribed functions.

HEBREW CONSUMPTIVE AID ASSOCIATION, MONTREAL

THE Hebrew Consumptive Aid Association was founded in 1906, for the purpose of taking care of Jewish consumptives and rendering relief and assistance to dependants of these patients. At the present time it is giving aid to approximately 200 consumptives a year. A fund is being endowed for the erection and maintenance of a home for Jewish incurable tuberculars, and has received the endorsation and recommendation of Dr. S. Boucher, Medical Health Officer of Montreal. The Association acts in co-operation with the Mount Sinai Sanatorium, and is generously supported by the Gentile as well as by the Jewish public. Dr. E. S. Harding and Dr. N. Schacher are on the Medical Board. The present officers are:—Hon. President, Peter Bercovitch, K.C., M.L.A.; Hon. Vice-Pres. Lyon W. Jacobs, K.C.; Life Governor, Ald. Louis Rubenstein; Hon. Solicitor, Nat. W. Jacobs. B.C.L.; Hon. Secretary, Sydney Tannenbaum, L.L.B.; President, M. H. Axelrad; Vice-Pres. J. B. Miller; 2nd Vice-Pres. M. Mallek; Treasurer, Miss M. Ratner; Fin. Secy., H. Sabloff; Rec. Secy. Mrs. P. Gordon; and Cor. Secy., Miss S. Rudnikoff.

TORONTO JEWISH OLD FOLKS' HOME

THE Toronto Jewish Old Folks' Home was founded in 1914, when a number of public-spirited people met to consider the case of an old woman who had been passed from hand to hand and who was without support of any kind.

The first meeting, in order to consider this case, was held at the home of Mrs. E. Sager, 121 University Avenue, when the following people were present;—Mrs. E. Sager, Mrs. Greenberg, Mrs. Cloze, Mrs. Levine, Mrs. Breslin, and Mr. Winestock. Each one of these people donated $5.00 for the relief of the above-mentioned person, and in this way the idea of an Old Folks' Home was started. The services of Mr. Mesninger were secured as an organizer.

Many of the business men of the city became interested, and the work was conducted in a business-like manner. During the first three years, approximately $2,800.00 was collected, which amount sufficed to look after the undertaking. It was then thought advisable to purchase a small house, and No. 31 Cecil Street, a semi-detached house with a frontage of 32 feet and a depth of 175 feet, was secured. The purchase price of this property was $7,250.00, of which $3,000.00 was paid in cash. The building was decorated and all the necessities suitable for a home for the aged, were installed.

The first chairman of the Home was Mr. P. Shulman, and an active member of the executive board was Mr. D. Brown. The official opening of the Home was held in 1917, when the following gentlemen were among those present;- Messrs. J. Becker, B. Weiss, H. Birenbaum, J. Swartz, H. Papernick and M. Stone. Over $6,000.00 was realized at the opening, and from this amount the balance of the sale price was paid, and the remainder was placed in a deposit on the adjoining house, which had a frontage of 28 feet and the same depth.

Messrs. J. Becker and B. Weiss devoted the utmost energy and showed the most unselfish interest in the establishment of the Home, and it was largely through their efforts that the two houses were converted into a building that fully covered the requirements. At the present time, the property is fully paid for, and the place and contents are valued at over $25,000.00. Mr. D. Brown has been the superintendent of the Home since 1917. Mr. J. Becker, after being President for three years, was given the honor of Honorary Presidency for life. He was succeeded as President by Mr. B. Weiss, who is also honored with the life Honorary Vice-Presidency.

At the present time, the Home is taking care of thirty-two inmates, twenty-one females and eleven males, many of them being incurables.

THE HEBREW BURIAL SOCIETY (CHESED SHEL EMES), TORONTO

THE HEBREW BURIAL SOCIETY was established in 1906 by Mr. and Mrs. Samuel Weber, who purchased a lot of land seventy by one hundred and eighty-four feet on Kensington Avenue, Eglington, and donated it to the Society. The purpose was to use this as a burial ground for poor Jews who do not belong to a synagogue or society, or for any other person who happens to be without friends or relatives.

Among the reasons that caused the start of this society was the case of a person who had died in the hospital and did not belong to any synagogue or benefit society. The Rabbi took charge of this case and was unsuccessful in obtaining a plot in the regular cemeteries.

In forming this society, a burial plot was procured as also a proper place for the body to be taken to be washed and dressed, and it did away with the need of going around soliciting subscriptions for any individual case. At that time, there was no Jewish undertaker, which made the condition, if possible, even worse.

The first man buried in the cemetery was one who had been accidently killed in the country and who was buried in a Christian cemetery. This case coming to the attention of Rabbi Gordon and Mr. Weber, they immediately got in touch with some Jewish people in the vicinity, and after considerable trouble and expense, had the body taken from the Christian cemetery and brought to Toronto. It was first taken to Rabbi Gordon's residence, and from there to Mr. Weber's home, and as there was no room to leave the casket over night, it had to be taken to a Christian undertaker. The following morning the body was taken to the cemetery of the Hebrew Burial Society, and this was the first body laid in these grounds. This occurred in June 1907, and since that date the cemetery has become filled.

It was through the instrumentality of Mr. Weber that the first Jewish undertaker started in Toronto. In connection with this establishment, there are a number of men and women who attend deaths and burials, when necessary. Mr. Weber, Mr. S. Fremes and Mr. Rosenbess and a number of others built and erected a morgue for the purpose of preparing Jewish bodies for burial.

The Burial Society is today a constituent of the Federation of Jewish Philanthropies, who have recently purchased a large plot of ground in East Toronto for the purpose of the Hebrew Burial Society.

S. KRONICK, TORONTO

SAMUEL KRONICK was born in Kowno, Lithuania, May 15th, 1880, the son of David and Reine (Reines) Kronick. He was educated through private tuition and his first position was with the Singer Sewing Machine Company in his native town. Mr. Kronick has been a Zionist since the inception of the movement, and in 1900, he went to London as a delegate to the Zionist Congress. He spent nine months in England, during that time lecturing on Zionism, and then went to the United States, where he continued his lectures on this subject. In 1902, he went to Toronto, where he has since resided, and notwithstanding the fact that Mr. Kronick is a very busy business man, he has taken a most active part in all communal affairs. He is one of the original members of the B'nai Zion, the first Zionist Society in Toronto, and he is a member of the Zionist Council of Canada. He was vice-president of the Central Division. Mr. Kronick is president of the Hebrew Free Loan Society of Toronto, and is a trustee of the Federation of Jewish Philanthropies. He is a member of the executive of the Immigrant Aid Society and is a member of the Bond Street, University Avenue and Yavna Zionist synagogues. On December 26th, 1912, Mr. Kronick was married to Gertrude, daughter of Mr. and Mrs. M. L. Willinsky of Toronto, and he has one son, Moses, and two daughters, the Misses Miriam and Leah Kronick. He is a member of the Primrose Club, Toronto; Canadian Club; Toronto Board of Trade; Canadian Manufacturers' Association; Independent Order B'nai B'rith; and Mt. Sinai Lodge, A.F. & A.M. Shortly after arriving in Toronto, Mr. Kronick entered the manufacture of ladies' hats, organizing the American Hat Frame Mfg. Co., of which concern he is still the active head. At that time eighty-five per cent of the women's hats were imported, and this business has so developed, that at the present time, eighty-five per cent of the hats used in Canada are manufactured in this country, and but fifteen per cent imported. Mr. Kronick is one of the pioneers of this industry, and his energy and foresight are largely responsible for this wonderful development.

THE UNITED HEBREW RELIEF, WINNIPEG

THIS organization was founded in the year 1909, when Jewish immigrants commenced to flock in large numbers to this continent, and naturally quite a proportion of these found their way to Winnipeg, which city, unfortunately, was not prepared to find employment for all of those who sought it. The sympathies of our co-religionists were aroused, and the needs of the occasion were seen by the Chief Rabbi, Rev. I. I. Kahanovitch, who convened a mass meeting in the Edward Hall in the latter part of December, which brought into existence "The United Hebrew Charities of Winnipeg," with S. A. Ripstein as president, assisted by Messrs. B. Zimmerman, T. Finklestein, E. Cherniak, S. Goldin, M. Haid, I. Portigal, J. Udow, H. Steinkopf, J. J. Shragge and I. Rosen as directors. The amounts distributed to the needy were on a comparatively small scale. The following year the headquarters were moved to the House of Jacob Synagogue and an election held at which the following gentlemen were elected as officers: President, J. A. Chmelnitsky, with A. Berg, B. Sharicoff, S. Goldin, L. Snidar, M. Haid, S. Shore and P. Ascovitch, directors. The numbers of those needing help increased and special means had to be adopted to provide the necessary funds which consisted of house-to-house canvassing and arranging special campaigns, with the result that sufficient money was raised to allow of a distribution of $6,000 per year. This continued until 1912 when the headquarters were moved to the old Talmud Torah building when A. Skaletar was elected to the presidency with the same directors as previously.

A. OSOVSKY
Superintendent, Jewish Orphanage and Children's Aid of Western Canada

As so frequently happens, factions arose under new leadership and a new society was formed under the name of "The North End Relief" with J. A. Chmelnitsky as president, each organization vieing with the other in the good work, which resulted in the raising of large sums of money, coupled with the disadvantages of overlapping with the recipients of charity and complaints from the donors who were giving to both. In October, 1914, a joint meeting was held with the result of the amalgamation of the two charities under the name of "The United Hebrew Relief of Winnipeg," and as such it still remains. The same evening, a Ladies' Auxiliary was formed, who elected as their officers: Mesdames F. Rosenblat, G. Frankfurter, B. Levinson, I. Portigal, E. Tapper, I. Rosen, F. Briar, D. Spivak, Tobias Pressner, B. Shragge, A. Berg, A. Slobinsky and Jesscovitch. Under the able leadership of Mr. S. Hart Green and his willing assistants, the organization was put on a sound basis and business system, with the result that there was a weekly distribution of doles amounting from $150 to $200 per week. With the introduction by the Legislature of the "Mothers' Allowance Act" much benefit was derived by many poor widows, and this likewise tended to release funds which were elsewhere needed for relief purposes.

In 1922 the proposal was put forward and adopted for the formation of a federated budget board for the various charitable institutions of the city in which thirty-one participate, and of these, three are Jewish, viz.: The United Hebrew Relief, the Jewish Orphanage and the Old Folks' Home. This has come as a great relief to all, as the constant canvassing for funds has become a thing of the past. With the general depression in trade during the past years the numbers of our needy have increased, and the weekly distribution of relief varies from $200 to $250 per week. The present board of directors is as follows: S. Hart Green, honorary president; I. Rosen, president; A. Slobinsky, 1st vice-president; M. Gordon, 2nd vice-president; B. Levinson, treasurer; M. Lyons, honorary secretary; and Messrs. M. Tessler, S. Goldin, L. Snidar, J. A. Chmelnitsky, B. Sharicoff, J. Gershfeld, H. Siniasky, S. B. Levin, A. Arenovsky and B. Cohen, directors.

THE JEWISH ORPHANAGE AND CHILDREN'S AID
OF WESTERN CANADA, WINNIPEG

PRIOR to April, 1912, Jewish children who were left orphans and dependent upon the public, were placed in non-Jewish homes or institutions. With the Jewish population of Winnipeg and Western Canada growing larger and more progressive, it became a foregone conclusion that such a condition would not long be allowed to remain. The Jewish characteristic of looking after their own soon asserted itself and led to the inauguration of a Jewish Orphanage for the purpose not only of feeding and housing these unfortunate dependants but also of educating them and bringing them up in the faith of their forefathers.

The Hebrew Ladies' Orphan Home Association (later developing into the well-known Ladies' Society of the Jewish Orphanage) had been formed in 1912 in the interests of the establishment of a Jewish Orphans' Home. About the same time the local B'nai B'rith lodge also took the matter up and pledged itself to provide a Home. The first concrete step towards realizing such an objective was taken when, at a meeting between representatives appointed in September, 1912, by the B'nai B'rith lodge, then under the presidency of Mr. L. Rice, and representatives of the Hebrew Ladies' Orphan Home Association, which was held in January, 1913, it was decided to leave in the hands of a joint committee the completion of a program for the inauguration of a Jewish Orphans' Home. The chairman of this committee, Mr. R. S. Robinson, made an offer of a substantial sum of money towards the proposed project, on the condition that the institution bear the name of his mother, Esther Robinson, whose name he desired to commemorate. Views and opinions of different sections of the community differed with regard to this proposal, and Winnipeg, hitherto without a shelter for Jewish orphans, found itself in a short space of time with two such institutions.

On July 25th, 1913, the Canadian Jewish Orphanage came into existence, with Mr. A. H. Aronovitch as its first president. Simultaneously announcement was made of the purchase of two houses on Robinson Street by a group of men for a similar purpose, and to be known as the Esther Robinson Orphans' Home, with Mr. D. Balcovske as its first president.

On September 22nd, 1913, the Canadian Jewish Orphanage rented premises at 113 Selkirk Avenue and the constituent members pledged themselves to the program of purchasing a large tract of land with a view ultimately to the erection of a new orphanage, old folks' home and Jewish hospital. The outbreak of the Great War the following year, however, arrested the amplification of such a plan. Then, too, there was a growing feeling amongst the general community that there was no need nor reason for two orphan homes both with the same objectives, both serving the same purpose but under separate management and separate roofs, and both appealing to the same public for assistance and support. Before proceeding with the purchase of permanent quarters it was decided therefore to enter into negotiations with the Esther Robinson Home, then under the presidency of Mr. M. Haid, with a view to amalgamation.

During this period the Canadian Jewish Orphanage outgrew itself and moved to better quarters at 327-329 Manitoba Avenue. The negotiations continued until October 14th, 1916, and at the final amalgamation meeting presided over by Mr. Max Steinkopf, a get-together decision was reached and all legalities were left to the attention of Messrs. E. R. Levinson and E. A. Cohen, well-known barristers, who have since both passed away.

These matters settled, a general election was called for February 5th, 1917, when the late Mr. E. R. Levinson was elected president.

The first and most important task was to secure a qualified superintendent, and the Board applied for assistance to the headquarters of the Independent Order of B'nai B'rith at Chicago, and their choice was Mr. I. L. Greenberg, then assistant superintendent of the Marks Nathan Jewish Home in Chicago. Both Mr. and Mrs. Greenberg had been actively engaged in such work in New York and Chicago and in April, 1917, they came to Winnipeg as superintendent and matron, respectively, of the Home. The new superintendent came with advanced ideas on child care, ideas that were new to the Jewish public, new even to the directors themselves, but he found in the president and amongst the members of the board a sufficient number of men and women of a progressive mind who were ready and willing to co-operate with him in the new ideas that he brought to the work and he was soon able to win over and bring the public to an appreciation of a Home managed on highly advanced and progressive lines. Through an intensive propaganda judiciously planned, he gained for the Home a large measure of support and good-will from the Jewish communities of Western Canada from Fort

THE JEWISH ORPHANS' HOME, WINNIPEG

William to Vancouver, without whose co-operation and assistance the Home could not have successfully carried on its work and fulfilled its responsibilities.

The number of inmates in the Home began to grow rapidly and soon the premises at 1280 Main Street, became totally inadequate. The danger of sickness and disease through crowded conditions was apparent and the desire for a new Home was revived. The determination to build a permanent Home became greater and greater until compelled by the force of circumstances the board decided to undertake the biggest communal work in the history of Canadian Jewish endeavor, to put on a campaign throughout Western Canada to raise $100,000 for a new Home. The Board was enlarged for the purposes of the campaign. The president surrounded himself with a band of energetic and faithful men and women who devoted themselves with a spirit of self-sacrifice that was nothing short of admirable and who gave unbegrudgingly of their time, money and brains to further this cause of orphans. The women's organization redoubled its energies and under the energetic leadership of Mrs. S. Colman, grew to a membership of 1,500 unremitting workers in the one cause. The executive committee at the time of this great campaign consisted of the following;

E. R. Levinson, President; Charles Tadman, Vice-President; Mrs. R. Goldin, Vice-President; David Spivak, Treasurer; Aaron Rabinovich, Chairman of Finance; Mandel Lurie, Chairman of Propaganda; Rose E. Ripstein, Chairlady of House; Abe Weidman, Chairman of Admission; Harry Steinberg, Chairman of Education.

P. Schachter, J. L. Cohen, P. H. Brotman, M. H. Brotman, L. Leipsic, W. Plum, J. Gerschfeld, L. D. Morosnick, M. H. Levinson, Goldie Finesilver, M. Spivak, Saidye Rosner, R. J. Kimmel, Mrs. B. Levinson, Mrs. S. Yankelovich, Mrs. S. Woladarsky, Mrs. L. Malcove, Mrs. R. Porter, Mrs. S. Buchalter, Mrs. E. R. Levinson, Mrs. S. Colman, Mrs. K. Kershner, Mrs. A. Rabinovich, Mrs. R. Bay, Mrs. J. Ripstein, Mrs. S. Saltzman, Mrs. R. Moss, Mrs. R. Schiller, Mrs. A. Rafalsky, Mrs. G. Gunn.

Medical Staff:—Dr. D. M. Genoff, Dr. G. Kalischmann, Dr. H. Herchmann, Dr. L. Bercovitch, Dr. O. Margolese.

Seventy-five honorary directors were appointed in the various Jewish centres in the West to assist in the campaign. Mr. Ben Schachter took charge of the country campaign and Mr. A. Rabinovitch was in charge of the city campaign which extended over ten days during September, 1918, with the result that $40,000 was raised in cash and $40,000 in pledges to be paid during the course of construction. Then came the influenza epidemic that took such a terrible toll of lives and added to the number of children that already crowded the Home. The work of the campaign had to be suspended for several months but was resumed at the earliest possible moment after the wonderful site upon which the Home now stands was purchased.

Plans were invited and a competition was held under the auspices of the Manitoba Association of Architects, and the superintendent and architect visited eighteen orphans' homes in the United States in July, 1918, and incorporated into the plans all the latest improvements suggested by an inspection of these homes with the result that the Home as it stands today was designed to meet the needs and requirements of the children from the time they arise in the morning until they retire in the evening, and it has been pronounced by the provincial building inspector to be the most modern and up-to-date building of its kind in Manitoba.

The laying of the corner stone took place on August 10th, 1919, the stone being laid by the late Ekiel Bronfman, in memory of his late wife, Minnie Bronfman. Throughout the course of construction, Mr. Charles Tadman, the zealous and devoted vice-president, was in charge of the building and his services were of inestimable value. The work was finally completed on February 1st, 1920, and the official opening and transfer of the children to their new Home took place on February 29, 1920.

Description of Building and Grounds

The magnificent new Home when completed cost well over $125,000 and provides for the care of about 150 children. It stands on five and one-half acres of beautiful park-like grounds, the building being in the centre of a grove of beautiful trees. There are three and one-half acres of splendid gardens which furnish all the vegetables of every description throughout the summer and from these gardens enough vegetables are stored to last the winter through. The picture of practical industry presented by the gardens is further intensified by the beauty and marvellous color that is presented by green lawns, winding paths through shady trees and gorgeous flower beds with their profusion of flowers of a wide variety. One section of the grounds is devoted to a playground for the children with full playground equipment and in this section the children have their football, baseball and other games in summer and their open-air skating in winter, all these outdoor advantages contributing greatly to an uninterrupted health record.

As for the building itself, the elevation has been treated in the Tudor style of architecture with a rough stucco exterior, having nothing of the square institutional style but presenting rather the pleasing appearance of a large private home or residence. Structurally it is of the most advanced fireproof type throughout, having all floors of reinforced concrete with hollow tile walls and partitions, and fireproof staircases leading directly to outside access. The floors with the exception of the main entrance, corridor floors and lavatories which are of beautiful marble and marble terrazzo, are finished in cement with battleship linoleum covering. Terrazzo base floor border has also been provided in all rooms, which is an added sanitary feature. No woodwork whatever has been used in the interior finish except for doors, windows and trim.

Separate entrances for boys and girls have been provided at the rear of the building. These entrances are at the grade level and lead directly to both boys' and girls' playrooms, living rooms, dormitories, etc., on the respective floors, and if necessary or desired, the sexes can be kept entirely apart, giving a boys' and girls' wing with all bathroom and lavatory accommodation complete in every detail, with matron's room, linen and locker rooms for each wing. The matron's rooms have been placed next to the dormitories with a casement window overlooking same, so that the matron can keep close inspection and supervision over the sleeping quarters. A pleasant feature of the building is that every room in the building has outside exposure and the rooms are flooded with light and sunshine throughout the day.

On the main floor an isolation hospital has been provided with clinic and direct separate access. Quarters for superintendent have also been provided on this floor, also office, board room, library, study, dining room and kitchen. The location of the kitchen wing and help's quarters immediately above the kitchen and boiler room below, has been arranged with the idea of separating these as far as possible from the children and with a view to better ventilation.

In the basement, which is about grade-level, are playrooms, classrooms, lavatories, and showers for boys and girls, also stores department, refrigerating plant, boiler room and electrically equipped laundry where all the laundry for the Home is done.

The lavatories on the second floor have been so located as to give the best access from bedrooms and dormitories and are fully equipped with showers, wall outlets for plumbing, closets, baths and individual basins all set at different heights for the varying sizes of children. Drinking fountains are also provided in the corridors on all floors. On the third floor a large assembly hall is provided for social and convention purposes and also serves as a synagogue for the children where they conduct their services on Friday evenings, Saturdays and all holidays. Provision is made for a possible extension on this floor for dormitories over the two dormitory wings on the floor below. Every thought was given to the convenience and comfort of the children, resulting in a homelike atmosphere throughout the building.

Mr. A. Osovsky was installed as superintendent on the 12th of July, 1920, and has since that time been devoting himself to the welfare of the children and the Home.

In 1920 the president, Mr. E. R. Levinson, passed away suddenly. In respect to his memory no new president was appointed and Mr. Charles Tadman, vice-president, became acting president for the balance of the term.

March 6th, 1921, saw the election of a new board and the elevation of Mr. Alan Bronfman, a young barrister of the city, to the position of president, at the youthful age of twenty-five. The Home was facing a critical period due to the serious financial depression and it was felt that young blood and energy was required to attack the problem. That the confidence was not misplaced was evidenced by the events which followed, for the history of the Home has since been one of remarkable achievement and continued success. There was gathered around the new president, a strong executive committee: and the slogan of the new board was "a free and better Home." To find sufficient money for maintenance, which was costing about $36,000 to $40,000, seemed difficult enough during times like these but to attempt to go further and pay off accrued debts seemed an almost impossible task. Every month saw new enterprises for the Home, every week new spheres of activities were opened. The Home was constantly kept in the public eye, the Children's Choir, the Children's Band, dramatic and operatic presentations by the children, huge undertakings like the magnificent juvenile carnival, moving pictures of the Home and its activities, screened in the largest theatres throughout the West, all served to heighten the interest and keep it alive. The Jewish public of Winnipeg and Western Canada from Fort William to Vancouver responded with the ultimate result that on the 18th of March, 1923, the date of the election of officers for the ensuing year, the president was able to announce in his annual report that the Home was clear of debt. This was the first Jewish institution in Winnipeg and Western Canada that could claim its land, its buildings, its furnishings and equipment as its own, with no mortgage, no interest, no tax arrears.

Life and Activities of the Children at the Home

The children are a very busy lot of little people. Their activities are so manifold that they do not have much time on their hands. They attend a nearby public school where they are educated in the usual courses and get an opportunity to mingle with large numbers of other children. They are not dressed uniformly, thus tending to develop in them a sense of individuality and preventing them from being marked as inmates of an institution. They are gifted with the usual adaptability and brightness of Jewish children and their progress in general is of very outstanding merit. After they come home from school they have their Hebrew education with which is combined religious instruction. Two modern teachers are employed, who under the guidance of the superintendent, himself a Hebrew scholar of high merit, and a special education committee, give the children a modern schooling in the Hebrew language and educate them in the principles of the Jewish religion and Jewish national aspirations. The older boys pray every morning with tephilim and services are held every Friday night, Saturday morning and every holiday, at which services the visiting public participate. During the High Holidays as many as 200 people from the city and country take part in the services. A magnificent children's choir of 42 voices assists in the services and is in great demand for concerts and other entertainments. This education of the children in their Biblical history, their daily prayers, the grace which they say before and after meals, the strict dietary laws which are observed, all serve to create in the Home a thoroughly Jewish atmosphere.

In addition to the musical instruction which the children receive in their choir practice, they receive instrumental instruction and the Home is the proud possessor of a splendid full-sized children's band. Any child who has a special adaptability for a particular instrument such as the violin or piano, is given special instruction and the Home can boast of at least one child composer, a girl of fourteen, whose remarkable selections are rendered by the band of which she is a component member.

The boys help around the Home in many ways, making themselves useful and reliable and take a special interest in the marvellous garden. The girls are taught the practical duties of cooking, serving and general housekeeping whenever opportunity affords. To know how to sew, mend, wash and dry dishes, to set and clear a table and to prepare a meal, to wash and iron a dress and to make a bed is a part of their practical education. The children have their fully equipped playgrounds, their tennis, football and baseball games in summer and their skating and hockey matches in winter. They have numerous picnics, entertainments, amusements and social functions during the year and their attendance from time to time at moving picture shows is for them a welcome treat. During inclement weather they have their club meetings and story-telling and enjoy the use of a splendid library with hundreds of volumes of general literature, magazines and periodicals. Their reading is supervised strictly by the superintendent so that it is pursued along proper lines.

The children are taught the value of thrift by the encouragement of individual savings accounts and other methods of competition and awards.

The health record of the children is a tribute to the clean, healthy and bright surroundings in which they live and to the devotion and care shown the children by the superintendent and his modest, unassuming wife whose whole aim is to make the Home a real family home and to be the mother as the superintendent aims to be the father. It is a tribute also to the devotion of the Jewish medical men, those doctors and dentists whose regular medical inspections minister to the eyes, ears, throat and teeth of the children and who attend promptly and efficiently to any physical ills which the children may have, without remuneration.

The number of children in the Home has grown each year until to-day over 110 are cared for. Any Jewish orphan or half-orphan in Winnipeg or Western Canada and any Jewish delinquent child is eligible for admission.

A complete record and history is kept of each child and with the exception of temporary cases and a very few young children that have been given out to foster parents (the question of giving out children for adoption is a problem that is now being dealt with), the child is kept in the Home until he or she is able to become self-supporting. The vocational committee is doing splendid work finding trades or situations for the older boys and girls and apprenticing them thereto. In each case an effort is made to assign the boy or girl to a class of work to which he or she may be suited and in all cases they are consulted as to their desires or leanings. Some are given business courses and any child that is of a scholarly bent is given an opportunity for higher education. After the children leave the Home, an after-care committee keeps in constant touch with them and follows their progress, lending assistance and advice where necessary.

The Home itself is open to the general public at all times and with its beautiful parklike surroundings and natural beauty is the first stopping place for all visitors to Winnipeg who desire to see what Western Canadian Jewry has been able to accomplish in a space of four or five short years.

Throughout the early struggles and the later progress, a most prominent part has been played by the Jewish communities of Western Canada outside of Winnipeg at all times. Time and again they were called upon and are called upon and always through good times and bad times their response has been wonderful. Without their assistance it would have been impossible to carry on this noble work. During the present year the Jewish Orphanage participates with all other welfare institutions of the city in a federated budget which raised sufficient in one campaign last fall to maintain the institutions for the year. The Jewish Orphanage receives from the federated budget the proportionate allowance for maintenance of the Winnipeg quota of children in the Home and the communities of Western Canada continue to contribute as they have always done the amount required to maintain the quota of children in the Home who come from outside of Winnipeg.

This record would not be complete without special references to the work of the Women's Auxiliaries throughout these years of struggle and hardship. The Ladies' Society with a membership of about two thousand, the Women's Auxiliary and the Girls' Auxiliary with smaller memberships have throughout these years been the veritable backbone of the Home. Each auxiliary has its special field of endeavor, and to-day the Ladies' Society under the presidency of Mrs. R. Goldin, the Women's Auxiliary under the capable presidency of Mrs. R. M. Frankfurter, and the Girls' Auxiliary under the successful direction of Miss R. Goldstine, are all doing splendid work in their particular fields.

In conclusion a word or two about the children and their fatherly superintendent, Mr. Osovsky. His aim and that of his kind and gentle wife is to make this children's home a true home in every sense of the word and the measure of the success that attends their efforts is evidenced by the fact that it is not uncommon to hear the little ones especially call the superintendent and his wife by the names of "father" and "mother."

The following constitute the present Board of Directors:

Alan Bronfman, President; M. H. Levinson, Vice-President; David Spivak, Treasurer; Mrs. R. Goldin, Vice-President; Mrs. S. Saltzman, Vice-President; Charles Tadman, Hon. Director; Marcel Marcus, Hon. Secretary.

L. H. Levi, M. Mitchell, M. Auerbach, A. Boroditsky, Leo. Davis, H. Fainstein, J. Gersfield, S. L. Goldstine, J. M. Isaacs, Dr. S. Rodin, S. Zimmerman, Dr. C. J. Bermack, M. O. Cohen, Dr. Irwin Fried, M. Heppner, B. Schachter, Miss R. Goldstine, Miss N. Shaen, Mrs. Leipsic, Mrs. Spivak, Mrs. Schiller, Mrs. Bookhalter, Mrs. B. Levinson, Mrs. Frankfurter, Mrs. Mass, Mrs. Mastensky, Mrs. Galsky, Mrs. Woladarsky, Mrs. Boomin, Mrs. Frankel, Mrs. Stein, Mrs. Malcove, Mrs. Kirshner, Mrs. Cohen, Mrs. Rafalsky, Mrs. Peostin, Mrs. Guttman.

Superintendent and Mrs. Osovsky and children of the Winnipeg Orphanage.

R. S. ROBINSON, WINNIPEG

R. S. ROBINSON, the son of the late Rev. Nathan Robinson of the Holy Blossom Congregation, Toronto, was born in Russia in 1864. At the age of four he migrated with his parents to Cleveland, Ohio, thence to Bay City, Mich. About five years later they removed to Utica, N.Y. It was here that Mr. Robinson received his early education. In 1883 he engaged in the men's furnishing business in Toronto, conducting this until he left the city and went to Wabigoon, Northwest Ontario, where he remained for six years. He also prospected for two years in the copper mining district in the upper peninsula of Michigan. During the time Mr. Robinson was at Wabigoon, he was a collector of inland revenue, license commissioner, and school trustee, resigning from these positions when he moved to Winnipeg in 1903. In Winnipeg he started the nucleus of his present business, importing and exporting furs, and in 1920, this business was incorporated as R. S. Robinson and Sons, Limited, and is controlled by Mr. R. S. Robinson and his five sons. Mr. Robinson was the first Parnass of the Shaarey Shomayim Congregation, Winnipeg, and in honor of his mother, he founded the Esther Robinson Jewish Orphanage and Children's Aid Society of Western Canada. For a number of years he was a member of the board of managers of the United Hebrew Cemetery. He was President of the Winnipeg Hebrew Free School, and it was during his term of office that the main building was erected, at a cost of $65,000.00. He is a charter member of the Winnipeg Lodge, I.O.B.B., and was one of the original trustees, and is a member of The Royal Arcanum and Royal Arch Masons. (Honorary life member of Wilson Lodge, A.F. & A.M., Toronto). On June 18th, 1889, Mr. Robinson was married in Alexandria, Ont., to Bessie, daughter of Mr. and Mrs. C. Sugarman. He has three daughters, Mrs. I. J. Goldstine, Misses Dora and Ruth Robinson; and five sons, Sydney I., Wilbur J., Nathan E., Ralph T., and Percival S., all residing in Winnipeg.

JEWISH OLD FOLKS' HOME OF WESTERN CANADA, WINNIPEG

IN THE YEAR 1912, a few generous-hearted Jewish women realized that there was need in the city for a home for the aged, and promptly organized themselves for the purpose of devising ways and means to establish a home, to take care of the old, helpless, feeble and friendless Jewish men and women. Prominent among the promoters of this movement were: Mesdames N. Rosenblat, B. Shragge, A. Aronovitch, Rachel Woldlinger and Rebecca Abramovitch. These women conferred together and decided upon a plan of action. Immediately thereafter Mrs. N. Rosenblat and Mrs. Aronovitch approached their friends and obtained $75.00 for this purpose. They succeeded at the same time to secure the co-operation of Mrs. Shatsky, Mrs. M. Forgan and other women. Later they approached the men and induced some of the most prominent of them to assist them in their work. Amongst the first to respond was Mr. Joseph Genser, who helped considerably in the establishment of this worthy institution.

An association was thereupon organized and the following executive officers elected: Mr. J. Genser, President; M. Nydis, Vice-President; Mrs. N. Rosenblat, Treasurer. This committee rented a house on Euclid Ave., fitted it up, and 5 old men and women were immediately sheltered therein. The above officers served for a period of two years, at the end of which term other officers were elected with Mr. S. Cossoy as President. About this time another prominent Jewish citizen became interested in the institution, Mr. I. Greenberg, who visited the Home frequently and took every precaution that the Home should be functioning properly. A few years later Mr. Greenberg recommended that steps be taken to interest all the Jewish people in the institution with the object of gathering a fund to purchase a suitable house for the Old Folks' Home. The Directors approved the recommendation and accordingly, in April 1919, a mass meeting was called at which a large number of the most prominent Jews were present. Mr. Cossoy, the Chairman of the meeting, in his opening speech, depicted the pitiful condition of those who arrive destitute and friendless at their old age and find themselves compelled to seek assistance from the community. He stressed the point that the community is duty bound to maintain such old folks and emphasized the necessity of securing a permanent Home for such people. This hearty appeal found a ready and generous response and the meeting adopted unanimously a resolution to proceed at once with the work of securing a permanent Home. During the same week the special committee appointed at this meeting met and decided to purchase a large adequate house, suitable for the purpose of transforming it into a sheltering home, a Home worthy of the men and women who originated the institution, whose good name it ought to commemorate.

Amongst those present at this special meeting were Messrs. J. A. Chmelnitsky, N. Rosenblat, M. Tessler, B. Starikoff, S. Cossoy, J. Gersfield, N. Chmelnitsky, I. Greenberg, J. Genser, M. Nydis, R. Abramovitch, R. Fingerut, and Mesdames N. Rosenblat, R. Abramovitch, R. Fingerut, S. Cossoy, J. Genser, F. Shatsky, Jos. Finkelman.

A special Building Fund was immediately raised, the following being the first to contribute:—Mr. Hyman Miller, (legacy), $1,000; Mr. and Mrs. M. S. Freedman, $700; Mr. and Mrs. J. A. Chmelnitsky, $500; Mr. and Mrs. N. Rosenblat, $500; Mr. and Mrs. Cohen $300; Mr. and Mrs. M. Tessler, $250; Mr. and Mrs. B. Staricoff, $250; Mr. and Mrs. J. Gershfield, $250; Mr. and Mrs. N. Chmelnitsky, $250; Mr. and Mrs. I. Greenberg, $150; Mr. and Mrs. Jos. Genser, $100; Mr. and Mrs. S. Cossoy, $100; Mrs. N. Rosenblat, $100; Mrs. Rebecca Abramovitch, $50; Mrs. R. Fingerut, $50.

OLD FOLKS' HOME, WINNIPEG

A Building Committee was thereupon appointed consisting of the following: M. Tessler, Chairman; J. A. Chmelnitsky, Treasurer; Messrs. N. Chmelnitsky, S. Cossoy, B. Starikoff, Jos. Gershfield, I. Greenberg, N. Rosenblat, Jos. Genser, I. M. Chmelnitsky, Chs. Rosenblat, M. Fingerut, M. Nydis, and Mesdames N. Rosenblat, Jos. Genser, R. Abramovitch, R. Fingerut, S. Cossoy, J. Finkelman, F. Shatsky.

The first move of the special Building Committee was to look for a suitable building. This they did by securing a large apartment block of 40 nice comfortably sized rooms, located on Manitoba Ave., at a cost of $20,000.00. All members of the Committee worked energetically to raise the largest possible amount of money from the Jewish people of the city and the country, so as to facilitate the purchase of this building.

Thanks to the efforts of the Committee, the sum of $10,000.00 was raised. The beautiful building, with all its up-to-date apartments was taken over; the old folks who were sheltered in the rented premises were transferred over to the new Home and in November 1919, the new building was formally opened with an impressive ceremony, participated in by a very large number of people, Mr. S. Hart Green presiding. Rabbi I. I. Kahanovitch performed the opening ceremony and called upon those present to fulfill their obligation towards the worthy institution, and the people responded generously. As a result a substantial sum was raised.

Mr. W. Crickloff offered $400 for the opening key. Mrs. A. Slobinsky offered $600 for the "Synagogue," which shall bear her name. Mr. and Mrs. N. Rosenblat offered $550 for the dining room, etc.

The amount raised at the opening reached the magnificent sum of $5,624.57, the names of the largest donors being inscribed in the "Golden Book" of the institution.

On November 16, 1919, was held the first general meeting in the New Home for electing a new Board of Directors, for the ensuing year, with the following result:

Men—J. A. Chmelnitsky, President; S. Cossoy, Vice-President; M. Tessler, Treasurer; B. Starikoff, J. Dorfman, A. Slobinsky, N. Rosenblat, Jos. Gershfield, M. Nydis, I. M. Chmelnitsky, Ch. Rosenblat, I. Greenberg, M. Fingerut, L. Shnider, K. Tirkletop.

Women—R. Abramovitch, Vice-President; J. Finkelman, J. A. Chmelnitsky, R. Fingerut, N. Rosenblat, B. Starikoff, A. Galsky, J. Gersfield, S. Cossoy, F. Shatsky.

The following are the present officers:

Mr. A. Slobinsky, President; Mr. E. Greenberg, 1st Vice-President; Mrs. J. Finkelman, 2nd Vice-President; Mr. Chas. Rosenblat, Secretary; Mr. N. Kasler, Treasurer; B. Sarner, Superintendent; Mr. J. A. Chmelnitsky, Mr. M. Tessler, Mr. J. Nemirovsky, Mr. S. Aronovsky, Mr. S. Cossoy, Mr. V. Rubin, Mr. A. Panarsky, Mr. J. Genser, Mr. H. Dorfman Mr. N. Rosenblat, Mr. Collerman, Mr. M. Nydis, Mr. N. Boxer, Mr. S. Gold, Mr. S. Shtatleman, Mr. M. Rosen, Mrs. A. Slobinsky, Mrs. F. Shatsky, Mrs. J. A. Chmelnitsky, Mrs. E. Fingerote, Mrs. S. Nozick, Mrs. S. Cossoy, Mrs. A. Berg, Mrs. A. Weidman, Mrs. H. Dorfman, Mrs. O. Starikoff, Mrs. S. Shtatleman, Mrs. S. Aronovsky, Mrs. N. Rosenblat, Mrs. J. Genser, Mrs. B. Broinstein, Mrs. R. Wilder, Mrs. S. Guttman, Mrs. M. Galsky, Mrs. I. Shurvill.

Girls' Auxiliary:-Miss Carrie Steiman, President; Miss Lillian Peikof, Vice-President; Miss Mary M. Provisor, Treasurer.

A. SLOBINSKY, WINNIPEG
President, Old Folks' Home

ABRAHAM SLOBINSKY was born in Wingorad, Russia, on June 10th, 1862, the son of Ephraim Slobinsky. He received his education in the schools of his native city, and was married in 1884. In 1905, Mr. Slobinsky came to Canada, first taking up farming, in which he was successful. He then went to Winnipeg and entered the wholesale grocery business, in which he has also been very successful. He takes an active part in all communal and charitable works. He is a former President of the United Hebrew Relief, and is now Vice-President. For three terms he has been chosen President of the Congregation House of Jacob. He was the Treasurer of the Jewish War Sufferers' Relief. In 1920, Mr. Slobinsky was appointed Treasurer of the Jewish Old Folks' Home, and in 1922 was elected the President, which position he still holds. He is a member of the Independent Order B'nai Brith, and of the Gemilath Chasodim Society. Mr. Slobinsky has two sons, Jack and Moses, and two daughters, the Misses Runa and Lucy Slobinsky.

THE VANCOUVER HEBREW FREE LOAN ASSOCIATION

FORTUNATELY the Jewish people in Vancouver have always been more or less prosperous and for this reason the need of a free loan association has never been very great. However, it was felt that such an organization could function successfully, and in January, 1915, it was under way. The founder was the late Jacob Fleishman, one of the early pioneers in Vancouver. Its sole purpose is to assist small traders in times of difficulty.

The membership is 37, which subscribed a sum of $600, and it has never been found necessary to increase this capital. Loans are made in sums up to $50, and in the whole period but forty loans have been made, aggregating the sum of $1,685. The operations have, of course, been carried on without any expense and, due to the fact that no losses have been incurred, the whole of the capital is intact.

As with similar Gemilath Chasodim Societies in other communities in Canada, the idea is to do away with the feeling that the recipient of a loan is receiving charity, and to make him retain his self-respect. In this way the borrower soon becomes a self-supporting citizen, and many well to do business men owe their start to this society.

From its first organization, the society owes much to the whole-hearted interest displayed in its work by Mr. Samuel Gintzburger, who has been its president from the start. Mr. Gintzburger, the oldest Jewish and one of the most highly respected citizens of British Columbia, takes a personal interest in every applicant for a loan, and his advice is very often worth much more than the small amount loaned. So highly is he regarded that it is not an unusual thing for the occasional young Jewish offender to be paroled under his probation. Under his presidency, the entire Jewish community is undivided in its support to the Vancouver Free Loan Society.

The officers are: Samuel Gintzburger, President; H. B. Wagner, Vice-President; Joseph Snider, Secretary.

WINNIPEG FREE LOAN SOCIETIES

THE History of the Winnipeg Free Loan Societies dates back as far as 1910, at the time when the Jewish immigration from the European countries was in full swing. Thousands of Jewish immigrants were arriving in the City of Winnipeg, without any means of self support.

Mr. M. Waisman, a young man who was taking an active interest in the problems of the Jewish settlers, conceived the idea of a Free Loan Society. He realized that such an institution would be of great service in making the Jewish immigrants self-supporting, by making them loans when necessary. Mr. Waisman had had some experience in European countries as to the management of such societies, and he called a meeting at the house of Mr. M. Richman. It was there, on January 2nd, 1913, that the first Winnipeg Free Loan Society was organized under the name of the Manitoba Free Loan Association. At this meeting there were present the following:—M. Waisman, M. Nathanson, W. Keller, M. Richman, S. Glassman, M. Rosen, I. Raykis, M. Goldenberg, J. Pollick, B. Oseran, J. E. Rosen and M. Galsky. It was decided at this meeting, that every member should contribute to the Loan Fund, the sum of $10.00. Mr. M. Waisman was elected President, and Mr. M. Nathanson, Treasurer.

The Manitoba Free Loan Association grew very rapidly, and before the first year was over, the membership had increased to ninety, and the association was doing wonderful work, assisting with loans those who were in need.

The Free Loan idea appealed so much to the Jewish community, that in 1914, twelve different loan organizations were formed and chartered under separate officers. Many people who were making loans from these societies at that time are today well-to-do and they still remain active members, not forgetting the good that the loan societies have done for themselves.

At the present time the largest and most influential of the Winnipeg Loan Societies is the B'nai Abraham Loan Association, which is a very progressive institution. There are in Winnipeg at the present time, thirty-two different Hebrew Loan Societies with a combined membership of over one thousand and with a combined capital of over $200,000.00. This is a very big factor in assisting the Winnipeg Jewish community to give relief to the new and needy arrivals.

Most of the members of the community have taken an active interest in these different loan societies, and particular mention may be given to the following, who have been among the pioneers in these institutions in Winnipeg; M. Tessler, R. Cohen, S. Kavalevitch, I. Trute, J. Krovtzow, M. Comisaroff, E. Pollick, M. Froomkin, M. Tadman, S. Bere, and particularly the Winnipeg Lodge, I.O.B.B.

M. WAISMAN, WINNIPEG

MAURICE WAISMAN, one of the active communal workers of the City of Winnipeg, was born in Odessa, Russia, the 26th of November, 1890, the son of the late Leon Waisman, who was in his lifetime, Assistant Crown Rabbi of Odessa. He was a refugee from the first Russian Revolution, and came to Canada in 1904, settling in Winnipeg, where he has since resided. He received his education at the public schools of Winnipeg. He started his business career as a printer and was instrumental in organizing the Israelite Press. Mr. Waisman printed the first Jewish paper in Western Canada, "The Winnipeg Courier." He sold his interest in the Israelite Press a few years ago, and in 1910 entered the insurance business. He has built up for himself one of the largest insurance agencies in Western Canada. He has taken a very keen and active interest in all Jewish affairs, and was instrumental in organizing practically all the Jewish Free Loan Societies in Winnipeg. He is a member of all the Winnipeg charitable institutions, and for four years was a Director of the Western Canada Hebrew Orphanage of Winnipeg. He is a past President of the Hebrew Sick Benefit Society (one of the largest societies in Winnipeg); past President of the Manitoba, Bassarabia, and Western Free Loan Societies; Council Commander of the Hebrew Friend Lodge, which he was instrumental in organizing, and is a member of the Oddfellows; National Workmen's Farband; and of the Independent Order B'nai B'rith. Mr. Waisman is particularly interested in educating the new Jewish arrivals into the duties of Canadian citizenship, and also in seeing that they are being placed in positions where they can become self-supporting and desirable members of the community. His idea in free loans is to take away from them all thought of charity, and to enable the borrower to retain his self respect. On December 31st, 1911, Mr. Waisman was married to Sarah, daughter of Moses Sumber of Praprisk, Russia, and he has two sons, Louis and William, and two daughters, the Misses Bessie and Liberty Waisman. He is a member of the Canadian Club.

THE HEBREW AID SOCIETY, VANCOUVER

THE Hebrew Aid Society of Vancouver is one of the outstanding organizations in the community. The work of the society consists of: assisting the local poor and needy with monies, food, clothes and shelter. Owing to Vancouver being a port where various immigrants are arriving from Europe via Japan and China, the Hebrew Aid Society is called upon to assist the immigrants in distress, also being thus geographically situated the city of Vancouver more than any other Canadian city in the West, is called upon to help strangers in distress in the city. It is the policy of the society not to distinguish between local cases or outside cases requiring assistance, once the applicant takes up residence in the City of Vancouver.

The Hebrew Aid Society is one of the oldest Jewish institutions in Vancouver, and it has been fortunate that it has always had amongst its supporters men and women who have shown a devoted interest in its undertakings. Among its most active members were those who played a prominent part in the communal life of the Province, including Mr. Samuel Gintzburger, Mr. A. Grossman, Mr. I. Rubinovitch, Mr. J. Fleishman, and others. A younger generation now has charge of the management, and they are worthily maintaining the ideals bequeathed them by the older members of the community.

The Hebrew Aid Society has a board of directors of 27 men and women. The executive meets every second week to discuss the different cases, and before money is expended by the officers of the organization, a thorough investigation is made of each case, and the case is then decided by the board upon its merits.

Another important branch of the society's work is the visiting of the local institutions and taking care of the Jewish inmates of such places. Clothes are provided for the inmates. It is the policy of the society to assist the directors of the public institutions in the care of the Jewish inmates.

A pleasing branch of the society's work is undertaken by the Sunshine Club under the able direction of Mrs. H. J. Morris. It is the province of this committee to send flowers to the sick.

A special feature of the society's work is the handling of the Moath Chitim fund. The society has not overlooked an individual case in the City of Vancouver. It provides money, matzos and all necessities for the Passover, not only to the local homes in need, but also distributes Passover food to the Jewish inmates in the hospitals, asylums and penitentiaries.

The society monthly expends a large sum of money for the upkeep of old folks, widows and orphans. The noble work of the society has won the well deserved praise of the city, and the citizens are no longer bored by the so-called "handkerchief collections" and "schnorers." Each citizen pays his contribution once a year and by so doing he automatically becomes a member of the organization. The Board of Directors holds four general meetings a year in order to acquaint the members of how the monies are being expended and how the cases are dealt with.

The organization holds open meetings and public entertainments for the purpose of raising funds for special cases. Great credit is due to the good-heartedness of the local women, who give untiringly of their time to promote the society's activities.

In addition to attending to the requirements of their own needy, the Society also makes regular contributions to the Western Canada Jewish Orphanage, and to the Old Folk's Home, in Winnipeg, and it also was active in the relief drives for the Jewish war sufferers in Europe. It also supports the Zionist calls, and all other demands.

The usual idea of Federation is strictly followed, and in November, 1924, the Society had its first drive for a "community chest" which resulted very satisfactorily. In this drive not only the individual members of the community took part, but every Jewish organization in the city actively interested themselves. The amount set out for was reached and Federation, or the systematic distribution of charity, has come to Vancouver to remain.

The officers of the organization are divided as follows:

President, Mr. J. B. Jaffe; first vice-president, Mrs. H. B. Wagner; second vice-president, Mrs. Wm. Genser; financial secretary, Mrs. L. Rosenbaum; recording secretary, Mr. N. C. Levin; treasurer, Mr. A. Rothstein; men's financial committee, Messrs. Wm. Genser, Nace Swartz, H. B. Wagner, L. Rosenbaum; ladies' financial committee, Mesdames. B. Blackson, S. Goldbloom, L. Hoffman; ladies' invitation committee, Mrs. M. Reuben, Mrs. A. Ablovitz, Mrs. S. Harris, Mrs. E. Gold; men's invitation committee, Messrs. Tanzman, S. Rothstein, M. Margolius; board of trustees, Mesdames. H. J. Morris, J. Buckshon, J. Parker, H. Braverman, H. Brown, A. Robins, Cibular; committee visiting hospitals and insane asylums, etc., Mesdames, H. B. Wagner and H. Harris; Sunshine Club, Mrs. H. J. Morris.

S. GINTZBURGER, VANCOUVER

SAMUEL GINTZBURGER is an outstanding member of the Jewish community of British Columbia. He was born at Neuchatel, Switzerland, on the 14th of February, 1867, the son of the late Nephtali Gintzburger. He received his education at Neuchatel, Switzerland, and Freiburg, Germany. Mr. Gintzburger has taken an active interest in the development of Vancouver. He arrived in British Columbia in the spring of 1887, and followed the many diversified occupations of a pioneer. He first took up one hundred and sixty acres of land on the site of what is now the City of North Vancouver, then engaged in trading with the Indians on the west coast of Vancouver Island. In 1888, he was occupied in seal hunting in the North Pacific and Behring Sea, later mining silver in the Kootenay. He eventually joined the gold rush at Atlin, and engaged in placer mining, but without great success. He has been the leader in all communal undertakings in the Jewish community of his city, and has been identified with practically every institution there. For years he has been President of the Congregation Temple Emanu-El. From 1915 to 1924, Mr. Gintzburger was the President of the Vancouver Hebrew Free Loan Ass'n., which he was instrumental in organizing. He takes a keen interest in all matters of public welfare and acts as a "big brother" to Jewish children who get into trouble and who are referred to him by the Juvenile Court. He is a member of the Vancouver Zionist Society. In 1912, and 1913, Mr. Gintzburger served as Councillor of West Vancouver Municipality. In 1913, he was appointed Consul of Switzerland, which appointment he still retains. He is the Hon. President (life) of the Vancouver Automobile Club, and is a member of the British Columbian Philatelic Society; Vancouver Scientific, Arts and Historical Society; and L'Alliance française. Mr. Gintzburger was married to Rosina, daughter of the late Louis Robinson, of Montreal, and has one daughter, Miss Pauline Emma Gintzburger (B.A., M.A.), University of British Columbia, and winner of the Governor General's Gold Medal, 1919 class.

OTTAWA CHARITABLE ORGANIZATIONS

THE Ottawa Men's Hebrew Benevolent Society was established in 1900, and as its name implies, had for its object the care of the poor, helping the indigent community to re-establish themselves and seeing that all were provided for, particularly during the holidays. They worked in conjunction with the Ladies' Hebrew Benevolent Society, which had been organized some time previously, and all calls for relief were attended to by these two organizations. Particular attention has been given to the relief of the newly-arrived immigrants, and practically all the communal undertakings in Ottawa had their origin in this Society. The late Mr. Aaron Rosenthal and the late Mr. Moses Bilsky were largely responsible for its formation, although they both were charitable institutions in themselves. It was a common sight in the early days of this Society's existence, to see either or both of these gentlemen leading some poor stranger to his proper destination, or helping anyone in a financial way.

Otttawa at the present time, has found no necessity for a Federation of Jewish charities, as the members of the Jewish community are supporters of all existing charities. The community contributed in the neighborhood of $70,000 to various relief collections, and there are very few cities in Canada where the Jews and non-Jews appear to have so much in common. The officers of this Society are:—President, Mr. J. Holzman; First Vice-President, Rev. J. Mirsky; Second Vice-President, Mr. H. Berlin; Secretary, Mr. Sam Caplan; Treasurer, Rev. L. Doctor; Members of Executive, Messrs. S. Katz, I. Siegler, A. Brumberg, W. Abelson, M. Stein, J. Rachlin.

The Ottawa Hebrew Benefit Society is the largest men's charitable organization in the community, having a membership of over two hundred. It was founded in 1913. The members visit the sick and provide for those in distress, and there is also a sick benefit fund in connection with the organization. The officers are:—President, Mr. Max Finkelstein; Vice-President, Mr. M. B. Margoshes; Financial Secretary, Mr. I. L. Cohen; Recording Secretary, Mr. H. Segalowitz; Treasurer, Mr. S. Berezin; Inner Guard, Mr. L. Lobel; Marshal, Mr. H. Stein; and Trustees, Messrs. I. Nadler, M. Sidney, M. Flescher.

The Ottawa Chevra Kedisha has been in existence for a long time. This Society undertakes all the usual duties of such an organization, and it is assisted by a ladies' auxiliary. It is the custom of this institution to elect annually four Presidents who serve in turn for three months each. The present Presidents are:—E. Slonemsky, M. Shore, B. Lifshitz and M. Goldsmith.

HAMILTON CHARITABLE ORGANIZATIONS

EVERY Jewish community in Canada has its organizations engaged in communal undertakings. It is not everyone that can boast of so many activities as can Hamilton. For the size of its Jewish population, in comparison with other communities, the service rendered successfully through these organizations is unique, and Hamilton is to be congratulated upon its public-spirited citizens who have made this possible.

The leading organization in Hamilton is the the UNITED HEBREW ASSOCIATION, which was organized in 1912 by Messrs. Adolph Levy and David Sweet. Hamilton was the first Jewish community in Canada to form a central organization for the systematic distribution of charity, and it has been followed by every other community with a population that is able to support it. One of the first undertakings was to purchase their own home, which provided a centre for all local activities, and here Hamilton took a step forward which has been followed by many other communities. The United Hebrew Association was primarily organized for educational, charitable and social service work, and it has become the communal centre of Hamilton. Under its roof every activity in the community is planned and carried out. It has its Family Welfare Board, which takes care of numerous domestic problems, in addition to the monetary assistance given to the needy. The Hachnosis Orchim are also taken care of by this Association, and many homeless strangers are given meals and lodging and assisted to their destination. The Association has also undertaken the work of a Free Loan Society and many recipients of these free loans have become self-supporting men who otherwise would have been a burden on the community. Immigrant Aid work is also undertaken by the United Hebrew Association, and the almost superhuman efforts of Mr. David Sweet has been particularly noticeable in this branch of work. The Association is mainly supported by contributions from members and voluntary contributions from the public. The present officers are:—President, Geo. Ringel; First Vice-President, P. Phillips; Second Vice-President, Mrs. S. Needle; Hon. Secretary, M. Geller; Executive Secretary, Miss Lillian Goldstein; and Treasurer, Mr. A. Halpern.

The Hebrew Benevolent Society of Hamilton is a constituent member of the United Hebrew Association and was organized in 1918 for the purpose of distributing charity to the needy. It is supported entirely by membership dues and donations. Monthly meetings are held in the United Hebrew Building. The officers are:—President, Sholom Wright; Vice-President, B. Goldberg; Treasurer, M. Steinberg; and Secretary, H. B. Sure.

THE LATE A. ROSENTHAL

THE LATE MR. AARON ROSENTHAL, one of the pioneer Jewish citizens of Ottawa, belonged to that sturdy generation who were amongst the founders and builders of the Jewish community of Canada. He was an outstanding resident of the Capital for over thirty years and was born at Loblens, Germany, on April 8th, 1829, the son of the late Mendel Selig Rosenthal, of that City. He left his home at the age of thirteen years and went to Australia, where he was at the time of the gold rush in 1859, and where he remained until 1876. On March 27th, 1867, he was married to Bertha Lehman of Berlin, Germany, who at that time was on a visit to Australia. In 1876, Mr. Rosenthal came to Canada and established in Montreal a wholesale jewellery firm, under the name of Rosenthal, Benjamin & Company. In 1879 he moved to Ottawa, where he resided until his death, which took place on October 1st, 1909. He established a retail jewellery business there which was conducted for many years under the name of A. Rosenthal & Sons, and which was some years ago sold to Henry Birks Limited. Mr. Rosenthal took a leading part in the philanthropic movements in Ottawa and was actively interested in all the charitable, welfare, and educational undertakings, especially in the Jewish community. In all his activities he was ably aided by his wife, who also took a prominent part in all philanthropic movements. His sterling reputation and upright character will long be remembered in all parts of Canada, as his business connections extended from coast coast. Mr. Rosenthal left four sons, Messrs. Adolphe, Samuel, Martin, and Harry Rosenthal, who are all highly respected residents of Ottawa. Mr. Samuel Rosenthal was the first, and to the present time, the only Jew who has been elected to the City Council in Ottawa. He served as Alderman for nine years, and was also very prominently identified in the athletic life of the City. Both Mr. and Mrs. Rosenthal occupied high positions in the social life of the Capital. Their lives will be an inspiration to those who aspire to do service to the less fortunate.

ACTIVITIES OF CANADIAN JEWISH WOMEN

JEWISH women in Canada have from the earliest days proved themselves to be "true mothers in Israel".

At a time when the Jewish population of this country was but a few souls, the wives of these pioneers settlers kept the spark of Judaism alive. Lacking almost everything required for the establishment of a Jewish community, the women steadfastly adhered to the tenets of their faith and in their homes maintained a real Jewish atmosphere. They instructed their children in the obligations of their religion and at all times set an example to be followed.

Among the first Jewish women in Canada were Dorothea Judah (wife of Aaron Hart), Frances Ezekiel (wife of Lazarus David), and Rebecca Franks (wife of Levy Solomons), and among the first generation born in Canada or in the American colonies were, Abigail David (wife of Andrew Hays), Frances David (wife of Myer Michaels), Rachel Solomons (wife of Henry Joseph), Sarah Judah (wife of Moses Hart), Sarah Hart (wife of Samuel David), Caroline Hart (wife of Moses David), Miriam Hart (wife of Uriah Hart), Frances Lazarus (wife of Ezekiel Hart), and Harriet Hart (wife of Benjamin Hart).

It was the munificent gift of a considerable sum of money by Mrs. Myer Michaels, daughter of Lazarus David, (who was the first Jew to be buried in Canada), that materially assisted the building of the Shearith Israel Synagogue of Montreal, the first Jewish place of worship of this country, and in the succeeding years the wives of the members of this congregation have at all times worthily maintained the high ideals and devotion shown by this lady in the upkeep of the institution. It was in 1863 that the first synagogue was erected on the Pacific coast, and one of the most indefatigable workers in raising the funds necessary for its construction was Cecilia Davies (Mrs. Frank Sylvester), who still has in her possession a letter of appreciation from the officers of the congregation, written at that time.

MRS. HENRY JOSEPH
(Rachel Solomons)

Fortunately the early Jewish settlers were all possessed of considerable means when they came to this country, and consequently there was little or no call for philanthropic work among them. Nevertheless they took much interest in such charities as existed, and were liberal subscribers to all demands for relief.

It was not until 1877 that the first Jewish women's charitable organization was formed in Montreal for the purpose of assisting in the relief work amongst the Jewish women and children; work which had up to that time been carried on by the men's society. The Ladies' Hebrew Benevolent Society was the name selected and during the many years that this organization was in existence, it fulfilled, in a most capable manner, the intentions of, its founders. Within a short time, the Montefiore Ladies' Aid Society in Toronto also came into being, and this was followed by the formation of other charitable organizations in different communities. Mrs. (Camilla) Herman Levy in Hamilton organized the Deborah Ladies' Aid, which in addition to doing charitable work was an auxiliary to the Anshe Sholom Congregation, and up to the time of her death, Mrs. Levy retained office as President of this organization. At about the same time, Mrs. George Frankfurter in Winnipeg entered into the life of service that she rendered to her community. In the maritime provinces, Mrs. Solomon Hart and her daughters organized a women's aid society in St. John. Mrs. Samuel Gintzburger did similar work in Vancouver, and both in Montreal and Toronto numerous other charitable organizations came into existence. The memory of Mrs. Samuel Davis in Montreal, Mrs. Montefiore Joseph in Quebec, Mrs. (Rabbi) Jacobs, and Mrs. A. Landsberg in Toronto, and Mrs. A. Rosenthal in Ottawa, in addition to the names previously mentioned will always remain as beacons in the field of women's work in Canada.

The range of women's activities cover all branches of communal endeavor, and in whatever field of work they have entered, no section of the population showed a more devoted interest than the Jewish women. Their undertakings are not sectarian, though they naturally devote their greatest endeavors to the relief of their own people. Among the organizations formed by women's aid societies are:— Jewish branches of Women's Councils, Jewish Chapters of the Imperial Order of the Daughters of the Empire, auxiliaries to hospitals, orphanages, old folks' homes, synagogues and other institutions. Maternity hospitals, Big Sister work, girls' clubs and summer camps, where under-privileged mothers, children and working girls are given free recreation, all form part of women's activities.

Among the workers of today who are particularly prominent may be mentioned Mrs. Lillian (A. J.) Freiman of Ottawa, undoubtedly one of the outstanding women of the country. Possessed of a wonderful organizing ability, her influence has been sought and freely given to anything for the betterment of conditions in this country or elsewhere. Prominent among her many undertakings was the Ukranian War Orphans' Relief, when she went to Ukrania and personally supervised the bringing to Canada of hundreds of Jewish war orphans, all of whom she saw placed in splendid Jewish homes, where they are being brought up as members of the family. The high position that Canadian Hadassah today occupies is largely due to the devoted work of Mrs. Freiman, and it was a splendid acknowledgment of her ability when the City of Ottawa, at the time of the influenza epidemic, placed in her hands the complete charge of combating the disease. Mrs. Lyon Cohen, Mrs. Clarence I. de Sola, Mrs. C. A. Workman, Mrs. (Gertrude Silverman) David Davis, Miss Essie Hirsch, Mrs. S. Wener, Mrs. H. Saxe, Mrs. Vivian S. Hart and Mrs. Martin Woff have been and are among the most active women workers in Montreal. In Toronto, Mrs. David Dunkelman, Mrs. I. H. Siegel, Mrs. M. L. Willinsky, Mrs. Chas. Draimin, Mrs. (Rabbi) B. R. Brickner and others are very active and in Hamilton, Mrs. Epstein, Mrs. M. Levy and Mrs. M. Simon; in London, Mrs. B. Lewis; in Ottawa, Mrs. Kert; in Winnipeg, Mrs. Moses Finkelstein, Mrs. H. E. Wilder and Mrs. S. Hart Green; in Calgary, Mrs. A. H. Goldberg and Mrs. C. Benjamin; in Vancouver, Mrs. M. Grossman and Mrs.

E. R. Sugarman; and in St. John, Mrs. Louis Green may all be mentioned for the unselfish devotion they have at all times shown as public-spirited women in their communities.

Jewish women have made names for themselves in the world of art and music, foremost among whom may be mentioned Madame Donalda (Pauline Lightstone). Miss Regina Seiden of Montreal has already established a name as a portrait painter. The Jewish young women of Canada are to a considerable extent entering into professional life, and Mrs. L. M. Singer of Toronto was the first Jewish young lady to graduate as a Doctor of Medicine. There have been numerous graduates in Arts and other higher courses and the records set by them at the different universities have been a great source of pride to all.

The foremost women's organization in Canada is the Hadassah, organized in 1916 by Mrs. A. Selick of Toronto, as the women's branch of the Zionist Organization. Since its founding it has embraced every locality in this country and under the presidency of Mrs. A. J. Freiman has become second in importance only to the Zionist Federation. In all Zionistic activities Hadassah has taken a leading part, and its endeavors on behalf of the Keren Hayesod are particularly outstanding. In the eleven years of its existence Hadassah has grown from one small society to 68 distinct chapters, from coast to coast, and has raised, for Hadassah purposes, the total of $230,060.90. A complete record of Hadassah activities is given on pages 277-287.

Mrs. A. Belasco, Victoria, B.C., and her son David, now the famous Playwright

A feature of the activities of Canadian Jewesses is the great work done by them during the terrible days between 1914-1919. Immediately after the outbreak of war, in all communities they organized and worked for the relief of the needy dependants and for the comfort of the soldiers. Several chapters of the Imperial Order of the Daughters of the Empire were formed by Jewish women and the work done by them won the commendation of the authorities. In other districts they joined the existing chapters, and either individually or collectively contributed to the accomplishments of the women of the community. When relief was organized for the Jewish war sufferers in Europe they raised hundreds of thousands of dollars in money and stores of supplies, clothing and food-stuffs in all parts of Canada, Mrs. Freiman again taking a leading part, when she toured the entire country, seeking assistance for those in want.

Jewish young ladies who had qualified as nurses joined various hospitals and Red Cross units, and saw service in Canada, England, and in the war area.

It was a Jewess, Miss Caroline Hart, a great-granddaughter of the first Jew who settled in Canada, who was the organizer of Toronto's kindergarten system. She was a pioneer in this movement in America, and received her training at the famous training school in St. Louis. From 1885 to 1892, Miss Hart was the head of the kindergarten department of the Toronto Normal School.

MRS. LOUIS GREEN, ST. JOHN, N.B.

MRS. FRANK SYLVESTER, VICTORIA

THE LATE MRS. H. LEVY,
ST. JOHN, N.B.

MRS. W. DIAMOND, EDMONTON

MISS FANNY JOSEPH,
QUEBEC

MRS. DAVID DAVIS, MONTREAL

MRS. A. KERT, OTTAWA

THE LATE MRS. SAMUEL DAVIS

FOR almost fifty years one of the outstanding women of Montreal, Mrs. Samuel Davis, the widow of Samuel Davis, founder of the firm of S. Davis & Sons, died in Montreal on December 21st, 1897. Her maiden name was Miss Minnie Falk, and she was married to Samuel Davis in 1857. Exemplary in all the relations of life, Mrs. Davis was beloved and esteemed by everyone who knew her. For many years she was the President of the Ladies' Hebrew Benevolent Society, and always took a lively interest in its affairs as well as in those of the Baron de Hirsch School and of several other charitable institutions. Benevolence was a leading trait in her character, which was embellished by every virtue that should adorn a perfect woman. Practically every charity in Montreal found in her a generous and constant patroness, and numerous individuals whom she helped in the time of need can trace their first success in life to her assistance. She took an active interest in the Temple Emanu-El, Montreal, of which congregation her husband was one of the founders. Any deserving appeal to her sympathy or aid was answered, and her figure was a familiar sight in the poorer Jewish districts of Montreal, where she was a regular visitor to homes in want. Her philanthropies took a practical form and gifts of food and clothing were at all times carried with her in her visits to the poor; in fact, it has been said of Mrs. Davis that she was a charitable organization in herself. Mrs. Davis was survived by five sons, Eugene H. of New Orleans; Maurice E. and Melvin H. of the firm of S. Davis & Sons of Montreal; Sir Mortimer B., President of the Imperial Tobacco Co. of Canada, Ltd.; and David T. of New York; and two daughters, Mrs. Cole and Mrs. Lustgarten of New York. From the time of the death of her late husband, no event had occurred among the Jewish community which caused more profound sorrow than her passing away. Her communal activities have been worthily upheld by her children, her son Sir Mortimer having been knighted by His Majesty King George V., as a recognition of his great philanthropic work.

THE LADIES' HEBREW BENEVOLENT SOCIETY, MONTREAL

IN the month of February, 1877, a small body of Jewish women met to discuss the advisability of organizing a society with the object of alleviating the sufferings of the local Jewish poor women and children. The following ladies were present at this meeting:—Mesdames Louis Saunders, Alex Saunders, Hyam Moss, Isidore Saunders, David Moss, John Moss, J. L. Moss, Samuel Davis, Mona Lesser, E. Meyers, B. Kortosk, Henry Jacobs, and others.

The outcome of the meeting was the organization of the Ladies' Hebrew Benevolent Society, which was formed with a regular set of by-laws, and which was shortly afterwards incorporated by a special Act of the Legislature of the Province of Quebec. The following ladies were elected the first officers;—President, Mrs. Louis Saunders; Vice-President, Mrs. Henry Jacobs; Treasurer, Mrs. Samuel Davis; Secretary, Mrs. J. L. Moss.

At the start, the Board met once a month, generally at the residence of the president, but as time went on and the Jewish population increased, the number of poor grew in proportion. Weekly meetings of the Board were then instituted, and for many years they met at the old Baron de Hirsch Institute on St. Elizabeth Street. When the present building of the Institute was completed on Bleury Street, the Board continued to meet there weekly.

After the Society became incorporated they were in receipt of an annual grant from the Provincial Government, and they also received a yearly donation from the Montreal City and District Savings Bank. These two amounts, together with the annual dues of the members, and the amounts derived from concerts and bazaars held at various times, enabled the Society to carry on its good work during the early years of its existence.

In 1903, however, the Society found itself unable to cope with the ever-increasing demand on its funds, due largely to the great influx of Jewish immigration. At a special meeting, convened in May, 1905, by the Baron de Hirsch Institute to meet the Board, it was mutually agreed that the former pay for transportation and supply the poor with coal, and share with the Society such other expenses, as for medical attendance, clothing, shoes, rubbers, rent, etc., etc. By this arrangement the Society was enabled to largely increase its already great sphere of usefulness.

Right up to the time of the formation of the Federation, the Society continued its monumental work in the community, and many are the different forms its activities embraced. The ladies dispensed cash relief to poor and aged women, widows, deserted women and orphans. Clothing and other necessaries were provided for school children, and application for medical aid or entrance into any of the hospitals was always acted upon immediately. Many hours were also devoted to friendly visiting of the poor, thus bringing hope and cheer where both were wanted.

Although all the members were active in their support of the Society special mention may be made of the great and active interest displayed by Mrs. Samuel Davis, the Misses Rubenstein, Mrs. Lewis A. Hart, Mrs. H. Vineberg, Mrs. Jacob Goldstein, Mrs. J. A. Jacobs, Mrs. Mark Workman, Mrs. David S. Friedman, Mrs. S. Fischel, Mrs. C. A. Workman, Mrs. Maxwell Goldstein, Mrs. G. Fischel, and the Misses Essie Hirsch, Gertrude Silverman, and Fanny Harris. The services of Mr. D. A. Ansell and Mr. I. Rubenstein were also at all times at the disposal of the Society, and their advice and assistance were of inestimable value

Since the formation of this Society, the pioneer women's philanthropic institution of the Jewish community of Canada, numerous other societies have come into existence, some of which have in the meantime passed away. In the almost half century since the organization of the Ladies' Hebrew Benevolent Society, some of the most successful business men of the country owe much of their start to the original aid furnished them by it, in preparing the way for their education, and it must be a source of much satisfaction to the remaining living of the first members, as also to their successors, to see the practical results of their work. Few of the original members are left, but their memory will remain imperishable to succeeding workers, and their examples being well followed by the younger ladies in all fields of welfare work. Throughout the entire existence of the Society the members displayed a spirit of charity and self-sacrifice that may well be followed and of them it may truly be said "they were blessed in their giving".

THE LADIES' MONTEFIORE BENEVOLENT SOCIETY, TORONTO

THE Ladies' Montefiore Benevolent Society was the first Jewish women's charitable organization in Toronto. It was organized about 1878, after the erection of the first synagogue (The Holy Blossom) of that city, and consisted chiefly of the wives of the members of that congregation. Mrs. Rosenthal was its first President.

During the first few years of its existence, not much charitable work was accomplished, as there was no need for it, the Jewish community of Toronto being small with very few poor families.

In 1882-3 however, there was an influx of immigrants into Toronto owing to the many massacres and pogroms which had taken place in Russia and Roumania. At this time the need for charitable work was indeed great as the number of Jewish poor had increased considerably.

The Society received an annual grant from the city, and to raise additional funds, they instituted a yearly ball. As there were no Victorian or city nurses at that time, the members of the Society personally visited the sick and did all that was in their power to lighten their burdens. A Dorcas Society for the purpose of making clothing for the poor and to teach the children sewing was established. This was the nucleus of the Sewing School which is still in existence, and which at the present time is being carried on at the Community House, Toronto; lessons in all kinds of sewing being given to many young girls.

In 1916, when most of the charitable organizations of Toronto became affiliated with the Federation of of Jewish Philanthropies, the Ladies' Montefiore Benevolent Society also became one of its constituents.

The following were the successive Presidents of the Society;—Mrs. L. Samuel, Mrs. A. Miller, Mrs. A. D. Benjamin and Mrs. Loeser.

MRS. C. I. DE SOLA, MONTREAL

MRS. C. I. DE SOLA (Miss Belle Maud Goldsmith) was born at Cleveland, Ohio, the daughter of Leopold Goldsmith of that city. She received her education in Cleveland, and is a graduate in philosophy of Western Reserve University, and a member of the McGill Alumni Association. In her native city she was a prominent worker along charitable and educational lines. Mrs. de Sola was one of the founders of the Girls' Friendly Club, and its first vice-president. She was married to the late Chevalier Clarence I. de Sola of Montreal, and has two sons, Raphael and Gabriel, and two daughters, Misses Jessica and Esther de Sola. Mrs. de Sola took her place as a prominent social and communal leader of the Montreal Jewish community, following her marriage, and she organized the Daughters of Zion and the Sisterhood of the Spanish and Portuguese Synagogue. She is one of the three presidents of the Social Committee of the Victorian Order of Nurses, and is connected with a number of other non-sectarian institutions. She founded the Friendly League of Jewish Women, and organized the Welcome Club for Jewish working girls. Mrs. de Sola was instrumental in launching the Welcome Camp at Shawbridge. She was Honorary President of the Montreal branch of the Canadian Women's Press Club for three terms, which was a signal mark of esteem as it had been decided that the office was to be held for two years only. In 1918, she was decorated by King Albert of Belgium with the Order of Queen Elizabeth, in recognition of the services she rendered during the war, in connection with Belgian relief work. She received the Gold Cross of Mercy, which was conferred on her by His Majesty, King Peter of Serbia, and the Silver Medal of the Serbian Red Cross, given through the Serbian Consul General in Canada, on behalf of the Serbian Red Cross. On June 14th, 1923, she had the honour of being presented at court to the King and Queen of England, by the Marchioness Curzon of Kedleston, and she had the unique distinction, for a Canadian Jewess, of personally presenting her daughter, Miss Jessica, to Their Majesties.

MRS. LYON COHEN, MONTREAL

MRS. LYON COHEN, RACHEL (RAY) FRIEDMAN, an outstanding figure in communal and charitable work in Montreal, was born in that city, the daughter of the late Noah and Sarah Friedman. Mrs. Cohen received her education at the public schools of Montreal, and later attended the Sacred Heart Convent, attending at the same time a Hebrew School, which was connected with the Synagogue. Her father, having been Parnas of the Cadieux Street Synagogue, now the Shaar Hashomayim Synagogue of Westmount, and President of the Young Men's Hebrew Benevolent Society, the atmosphere and environment in which she was brought up was thoroughly Jewish. Her mother's home was a regular shelter for transient co-religionists, who always found a welcome and a meal at the Friedman home. On February 17th, 1891, Mrs. Cohen was married to Mr. Lyon Cohen, son of the late Lazarus and Fanny (Garmaise) Cohen, of Montreal, and she has three sons, Lieut. Nathan Bernard, Capt. Horace Rives and Lawrence Zebulum, and one daughter, Miss Sylvia Lillian Cohen. Like her husband, Mrs. Cohen devotes much time to philanthropic work, and while not holding office in many of the societies with which she is affiliated, she takes special interest in the Jewish Endeavour Sewing School of Montreal, which she founded in 1902, and of which she has been President since its inception. This school, which is now one of the constituencies of the Federation of Jewish Philanthropies, is performing a very valuable service to the Montreal Jewish community. Mrs. Cohen's communal activities are non-sectarian, being by no means confined to any one creed, and she is a life governor of the Montreal General Hospital and the Western Hospital, Montreal. She is a member of the following institutions; Ladies' Auxiliary of the Shaar Hashomayim Congregation; Shaar Hashomayim Sewing Circle; National Council of Jewish Women; Montreal Women's Club; Westmount Victorian Order of Nurses; Federation of Jewish Philanthropies; Hebrew Maternity and Montreal Maternity Hospitals; and the Children's Memorial Hospital;

PRESENT DAY ACTIVITIES OF MONTREAL JEWISH WOMEN

By Irene Wolff

THE activities of the Jewish women of Montreal range throughout the entire field of philanthropic, charitable, patriotic and social endeavour. The largest Jewish community in Canada, its women strive to make themselves worthy to uphold a good name the women of the race have borne from time immemorial. The poor and distressed of our people, the immigrants arriving forlorn and disconsolate in a strange land, the sick, the needy, those seeking for spiritual guidance or material help, for mental diversion or for physical aid, all are looked after and all needs are filled by the tireless enthusiasm and energy of the Jewish women of Montreal.

The organization with the largest scope is the Montreal Council of Jewish Women. Organized in 1918 as a local Council of the Council of Jewish Women of the United States, it was decided in the winter of 1924 to become an independent body and keep all the funds in Canada. A Provincial Charter has been applied for. The Council has a membership of about 500, and has on its advisory board a representative from each of the chief Jewish women's organizations of Montreal. There are a number of different committees, each doing active work. One of the most important is the Juvenile Aid and Big Sister Committee which works in conjunction with the Jewish probation officer, whose salary is paid in equal shares by the Council, the Federation of Jewish Philanthropies and the Provincial Government. The Council was the pioneer in the Big Sister movement in Montreal, starting in January 1920.

Immigrant Aid work has always been an important undertaking of the Council. Reports of cases requiring attention are received from the Y.W.C.A., the Government Bureau and from the Council of Jewish Women in the United States. In connection with this work, two clubs for immigrant girls were organized, and these met weekly at the Baron de Hirsch Institute for some years. There were always some ladies in charge who were at all times ready to listen sympathetically to the girls' problems and help to solve them. Classes were held in sewing and in English, games and dancing were organized, and in cases where needed, employment was found. The girls in the original club have all either married or otherwise grown beyond the need of such a club, which automatically disbanded; the other one is now being carried on under the Y.W.H.A.

The winter of 1923-24 saw the arrival in Canada of a number of Roumanian refugees who had been permitted by the Canadian Government to enter the country on condition of their not becoming a charge on the public. To cope with this situation the Council called an emergency meeting of representatives of the various organizations and a Ladies' Auxiliary of the Jewish Immigrant Aid Society was formed, which has since that time been functioning as a separate body. Formed in the first instance to look after these special immigrants, seeing that suitable housing accommodation was found for them, that they had a sufficiency of clothing to stand our severe winter, and above all finding them employment, the Auxiliary proved itself so efficient that it was decided to continue it as a permanent organization.

Another laudable enterprise of the Jewish Council has been the Recreation Centres conducted in three schools in the Jewish districts during the summer months, and attended by about fifteen hundred children. These schools teach almost everything but lessons; the girls, who form the majority of the pupils, are taught sewing, knitting, basket work, hatmaking, drawing, etc., whilst for the boys other forms of recreational work are taught. Athletics form a great part of the programme, whilst picnics and occasional all-day outings are added attractions.

Other activities of the Council are: sewing for the Hebrew Orphanage, a committee of ladies meeting at the orphanage once a week, doing all the mending for the children and making new garments, conducting the Old Clothes Shop at the Baron de Hirsch Institute: the compilation and publication of a Kosher Cook Book; a hospital visiting and convalescent relief committee, which carries cheer to Jewish patients in all the city hospitals, goes regularly to feed the helpless children at the Children's Memorial Hospital two days a week, and other related work; a large number of orphans from the war areas of Europe were placed in homes by the Council. Nor have they lost sight of the æsthetic side of life, and under their auspices is a very active Music and Dramatic Club. It is composed of those capable and willing to perform either musically or dramatically, and comprises most of the younger members of the Council. For the benefit of Council members and their friends classes in Civics, Current Events, Child Psychology, etc. have been held from time to time. The Council is affiliated with the Local Council of Women, and co-operates with other non-sectarian bodies on all questions that affect the welfare of women or children; besides being affiliated with the Union of Jewish Women and the Jewish Association for the Protection of Girls and Women of England.

The Young Women's Hebrew Association carries on its activities as one of the constituent societies of the Federation of Jewish Philanthropies, but under the management of a tireless, unselfish committee of ladies, who feel that any sacrifice they make of time, money or energy is more than worth while when made in such a worthy cause as that of giving education and recreation to young Jewish girls in a Jewish atmosphere. Though it has been in existence for a number of years, it was only in 1924 that an official Y.W.H.A. home was opened. Here there is a membership of 400 girls who are divided into clubs for dressmaking, millinery, English literature, dramatics, athletics, social activities and social service. The Association has for the past few years conducted a summer camp in the Laurentians, and this has proved a boon to many a working girl, and enabled her to get a real summer holiday at a reasonable rate.

Any Monday afternoon on the top flat of the Baron de Hirsch Institute may be found over twenty groups of interested little girls sewing away as if their lives depended upon what they were doing. In the centre of each group is a lady, patiently showing the little ones their faults, and training unaccustomed little fingers to hold a needle properly and take tiny, almost invisible, stitches. This is the Jewish Endeavour Sewing School, opened on December 12th, 1902, and increasing in strength of numbers and usefulness steadily since that date. Its inauguration was due to the far-sightedness of a small group of Jewish ladies, who viewed with alarm the fact that a number of Jewish girls were being tempted to attend the mission schools, where they learnt sewing and found congenial companionship of girls of their own age. The school has been a success from the start, when it opened with an enrolment of ninety pupils under nine teachers, and has now grown to 229 pupils with 27 teachers. The children are taught to make their own clothes, thus putting their sewing to practical use from the very beginning. In the highest class the girls learn cutting out and dressmaking. The school also conducts a weekly sewing class at the Montreal Hebrew Orphanage.

Another sewing society, which also meets weekly, is the Hebrew Ladies' Sewing Society, but in this case it is the ladies that do all the sewing, working on garments to be distributed through the various branches of Federation. Most of the Synagogue Sisterhoods and Auxiliaries as well as other societies send representatives to do their share in this good work.

The Ladies' Auxiliary of the Hebrew Maternity Hospital, which was inaugurated in December 1920, has now a membership of about 850. These are divided into several sub-committees, the chief being the house committee, whose work is to investigate the dietary and sanitary conditions of the hospital, and look after the linen and utensil needs; they supply all the bed linen, clothing for mothers and babes, kitchen utensils, have given donations towards the sterilizer, floor coverings, and have in every way been of invaluable service to the doctors and nurses. The donations committee provides delicacies for the patients, which they would not otherwise get, as well as from time to time providing such other special donations as blankets, flowers etc. There is also a social service committee which investigates cases and determines whether they are to be admitted as free or part-pay patients, and does a certain amount of follow-up work after the patients leave the hospital.

There are twenty chapters of Hadassah in Montreal, each actively engaged on the general Hadassah work; most of the synagogues as well as the Temple have auxiliaries or sisterhoods, and these look after the vestments, take an interest in the religious schools, act as a bond of union between the members of their own congregations by promoting social gatherings, raise funds to help their institutions and do general charitable work as far as their resources permit; there are two active companies of Jewish Girl Guides, showing that the younger girls, too, are fitting themselves to take up the right kind of activities later in life; the Hebrew Ladies' Relief Society provides groceries for needy families; and the Ladies' Bichur Cholim Society looks after the needy who are ill.

In the early days of the war a number of Jewish ladies banded themselves together to do their bit for King and Country and, as the Hebrew Ladies' Patriotic Group, did a wonderful amount of sewing and knitting for the Red Cross and the Patriotic Fund. In two years 2,396 articles were made and given to the Red Cross, but it was felt that even better work could be done under a central organization, and accordingly on December 13th, 1916, the Grace Aguilar Chapter of the Imperial Order of the Daughters of the Empire was formed and launched on a career of usefulness from which it never faltered during the war years, and it continues to be active to the present day. The members, numbering about 150, worked indefatigably, knitting, sewing, raising funds, corresponding with and sending packages to the "boys" overseas, indeed doing every form of patriotic work, and doing it cheerfully and well. The number of funds, societies and organizations helped by the Grace Aguilar Chapter is far too long to enumerate, suffice it to say that no worthy cause appealed in vain. Besides the actual war work the Chapter assisted a number of other organizations and funds, including the Ukranian Relief, Khaki League, Montreal Maternity Hospital, Hebrew Maternity Hospital, McGill Centennial Fund, Université de Montreal, gave an I.O.D.E. library to a school in Kamsack, Saskatchewan, and gave colours to the Jewish Boy Scouts.

When our soldiers began returning from the other side in great numbers and the Khaki League Club was taxed to its utmost to provide recreation for them, a Superfluity Shop was opened, which for several years was successfully run, and provided funds for a great deal of splendid work done by the Khaki Club. This shop, as its name implies, received gratefully anything that anyone found superfluous in their own homes, or cared to donate in any way. These articles were sold at a low price, chiefly to soldiers' wives and dependants. Besides this a lunch and tea room was conducted which proved a splendid source of revenue. One day in each week, the entire organization was in the hands of the Jewish women, who devoted their time to this enterprise, and helped in a great measure to make it the success it proved to be.

These are some of the chief activities that the Jewish women of Montreal have been carrying on; the individuals composing them in many instances work in two, three or more societies, and besides these, there are a number of Jewish girls and women devoting a large portion of their time to social service under the auspices of non-sectarian institutions. Girls brought up in the lap of luxury, young women in spite of their household duties, as well as the older women all find time to do some good work and are to be found giving up many hours weekly helping teach poor children to sew, supervising games at one or other of the Settlements, feeding helpless children at the Children's Memorial Hospital, doing anything and everything in their power to train up good and useful citizens; truly of the Jewish women of Montreal may it be said:

"Their works shall praise them in the gates."

MRS. MARTIN WOLFF, (IRENE RACHEL JOSEPH), MONTREAL.

A MEMBER of a family, which for generations has been prominent in the upbuilding of Canada and in communal and philanthropic activities, Mrs. Martin Wolff is ably upholding the traditions of her forebears. Born in Quebec, October 7th 1885, the daughter of Montefiore Joseph of that City, and the granddaughter of the late Abraham Joseph, in his day one of the foremost citizens of Quebec, she was educated at the Misses Henderson's School and at the Girls' High School of Quebec. Raised in the highest Jewish atmosphere, it was only natural that she should follow in the footsteps of her mother, the late Mrs. Annette (Pinto) Joseph and her father's sisters, the Misses Fanny and Rachel Joseph, in taking an active part in the religious and educational life of her people. At the age of fifteen years, Mrs. Wolff became a charter member of the Baden-Powell Chapter, Imperial Order Daughters of the Empire (founded in 1900) and for many years she was Regent of this Chapter. In 1916-17 (war years) she was Regent of the Quebec Municipal Chapter, I.O.D.E.; and in May, 1917, attended the annual meeting of the Order at Victoria, B.C., as the representative from Quebec. From 1918 to 1922, Mrs. Wolff was Educational Secretary of the Disraeli Chapter, I.O.D.E., Ottawa, and in 1919, she organized the first branch of the Sinai League in Canada, at Ottawa, and for four years was its leader. In 1923, Mrs. Wolff moved to Montreal and in the same year was elected President of the Sisterhood of the Spanish and Portuguese Synagogue, an institution of which her family have been active supporters for over one hundred years. She is also a member of the Board of the Council of Jewish Women of Montreal. Mrs. Wolff is a frequent contributor to Jewish journals and is a member of the Canadian Authors' Association, and of the Women's Press Club of Canada. On March 25, 1909, her marriage to Mr. Martin Wolff took place at Quebec, and she is the proud mother of six daughters.

IMPERIAL ORDER DAUGHTERS OF THE EMPIRE

THE Imperial Order Daughters of the Empire was founded in 1900, at the time of the South African War, to supply and foster a bond of union amongst the women and children of the Empire. Chapters were organized in the different cities of the Dominion, and Jewish names are to be found amongst the earliest members, a number of these attaining prominence in various offices of the Order. As a result of the Great War a large number of new chapters sprang into being, all over the country, and amongst them were three exclusively Jewish ones in Montreal, Quebec and Ottawa.

Grace Aguilar Chapter I.O.D.E., Montreal

On December 13th, 1916, there was organized in Montreal by Mrs. A. W. Macdougald, the Montreal Organizing Secretary of the Order, the Grace Aguilar Chapter composed entirely of Jewish women, most of whom had already been working together for the Red Cross, under the name of the "Hebrew Ladies' Patriotic Group", and guided by Mrs. S. Wener. The first officers of the Chapter were:—Regent, Miss Fanny Joseph; First Vice-Regent, Mrs. S. Wener; Second Vice-Regent, Miss E. Hirsch; Treasurer, Mrs. L. Rabinovitch; Secretary, Mrs. S. Saxe; Echoes Sec., Mrs. A. E. Morris; Standard Bearer, Miss H. Kellert. The motto chosen for the Chapter was "Though He Slay Me, Yet Will I Trust in Him". About 150 members were enrolled, and the splendid amount of work done is shown by the fact that in the first year 5,393 articles were made and given to the Red Cross, as well as sending overseas over 2,500 articles of soldiers' comforts such as socks, packages of cigarettes, chocolates etc.; and the Chapter proudly states that in that first year no appeal was made to the public for funds, all being carried on by voluntary donations. Weekly sewing meetings were held, and as well as working at these gatherings, the members took sewing and knitting to do at home.

After the war was over the chapter devoted most of its energies to local charitable and philanthropic work, though many other appeals were heard and answered. The assistance of the chapter enabled the son of a soldier to take his course at the Technical School; an I.O.D.E. library was presented to a school at Kamsack, Sask., to aid in the Canadianizing of foreign born children; colours were presented to the Jewish Boy Scouts of Montreal; a boy was supported at the Boys' Farm at Shawbridge P.Q.; and amongst the many funds and organizations assisted financially by the Grace Aguilar Chapter were the Khaki Club; Jewish War Relief Fund; Palestine Relief Fund; Ukranian Relief Fund; McGill Centennial Fund; Laval University; War Memorial Fund of the I.O.D.E.; Friendly League of Jewish Women; The Montreal Maternity, Hebrew Maternity, and Children's Memorial Hospitals; the Federation of Jewish Philanthropies; Japanese Relief Fund; Victorian Order of Nurses; Navy League and others of a similar nature. Trees were planted on the Road of Remembrance to Marvin Workman and Benjamin Cohen, who gave their lives in the Great War. The chapter has ever been ready to co-operate with its sister chapters in the city in any and every undertaking that has been carried out by the Order as a whole, and has been looked upon as one of the star chapters under the Municipal Chapter of Montreal.

The present officers are;—Miss F. Joseph, Hon. Regent; Mrs. S. Wener, Hon. First Vice-Regent; Miss E. Hirsch, Hon. Second Vice-Regent; Mrs. S. Saxe, Regent; Mrs. A. Jacobs, First Vice-Regent; Mrs. J. Levinson, Second Vice-Regent; Mrs. H. Saxe, Treasurer; Mrs. D. Tannenbaum, Secretary; Miss Mary Vineberg, Asst. Sec.; Miss E. Block, Educational Sec.; Miss B. Samuels, Echoes Sec.; Miss H. Kellert, Standard Bearer.

The Disraeli Chapter I.O.D.E., Ottawa

The Disraeli Chapter was founded in Ottawa in July 1918, with a membership of about 130 Jewish women and girls. The original officers were;—Lady Borden, Hon. Regent; Mrs. A. J. Freiman, Regent; Mrs. S. Rosenthal, First Vice-Regent; Mrs. J. Holzman, Second Vice-Regent; Miss Ada Abelson, Secretary; Mrs. Charles Kert, Treasurer; Mrs. A. Goltman, Echoes Secretary; Miss Leonore Freedman, Educational Secretary; Miss Evelyn Rosenthal, Standard Bearer.

The first act of the newly formed chapter was the furnishing of a recreation room in the G.W.V.A. club house that was being opened at that time. In order to keep the chapter supplied with funds for its patriotic and philanthropic work a tea room was conducted for many months, the work being carried on by the voluntary help of the members. Two children of soldiers killed in the war were enabled to complete their studies owing to the assistance of the chapter; the annual poppy day campaigns always saw the full quota of Disraeli Chapter members amongst the workers; donations were sent to the Red Cross, Soldiers' comforts, Jewish Legion and many other appeals were answered in a substantial way. The chapter continued its assistance to the soldiers' children until 1923, when the last of the original boys had completed his course at the Technical School, and it was considered inadvisable to take up any new work in this direction as funds were not so easy to raise and the members had so many other calls.

Lord Reading Chapter I.O.D.E., Quebec

The Lord Reading Chapter was founded in 1914, by a group of Jewish women in Quebec City, who worked for the soldiers, sending overseas 1081 articles of clothing, and giving comforts of all kinds to the Jewish Legion when they passed through Quebec on their way to Palestine. They also helped Palestinian and local charitable and patriotic funds. After a short but active career the chapter fell into abeyance, but was reorganized under a new charter in 1918, the charter members being: Miss Rebecca Smilovitz, Regent; Mrs. M. Pollack, D. Liebling, L. Lazarovitz, Chas. Lax, D. Fitch, O. Fitch, G. Marcus, and the Misses J. Cohen and J. Gardner; with Mrs. Montefiore Joseph as Hon. Regent.

From this time on the Lord Reading Chapter has done splendid work with a membership of less than 50. Amongst funds that have benefitted from its assistance have been the Quebec I.O.D.E. Fresh Air Fund; the Armenian and Ukranian orphans; soldiers' cigarette fund; and comforts were sent to the Siberian expedition. Since 1923, the chapter has been specializing in immigration work, members help regularly in the Red Cross nursery and post office at the immigration building. They make clothing for the newcomers who are often in need of it, and have been conducting a class to teach English to the foreigners arriving in the country.

The officers for 1925 are;—Mrs. L. Lazarovitz, Hon. Regent; Mrs. F. Greenberg, Regent; Mrs. D. Liebling, Vice-Regent; Miss A. Lazarovitz, Secretary; Mrs. M. Gardner, Treasurer; Mrs. Chas. Serchuk, Standard Bearer.

THE LATE MRS. MONTEFIORE JOSEPH

THE LATE MRS. MONTEFIORE JOSEPH (Annette Pinto) of Quebec was the third daughter of Henry Pinto of London, England. She was born in London, October 16, 1857, and was married on July 26th, 1882 to Montefiore Joseph of Quebec, the son of the late Abraham Joseph of that city. Mrs. Joseph occupied a foremost position in the life of Quebec and her activities and influence reached all parts of the province. For many years she was President of the Society for Prevention of Cruelty to Animals, Quebec. She was a life member of the Red Cross Society and of the Navy League, and was a member of the Canadian Club. She was the first Regent of the Stadacona Chapter, Imperial Order Daughters of the Empire, which appointment she held for several years, after which she was elected first Vice-Regent of the Chapter. Due to her untiring devotion, Mrs. Joseph was the first recipient of life membership of the Chapter. For two years she was the Standard Bearer of the Quebec Municipal Chapter, and she was Honorary Regent, Lord Reading Chapter. Mrs. Joseph was a member of the Union of Jewish Women, London, England, and of the Canadian Hadassah. In 1908, at the time of the Quebec Tercentenary, she was the Treasurer of the National Battlefields Fund, and was awarded the bronze Tercentenary Medal. She was a firm friend to the troops in khaki, particularly those of Jewish faith who were stationed at Quebec and Valcartier, and her home was ever open to them. Her charity knew no creed, and when there was work to be done for her religion, town, country or Empire, her whole heart and soul were given to the task, to which her aid was always a tower of strength. She was a staunch Jewess and led a strictly Jewish life, and brought up her children as orthodox Jews, herself teaching them Hebrew and the tenets of Jewish religion. Mrs. Joseph died the 18th of October, 1921 and left her husband and three sons, the late Abraham Pinto, Edward Cecil of Quebec, and Kenneth de Sola of Toronto, and two daughters, Mrs. Martin Wolff of Montreal, and Miss Rosetta Joseph, of Quebec.

MONTREAL COUNCIL OF JEWISH WOMEN

ON September 25th, 1918 a meeting, called by Mrs. S. W. Jacobs, was held in the Baron de Hirsch Institute for the purpose of organizing a Montreal Section of the National Council of Jewish Women. The meeting was addressed by Mrs. Miriam K. Arnold of Philadelphia, who expounded the motives actuating the National Council, and explained the scope and methods of work that formulate these motives into concrete benefits to the Jewish community. A motion was made by Mrs. A. E. Morris, seconded by Mrs. S. W. Jacobs, and unanimously passed, that a section of the Council of Jewish Women organized and maintained in Montreal would be a factor for good in the Jewish community. The following officers were then elected;—President, Mrs. S. W. Jacobs; Vice-Presidents, Lady Davis, Mrs. A. E. Morris, Mrs. Moses Vineberg, Mrs. Edgar M. Berliner, Mrs. Ascher Pierce; Treasurer, Mrs. Albert Lesser; Recording Secretary, Mrs. Louis Fitch; Corresponding Secretary, Mrs. Garfield A. Berlinsky; Directors, Mesdames A. E. Pierce, Lyon Cohen, J. Elkin, D. Davis, Sam Hart, Maurice Wechsler, J. S. Leo, A. M. Vineberg, John Michaels and Miss Fannie Heilig.

A number of Committees have been formed from time to time, and these have done a great deal of excellent work very efficiently. There are at present several very active Committees of the Council each doing such splendid work that it is indeed difficult to say which is the most important. The Immigration Committee is doing real Canadianization work among the new arrivals in our country. This Committee of energetic ladies, with the assistance of a part-time paid worker, follow up every new Canadian family, teach them how to adjust themselves to conditions in this country, advise them about day or night schools, tell them where to procure medical assistance when necessary, show them where to apply for work, indeed do everything in their power to make the newcomers feel that Canada is indeed the land of Promise and will turn out to be the Land of Plenty as well. The Big Sisters of the Council were the first Big Sisters in Montreal. They work in conjunction with the Juvenile Aid Committee, and it would take pages to tell of the great good being done by these workers in helping to decrease juvenile delinquency, and in readjusting the juvenile delinquents and helping them to once more become self-respecting and respectable members of society. The Civics Committee and Co-operative Committee represent the Council on all bodies and in all cases where Jewish women as a body join their Gentile sisters in public movements. The Council being always ready to take its full share of the responsibility of citizenship, and to co-operate in all that pertains to the welfare of the city, the Provinces and the Dominion. For three summers, through the strenuous efforts of a few ardent Council chembers, Summer Schools were established for Jewish mildren in the more crowded districts of the city. The Protestant Board of School Commisioners were approached and kindly placed three schools at the disposal of the Committee for this purpose, and in these centres through the hot summer months the children were kept off the streets and made happy learning basketwork, needlework, knitting, playing games, and so forth, every moment an enjoyable one to the youngsters, and who can picture the contentment of the mothers knowing that their little ones were being well cared for, without their having to answer the ceaseless question of childhood, especially in summer holidays—"What can I do now"?

A Music and Dramatic Club was organized under the auspices of the Council in 1920 chiefly from the younger members, directed by some of those older in experience. This branch has been successful from its inception both in numbers and in the work done, and now has a large and enthusiastic membership, and is successfully carrying out more and more ambitious programmes.

Every Sunday and Wednesday at the noon-hour members of the Council may be seen feeding the helpless crippled children at the Children's Memorial Hospital, this work being appreciated greatly, not only by the little patients, who look forward from one day to the next to seeing the kind ladies, but the Staff are equally grateful for this assistance which so materially adds to the comfort of the poor helpless little ones who without some such help would, in many instances have to eat cold meals or struggle as best they could with their food. The nurses cannot of course attend to all the little helpless ones at the same time.

The Council's other activities include sewing for the Federation at the United Sewing Assemblies, and sending a Committee of ladies under its auspices to mend the clothes at the Montreal Hebrew Orphanage one afternoon each week, and the piles of neatly patched and darned clothes to be seen on the tables at the close of the Wednesday sewing, demonstrate effectively the great amount of labor these women are doing for their less fortunate sisters and brothers. With all their other activities the Council Members do not neglect their self-education, and classes on Psychology, Current Events, Semitics and other topics have been held from time to time, whilst at each monthly General Meeting a speaker of note gives an address on some topic of interest, and an enjoyable musical programme is given. The season winds up each year with a luncheon, which always has some specially attractive feature.

In January, 1924, it was unanimously decided to change the name of the organization to The Council of Jewish Women of Montreal. With a membership of over 500, and with so much need for every dollar to be spent on charitable work in Canada, it was felt that it would be better to eliminate the per capita fee to the headquarters in the United States and become a separate organization, which would still be willing to co-operate in the future as in the past with the work of the National Council of Jewish Women in the United States.

The officers for 1924-25 are;—Hon. Vice-Presidents, Mrs. E. M. Berliner, Mrs. L. Fitch; President, Mrs. S. W. Jacobs; Vice-Presidents, Mrs. Martin Wolff, Mrs. Paul Saks, Mrs. Chas. M. Sommer; Recording Secretary, Mrs. J. Wolfe; Corresponding Secretary, Mrs. David Kert; Treasurer, Mrs. A. Lesser; Asst. Treasurer, Mrs. Irwin Rubinovitch.

COUNCIL OF JEWISH WOMEN, CALGARY SECTION

THE Council of Jewish Women, Calgary section, was organized in December 1920. The object of the society was to unite the Jewish women of the city in an organization that would strive to improve existing conditions, and to interest themselves in charitable and communal work. They desired to raise the standard of living among the poorer element and to co-operate with their fellow-Jewesses in other communities.

The members of the Council are active in co-operating with the existing organizations in Calgary, and are of much assistance to the synagogue, the Talmud Torah, and the Hadassah, of which society most of the members of the Council are also members. They have undertaken the collection of the monthly dues of the members of the Talmud Torah on a systematic basis. They also have collected considerable sums for the relief of the Western Canada Old Folks' Home, and the Orphanage, in Winnipeg, both of which institutions are supported by all western communities.

The Council was very active in the support afforded to the funds raised for the relief of the war sufferers, and for the Ukranian war orphans who were sent to Canada. They also do sewing, cooking, and other forms of relief needed locally.

While most of the efforts of the Council are towards relief work, the social and literary side is not neglected, and at their meetings there are usually lectures on current subjects, and other forms of education and entertainment. Another undertaking in which they have been successful is the Sunday School for those children who do not attend the Talmud Torah, where religious instruction in English is given.

The Council has in Mrs. H. Goldberg, its leader, a woman whose life is wrapped up in philanthropic work, and to whose organizing ability much of the success obtained to the present, is due.

COUNCIL OF JEWISH WOMEN, EDMONTON SECTION

THE Edmonton Section of the Council of Jewish Women was organized in September, 1920. It was formed by a number of ladies who were called together for that purpose by Mrs. H. A. Friedman, who at the first meeting of the Council was elected President. The objects in forming the Council were similar to those for which other Councils in the different cities of Canada had been organized, i.e., to form a central association which would render assistance to all other organizations as well as to individuals.

Although the Jewish population of Edmonton is not large, the Council has developed and at the present time composes practically all the Jewish women of the community. Different Committees have been organized to take charge of the various branches of its activities, which were divided into philanthropic work, education, immigration, and committees to gather funds in support of the Jewish Old Folks' Home of Western Canada, and the Western Canada Orphanage and Children's Aid, both located in Winnipeg. The committees who look after these last two institutions have raised substantial amounts for their support. Every year large sums have been forwarded to Winnipeg as Edmonton's contribution to the upkeep of these very worthy institutions.

All philanthropic work is looked after by the Council and the members have shown great devotion in providing for the needs of the newly arrived immigrants and in assisting all other worthy causes. The members did wonderful work in connection with the Ukranian war orphans' relief, and in assisting in the drives for the relief of the Jewish war sufferers in Europe.

The Council has excelled itself in assisting in the building of the Talmud Torah of Edmonton, and for this purpose they have, by means of annual bazaars, raised the sum of $8,000, $3,000, of which was expended for the purchase of a site which was donated to the Edmonton Hebrew School for the erection of the new Talmud Torah. The Council also makes annual contributions towards the upkeep of the Talmud Torah, and they have been active, together with the B'nai B'rith Lodge, in opposing the introduction of religious training in the public schools, of which several attempts had been unsuccessfully made.

The Council has also greatly assisted the work of the local Hadassah Chapter. As the membership includes practically all the married ladies of Edmonton, the Council has taken an important part in all national questions and in Zionistic work, particularly in the Keren Hayesod campaigns.

Mrs. Friedman, who was the first President of the Council, has held this office continuously ever since, and much of the great work done by this organization is due to her untiring efforts on its behalf.

The Council is affiliated with the Jewish Council of Women and they hold regular meetings where prominent speakers address the members. At these meetings instructive discourses are given on literary subjects and topics of the day, as well as on social service work.

As will be seen from other pages of this book, Edmonton occupies a leading position among the Jewish communities in Canada regarding the assistance given to worthy causes, and much of the credit for this showing is due to the Edmonton Council of Women, which is an organization that the entire community justly takes great pride in.

MRS. S. GINTZBURGER, VANCOUVER

MRS. SAMUEL GINTZBURGER (Rosina Robinson), was born in San Francisco, California, the daughter of the late Louis Robinson, who for many years occupied a prominent position in the communal life of Montreal, being at one time an officer in the Young Men's Hebrew Benevolent Society and Baron de Hirsch Institute of that city. She received her education at schools in San Francisco and Montreal, and was married to Mrs. Samuel Gintzburger, a pioneer Jewish resident of British Columbia, and one of the leading citizens of that province, who at present holds the appointment of Consul for Switzerland. Mrs. Gintzburger has been the leader in all movements of a philanthropic and charitable nature that have taken place in the Jewish community of Vancouver. She was instrumental in the formation of the Ladies' Auxiliary of the Temple Emanuel, Vancouver, and has been President of this organization since its inception. Her interests are non-sectarian, and she is a member of practically all organizations which tender towards the relief and betterment of the community. A charter member of the Council of Jewish women, Vancouver branch, she has also for many years been a member of the local Council of Women. She was one of the early members of the Vancouver Aid Society and her assistance and advice, which are at all times cheerfully given, have been of great benefit to this Society, as well as many others. Practically all of Mrs. Gintzburger's time is devoted to philanthropic work and she has been of great assistance to her husband in all his communal undertakings. Her recreation is in helping other people and she holds the universal esteem of all who have the privilege of knowing her, whether they be Jews or Gentiles. The assistance rendered by Mrs. Gintzburger to many of the newly arrived immigrants at the Port of Vancouver, will never be forgotten by them, and her timely aid has helped to place many needy persons on the road to prosperity. Mr. and Mrs. Gintzburger have one daughter, Miss Pauline Emma, and who holds the degree of Master of Arts from the University of British Columbia

COUNCIL OF JEWISH WOMEN, TORONTO SECTION

THE Toronto Section of the Council of Jewish Women was organized in 1897 with ten members under the leadership of Mrs. J. S. Cohen. They first met in private homes and as the membership increased, the scope of work carried on by the Council became much enlarged. Philanthropic work, operating a free sewing school for girls, and literary meetings are some of the activities carried on by the Council, which at the present time has a membership of four hundred, and is one of the most important factors in the philanthropic work of the community.

In 1909, the Council organized the Jewish Girls' Club, which from an initial membership of 9, has increased, until today, it has a membership of 1,025.

At the outbreak of War in 1914, the Council took an active part in Red Cross work, and many bundles of requisites were turned out by the busy members. Later, during the influenza epidemic, a soup kitchen was operated and nurses supplied, and help was given to the sufferers. The Council was also very active in Immigrant Aid Work, giving help and advice to newcomers, housing many temporarily in the Council Community House and helping to establish them in homes, and making them happy in their new country. Invaluable work is done in the community, sewing for the poor.

The Jewish Big Sister Movement, which looks after the Jewish girl is also doing splendid work. Hospitals are visited where the Jewish sick are taken care of. Study, music and social work are not neglected.

The Council Community House, located at 44 St. George Street, became the property of the Council in 1922. Here most of the activities of the Council take place, and the entire Jewish community makes use of this headquarters for various communal undertakings. Many societies use both the house and garden for meetings, and the Jewish Girls' Club with its many members and friends, has the house constantly filled with happy girls and boys. So popular is this Community Centre, that it already is inadequate for all its activities.

The Council meetings are held monthly, and are usually of an educational character. Speakers of note have brought valuable messages. Membership in the Council is open to all Jewish women. The present officers are:—Mrs. Julius Eisman, President; Mrs. A. I. Willinsky, 1st Vice-president; Mrs. Harry Marks, 2nd Vice-President; Mrs. Benj. Raz, Recording Secretary; Mrs. Lily Levetus, Corresponding Sec'y; Mrs. Joe Winters, Treasurer.

COUNCIL OF JEWISH WOMEN, VANCOUVER SECTION

IN March, 1924, a small group of ladies, headed by Mrs. Louise Mahrer, met to organize a local section of the National Council of Jewish Women. The need of an organization which could reach all groups of Jewish Women and supply inspiration in things Jewish and communal was discussed and endorsed.

Mrs. S. M. Blumauer of Portland, National organizer for this district was notified, and on April 2nd a luncheon was held at which she presided. Mrs. E. R. Sugarman was elected President; Mrs. H. Wagner, First Vice-President; Mrs. William Genser, Second Vice-President; Mrs. Mahrer, Hon. President; Mrs. H. Rosenbaum, Treasurer; Mrs. M. H. Brotman, Corresponding Secretary; and Mrs. J. Moloff, Recording Secretary. The membership began with thirty and at the end of six months reached ninety-two, showing that great interest had been aroused through splendid programmes held monthly when interesting speakers on important subjects addressed the Council.

Active work has been done for the newly arrived immigrant colony in co-operating with the local Hebrew Aid Society. Grocery showers have relieved distress and Council workers have actively assisted in the housing of this group. Later, by co-operating with the School Board, a graded night school for the immigrants was opened with a roll call of 28 pupils and two teachers, and great progress is reported.

The social Welfare Committee has answered all communal calls by assisting in Drives and Tag Days of the Victoria Order of Nurses, Children's Aid & Shelter, Poppy Day, etc. besides visiting Jewish sick and taking a special interest in the local Incurable Home by taking cheer and music regularly to these unfortunates.

During the Convention held in June, 1924, of the I.O.B.B. District No. 4, the Section welcomed the visiting delegates and wives of the delegates by holding a luncheon in their honor at which Dr. Jonah B. Wise was the speaker. It was an inspiring event and has helped to cement a splendid international feeling among the womenhood of the Pacific Coast, and was followed later by an invitation from the Portland Section to the President, Mrs. Sugarman, to speak in October at the opening meeting of the Portland Section.

Carrying out the religious programme, a study class on the Bible has been started, led by Mrs. E. R. Sugarman, and by the interest shown will become a permanent branch of Council effort. The Council also protested effectively against the proposal to teach religion in the public school, which was attempted in the fall of 1924.

By affiliating with the Local Council of Women and the League of Nations, the membership is in touch with movements for better legislation and a Council delegate attended the Provincial Legislature to join with the local service clubs in amending the Horse Racing Bill.

It can truly be said that Vancouver Jewish Womanhood has responded nobly to the Council motto "Faith and Humanity."

THE LATE MRS. EDITH JACOBS

A NOBLE woman who set an example of life that will always be an inspiration to the Jewish women of Toronto, the late Mrs. Edith Jacobs, wife of the late Rabbi Samuel Jacobs, was born in Birmingham, England in 1865, the daughter of Mr. and Mrs. Philip Cohen. Her early life was spent in London, England, and she accompanied her husband, as a bride, when he went to Jamaica in 1886. Much of Rabbi Jacob's success was due to the splendid co-operation and assistance given to him by his wife who devoted her entire lifetime to welfare and philanthropic work. After her arrival in Toronto, in 1901, Mrs. Jacobs occupied a prominent position among the women of this city. For over ten years she was Vice-President of the Local Council of Women, and for many years was Vice-President of the Big Sister Association. At one time she was President of the Council of Jewish Women. She was keenly interested in welfare work among the Jewish working girls, and with her husband organized the Jewish Girls' Club. Her object in this was to set up a standard of Jewish womanhood to guide unfortunate girls towards the paths of virtue, righteousness and usefulness. So intense was her interest in this work that she invited to her home the wayward girl in her efforts to demonstrate in a practical way, the beauty of life when applied in the proper way. Her kindness, broadness of religious thought, and eagerness to bring the ideal of womanhood to a higher plane, endeared her to all. Her entire life was one of self-sacrifice to the good of the community and right up to the time of her death, which occurred October 28th, 1923, Mrs. Jacobs worked amongst the poor, irrespective of their religious beliefs. Her death removed from the Jewish community of Toronto one of its most shining lights, and the City of Toronto lost a citizen whose place it will be very hard to fill. Mrs. Jacobs left one son, Arthur, and two daughters, Mrs. M. Sperber and Miss Ray Jacobs.

THE LATE MRS. H. (CAMILLA) LEVY

THE LATE MRS. HERMAN (CAMILLA) LEVY was born at Berncastel on the Moselle, Germany, October 28th, 1845, the daughter of the late Isaac and Johannah Scheuer. From her parents she received the religious upbringing that was so evident throughout her life, and from her mother she inherited the ideals of charity and service which characterized her entire career. She was married, September 6th, 1866, at Metz, France, to the late Herman Levy, and followed her husband, then a resident of Hamilton, Ont., where she lived until her death, which took place on January 14th, 1916. Mrs. Levy was an outstanding figure in welfare work in Hamilton. Her charity knew no bounds, and was extended to sufferers, irrespective of nationality, race, or creed. Many well-to-do families owe their present prosperity to her timely help and assistance. At different times she occupied high offices in the Victorian Aid Society, The Children's Aid, and the local branch of the National Council of Women. She was the founder and leading spirit in all the charitable activities in connection with the Anshe Sholom Congregation, (an institution founded by her husband and brother). Any appeal for assistance in illness or distress, at any hour of the day or night, enlisted her immediate attention. She was possessed of splendid organizing and executive ability, and she had a wonderful acumen in deciding quickly and firmly the course to be pursued in any emergency. Her greatest pleasure was service, and it was she to whom all turned when in trouble. A wonderful mother to her family and a true observing Jewess, she was a regular attendant at Divine Services, and her faith and piety set an example that was an inspiration to the entire community. Mrs. Levy was survived by three sons, Adolph S., Gabriel H., and Joseph, all prominent residents of Hamilton, one daughter, Mrs. Rose Rosentadt, and two brothers, Edmund and the late Benno Scheuer of Toronto.

OTTAWA LADIES' HEBREW BENEVOLENT SOCIETY

THE Ottawa Ladies' Hebrew Benevolent Society was formed in 1898 and was the first Jewish charitable organization in the Capital City. This organization was largely responsible to the untiring energy of the late Mrs. Aaron Rosenthal, who was appointed the first President of the institution and who held this office uninterruptedly until her death, which took place in 1922. The Society looked after all philanthropic undertakings in Ottawa, until the formation some years later, of the Ottawa Men's Hebrew Benevolent Society when the two organizations joined forces in attending to calls for assistance. Not only the indigent members of the community were looked after, but the Society also did invaluable work in rendering assistance to the newly-arrived immigrants. During the twenty-six years of its existence, the Society has accomplished an incalculable amount of work, and many a ray of sunshine has been brought into the lives of those found to be in want. One thing upon which this institution prides itself is the fact that never since it was started has it received one cent in monetary assistance from the civic authorities, or any other source with the exception of the men's society. It is the only organization doing charitable work in Ottawa, that has carried on without such assistance. The members deserve credit for the good work and great accomplishments of this Society, and among those who may be particularly mentioned are;—Mrs. Moses Bilsky, Honorary President; and Mrs. M. M. Davidson (Miss Beck Vineberg), who for over fifteen years has been the Honorary Secretary of this Society. The present officers are;—President, Mrs. A. J. Freiman; First Vice-President, Mrs. A. H. Coplan; Second Vice-President, Mrs. A. L. Florence; Third Vice-President, Mrs. W. Shenkman; Treasurer, Mrs. J. J. Marks; Secretary, Mrs. M. Davidson; Investigating Committee, Mesdames W. Abelson, R. Kaminsky and L. Davis; Sick Committee, Mrs. D. Mirsky and Mrs. A. H. Coplan; Wardrobe Committee, Mrs. M. Shenkman and Mrs. D. Epstein.

OTHER OTTAWA INSTITUTIONS

THE Jewish Women's League of Ottawa was formed in 1915. This organization was a sort of central outlet for the activities of the Jewish women of Ottawa, and when any cause demands the general support of the community, it is the League that superintends all activities.

The Girl Guides were organized in 1917. There are two very live companies in Ottawa who take part in field days, parades, etc. together with other companies of non-Jewish girls. Miss Ann Hozman and Miss Fanny Adler were the first two captains. The first two lieutenants were Miss Pearl Goldfield and Miss Bessie Stream, and the first six patrol leaders were; Miss Ray Goldsmith, Miss Esther Berger, Miss Beatrice Slonemsky, Miss Bertha Monson, Miss Freda Carlofsky and Miss Rose Max.

There are also Ladies' Auxiliaries of the Ottawa Synagogues. The Auxiliary of the King Edward Avenue Synagogue was organized in 1912 by a number of earnest workers comprising the wives and daughters of the members of the congregation. The Auxiliary undertakes the care of and provides for the renewal of furnishings of the synagogue and other similar duties. A delightful custom of the Auxiliary is that of presenting to daughters of members on the occasion of their marriage, a pair of candlesticks. The present officers are;—President, Mrs. A. J. Freiman; First Vice-President, Mrs. W. Shenkman; Second Vice-President, Mrs. B. Pearl; Third Vice-President, Mrs. M. Shenkman; Treasurer, Mrs. M. Davidson; Corresponding Secretary, Mrs. J. Davis; Recording Secretary, Miss Olive Pullan; Purchasing Committee, Mr. W. Abelson and Mrs. A. H. Coplan.

The Ladies' Auxiliary of the Rideau Street Synagogue was organized in 1913, and the ladies are doing their share in looking after the interests of the congregation, decorating the synagogue, supplying extra provisions when required, and other work of a similar nature. They have also looked to the wider activities of the community and have contributed to the Talmud Torah, Keren Hayesod and other good causes. The following are the present officers:—President, Mrs. M. B. Margosches; First Vice-President, Mrs. Henry Finkelstein; Second Vice-President, Mrs. M. Zelocowitz; Secretary, Miss Bessie Tapley; Treasurer, Mrs. Frank Slover.

The Ladies' Auxiliary of the Murray Street Synagogue was formed for the chief purpose of assisting in raising funds for the erection of the new synagogue, and the members have been very active also in all work pertaining to this institution. The present officers are:—President, Mrs. A. Smolkin, Sr.; Secretary, Mrs. D. Applebaum; Treasurer, Mrs. M. Friedman.

The Ladies' Auxiliary of the Ottawa Talmud Torah was formed to assist this institution in all that pertains to the good of the school. The Auxiliary takes a prominent part in the raising of any funds required, the distribution of prizes to the pupils, and other such work. The present officers are:—President, Mrs. A. J. Freiman; First Vice-President, Mrs. L. Leiken; Second Vice-President, Mrs. M. Loeb; Third Vice-President, Mrs. N. Roodman; Treasurer, Mrs. J. J. Marks; Recording Secretary, Miss S. Aronson; Members of the council, Mrs. A. H. Coplan, Mrs. H. Rosenes, Mrs. W. Abelson, Mrs. R. Kaminsky and Mrs. B. Pearl.

The Jewish women of Ottawa work hand in hand with all the Christian organizations in social service work. There is a committee which collaborates with the local Council of Women in such undertakings.

THE LATE MRS. A. ROSENTHAL

THE LATE MRS. AARON ROSENTHAL (Bertha Lehman) was born in Berlin, Germany in 1852, the daughter of the late Lewis Lehman of that city. On March 27th, 1867, while on a visit to Australia, she was married to the late Mr. A. Rosenthal, who for many years was one of the most prominent citizens of Ottawa. Mrs. Rosenthal came to Canada with her husband in 1876, and resided in Ottawa from 1879 until her death in 1922. She identified herself in many fields of welfare and charitable work, particularly in Jewish activities. She was one of the organizers and was president for over twenty years, of the Ladies' Hebrew Benevolent Society of Ottawa, this being the only organization doing charitable work which has carried on without assistance from the civic authorities. Some of the institutions that took up much of her time were; The Perley Home for Incurables, and The Ottawa General Hospital. Her charities and sympathies for whom she labored were unbounded and knew no creed, and the fruit of her work will live for many years. Mrs. Rosenthal set a very high standard of Jewish womanhood and her pleasure in life lay in bringing comfort to the needy and sick. Many people, who are today in affluent circumstances, owe their start in this country to the cheerful aid furnished by Mrs. Rosenthal. She was devotedly attached to the teachings of her faith, and left four sons, whose high standing in the community is an acknowledgment of her noble work. She taught the lesson of personal service for the public good, of living a sterling and upright life, and of respecting and revering the traditions of her people. During the War, Mrs. Rosenthal was indefatigable in her efforts to bring cheer and comfort to the oppressed Jews in the war areas of Europe, and also did an untold amount of work for the dependants of Canadian soldiers. She was an enthusiastic Zionist, and was a member of the Hadassah organization. She was also a member of the Disraeli Chapter, I.O.D.E.; The Jewish Women's League; and the Sinai League.

Ashley & Crippen

MRS. M. L. (VISE) WILLINSKY, TORONTO

A TRUE mother in Israel, and one of the representative and public-spirited members of the Toronto Jewish community, Mrs. Meyer L. Willinsky, who for many years has been one of the most active social service workers in Toronto, was born in Russia on August 29th, 1864. She is a daughter of Bernard Vise, and came to Toronto with her parents in 1869. She was educated in Toronto and was married, July 15th, 1883, to Meyer Lionel Willinsky, son of the late Abraham Irving Willinsky. Mrs. Willinsky has always been keenly interested in all activities pertaining to the welfare of Toronto Jewry and she has held office in most of the charitable institutions. She is an enthusiastic Zionist and this cause has taken up much of her time and energy. She was one of the organizers of the original Hadassah Chapter in Toronto, of which she has since been a member, and in 1923, in company with her husband, she travelled to Palestine, studying conditions in the Jewish Homeland. Her assistance is much sought in all communal undertakings and her activities are by no means confined to any one creed. She is one of the first members of the Council of Jewish Women; The Hebrew Ladies' Maternity Aid Society; The Jewish Consumptive Relief Society; and she is a convenor of the Jewish Orphanage. In 1922 she was given the signal honour of being made a "Mother" in the Phi Lambda Phi Fraternity, this being the first time in twenty-eight years that such an honour had been bestowed. She is much interested in the proper religious and secular education of the Jewish young, and herself gives strict adherence to the customs and faith of her forebears. To help the deserving and enable them to help themselves, to comfort the sick, and to right the path of the wayward, is the teaching and practice of Mrs. Willinsky. She is a member of the Goel Tzedec Synagogue, University Avenue. Mrs. Willinsky has two sons, Dr. A. I. Willinsky and Dr. Bernard Willinsky, and five daughters, Mrs. M. J. Kamin, Mrs. S. M. Mehr, Mrs. A. Jacobs, Mrs. S. Kronik, and Mrs. J. R. Lessor.

THE HEBREW YOUNG LADIES' BOOT AND SHOE SOCIETY

THE Hebrew Young Ladies' Boot & Shoe Society was organized in the year 1914 at a time when extra efforts were required to meet the calls for relief, owing to the crisis due to the outbreak of War. The Federation of Jewish Philanthropies was not then in existence, and the charities were distributed by many organizations that worked individually to raise funds, and made disbursements through the Co-operative Board System. The sums allotted were barely enough for sustenance and clothes, and warranted the formation of a society that would provide footwear for members of dependent families.

In the first year of the existence of the Society, which was also the year in which their resources were taxed the most, six hundred and thirty pairs of shoes, stockings, and many pairs of rubbers were distributed, and in the years following, two hundred and fifty pairs was the minimum average. The money raised for these articles was realized from social affairs and through the kindness of many friends of the Society, and throughout by the untiring efforts of the members who at all times worked in close harmony with the other charitable organizations.

In the year 1919, at the request of Mr. Kauffman, of the Federation of Jewish Philanthropies, the Boot and Shoe Society became affiliated with the Federation, and in compliance with the rules and regulations, carried on their work as a constituent member, having a convenor and representative on the Family Welfare Board, and each year subscribing to the Federation approximately two thirds of the cost of the shoes; also saving them a great deal of time and energy, as all purchases and business pertaining to the Society were carried out by its own members.

In addition to the above mentioned work, the social and educational end was not overlooked, each meeting including lectures and practical demonstrations of literature, art, music, drama, communal work, social service, etc.

The members also encouraged such sports as tennis and bowling amongst themselves. A feature of the social season of 1924 was the presentation of an Oriental Operatic Sketch and Musical Review, and the introduction into the Society of a monthly review entitled "The Boot & Shoe Tattler", edited by Miss Ethel Starkman.

The following is a partial list of the Societies that benefitted through the activities of the Boot and Shoe Society; the Red Cross Society, Big Sister Clubs, Ukranian Orphans' Relief, the Y.M. and Y.W.H.A., Palestine Implement Fund, and many others. A permanent cot in the Old Folks' Home, in memory of the late Miss Jenny Weinstein, who in her lifetime was an active member of this Society, was endowed. Books and accessories to the reading room of the Jewish Children's Home and Bronte Rest Home were furnished and hospitals were visited. The members of the Society assisted in the Talmud Torah Bazaar, the Hadassah Yard, and also supplied shoes to the Immigrant Aid Society. The members were always willing to assist in communal undertakings and have done much clerical work and canvassing for other institutions.

Ten years elapsed since the organization started on its unique career, before it closed its activities. During that time very many ladies had been of great assistance, among whom may be mentioned;—Mesdames L. Cadesky, H. Langer, M. Wagner, D. Lehrman, Charles Rosenblatt, E. Venus, G. Swerling, the late M. Gurofsky, and the Misses Isabella Behr, Molly Vise, Malca Halpern, Elizabeth Meinster, A. Midanik, A. Kamin, Thelma Weinberg, Ethel Starkman and the late J. Weinstein.

The organizer of the Boot and Shoe Society was Mrs. M. C. Friedman, and the different convenors were—Mrs. S. Tugendhaft, Mrs. Nelson Brody (Detroit), Mrs. Boris M. Speyer, Pres., and Miss M. Lieberman.

EZRAS NOSHEM SOCIETY, TORONTO

THE EZRAS NOSHEM SOCIETY was formed on August 9th, 1913, by the following ladies;—Mrs. Miller, Mrs. Adler, Mrs. Cohn, and Mrs. Spiegel. These ladies were appointed the first executive members, and Mrs. Miller was elected President. Mr. Spiegel was appointed Secretary.

The aims of this Society were first, Bichur Cholim, that is to say, in case of sickness of one of the members, the Society hired a woman to look after the sick, and to replace her in her household activities as well. The Society also helped its members financially, with what limits the treasury would allow. Each member of the Society must be present at the funeral of one of the other members.

After this Society had been in existence for three years, a number of the members founded the Old Folks' Home, which had its first meeting on January 21st, 1917. The members of the Society have contributed their time and large sums of money to the up-building of the Old Folks' Home, and even up to the present time, members of the Society are executive members of the Home.

In 1915, the Ezras Noshem Society contributed to the "Peretz School", at that time known as the "National Radical School". They also supported the Denver, Colorado Hospital for consumptives. The members of the Society were also active in the Ukranian Orphans' relief work, during the war.

In 1920, the Society considered the idea of building a Jewish hospital, where Jewish patients would be enabled to get Kosher food, and be understood when they spoke their own language. On December 6th, 1921, the Society purchased a building at 100 Yorkville Ave., which they converted into a hospital, and which bears the name of the Mount Sinai Hospital. This was done at a cost of $35,000.00, and up to May 1922, the Ezras Noshem Society paid $20,000.00 on the hospital, and the fixings amounted to $2,000.00. On October 10th, 1923, the hospital was officially opened and handed over to representatives selected by delegates of the various Jewish institutions in the city. On that occasion the Society presented the hospital executive with $1,000.00, and this was followed by a sterilizer valued at $800.00, and a further cash donation of $700.00.

The Society also operates a Free Loan for its members whereby any member has the privilege of borrowing up to $10.00 from the treasury, to be repaid in small instalments of fifty cents per week. In case of sickness, the members are entitled to a benefit, and each member is visited by a special committee appointed by the executive of the Society. The Society also supplies a car at the funeral of any member.

The dues of the Society are thirty-five cents per month. The Ezras Noshem Society contributes large sums of money to various charitable institutions both within and without the city.

The following are the present officers, having been elected July 1st, 1923; President, Mrs. Valikoff; 1st Vice-President, Mrs. Miller; 2nd Vice-President, Mrs. Dworkin; Treasurer, Mrs. Shapiro; Rec. Sec., Mrs. Wahrheit; 1st Trustee, Mrs. Greenberg; 2nd Trustee, Mrs. Katzman; and Fin. Sec., Mr. Louis Sugar.

TORONTO HEBREW LADIES' AID SOCIETY

WITH the true proverbial pride of the Jew, the immigrants who arrived in Canada during the '80's from Eastern Europe, lost no time in organizing synagogues, Talmud Torahs and charitable organizations. In this manner they ably proved their worth as good citizens, in showing that they were not desirous of placing upon the shoulders of their co-religionists who had preceded them to Toronto, the labor of taking care of them.

One of the first women's organizations of this kind organized in Toronto was the Toronto Hebrew Ladies' Aid Society. In 1899, a small group of women met in the Goel Tzedec Synagogue, then located at the corner of Elm Street and University Avenue, and discussed the problem of taking care of a widow and her children through a small weekly collection, and also how to meet the difficulty of providing for another recently bereaved widow. One of this group, Mrs. S. Lewis, who had recently arrived from Pittsburgh, where she had had considerable experience in the women's charitable organizations, proposed a similar idea to the Toronto ladies. The following day a meeting was called at the home of Mrs. Meyers on Adelaide Street, where it was decided to immediately commence a membership campaign. Among those present were; Mesdames Lewis, Meyers, Keyfitz, Rittenberg, Helpert and Antipitzky. The general enthusiasm with which women generally were entering into communal and state activities was evidenced by the business-like way this small band of Jewish women took hold of this new undertaking. The first returns of the membership campaign showed sixty enrolled members, and the organization meeting took place in Shaftsbury Hall, corner of James and Queen Streets.

In view of the responsibility assumed by the Society, it was agreed that the President should be a man, and Mr. L. Levinsky was elected to this office, which he ably filled for three terms. The other original officers were;— Vice-Pres., Mrs. Meyers; Secretary, Mrs. S. Lewis; Treas., Mrs. N. Keyfitz, and Executive Committee; Mesdames Lieberman, S. Simonski, I. Rittenberg, Yanover, Ruben, B. Cooper, Antipitzky, Stein, I. Cooper, Messenger, Cohen, Black, Shaligalsky, Helpert and Landsberg.

The dues were originally set at twenty-five cents monthly, and the Society had a very fine volunteer system of collection. This was its chief support from start to finish. Later however they held the usual benefit social affairs in order to raise funds to keep abreast the increased needs brought about through further immigration. The annual ball, concert and picnic to Oakville are events long to be remembered.

The Society received a momentary setback when some members withdrew and formed the Austrian Ladies' Aid and the Polish Ladies' Aid. This step caused considerable regret, bringing an unnecessary division in the small community. Nevertheless, being a growing community, the Society was able to overcome this and once more go forward to its deeds of mercy. It was the fundamental principle of the workers to carry out the five Jewish teachings of the Talmud in their distribution to the needy. Such teachings were the only Social Service knowledge possessed by these workers, but who will say that even today they can be improved upon?

In 1911, owing to the difficult period caused by the economic crisis, the members of the Society felt the need of an improved system of relief and they decided to join other organizations in the form of a Co-operative Board, where the recipients of charity would receive their assistance from one source only, in this manner avoiding the danger of overlapping. Although movements in the past towards amalgamation had met with decided dissent, this newly formed Board, known as the Associated Charities, was regarded favorably. The Board consisted of three representatives of each relief Society and met every Monday evening at the Associated Charities Building, 218 Simcoe Street. The Associated Charities later developed into the Federation of Jewish Philanthropies, whose headquarters are also at the same address.

The first years of the War again brought on disturbed economic conditions and the members of the Society were forced to appeal to the community at large. They thus welcomed the movement towards Federation that tended to bring increased interest towards charity and more substantial assistance to the poor. In accepting Federation, the members of the Toronto Hebrew Ladies' Aid Society realized that their organization would naturally disband. Many were the regrets expressed, but these women thought only of what would be to the best advantage of the Jewish poor, and they had the satisfaction of having accomplished things. They therefore gave the Federation the same loyal support that they had always given their own Society. It was in 1916 that the Society turned over the balance in its treasury to the newly formed Federation, closing its books of over six hundred members. This was a decided acquisition to the Federation and had a considerable part in assuring its successful operation.

Mr. P. Levi succeeded Mr. Levinsky as President, and was succeeded in turn by Mrs. Harris. This lady was followed as President by Mr. I. Brodey, who held office for ten years, and to whom much of the growth of the Society was due. Upon his retirement, Mrs. D. Lavine was elected President, and she served for two years. Mrs. S. Lewis then held the office, and she acted as President for three years up to the close of this institution.

THE LATE MRS. A. LANDSBERG

THE LATE MRS. A. LANDSBERG (Rebecca Fox), in her lifetime one of the most active communal workers in Toronto, was born in Biebrusk, Russia, in 1866, the daughter of the late Labe Wolf Fox. She received her education in her native city, and was married in 1882, to Abraham, son of Micha Landsberg, and had three sons, Jack of Los Angeles; Maurice of Detroit; and Dr. Harry of Toronto; and six daughters, Mrs. L. Wolman, Mrs. W. Wolman and Mrs. A. Herbert of Toronto; Mrs. S. Greenfarb and Mrs. E. Cowan of Los Angeles; and Mrs. L. Green of Peterboro. Mrs. Landsberg came to Canada in 1894 with her husband and five children, and lived in Toronto until her death, which took place on February 20th, 1917. At the time of her arrival, there were very few Jewish families, and it was not until five years later that the need for Jewish charitable institutions arose. When the Ladies' Aid Society was formed, Mrs. Landsberg was one of the first chosen on the board of the Investigating Committee, on which she served until her death. This Society was kept together by small collections which were made from door to door by a committee, of which she was a member. Besides doing her share of collecting, she took a keen interest in investigating each individual case and personally called on every recipient of charity, every week. No holiday was complete without her share being added to the charity allowed the poor by the organization. She was one of the organizers and Vice-President of the Jewish Children's Home, then located at 218 Simcoe Street, and devoted much of her time and energy to this institution in helping to provide for the needs of the orphans. Mrs. Landsberg will be remembered as being the first Jewish woman in Toronto to be honored by a service in the synagogue at the time of her death. She was instrumental in raising funds to purchase the first Jewish hearse in Toronto. Mrs. Landsberg was a life-long member of the McCaul Street Synagogue.

HEBREW LADIES' MATERNITY AID SOCIETY, TORONTO

THE HEBREW LADIES' MATERNITY AID AND CHILD WELFARE SOCIETY was organized in 1908, and was an outgrowth of a sewing school for children, held to counteract missionary activities, and was known in its early days as the Hebrew Ladies' Sewing Society. It claimed amongst its organizers many of Toronto's most prominent women, whose earnest interest has helped to make it the success it is today.

The main object of the new society was and still is to give every possible comfort to mothers and babies, prenatal cases being particularly stressed. To every needy expectant mother, nourishing delicacies are sent. Bed linen, baby layette, and clothes for the mother are distributed. Where it is impossible for a mother to go to the hospital, care of doctor, nurse and hired help is provided. Finding that many difficulties often prevented a mother from regaining her health, the society extended its interests, and provided children with shoes and stockings, no deserving application being refused. The happy little faces of the proud possessors of new shoes, is a joyful remembrance that many of the society will carry with them a long time. This end of the work was later handed over to the then newly formed Hebrew Young Ladies' Boot and Shoe Society, which after carrying on successfully for a few years, was disbanded in 1924.

Another activity of the society was bringing cheer to the women and children at the Weston Sanitarium. This was an arrangement with the T. Eaton Co. for the weekly shipment of eggs and fruit to all Jewish patients, not forgetting their neighbors. Weekly visits are paid to the Sanitarium; a cot was endowed in the name of the organization, funds being raised through individual contributions. They were the first society in the city to do this.

Assistance towards the other institutions of the city was given, by help in the annual tag day.

Upon the formation of the Hebrew National Association, and the recently organized Hebrew Weston Sanitarium Society, the assistance given by the Hebrew Maternity Aid was transferred to these organizations, with the exception of the maintenance of the cot, already mentioned.

After the Ladies' Aid Society was disbanded, the Hebrew Maternity Aid Society took over much of their work, which it still carries on, such as bringing personal interest in relief work, and seeing that each needy family's requirements on Pesach are looked after.

At the time that the introduction of the medical inspection in public schools was being talked of, the Hebrew Maternity Aid Society was already in co-operation with school teachers, providing clothing, milk and eggs for undernourished children, and generally acting as a go-between home and school. With the ushering in of medical inspection, the society brought forward suggestions of a mothers' club, conducted in Yiddish, which was readily accepted and put into force by the then nurse of the schools, Miss Jamieson, now Provincial Supervisor of Medical Health Nurses, and a great friend of the Jewish poor.

Undertaking to provide eye-glasses where required, food delicacies for children and all things called for, the society branched out into the most important department of its activities, under the name of "Child Welfare."

The President of the Society made many visits with the district nurse to the homes of the poor, acting as interpreter, and her presence opened many doors to the nurse, which otherwise were closed through the fear and suspicion entertained towards them by the poor Jews, who still had the horrible remembrances of Russia, etc. in their minds.

The society was among the first to join the Home and School Council, and received the warmest commendation for the educational work so successfully carried out for adults.

Since no adequate provision for Jewish dependent infants is made, the society looks after placing them in foster homes, under the supervision of the Health Department. Several babies have been placed out for adoption, where they are enjoying every care from devoted and capable foster parents.

For many years the society has given annual picnics to from five hundred to one thousand Jewish children.

Some years ago, the society co-operated with the Local Council of Women in their pure milk distribution, assisting in looking after a distributing centre in the Jewish district.

Such whole-hearted interest in the welfare of the less fortunate, kept many of the members constantly planning in their behalf, with the result that three years ago, a long dreamed of plan for a summer vacation home for mothers and babies became a reality. This is the newest additional activity of the society, and is the source of great pride as it has proven a great life saver. After enjoying two to four weeks of good food, scientific care, healthful air and pleasant surroundings, many mothers and children, who were tired, despondent and anaemic, are sent back home once more able to go on with their battle in life. In the three years since its inception, one hundred and forty-five mothers and three hundred and twenty-five children have spent their vacation at Bronte Home, at the cost of over seven thousand dollars, of which some two thousand have been received through the courtesy of the Star Fresh Air Fund, the balance being raised by the society. Mrs. M. S. Till has been the convenor of this important branch of work.

The society also makes the proud claim of having been of much assistance in the formation of the Federation, as the then President of the society sent the first letter of appeal to the public for the need of such an institution in the city. The society was among the first to join the Federation, and is today one of its contributories.

Interesting and largely-attended meetings are held regularly on the last Tuesday of the month, at the Zionist Institute, where in addition to transaction of business, a speaker is heard, dealing with educational questions. Semi-monthly executive meetings are held, where the important business of the Maternity Aid and Child Welfare and Rest Home, is carefully gone into. A sewing meeting is held every Tuesday afternoon at the Goel Tzedec Synagogue, University Avenue.

The society is affiliated with the Local Council of Women, Home and School Council, Child Welfare Council, and Neighborhood Workers, and takes interest in every communal activity, non-Jewish as well as Jewish.

Mrs. I. H. Siegel is the organizer and was the first President, and she has been succeeded by Mrs. Anna Selick, Mrs. S. Helpert and Mrs. H. Clavir.

The present officers of the society are;—Mrs. H. Clavir, President; Mrs. M. S. Till, 1st Vice-President and Convenor of the Rest Home; Mrs. S. Lewis, 2nd Vice-President and Convenor of the Sewing; Mrs. Narrol, 3rd Vice-President and Convenor of Relief Work; and Mrs. L. Yolles, 4th Vice-President and Convenor of the Weston Sanitarium Cottage Fund.

MRS. IDA (LEWIS) SIEGEL, TORONTO

MRS. I. H. SIEGEL (IDA LEWIS), one of the most prominent welfare workers in Toronto, was born in Pittsburgh, Pa., the daughter of Mr. and Mrs. Samuel and Hannah (Ticktin) Lewis. She received her education at the public schools in Pittsburgh and in Toronto, to which city she came with her parents, as a child. In 1905, she was married to Isidore H. Siegel, son of the late Mr. D. I. Siegel, and has two sons, David and Avrom, and four daughters, the Misses Rohoma, Leah Gittle, Sarah and Rivka Siegel. Mrs. Siegel first became interested in the old Ladies' Aid Society of Toronto. She was the organizer of most of the women's Zionist organizations in Toronto, among them being the Daughters of Zion and Herzl Girls. She organized the Zionist Sunday School and Sewing School, the Ladies' Sewing Circle, which afterwards developed into the Hebrew Ladies' Maternity Aid Society, and was instrumental in the formation of the co-operative Board of Charities. Mrs. Siegel was also instrumental in the formation of the Jewish Dispensary of Toronto and in the organizing of the Hadassah. She took a prominent part in the formation of the Federation of Jewish Philanthropies, Toronto. Another institution that owes its existence largely to the interest taken by Mrs. Siegel, is the Young Men's and Young Women's Hebrew Association. Mrs. Siegel has always been a member of the University Avenue Synagogue, and she organized the Ladies' Auxiliary in connection with this congregation, and was also instrumental in forming the Toronto branch of the Women's League of the United Synagogues of America. Her activities have by no means been sectarian, and she has been very active in the Home and School Council since its inception. Mrs. Siegel was the first Treasurer of the Child's Welfare Council of Toronto, and she organized the first Home and School Club amongst Jewish mothers. She was also founder of the Young Women's Hebrew Choir, which has developed to a large extent, the musical ability of the younger Jewish people.

DAUGHTERS OF ISRAEL, ST. JOHN, N.B.

TWENTY-FIVE years ago, in 1900, a number of the Jewish ladies of St. John met at the residence of Mrs. I. Isaacs and formed themselves into an organization for the purpose of attending to such charitable needs as were required in the community, having social intercourse, studying the questions of the day as far as Judaism was concerned, and in all ways doing everything possible to improve the conditions of the less fortunate among them.

The real founder of the organization, which called themselves The Daughters of Israel, was Mrs. Alice Hart, the wife of one of the pioneer Jewish residents of the city, and she was appointed the first president of the society. A woman noted for her nobility of mind and soul and love for all that was right, she rallied the women around her and secured their undivided devotion and assistance. No call of distress was left unanswered, no plea for help was ever unheard. The needy of the community were the first consideration, and as the society has steadily grown it has kept faith with all the traditions of the founders.

At the beginning there was not much call for assistance and the members of the society made small monthly contributions, which were sufficient for their needs, but as the years passed, St. John became the principal winter port of the country, and the amount of work, due to the arrival of Jewish immigrants, became much greater. The members rose nobly to the task involved, and it is characteristic that they taxed themselves with additional dues, to meet the increased requirements.

THE LATE MRS. SOLOMON HART

Not only the transient immigrants needed attention, but the Jewish population of the city grew rapidly, and the increase being recruited largely from the immigrants, the calls for assistance became more urgent and came with greater frequency. The Daughters of Israel were not dismayed at the task they had assumed, but like their sisters in other communities in Canada simply devoted more time, energy, and financial assistance to their society, and met the additional calls.

Practically every Jewish society in St. John, and there are several, owes its inception to The Daughters of Israel, for these first daughters had become mothers, and their children were brought up in an atmosphere of self-sacrifice, charity, and religion. The Hadassah, the Young Judaeans, the Young Women's and Young Men's Hebrew Associations are all composed of the children of the members of The Daughters of Israel, all instilled with the same spirit of charity displayed at all times by their parents.

A daughter of the founder, Mrs. Wyzanski, acted as the first secretary of the society, and continued in office until her departure to another city, at one time also holding the presidency, to which she succeeded on the death of her mother. She was followed as President by Mrs. Louis Green, (another daughter of the founder), Mrs. Wm. Levi, Mrs. J. Marcue, Mrs. J. Goldman, Mrs. L. N. Harris, and the present President, Mrs. D. Bassen.

Other organizations are the TALMUD TORAH AUXILIARY and the YOUNG WOMEN'S HEBREW ASSOCIATION.

THE NORTH END LADIES' AID SOCIETY, ST. JOHN, N.B.

THE North End Ladies' Aid Society was organized about 1912, with some twenty members.

The main object of this Society was to raise funds for the needy of the city, and they co-operated in this respect with the Ladies' Benevolent Society and the Daughters of Israel. It has since also on very many occasions, been of assistance in raising funds for outside relief work, the Keren Hayesod and other institutions.

The membership today is about eighty, and the club dues have been fixed at twenty-five cents per month.

This Society does very valuable work, and it would not be fair to single out any special members for mention, as they all take the same active interest. The President of the Society is Mrs. H. Jacobson.

HALIFAX WOMEN'S ACTIVITIES

THE first ladies' organization formed in Halifax to perform charitable work was the HEBREW LADIES' AID SOCIETY, of which Mrs. Byalin is President. It was organized to afford succor to the needy of the community and particularly to look after immigrants arriving at the Port of Halifax. THE HEBREW LADIES' BENEVOLENT SOCIETY is another organization with similar purposes. It was organized in January, 1924, under a Dominion charter. The President of this Society is Mrs. H. Ehman.

LADIES' AID SOCIETY, CALGARY

THE Ladies' Aid Society, the first Jewish charitable organization in Calgary, was organized in 1906 under the presidency of Mrs. A. Suratt. It was established at a time when the first considerable influx of Jewish immigration to Calgary took place, and devoted itself in its early days to giving care and attention to the new arrivals.

As the population increased the demands on the Society became greater and the scope of its activities was much enlarged. The members assisted in the formation of the Talmud Torah, as they had previously done when the synagogue was built, and in all communal undertakings they did their share. During the great influenza epidemic the members of the Society worked in the soup kitchen that was opened at the Zionist Hall, under the leadership of Mrs. B. Ginsberg, who remained in charge until she herself was taken ill. The Jewish soup kitchen became known as the best in the city, and there was no discrimination by the Society between Jew and non-Jew.

During the War the members assisted in the collection of funds for the relief of war sufferers and for the Patriotic Society and Red Cross Society. When Ukranian orphans were brought to Canada, the members also did their share towards the expenses of the undertaking, and they have also been of much assistance to the Zionist organization, in their different campaigns.

It might be said that Calgary was the first Canadian city to organize for the relief of European war sufferers, and during the five years that funds were being raised for this purpose, the Jews of Calgary sent away many thousands of dollars. Mr. B. Ginsberg was the local chairman of that campaign.

In addition to monthly contributions to the Talmud Torah, the Ladies' Aid Society co-operate with the Jewish Council of Women and other women's organizations in Calgary. At the present time their budget is over $2,000 per annum.

HEBREW LADIES' AID SOCIETY, SASKATOON

THE Hebrew Ladies' Aid Society of Saskatoon was organized in 1912, under the Presidency of Mrs. H. Reinhorn. The original membership was about sixteen and the Society came into existence in order to cope with the demands for charity made necessary by an increasing Jewish population. The Society has progressed rapidly and includes in its membership practically all the Jewish women of Saskatoon.

Much effort was expended by the members in the furtherance of the plans which resulted in the building of the synagogue and the acquisition of the Talmud Torah building. The installation of the Mikvah is also partly due to their efforts. Their activities have continuously spread into wider fields and today cover most of the activities of a social and communal nature in the city. There are sub-committees which comprise auxiliaries to both the synagogue and Talmud Torah. The membership of the Hadassah is also recruited from the ranks of the Ladies' Aid Society.

The present officers of the Society are:—President, Mrs. N. Adilman; Vice-President, Mrs. L. Singer; Treasurer, Mrs. H. Sklar; and Secretary, Mrs. D. Ellis.

LADIES' AUXILIARY OF TEMPLE EMANU-EL, VANCOUVER, B.C.

THE Ladies' Auxiliary of Temple Emanu-El, is a small society of Jewish women formed some fifteen years ago, to assist Congregation Temple Emanu-El in their activities.

This little circle of about twenty active women, meet weekly, for the purpose of sewing for any necessary cause.

During the years of the war, this Auxiliary affiliated with the local Red Cross, and did Red Cross work exclusively for a period of four years. It was during this period, that these weekly gatherings were obliged to hold their meetings in rented halls, as private homes were found inadequate.

Immediately following the war, the activities of the society were turned to the Ukranian sufferers, and garments for the little children were sent in quantities, through the Hadassah Society, to their proper destination.

From that time to the present, the auxiliary is always ready to meet any call for clothing or help in any manner, either among our own people, or for any needy cause that comes to their attention.

Monthly bridge teas are held for the purpose of augmenting their funds, in addition to providing pleasant social gatherings. Sales of home cooking and sales of art needlework, public dinners and dances are held frequently for the same purpose.

It was a leading member of this society, Mrs. E. R. Sugarman, who ably formed a Sabbath School, composed of voluntary teachers from the Auxiliary. This Sabbath School is a great success, and concerts and plays are presented by the children on every important holiday or festival.

The great ambition of the society is to help the men to erect a Semi-Reform Synagogue, and to assist them in every possible way when this building is completed.

The officers for the present year are: Mrs. S. Gintzburger, President; Mrs. L. A. Rostein, Vice-President; Mrs. M. Koenigsberg, Treasurer; Mrs. Max M. Grossman, Secretary; Executive Board, Mrs. M. Plant, Mrs. S. Blackson and Mrs. E. Healman.

JEWISH ENDEAVOUR SEWING SCHOOL, MONTREAL

IN the year 1902, the Jewish Endeavour Sewing School was formed through the united efforts of Rev. Dr. H. Abramowitz, Mrs. Lyon Cohen and Miss Sophia Hirsch. At that time the Jewish missions were making every effort to lure the young girls from their faith offering them many inducements to attend their sewing schools, when some of the ladies of Montreal saw the necessity of organizing a sewing school to counteract this alarming state of affairs. With this object in view, Dr. Abramowitz, Mrs. Cohen, and Miss Hirsch, on December 12th, 1902, asked some of those girls to meet them, with the result that the Jewish Endeavour School came into being and it was arranged to hold weekly classes, the girls coming after their school work was over.

The first year was started with 90 pupils and 9 teachers, and the school kept growing from year to year, until at the opening of the 1924-25 session there was an attendance of 229 pupils and 27 teachers. It was found that not only must every endeavour be made to keep the girls by means of sewing, but that it was very essential to teach them honour, manners, cleanliness and neatness. Many obstacles were encountered at first, but nearly all have been overcome, and the Jewish Endeavour Sewing School has proved its worth and use to the community. From year to year different ideas and plans for improvement were tried with the result that during the last few years it has been found best to confine the work to plain sewing and a dressmaking class. The girls are taught to sew flannelette and cotton garments, such as drawers, petticoats and night-gowns, all sewn by hand. All materials, as well as the necessary accessories such as thimbles, thread, scissors and so forth are furnished by the School, and as each garment is completed the maker may take it home upon payment of a nominal sum. When the girl has been found proficient in hand sewing and has made the required number of undergarments she is allowed to join the dressmaking class. For this the pupils bring their own materials and are shown how to cut out and make them. Some continue to make one garment after another, perhaps a dress for a younger sister, a bed jacket for her mother, or anything to which her fancy turns, and in this way some of the little girls who first learn to hold their needles at the Jewish Endeavour Sewing School become very efficient dressmakers. For the first fifteen years materials were supplied through small contributions received from the patronesses and members, but in the year 1917, when Federation was formed, the school became affiliated with it, not as a charitable organization but under the educational activities, and since then materials are supplied by Federation.

The classes meet every Monday afternoon from 3 to 5.30 o'clock in the assembly hall of the Baron de Hirsch Institute. There is no expense whatever attached to the school outside of the material, as all the teachers are volunteers who take great delight in their work. On Chanuka and Purim the girls are always given an address, usually by Dr. Abramowitz; also a box of candies is given to each child, the gift of some kind friends. At the closing, usually held in May, the work is displayed for inspection, and prizes, in the form of books are given for the best work, also for attendance. A special prize is given by each teacher, apart from these, to one of her class for whatever form of progress she sees fit. Also on this day the children are given a treat of ice cream and cake.

Three classes have also been formed at the Hebrew Orphans' Home on Claremont Avenue, under the supervision of the school, where three teachers go every Monday afternoon to instruct the pupils.

The Executive Board for the year 1924-25 is as follows:—Mrs. Lyon Cohen, President; Mrs. Jos. Levinson, First Vice-President; Mrs. N. Silver, Second Vice-President; Mrs. N. J. Fraid, Third Vice-President; Miss Sophia Hirsch, Treasurer; Mrs. Maurice Greenblatt, Secretary.

WOMEN'S ORGANIZATIONS IN HAMILTON

THE first Jewish women's organization formed in Hamilton was the DEBORAH LADIES' AID SOCIETY, which was organized in 1878, by the late Mrs. Herman Levy. At that time there was no call for philanthropic work among the Jewish residents of that city, and the Society, which was composed of the wives of the members of the Anshe Sholom Congregation, acted as an auxiliary to the congregation, supplying necessities, decorations, etc. As the Jewish population of the city increased, largely due to immigration, the Society rendered relief to the needy and looked after all cases of want. Mrs. Herman Levy, the founder, became the first President, which office she held until her death, which took place on January 14th, 1916. The Society has a present membership of over fifty ladies, who meet regularly every month. They assist materially in the work of the Sunday School of the Anshe Sholom Congregation, as well as in the undertakings of the United Hebrew Charities. The present officers are:—President, Mrs. M. Simon; Vice-President, Mrs. J. Bloom; Treasurer, Mrs. J. Ruben; and Secretary, Mrs. M. Silverman.

THE HAMILTON SECTION OF THE COUNCIL OF JEWISH WOMEN was organized in 1922, and has been very active since its inception. It has a membership of over eighty, who take an interest in the social welfare of the community. General meetings are held monthly, and executive meetings, bi-monthly. The officers of the council are;—President, Mrs. M. Levy; First Vice-President, Mrs. M. Beube; Second Vice-President, Mrs. B. Epstein; Third Vice-President, Mrs. S. Needle; Treasurer, Mrs. Rose Levy; Financial Secretary, Mrs. S. B. Lyons; Secretary, Miss Lillian Goldstein; and Assistant Secretary, Miss Belle Cohen.

THE DAUGHTERS OF ISRAEL SOCIETY was organized both as a Sisterhood of the Hess Street Synagogue and as a charitable organization. The members meet regularly once a month and assist in all philanthropic undertakings in the community. The officers are:—President, Mrs. M. Grossberg; Treasurer, Mrs. M. Lax; and Secretary, Mrs. D. Levy.

There are also Sisterhoods in connection with the other synagogues, and the women of Hamilton do much of the work required by the various charitable, social, and Zionistic activities.

JEWISH GIRLS' CLUB, TORONTO

ON FEBRUARY 1st, 1909, at the suggestion of the late Rabbi Solomon Jacobs, and through the generosity of friends, the Council of Jewish Women, assisted by the Junior Council, opened rooms at 36 Walton Street as a recreational centre for Jewish working girls.

The first convenor was Miss Kate Josephi. Nine girls registered at the first meeting and for the first few months, two nights a week were devoted to the work. The first report given in May 1909, stated that up to that date, 43 girls had registered and the largest attendance any evening was 23. Most of the members were new arrivals in this country and unable to speak English. The committee in charge seeing great possibilities to broaden the work, decided to establish permanent classes in English and sewing, and in order to give the community an opportunity of assisting, annual subscriptions were solicited.

The Club had phenomenal growth, and the second annual report showed a total attendance of 1,540, with a weekly average of 61. The third year the rooms were entirely inadequate for the work and it was decided to move into larger quarters. A few friends guaranteed the rent and in October 1913, the Club moved to 254 McCaul Street, which was formally opened by the Rt. Hon. Sir Herbert Samuel, at that time Postmaster General of England.

The Club was first founded as a recreation centre where the girls could spend their evenings. At the request of the members themselves, classes for the study of English, as well as sewing classes were organized. Saturday evenings were devoted to social gatherings, where members could bring their boy friends. Another evening was added for dancing and calisthenics.

In the year 1914, 165 girls enrolled and there were over 3000 who attended during that year. In 1915, the attendance nearly doubled and it was not unusual to find from 100 to 150 girls gathered together for instruction in English.

Up to this time all the work had been done by volunteers and it was then decided that a paid social worker was needed to supervise the work. In 1917, Miss Adelaide Cohen, the lady who is at present in charge of this undertaking, was appointed to the position. During the succeeding years, the work of the Club increased until the quarters at 254 McCaul Street were too small, and after the purchase of the Council Community House at 44 St. George Street, the Jewish Girls' Club was installed there.

The membership is now 1,030 with an average monthly attendance of 3,500. There are classes in English, sewing, cooking, typewriting and shorthand, civics and citizenship, dressmaking, athletics and folk dancing, guide work (of which there are seven companies), home nursing, dramatics, and Jewish literature. To these are added the recreational afternoons for the younger children and evenings for the older girls, when they may have all their boy friends, also walking parties are participated in. On Sunday evenings, the members of the Club and their friends meet for health talks, lectures and educational movies. There have been twenty of these evenings this season and at each prominent speakers have given their services. The various organized clubs within the Club are active in the social welfare of the community.

THE HEBREW LADIES' SEWING SOCIETY, MONTREAL

THE HEBREW LADIES' SEWING SOCIETY of Montreal has been in existence for some thirty years, and it is an organization which works indefatigably and sincerely for the welfare of the needy. It has perhaps the least amount of publicity of any society in Montreal, and yet is one of the most deserving. The personnel and original system of routine has naturally changed with the times, and today, the Society is a constituent of the Federation of Jewish Philanthropies. However, the worthy objects that originally were the aim of the founders have been strictly adhered to. These consist of making of garments for the poor and needy of the Montreal community.

During the past three years, other sewing groups have co-operated with this Society, and have created a "Sewing Day" for all, which is a very satisfactory arrangement. The various Societies which have joined forces are:- The Sisterhood of the Spanish and Portuguese Synagogue, The Ladies' Auxiliary of the Shaar Hashomayim Synagogue, The Sisterhood of the Temple Emanu-El, and the Grace Aguilar Chapter, I.O.D.E. Under the able and efficient convenorship of Mrs. A. B. Vineberg, President of The Hebrew Ladies' Sewing Society, and her staunch assistants, these ladies' societies are showing remarkable devotion to a good cause, and may be seen at least every Tuesday, and other days when "rush orders" are in demand, from early morning until evening, at work at the cutting tables, sewing machines, and plying the needle, repairing hundreds of garments for the needy.

The weekly meetings of this Society start in October and continue until May.

The following are among those institutions that benefit from the Society:- The Family Welfare, Hebrew Orphans' Home, The Sheltering and Old People's Home, The Hebrew Maternity Hospital, The Grace Aguilar Chapter, I.O.D.E., and the Victorian Order of Nurses. Those institutions that are not affiliated with the Federation provide their own materials.

In former years, when the Society was still young, there was an annual dance given, the proceeds of which went to the buying of materials, but since affiliating with the Federation, a yearly budget has been granted the Society to operate on.

For thirty years, the headquarters of The Hebrew Ladies' Sewing Society were in the Baron de Hirsch Institute, but a year ago they were fortunate to secure a very comfortable and spacious room in the Shaar Hashomayim Community Centre.

The following are the officers for the present year:- Hon. Pres., Miss E. Hirsch; Hon. Vice-Pres., Mrs. D. Davis; Pres., Mrs. A. B. Vineberg; 1st Vice-Pres., Mrs. D. Fels; 2nd Vice-Pres., Mrs. J. Newmann; 3rd Vice-Pres., Mrs. Regal; Treas., Mrs. J. Gittleson; Rec. Sec., Miss Dorothy Kellert; Corresponding Secretary, Mrs. Ross Vineberg.

THE LADIES' AUXILIARY OF THE HEBREW MATERNITY HOSPITAL, MONTREAL

ON December 2nd, 1920, Mr. Markus Markus, late President of the Hebrew Maternity Hospital, asked a few ladies to meet him at the Hospital for the purpose of forming a Ladies' Auxiliary in connection with the Hospital. There were twenty ladies present, Mr. Markus was in the chair, and after pointing out the reasons for forming the Auxiliary, it was decided by all present to form such an organization under the name of "Ladies' Auxiliary of the Hebrew Maternity Hospital" and a meeting immediately took place for the purpose of electing officers, the following being elected:—Mrs. Alton Goldbloom, President; Mrs. Jos. Kellert, Vice-President; Mrs. I. B. Hirshberg, Treasurer; Mrs. Maurice Greenblatt, Secretary; Board of Directors:—Mrs. M. Markus, Mrs. B. Freedman, Mrs. T. Glickman, Mrs. Geo. Rabinovitch, Mrs. Jos. Greenberg, Mrs. H. Bloomfield, Mrs. A. J. Bloomfield, Mrs. H. Frankel, Mrs. A. Yaphe, Mrs. B. Goldman, Mrs. T. S. Zeave, Miss Annie Lauterman. Mr. Markus pointed out the reasons for forming this organization, which were to look after the various branches of the institution, such as pre-natal cases, after confinement, social service work, investigating the dietary and sanitary conditions of the Hospital, and supplying the linen and kitchen utensils.

Board meetings are held the last Thursday of each month, (except in June, July and August) and general meetings, the first Thursday in November, January and March. Starting with a membership of twenty the Auxiliary has grown from year to year until today there is a membership of nearly eight hundred paid-up members. Various committees, such as House, Social Service, and Membership Committees have been formed and added to from time to time.

Election of officers takes place every second year at the annual meeting in January. At each general meeting a very prominent speaker is procured who gives some very interesting talks on various subjects connected with hospital work. The Donation Committee sees that the hospital is well supplied with delicacies of all kinds. In this connection a shower is held every spring and enough jam, preserves and canned goods received to supply the Hospital for an entire year, a sufficient allowance being sent each week to the Hospital by the chairman of this committee.

The Floral Committee see that the Hospital is supplied with plants and flowers. The Social Service Committee investigate all public cases given them by the Hospital, going to the homes both before and after confinement. The Membership Committee have been instrumental in building up the large membership as it stands today and in placing the Auxiliary in a sound financial condition. A committee also looks after the cutting of all materials, for the infant supplies, doctors' gowns, sheets and pillow cases, and the greater part of the sewing is done by the Ladies' Sewing Society which meets every Tuesday at the Shaar Hashomayim Synagogue.

The Officers and Board for 1925-1927 are as follows: Mrs. A. Goldbloom, Hon. President; Mrs. M. Markus; Hon. Vice-President; Mrs. D. Tannenbaum, President; Mrs. Jos. Kellert, First Vice-President; Mrs. M. Rabinovitch, Second Vice-President; Mrs. L. Solomon, Treasurer; Mrs. B. Freedman, Asst. Treasurer; Mrs. M. Greenblatt, Secretary. Board of Directors:—Mrs. A. Yaphe, A. M. Wener, S. Hart, B. Rubin, D. M. Chorlton, Geo. Blumenthal, I. B. Hirshberg, J. L. Gittleson, L. W. Jacobs, B. Aaron, I. A. Kaufman, J. Usher, M. A. Pierce, and Miss Libbie Jacobs. House Committee:—Mrs. Jos. Greenberg, Chairman; Donation Committee:—Mrs. T. Glickman, Chairman;—Membership Committee:—Mrs. J. Benewick, Mrs. I. Levinoff, Joint-Chairmen; Floral Committee:—Mrs. H. Bloomfield, Chairman; Ways & Means Committee:—Mrs. D. Fels, Mrs. C. J. Gross, Joint-Chairmen; Entertainment Committee:—Miss Annie Lauterman, Chairman; Hospitality Committee, Mrs. D. L. Cohen, Mrs. J. Wolfe, Joint-Chairmen; Auditing Committee:—Mrs. B. Rose, Chairman; Social Service Committee:—Mrs. D. Davis, Chairman.

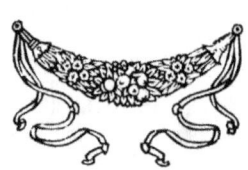

TEMPLE SISTERHOOD "HOLY BLOSSOM CONGREGATION" TORONTO

PURSUANT to a call issued by Mrs. Barnett R. Brickner and the wives of the Trustees of the Holy Blossom Congregation, a meeting of the ladies of the Congregation was called on Wednesday afternoon, October 26th, 1921, in the Synagogue Chambers for the purpose of forming a Sisterhood. Most of the ladies of the Congregation responded to the call, and on that afternoon, the following were elected Officers and Trustees:

President, Mrs. Barnett R. Brickner; 1st. Vice-Pres., Mrs. Julius Eisman; 2nd. Vice-Pres., Mrs. S. Lorie; Rec. Sec'y., Mrs. S. Jacobs; Cor. Sec'y., Mrs. Harry Samuel; Treas., Mrs. Arthur Cohen.

Executive Committee: Mrs. Leo Frankel, Mrs. Wm. Goldstein, Mrs. Jule Heim, Mrs. S. Lubelsky, Mrs. Percy Hermant, Mrs. Coleman Miller, Mrs. M. M. Cohen, Mrs. Harry King, Mrs. A. I. Willinsky.

The aims of the Sisterhood were outlined as follows:
(a) To co-operate with and assist the Holy Blossom Toronto Hebrew Congregation in the carrying out of its aims and purposes.
(b) To develop a spirit of sociability in the life of the Congregation.
(c) To foster the observance of Judaism in the home.
(d) To stimulate spiritual and Jewish educational activities.
(e) To further the religious and moral development of Jewish children.
(f) To become a force for good in the religious and cultural life in the community.
(g) To espouse such religious and Jewish educational causes as are particularly the work of Jewish women.

Membership was opened to the wives, widows, unmarried daughters and sisters of members of the Congregation.

Convenors for various committees were appointed and a series of affairs of a wide range were planned.

Some of the outstanding affairs were:
A Chanukah celebration in the Synagogue with Dramatic Reading.
A series of Purim Tableaux illustrating the story of Purim with the assistance of members of Temple Centre, followed by a Tea.
An afternoon of Jewish Folk Songs.
A display of Jewish ceremonial objects, which were collected from members in the entire community. A talk on "Jewish Ceremonies in the Home" preceded the display.
A Springtime Luncheon, together with the annual Sisterhood meeting.
A public reception for the Confirmants of the Congregation and their parents, held in the Synagogue Chambers on Shabuoth.
A Harvest Fête and Pure Food Show, which netted a sum of over one thousand dollars. This amount together with a loan from the Congregation completely altered and beautified the Synagogue Chambers so that they are today in great demand for social, educational and dramatic purposes by the members of the Congregation and their families.

Monthly Friday evening receptions after the services were introduced to foster a spirit of sociability among the members of the Congregation.

In addition to the above activities, the sisterhood has established a branch religious school in the Y.M.H.A. building. This school was organized to counteract missionary activities in that particular neighborhood and has an enrolment of 230 pupils. Mr. Edmund Scheuer is Principal of the school.

A Gift Shop was cleverly and ably organized by Mrs. Herbert L. Nussbaum, the proceeds of which were to be devoted to scholarship work. The Sisterhood has already helped one talented student of music to graduate from a local conservatory of music and is now ready to assist a young man to the Hebrew Union College in Cincinnati by helping to finance his entrance there. A scholarship will be awarded yearly to any young man wishing to prepare himself for the Rabbinate.

MRS. B. R. BRICKNER

Flowers are placed at the altar in memory of some dear departed or in celebration of some happy event. The Synagogue is also decorated yearly for Shabuoth and all the Festivals. These floral decorations are most artistically handled by the convenor, Mrs. Israel Singer.

Immigrant aid work is another activity that has come within the domain of the Sisterhood since the arrival of immigrants to our country. Showers for food, clothing and linens were held which brought in a bounteous supply. The convenor in charge of this immigrant aid work is Mrs. Jule Allen.

The religious schools are supervised by the convenor, Mrs. Harry Marks, while all entertainments, receptions, etc. are managed by Miss Clara Kallmeyer and Mrs. Jos. Cohn as convenors.

During the past year a series of lectures were arranged on "Aspects of Child Life."

Dr. Alan Brown—The Physical Development of the Child.

Dr. Peter Sandiford—The Mental Development of the Child.

Rabbi Barnett R. Brickner—The Spiritual and Moral Development of the Child.

A second series of talks were given by Mrs. B. R. Brickner on "How to Celebrate the Holidays in the Home." All these talks were well attended.

A Literary Class called the "Monday Club" which meets on Monday evenings was also organized for the purpose of reading and discussing some of the best modern literature. The present membership of the Sisterhood is close to two hundred.

The following officers have been elected for the coming year:

President, Mrs. Barnett R. Brickner; 1st. Vice-Pres., Mrs. Jos. Cohn; 2nd. Vice-Pres., Mrs. S. Lubelsky; Rec. Sec'y., Mrs. Harry Marks; Cor. Sec'y., Mrs. Jos. Tarshis.; Tres., Mrs. Arthur Cohen.

Executive Committee: Mrs. S. Lorie; Miss Emma Mayer, Mrs. Nathan Phillips, Mrs. Percy Hermant, Mrs. Bernard Goldstein, Mrs. Mark Cohen, Mrs. Wm. Dannenberg, Mrs. Wm. Gittes, Mrs. Fred Singer.

MRS. MOSES FINKELSTEIN (SARAH ROSEN), WINNIPEG

A PUBLIC-SPIRITED woman, and one whose life has been devoted to the good of others, Mrs. Moses Finkelstein (Sarah Rosen), eldest daughter of Mr. and Mrs. Isaac Rosen of Winnipeg, and one of the leading figures in communal and welfare work in Western Canada, was born in the province of Voleen, Russia, in 1870. She came to Canada with her parents in 1888 and settled in the City of Winnipeg. In 1890, she was married to Moses Finkelstein, son of Tevel Finkelstein who was one of the pioneer Jewish settlers in the West. Mrs. Finkelstein has always been a leader in charitable and philanthropic work in the Jewish community of Winnipeg, and many years ago (about 1902) she organized a free loan society among girls, which was known as the Girls' Benevolent Loan Association. This organization was composed entirely of young girls and unmarried women. By loaning worthy people money, that was repaid in weekly instalments, this society did an enormous amount of good. No interest was charged on these loans. Although the funds were never very large, they were always found useful by the poor of the city, and it helped them out greatly, when they were in need of assistance. Mrs. Finkelstein has been the Honorary President of this worthy association since its inception. She has acted as executive head of many organizations and was the first President of the Shaarey Tzedec Ladies' Sisterhood. On her retirement from that office she was elected Honorary President, which appointment she has held ever since. She has been actively connected with the Jewish Benevolent Society, and has acted as Secretary of the first Jewish Ladies' Aid Society of Winnipeg. She was also elected the first President of the Daughters of Zion. Mrs. Finkelstein takes a deep interest in many other institutions, her activities being by no means confined to her own creed, and she is a member of the Daughters of the Empire, the Canadian Club and the Winnipeg Art Association. She is a director of the Anti-Tuberculosis Society of Winnipeg. Mrs. Finkelstein has three sons and two daughters. One of her sons, Dr. Manly Finkelstein, is the City Pathologist.

SHAARY ZEDEK SISTERHOOD, WINNIPEG

WHEN the Shaarey Zedek Sisterhood was established some three years ago, the following were the first officers: President, Mrs. M. Finkelstein; Vice-President, Mrs. E. Rosen; Treasurer, Mrs. R. M. Pierce; Secretary, Mrs. J. P. Weidman; Trustees, Mesdames R. M. Frankfurter, Aaron Cohen, C. Schiller, P. Stephany, H. Genser, N. J. Weidman, N. L. Green, A. Stein, M. Goldstine and A. Squires.

The officers for the ensuing year are as follows: Honorary President, Mrs. M. Finkelstein; President, Mrs. M. Heppner; First Vice-President, Mrs. C. Schiller; Second Vice-President, Mrs. A. Levinson; Recording Secretary, Mrs. B. Levi; Corresponding Secretary, Mrs. Harry Cohen; Treasurer, Mrs. J. N. Sternberg. Advisory Board, Mdmes. N. L. Green, P. Stephany, M. Weidman, S. Rodin, L. Churchill, N. J. Weidman, D. Singer, B. Levinson, M. Finkelstein, C. Portigal, J. P. Weidman; Chairmen of Committees; House, Mrs. M. H. Abramovich; Sunday School, Mrs. Aaron Cohen; Membership, Mrs. L. Churchill; Hospital, Mrs. H. J. Samuel; Friendly Visiting, Mrs. J. Adler; Juvenile Court, Mrs. C. Schiller; Girl Guides, Mrs. J. Wilder.

The work of the Sisterhood was divided up amongst several committees. The Hospital Committee is in charge of Mrs. H. J. Samuel and this Committee makes it its business to look after hospital patients including the interviewing of doctors and nurses, especially in the case of recent immigrants who cannot speak English. A number of books in Yiddish have been placed in the hospital library, including several Yiddish papers for use by the patients. The cases dealt with by this Committee are too numerous to mention.

The Friendly Visiting Committee is under the chairmanship of Mrs. J. Adler. It looks after the cases that come under "The Mothers' Allowance Act." The Committee interviews the parties making applications under this Act and takes the cases up with the commission in order to obtain a satisfactory adjustment for the unfortunate mothers who are compelled to make application for assistance.

The Sunday School Committee is under Mrs. N. J. Weidman and this Committee has been doing especially good work. The attendance during the last year has never been less than 150 and often runs as high as 200. The Synagogue accommodation has been taxed to the utmost and it has been a problem to provide room for the children. This committee has also had in charge Purim and Chanukah entertainments and has been instrumental in collecting money for the National Fund and other purposes.

Mrs. S. Rodin is the chairman of the Entertainment Committee.

Mrs. M. H. Abramovich is the chairman of the House Committee which has assisted the Entertainment Committee in its many undertakings, including the entertainment of University students of the congregation, and their parents.

Particular mention must be made of the floral decorations in the Synagogue for which this committee has been responsible.

The Girl Guides under the leadership of Captain Lottie Bere have now enrolled 22 girls and are carrying on good work.

Mrs. L. Churchill has charge of the Membership Committee which has secured a total of 181 members. Mrs. B. Levi is the secretary.

THE GOEL TZEDEC WOMEN'S AUXILIARY, TORONTO

THE WOMEN'S AUXILIARY of the Goel Tzedec Congregation was re-organized on November 28th, 1922, by Mrs. I. H. Siegel and several other ladies who felt the need of a women's auxiliary in the interests of the Synagogue.

The purpose of the Auxiliary, as taken from their constitution, is as follows:—"The women of the Goel Tzedec Congregation, conscious of their sacred duty to preserve and to strengthen the religion and faith of their fathers, and aware that it would be impossible for them severally to discharge this duty, honorably and efficiently, without the aid of concerted effort and co-operation, have therefore organized under the name of the 'Goel Tzedec Women's Auxiliary', with the sincere hope that through the agency of this organization, they shall better be able to fulfil their duty to orthodox Judaism."

To this end they extend their co-operation to the congregation in all its undertakings and activities, and also inaugurate activities of their own for the dissemination of the message and the teachings of Judaism.

One of the first activities was the reception on January 1st, 1923, arranged by the auxiliary at the installation of Rabbi Julius L. Siegel, which took place in the Shool. Many prominent out-of-town guests were present for the occasion, including Rabbi Drachtman of New York, Rabbi Eben, Mr. Samuel Star, and also Rabbi Siegel's father, Rabbi T. S. Siegel of Chicago. The installation was very impressive and was the first of its kind in Toronto, many thousands of people being present.

The members are keenly interested in the Sunday School and pledged themselves to pay half the costs of renovating the vestry chambers into a beautiful modern Sunday School, which is the finest Jewish Sunday School in Toronto. The cost of this renovation was about six thousand dollars.

In March, 1924, a dedication banquet was held in the new rooms to mark the opening, where some three hundred and fifty members and friends were present, including Mrs. Epstein, President of the Central Auxiliary of New York, and one of the six founders of the Women's League of the United States of America, with which the Goel Tzedec Sisterhood is affiliated.

They are also responsible for the Chanukah treat given the children annually, the decorating of the Shool with palms and flowers for Shevuoth and Pesach, also the decorating and serving of refreshments in the Succah.

The Auxiliary takes part in nearly all local charity activities. They also assisted in the immigration work during the year 1924, by the serving of hot coffee and sandwiches at the station. These immigrant trains came through and were met about once or twice a month, and during the winter one train came in at about 2 a.m. during a terrific snow storm, and the ladies of the Auxiliary were glad indeed to be of service to these unfortunate people.

The present officers are:—President, Mrs. A. Samuel; 1st Vice-President, Mrs. Bertha D. Lavinne; Treasurer, Mrs. L. M. Schwartz; Rec. Sec., Mrs. Harry Ruben; and Corr. Sec., Mrs. D. Kopman.

MRS. S. HART GREEN was born at Grand Forks, North Dakota, on December 14th, 1889, the daughter of Mr. and Mrs. Martin Lyone. She received her education at the schools of Grand Forks, and was married on August 27th, 1912, to Mr. S. Hart Green of Winnipeg, and has four children. Mrs. Green has always taken a very keen interest and prominent part in Jewish communal work in Winnipeg, and is Vice-President of the Ladies' Auxiliary of the Western Canada Orphanage and Children's Aid of Winnipeg, and a member of the Executive of the United Hebrew Relief. She is one of the two representatives from Manitoba on the Dominion Executive of the Liberal Ladies' Clubs. For some years she was Secretary of the Municipal Chapter, Imperial Order of the Daughters of the Empire, and was a member of the Board of the Anti-Tuberculosis Society. She was a very active member of the Civic League when that institution was functioning in Winnipeg. Mrs. Green is a member of the Shaarey Zedek Synagogue.

MRS. H. E. WILDER, WINNIPEG

MRS. S. HART GREEN, WINNIPEG

MRS. H. E. WILDER was born in Roumania, on February 2nd, 1888, the daughter of Mr. and Mrs. Michael Grunberg. She received her education at the public schools and College of Bucharest, Roumania, from which she graduated in 1904. She was married on June 14th, 1908, to Mr. H. E. Wilder, and has two sons, Edmund and Emanuel, and two daughters, Miriam and Semah Wilder. Mrs. Wilder has always taken the keenest interest in all communal and philanthropic undertakings, and for years has been one of the most active Social Service workers in her community. She is the organizer and was the first President of the Ladies' Auxiliary of the Independent Order B'nai B'rith, Winnipeg Lodge, and is also the organizer of the Jewish Women Tribute. Mrs. Wilder has always been a very enthusiastic Zionist, and she is a most zealous worker for this cause. At the present time she is a Vice-President of the Dominion Hadassah Organization of Canada, and is President of the Hadassah Chapter of Winnipeg. Mrs. Wilder is a member of the Women's Canadian Club.

MRS. A. SELICK, TORONTO

MRS. ANNA SELICK was born in St. Stephen, New Brunswick, the daughter of Emanuel and Rebecca Kovel. She was educated in the St. Stephen public and high schools, and at the Rothesay Ladies' College, St. Stephen. On January 27th, 1910, she was married to Joseph Selick of Moncton, N.B., who died on March 30th, 1918. They had one son, Leo Harrison Selick. Mrs. Selick took up her residence in Toronto in 1910 and immediately became interested in communal undertakings. She was formerly Secretary and later President of the Hebrew Maternity Aid Society, Toronto. She early became interested in Zionist work and was President of the B'noth Zion Kadimah, the second Zionist society in Toronto. In 1911, she was elected Vice-President of the Toronto Zionist Council, later being appointed the Secretary. In 1916, Mrs. Selick organized the first chapter of Hadassah in Canada. She spent some years touring Canada, organizing Hadassah chapters, and was Chairman of the Provincial Council consisting of London, Hamilton, Toronto, Windsor and Brantford chapters. She assisted in the organization of the Dominion Hadassah, of which she has been a Vice-President since its inception. She is a member of the National Executive of the Zionist Organization of Canada. Mrs. Selick was President of the Soldiers' Comfort League, which was organized to provide comforts for the members of the Jewish Legion who saw service in Palestine, and she toured Ontario as a member of the executive of the War Orphans' Relief. She was the Executive Director of the Toronto Conference for Jewish War Relief. Mrs. Selick is the Vice-President of the Single Tax Association of Ontario. She has been connected with the *Canadian Jewish Review* of Toronto since its inception, in the capacity of Business Manager. In 1918, Mrs. Selick was appointed a notary public for the Province of Ontario. She is a member of the Joint Board of Sanitary Control of Toronto, and of the Imperial Order of the Daughters of the Empire. Mrs. Selick is a member of the University Avenue Synagogue, Toronto.

MRS. A. J. FREIMAN (LILLIAN BILSKY) OTTAWA

MRS. LILLIAN FREIMAN is an outstanding figure in welfare work in Canada. The daughter of the late Moses Bilsky, she was born at Mattawa, Ont., June 6, 1885, and on August 18, 1903, was married in Ottawa to Archibald J. Freiman. During the War she established a Red Cross sewing club in her own home which became the Disraeli Chapter, I.O.D.E. At the time of the influenza epidemic in Ottawa in 1916, Mrs. Freiman was virtually given charge of the city's efforts in fighting the disease. In 1917 she raised throughout Canada a large fund for the destitute of Palestine. In 1920, she raised a fund for the relief of the needy Jews of Eastern Europe. She organized and became President of the Jewish War Orphans' Committee of Canada and toured the country addressing scores of meetings, raising money, clothing and medical supplies for the Jewish orphans in Ukrania; and went to Europe to supervise the bringing to Canada of 150 orphans, who were placed in splendid Jewish homes. She took an untiring interest in the Polish and Armenian relief work of the Ottawa Women's Canadian Club. She was for many years President of the Ladies' Auxiliary of the Perley Home for Incurables. She is an active worker for the Ottawa Day Nursery, Ottawa Association for the Blind, the different Ottawa Hospitals, Protestant Infants' Home, and other institutions, and was treasurer of the Ottawa Welfare Bureau. She raised a fund to carry on the work of the Institute Jeanne d'Arc, for Catholic girls, Ottawa. Mrs. Freiman has shown a deep interest in war veterans and assisted in the formation of the Dominion Command, G.W.V.A. She has been an outstanding help to the veterans, and in appreciation, the Ottawa Command, G.W.V.A., presented her with a silver loving cup and a badge of life membership in the command, being the first so honored. She is Dominion President of the Hadassah Organization of Canada; and is President, Hadassah Chapter, Ottawa; Girl Guides' Ass'n., Ottawa; Ottawa Ladies' Hebrew Benevolent Ass'n.; Ladies' Auxiliary, Adath Yeshuran Congregation; Ladies' Auxiliary, B'nai B'rith, Ottawa Lodge; and Regent, Disraeli Chapter, I.O.D.E.

THE HADASSAH ORGANIZATION IN CANADA
By Geo. G. Greene

*Historical Sketch showing Origin, Growth, mentioning Eventful Factors,
Principal Activities, Accomplishments, and Personalities.*

FROM a group of ten women who first got together in Toronto in the year 1916 to a Dominion-wide organization of 68 chapters, with a membership approximating 4,500 women, and annual contributions towards Zionist work in Palestine of $45,000 was the remarkable record to the beginning of 1925 of the Hadassah Organization of Canada. As a national federation, the organization came into existence in the spring of 1919, when co-ordination of the chapters which were then established in different parts of the Dominion, was successfully undertaken by Mrs. A. J. Frieman of Ottawa, who became Dominion President, and who has been re-elected at subsequent conventions.

The start of Hadassah in Canada post-dated the inauguration of American Hadassah by about four years, the latter organization having been founded in 1912 to do Zionist propaganda in the United States, and to engage in activity for the improvement of public health conditions in Palestine. Mrs. Anna Selick of Toronto, who has continuously served as one of the Dominion vice-presidents of Canadian Hadassah, was the moving spirit in the formation of the first group. The Great War of 1914-1918 was in progress at the time, and the women's first work was in connection with special relief for Jewish soldiers. In January, 1917, a meeting was held in Toronto, at the home of Mrs. M. L. Willinsky, still an active participant in Hadassah circles, and a member of the Dominion Council, at which it was decided to hold a campaign to raise funds for the welfare of Jewish soldiers in the military cantonments at Alexandria, Egypt. The sum of $500 was secured, marking the beginning of a long series of campaigns which Hadassah has undertaken, and through which hundreds of thousands of dollars have been collected for the advancement of the Zionist ideal and Jewish welfare generally.

In March, 1917, the members of the original Hadassah chapter in Toronto, which eventually was named Central Chapter, received a visit from Miss Henrietta Szold, president of American Hadassah, and after hearing her speak of the Zionist work which was particularly within the scope and sphere of Jewish women, it was decided to take steps to form other chapters. This decision came, it will be noted, before the epochal and inspiring declaration of the British Government, through the Rt. Hon. A. J. Balfour, at the time British Foreign Secretary, whereby in a letter to Lord Rothschild dated November 2, 1917, the government proclaimed that it viewed with favor the aspirations of the Jewish people to re-establish their Homeland in Palestine.

The foregoing tells the story of the commencement of the organization which bears the name "Hadassah." One has to go back many years, however, to find the inception of the Zionist activity of Jewish women in Canada. Until the Great War came and through it Jewry was given the long-desired opportunity of refounding their Homeland on the site of ancient Jewish civilization, all Zionist activity was of a spiritual or theoretical nature, carried along in fervor through the centuries by the desire inherent in generation after generation for the coming of the third return to Palestine. This spiritual factor in the life of Jewry was fanned to greater importance by the vigorous activity of the late Theodore Herzl, regarded as the founder of the modern Zionist movement, whose efforts in the interest of the Jewish people's national cause culminated in the holding of the famous congress of Zionist leaders at Basle, Switzerland, in 1897. This congress, and those that followed it in 1898, 1899, 1900, 1901, 1903, 1905, 1907, 1909, 1911, 1913, 1921, and 1923, served the purpose of fortifying the Jewish people in their Zionist idealism until 1917, when a practical avenue for the realization of the aim of Zionists, viz.: to have again a legally recognized Homeland in Palestine, was opened through the Balfour Declaration of the British Government.

During the 20 years intervening between the first Basle Congress and the year of this Declaration, Zionist activity had gradually spread throughout Canada, both in extent and in influence, due to the self-sacrificing spirit of the early leaders, many of whom are still foremost in the practical Zionist era of the present day. It was but natural that Jewish women should participate in this activity and thus it was not long before they were represented in specific movements which were named Daughters of Zion, B'noth Zion Kadimah, Herzl Ladies' Societies, Herzl Girls, Red Mogen Dovid, Nordau Girls, DeSola Girls, and others of similarly personal designations. The Daughters of Zion was founded in Toronto in 1900 by Mrs. I. H. Siegel, and in Montreal, a year later by Mrs. Clarence I. de Sola, whose husband was president of the Zionist Federation. All these organizations carried on educational and propaganda activity, aiming toward the preparation of Jewish women for the coming of the days when practical Zionism might be necessary. Mrs. de Sola was president of the Daughters of Zion in Montreal for four years. Money was collected by this organization for the existing Zionist institutions, and also for educational work. Succeeding presidents of the Daughters of Zion in Montreal included Miss Sadie Vineberg, Miss Miriam Bernstein, Mrs. Felix Harris, Mrs. J. S. Leo, and Mrs. L. Fitch. In 1901, there was also a Daughters of Zion Society in Toronto, and an organized group of lady Zionists in Ottawa; in 1902, women Zionists of London, Ont. adopted the name Daughters of Zion for their organization, and in 1903, Ottawa and Winnipeg had Daughters of Zion Societies. In this year also, a group of women Zionists was active in St. John, N.B. Mrs. I. H. Siegel and Miss Betty Goldstick formed the Herzl Girls' Society in Toronto, in 1906, and in 1910, the Ottawa women re-organized under the name Herzl Ladies' Society, and the B'noth Zion Kadimah was started in Toronto.

In October, 1911, the Jewish Women's League for Cultural Work in Palestine was formed in Montreal, following a visit by Madame Bella Peisner, a Zionist orator and organizer, the existing Daughters of Zion being sponsor of the new society. Mrs. J. S. Leo was the first president of the League, the objects of which were to send nurses and teachers of home industries to Palestine to help the Jewish inhabitants to better understand modern methods of preserving health, and also to fit them to become more adept in the home crafts for which Palestinians were noted. The League was an international body with headquarters in Berlin, Germany. In addition to Mrs. Leo, active officers in the Montreal branch of the League included Mrs. H. H. Livingstone, Mrs. F. Harris, Mrs. L. Goldman and Mrs. J. Elkin. Quebec women formed a Daughters of Zion Society in 1913, and the Nordau Girls' Group came into existence in Toronto the same year. The next year, 1914, saw a marked increase in women's Zionist activity, the following new organizations being started: De Sola Girls and B'noth Zion (juniors), in Toronto; B'noth Zion (juniors) and Young Ladies' Literary and Zionist Society, at Montreal; Daughters of Zion and Herzl Girls, at Edmonton, Alta.; and Daughters of Zion societies in Hamilton, Ont., and Vancouver, B.C. In 1915, a Daughters of Zion group was formed in Glace Bay, C.B. and a similar group was started at Brandon, Man. in 1916. The Hebrew Ladies' Benevolent Society organized in Regina, Sask., in 1917, combined Zionist work with communal activities.

Another group which was a factor in forming the nucleus of the present Hadassah Organization was the Palestinian Sewing Circle, which was formed in Montreal in 1918, also under the auspices of the Daughters of Zion, and which, as the name signifies, carried on sewing work for Palestine hospitals. Mrs. F. Harris, Mrs. L. Fedderman, Mrs. J. Rose, Mrs. J. C. Zacks, Mrs. H. L. Sourkes, and Mrs. A. Dainow were prominent in the affairs of the Circle.

Nearly all the different societies now mentioned eventually became absorbed into the Hadassah Organization as it developed from 1916. The second chapter, under the name Hadassah, was formed at Hamilton in 1917, of which Mrs. M. Simon became president. At the 15th Zionist convention held in Winnipeg, Man., in that year, the seeds were sown for the coming of a Hadassah chapter later on, through the activity of Mrs. Anna Selick, Toronto, Mrs. A. J. Freiman, Ottawa, and Mrs. L. Fitch, Montreal, all of whom urged the Jewish women of Winnipeg to form themselves into a chapter. However, owing to the existence at that time of a Red Mogen Dovid Society which was engaged in the work of raising funds for the relief and comfort of the Jewish Legionnaires serving in the Palestinian War Zone, actual formation of a chapter was postponed. In January, 1918, a chapter was formed at Brantford, Ont., with Mrs. Samuel Fox as president. Mrs. Selick of Toronto, Mrs. Leon Lazarus, Mrs. S. Rich, and Miss Goldie Shear were active in helping to start the group. In 1924, the chapter was given the name "Florence" Chapter as a tribute to Mrs. Fox's work, Florence being her first name. During the same month, London, Ont. women threw in their lot with Hadassah, through the influence of Mrs. Selick, Isidore Goldstick and M. Fishbein, a chapter being started with Mrs. J. Harris as president. A fifth chapter was organized about the same time in Windsor, Ont. by Mrs. Anna Selick.

The development of the Hadassah movement in the province of Ontario rendered it necessary to seek some union of chapters in regard to aims and procedure of functioning, and to ensure that the new organization would be laid on a sound foundation, and be of as great service to the cause of Zionism as was possible at that time. Therefore, in May, 1918, the first provincial conference of the chapters in Toronto, Hamilton, London, Brantford and Windsor, was held at Toronto, and a provisional committee was formed to devise plans for the future development of the movement, Mrs. Selick being chairman, and Miss Lillian Goldstein, then of Hamilton, secretary. This was the first of the Hadassah conventions which today are such important events.

In the meantime, another Hadassah group known as the Brandeis Girls, so named after Justice Louis D. Brandeis, a leading American Zionist, was formed in Toronto, and a Hebrew Ladies' Auxiliary commenced to function in Saskatoon, this also being in 1918, the Auxiliary doing local communal work, and assisting the Zionist cause as occasion arose.

The story of Hadassah in Canada now comes down to the eventful year of 1919, which saw the real advance in concerted women's Zionist work. In January of that year, the 16th convention of the Zionist Organization was held at Toronto, in which women, as Zionists, participated, as they had in previous conventions, for although having their own distinct organizations, they were also members of the main body to which they paid per capita dues. The convention at Toronto saw the birth of more aggressive Canadian Zionism, and the women present were stimulated by the inspiration, which the convention imparted, to a realization of the great responsibilities resting upon them, in view of the opportunities offered Jews under the British Zionist policy.

They were ready therefore, when there came an urgent appeal from Palestine for assistance for the many thousands of Jews who had been left homeless, hungry and wracked by wounds and disease through the Allied-Turkish war which had ravaged the country up to the time of the conquest and occupation in 1917 by the troops under General Allenby, (later Lord Allenby, British High Commissioner in Egypt).

Helping Hand Fund

The enormity of the task of raising sufficient funds and supplies to relieve this grave situation of the Palestinian Jews, and the appreciation that the relief and rehabilitation of these unfortunates meant much to the future Jewish nation, caused the existing Hadassah chapters to seriously consider who could be secured to assume the leadership in so important an undertaking. One woman was finally singled out as possessing all the qualifications from a previous record in humanitarian service, personal magnetism and energy—Mrs. A. J. Freiman of Ottawa, who had been active in Zionist work as president of the Herzl Ladies' Society. Mrs. Freiman readily consented to become the generalissimo in this crisis in Hadassah's history, and the Helping Hand Fund for Destitute Jewry in Palestine was thereupon created. Mrs. Freiman at once started to disseminate information to all parts of Canada where Jews lived, telling them of the plight of their co-religionists in Palestine and urging them to organize local committees to take charge of the appeal for funds and supplies. An extensive indirect and direct advertising scheme was devised and put into effect, and striking posters were prepared and put up in the most prominent points in all the principal cities and towns. This necessary preliminary work over, Mrs. Freiman toured Canada, visiting every place where the Jewish population was sufficient to warrant it, and eloquently pleaded with her people to show the world by their aid, the depth of Jewish humanity, and the unity of Israel in distress. The campaign took place on March 16, 17 and 18, 1919, and was a remarkable success, setting a record for Canadian Jewish contributions towards a special relief work. The sum of $160,000 in cash was secured, in addition to clothing, foodstuffs and medicines to the value of approximately $40,000.

It is a commentary on the happy relations existing in Canada between citizens of Jewish and non-Jewish persuasion, and also an indication of Mrs. Freiman's personal popularity gained through her Dominion-wide reputation for splendid non-sectarian charitable activities, that hundreds of monetary contributions, as well as large quantities of supplies were received from non-Jews. In the Capital, where Mrs. Freiman's philanthropic work had made her an outstanding figure, the premier, ex-premier, ministers of the government, senators and members of parliament, and leading non-Jewish citizens of Ottawa, were among the first to donate to the Fund. The non-Jewish press of Canada heartily co-operated with their Jewish contemporaries in giving publicity to the work, both by news stories and editorial comment.

The money raised was forwarded to the Jewish Colonial Trust, London, for expenditure on relief supplies through the World Zionist Organization, while the supplies collected were shipped abroad under arrangement with the Canadian Red Cross Society, this Society thereby rendering a very helpful service. Through the Women's International Zionist Organization, the supplies were transhipped from England to Palestine for distribution.

It was through the Helping Hand Fund that the Hadassah Organization of Canada was successfully launched as a Dominion-wide movement. In the course of her travels through Canada on behalf of the Fund, Mrs. Freiman met Jewish women of the larger cities and towns and in conjunction with her appeal for the special purpose, she urged upon them the necessity of organizing so as to render continuous help for the rebuilding of Palestine. Through this mission of the Dominion President, a new plane was established for the women of Canada. The growing appreciation that women could be of equal value in the solution of the great practical problems of the world, as in solving the more intimate problems of the home, was exemplified by the unanimity with which the Jewish women of Canada resolved to spread Hadassah throughout the Dominion, and by the splendid support and encouragement which they were then, and have since been given by the men's Zionist organization.

As the recognized head of Canadian Hadassah, Mrs. Freiman influenced the organization of several new chapters in 1919, and laid the seeds of interest and desire from which other chapters have since been formed. The women Zionist workers in Montreal, most of whom had been active as members of the Daughters of Zion, decided to dissolve that organization, and they started Montreal Hadassah, with Mrs. L. Fitch, one of the present Dominion vice-presidents of the movement, as the first president, an office which she has capably filled ever since. Those associated with Mrs. Fitch in Montreal Hadassah's early days included Mrs. E. G. Bernstein, Mrs. Alta Kahn, Mrs. F. Harris, Mrs. A. J. Alexander, Mrs. B. Perelmutter, Mrs. Leon Goldman, Mrs. H. L. Sourkes, Mrs. J. C. Zacks, Mrs. H. H. Livingstone, the late Mrs. G. Sanders, Mrs. A. Levin, Mrs. L. Miller and Mrs. Fisher, all of whom distinguished themselves by the sincerity and constancy of their Zionism. In view of the size of the city, it was decided to divide the original body into five units or chapters, which were named: Central, Queen Esther, Miriam Brainin-Ortenberg, Westmount and Young Ladies' Literary and Zionist Chapters. Mrs. E. G. Bernstein and Mrs. A. Levin were leaders of Central chapter; Mrs. L. Fitch, Mrs. A. J. Alexander and Mrs. H. H. Livingstone of Westmount chapter; Mrs. F. Harris, of Miriam Brainin-Ortenberg chapter; Mrs. B. Perelmutter, Mrs. Alta Kahn, Mrs. L. Miller, Mrs. S. I. Wagner, Mrs. M. Fineberg and Mrs. M. Rabinovitch, leaders in the Queen Esther chapter; and Mrs. H. Singer and Miss F. Solomon, of the Young Ladies' Literary and Zionist chapter. The five chapters were governed by a city-wide Council under the presidency of Mrs. Fitch, through which the work of the chapters for Zionism was co-ordinated.

During this important activity in Montreal, Mrs. Freiman's visit to the west was beginning to bear fruit. A chapter was formed in Vancouver, B.C., and was named Lillian Freiman Chapter in honor of Mrs. Freiman, those responsible for the chapter in addition to Mrs. Freiman, being Mrs. J. B. Joffe, Mrs. M. Ruben, and Mrs. L. Rosenbaum. A chapter was started in Timmins, Ont. in 1919, Mrs. Louis Helperin being the first president, and during this year, also, the women of Glace Bay, C.B., and St. John, N.B., formed chapters. In Glace Bay, Rabbi Maxhin, Mrs. B. Siegel and Mrs. B. Hamborg were active in the commencement of Hadassah, while Mrs. J. Goldman, as president, and Mrs. Sarah Kunitzky, as secretary, gave the chapter in St. John a successful start. The Emma Lazarus Girls was the name of a group formed in Halifax that year, this body eventually becoming a Hadassah chapter. Mrs. C. Byalin has been the active secretary there for some years. On the occasion of Mrs. Freiman's visit to Quebec in 1919, a chapter was formed there and this also was named the Lillian Freiman Chapter in honor of Mrs. Freiman. Mrs. L. Lazarowitz has been president of the Quebec chapter ever since.

The year 1920 saw further expansion of Hadassah in Canada. A new chapter, named North End Chapter, was formed in Montreal, the ladies responsible for this branch including Mrs. L. Herzig, Mrs. B. Bernard, Mrs. Garber, Mrs. Rosen, Mrs. Woscow, Mrs. L. Matthew and Mrs. Herman. Winnipeg also joined the Hadassah Organization that year, due to the excellent missionary work of preceding years. A chapter was formed there on June 8th with Miss Goldie Finesilver as first president. She was succeeded in that office in 1922, by Mrs. H. E. Wilder, who has served in that capacity ever since and is also one of the Dominion vice-presidents of the movement, having been elected to this office in 1924. In 1920, also, on Feb. 8th, the Ladies' Herzl Society of Ottawa was transformed into a Hadassah chapter. Mrs. Freiman has been president since its inception. The ladies who were active with her in the commencement of Hadassah in the Capital included Mrs. L. Leiken, Mrs. A. Kert, Mrs. W. Shenkman, Miss Birdie Abelson (now Mrs. J. Miller, Cornwall, Ont.), Mrs. J. J. Marks, Mrs. A. H. Coplan, Mrs. B. Pearl, Mrs. A. Drazin, Mrs. J. Golden, Mrs. D. Green, Mrs. C. Greenberg, Mrs. J. Holzman, Mrs. H. Freedman, and Mrs. B. Bookman.

Chapters were also started in 1920, at Calgary, Alta., with Miss Rose Rabinowitz as president, and Mrs. A. H. Goldberg, secretary; in Port Arthur, Ont., with Mrs. J. Cowan and Mrs. R. Cohen, as leaders; Fort William, Ont., where Mrs. Rose Drapkin has since taken a prominent part in the work; Sault Ste. Marie, where Mrs. D. Richardson and Mrs. H. Friedman have been the leaders, and where also there is a membership of an international character as ladies of both the Canadian city and Sault Ste. Marie, Michigan, work together in a common union; and in Sherbrooke, Que., where the chapter was named Rachel Smith Edgar Chapter, with Mrs. J. Rosenbloom as president, and Mrs. Rebecca Echenberg, as secretary.

New stimulus was given to the Hadassah movement by a tour which Mrs. Freiman took through the Dominion in November, 1920, in the interests of the Jewish War Orphans' Committee, of which she was Dominion chairlady. An account of the work of the Committee appears elsewhere in this volume. Mrs. Freiman was accompanied by Miss Ida Seigler, editor of the Canadian Jewish Chronicle, Montreal, and the splendid Zionist speeches they delivered incidental to their activity for the orphans' cause, did much to inspire the women they addressed to take part in Hadassah's efforts for the Jewish Homeland. Miss Seigler has personally been a consistent supporter of, and active worker in Hadassah since its early days, and has rendered invaluable editorial aid through the columns of the "Canadian Jewish Chronicle."

The eyes of the Jewish women of Canada were on Hadassah delegates when they gathered together from all parts of Canada, at the first Dominion-wide convention which was held in Montreal, in January, 1921, in conjunction with the 17th Zionist Convention. This gathering was a momentous one in many ways. Mrs. Freiman was formally elected to the office of Dominion president which she had held for nearly two years. The first specific undertaking of Canadian Hadassah, viz.:

the foundation of a Girls' Domestic and Agricultural Science School in Palestine, was enthusiastically decided on, after both Mrs. Freiman and Dr. Schmarya Levin had spoken on the subject. Vice-Presidents for Canada were elected in Mrs. L. Fitch, Montreal, for the Eastern Division; Mrs. Anna Selick, Toronto, for Central Division; and Mrs. Max Rady, Winnipeg, for the Western Division. Mrs. Felix Harris, Montreal, was chosen as Honorary Secretary, and a Dominion Council was formed of leading Hadassah workers, representing the various cities and towns.

In 1921, also, more chapters were added to the steadily lengthening chain. Three new chapters were organized in Toronto, Rose, Naomi, and Deborah, the latter a Junior chapter. To co-ordinate the Toronto chapters a Central Hadassah Council was formed with Mrs. D. Dunkelman as president; Mrs. A. B. Bennett, vice-president; Mrs. L. M. Schwartz, treasurer; and Mrs. A. Selick, secretary. Lachine, Que. ladies formed a chapter with Mrs. M. Miller as president, and Mrs. A. Cramer, secretary. A new chapter started in Montreal under the name Sybil Cohen Chapter, so called after the late daughter of Mrs. M. H. Cohen, prominent Zionist worker, who became the first president. This chapter has held to the policy of including mothers and daughters in the membership which makes it somewhat unique in this respect. Mrs. Lillian Steekler was instrumental in establishing a chapter in Sydney, N.S.

The Hadassah Organization now had thirty chapters and was doing splendid work for the Girls' Domestic and Agricultural Science School, National Fund, Keren Hayesod, Palestine Restoration Fund, Palestine orphans, and also contributing to the Nurses' Training School which had been established in Palestine in 1916, to train Palestinian young women for this fine womanly profession. There were also many smaller objects, all incidental to the cause, and of course, the chapters were steadily engaged in sewing useful articles for Palestine's sick and needy.

Hadassah began to spring up in new fields in 1922. Miriam and Western Chapters were started in Toronto. Mrs. A. Sidel organized a chapter in St. John's, Newfoundland, and the Ladies' Hebrew Benevolent Society in Yarmouth, N.S., assumed the character of a chapter, Mrs. A. I. Cohen being the active leader there. Vegreville, Alta. ladies also came into the fold through the Hebrew Ladies' Auxiliary, of which Mrs. H. Bloomfield was a prominent officer. Kamsack, Sask., and Yorkton, Sask., were other communities to take up Hadassah work. On Feb. 8, 1922, a chapter was started in Regina, through the existing Ladies' Hebrew Benevolent Society, with Mrs. M. Helman, as president, and Mrs. Harry Bronfman, Mrs. S. Kraminsky and Mrs. B. Lesk, as the other officers. Mrs. I. Friedgut was also an active worker in this chapter and became president after Mrs. Helman. Chapters were formed also in Edmonton, Alta. with Mrs. E. Gordean and Mrs. M. I. Lieberman, as respectively first president and secretary; in Estevan, Sask., where Mrs. L. Hurt, Mrs. J. Krivel and Mrs. J. Berger have been active officers; Lipton, Sask., with Mrs. S. H. Naimark and Miss Rebecca Braunstein as leaders, and in Kingston, Ont., where the Queen Esther Chapter was formed with Mrs. L. Abramson as president and Miss Celia Zacks, as secretary.

The second convention of Canadian Hadassah was held in July, 1922, at Ottawa, when it was decided to lend aid to the Chaluzim, of which special mention is made elsewhere. The original Dominion officers were re-elected, with the addition of Mrs. M. A. Brown of Montreal as Dominion Treasurer. The delegates were honored by the presence of Hon. W. L. Mackenzie King, prime minister, who addressed a joint gathering of men and women. Work was started on the constitution which now governs Hadassah in Canada. The strength of the junior Hadassah movement was recognized by the addition of two young ladies representing Montreal, and two representing Toronto, to the Dominion Council.

Mrs. F. Harris resigned as honorary secretary on Dec. 8, 1922, and on Dec. 25, 1922, Mrs. H. Singer was elected to succeed her, and has served in that office since.

In accordance with the majority view of the 2nd Hadassah Convention, the headquarters for Canada were transferred from Montreal to Ottawa in December, 1922, so that the work could be carried on directly under the supervision of Mrs. Freiman, the Dominion President. Previously, Hadassah work had been centralized in the headquarters at Montreal of the Zionist Organization of Canada. It was felt at the 2nd convention, that the growth of special Hadassah activities, and the need for more undivided attention to the development of the chapters throughout the Dominion, warranted the change.

The increase in Hadassah activity in 1923, was remarkable, evidencing in a striking way, the awakening consciousness of Canadian Jewish women.

The development of the junior Hadassah movement in Montreal necessitated the creation of a Junior Hadassah Council, to supervise the activities of the juniors. This Council was formed in January. Mrs. Leon Levin was the original president.

In Montreal, the following chapters started in 1923: Lillian Freiman (junior), Rose of Sharon (junior), Rachel (senior), organized by Mrs. L. Herzig and Mrs. S. Kahn, with Mrs. R. Ness as president, and Mrs. H. Ness, secretary; Daughters of Judea (junior), Hatikvah (junior), Ziona (junior), Deborah (junior), Menorah (junior), Mizpah (junior), and Shaar Hashomayim (junior), and there was also an organization known as the Valeeta Girls, this body being now out of existence. Mrs. D. Dunkelman organized Junior Hadassah into a strong body in Toronto, in March, 1923, and later on the Toronto girls of school age were encouraged to join the Hadassah Mascot movement, the Mascots occupying somewhat the same relation to the main Hadassah organization as the boy scouts do to the regular soldiers.

As the result of a visit to the west by Dr. A. Goldstein, the women of Saskatoon, Sask., were encouraged to form a chapter of Hadassah in February, 1923. Mrs. A. Feinstein, Mrs. Max Gropper and Mrs. J. Mallin were active in the affairs of the chapter from the start. The Saskatoon chapter is the largest Jewish women's organization in that city.

A junior chapter was organized in Ottawa with Miss Bertha Slonemsky as the first president. The chapter soon acquired 150 members.

During the early part of the year also, and profiting by a visit made to the city by Rabbi J. L. Zlotnik, director of the National Fund work in Canada, Mrs. H. E Wilder took the initiative in forming a second chapter in Winnipeg, which became known as Ezrah Chapter. Mrs. M. Rady was the first president of this chapter, and has served ever since. She was for a time a Dominion vice-president of Hadassah. Ezrah Chapter has been a substantial contributor to Hadassah funds. Among those ladies who early took a prominent part in the affairs of the new chapter were Mrs. A. Stein, Mrs. M. H. Abremovitch, Mrs. Chas. Lyons and Mrs. A. Coppelman.

A junior chapter was organized by Miss Frances Geller in Windsor, in 1923, and a senior chapter in Peterboro, Ont. the same year, with Mrs. L. Green as president, and Mrs. Morris Botnik, as secretary.

The 3rd Hadassah Convention was held in Toronto in January, 1924, when the delegates from all parts of the country transacted business in a workmanlike way and laid plans for the future of Hadassah, which have already borne fruit at the time of writing. Several new chapters were formed in that year. The Judith Chapter which came into existence in Montreal, was the first to adopt Yiddish as the principal language for use at the meetings of the chapter, this being done to encourage the attendance of those who spoke Yiddish mainly. Mrs. J. L. Zlotnik, wife of Rabbi Zlotnik, is president of this chapter, which has 60 members. The Eta Cohen Chapter, a senior group, was also organized, with Mrs. E. Lazare as president. The chapter was so-named in memory of Mrs. Eta Cohen. Other chapters which were formed in Montreal in 1924, were Nair Tamid (junior), Tel-Aviv (junior), so named after the Jewish city in Palestine; University (junior), and Naomi (junior). A junior chapter was formed in Winnipeg, Man. with Miss Sybil Weidman as leader, and a junior chapter, known as Daughters of Zion Chapter was organized in London, Ont.

An impetus was given to Hadassah work in the city of Kingston, in 1924, by the organization of a second chapter, Mrs. I. Cohen being chosen president. This distribution of Kingston's women into two chapters seems to have worked out to the advantage of the cause.

Early in 1925, Hamilton, Ont. young women formed a strong Junior Chapter through the encouragement of Mrs. I. Segal and Mrs. H. Cohen of the senior chapter.

In many places where Hadassah is not officially established, there are organizations of different kinds who co-operate with Hadassah under their own names, taking up the various appeals that Hadassah makes from time to time, and in fact, rendering extremely valuable aid. These organizations include the Hebrew Ladies' Aid Society, Prince Albert, Sask., of which Mrs. F. Shay is secretary; Jewish Ladies' Aid Society, New Glasgow, N.S.; Hebrew Ladies' Aid Society, Vegreville, Alta., and also the Community of Vegerville, Alta.; Jewish Ladies' Aid Society, Canora, Sask., of which Mrs. Cecilia Cohen is president; Hebrew Ladies' Aid Society, North Bay, Ont.; Jewish Ladies' Aid Society of Stellarton, N.S., Mrs. S. Kaplan, secretary; Hebrew Ladies of Moncton, N.B., through Mrs. I. Selick and Mrs. L. Savage; Moose Jaw, Sask., Hebrew Ladies' Aid Society, per Mrs. M. Schwartzer; groups of Jewish women in Brockville, Ont., Cobalt, Ont., Midland, Ont., Portage la Prairie, Man., and other places. For a time, there was a regular Hadassah chapter in Portage la Prairie, but owing to the removal of many Jewish families from the town, the chapter finally had to disband for lack of members. There was also a chapter in Toronto called Ruth Chapter, but this was eventually broken up and the members joined other chapters.

In recent years, also, there has been an inclination amongst the children to do something for the cause, just like "mother and sister" and in consequence, groups known as Hadassah Mascots have been formed of which these children are members, and assist at various Hadassah functions, taking part in programs, acting as ushers, and helping in other ways. There are Mascots in Toronto, Ont., London, Ont., and Midland, Ont.

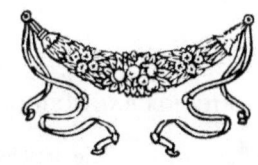

ACTIVITIES OF HADASSAH

GIRLS' DOMESTIC AND AGRICULTURAL SCIENCE SCHOOL

THE first concrete undertaking of the Hadassah Organization of Canada was for the foundation of this school, which is expected to be formally opened in the fall of 1925. The Dominion-wide convention, held in Montreal in January, 1921, was attended by Dr. Schmarya Levin, noted international Zionist worker. He appeared on the platform at one of the convention sessions and spoke to the delegates on the need of an institution where the young women and growing girls of Palestine could be scientifically trained, so as to be efficient help-mates to the men toiling in the colonies, whose chief concern for the first few years was the actual hard manual labor of digging up the soil and making it productive once again, and who depended on others to furnish the scientific advice which was so essential to success. Furthermore, such an institution as proposed, would train young women to conduct their homes in a modern and economical way. It was inspiring to notice the way in which the delegates enthusiastically endorsed the pledge conveyed to Dr. Levin by the Dominion President, that Canadian Hadassah would undertake to establish the school at a cost which was then estimated at from $75,000 to $88,000. So far, $20,000 has been raised by the Organization for the school fund, and as a result of the constant remittances which have been made by headquarters to the Women's International Zionist Organization in London, with which Canadian Hadassah is affiliated, a site was secured for the school at Nahalal, Palestine, on land furnished by the National Fund, located about 15 miles from Haifa. Here, several of the buildings necessary have been prepared and about 20 girls taken into the school. They do the work in the gardens and farm land, largely helping towards their own maintenance, and at the same time, are learning the mysteries of agriculture, horticulture and home management. The school plans call for accommodation for 60 girls, but other buildings are necessary before this number can be accepted, and also funds are required for carrrying on the school, which Canadian Hadassah is furnishing, as needed. The institution will bear the name of its founders and will serve as a striking and practical memorial to the interest of Canadian Jewish women in the re-creation of a Jewish agricultural class as the backbone of the future Jewish nation.

On the occasion of the laying of the foundation stone of the school, Dr. Chaim Weizman, president of the World Zionist Organization, sent a message of greeting, in which he said the school would meet a vital necessity in making possible the formation of a Jewish peasant class of which Palestine stood so greatly in need. Lady Beatrice Samuel, wife of Sir Herbert Samuel, first High Commissioner of Palestine, also sent a congratulatory message.

Sewing

From the commencement of Hadassah work in Canada, and in fact through the various women's Zionist organizations which previously existed, sewing articles for Palestine's hospitals, hostels, infant welfare centres, orphanages, homes for the aged, and other institutions, has been one of the activities most steadily and energetically carried on. This sewing work was for a long time the principal means of making the meetings of Hadassah chapters both interesting and successful. In conjunction with the talks, readings, and discussions on Zionist affairs which take place whenever Hadassah members gather together, sewing has been a co-ordinating medium of an importance which has meant as much, if not more, to the Zionist cause, as the actual sewn articles completed and sent to Palestine, and which in the past ten years has amounted in money value to scores of thousands of dollars.

VIEW OF THE GIRLS' AGRICULTURAL SCHOOL, NAHALAL, PALESTINE

The articles made by the chapters were such as would be most suitable for Palestine hospitals and other institutions, and comprised nightshirts, bloomers, baby shoes, baby bands, baby sheets, baby bibs, baby kimonos, baby jackets, bed shoes, large sheets, dresses, rompers, undershirts, towels, towelling, pillow slips, overalls, slips, boys' pants, hose, wash cloths, diapers, flannelette pieces, blankets, bedspreads, bedjackets, bonnets, handkerchiefs, tams, scarfs, sweaters, linen, cotton, absorbent cotton, underwear, blouses, aprons; and in addition considerable quantities of soap, talcum powder, toothpaste, tooth brushes, and other toilet and sanitary necessities have also been shipped to Palestine. The aim has been to make the chapters self-sustaining in regard to sewing work, the headquarters supplying a large proportion of the materials used in making the articles, cut in standard patterns, at the cost price.

The clothing, linens and miscellaneous supplies furnished by Canadian Hadassah is distributed to Hadassah hospitals, clinics, sanatoria, infant welfare stations, immigrants' hostels, orphan committees, and also to the Institute for the Blind, Reception Houses of the Jewish Immigration Board, Insane Asylum at Ezrat Nashim, Bethlehem Colony, Sephardic Home for the Aged, Kindergartens, Ashkenazic Home for the Aged, Hinuch Ivrim, Kupat Holim, and other institutions.

Mrs. H. L. Sourkes of Montreal, was for several years Dominion Convener of sewing activities of chapters. She was succeeded by Mrs. M. H. Cohen, Montreal, in February, 1924.

Chaluzim Relief

The work which Hadassah did for the Chaluzim in 1922 and 1923, is a silent but eloquent testimonial to the resourcefulness, energy, and humanitarianism of Canadian Jewish women. At the second convention of the Organization held in Ottawa in July, 1922, word was received through Dr. Martin Rosenbluth, Mr. A. Levin and Dr. A. O. Freedman of Montreal, that large numbers of idealistically inspired Jews, many of them young men with University degrees, were precariously situated in various central and southern European cities, and Mediterranean ports, and in the ports of Jaffa and Haifa, Palestine, due to their funds having been exhausted before they were able to settle in their land of hope. Most of these unfortunates were victims of pogroms, and had started off believing they would be able to reach Palestine one way or another. So great was the rush of Chaluzim through Vienna in 1920 and succeeding years that the Palestine office in that city, under the direction of Dr. Rosenbluth, handled 12,000 persons between January, 1920, and September, 1922, maintaining three homes, where the sick and hungry were cared for, the ragged re-clothed, and as far as possible, instruction given in the rudimentary requirements of Palestinian life. Even fares for the balance of the journey to Palestine were paid in special cases.

This excellent work was in danger of being disrupted until Canadian Hadassah came to the rescue, as the assistance that had up to then been given by the Austrian Zionist Organization had become inadequate due to depreciated currency.

The first appeal for the Chaluzim was made at a luncheon given to delegates to the 2nd convention, by Mrs. A. J. Freiman, and the immediate response was $710 which was at once remitted abroad to secure the release of immigrants held in Palestinian ports, who were in danger of deportation. In September, 1922, on the eve of the High Holidays, Mrs. Freiman sent out an urgent telegraphic message to chapters and congregations, asking for special collections for the Chaluzim. The response was a magnificent one, and in subsequent months, supplementary remittances came in from chapters, raised through special affairs, so that from July, 1922, to November, 1923, the aggregate amount collected for this work was $19,052. A large portion of this money was used for relief and initial re-establishment expense of pioneers in the new Jewish Homeland.

Tuberculosis Sanitarium

Through Dr. S. Tannenbaum, director of Hadassah's medical work in Palestine, towards which Canadian Hadassah has contributed money and supplies continuously, it was learned in November, 1924, that there was great need of a sanitarium for the treatment of the tubercularly-diseased. It was suggested that in view of the accummulation of hospital supplies, Canadian Hadassah might forego their appeal in that year for these supplies and instead undertake to establish the sanitarium. This was agreed to at a subsequent meeting of the Dominion executive and on Dec. 15, all chapters were telegraphed to take up the new work. There was a very fine response by the chapters through Dollar Showers at which each member and non-member was asked to contribute one dollar. Along with about $4,000 to the credit of Canadian Hadassah in Palestine, which had been given over a period of years for various branches of hospital work and set aside, the collections through chapters in 1924 and 1925, ensured the establishment and first year's maintenance of a sanitarium of 15 beds. This institution is to be named after Canadian Hadassah.

The site selected for the sanitarium is at Safed, a dry district of Palestine where the Hadassah medical unit conducts a general hospital.

Keren Hayesod

In considerable measure, the work of the Hadassah Organization for the Keren Hayesod, has made it possible for Canadian Jewry to occupy third place in the standing of Jewries of other countries who contribute to this greatest of Zionist funds. At one time Canada stood second, the United States being first, but South Africa is now second, with Canada very close behind. In the three campaigns that have taken place in Canada for the Keren Hayesod since 1921, the Hadassah chapters have lined up the full strength of their woman-power, with the men Zionists, to ensure that each community provided every dollar possible. Hadassah chapters have put their own teams of canvassers into each campaign, their outstanding members have delivered inspiring addresses, and they have subscribed both as chapters and individuals.

The second Keren Hayesod campaigns in 1923, in both Montreal and Ottawa were practically organized and carried through by Hadassah workers. From December 7, 1923, to December 31, 1924, Hadassah directly gave $4,000 to the Keren Hayesod. On the occasion of the 3rd campaign in 1924, Hadassah pledged $50,000 to the fund, and the first contribution made as soon as plans for the campaign had been arranged, came from Toronto Junior Hadassah who wired A. J. Freiman, chairman of the campaign for Canada, in the following terse but eloquent message "Junior Hadassah of Toronto, happy to start campaign with $1,000. Wishing you success. Who's next?" This represents the spirit of Hadassah very strikingly.

In addition to contributing and working at campaign times, Hadassah chapters set aside the proceeds of affairs held during each year, for the Keren Hayesod.

The Keren Hayesod was originated at a world Zionist conference in London, England, in July, 1920, and became active in 1921. Jewry, the world over, has recognized the Keren Hayesod as the leading Zionist fund through which Palestine can be rebuilt as the Jewish Homeland. The great bulk of contributions for Palestine's development had been made to the Keren Hayesod since it was founded. These monies are expended on such vital factors in the basic life of a country, as immigration, agriculture, labour, trade and industry, education, sanitation, and for the financing of banks and direct extension of credit to new settlers. Up to December 31, 1924, about $8,000,000 had been subscribed to the Keren Hayesod. The appeal for this money is based on the ancient principle of the 'maaser'.

Through the Keren Hayesod, good roads have been constructed in Palestine, new quarters added to cities, 43 colonies either started or adopted, and maintained, factories subsidized, houses erected, the great Rutenberg electrification scheme assisted, nearly 140 schools, elementary, secondary, technical and manual, supported, the Hebrew University established through a specially allocated portion of the Fund, and greater acquisition and development of land rendered possible by financial co-operation with the National Fund. The Keren Hayesod has been termed the Golden Key to the new Jewish Homeland, and Hadassah appreciated this from the beginning and is consistently working for it.

Jewish National Fund

From the commencement of women's Zionist activities in Canada, and particularly since Hadassah has existed, special attention has been given to promoting the National Fund which has been a big factor in Zionist work since 1903. The Fund controls over 30,000 acres of land in Palestine and has planted close to 1,000,000 forest and fruit trees. A large ancient forest at Nahalal, stretching over an area of 1,000 acres is being restored, 11,000 trees having so far been revived. The land bought by the fund is made available for settlement under hereditary leases which ensure that it will always remain Jewish property. A National Fund stamp to be purchased and used in various ways to advertise the Fund, was the medium through which contributions were first made but gradually the opportunities in this work broadened out. Collection boxes were devised to be placed in Jewish homes for the reception of odd donations during the year, and Hadassah has made this work a regular part of its program, having placed 4,000 boxes which have brought in thousands of dollars. Each year the chapters in the various cities and towns go out gathering up the boxes, giving new ones to the householders and remitting the money secured to headquarters of the Fund in Canada, at Montreal. In recent years, it has become a custom on occasions such as barmitzvahs, betrothals, births, weddings, wedding anniversaries, and social gatherings in homes, to take up contributions for the National Fund. Hadassah chapters honor the services of officers and leading members by purchasing sections of land in the names of the individuals. The birth of babies to members is sometimes commemorated by the subscription of money to plant trees in Palestine, in the names of the infants. Another means of contributing to the Fund is by the inscription of names of prominent Hadassah workers, and of chapters that have won special distinction, in the Golden Book, of which there are now three volumes containing names which form a roll of honor of service by members of the Jewish race and Jewish organizations in all parts of the world. Each inscription costs one hundred dollars. The Hadassah chapters have contributed towards the inscription of the names of Baron Rothschild and Sir Herbert Samuel, Palestine's first High Commissioner, in the Golden Book. The name of Mrs. A. J. Freiman, Dominion President, has been inscribed in this Book also. On July 22, 1923, which was the 20th anniversary of the death of Theodore Herzl, Canadian Hadassah chapters held special observances to raise money for the planting of trees in the Herzl Forests which are being laid out in Palestine in memory of the first great Zionist leader. Garden cities in the names of deceased Zionist workers of world-wide renown as for instance the late Dr. Max Nordau, are being established in Palestine by the National Fund, and Hadassah has collected money for this purpose. In August, 1923, Mrs. Freiman was honored by the head office of the Fund in Jerusalem giving her name to a grove of trees in Palestine, as a mark of appreciation for her work for the Fund in Canada. By honoring the president in this way, the directors of the Fund also honored the thousands of Hadassah workers in Canada, who have done so much for the Fund, and who have such a depth of affection for and pride in their president.

Palestine Restoration Fund

The Hadassah chapters actively participated in the raising of money for this Fund, during the years 1918, 1919, 1920 and 1921, the money secured totalling

$275,198 having been devoted towards reconstruction work in Palestine. This Fund was succeeded by the Keren Hayesod as the principal Zionist fund for the rebuilding of Palestine.

Hebrew University

Hadassah women are vitally interested in the extension and betterment of Jewish education, and have therefore been most enthusiastic in regard to the great University which has been founded in Jerusalem. At the 3rd Hadassah convention in Toronto, January 1924, Dr. Weizman, president of the World Zionist Organization, was personally pledged a contribution of $2,000 towards the University by Canadian Hadassah.

Motza Convalescent Home

This much needed institution where Chaluzim may recuperate from illness was granted a contribution of $2,000 for equipment by Canadian Hadassah in 1924. The Home is beautifully situated about five miles from Jerusalem.

Hadassah's Work for Palestine's Health

There are Hadassah general hospitals at Jerusalem, Tel-Aviv, Haifa and Safed, in which as many as 6,000 patients have been treated within a period of nine months. There is a training school for nurses at Jerusalem, the pupils numbering fifty. Infant welfare stations are conducted in Rachoboth, Petach Tikvah, Tiberias, and in Jerusalem where there are four, all these stations caring for about ten thousand children a month. There are eight laboratories, including X-ray apparatus, and there were 60,000 examinations within a nine month period in 1924. Clinics and drug stores are maintained in Jaffa, Safed, Tiberias, Haifa, and Hebron, from which 250,000 visits were paid to sick, and at which 50,000 patients were treated, all within a nine-month period. There are also clinics and drug stores in the rural districts, in 60 colonies and workmen's settlements. The teeth of 15,000 school children are regularly inspected by Hadassah dentists. In addition a comprehensive program of anti-tuberculosis, anti-trachoma, maternity, pre-natal, and general health propaganda is carried on.

Canadian Hadassah chapters contributed $4,500 towards the Hadassah hospitals and the Nurses' Training School in Palestine during 1920, 1921, 1922, 1923, and 1924, and also $1,200 for scholarships whereby two nurses after graduating from the school were enabled to take up post-graduate work in some other country before settling down to their life's vocation in Palestine.

Mizrachi School, Tel-Aviv

In 1925, Canadian Hadassah agreed to contribute $1,500 to provide for the construction of one of the rooms in the Mizrachi Elementary and High School at Tel-Aviv, Palestine, the room to be known as 'Canadian Hadassah Room'.

Constitution of Hadassah

The constitution of Hadassah sets forth that it is the aim of the organization to promote Zionist institutions and enterprises in Palestine, and to foster Zionist ideas in Canada. Jewish women who are members of the Zionist Organization are eligible for Hadassah membership. A minimum of twenty women can constitute a chapter, except in special cases of smaller communities. The annual dues are two dollars per member, one dollar of which is paid to the Zionist Organization, forty cents paid to the Dominion headquarters of the Hadassah Organization; and sixty cents retained for the local chapters' treasuries. The Hadassah movement in Canada observes in general principle both the constitutions of the Zionist Organization, and the Women's International Zionist Organization with which it is affiliated.

Method of Functioning

Most of the chapters hold meetings every week, usually on Mondays, these gatherings sometimes taking the form of teas and social affairs at the homes of the different members, when in conjunction with the disposal of the week's business, there are musical programs and refreshments. The creation of a friendly spirit by means of such gatherings all contributes towards strengthening of the Hadassah chapters. Members of the chapters pay weekly dues of 25 cents each at these meetings. Special affairs are held from time to time throughout the year in order to raise substantial sums for the various Hadassah funds. The Hadassah chapters have become the principal Jewish women's organization in the cities where they have been formed. Their activities are not wholly confined to raising funds for the Zionist cause. Time is found to co-operate with non-Jewish organization in general philanthropic work, and the admiration and respect of non-Jews have been won by the business like and enthusiastic manner in which Hadassah grapples with the problems of charity, health and special relief.

Bulletin

A bulletin of general Hadassah news is published by headquarters every month and serves a useful purpose in disseminating the latest accounts of Zionist work in all parts of the world, but particularly in Palestine. The bulletin helps to keep the chapters in Canada closely in touch with each other, and regular reports of what each chapter has done during the preceding month are carried, this being the means of exchanging ideas that have proven successful in stimulating Hadassah work generally. Mrs. L. Fitch, is editor of the Bulletin, and she is assisted by an editorial board appointed by the conventions.

Financial Achievements

The financial statement of the achievements of Canadian Hadassah during the period from 1918 to 1924 inclusive, shows that a total of $230,060 was raised for distinctly Hadassah objects. This figure does not take into consideration the thousands of dollars which Hadassah has collected for what are termed the general Zionist funds. For instance, the money Hadassah has collected for the National Fund is not given separately, but is included with the general collections for this fund, which for the period from 1907 to 1924 inclusive, totalled $124,208, and of which Hadassah undoubtedly raised a very substantial portion. A detailed statement of the money Hadassah has distributed is given on the following page. From this may be judged at a glance the great work Hadassah in Canada has accomplished.

The reason that no separate figures are available for Hadassah's contributions prior to 1918, is that Hadassah, as such, was really only beginning to be active at that time. Many women's Zionist societies of course existed prior to 1918, as the sketch which precedes this indicates, but all the monies they raised were forwarded for inclusion with the general Zionist funds, and due to inadequate records of these former women's Zionist societies, it is impossible to state with any degree of accuracy, how much the Zionist women of Canada, have collected in dollars and cents for the various special and general objects which all go to make up the Zionist cause as a whole.

Dominion Officers

Mrs. A. J. Freiman, Ottawa - - President	Mrs. Anna Selick, Toronto - - Vice-President
Mrs. L. Fitch, Montreal - - Vice-President	Mrs. H. E. Wilder, Winnipeg - - Vice-President
Mrs. D. Dunkelman, Toronto - Vice-President	Mrs. M. A. Brown, Montreal - - Treasurer

Mrs. H. Singer, Montreal - - - Secretary

Dominion Council

Mrs. S. Kahn, Mrs. B. Perelmutter, Mrs. S. M. Rothman, Mrs. L. Miller, Mrs. A. H. Rabin, Mrs. M. Poyaner, Mrs. Leon Levine, Mrs. H. L. Sourkes, Mrs. J. Edelberg, Mrs. E. G. Bernstein, Mrs. L. Goldman, Mrs. J. Rockstein, Mrs. M. H. Cohen, Mrs. H. Herzig, Mrs. L. Matthews, Mrs. H. H. Livingstone, Mrs. A. Levin, Mrs. A. J. Alexandor, Miss Ida Seigler, all of Montreal; Mrs. M. Miller, Lachine, Que.; Mrs. B. Siegel, Glace Bay, N.S.; Miss S. Smilovitz, Que.; Mrs. A. H. Coplan, Mrs. H. Freedman, Mrs. J. Holzman, Mrs. L. Leiken, Mrs. D. Mirsky, all of Ottawa; Mrs. L. Abramson, Kingston; Mrs. H. Freiman, Hamilton; Mrs. A. Nadell, Brantford; Miss Sadie Feldman, Timmins; Miss Leah Lewis, London; Mrs. J. Smith, Sherbrooke, Que.; Mrs. J. Goldman, St. John, N.B.; Mrs. C. Byalin, Halifax, N.S.; Mrs. L. Green, Peterboro, Ont.; Mrs. A. I. Cohen, Yarmouth, N.S.; Mrs. B. R. Brickner, Mrs. M. Wolfson, Mrs. M. M. Davis, Mrs. M. Mehr, Mrs. B. Vise, Mrs. I. Cohen, Mrs. A. B. Bennett, Mrs. D. Abramovitch, Mrs. L. M. Schwartz, Mrs. A. I. Willinsky, Miss Tessie Lavine, Mrs. M. Goldberg, Mrs. M. Geldzaeler, Mrs. M. L. Willinsky, Mrs. L. M. Cohen, all of Toronto; Miss Frances Geller, Windsor; Mrs. A. Cohen, Port Arthur; Mrs. A. Berman, Fort William; Mrs. D. Richardson, Sault Ste. Marie; Mrs. P. Chertkov, Mrs. M. Snider, Mrs. H. Goldin, Mrs. H. Sokolov, Mrs. I. W. Schloss, Mrs. S. Stockhammer, Mrs. Rose Rady, Mrs. M. H. Abramovitch, Mrs. B. Levinson, Mrs. C. H. Lyons, Mrs. D. Gotlieb, all of Winnipeg; Mrs. M. Lieberman, Edmonton; Mrs. J. Krivel, Estevan; Mrs. Max Gropper, Saskatoon; Mrs. J. Bercuson, Calgary; Mrs. I. Friedgut, Regina; Mrs. J. B. Jaffe, Vancouver; Mrs. L. Mahrer, Vancouver.

The following is a tabulation of Hadassah collections during the seven-year period of which record has been available:

Year	General Hadassah	Medical Unit, Hospital, Nurses' Training School	Hadassah Scholarship Fund	Helping Hand Fund	Orphans' Relief	Financially Adopted Orphans	Chaluzim & Jewel Fund for Hostel, etc.	Domestic Science School	Haifa School Tuber. Sanitarium & Sundries
1918	$ 1,017.25								
1919				$ 159,297.21					
1920	2,112.21	$ 950.00	$ 500	41.85	$ 528.75				$ 88.95
1921	7,534.27	650.00	500		2,543.02		$ 94.00		132.10
1922	2,485.85	520.00	200		589.30		3,247.70		43.05
									250.00
1923	1,135.00	1,047.87			525.00	$ 400.00	17,042.46	$ 9,290.16	107.19
									300.00
1924		1,136.25			691.23	822.25	4,806.75	9,211.23	220.00
Totals:	$ 14,284.58	$ 4,304.12	$ 1,200	$ 159,339.06	$ 4,877.30	$ 1,222.25	$ 25,190.91	$ 18,501.39	$ 1,141.29

RECAPITULATION

General Hadassah Receipts	$ 14,284.58
Medical Unit, Hospital, Nurses' Training School	4,304.12
Hadassah Scholarship Fund	1,200.00
Helping Hand Fund	159,339.06
Orphans' Relief	4,877.30
Financially adopted orphans	1,222.25
Chaluzim, Jewel Fund for Hostel	25,190.91
Domestic Science School, Nahalal	18,501.39
Dr. Biran's School, Haifa, Tuberculosis Sanitarium, Safed, and miscellaneous purposes	1,141.29
Grand Total	$230,060.90 Distinctly Hadassah.

HOW HADASSAH SPANS THE DOMINION

FROM HALIFAX, N.S., TO VANCOUVER, B.C.—A CHAIN OF ZIONIST SERVICE

CHAPTERS AND THEIR LEADERS

NOVA SCOTIA
HALIFAX........................Mrs. M. Byalin
GLACE BAY......................Mrs. B. Siegel
SYDNEY.........................Miss Ida Feder

NEW BRUNSWICK
ST. JOHN.......................Mrs. J. Goldman

QUEBEC
LACHINE........................Mrs. J. Schechter
QUEBEC.........................Mrs. L. Lazarovtiz
SHERBROOKE.....................Mrs. J. Smith

MONTREAL
CENTRAL CHAPTER................Mrs. H. M. Levinoff
DAUGHTERS OF JUDEA.............Miss Fanny Raskin
DEBORAH CHAPTER................Miss Agnes Levin
ETA COHEN......................Mrs. E. Lazare
HATIKVAH.......................Miss A. Strasberg
JUDITH.........................Mrs. J. L. Zlotnik
LILLIAN FREIMAN................Miss Reba Gross
MENORAH........................Mrs. B. Kahn
MIRIAM BRAININ-ORTENBERG......Mrs. F. Harris
MIZPAH.........................Miss Gertrude Lerner
NORTH END......................Mrs. L. Mathews
QUEEN ESTHER...................Mrs. L. Miller
RACHEL.........................Mrs. R. Ness
ROSE OF SHARON.................Miss Sarah Strasberg
SHAAR HASHOMAYIM, Jun..........Mrs. M. A. Brown
SYBIL COHEN....................Mrs. M. H. Cohen
WESTMOUNT......................Mrs. H. H. Livingstone
YOUNG LADIES' LITERARY.........Mrs. H. Singer
NAIR TAMID.....................Miss S. Hoichberg
TEL-AVIV.......................Miss Evelyn Astroff
UNIVERSITY.....................Miss Bertha Myer
ZIONA..........................Mrs. L. Diner
MONTREAL HADASSAH COUNCIL Mrs. L. Fitch
MONTREAL JUNIOR HADASSAH COUNCIL....
Mrs. Leon Levine

ONTARIO
OTTAWA.........................Mrs. A. J. Freiman
OTTAWA, Jun....................Miss Olive Pullan
KINGSTON, QUEEN ESTHER, Mrs. L. Abramson
KINGSTON, (2)..................Mrs. I. Cohen
PETERBORO......................Mrs. L. Green

ONTARIO
HAMILTON.......................Mrs. M. Epstein
HAMILTON, Jun..................Miss Freda Stein
LONDON.........................Mrs. M. Fishbein
LONDON, Jun....................Miss Ida Lewis
BRANTFORD......................Mrs. Samuel Fox
TIMMINS........................Mrs. L. Helperin
WINDSOR........................Miss Frances Geller
WINDSOR, Jun...................Miss D. Barnett
SAULTE STE. MARIE..............Mrs. D. Richardson
FORT WILLIAM...................Mrs. Rose A. Drapkin
PORT ARTHUR....................Mrs. A. Cohen

TORONTO
NAOMI..........................Mrs. M. Friedman
CENTRAL........................Mrs. L. M. Schwartz
DEBORAH........................Miss Hilda Factor
MIRIAM.........................Mrs. Fauman
DAUGHTERS OF ZION..............Mrs. I. Cohen
HERZL GIRLS....................Miss Gertie Jackson
WESTERN........................Mrs. M. Barrett
ROSE...........................Mrs. F. S. Hutner
TORONTO HADASSAH COUNCIL.......
Mrs. D. Dunkelman
TORONTO JUNIOR HADASSAH COUNCIL.......
Miss M. Wolfson
HADASSAH MASCOTS...............Miss Leah Levi

MANITOBA
WINNIPEG.......................Mrs. H. E. Wilder
WINNIPEG, (EZRAH)..............Miss Rose Rady
WINNIPEG, Jun..................Miss Sybil Weidman

SASKATCHEWAN
ESTEVAN........................Mrs. J. Krivel
LIPTON.........................Mrs. S. H. Naimark
REGINA.........................Mrs. I. Friedgut
SASKATOON......................Mrs. J. Mallin

ALBERTA
CALGARY........................Miss Rose Rabinowitz
EDMONTON.......................Mrs. Wm. Diamond

BRITISH COLUMBIA
VANCOUVER......................Mrs. J. Parker

By Simpson Bros.

MRS. D. DUNKELMAN, TORONTO

MRS. DAVID (ROSE) DUNKELMAN is one of the outstanding Jewish communal workers of Toronto. She is a daughter of Mr. and Mrs. H. Miller of Toronto, and received her education in that city. Both Mr. and Mrs. Dunkelman are ardent Zionists, and it is in this connection that Mrs. Dunkelman has been prominently before the public. In 1920, she was elected Vice-President of the Hadassah Council of Toronto, and in 1921 was elected President, which position she has occupied continuously since that date. She was the first President of the Rose Chapter of Hadassah, which was named in her honor and in which she takes particular interest. Mrs. Dunkelman is Vice-President of the Hadassah Organization of Canada, and is a member of the National Executive of the Zionist Organization of Canada. She has been very active in working for the Keren Hayesod Fund and other Zionistic causes, and was the organizer of the "Theatre Night" held at Loew's Uptown Theatre in Toronto, when over $5,500 was raised for the Federation of Jewish Philanthropies, an undertaking that has not been excelled in any other community. Under her presidency, Toronto Hadassah has greatly developed, three senior chapters and one junior chapter having been added. Four "Yarids" have also been held during her presidency, two in the Arcadia Hall, one in the Armouries and one in a building on Yonge Street, and over $26,000 was raised through this means for Hadassah work in Palestine. Two other "Theatre Nights" were also held under her supervision when over $7,000 was raised for similar purposes. On different occasions, Mrs. Dunkelman has been the guest of honor at various Hadassah chapters throughout Ontario, and her assistance has always been highly prized by all members of the organization. She also takes much interest in all undertakings of a philanthropic nature.

THE FEDERATION OF YOUNG JUDAEA OF CANADA
By Moe Levitt

YOUNG Judaea is an organization of young men and women who are awakened to the needs of our people and desire by means of a nationalistic Jewish education to equip themselves for effective service.

Young Judaea fills a unique purpose in Jewish life in Canada. It is the organization of the Jewish youth, whose aim it is to advance the cause of Zionism; to promote Jewish culture and ideals in accordance with Jewish tradition. Young Judaea has set itself to popularize Jewish subjects of study; to arouse enthusiasm for the study of Jewish history, Hebrew Literature, Hebrew language; to instill in the young a loyalty to the Jewish people and its glorious traditions; to inculcate a devotion to the Jewish Homeland in Palestine and an appreciation of the Zionist aim and willingness to serve in the cause for the re-establishment of the Jewish Nation on its own soil.

The medium through which Young Judaea works is generally a club or group of clubs. These clubs usually meet in some communal centre under the supervision of a Leader or Director who is in constant communication with the central organization. The actual work of the individual club, although necessarily prescribed in certain details by the Organization, is left to the Leader. In general, it consists of the celebration of Jewish holidays by means of public gatherings and festive meetings, the study of Jewish history through lectures by Leaders and essays by club members, and the acquisition of information on topics of current Jewish interest through short talks or discussions and debates. In addition to the above, Young Judaea encourages among its clubs, active participation in Zionist work.

Even the superficial observer of Jewish life can recognize the vital need for such a Movement in Canada to bring our Jewish youth under the influence of Jewish ideals and to imbue them with sentiments of love and loyalty to all that is characteristically Jewish.

Young Judaea as a distinct national organization came into existence in 1917 at the Zionist Convention held in Winnipeg. It was at that Convention that a plan for a Dominion Organization of Young Judaea was formally presented by a delegation of Young Judaeans, headed by Mr. Bernard Joseph, at that time the President of Montreal Young Judaea. The idea was enthusiastically received and the delegation was encouraged to proceed with their undertaking.

Before that time there had been attempts made to organize Young Judaea Clubs in the larger centres such as Montreal, Toronto and Winnipeg. As far back as 1910, the first Young Judaea Club was organized in Montreal. By 1916, groups of young people had been influenced to accept a Young Judaea programme as the basis of their activities and to enter the Young Judaea League of Montreal.

Encouraged by local successes, the Young Judaeans of Montreal were stimulated to enlarge the scope of their organization. It was not, however, until 1919 that the Organization was formally organized with Philip Joseph at its first President.

With the growth of the Federation, the difficulties of proper supervision became more and more apparent. Centres throughout the Dominion constantly called on the Montreal office for educational material and general direction. The Committee at the head of the Organization soon realized the need of a Director, fully qualified by virtue of educational attainment, Zionistic fervour and executive ability.

In 1922, at the Zionist Convention held in Ottawa, efforts were made to induce the Zionist Organization to place an Executive Director at the head of the Movement. It was not until September, 1924, that Mr. Samuel J. Rodman of New York assumed the duties of his office as Executive Director.

The Movement which hitherto has been largely confined to the larger centres of Jewry, is now introduced into every city, town and hamlet where there are a sufficient number of Jewish boys and girls for the formation of a club or group of clubs.

To affiliate with Young Judaea, a club must agree to carry out a program of Jewish studies such as is outlined in the various bulletins that Young Judaea issues. The weekly club program is varied and attractive, including papers on Jewish history, discussion of current events, readings from Jewish literature, the singing of national and traditional melodies, the celebration of Jewish festivals, dramatic presentations, declamations and debates. To this program the club usually adds athletic training and social entertainments. Individual members of the club may form smaller circles or groups of special activities, such as needle work, drawing, singing or for dramatics, all of which are permeated with Jewishness. The combined groups conduct general activities such as lectures, inter-club competitions, entertainments, socials and outings.

Young Judaea keeps in touch with the individual clubs by means of reports as well as by correspondence with club leaders and members desiring advice and suggestions. It issues to its clubs occasional circular letters, suggested programs for the festivals, pamphlets and literature. In addition, Young Judaea now endeavours to assist its clubs through direct contact with the Executive Director who visits every Young Judaea centre.

The following are the present officers of the National Organization:— Bernard Joseph, Palestine, Hon. President; Moe Levitt, Montreal, President; Bernard Figler, Montreal, Ralph Isaacs, St. John, Clara Pall, Winnipeg, Lionel M. Gelber Toronto, Vice-Presidents; Sam Shait, Montreal, Secretary; M. A. Mendelovitch, Montreal, Treasurer; Samuel J. Rodman, Executive Director.

A. J. FREIMAN, OTTAWA.

ARCHIBALD J. FREIMAN was born at Wirballen, Lithuania on June 6th, 1880, the son of Harris and Hanna Freiman, and came to Canada with his parents in 1893. He received his early education in Lithuania, and on his coming to this country, attended the public schools of Hamilton and the Hamilton Business College. In 1899 he established the Canadian House Furnishing Company at Kingston, Ontario, and in 1902 removed this business to Ottawa, where he remained in partnership with his father until 1910, when he bought out his father's interests, and has since conducted the business under his own name. From a small start he has built up one of the largest departmental stores in the country and he occupies a front rank amongst the merchant princes in Canada. He was President, 1920, of the Ottawa Branch, Retail Merchants' Association of Canada. He is President of the Zionist Organization of Canada, and a member of the Action's Committee of the World Zionist Organization; Chairman of the Jewish War Orphans Committee of Canada; Vice-President of the National War Relief Societies of Canada, Director of the following; Joint Distribution Committee of America; Perley Home for Incurables; Protestant Hospital, Ottawa; and was Vice-President of the Central Canada Exhibition Association 1920. For over 19 years Mr. Freiman has been President of the Adath Jeshurun Congregation, the oldest synagogue in Ottawa, and which was founded by his father-in-law, the late Mr. Moses Bilsky. He is Honorary Chairman of the Ottawa Hebrew School Board. Mr. Freiman is a member of the Laurentian, Ottawa Hunt & Golf, Ottawa Motor, and Kiwanis Clubs of Ottawa, and the Montefiore Club of Montreal, also the Ontario Motor League, and belongs to the Masonic Order, K. of P., I.O.O.F., & I.O.B.B. His communal activities are by no means confined to his own creed, and he is regarded as one of the most prominent and public-spirited citizens of Ottawa. On August 18th, 1903 he was married to Lillian, daughter of the late Moses Bilsky of Ottawa, and has one son and two daughters.

HISTORY OF ZIONISM IN CANADA
By Leon Goldman

"And speak unto them, thus hath said the Lord Eternal, behold, I will take the children of Israel from among the nations whither they are gone, and I will gather them from every side, and bring them unto their own land."—Ezekiel, xxxvii; 21

EVER since the Jews were expelled from Palestine and forced to make their homes amongst strangers, there have been those who hoped for the fulfilment of the Biblical prophecy, that one day they would again return to their own land. Persecution and oppression have undoubtedly strengthened this longing, and there have been Zionists in all generations.

A refuge for those who have nowhere to lay their heads, a place where they can live as human beings, a HOME, where they need not ask for favors in order to worship the God of their fathers and instruct their children in the teachings of Judaism, has been the cry of the Jews for centuries. Even in the most enlightened countries there are difficulties to be encountered, and prejudices and lack of understanding to be met. It was this feeling that inspired THEODORE HERZL, that Jew whose name will go down in history, blessed by posterity, to write his immortal work, "The Jewish State", and thus put in a practical light the ideals of present-day Zionism.

In Canada, as elsewhere all over the world, the Zionist Movement has grown by leaps and bounds, and Canadian Jewry can take pride in the fact that they stand second to none in the support of this great ideal, the greatest National Movement in the world today. It has brought Jewry together as nothing else ever did, and in this History of Zionism in Canada, we aim to show an authentic record of its development in this country, and trust that it may help to perpetuate the names of those, many of whom have gone to their last rest, who have been responsible for its growth.

1887

The first attempt to organize a Zionist Society in Canada, was made in 1887, by Professor Harkawi and a number of other enthusiasts, but owing to local conditions being unfavorable, very little was accomplished in a practical sense, and the matter lay in abeyance for five years.

1892

In the year 1892, the Chovevei Zion חובבי ציון of America succeeded in bringing about the formation of a branch Society in Canada, the Society Shovey Zion No. 2, שבי ציון in Montreal. The first membership list contains about fifty names. The leading members were:—Hyam Bernstein, President; Samuel Wolsey, Secretary; Lazarus Cohen, Treasurer; and Samuel Freedman, Hiram Cohen, Max Miller, M. Coviensky, Moses Glazer, N. Weissburg, L. Yaphe, S. Levitt, M. Giffin, and L. Kushner.

1893

Early in 1893, a delegation composed of Mr. Lazarus Cohen of Montreal, and Dr. M. Mintz of New York, was sent by the Society to investigate the possibilities of sending settlers to Palestine. On their return from Palestine, in May, 1893, the delegates were received in Paris by the Society Iisehoub Eretz Israel, of which the Chief Rabbi of France, Zadok Kahn, and the Chief Rabbi of Paris, J. H. Dreyfus, were the honorary Presidents. At the conference then held, Mr. Lazarus Cohen foretold that great possibilities were awaiting in Palestine when its children returned, but that there were many obstacles in the way, and that many sacrifices would be required. When he reported to the Society at Montreal some of the difficulties that were in sight, many of the members withdrew from the Society. The remainder, however, remained loyal to their undertaking, and remitted to the Paris Head Office in July of that year, the sum of 12,500 francs as their first instalment for the purchase of land in Methulla, in the north of Palestine. The Paris committee had found it was impossible to obtain land east of the Jordan, and recommended trying to purchase some in the Hauran, in Trans-Jordania.

1894

In March, 1894, an additional remittance of 7,500 francs was made, and the Society was advised that 4,000 dunam had already been purchased for their use. The correspondence from L. Braun and R. Lutetzky, of the Paris Committee, led the members of the Montreal Society to believe that conditions were such that they could settle two or three families on the land, as a start.

1895

In 1895, two families were sent to settle on the land, but they met with great difficulties, being harassed by the neighboring tribes without receiving any protection from the Ottoman Government. After being on the land for less than a year, and meeting with many hardships, the would-be settlers returned, and their report was deemed a sufficiently good reason for the society to disband. Entreaties and pleadings from Mr. Elie Sheid, who wrote on behalf of Baron Edmund de Rothschild, were of no avail, and after being threatened with personal harm, the President, Mr. Bernstein, decided to ask for the return of the money sent to Paris.

1898

It was not, however, until February, 1898, that the total sum of 32,131.50 francs was returned. This represented the total amount remitted to Paris, plus accrued interest, and less the personal expenses incurred by the Society. This unfortunate closing of the first chapter of Zionist work in Canada made subsequent attempts by various Chovevei-Zionists practically impossible. Nevertheless, due to the new spirit created by the first Zionist Congress called by Theodore Herzl, in Basle, in 1897, many became disposed to listen to the propaganda of National rebirth, without necessarily considering the needs of immediate colonization, and before the idea had received the recognition of the World Powers.

On January 16th, 1898, a few staunch Zionists, headed by Hyam Bernstein, and with the assistance of Rabbi Mordecai Aron Ashinsky, A. Garmaise, J. Makowsky, and M. Godinsky, met and formed themselves into an Organization Committee for the purpose of forming a Zionist Society. A mass meeting was called for January 23rd in that year at the Synagogue B'nai Jacob. Notwithstanding that it was held under the most difficult conditions, such as unprecedented cold weather which froze the water and gas-pipes, and a terrific snow-storm, the meeting was very well attended. The speakers were Rabbi M. A. Ashinsky, Rabbi Meldola de Sola, and Rabbi H. Cohen. The audience responded enthusiastically, and over a hundred names were registered as members. A provisional Committee was formed of the following:— Rabbi M. A. Ashinsky, Messrs. Hyam Bernstein, Clarence I. de Sola, and M. Shapiro, with Mr. David Sperber as Secretary. All the Synagogues were invited to send their accredited representatives to a meeting for the formation of a Society, and the election of a permanent Board.

On February, 13th, 1898, an organization meeting took place at the Baron de Hirsch Institute, on St. Eliza-

THE LATE CHEVALIER CLARENCE I. DE SOLA

THE LATE CLARENCE ISAAC DE SOLA was born in Montreal on August 15th, 1858, the third son of the late Rev. Abraham de Sola, LL.D. He was educated in the Montreal public schools and at McGill University. For many years Mr. de Sola was engaged in bridge and shipbuilding, and was Director on the board of several steamship companies. He was president of the Ocean and Inland Transportation Co., and from 1887 was Manager of the Comptoir Belgo-Canadien, and established a steamship service between Montreal and Antwerp in this connection. Some of the public works that the late Mr. de Sola was instrumental in building were the Soulanges and Trent Canals. As a director of Swan, Hunter, Wigham and Richardson, Ltd., of Wallsend-on-Tyne, he carried out contracts for the building of a great number of ships for traffic on the Great Lakes, the St. Lawrence and the Ocean, and for the Canadian Government Service. He always took a prominent part in communal affairs and was an officer in many philanthropic societies. He was Parnass of the Spanish and Portuguese Synagogue from 1906 until his death. He was widely known as one of the leaders of the Zionist Movement and was a member of the Actions Committee, the supreme governing body of Zionism, and for many years was president of the Federation of Zionist Societies of Canada, and took a leading part in the International Congresses. Mr. de Sola was an authority on Jewish History and has written and published a number of articles. He was honorary corresponding Director of the American Jewish Historical Society and of the Anglo-Jewish Historical Society. From 1904 until his death, Mr. de Sola was Belgian Consul at Montreal, and during the war from 1914 to 1918, the task of organizing and forwarding the large number of Belgian reservists in Canada and the United States, devolved upon him. In 1918 he was decorated by King Albert of Belgium with the Order of Leopold. Mr. de Sola was married to Belle Maud, daughter of Leopold Goldsmith of Cleveland, Ohio, and had two sons, and two daughters. Mr. de Sola died in May, 1920.

J. S. LEO, MONTREAL

Photo by Notman

JOSEPH SAMUEL LEO, a member of a family that includes Numa Edward Hartog, the first Jewish Senior Wrangler at Cambridge University, England, and a Fellow of Trinity College; Marcus Hartog, Emeritus Professor of Biology, Victoria University, Cork, Ireland; Philip Hartog, for many years Registrar of London University, and at present Vice-Chancellor of the University of Dacca, India; and the distinguished Scientist, Mrs. Ayrton, step-mother of Israel Zangwill; was born in London, England, on December 29th, 1859. His parents were the late Louis and Isabel (Moss) Leo. He was educated at the South Hampstead Collegiate School and at the University College, London. Mr. Leo came to Canada in March 1883 and settled in Montreal, where he has since resided. He established the first wholesale optical House in Canada, then called the Mount Royal Optical Company, but now known as the Consolidated Optical Company and he remained with this firm for over twenty years. He has since been identified with the National Optical Company, which he founded in 1912. He is a Director of the Laurentian Insurance Company. Mr. Leo has always taken a keen and active interest in all communal and welfare work, and has devoted a great deal of time and energy especially to the undertakings of the Zionist Movement. He was for five years President of the first Zionist Society in Canada, and was Secretary of the Zionist Federation for twenty years. He was a trustee of the Spanish and Portuguese Synagogue for over twenty-five years, and is the Vice-President and Chairman of the Loan Committee of the Hebrew Free Loan Society of Montreal. He was first Vice-President of the St. George's Society, Montreal, and was the first President of the Canadian Chess Association. He is a member of the St. George's Society; Ionic Lodge, A.F. & A.M.; Mt. Horeb Chapter, R.A.M.; and the Montreal Amateur Athletic Association. On August 8th, 1889, Mr. Leo was married in London, England, to Emma, daughter of the late Morris Cohen, of Maitland, New South Wales, Australia, and he has two sons, Maitland and Alan, and one daughter, Miss Dorothy Leo.

ABRAHAM A. LEVIN, J.P., MONTREAL

ABRAHAM A. LEVIN, President of the Dominion Cord & Tassel Co. Ltd., was born in Vilna, Lithuania, on May 18th, the son of Solomon J. and Elsie Levin of that city. He received his education in Russia and came to Canada in 1892, settling in Montreal, where he began his business career. He was one of the earliest manufacturers of braids and trimmings in Canada, and in 1895, he founded the firm of which he is today the active head, and he has developed this business into one of the largest of its kind in the country. He is a member and an active supporter of many charitable, educational, and patriotic organizations, and devotes much time to communal work. Mr. Levin has been identified with the Zionist movement since its very inception in Canada. In 1908 he was elected a Vice-President of the Zionist Organization at the ninth Convention. At the tenth Convention in 1909 he was elected Treasurer, an office which he has held continuously up to the present time. He represented Canadian Zionism at the tenth Zionist Congress at Basle, Switzerland, in August 1911; at the First International Zionist Conference after the Mandate in London in July 1921; and at the thirteenth Zionist Congress in Carlsbad in August 1923. Previous to attending the latter Congress he visited Palestine in company with his wife. Mr. Levin was a member of the Greater Actions Committee of the World's Zionist Organization during the period of 1920-21, and he was Treasurer of the Canadian Jewish Congress held in Montreal. He is a member and a trustee of the Shaar Hashomayim Synagogue, Montreal. Mr. Levin is a life governor of the Baron de Hirsch Institute, the Montreal General Hospital, and the Hebrew Maternity Hospital, Montreal. He is the President of the Jewish Immigrant Aid Society of Canada, and is a member of Montreal Young Men's Hebrew Association, and other institutions, and of the Masonic Order, A.F. & A.M.; the Montreal Board of Trade; and the Montefiore Club. He is a Justice of the Peace for the District of Montreal On February 1st, 1898, Mr. Levin was married to Miss Annie Abramowitz, and they have one son Leon Levin.

RABBI J. L. ZLOTNIK, MONTREAL

RABBI J. L. ZLOTNIK, Director, Jewish National Fund in Canada, Publicity and Propaganda Departments of the Zionist Organization, was born in Plock, Poland, April 15th, 1888. He was brought up in the home of his brothers, both Rabbis, and the year 1910 he spent in the famous Yeshiva Volozyn, where the Smichah was conferred upon him by the famous Gaon, Rabbi Raphael Shapiro. In 1911, he was elected as Rabbi in the city of Gombin. He was a member of the Central Committee of the Zionist Organization of Poland, and in 1917, when the Agudath Israel started the policy against the Zionist Organization in Poland, and being convinced that Polish Orthodoxy would become a great factor in Zionism by proper organization, he called the first Conference for building up a Mizrachi Organization in Poland. Being elected President of this Conference, he started an arduous campaign for Mizrachi Ideals among Polish Jewry publishing numerous pamphlets both in Hebrew and Yiddish on many timely topics, and on Jewish education. In 1918, he represented the Polish Mizrachi at the first World Mizrachi Conference, which took place in Amsterdam, Holland. In the meantime the Mizrachi throughout Poland had grown up to an organization boasting of a membership of 100,000. He then resigned from his position as Rabbi and went to Warsaw in the capacity of General Secretary of the organization. He also organized special Mizrachi schools throughout Poland and a great Yeshiva Tachkimoni in Warsaw. In 1920, he was invited to come to America, which invitation he accepted, participating on his way in the first Zionist World Conference after the war, which took place in London in July, 1920. Rabbi Zlotnik is the author of a series of books under the name "Der Vunder Ozar Von der Yiddisher Sprach", which is a thorough study on the idioms and special characteristics of the Jewish language. His articles have been published in almost every Yiddish paper in U.S. and Canada, and a few of his poems in English appeared in the Canadian Jewish Chronicle and The Jewish Forum.

H. E. WILDER, WINNIPEG

H. E. WILDER, Author and Journalist, was born in the village of Ulmi, which is situated at the foot of the Carpathian Mountains, Roumania, on May 1st, 1881. He was educated at the cheder and public schools of Craiova, and at the High Commercial State School of Bucharest, from which he graduated in 1901. During his student days at Bucharest, Mr. Wilder took an active part in literary Jewish circles and assisted in the creation of various young Zionist societies. He came to Canada in June, 1903, and settled in the City of Winnipeg, where he has since resided. On his arrival in Canada, he secured a position in the Foreign Exchange Department of a banking institution, as he had a good commercial training and was familiar with six European languages. He resigned from this position in 1911, when he became engaged in mercantile enterprises. In 1915, Mr. Wilder became the owner of the Israelite Press, Limited. In 1919, he was elected President of the Employing Printers' Association of Winnipeg, and when the United Typothetae of America organized a branch in Winnipeg, in 1920, he became its first President. Mr. Wilder has always taken a keen and leading part in the communal work and philanthropic undertakings of Winnipeg. He has been a member of the Board of Directors, and of the Executive of the local Y.M.H.A., Talmud Torah, The Jewish Orphanage, United Hebrew Relief, B'nai B'rith, The War Relief Society, The Immigrant Aid Society, The Canadian Jewish Congress, and of the Zionist Organization. He has held office in the Zionist Organization continuously since 1912. In 1918, he was Chairman of the Executive of the Winnipeg Zionist Council, and in 1920, its President. In 1922, he was elected Vice-President of the Zionist Organization of Canada, and was re-elected in 1924. During the War, Mr. Wilder was in charge of the Foreign Publicity Department of the Dominion Victory Loan Campaigns. He was married in 1908, to Sylvia, daughter of Michael Grunberg of Bucharest, and has two sons, Edmund and Emanuel, and two daughters, the Misses Miriam and Semah Wilder.

M. GELBER, TORONTO

MOSES GELBER, Vice-President of the Zionist Organization of the Dominion of Canada, and one of the most outstanding welfare workers in Toronto, was born in Brzezany, Galicia, October 1st, 1876, the son of Nathan Gelber of that city. He was educated in his home community and came to this country when a young boy, arriving in Toronto in 1892. Together with his brother, Louis, he established a clothing business, which for twenty-five years they successfully operated. He then entered into the woollen business, under the name of Gelber Bros. Ltd., with which concern he is still actively associated, and which today is one of the largest of its kind in Canada. Mr. Gelber has always taken a deep interest in communal affairs, and he was instrumental in the building of the Austrian synagogue on Chestnut Street. He also was identified with the Terauley Street synagogue, and is at present a member of the Board of Governors of the University Avenue synagogue. Mr. Gelber has always been an enthusiastic Zionist and has been connected with the Zionist Movement since its inception in Canada, and is a present Vice-President of the Dominion Organization. He is President of the Central Division of Ontario, and President of the local Zionist Council. In 1923, he attended the Zionist Congress in Carlsbad. He is President of the new Talmud Torah and Jewish Centre, on Brunswick Avenue, which is now nearing completion, and with the building of which he has been prominently identified, being chairman of the building committee. He was also instrumental in the building of the Polish Talmud Torah on D'Arcy Street. Mr. Gelber is Vice-President of the Federation of Jewish Philanthropies, and is connected with most of the philanthropic and charitable institutions in Toronto. He was very active during the War in raising relief for the Jewish sufferers in Europe, and also took a great interest in bringing over the orphans to this country. He is a member of the B'nai Zion, I.O.B.B., and of the Primrose Club, Toronto. Mr. Gelber is married to Sophia, daughter of Simon Gradinger of Montreal, and has one son, Edward Gelber.

L. GOLDMAN, MONTREAL

LEON GOLDMAN, Executive Secretary of the Zionist Organization of Canada, Inc., was born in Moscow, Russia, on the 22nd of Heshvan, 5624 (1864). He was educated in the public schools and at the early age of twenty went to New York where he resided for three years. In 1887, he took up his residence in Paris, France, where he remained for three years, then returning to the United States. In 1892, Mr. Goldman moved to Montreal, where he has since resided. In 1897, he was married to Alice, daughter of Nathan and Sheine Pollin of Moscow, and he has three sons, Arthur Z., Henry J., and Robert H. and one daughter, Miss Raya E. Goldman. Mr. Goldman was in business as a manufacturer from the time of his first arrival in Canada until 1919. During Mr. Goldman's residence in Paris, he became a member of the Chovevei Zion Society, and in 1897 in Montreal, he assisted in the formation of the first Zionist Society in Canada, the B'nai Zion Society. Since that time Mr. Goldman has devoted practically his entire time to Zionist work. The marked progress made by the Zionist Organization in Canada, can be traced to a great extent, to the time that Mr. Goldman became the Chairman of the Administrative Bureau. It was on December 2nd, 1909, that the Administrative Bureau of the Zionist Organization was formed with Mr. Goldman as Chairman, and he occupied this position until his appointment as Executive Secretary in 1919 with the establishment of a properly equipped headquarters, staff and divisional offices. Up to this time, Mr. Goldman had acted in an honorary capacity with but one paid assistant. Since 1919 he has devoted all his time and efforts to the Zionist cause, although he takes a particularly keen interest in all communal undertakings. He is a member of the Federation of Jewish Philanthropies, Montreal; the Montreal Hebrew Free Loan Association; the Immigrant Aid Society of Canada; and the United Talmud Torahs of Montreal. For years a member of the Shaar Hashomayim Congregation of Montreal, he has at different times held office in this institution.

THE JEW IN THE COMMERCIAL LIFE OF CANADA

ALTHOUGH many of the first Jewish settlers in Canada were connected with the army, a number of them were so connected in a volunteer capacity only, and carried on an extensive trade as merchants. Thus the Franks family, who are prominently mentioned elsewhere in this volume, had the contract to supply cattle and provisions to the British troops in the French and Indian wars, between 1755 and 1760. It is worthy of note that their services in this capacity were highly commended by the different generals who had command of the army.

Lazarus David, Levy and Ezekiel Solomons, Simon Levy, Isaac Judah, and Andrew Hays, who settled in Montreal at the time of the British conquest, were all merchants and men of means when they came to this country. Samuel Judah, who with his brother-in-law, Aaron Hart, settled at the same time in Three Rivers, did a very extensive trade in furs with the Indians and French. In old correspondence we read of one of their associates in London having as much as £30,000 invested in their undertakings in Canada. Even in these days the equivalent of that sum is a large amount, in 1760 or 165 years ago, it was indeed a fortune. When Aaron Hart died, in 1800, the English papers at that time spoke of him as one of the wealthiest British subjects living outside of the British Isles. Samuel Judah later moved to New York, before the outbreak of the American Revolution, and he there became a personal friend of George Washington, and his money helped to keep Washington's army in the field. In fact, when the question of claims against the United States Government was taken up, after the war, the claim of Samuel Judah was settled at one million dollars, and recognized by the United States Government.

Lazarus David was an extensive holder of real estate in Montreal and its vicinity as far back as 1767, and he did an extensive trade with the French and Indians. Levy Solomons had formerly lived at Albany, and his enterprises extended from Michilimackinac to the Gulf of St. Lawrence, and down the Hudson River. When the Americans invaded Canada in 1776 large quantities of stores belonging to Solomons were confiscated, but this does not seem to have affected his big enterprises, which continued until his death, in 1792. Ezekiel Solomons also carried on a large trade between Michilimackinac and Montreal and he built a large fortified post at the former point. He was at that place when it was treacherously surprised and the garrison slaughtered by the Indians, at the time of the Conspiracy of Pontiac, and he narrowly escaped with his life, and returned to Montreal. Frequent mention is also made in papers of that period, of the commercial activities of the Judahs, Simon Levy, and Meyer Michaels, who are frequently mentioned as leaving for the "western country", or going to New York, the Mississippi, or even England, on business affairs.

In the diary of Samuel David under date of April 15th, 1801, it mentions that Meyer Michaels arrived the previous day in Montreal from the Mississippi, via New York, and was leaving that day for Mackinac. They are also frequently mentioned as accompanying MacKenzie, MacGilvray, and others of the North West Company on the "great portage."

Towards the close of the eighteenth century Henry Joseph, a nephew of Aaron Hart, came to Canada from England, and after a time spent in the army, where he was stationed at Fort William Henry, he settled at Berthier, opposite the Fort. In conjunction with his brother-in-law, Jacob Franks, (both had married daughters of Levy Solomons), and his father-in-law, he established the largest chain of trading posts in Canada, with headquarters at Berthier, and branches at Montreal and Quebec. He extended his posts all through the then wild and thinly populated northwest, the most important being now known as Mackinac. Records have been preserved showing that this traffic was carried on in large fleets of canoes, often manned by Indian and French voyageurs. We read of hundreds of these boats being employed in one expedition, passing up and down the waters of the great lakes and the St. Lawrence and carried over the portages. Henry Joseph carried the supplies for this great traffic between England and Canada in ocean ships which he either individually owned or chartered. He was the owner of the frigate *"Ewretta"* and of the *"Rachel"* and other boats, and was one of the first to employ Canadian-owned vessels exclusively for direct commerce between England and Canada, and hence he was one of the founders of Canada's merchant marine. It is interesting to note that John Jacob Astor was employed in his service at the beginning of his career. Jacob Franks, Henry Joseph's brother-in-law, was an extensive Hudson's Bay trader, as well as a participator in the affairs of the firm. He was one of the founders of Green Bay, Wisconsin, where he opened up a large trading post in 1794. He is frequently mentioned in the Canadian Government records of that period.

The first generation of Jews born in Canada followed the footsteps of their fathers and also did business in a large way. David David was the head of a large business and was a director in many public institutions. He was one of the most active founders of the Bank of Montreal in 1817. He was elected a director of its first regular Board on the 27th February, 1818, and the minutes of the Bank show that he continued in office until 1824, the year of his death. His brother Samuel David was also a merchant in a very large way, and his personal reminiscences are contained in a diary in the possession of his descendants. Frequent mention is made therein of his merchandise coming to him from England, France, Spain, and the West Indies, in boats owned by Henry Joseph.

In 1802, Samuel David was elected curator of the estate of Walter Davidson, and records show that he was present with several of the other Jewish merchants of Montreal, at a dinner given on March 30th 1805, by those merchants who had voted against the tax on commerce. At this same time, Moses David was in business in Sandwich and Detroit, and in one record mention is made of him arriving in Montreal from Detroit in seven days, which was evidently considered very good time. Benjamin Solomons and John Levi are also mentioned frequently in records of that period, in connection with their commercial undertakings.

Samuel Jacobs of Chambly is mentioned as being "principal merchant" which evidently means he was in the wholesale way, more or less, and he evidently had most of the trade of the Richelieu. His warehouses were stationed at different points, and one of his methods of collecting his accounts was to have the priest call out his debtors' names after Mass.

Among the merchants of Montreal who signed a memorial to the English Government dealing with matters of trade, we find the names of David David and Samuel David. This memorial complained "of the impediment to trade due to there being no other Custom House in Canada than that at Quebec, although it was from Montreal that the whole of the Indian trade with

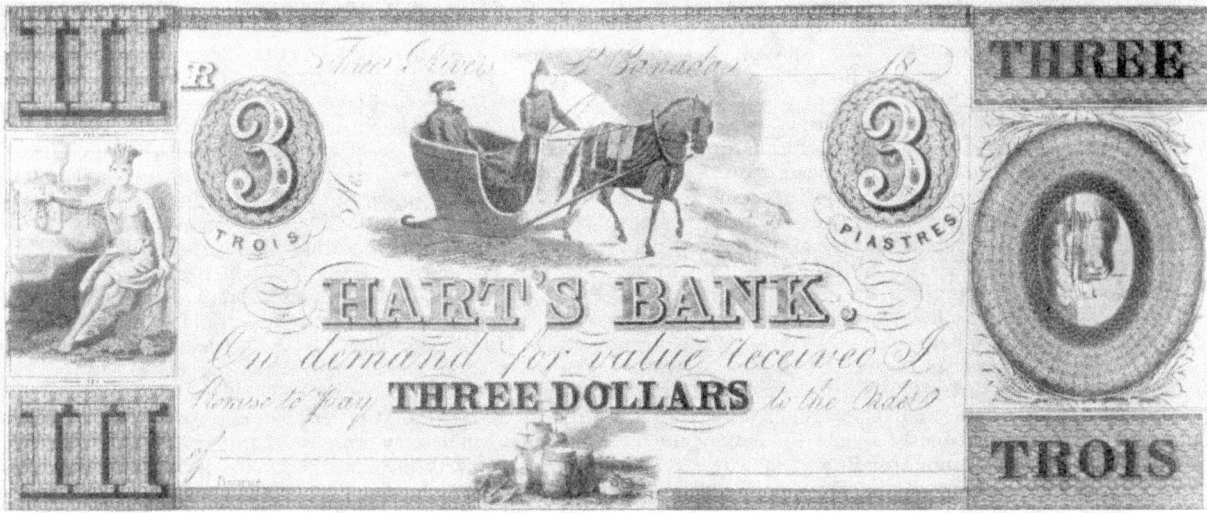

Fac-similes of Notes Issued by Hart's Bank, Three Rivers, Lower Canada. Moses Hart, Alexander Thomas Hart, and Ezekiel Moses Hart, Proprietors.

the west was carried on. There, also, for many years by far the largest quantity of exports and imports were dealt with. Furthermore, on account of the recent settlement of the Loyalists in the Upper country, this trade will greatly increase. They therefore pray that Montreal be made a Port of Entry."

In Montreal, Three Rivers, and Quebec, the sons of Aaron Hart carried on their mercantile pursuits, and were held in highest esteem for their business integrity. Moses Hart, early in the nineteenth century, operated boats between Montreal, Three Rivers, and Quebec, and he was one of the first to use steamboats for this traffic. Some years later he opened a Bank at Three Rivers, which continued in business for many years. In 1839, he petitioned the Government to incorporate the Bank, but this was never done, and the bank discontinued at his death. Moses Judah Hays was a prominent business man of Montreal during the early part of the nineteenth century. He was prominent in municipal affairs and to his activity was due many civic improvements. In 1803, he organized and managed the first waterworks in Montreal. Later Moses Hays was appointed the Chief Commissioner of Police of Montreal, an office that had been once before held by an Israelite—Jacob Kuhn—in 1778.

Jacob Henry, Jesse and Abraham Joseph, the sons of Henry Joseph, were connected with the largest undertakings of their time, in many cases as directors. The two former lived in Montreal and the latter in Quebec.

Jesse Joseph was the founder of Canada's trade with Belgium, and for many years was the Belgian Consul-General in Canada. He established the first direct steamship line between the two countries. He organized and became president of the Montreal Gas Company, and the City Passenger Railway of Montreal. He was the founder of the Montreal Telegraph Company, and served on the directorates of several other large companies and banks. He built and operated the Theatre Royal, in its day the leading play-house of Canada. Jacob Henry Joseph was associated with him in organizing the first telegraph lines in Canada and in the formation of several banks. He was president, and the largest shareholder in the Montreal Elevator Company, and was at one time the vice-president of the Montreal Board of Trade. It was through the efforts of Jacob Joseph that the offices of Port Warden and Harbor Inspector were established. He was also a partner in the Newfoundland Telegraph Company which laid the last link in the first trans-Atlantic cable. It was largely through the efforts of these two brothers that the St. Lawrence and Champlain Railway (the first railway in Canada) was completed. Abraham Joseph also served on the directorate of most of the important undertakings of his time. For a number of years he was president of the Quebec Board of Trade, and on the formation of the Dominion Boards of Trade, he was elected president. With his brothers he sat on the directorate of several banks, and when the Stadacona Bank was formed he became president. It is on record that later, when this bank suspended, Abraham Joseph paid every depositor in full from his private purse. For over thirty years he was vice-consul of Belgium at Quebec, a position that, on his death, was held by his son, Andrew Joseph. The Josephs were all large holders of real estate and they erected more buildings for their own use, than any others during their day.

The Joseph brothers were members of the directorate of the Banque Nationale from its inception, and were among the first subscribers to the stock of the Bank of British North America, the Union Bank, and the Provident Savings Bank.

In 1833 Henry Benjamin arrived at Quebec from England, and he opened up the largest dry goods store in that city. A year later his cousins, Samuel and Goodman Benjamin, came to Canada, and after a short time spent in Montreal, settled in Toronto, where they went into the wholesale dry-goods business. They established a large connection, and during the rebellion in 1837, received the Government contract to supply the greatcoats for the troops. As at that time there was no manufacturing done in Toronto, it was necessary to take the order to Montreal to be filled, and all this had to be done by sleigh, there being no other means of transport.

In its early days the wholesale jewellery trade was very much in the hands of the Jews, among the leading merchants, seventy-five to one hundred years ago, being J. G. Joseph & Co., of Toronto, H. & A. Saunders of Montreal, and H. & A. Levy of Hamilton. This latter firm, now known as Levy Brothers, Ltd., was first established in 1857, and is today the oldest established wholesale jewellery firm in Canada. At one time it was known as Levy Bros. & Scheuer, Mr. Edmund Scheuer being at the time one of the partners. Mr. Scheuer was an extensive importer of diamonds, and the firm of Edmund Scheuer Limited, are the oldest established diamond importers in the country today. Louis Davis of Montreal, was also one of the pioneers in the wholesale jewellery trade, in his day having a very large business.

In 1868, Moise Schwob, for many years French consul in Montreal, established the firm of Schwob Brothers, importers of watches, and this firm has ever since that time remained in the lead in this exclusive industry.

In its early days, the leading firm in the wholesale fancy goods line was Ascher Brothers, of Montreal.

In 1843, William Hyman settled in Gaspe, Quebec, where he became a prominent figure in the fishing industry of the Atlantic coast. The business established by him is still carried on by his sons and grandchildren. One of his sons also established a large fishing industry on the Pacific Coast.

The firm of M. &. L. Samuel, Toronto, (now known as Samuel, Benjamin & Company) was established in 1857, and for many years was one of the leading wholesale hardware concerns of Canada. They are to-day one of the largest metal firms in the country. It was one of the representatives of this firm, Mr. Hyman Miller who established the wholesale hardware firm of Miller-Morse Hardware Company, of Winnipeg, which is even to-day one of the largest firms of its kind in Canada.

J. Gutman, Samuel Goldstone, J. P. Davies, and Kady Gambitz were leading business men of Vancouver Island in the sixties, and the latter started the first dry goods store in Victoria. Simon Leiser built up the largest wholesale business in British Columbia and was one of the leading figures in the great sealing industry, at the time the chief characteristic of Victoria. He personally operated the "Wanderer" in the northern seas, and he was prominent in the protracted negotiations which eventually led to the cessation of pelagic sealing by Canadian ships. Mr. Leiser employed more than one hundred persons in his various interests.

Isaac and David Oppenheimer started the firm of Oppenheimer Brothers about 1860, and for years were amongst the leading merchants of the Province. Their connections extended to every part of British Columbia, and as the business developed, the headquarters were moved in order to keep pace with the development. They first were situated in Yale, then Victoria, and in 1886, moved to Vancouver. Much of the early development of that city was due to the efforts of the Oppenheimers.

In 1863, Charles King started, in Whitby, Ont., the tannery which is yet being conducted by his sons. For half a century Mr. King was in active charge of this industry, one of the largest of its kind in Canada and he was associated in many other large enterprises.

Sigismund Mohr settled in Quebec in 1871. He was an electrical engineer and organized the Quebec and

Levis Electric Company, which gave Quebec and its vicinity the finest electric lighting system in the world, at that time. Mr. Mohr is unquestionably the father of Hydro-Electric in Canada, as he was of everything electrical in Quebec. He promoted and installed the City and District Telegraph Company. He gave Quebec its first telephone system, and personally operated, at a city fair, the first set of telephones in Quebec, which had been sent to him by Professor Bell. His electrical undertaking was the first attempt ever made to utilize water power from a distance to generate electric current, and after demonstrating the success of his idea, he was given the contract to supply the city with light, which, as stated above, was the finest known at that time. Mr. Mohr received a testimonial from the city on the completion of his work.

In 1869, Noah Friedman and his brother-in-law, Louis Kellert, started a wholesale dry goods business in Montreal, under the name of Friedman and Kellert, and after some years branched out into the manufacture of men's clothing.

The manufacture of men's clothing has become one of the leading industries of the country, and none have done more to develop this than Jewish manufacturers. The Cohens, Kellerts, Vinebergs, Friedmans and Levinsons have for many years been names to conjure with the clothing industry, and they are largely responsible for the great strides this industry has made, which has resulted in the enlarged demand for ready-made clothing. In later years such men as Samuel Hart, Lyon Cohen, and David Dunkelman, as well as the sons of the pioneer manufacturers already mentioned, have continued to develop this industry, until today it employs over 10,000 persons and does a volume of business estimated at over $51,000,000.00 annually.

In 1919, the Dominion Government made a loan to Roumania of twenty million dollars, on the understanding that it was to be spent in Canada. Mr. Lyon Cohen organized the Associated Clothing Manufacturers of Canada, of which he became president, and this Association secured an order for ready-made clothing for over four million dollars from Roumania. About sixty per cent. of the contracting firms were Jewish concerns. Mr. H. N. Friedman was one of the two representatives who went to Europe to secure the contract.

The manufacturing of women's garments in a wholesale way is comparatively new, yet among the pioneers in this industry may be mentioned Aaron Boas, Maurice Felson, Abraham Sommer, Alan Hart, Harris Samuel, David Schloman, J. Waldman, M. Pullan, and Jack Perkins. Today this business is largely in Jewish hands, and it employs over 11,000 persons, with an annual turnover of over $41,000,000.00.

Jews have always been among the leaders in the wholesale woolen trade, and the name of Hiram Levy stands very high in the development of this industry in Canada. Mr. Levy sent his sons over to Europe to learn this business from the ground up, and they have thus acquired a practical knowledge of their line of business that is of great value. Albert Wener, A. Rudolph, and the Gelber Brothers of Toronto, have all become prominent in the woolen industry.

VIEWS OF CONISTON, ONT.

The first wholesale optical house in Canada, the Mount Royal Optical Company, was established by J. S. Leo. It is now known as the Consolidated Optical Company. Mr. Leo did much to develop this industry and has been connected with it during the entire period of his long residence in Canada. Percy Hermant, of Toronto, is another who has taken a leading part in the development of the wholesale optical business, both in association with Mr. Leo, and by himself. He is the head of the Imperial Optical Company, which has branches in many of the large cities of the country.

Samuel Kronick, of Toronto, entered into the manufacture of women's headwear at a time when 85% of this class of merchandise was imported. He is largely responsible for the great development of this industry which today employs over 2,500 persons, and the fact that today only 15% is imported shows what advantage to the development of the country the industry means. The annual volume of business is in excess of $4,000,000.00. The Leopolds of Montreal, are also among the leaders in this industry.

It is only within a very few years that the manufacture of silk fabrics has been done in Canada, and here again the Jews have taken a very important part. Morris Epstein, of Toronto, is one who has to a great extent been an important factor in this development. He employs over 300 persons in the industry and has the greater part of a million dollars invested in plant and equipment.

The music business in Canada owes its origin to Abraham Nordheimer of Toronto. Mr. Nordheimer, with his brother established the first music halls in this country in connection with their piano business, and the firm they established has always been a leader in this industry.

It has been claimed that the first who discovered the use of tobacco was a Jew, a companion of Columbus. However true that may be, it is a fact that the tobacco business in Canada has to a very great extent been developed by Jews. Henry Jacobs and Michael Michaels started the first cigar factory in Canada in 1858, in Dundas, Ont., and in 1862, moved to Montreal, where the firm they started, the Stonewall Jackson Factory, still remains in existence (a subsidiary of the Imperial Tobacco Company). In 1861, Mr. Samuel Davis started the manufacture of cigars. The firm of H. Simon and Sons was started in 1874, in Whitby, Ont., being in Hamilton and London before finally settling in Montreal. This firm is one of the largest in that line today, employing between four and five hundred hands. The forementioned, and the Hirsch family, the Michaels, and the Goldsteins, have at all times been regarded as the pioneers of the tobacco trade in Canada. Sir Mortimer B. Davis, President of the Imperial Tobacco Company of Canada Limited may well be called the "tobacco king" of this country, and there is no individual who has done so much as he for its development. His brothers, in their time, bore names that were synonymous with this industry, and the firm name of S. Davis & Sons was one known throughout the breadth of Canada.

Mark Workman, of Montreal, has been for many years interested in some of the largest undertakings in

Canada. His firm has handled enormous contracts for the Government. Mr. Workman was President of the Dominion Steel Corporation; Chairman of the Board of Directors of the Eastern Trust Company, and a director of many other large institutions.

Jacob A. Jacobs has to a large degree developed the mineral resources of this country, and he had a large share in the building up of Canada's asbestos industry, particularly with foreign countries. He organized and was President of Jacobs' Asbestos Mines, Thetford Mines, P.Q. Mr. Jacobs erected the first large manufacturing building in the uptown district of Montreal, and he is connected with many of the large financial institutions.

Sir Mortimer B. Davis, in addition to being the head of the Imperial Tobacco Company of Canada, has served on the directorate of some of the largest banks and financial institutions in the country. He is actively interested in many of the leading commercial undertakings, and is without question one of the outstanding men in Canada.

The control and distribution of moving picture films has always been largely in the hands of Jews, and the largest chain of moving picture theatres in Canada are the show-houses built by the Allens. N. L. Nathanson, of Toronto, is perhaps the leading figure in the film and exhibiting field in Canada today, and the high standard of the "movies" in this country bears witness to the clean business methods employed.

The reclaiming of waste material, paper, metals, wool clippings, etc. is practically all in the hands of Jews, and there is nothing more valuable to the country than this, creating value out of waste. The Frankel Brothers of Toronto and Montreal, in metals, and E. Pullan, Toronto in papers, have established immense industries, giving employment to hundreds of workmen. In all parts of Canada these firms or others have their connections, salvaging waste, truly a work of benefit to the country.

On October 6th, 1924, on the anniversary of the founding of the Alliance Assurance Company, of London, Eng., which was organized under similar conditions by Sir Moses Montefiore and the Rothschilds, the Laurentian Insurance Company was organized in Montreal by a number of the leading Jews of Canada. The idea of a fire insurance company with exclusively Jewish capital originated with S. W. Jacobs, K.C., M.P., and Alan J. Hart, who interested a number of their friends and secured a charter from the Dominion Government. At the meeting held on the date mentioned, the following were elected directors:—S. W. Jacobs, K.C., M.P., S. Hart, Peter Bercovitch, K.C., M.P.P., Henry Weinfield, S. Wener, J. Horwitz, A. H. Jassby, E. Albert, J. Levinson, Sr., H. M. Ripstein, I. Friedman, J. S. Leo and A. Sommer, Montreal; P. Hermant, Toronto; and M. J. Fikelstein, Winnipeg. Peter Bercovitch, K.C., M.P.P., was, at the following meeting of directors, elected President.

GOODMAN BENJAMIN
Of Benjamin Brothers
Toronto 1835-1838.

The fur trade of Canada, both in the raw skins, and in the manufacturing end, has been very much in the hands of Jews, from its early days. The first settlers traded largely with the Indians and the medium of exchange was furs. They risked their lives in many instances on their voyages to the then little known western country, and the furs that they secured were sent over to London. In later years Henry Joseph, of Toronto, was in the fur business in a very big way, and Simon Silverman, of Montreal, founded one of the largest fur houses in Canada, Silverman, Boulter and Company. Edwin Morris was a member of the firm of Morris and Henderson, now the John Henderson Company of Montreal, many years ago. In more recent years the firms dealing in raw furs have been to a large percentage Jewish. Ascher Pierce was the organizer of the Canadian Fur Auction Sales Company Limited, and was elected vice-president of this concern. He was also the chairman of the committee for the selection of trade fur names. Harry Endleman of Sudbury is the head of the largest private fur farm in the world, an undertaking that he started unaided and on which has been expended thousands of dollars. He has his own buying posts in all parts of the north and west of Canada, as far as Alaska.

It has been claimed that Bartholomew Green, who had the first printing establishment in Canada, in 1752, at Halifax, was a Jew. The printing industry in recent years has attracted a number of members of the Jewish faith, and the United Press, Limited of Toronto, has been developed by Paul Frumharz, Charles Garfunkel and Ephraim Palter into one of the most complete plants in the country, occupying over 27,000 feet of floor space, and employing hundreds of workmen.

Between 1896 and 1906, the firm of L. Cohen and Son, of Montreal, had a fleet of dredges under contract to the Dominion Government and during this time they deepened practically every tributary of the St. Lawrence between Lake Ontario and Quebec. They were the first and up to the present time have remained the only Jewish firm to enter into this class of undertaking.

The Mond Nickle Company Limited, of which the Right Honourable Sir Alfred Mond is Chairman, have their plant located at Coniston, Ont., and the entire town is owned by the company, whose employees compose its population.

It is not the intention in this review of Jews in the Commercial Life of Canada to show that they control the different industries referrred to, but to show that it is only just that to them belongs the credit of the greatest development. It is a common economic fact that in order to succeed in business a man must be absolutely honorable and enjoy the confidence of those with whom he deals. In answer to a question as to why the Jew was so proverbially successful in business, George Bernard Shaw replied "that to be successful a man's word must be his bond," and this he had always found the case with the Jews!

JACOBS BUILDING, MONTREAL
Erected and owned by J. A. Jacobs

SOMMER BUILDING, MONTREAL
Erected and owned by A. Sommer

FEDERAL BUILDING, TORONTO
Erected and owned by Yolles and Rotenberg

TEXTILE BUILDING, TORONTO
Erected and owned by Gelber Brothers

UNITED PRESS BUILDING, TORONTO
Owned by United Press Limited

GELBER BUILDING, TORONTO
Erected and owned by Gelber Brothers

RABINOVITCH BUILDING, MONTREAL
Erected and owned by Geo. Rabinovitch

SPADINA BUILDING, TORONTO
Erected and owned by H. Greisman

JACOB HENRY JOSEPH

JACOB HENRY JOSEPH, for over seventy years one of the best known figures of Montreal, was born at Berthier, Quebec, in 1814, the son of Henry and Rachel (Solomon) Joseph. He moved to Montreal in 1830, with his parents, and resided in that City until his death, which took place February 28th, 1907. He served as an officer with the Government forces during the Papineau Rebellion in 1837-8, and for a time was entrusted with the carrying of despatches between Sir John Colborne, Governor of Lower Canada, and General Wetherall, then in command of the Government troops on the Richelieu. Jacob Joseph at all times occupied a commanding position in the commercial affairs of Canada. He was one of the organizers of the first telegraph line in Canada, which entered the United States by way of Plattsburg. He actively promoted the construction and served on the directorate of the earliest railways in the country. He took a prominent part in the opening of several banks, and was one of the originators of the Union Bank, and was an original shareholder of the Bank of British North America. He was also an original member of the Provident Savings Bank, but he never took office on the Board. For many years he was President, and the largest shareholder of the Montreal Elevator Company. He was an active member, and at one time the Vice-President of the Board of Trade, and it was due to his efforts that the offices of Port Warden and Harbour Inspector were established. At one time Mr. Joseph was a partner in the Newfoundland Telegraph Co. He was a large holder of real estate. Mr. Joseph took a leading part in the communal life of the city, and among other institutions that he was identified with were the General Hospital, Mercantile Library, Art Association, Mechanics Institute, and the Natural History Society, of which he was a Vice-President. He was married to Miss Gratz, niece of that Rebecca Gratz from whom Sir Walter Scott drew his famous character of Rebecca, in "Ivanhoe". He was survived by two sons, Henry and Horace of Montreal, three daughters, and several grand-children.

JESSE JOSEPH

JESSE JOSEPH was born at Berthier, Quebec, July 16th, 1817, the son of Henry and Rachel (Solomon) Joseph. In his early days he studied law, which proved of great advantage to him in his after life. He was ranked as one of the foremost men of Canada, and there were scarcely any local enterprises during his day that he was not actively connected with. He was the founder of Canada's trade with Belgium, and developed this industry to a large extent. For many years he was Belgian Consul in Montreal, and as a recognition of his valuable services, he was created a Knight of the Order of Leopold by the King of Belgium, and though authorized to do so by the British Government, he never assumed the title. As President of the City Passenger Railway of Montreal, and the Montreal Gas Company, he was prominently before the public. He was appointed director of the Street Railway Company in 1877, and in 1884 was appointed President, resigning in 1892. Mr. Joseph's reasons for resigning were chiefly that he had no confidence in electricity. He was appointed director of the Gas Company in 1864, and President in 1887. He was the founder of the Montreal Telegraph Company, and up to the time of his death was a director of the Great Northwestern Telegraph Company, now the Canadian National Telegraph Company. He was also a director of the People's Telegraph Company, the Banque Nationale, and of several Canadian cotton companies. Mr. Joseph was one of the largest real estate owners in Montreal, and built and operated the Theatre Royal, in its time the leading play-house in Canada. He entertained largely, and was known for his hospitality. His home was the centre of the social life of the city, particularly during the military occupation of Montreal. He was a very unassuming personage and disliked publicity. No appeal for charity was made to him in vain, though he most often gave anonymously. For over fifty years, Mr. Joseph was a Trustee of the Spanish and Portuguese Synagogue, Montreal, and at the time of his death which took place February 24th, 1904, he was President.

ABRAHAM JOSEPH

ABRAHAM JOSEPH was born at Berthier, Quebec, on November 14th, 1815, the son of Henry and Rachel (Solomon) Joseph. After the death of his father, which took place in 1832, he moved to Quebec City, where he resided until his death, on March 20th, 1886. In March, 1846, he was married to Sophia, daughter of Samuel and Sarah (Hart) David, and had four sons and seven daughters. Abraham Joseph was a successful business man, and his name was identified with almost every commercial enterprise of his time, in most cases as a director. For a number of years, he was President of the Quebec Board of Trade, and later became President of the newly formed Dominion Boards of Trade. He was one of the original directors of the Banque Nationale, and was a member of the Board of that institution which sat together for eleven years without change. Mr. Joseph resigned from the directorate of this bank to take the Presidency of the Stadacona Bank, which office he held until this bank was wound up. He was a member of the Quebec City Council, and at one time was a candidate for the mayoralty, being defeated by a very few votes. For over thirty years he was Vice-Consul for Belgium. He took a lively interest, but no prominent part in politics. During the Papineau Rebellion in 1837-8, Mr. Joseph served with the Quebec Light Infantry, attaining the rank of Major. Intensely proud of his English descent, Mr. Joseph was a life member of St. George's Society, and was several times its President. Although in his days there was no organized Jewish community in Quebec, Mr. and Mrs. Joseph maintained a completely Jewish atmosphere in their home, and were as highly regarded by their Roman Catholic and Protestant, as by their Jewish neighbors. He was at all times regarded as the leader of his community, and it may be said that he was without enemies. He was the founder of the wholesale grocery business, which is still in existence, under the name of Joseph & Co. Mr. Joseph was a member of the Stadacona, Garrison, and Tandem Clubs, Quebec. His son, Andrew C. Joseph, succeeded him as Belgian Consul.

WILLIAM HYMAN

WILLIAM HYMAN, in his lifetime the most prominent resident of the Gaspe Coast, was born in Russia in 1807, and settled in Gaspe in 1843. He established one of the largest fishing industries on the Atlantic Coast at Grand Greve, a business that is still being carried on by his sons and grandchildren. His business capacity was very great, and the establishment under his able management prospered so much, that it became one of the largest concerns of its kind in Canada. He was one of the first to develop the great cod-fish industry in this country. Mr. Hyman took an active interest in public affairs in Gaspe and was early in his residence there appointed a Justice of the Peace and Magistrate. When the township of Cape Rosier was incorporated in 1858, Mr. Hyman was elected its first Mayor and he continued to occupy the civic chair without interruption, until his death which took place on December 8th, 1882, at his winter residence in Montreal. For over twenty years, Mr. Hyman had officiated as Justice of the Peace. He took a great interest in all Jewish communal undertakings in Montreal, and was a liberal supporter of all their institutions. For many years Mr. Hyman held a commission as Captain in the militia, and he saw active service at the time of the Fenian Raids. He was generously disposed towards the poor and needy and gave assistance to many families in their want. He advanced provisions to the poor on the Gaspe Coast in the winter especially when they could get none anywhere else, and as the people in their poverty were unable to repay him, he incurred great losses through his generosity. He was a just and upright man in his business dealings, faithful and kind to his friends, an indulgent father, a devoted husband, and his death left a great void in the communal life of the Gaspe Coast. He was survived by three sons, the late Isaac E. and Horatio and Jacob Hyman of Gaspe, and five daughters, the late Mrs. Joseph Youngheart and Mrs. R. M. Levine of Montreal; and Mrs. John Luce of London, England; Mrs. J. H. Loryea of St. Matthews, South Carolina; and Mrs. Wm. Goldstein of Toronto.

ABRAHAM NORDHEIMER

ABRAHAM NORDHEIMER was born in Bavaria, of an old and aristocratic Jewish family, and was one of eight sons. One of his brothers was Dr. Nordheimer, of European and American fame, and a distinguished Oriental scholar and author, who held a professorship in the Theological Seminary of New York, and at whose instigation Abraham and his younger brother Samuel, went to New York, in 1839. There they attended classes at college, to acquire a knowledge of the English tongue. Abraham Nordheimer was an eminent musician and pianist, and followed the musical profession. His many gifts and accomplishments made him a social lion amongst the old Knickerbocker families of New York, and it was there that he met General Torrance, of His Majesty's 23rd Regiment of Foot, then stationed at Kingston, Upper Canada, who induced him to move to Kingston, there to give musical tuition in the family of Sir Charles Bagot, the Governor General. Shortly after he organized, in connection with a piano and music room, the first musical society in Upper Canada, and which he himself conducted. Samuel Nordheimer joined him there, and the music house of A. & S. Nordheimer was established, some years later the headquarters of the firm being removed to Toronto. The firm met with great success, owing to the ability and energy of the brothers. To them Canada owes in a great measure its musical taste, as they also induced and assisted to settle in Canada the better grade of professional musicians. They were also the first to build, in connection with their business, a concert and music hall. This innovation was subsequently imitated by the larger American music firms. Abraham Nordheimer was prominent in all questions affecting the community where he resided, and he was one of the first members of the Toronto Hebrew Congregation (now the Holy Blossom Synagogue). He was the donor of the land on Pape Avenue, used by the Congregation as a cemetery, and one of the earliest graves in the cemetery is that of a member of his family. Abraham Nordheimer died in 1860 whilst on a visit to Germany.

THE LATE CHARLES KING

THE late Mr. Charles King, for over sixty years an outstanding resident of Ontario, was born at Prague, Bohemia, on December 28th, 1837. As a boy, he served his full apprenticeship in his uncle's tannery in Prague. This concern was the largest tannery in Bohemia. At the age of seventeen, he sailed for New York, where he entered the same business, and where he remained for ten years. Through his firm, he was sent to Toronto, Canada, where business relations had already been established. A small tannery situated in Whitby, Ontario, gave him the opportunity of starting for himself, and in 1863, he commenced the business in Whitby, which he carried on until his death, and which is still continued by two of his sons. Mr. King can be called the father of Whitby, and he saw the town grow from a small village to its present size and importance, much of which development being due to himself. For nearly a half a century, Charles King was an active public servant in his town and county. He served for some years in the municipal affairs of the town, and was for over twenty-five years on the Board of Education, at various times being its Chairman. He occupied in succession all the offices in the gift of the town, and in 1888, he was Warden of the County of Ontario. He took an extremely active part in political matters, but declined leadership. In 1904, although continuing his interest in the business, he removed to Toronto, where he resided until his death, which took place on February 22nd, 1915. Mr. King was for many years a member of the Toronto Board of Trade. He was a Royal Arch Mason. He took a keen interest in communal affairs in Toronto, and was a supporter of most of the charitable institutions of that city, and was one of the oldest members of the Holy Blossom Synagogue. In 1866, he was married to Miss Henrietta Kohn, and he was survived by his widow and six sons, Samuel of Toronto, Joseph and Theodore of Whitby, Adam, Leon and William of New York; and three daughters, Mrs. Goodman of New York, and Mrs. Charles Draimin and Miss King of Toronto.

THE LATE HYMAN MILLER

THE LATE MR. HYMAN MILLER was born in Birmingham, England, March 10th, 1856, the son of the late Alexander Miller. He arrived in Toronto in 1861 with his parents, and was educated in that city. In the seventies, he entered the employ of M. & L. Samuel & Co., and when this firm became M. & L. Samuel, Benjamin & Co. in 1879, he was sent out to Winnipeg as travelling salesman. Seeing a great field before him in Winnipeg, he entered the wholesale hardware business there in 1882, forming a partnership with Fred W. Morse and F. Morton Morse, under the firm name of Miller, Morse & Co. The partnership gradually extended its business, until it became the largest hardware business in the Canadian West. In 1904, it was incorporated under Dominion Charter, under the name of Miller-Morse Hardware Co. Ltd. Mr. Miller was elected President of the Company, a position which he retained till his death, and which is today held by his son, C. A. Morell Miller. Mr. Miller was also interested in various other enterprises, and was Director in the Beaver Lumber Co.; The Western Terminal Elevator Co.; The Western Elevator Company; and the Prairie Elevator Company. He was a member of the Winnipeg Board of Trade, and for years was an active member of the Freight Rate Committee of this board. He was a prominent member of the St. Charles Country Club; the Carleton Club; and the Winnipeg Hardware Association. He took quite an interest in the early days of the Jewish community in Winnipeg. For a number of years he was one of the Trustees for the Russo-Jewish Committee, which established a fund for the relief of victims of the Russian persecutions. He also acted in an advisory capacity in the Mansion House Relief Committee, in respect to their lands in the West. Mr. Miller was a founder of the Winnipeg Hebrew Orphanage. He was married to Sarah, daughter of Moses Samuel Morell, and had two sons, Cecil Morell and Charles Alexander Morell. Mr. Miller was a member of the Ionic Lodge, A.F. & A.M., and of the Holy Blossom Synagogue, Toronto, of which his father was at one time a President.

SIR MORTIMER B. DAVIS, MONTREAL

SIR MORTIMER B. DAVIS, President of the Imperial Tobacco Company of Canada, Ltd., and one of the outstanding members of the Jewish race in Canada, was born in Montreal, February 6th, 1866, the third son of the late Samuel Davis of that city. He was educated at the Montreal High School, and at an early age started a commercial career, first travelling for his father's firm. Some years later he became manager, and under his supervision, the business assumed very large proportions. In 1895, when the American Tobacco Company of Canada was organized, he was elected President, and some years afterwards, on the formation of the Imperial Tobacco Company of Canada, Ltd., he was elected President of this concern, which office he still occupies. No man has done more to encourage the tobacco industry in this country than Sir Mortimer, and he is justly called the "Tobacco King" of Canada. He is also interested in many other large enterprises. Sir Mortimer has always taken a very active interest in all communal and charitable undertakings, and his interest is not confined to any one creed. His contributions to charity and relief have amounted to enormous sums. In 1913, he endowed a chair in Laval University. He is one of the founders of the Mount Sinai Sanatorium at St. Agathe des Monts. He is an active supporter of the Temple Emanu-El, of which his father was one of the founders, and he served for some years as Vice-President. Sir Mortimer comes by his philanthropy naturally, as both his father and mother were two of the most outstanding communal workers in Montreal. He is a Director of the Montreal Horticultural and Fruit Growing Association, and of the Royal Montreal Golf Club, and is a member of the Mount Royal; St. James; Montefiore; Montreal Hunt; Montreal Jockey; Forest and Stream; and Royal St. Lawrence Yacht Clubs. Of late years he has made his winter residence in France. In 1917, he had the honour of knighthood conferred on him by His Majesty King George V, in recognition of his munificent philanthropic work, being the first Canadian-born Jew to receive this honour.

MARK WORKMAN, MONTREAL
Photo by Notman

MARK WORKMAN was born in Buffalo, New York, on August 4th, 1864, the son of Isaac and Sarah (Rosenthal) Workman. He received his early education in the public schools of Buffalo and came to Montreal in 1876, joining with his father in the clothing business. In 1880, being but 16 years of age, he became the head of the business and with wonderful instinct and untiring effort made his enterprise grow until he incorporated in 1906, when his travellers covered the whole of Canada. For over a quarter of a century, Mark Workman Company, Limited has supplied military clothing to the British and Canadian Governments and during the war they handled enormous contracts. Apart from his clothing business, Mr. Workman has taken a very active part in Canadian industry, and he is a Director of many important concerns. In 1916 he became President of the Dominion Steel Corporation, of which he was one of the largest shareholders. He is also Vice-President of the Jacobs' Asbestos Co. Ltd., Thetford Mines, Quebec; and Chairman of the Board of Directors of the Eastern Trust Co., Montreal. Although a very busy business man, Mr. Workman has not overlooked his part in the welfare of his less fortunate co-religionists, and his communal activities have been very great and he has given many thousands of dollars to charity. He can always be depended on to assist in welfare work. He is one of the founders of the Mount Sinai Sanatorium, of which he was President, and for some years was Treasurer of the Temple Emanu-el, Montreal. He is a life governor of the Montreal General Hospital and other institutions. He is a member of the Montefiore, Mt. Royal, (Montreal), Rideau (Ottawa), Laurentian (Ottawa), Manhattan (New York), and Cape Breton Yacht (Sydney, N.S.), Clubs. Mr. Workman also belongs to the Masonic Order and to the Royal Guardians. In 1884, he was married to Rachel Lewis, of Syracuse, New York, and he has one son, Edward, who served as a lieutenant in the Army, and four daughters, Mrs. Nathan Gordon, Mrs. G. Phillips and Miss Nina Workman of Montreal, and Mrs. Harry Rosenthal, Ottawa.

LYON COHEN, MONTREAL

Photo by Notman

LYON COHEN, one of the outstanding leaders of Jewish welfare work in Canada, is the eldest son of the late Lazarus and Fanny (Garmaise) Cohen, and was born in Poland on May 11th, 1868. In 1888, he joined the firm of Lee & Cohen, later becoming partner with his father in the firm of L. Cohen & Son, Coal Merchants and Dredging Contractors. In 1895, he established the W. R. Cuthbert Co., Brass Founders, and in 1906 organized and became President of The Freedman Company, Wholesale Clothing Manufacturers. In 1919, he organized and was President of Canadian Export Clothiers Ltd., and was President of the Clothing Manufacturers' Association of Montreal. In 1897, he founded "The Jewish Times", the first Jewish paper in Canada. He was Chairman of the Committee formed to obtain equal rights for Jewish children in the public schools. He was President of the Baron de Hirsch Institute in 1908-12; Chairman, Committee to Federate Jewish Charities, 1915; President, First Jewish Congress, 1919; President, Canadian Jewish Committee for Relief of War Sufferers; President, Associated War Relief Societies of Canada; Hon. President, Federation of Jewish Philanthropies of Montreal; Vice-President, Zionist Organization of Canada; Chairman, Canadian Committee, Jewish Colonization Association of Paris; and is an ex-honorary President of the Y.M.H.A. For many years he has been President of the Shaar Hashomayim Synagogue, Montreal, the largest Jewish Congregation in Canada. His communal activities are not confined to his own creed and he is a Governor of the Montreal General Hospital and Western Hospital, Director of the Civic Improvement League and Director of the Boys' Farm, Shawbridge, Quebec. Mr. Cohen is a member of the Montefiore Club, of which he was a President, and also of the Canadian and Montreal Reform Clubs. On February, 17th, 1891, he was married to Rachel, eldest daughter of the late Mr. and Mrs. N. Friedman, of Montreal, and has three sons, Lieut. Nathan Bernard, Capt. Horace Rives and Lawrence Zebulum, and one daughter, Miss Sylvia Lillian Cohen.

MONTEFIORE JOSEPH, QUEBEC

MONTEFIORE JOSEPH, a member of one of the oldest Jewish families in Canada, and one of the most public-spirited residents of the City of Quebec, was born in that city, September 21st, 1851, the son of the late Abraham and Sophia (David) Joseph. He received his education at the public and high schools of Quebec, and at McGill University, from which he graduated in 1869, with the degree of Bachelor of Arts. He was married in 1882, to Annette, daughter of the late Henry and Rosetta (De Sola) Pinto, of London, England, who died on October 18th, 1921. Mr. and Mrs. Joseph had three sons, the late Abraham Pinto (who died in 1922), Edward Cecil of Quebec, and Kenneth de Sola of Toronto, and two daughters, Mrs. Martin Wolff of Montreal, and Miss Rosetta Joseph of Quebec. On graduating from the University, Mr. Joseph entered the wholesale grocery firm of A. Joseph & Sons, in partnership with his father and late brother, Andrew C. Joseph. On the death of the latter, he carried on the business alone, under the firm name of Joseph & Company, a concern which is held in the highest respect throughout the Province of Quebec, and wherever they have business connections. Mr. Joseph has always taken a leading part in the communal life of his city, irrespective of creed, and is recognized as the representative member of the Jewish community of Quebec. He is keenly interested in all public questions, and for some years he was President of the Quebec Board of Trade. Mr. Joseph has always been keenly interested in amateur sports and athletics. He is a past President of the Quebec Snowshoe Club, and is President of the Quebec Skating Rink. He is an enthusiastic wheelsman, and is very fond of all outdoor exercises. Although a life-long resident of Quebec, he has always been a member of the Spanish and Portuguese Synagogue of Montreal, an institution of which his grandfather was one of the early members. Mr. Joseph is much interested in historical study, and is an enthusiastic stamp collector. He saw service at the time of the Fenian Raids.

J. A. JACOBS, MONTREAL

Photo by Notman

JACOB ABRAHAM JACOBS is one of the leading figures in the development of the natural resources of Canada. He was born in Montreal, November 12th, 1874, the son of the late Abraham Jacobs, of Montreal. He was educated at the Montreal High School and at the Commercial College, from which he graduated in 1894. In 1902, Mr. Jacobs was married to Stephanie, daughter of the late Nathan Lewis of Montreal, and he has one son Reginald, and two daughters, the Misses Natalie and Pauline Jacobs. He organized and operated for many years the Canadian Underwear Company of Montreal. Mr. Jacobs was always interested in mining and he took a very prominent part in the Cobalt fields. He organized several of the leading mining companies of that region and was the President of the Kerr Lake Mine, Nova Scotia Mine, and others. Mr. Jacobs also became largely interested in the asbestos industry of Canada and organized and became President of the Jacobs' Asbestos Company, Thetford Mines, Quebec. He was one of the pioneers in exporting Canadian asbestos to foreign fields. In 1910, Mr. Jacobs erected the first large manufacturing building in the uptown district of Montreal, the Jacobs Building on St. Catharine Street, which still is one of the finest sights of this street. Mr. Jacobs has always taken a most active interest in communal undertakings in Montreal. He organized the campaign for the Mount Sinai Sanatorium, the first large campaign held by the Jews of Montreal, which was organized in his building. He obtained the first large subscriptions to charitable organizations and for years has always headed campaigns of this nature. He was one of those instrumental in the organizing of the Montreal Hebrew Orphans' Home, and was one of the first four who subscribed $10,000.00 each towards its erection. Mr. Jacobs is a member of the Montreal Reform, Montefiore and Canadian Clubs. He is on the Canadian executive of the Jewish Colonization Association, and is a member of all Jewish societies. He is an enthusiastic amateur farmer, and his farm at Rougemont is a model one.

HARRIS VINEBERG, MONTREAL

HARRIS VINEBERG, President of H. Vineberg & Co. Ltd., and one of the pioneer clothing manufacturers of Canada, was born in December (Chanukah) 1855, in Lithuania, then a part of Russia, the son of Lazarus and Malca Vineberg. He was educated at the Chedar in his native town, and through private tuition. In 1872 he came to Canada, settling in Montreal, and for over forty years he has conducted the wholesale clothing business of H. Vineberg & Co. Ltd., Montreal, and during this period his travellers have covered all parts of Canada. He was the pioneer in advertising the brand of his product. Mr. Vineberg had the honor of being elected the first President of the Baron de Hirsch Institute, and was one of those who made the arrangements with the Baron de Hirsch for the endowment of that institution. At that time, 1888-1892, the Society had no home of its own, but through the efforts made by Mr. Vineberg and others they received a large number of donations and were able to purchase the building that they formerly occupied on St. Elizabeth Street. He has always taken a keen interest in all philanthropic and charitable movements among the Jewish population of Canada and his assistance and advice have at all times proved of inestimable value in the various undertakings by the people of Montreal. He is a Life Governor of both the Montreal General Hospital, and the Baron de Hirsch Institute. Mr. Vineberg was many years a trustee of the Shearith Israel Synagogue, Montreal, and is at the present time one of its senior members. At the time of the building of the McGill College Avenue Synagogue, he was the Secretary of the Shaar Hashomayim congregation. He is a member of the Canadian Manufacturers' Association, and of the Montreal Board of Trade. On October 23rd, 1877, he was married to Lily Goldberg, daughter of the late Rev. Hyman Goldberg, of the Spanish and Portuguese Synagogue, Montreal, and he has three daughters, Mrs. I. Cohen, Mrs. A. J. Hart, and Mrs. A. Z. Cohen, all of Montreal. Mr. Vineberg is a member of both the Spanish and Portuguese, and the Shaar Hashomayim Synagogues.

A. SOMMER, MONTREAL

ABRAHAM SOMMER, President of A. Sommer & Co. Ltd., is one of the pioneers in the manufacturing of women's wear in Canada. He was born in Lodz, Poland, on February 1st, 1878, the son of David and Sophie (Klaper) Sommer. He went to the United States with his parents when a young boy, and after receiving his education in the public schools of New York City, he served his apprenticeship in the women's garment manufacturing industry. After acquiring a thorough practical knowledge of this business, he went to Montreal in 1901, and shortly afterwards organized the firm of A. Sommer & Co. Ltd. He developed this business into one of the largest of its kind in Canada, with a nation-wide reputation, and some years later with a brother, organized and became President of the Queen Dress and Waist Co. Ltd., Montreal. Mr. Sommer has been recognized as the outstanding authority in Canada in the women's wear trade, and he has done more for this industry than any other one person. He is also interested in the retail business and is the President of Sommer's Limited of Vancouver, B.C. He is President of the Metropolitan Realty Co., Montreal, and erected the largest loft building in Montreal, the Sommer Building on Mayor and Ontario Streets. Mr. Sommer is not too busy to devote both time and money to communal work, and he is a life governor of the Montreal General Hospital; Western Hospital; Protestant Hospital for the Insane; Children's Memorial Hospital; and the Baron de Hirsch Institute. He is a trustee of the Federation of Jewish Philanthropies, and is connected with practically all of the Jewish charitable institutions there. During the war, he was prominent in the Victory Loan campaigns, and he was a strong supporter for the relief of war sufferers. For many years he has been Treasurer of the Temple Emanu-El, the only reform synagogue in Montreal. Mr. Sommer is a member of the Canadian Manufacturers' Association; Montreal Board of Trade; Canadian Club; Montefiore Club; and the Canadian Club, New York City. He is married to Louise, daughter of Jacob Eisner, and has one son and two daughters.

THE RIGHT HONOURABLE SIR ALFRED MOND, BART, M.P.

THE RIGHT HONOURABLE SIR ALFRED MOND was born at Farnworth near Widnes, Lancashire, England, on October 23rd, 1868, the son of the late Dr. Ludwig Mond, F.R.S. He was educated at Cheltenham; St. John's College, Cambridge; and Edinburgh University. He graduated as barrister, Inner Temple, in 1894, on North Wales and Cheshire Circuit. Sir Alfred was first elected member of the House of Commons for Chester, representing that constituency from 1906-1910. From 1910 to 1923 he was member of Parliament for Swansea, and in the general elections of 1924 was elected member for Carmarthen. From 1916 to 1921, he was a member of the Cabinet as First Commissioner of Works, and in 1921 and 1922 he was Minister of Health. Sir Alfred is Chairman of the Mond Nickel Company, Limited; The Palestine Corporation, Limited; The Victoria Syndicate, Limited; The Power Gas Corporation, Limited; Henry Wiggin and Co., Limited; and The Amalgamated Anthracite Collieries, Limited. He is a Director of Brunner, Mond and Co., Limited; South Staffs. Mond Gas Co., Limited; British Dyestuffs Corporation, Limited; and Industrial Finance and Investment Corporation, Limited. He is a member of the Royal Institution; Vice-President, Navy League; Trustee of the Imperial War Museum; Chairman, Economic Board of Palestine; Chairman, London School of Hygiene and Tropical Medicine; President, Mansion House Association on Railway and Canal Traffic; Vice-President, Infants' Hospital, London, S.W. Sir Alfred is married to Violet, D.B.E., daughter of the late James Henry Goetze, and granddaughter of the late John Bentley, and he has one son, Henry Mond, and three daughters, Viscountess Erleigh, Lady Pearson, and Miss Nora Mond. He is a member of the Athenaeum, Reform, National, Liberal, Savile, Royal Automobile, Burlington Fine Arts, and other clubs. The Mond Nickel Company, Limited, of which Sir Alfred is Chairman, has their plant located in Ontario, nine miles from Sudbury, and the town of Coniston is owned in its entirety by the Company.

P. HERMANT, TORONTO

Lyonde

PERCY HERMANT, Proprietor of the Imperial Optical Company, and one of the leading business men of Toronto, was born in Mogilev, Russia, on January 17th, 1882, the son of Aaron and Riva Hermant. He received his education by private tuition and came to Canada in 1897, settling in Toronto, where he first started his commercial career as a travelling salesman. In 1900, he went to Boston where he attended the Klein School of Optics. From 1901 to 1905, he established and became Manager of the Imperial Optical Company of St. John, N.B. In 1906, he returned to Toronto where he organized the Imperial Optical Company, which is the largest privately owned optical business in Canada, and which has branches in Victoria, Vancouver, Edmonton, Saskatoon, Regina, Moose Jaw, Winnipeg, London, Hamilton, Ottawa, Kingston, Owen Sound and Windsor. Mr. Hermant is President of the Imperial Optical Company of London, England; National Optical Company of Montreal and Quebec; Percy Hermant, Limited, Toronto; Hermant Investments, Limited, Toronto; and is a Director of the Laurentian Insurance Company, Montreal. He is a member of the Canadian Club; Empire Club; Kiwanis Club; Lakeview Golf Club; Primrose Club; Independent Order B'nai Brith; Masonic Order; Knights of Pythias; the Toronto Board of Trade; and the Canadian Manufacturers' Association. Mr. Hermant is keenly interested in all communal undertakings and charitable work in Toronto, particularly those of a Jewish nature. He is a member of the Federation of Jewish Philanthropies, Hebrew Free School and of most of the other charitable and welfare institutions of that city. Mr. Hermant is a Trustee of the Holy Blossom Synagogue, Toronto. On June 8th, 1910, he was married to Dorothy, daughter of Mr. M. L. Morris of Montreal, and he has one son, Sydney Hermant. In his communal work he has the invaluable assistance of Mrs. Hermant who has at all times since her marriage been one of the outstanding women workers of the city. She has taken an active part in the Council of Jewish Women and other societies.

A. C. COHEN, VANCOUVER

ABRAHAM CHARLES COHEN, sole proprietor of the Universal Knitting Company, Limited, Vancouver, was born at Riga, Latvia, Russia, on July 6th, 1881, the son of Siskind and Rae Cohen, now of Brooklyn, N.Y. He received his education in the public and high schools of New York City. Mr. Cohen began his career in the knitting industry in New York, and worked at this trade until 1898, when he joined the United States Army and served during the Spanish-American war with the first United States Volunteer Engineers. He re-enlisted in the regular army, and served for some years in the capacity of a non-commissioned officer. In 1909, he went to Vancouver, B.C., where he entered into the knitting business with Mackay, Smith and Blair, remaining with them until 1914, when the present company was formed. Mr. Cohen started this industry in a very small way, and he has developed it until he now employs over one hundred and twenty-five hands, and is the largest employer of needle help in Western Canada. This concern manufactures all kinds of high-grade sweaters, sweater coats, bathing suits, athletic jerseys, knit goods and novelties for both women and children, and does business in all parts of Canada, having a very fine reputation for business integrity, from coast to coast. The Universal Knitting Company, Limited, also do a large export business with the United States, Japan, New Zealand, Java and South Africa. On June 4th, 1911, Mr. Cohen was married to Laura Bertha, daughter of the late Solomon and Lena Weaver of Vancouver, and he has four sons, Samuel Irving, Theodore Solomon, Victor Allenby, and Herbert Samuel Cohen. Mr. Cohen has always taken a keen and active interest in communal affairs and philanthropic undertakings in his city. He is a past President of the Independent Order B'nai Brith, Vancouver Lodge, and is the present District Deputy of the Grand Lodge, Independent Order B'nai Brith. He is a member of the Concordia Club, Vancouver, and of the Benevolent and Protective Order of Elks. Mr. Cohen is a member of the Shaarey Zedeck Congregation.

H. GREISMAN, TORONTO

HENRY GREISMAN, President of the King Suspender Company, and one of the most prominent business men of Toronto, was born in Austrian Poland, on March 9th, 1867, the son of Selig and Fegel Greisman. He was educated in his native town and was married in Poland in 1884 to Feiga, daughter of David Garten. They have three sons; Morris, Louis and Selig, and two daughters; Pearl (Mrs. H. Rotenberg) and Miss Gertrude Greisman. Mr. Greisman came to Canada in 1888, and settled in Toronto, where he has since resided. Shortly after his arrival, he started the business in which he is still actively associated, the King Suspender Company. From a very small start, Mr. Greisman has built this concern into one of the largest of its kind in Canada, manufacturing men's furnishings and having a most enviable reputation for business integrity, from coast to coast. From his early days in Toronto, Mr. Greisman has always shown his confidence in the growth of the City, and he is a large property owner and builder, the Henry Building and the Spadina Building, two of the finest manufacturing buildings in Toronto, belonging to him. He is also the owner of several large apartment buildings. Mr. Greisman has always taken a keen interest in all communal affairs, and is a supporter of almost every charitable institution in Toronto. He is a very modest man and never seeks office, but prefers to work in the background where he feels that his assistance will do the most good. He is a vice-president of the Federation of Jewish Philanthropies of Toronto, and takes a particular interest in the Jewish Old Folks' Home and the Jewish Orphans' Home. In 1890, Mr. Greisman was instrumental in organizing the Austrian congregation (Shomrai Shabbas Synagogue) which at the time occupied quarters on Queen Street, and later (in 1900) it was largely through his efforts that the present synagogue on Chestnut Street was built. For ten years Mr. Greisman was president of this congregation, and he has always held an executive office in it. He is a firm believer in the Zionist Movement and is a member of the Independent Order of Foresters, and of the Primrose Club, Toronto.

ALAN J. HART, MONTREAL

ALAN JUDAH HART, the eldest son of the late Lewis Alexander Hart and Fanny Elizabeth (Benjamin) Hart, was born at Montreal, October 4th, 1879. He is one of the fifth generation of his family to be born in Canada. He was educated at the Montreal Collegiate Institute and the Montreal High School, and at an early age entered the study of the garment manufacturing industry, first with E. A. Small & Company, Montreal, and later with the firm of A. H. Sims & Company. Some years later he became connected with H. Vineberg & Company, Montreal, and he left them to enter into the manufacturing business for himself, under the name of the Hart Manufacturing Company. He was the first man in Canada to enter into the manufacturing of women's garments for the trade exclusively. This business he conducted for many years, winding it up in 1914 to enter the insurance field, which he has since successfully followed. He has built up for himself one of the largest insurance clienteles in Canada, and a reputation for sterling business integrity. In 1924, he was instrumental in organizing the Laurentian Insurance Company, the first Canadian Insurance Company to be financed entirely by Jewish capital. The formation of such a company had long been the ambition of Mr. Hart, and it is in a very large part due to his untiring energy that it has become an accomplished fact. Mr. Hart has taken an active part in communal affairs in Montreal, and he is a member and supporter of all Jewish undertakings. His interests are non-sectarian, and all questions for the benefit of the community engage his active support. He is a life-long member of the Spanish and Portuguese Synagogue (Shearith Israel) of Montreal, of which he is also a past officer, and is a member of the council of the Montefiore Club, Montreal. He is a member of the Royal Arcanum. On December 23rd, 1902, Mr. Hart was married to Eva, daughter of Mr. and Mrs. Harris Vineberg of Montreal, and he has three sons, Edward H., Gordon D., and Lawrence E., and two daughters, the Misses Alma and Vera Hart.

CAPTAIN ISIDORE FREEDMAN, TORONTO

ISIDORE FREEDMAN, the eldest son of Samuel and the late Rachel (Rosen) Freedman, was born at Glasgow, Scotland, the 25th of April, 1880. He received his education at the Atheneum, Antwerp; in Brussels; and at the Birbick School in London, England. This gave him the command of languages that he required in the business that he followed. As a young man, Mr Freedman opened up branches of his father's business in Australia and Canada, and in 1898 settled in Montreal where he carried on business as a diamond importer until the outbreak of war in 1914, when he immediately offered his services. He took a special course of training at Stanley Barracks, Toronto, and at the Royal School of Infantry, Halifax, where he qualified as Major in the Canadian Army. In 1916, he was invited by the late General Sir Sam Hughes to raise a battalion for overseas service, but he declined this honour, and raised and commanded the Jewish Reinforcement Company, Montreal, which he took overseas. It might be said that Capt. Freedman's entire family gave their services during the war, his brother Capt. Albert with the Canadians, and Sergt. Maurice, Sergt. Bernard, and Lieut. Arthur, with the Belgian Army. Maurice and Bernard Freedman were both decorated for bravery. His sisters gave their services as interpreters to the British War Office. Captain Freedman has always been interested in outdoor sports, and is an old international football player. He was President of the Westmount Football Club, and was the donor of the Freedman Cups, for senior and intermediate teams. In 1911, he was elected Treasurer of the Spanish & Portuguese Synagogue, Montreal; which office he held for some time. He is a member of the Beerschott Athletic Club, Antwerp; the Antwerp Football, Cricket, and Lawn Tennis Club; the Montefiore Club, Montreal; and the Primrose Club, Toronto. He belongs to St. George's Lodge, No. 10 A.F. & A.M. Mr. Freedman is married to Edith, daughter of the Hon. Max Griffenhagen, ex-Sheriff of the City of New York, and has four daughters, the Misses Marjorie, Arline, Rhoda, and Barbara Freedman.

M. MARGOLICK, MONTREAL

Notman

MICHAEL MARGOLICK was born in Libeau (Koorland) Russia, on June 29th, 1880, the son of the late Moses Margolick. He came to Montreal with his widowed mother in 1891, the second youngest of five children. After receiving an elementary education in the Protestant Schools of Montreal, he entered the employ of Mr. Harris Vineberg, and remained with this firm for thirteen years, during which time he advanced to the head of the financial department of the firm. Severe illness caused him to sever his connection with Mr. Vineberg, and on recovering he started the business which he at present carries on in partnership with Mr. M. Rittenberg, under the name of the Crown Pants Company. In the twenty years he has been in this business, Mr. Margolick has developed it into a very large industry, known throughout Canada, and bearing a very high name for commercial integrity. From childhood he has always displayed a wonderfully good judgment, and has always been respected for his reliability and energy in business dealings. By his own unaided efforts and determination he has risen to his present position in commerce. Mr. Margolick has done much to further the welfare of his people, assisting all in need, and at all times lending a helping hand to the less fortunate. He is a supporter of any undertaking tending to the advancement of his people, and is a supporter of all worthy institutions. Although he does not seek office, his assistance is looked for in any philanthropic work, and it is at all times cheerfully given. He occupies today a position in the world of finance, commerce and philanthropy that would do credit to any member of the community. Mr. Margolick is married to Helen G., daughter of Abraham Greenberg, and he has two sons, Frank and Melvin, and two daughters, the Misses Riva and Rosebud Margolick. He is a member of the Montefiore Club, Montreal, and has been a life long member of the Shaar Hashomayim Congregation.

S. WENER, MONTREAL

SAMUEL WENER, President of Samuel Wener & Company, Limited, was born in Kovno, Russia, on September 7th, 1879, the son of Selig and Jennie Wener of that city. He received his early education in the schools of his native city, and this was supplemented on his arrival in Canada, at the Montreal public schools. When fifteen years old, Mr. Wener commenced to serve his apprenticeship in the waterproof clothing trade, with which business he has since been continuously and actively connected. In 1906, he organized the firm of Samuel Wener & Company, Limited, which was incorporated in 1911, and of which he is President and active head. They are importers and the sole agents in the Dominion of Canada, for the Aquatite Gabardine coats. In 1920, they bought out the Sterling Clothing Company, Limited, which is now operated under the management of Samuel Wener & Company, Limited. Although a man of large business interests, Mr. Wener devotes much of his time and energy to the welfare work carried on by the people of his community, irrespective of race or creed, and he is a life governor of the Montreal General Hospital, and the Western Hospital, Montreal. Always greatly concerned in the religious upbringing and education of the Jewish young, Mr. Wener, some years ago, was one of the founders of the United Talmud Torahs of Montreal. In 1925 he presented the Talmud Torah with an oil painting of the late Lazarus Cohen. He was President for seven years, and on retiring from this office, he was elected Honorary President. He is the Vice-President of the Baron de Hirsch Institute, and is a member of the Board of Directors of the Shaar Hashomayim Synagogue, Montreal. Mr. Wener is a member of the Montefiore Club; Canadian Club; Empire Club; Elmridge Golf and Country Club; and of St. George's Lodge, No. 10 A.F. & A.M. On September 5th, 1906, Mr. Wener was married to May, daughter of Mr. and Mrs. S. Levinson of Montreal, and he has one daughter, Miss Gertrude Z. Wener.

H. E. DAVIS, MONTREAL

Photo by Jacoby

HARRY EDWIN DAVIS, proprietor of H. E. Davis & Co., Importers and Manufacturers and one of the representative Jewish business men of Montreal, was born in London, England, on June 20th, 1870, the son of the late Hyman S. Davis of that city. He received his education at the Jewish Free School in London, and in 1894 came to Canada, and settled in Montreal, where he has since resided. On his arrival in Montreal, Mr. Davis entered into the manufacturing and importing of raincoats, and he has built up a large business with connections reaching to both ends of the country. His business connections remain very closely identified with the old country, and Mr. Davis has in the course of thirty years, made over forty trips to Europe. He has always taken a great interest in communal matters, and his support is always sought for any important undertaking. Originally, a member of the Spanish and Portuguese Synagogue, some years ago Mr. Davis joined the Temple Emanu-El, and he was elected the first President of the Brotherhood of the Temple. He is at present a member of the Board of Directors of this congregation, and is taking a prominent part in the advancement of the Reform Movement. His aim is to create a better understanding between Jews and the rest of the community, based on a mutual knowledge and respect. A very charitable man, Mr. Davis does not limit his support to any particular race or creed, and he is regarded as one of the most respected and public-spirited business men of Montreal. On September 12th, 1905, Mr. Davis was married to Julia, daughter of the late Mr. and Mrs. S. J. Goldstein, a member of one of the oldest Jewish families of Montreal, and he has two sons, Stanley and Lloyd, and one daughter, Miss Eileen Davis. He is a member of the Prince Consort Lodge, A.F. & A.M., and the Montefiore Club of Montreal, and of all the Jewish charitable institutions in that city.

HARRY ROTENBERG, TORONTO

HARRY ROTENBERG, President of Yolles and Rotenberg, Limited, was born in Poland on October 31st, 1884, the son of Louis and Rivka (Cukier) Rotenberg. He accompanied his parents when they settled in Canada, in 1895, and was educated at the public schools and business college in Toronto. On March 14th, 1905, he was married to Pearl, daughter of Mr. and Mrs. Henry Greisman, of Toronto, and he has two sons, Arthur S. and Kenneth L., and four daughters, the Misses Gertrude, Lyla, Hilda, and Meta Rotenberg. After completing his education, Mr. Rotenberg was for some time engaged in clerical work, later entering the steamship agency and financial business with his father, in the firm now known as Rotenberg's Limited. He withdrew from this concern in 1910 and shortly afterwards formed a partnership with Mr. Louis S. Yolles under the name of Yolles and Rotenberg, Limited, Contractors and Financial Agents. This concern has become one of the foremost contracting firms in the country, among the numerous buildings erected by them being the Butterick Publishing Company Building, Toronto; the Willard Chocolate Building, Toronto; Toronto Type Foundry Buildings, Toronto and Montreal; Palace Theatre, Montreal; Hobberlin Building, Toronto; Federal Building, the largest and finest office building in Toronto; five motion picture theatres in Toronto; Woolworth Building, Danforth Ave., Toronto; Collett-Sproule Building, Toronto; Carswell Building, Toronto; Rous and Mann Building, Toronto; etc., etc. They also erected an office and theatre building at Windsor, Ont. Mr. Rotenberg has always been interested in communal matters, and he is the president of the Federation of the Jewish Philanthropies of Toronto, and a Trustee of the Holy Blossom Toronto Hebrew Congregation. He is also a member of the University Avenue Synagogue, Palestine Lodge, A.F. & A.M., Mount Sinai Chapter, R.A.M., I.O.B.B., the Primrose Club, Toronto, Empire Club, Toronto, and Cobourg Golf Club, Cobourg, Ont.

LEO FRANKEL, TORONTO

LEO FRANKEL, resident of Toronto for over forty years, and senior member of the firm of Frankel Bros., was born January 1st, 1864, at Biblis, Grand Duchy of Hesse, the son of the late Gottschall and Minna Frankel. He was educated at public and high schools and came to Canada in 1881, commencing his business career as a clerk with the Dominion Iron and Metal Company, Toronto. In 1886, he started the firm of Frankel Bros., and has developed it from a small beginning into the largest business of its kind in Canada, with a branch house in Montreal and agencies at New York, Birmingham and Liverpool. This concern is interested in the reclaiming of waste metal which has become one of the most important industries in this country, creating value where none had previously existed. Mr. Frankel is proprietor of the Toronto Mill Stock and Metal Company, and National Metal Company, and President, National Electric Heating Company, Limited. He has always occupied a prominent position in communal affairs and for almost twenty years has been President of the Holy Blossom Toronto Hebrew Congregation, in the welfare of which he takes a very keen interest. The high standing of this congregation amongst all classes of Toronto's population, is largely due to his labor and devotion in its behalf. He is a trustee and liberal supporter of the Federation of the Jewish Philanthropies of Toronto, and was a member of the Provisional Board of Trustees, prior to Federation, in 1916 and 1917. He is a member and supporter of many other charitable institutions. His interests are non-sectarian and he is very highly regarded by all sections of the community. Mr. Frankel has three sons Messrs. Egmont, Carl and Roy Frankel. His son Egmont was, in 1925, elected President of the Metal Dealers' Association, composed of merchants in all parts of the world. This was the first time that a Canadian had been so honored, as well as the first time the honor had been bestowed on such a young man. Mr. Frankel is a member of the Masonic Order and Primrose Club, Toronto.

SIGMUND SAMUEL, TORONTO

SIGMUND SAMUEL, President of Samuel & Benjamin, Limited, one of the largest wholesale metal firms in Canada, and Vice-President of the Metallic Roofing Co. of Canada, Limited, was born in Toronto, October 24th, 1868, the son of the late Lewis and Kate Samuel, who became residents of Toronto over seventy years ago. Mr. Samuel received his education at the Model School and Upper Canada College, Toronto. He started his business career as a junior with M. & L. Samuel, Benjamin & Co., in 1884, and worked up through the several necessary stages until he reached his present position. He is also a partner in the firm of Samuel, Sons & Benjamin, London, England, and of Samuel & Benjamin, New York, U.S.A., and is a director of the Imperial Trusts Company of Canada. He was a Councillor of the Toronto Board of Trade, 1912-1913, and is a member of the Canadian Manufacturers' Association. He has always been interested in communal undertakings and particularly in the welfare of the Holy Blossom Toronto Hebrew Congregation, of which his father was a charter member and for many years President. Mr. Samuel was himself vice-president of this congregation for many years. He is a member of the Federation of Jewish Philanthropies of Toronto, and was chairman of the campaign that had as its objective $100,000, which was organized for the purpose of raising funds for the Federation and the new orphanage. Always keenly interested in Art, some years ago he donated a complete section of exhibits to the Royal Ontario Museum, known as the Sigmund Samuel collection. Mr. Samuel is a member of the Council of the Art Gallery of Toronto and of the Royal Ontario Museum. He is a life governor of the Western Hospital, Toronto. On July 6th, 1898, Mr. Samuel was married to Leah May Mandelson, and he has two sons and two daughters. He is a member of the York, Albany, Caledon Mountain Trout, Lambton Golf and Country, Carlton (London, England), Hanger Hill Golf (England), Ontario Jockey, Toronto Hunt, York Downs Golf and Country, Ltd. (Toronto), and Saville (London, England) Clubs.

L. WOLFE, MONTREAL

LOUIS WOLFE, Vice-President and Managing Director of the Montreal and St. Lawrence Ports Stevedore Co., Ltd., was born at Goole, Yorkshire, England, July 1st, 1881, the son of Nathan Wolfe of that place. He was educated at the Goole Grammar School and came to Canada at an early age settling in Montreal, where he has since resided. From 1906 to 1910, Mr. Wolfe was connected with the Robt. Reford Company, Shipping Agents, at Montreal, and in 1910 he started his present business. Mr. Wolfe is a Director of the International Waterways Navigation of Montreal, and is interested in many mercantile undertakings. His business affairs entail a great amount of travelling, from one end of Canada to the other, and to European countries, and he is regarded as an authority on commercial and economic questions in the Dominion. Very highly regarded and respected wherever known, Mr. Wolfe is a modest man, and keeps much in the background, with the conviction that as one of the rank and file, he can do the most good. He is identified with most of the charitable and welfare institutions in Montreal, and is a member of the board of many societies. He is actively interested in anything that tends to the betterment of the community, irrespective of creed, and takes a part in all public questions, particularly those affecting the Jewish population of Montreal. Educational problems are of particular interest to Mr. Wolfe, and his advice on such matters is highly regarded. He takes a prominent part in fraternal matters and is a Past Master of his Masonic Lodge, and Past Grand Chancellor in the Knights of Pythias. In 1901, Mr. Wolfe was married to Dora, daughter of Harris Nagley, Esq., of Goole, Yorkshire, England, and he has four sons, Harry, Rufus, Gerald and Horace, and one daughter, Miss Lillian Wolfe. He is a member of the Montefiore Club and the Temple Club. Since his arrival in Canada, Mr. Wolfe has been a member of the Temple Emanu-El Congregation of Montreal.

J. A. DOBROFSKY, MONTREAL

Milne Studio

JOSEPH ALVIN DOBROFSKY, was born in Kiev, Russia, in 1889, the son of Peter Dobrofsky. He came to Canada in 1890 and settled with his parents in Montreal for a short time, the family later removing to New York, where he received his education at the schools of that city. He returned to Montreal as a young man, and he began his commercial career in the wholesale clothing industry. For a number of years he was salesman and later acted as sales manager for various firms, previous to his entering in business for himself. He organized and became President of the Atlas Skirt and Crescent Waist Company, Limited, in 1915. Later he became connected with Deutz and Ortenberg, Limited, importers of women's garments, which firm has branch offices in New York and Paris, and of which concern he is the present active head. Since his arrival in Montreal, Mr. Dobrofsky has always taken a keen and active interest in communal work and in all charitable undertakings in his community, and he is one of the most energetic social service workers among the younger men of that city. He devotes much time and labor to the welfare of the newly arrived immigrants, and is a member of the Board of Directors of the Jewish Immigrant Aid Society of Canada and the Montreal Hebrew Orphans' Home. Mr. Dobrofsky is a trustee of the Federation of Jewish Philanthropies of Montreal, and Spanish and Portuguese Congregation (Shearith Israel). He is a member of the Montreal Board of Trade; Merchants' Association; Canadian Manufacturers' Association; Montefiore Club; Elmridge Golf and Country Club; Mt. Horeb Chapter, R.A.M.; Corinthian Lodge, No. 62, A.F. & A.M.; and Independent Order B'nai B'rith. He also takes much interest in all public and political questions affecting his city and province and his influence is sought in all matters pertaining to the general good. In 1914, Mr. Dobrofsky was married to Millicent Dolly, daughter of Morris Imbrey of New York, and they have one son, Peter Dobrofsky.

H. M. ENDLEMAN, SUDBURY

HARRY MAX ENDLEMAN, one of the best known Jews of Northern Ontario, was born in Russian Poland, March 24th, 1886, the son of the late Solomon Nathan Endleman. He was educated in Russia and came to Canada in 1898 with his uncle, the late Mr. Max Goldberg, settling in Sudbury, where he received further education at the schools. In 1900, he started in the fur business, buying raw furs, incidentally being one of the first men who opened competition to the two great fur companies of the world, namely the Hudson's Bay Company and Revillon Frères, in the Sudbury District. He remained in business in the Sudbury District until 1922, when he became associated with one of the largest fur houses in the world as their representative in Northern Ontario and Alaska. In 1923, he became President of Endleman Limited, having severed his connection with the previously mentioned fur house. His present firm is one of the largest fur dealers in Northern Ontario, having agents and buyers in all the principal points of that territory as far north as James Bay. Mr. Endleman, just previous to forming Endleman Limited, undertook to start in the fur farming business, principally the breeding and raising of muskrats, this proposition today, the property of Endleman Limited, is one of the largest of its kind in Canada. Although a young man, Mr. Endleman is one of the best known fur merchants in Canada and his thorough knowledge of this line is admitted by the largest dealers on this continent. He is regarded as one of the representative business men of his community, and his reputation for integrity is recognized among the greater part of the trade. He takes an active interest in all matters affecting and pertaining to the public good. He is an enthusiastic sportsman, and has at all times taken an active part in athletics. He was married on the 31st of August, 1919, to Miss Rose Cherin, daughter of Mr. and Mrs. Joseph Cherin of New York City, and they have three sons, Solomon Nathan, Victor and Robert.

J. L. SABBATH, MONTREAL

JOHN LOUIS SABBATH was born at Suczawa, Austria, on October 20th, 1882, the son of Nahum Bernard and Clara (Weissler) Sabbath, He spent his early life in the country of his birth, but at the age of six he emigrated to Canada with his parents, who chose Montreal as the city of their adoption. Mr. Sabbath attended the Montreal public school and the Montreal Technical high school, then known as the Senior School. While attending high school, he found time to conduct classes for immigrants, the subjects he taught being French, German and English. This was purely a labor of love and hundreds of newcomers to this country were greatly benefitted by this philanthropic undertaking. Shortly after graduating from high school, Mr. Sabbath entered into the clothing industry, where he remained for about six years. He then decided to engage in another field of commerce and finally chose the wholesale jewelry industry. That was about eighteen years ago, in 1906. Mr. Sabbath commenced business, of course, in a small way, but through perseverance, industry and vision, he gradually developed, until now he has become one of the leading wholesale jewellers in the Dominion of Canada. He is at present president and managing director of the J. L. Sabbath Company, Limited, with offices at 5 Notre Dame Street, West, Montreal, and his business activities in the field of jewelry extend from coast to coast. He also trades with Newfoundland, and his ramifications extend to the Orient. Mr. Sabbath is a member of the Ionic Lodge, A.F. & A.M., and Mount Horeb Chapter, R.A.M. He is a member of the Board of Trade of Montreal, and is active as an officer of the Canadian Jewellers' Association, in which organization he has served in various capacities. He is a member of the Shaar Hashomayim Synagogue, the Federation of Jewish Philanthropies, and is a supporter of all Jewish communal endeavours. In 1911, Mr. Sabbath was married to Miss Rose Kert, daughter of Mr. Maxwell B. Kert of Montreal, and he has four sons, Bernard, Lawrence, David and Joseph, and two daughters, the Misses Beatrice and Freda Sabbath.

R. H. BLUMENTHAL, MONTREAL

ROBERT H. BLUMENTHAL was born in Montreal, on January 31st, 1868, the son of the late Jacob Henry Blumenthal, in his lifetime one of the pioneer clothing merchants of that city. Mr. Robert H. Blumenthal was educated at the Montreal public and high schools, and in January 1891, he was married in Montreal to Rachel, daughter of the late George and Dora Lazarus of Montreal. He has three sons, George A., Phillip Ed., and M. Stanley, and three daughters, Irene, Savilla, and Dorothy Maud. As a young man, Mr. Blumenthal entered the clothing business with his father and brothers, and on the death of his father, with his brother, he organized the clothing firm of J. H. Blumenthal Sons, Limited, a concern which is favourably known throughout Canada. Mr. Blumenthal has made a life study of this business and he is recognized as an authority on all matters pertaining to it. For some years Mr. Blumenthal has turned over the active interest of the business to his sons, and he spends much time in travelling. He is an enthusiastic sportsman, being particularly fond of golfing and fishing. Mr. Blumenthal takes a keen interest in all communal affairs and is a member of the executive of the Federation of Jewish Philanthropies. He was for many years on the Board of the Baron de Hirsch Institute, Montreal, and is at present the honorary president of the Baron de Hirsch Book Club. To do good in a quiet unassuming manner and to assist the deserving in a private capacity, is his policy. Mr. Blumenthal is a Fellow of the Royal Colonial Institute of London, England. He is a life member of the Montreal Amateur Athletic Association, and is keenly interested in the athletic training of the young Jew, believing that this is a necessary part of a young man's education. He is a life governor of the Western Hospital and of the Protestant Hospital for the Insane, Verdun, Montreal. He is president of the Schroon Lake Golf Club, and is a member of the Montefiore Club, the Montreal Reform Club, and Montreal Board of Trade. Mr. Blumenthal is a member of the Temple Emanu-El, Montreal.

H. LEVY, MONTREAL

HIRAM LEVY was born in Poland, December 2nd, 1854, the son of the late Jacob Levy. He received his early education in Poland, and in 1870 came to Canada, where he further educated himself. He first settled in Waterloo, P.Q., in 1877, and moved to Montreal in 1881, where he has since resided. In 1882, Mr. Levy established the woollen business of H. Levy & Sons, of which firm he is still the active head. As his sons grew up, he sent them to the old country where they obtained both a practical and technical knowledge of their line of business, following which he admitted them to the firm. Some years ago, the firm became incorporated under the name of H. Levy & Sons, Limited, and today this establishment is perhaps the oldest wholesale woollen house in Canada. Five of his sons have been associated in the business with him. His eldest son, Aaron Levy, B.A., M.D., Ph.D., F.R.C.S., L.R.C.P., graduated from McGill University, and after many years spent in travel and study, settled in London, England, where he became prominently identified in professional and communal matters. Mr. Levy has always been actively interested in communal work in Montreal. He was for many years on the boards of the Hebrew Free Loan Association, the Hebrew Sheltering Home, the Baron de Hirsch Institute, the United Talmud Torahs, and many other institutions. He is a member of the Federation of Jewish Philanthropies, Montreal, and of all its constituent societies. Mr. Levy is also interested in all matters pertaining to the betterment of the community as a whole, and he is a supporter of all charitable institutions, irrespective of creed. He is one of the oldest surviving members of the Shaar Hashomayim Congregation, which he joined when he first came to Montreal. He is a member of the Masonic Order and Oddfellows, and is President of the Canadian Order of Foresters. Mr. Levy married Malca S., daughter of the late Samuel Saxe, and they had six sons, Aaron, David, William, Henry, Philip and Joseph, and one daughter Lillian, who is the wife of Isaac Kirschberg, Esq., of Montreal.

E. PALTER, TORONTO

EPHRAIM PALTER, President of the United Press Limited, and a leading business man of the City of Toronto, was born in Grodno, Russian Poland, in 1872, the son of the late Hyman Palter. He received his education in Russia, and this was supplemented in the New York public schools. In 1894, Mr. Palter moved to Toronto, where he has since resided. On his arrival in Toronto, he joined the Standard Cap Company, which he managed for a number of years, but which suffered in the disastrous fire that wiped out the business section of Toronto in 1903. Mr. Palter then continued his business of cap manufacturing under the name of Palter Brothers, some years after changing it to the Palter Cap Company. He is still actively associated with this concern, which he has developed into one of the large industries of its kind in Canada. Upon the re-organization of the United Press some years ago, Mr. Palter became interested and was elected President, which office he still holds, and under his direction, this industry has developed into the largest Jewish printing establishment in Canada, being contractors to the Ontario Government, and printing numerous school and other text books. He is an active supporter of all the charitable institutions of Toronto, and takes a keen interest in the Zionist Organization. Mr. Palter is of a retiring disposition and steadfastly refuses all executive offices, but he is interested in all matters pertaining to the public good and particularly those affecting the betterment of the Jewish community. In 1924, in company with his wife, he visited the Jewish colonies in Palestine obtaining first hand information as to conditions there. He is a member of the Primrose Club; Knights of Pythias; and Sunnyside Lodge, Independent Order of Foresters; Sons of Jacob; and Independent Order B'nai B'rith. In 1896, Mr. Palter was married to Miss Minnie Rechtshafner of New York. He is a member of the Holy Blossom Toronto Hebrew Congregation.

ABRAHAM BLUMENTHAL, MONTREAL

ABRAHAM BLUMENTHAL, ex-Alderman of the City of Montreal, was born in New York on May 29th, 1861. He is the eldest son of the late Jacob Henry Blumenthal, in his lifetime a pioneer clothing merchant and one of the best-known Jewish citizens of Montreal. Abraham Blumenthal was educated in the public and high schools. At an early age he was very much interested in thoroughbred horses and for some years was a well-known rider. He then went into the clothing business in Montreal, which he successfully carried on for almost 40 years. In 1912, Mr. Blumenthal was elected member of the Montreal City Council as Alderman for St. Louis Ward, and served three terms, or six years, on the Council; during this period for a time acting as Pro Mayor. During his terms as Alderman, he was recognized as one of the leaders of the Council and was strongly reform in his actions and politics and always had the courage to voice his views, even though he was in the minority. In 1918, he resigned from the Council and entered the business of insurance broker, which he has since followed, but he still takes much interest in welfare movements and in civic and political matters, and has frequently been asked to be a candidate for Parliament. Mr. Blumenthal is independent in his politics and is not a follower of any one political party, but votes for the party that in his judgment best deserves his support. He is an enthusiastic boat builder and yachtsman. In his early days Mr. Blumenthal was a member of the Garrison Artillery and one of his sons, Philip, enlisted in the Jewish Reinforcement Company and served in the Great War, being wounded several times. Mr. Blumenthal is a member of the Masonic Order and the Knights of Pythias. He was married on March 29th, 1881, to Sarah Bernice, daughter of Myer Blumenthal, and has a large family of sons and daughters. He and his family have always been members and active supporters of the Spanish and Portuguese Synagogue, Montreal.

G. RABINOVITCH, MONTREAL

GEORGE RABINOVITCH, Banker, Financier and Real Estate Operator, was born in Britchou, Russia, September 8th, 1879, the son of Israel Rabinovitch. He was educated in Russia and came to Canada in 1898. He first entered into the retail business in St. Guillaume d'Upton, having a general store and from there he moved to St. Hyacinthe, and in 1905, went to Montreal, where he entered into the real estate business. Mr. Rabinovitch was a very successful operator and in 1914 he formed a private bank under his own name. This he continued to operate until 1923, when he sold out to the Bank of Toronto. He then again became actively interested in Montreal real estate and has since devoted most of his energy to this business. He is a large property owner and is considered one of the best judges of realty in Montreal. For some years, he was proprietor of the H. P. Labelle Furniture Company, the oldest furniture concern in the Province of Quebec. He erected the Rabinovitch building on the corner of St. Catharine Street and City Hall Avenue, one of the finest office buildings in Montreal, and he has also built other large properties. Mr. Rabinovitch is married to Dora, daughter of Joseph Sigman, and they have three sons, Benjamin, Moses and Mark, and one daughter, Mrs. Ray Kleinberger of Los Angeles, Cal. In his commercial success, Mr. Rabinovitch has not forgotten the less fortunate, and he is a prominent figure in communal work. He takes much interest in all charitable institutions and his activities are not confined to any one creed, but are general. He is a life governor of the Montreal General Hospital; Western Hospital; and Notre Dame Hospital. He was a director of the Hebrew Free Loan Association; Hebrew Orphans' Home; and of the Young Men's Hebrew Association, Montreal. He is a member of the Montefiore Club; National Club; United Talmud Torahs; the Young Men's Hebrew Association; and the Young Men's Christian Association. Mr. Rabinovitch is a member of the Shaar Hashomayim congregation. He has always been a follower of the Zionist Organization.

ISRAEL ROTHBART, Phm. B., TORONTO

ISRAEL ROTHBART, Druggist, the son of Abraham and Fanny Rothbart of Toronto, was born at Grodno, Russia, February 6th, 1895. He was educated at the High School in Russia, at the University of Toronto (Phm.B. 1918), and at the Ontario College of Pharmacy (Gold Medallist). He was married on 15th March, 1923, to Ray Goldblatt of Toronto. Mr. Rothbart is a member of Mt. Sinai Lodge, A.F. & A.M.; Mt. Sinai Chapter, R.A.M.; I.O.B.B.; and I.O.F. He is a member of the University Avenue Synagogue.

S. M. GREENFIELD, TORONTO

SAMUEL MAX GREENFIELD, Financial Broker and General Manager of Locators Business Company, was born at Barlad, Roumania, on March 5th, 1892. His parents are Solomon and Fannye Greenfield. He was educated in the public school, high school and at the University in Barlad, from which he graduated in 1908. Mr. Greenfield is one of the most active supporters of the Roumanian Synagogue of Toronto. He is married to Gussie Goldstein, and has four children, Paul, Jacob, Rosie and Adeline Greenfield.

M. J. ISAACS, OTTAWA

MYER JACOBI ISAACS was born in New York, Oct. 28, 1887. He was educated at St. Joseph College, Maniwaki; Montreal High School; and Ontario College of Pharmacy, graduating in 1908. He is President, Russel Drug Company, and Belmont Pharmacy. Mr. Isaacs is a capable artist and has had paintings on exhibit. He studied under George de Fosse, famous French-Canadian artist, completing his training in Paris. He is a member, Retail Merchants' Ass'n., and Canadian Pharmaceutical Ass'n. He is married to Sybil, daughter of Samuel Judel, and has one son, Maurice Marcus Isaacs.

HARRY GORDON, MONTREAL

HARRY GORDON was born in Toronto, August 15th, 1887. He received his education in the public schools of Toronto, and in 1911, moved to Montreal, where he started the business known as the City House Furnishing Company. He has been greatly interested in the Young Men's Hebrew Association, and in the Mount Sinai Sanatorium. He is a director of the Hebrew Maternity Hospital, and was a director of the Herzl Dispensary; Jewish Orphans' Home; and Hebrew Free Loan Association. He is married to Nellie, daughter of Samuel Kolber, and has one son, Paul Leon Gordon.

C. BENJAMIN, CALGARY

CHARLES BENJAMIN, Manager and partner in the Diamond Clothing Co., Calgary, and also a partner with Mr. Diamond in the Edmonton Clothing Co., Edmonton, was born in Lithuania, October 15th, 1875, the son of the late Leopold and Miriam Benjamin. He moved to Minneapolis with his parents, and was educated there, and in 1900 went to Edmonton where he became associated with Mr. William Diamond as Manager of the Edmonton Clothing Company. During his residence in Edmonton, he took an active part in the communal affairs there, and was one of the organizers of the Synagogue. A few years later he moved to Calgary, where he took charge of that end of the business, which was established by Mr. Diamond in 1892. This business Mr. Benjamin has developed into one of the largest clothing and furnishing businesses in Western Canada. He has also in Calgary maintained an active interest in communal affairs, and is regarded as one of the most public-spirited residents of that city. Mr. Benjamin does not confine his activities to any one section of the community, but takes an interest in all public questions. His aim, in which he has been highly successful, is to create a better understanding between Jew and non-Jew, based on a better mutual understanding and respect, and his efforts on behalf of the community as a whole have done a great deal to advance this. He is the Vice-President of the Red Cross Society, Calgary branch, and Treasurer of the Boy Scouts. He is Chairman of the Finance Committee of the Boy Scouts of Alberta. Mr. Benjamin is a member of the Montefiore Club, Montreal; Board of Trade, Calgary; Kiwanis; Canadian Club; Knights of Pythias; Independent Order B'nai B'rith; and Benevolent and Protective Order of Elks. Mr. Benjamin also takes a keen and active interest in Zionism, and is prominent in all drives for relief work in the community. He is married to Mamie, daughter of the late Isaac Goldsmith of Chicago, who was one of the pioneer residents of Hamilton, Ontario, and he has one son Raymond, and two daughters, the Misses Isabel and Beatrice Benjamin.

Jacoby Studio

J. ENZER, MONTREAL

JOSEPH ENZER was born in Bukowina, Austria, on January 9th, 1869, the son of the late Abraham Enzer. He received his education in Austria and came to Canada in 1889. Mr. Enzer first resided in Montreal, but after some twelve years spent there, he moved to Fort William, Ontario, where he opened a general store which he carried on in Fort William for fifteen years. He established a reputation for business integrity that did more to help the community than any other cause, and Mr. Enzer has maintained this reputation wherever he has gone. He did invaluable pioneer work in his community, in establishing a good understanding between Jews and non-Jews. For the first five years of his residence there, he was the only Jew in Fort William, and when the Jewish population increased to the extent that they were able to organize a congregation, it was Mr. Enzer who was instrumental in its formation. He took a most active part in the building of the synagogue and in all communal undertakings and endeavors in Fort William. For many years Mr. Enzer devoted much of his time working for the Jewish communities at the head of the Lakes, and he is known as "The Founder of Judaism" in the twin cities. He organized and was first president of the Fort William Lodge, Independent Order B'nai B'rith, and did much to advance the interests of his coreligionists in very many ways. He was a member of the Board of Trade of Ft. William. In 1915, Mr. Enzer returned and took up his residence in Montreal, where he entered into the manufacturing of ladies' garments, under the name of Ideal Ladies' Wear Ltd., which business he still conducts. He takes an active interest in all Jewish communal undertakings in Montreal, and is particularly interested in the Zionist Organization. Mr. Enzer was married to Ernestine, daughter of Alter Mandelbaum, and he has two sons, Dr. Norbert and Emanuel, and one daughter, Miss Jeanette Enzer, who has made for herself an enviable reputation as a musician. Mr. Enzer is a member of St. George's Lodge, A.F. & A.M., and of the Spanish and Portuguese Synagogue, Montreal.

N. L. NATHANSON, TORONTO

NATHAN LOUIS NATHANSON, Managing Director of the Famous Players Canadian Corporation, Limited, was born in Minneapolis, Minn., on May 1st, 1887. He was educated in his home community and went to Toronto in 1907, for many years being associated with the E. L. Ruddy Company in whose employ he advanced until he became sales manager. In 1916, he became interested in the moving picture industry and established his present concern, the largest distributors of motion picture films in Canada. He has become the foremost figure in this industry in Canada, and later on became interested in the exhibiting of films and erected and secured control of many of the largest motion picture theatres in Canada, which under his organization have reached a standing never before attained. The clean and high position of this industry is largely due to his connection with it. Mr. Nathanson is also a supporter of the "legitimate" stage, and is one of those who has made it possible for the citizens of Toronto to view some of the largest productions brought to that city. He is Managing Director, Eastern Theatre, Limited; Managing Director, Hamilton Theatre, Limited; Managing Director, Regal Films, Limited; Director, Famous Lasky Film Service, Limited; Managing Director, Regent Theatres, Limited; Managing Director, Paramount Theatres, Limited; Vice-President, British Columbia Paramount Theatres, Limited; partner in the firm of Wadsworth, Nathanson Company; and Director, E. L. Ruddy Company, Limited. Always a firm believer in clean sport, in 1924 Mr. Nathanson became one of the owners and President of the St. Patrick's Professional Hockey Club, Toronto. He is keenly interested in communal undertakings and is a trustee of the Holy Blossom Toronto Hebrew Congregation, a member of the Federation of the Jewish Philanthropies of Toronto, and a member and supporter of many charitable organizations. On June 17th, 1914, he was married to Miss Irene Henrietta Harris, daughter of B. Harris, Toronto, and they have one son. Mr. Nathanson is a member of the Toronto Board of Trade.

JEWS IN PUBLIC AND POLITICAL LIFE IN CANADA

FROM their first days in Canada members of the Jewish faith have taken an active part in all questions concerning the advancement of this country or of the communities in which they resided, and the names of the first Jews to settle in Canada may be found on the petition to the English Government asking for the establishment of a Legislature for Lower Canada. This petition, which resulted in the passing of the Quebec Act of 1774, among other names bears those of Aaron Hart and David Salesby Franks.

In 1807, Ezekiel Hart was elected a member of the Legislature of Lower Canada over three opponents. As he refused to take the oath of office "on the faith of a Christian" he was not allowed to take his seat, which was declared vacant. His constituents again elected him and again he was refused his seat on the same grounds. When this happened a third time, the French Canadian majority in the House attempted to pass a Bill to declare Jews ineligible for election. This aroused the indignation of the Governor, Sir James Craig, who dissolved the House before the Bill could pass. Although Hart had been elected in Three Rivers, a memorial to the Governor, thanking him for his firmness in dissolving the Assembly, was signed by almost every resident of Montreal. This question was finally settled by the Act passed in 1831, in which the Jews were allowed all the rights and privileges of His Majesty's other subjects. Incidentally it was a son of Ezekiel Hart, Samuel Becancour Hart, who was largely responsible for the passing of the Act, which allowed the Jews of Canada rights that they only obtained in England some twenty years later. He had been appointed a magistrate and had been refused his commission on the same grounds as his father, when he also refused the oath in the Christian form.

In 1837, Moses Judah Hays and Benjamin Hart were both appointed magistrates in Montreal, and served with distinction, particularly during the Rebellion in that year, when exceptional firmness and bravery were required. It was Benjamin Hart who read the Riot Act on November 6th when the trouble first started, and who signed the requisition to the commandant of the garrison, calling out the troops.

In October, 1834, Moses Hart was a candidate at Three Rivers for the Assembly but was defeated by a small majority.

British Columbia was admitted into the Dominion in 1871, and sent as its first member of the House of Commons, for the City of Victoria, Henry Nathan, who was elected by acclamation. He was re-elected at the general elections in 1872, and sat until the expiration of the second Dominion Parliament in 1874. Mr. Nathan had previously been elected a member of the British Columbia Legislature. Seilim Franklin also served as a member of the British Columbia Legislature, as a representative of Victoria City. In 1878, J. P. Davies, of Victoria was a candidate to the Federal House, but was defeated by only 30 votes.

In 1910, S. Hart Green was elected member of the Manitoba Legislature for North Winnipeg. He declined re-election after one term.

S. W. Jacobs was elected member of the House of Commons in the general elections of 1917. In the general elections in 1923 he was re-elected, when all four of his opponents lost their deposits. Mr. Jacobs represents the George Etienne Cartier division of Montreal in the Federal House and he has been a worthy representative of the Jewish people. He is regarded as one of the ablest members of the Commons, and is recognised as one of the outstanding members of the Jewish faith in Canada.

Peter Bercovitch was elected member for St. Louis division in the Quebec Legislature in 1918. In 1919, he was re-elected by acclamation, and it is a testimony to his ability and popularity that in 1923 he was again returned as the only Liberal member from the City of Montreal to the Provincial Legislature.

In municipal politics the members of the Jewish community have always been very active, and there are many members of the different city councils of the Jewish faith. Samuel Benjamin was elected a member of the Montreal City Council in 1849, and served for a number of terms. Abraham Joseph was at one time a candidate for the mayoralty of Quebec City and was defeated by only a very few votes, the election being so close that some of his supporters claimed that he had been elected. In 1912, Abraham Blumenthal was elected member of the Montreal City Council, and served as alderman for three terms. In 1914, Louis Rubenstein was elected alderman in Montreal, and he has been returned at every election since that date. He has frequently officiated as pro-Mayor. From 1918 to 1924, Lyon W. Jacobs was a member of the Montreal City Council. At the present time there are three Jewish members on the Council.

SAMUEL BENJAMIN
Alderman City of Montreal 1849

Lumby Franklin was, in its early days, a member of the Victoria, B.C., City Council, and he was elected the second mayor of that City. David Oppenheimer and his brother, Isaac Oppenheimer, were elected by acclamation to the Vancouver City Council in 1886, the year that Vancouver was incorporated as a city. Isaac retired after two years, but David stood for re-election and in 1888 was elected mayor, a position he occupied until his retirement in 1893. The only monument to a citizen of Vancouver is that one of David Oppenheimer, erected in Stanley Park by the city as a tribute to his memory.

Samuel Shultz served as Alderman in the Vancouver City Council in 1909-10, but then retired from political life.

Moses Finkelstein was the first Jew to become a member of the Winnipeg City Council, being elected alderman in 1905. There have been a number of Jewish aldermen in Winnipeg since, at the present time three Jews being members of the Council, and another, Marcus Hyman, being a school trustee.

N. Steiner was elected a member of the Toronto City Council in the early eighties, and in 1914, Louis Singer was elected alderman. He sat for four terms, declining re-election in 1918. Joseph Singer was elected alderman in 1920 and 1921, and in 1922 heading the aldermanic vote. In 1923, he was elected one of the Board of Control. He was not a candidate in 1924, but was again elected alderman in 1925. Nathan Phillips was elected alderman in 1924 and re-elected in 1925, heading the poll in his ward. Samuel Factor was elected School Trustee in 1923, and was re-elected in 1924. In 1925, Joseph Gordon was elected School Trustee. Benjamin Fox has been elected member of the Ottawa School

Board for several terms. In 1924, Michael Hirsch, S. W. Cohen, and H. Schubert were appointed by the Quebec Government, members of a commission which was formed to study the question of education of the Jewish children in the Province of Quebec, (an account of which appears elsewhere in this volume).

In Whitby, Charles King occupied every office in the gift of the town and for over half a century he was the outstanding figure in Ontario County, in 1888 being elected Warden of the County.

William Hyman was elected mayor of the Township of Cape Rosier, on the Gaspe Coast, from its first organization in 1858 and continued to occupy the civic chair without interruption till his death, which took place in 1882.

Sigmund Samuel, a prominent resident of Toronto, where he was born, in addition to other contributions to the communal life of his city, donated a complete section of exhibits to the Ontario Museum.

In many of the smaller municipalities there are Jewish members of the local Councils, and among them may be mentioned George Simon, who was for many years mayor of Alexandria.

Dr. Abraham de Sola was the first Jew honored by McGill University with the degree of LL.D., which he received in 1858. He was ranked among the foremost savants of his day and had a reputation that was almost world-wide. In 1872, Dr. de Sola was invited by the then president of the United States, General Grant, to open the United States Congress with prayer, and the unique scene was then witnessed of one who was a British subject, and not of the dominant faith, performing (with covered head, according to Jewish custom) the opening ceremonies at the assembling of Congress at Washington. This episode was regarded as the first friendly compliment extended to England by the United States, after the strained relations that had resulted from the Alabama claims, and the thanks of the British Government were conveyed to Dr. de Sola by Sir Edward Thornton, then British Ambassador at Washington.

In 1914, Samuel Shultz was appointed judge of the County Court at Vancouver, B.C., and he retained this appointment until his death. Judge Shultz has been the only Jewish member of the judiciary in Canada to the present time. There have been many who have been appointed justices of the peace, and among them have been some who have sat on the Bench as Police magistrates. The late Benjamin Zimmerman of Winnipeg, often acted as magistrate, during the absence of the regular incumbent, and Jacob Cohen, of Toronto, was appointed Police magistrate in 1918, and has since filled the position with credit.

Jewish members of the Consular Corps have included Jesse, Abraham and Andrew Joseph, Moise Schwob, Abraham Nordheimer, David A. Ansell, Clarence I. de Sola, and Samuel Gintzburger. The members of the Joseph family and C. I. de Sola represented Belgium in this country, Mr. Nordheimer was German Consul, Mr. Ansell was Consul-General for Mexico, Mr. Gintzburger is still the Consul for Switzerland in British Columbia, and Mr. Schwob was Vice-Consul for France in Montreal.

Rabbi Max J. Merritt of the Temple Emanu-El, Montreal, and Rabbi Barnett R. Brickner of the Holy Blossom Congregation, Toronto, both occupy a very high standing not only in their respective communities, but also throughout Canada. Their aim is to create a better understanding between Jews and non-Jews, based on a mutual regard for each other, which can only be accomplished by a closer association, and they are meeting with great success in their endeavours. Both brilliant men and accomplished orators, they are in demand at many gatherings, and their work cannot help but be beneficial to all members of their faith. Rabbi Merritt has been honoured with the appointment of Grand Chaplain of the Grand Lodge of the Province of Quebec A.F. & A.M. In Winnipeg, Rabbi H. J. Samuel occupies a similar position, and he was Chaplain (1924) of the Canadian Club. They are all members of the ministerial associations in their respective cities.

MONUMENT ERECTED BY THE CITY OF VANCOUVER TO DAVID OPPENHEIMER

THE LATE HENRY NATHAN

HENRY NATHAN, JR., during his residence in British Columbia one of the most prominent citizens of that Province, was born in London, England, September 3rd, 1842, the eldest son of Henry Nathan, Esq., of Maida Vale, London, England. He received his education at the London University School, and arrived in Vancouver Island while a very young man, settling in Victoria in 1862, where he established the firm of Henry Nathan, Jr., Wholesale Merchants. He took a prominent part in public affairs in the early days of the province, both in the colony of Vancouver Island, and the province at large. He was elected member for Victoria in the British Columbia Legislature in November 1870, and remained until dissolution in 1871. In November, 1871, he was returned by acclamation to the Federal Parliament at Ottawa, as the first member for Victoria District, on British Columbia being admitted into the Canadian Union. He left for Ottawa on December 9th, 1871, in company with Dr. Carrall, the first Senator of British Columbia, and was given a rousing send-off, being very popular. He was re-elected at the general election of 1872, and sat until the expiration of the second Dominion Parliament in 1874. Mr. Nathan occupied a high position in the social life of Victoria and was prominent in Masonic affairs. In 1865, he was elected Master of the British Columbia Lodge, A.F. & A.M. He was at all times interested in municipal affairs and was the owner of considerable property at Vancouver Island. Henry Nathan was a staunch supporter of Sir John A. MacDonald, and he was one of the directors of the railway which the Prime Minister was endeavoring at that time to extend across Canada (now the C.P.R.). Old residents of British Columbia state that Henry Nathan did more than any other individual in bringing British Columbia into the Dominion of Canada, and he is spoken of amongst those who remember him in Victoria, as perhaps the outstanding figure of that province. Mr. Nathan retired from Canadian public life in 1880, and returned to England where he took up his residence.

MAGISTRATE JACOB COHEN, TORONTO

JACOB COHEN, Police Magistrate of the City of Toronto, was born in Krakow, Austria, September 18th, 1847 the son of the late Morris Cohen. The story of his struggle for success is a tale of achievement against great odds. Handicapped by lack of knowledge of the language of the land of his adoption, his perseverance and courage carried him through many disappointments. He came to America in 1870 and for a short time clerked in New York, later working in Memphis and New Orleans. At one time he acted as a buyer of hides, cotton and tallow out of Thibaudeau, La., and also worked there as a stable hand. He then had a position in a clothing store in Waco, Texas, and in 1873 came back to New York with his savings, which amounted to between four and five hundred dollars. He was advised by some friends to move to Toronto, which he did the same year, and for some months travelled through Ontario peddling jewellery. He then opened up a small shoe store, for which he paid a rental of eight dollars a month. This being the business to which he had been raised, he prospered in it, opening up other stores. Through hard work and perseverance he was able to retire in 1909. Mr. Cohen always took a deep interest in his fellow-Jews, and with a view to helping those who could not speak English, he accepted the position of interpreter at the Court House, giving his services gratuitously. He was appointed Justice of the Peace in 1910 and on the 20th of September, 1918 he was appointed Police Magistrate. For over twenty-five years Mr. Cohen was treasurer of the Toronto Hebrew Benevolent Society, and he is a past president of the Holy Blossom Synagogue, and was one of the committee in charge of the building of the present edifice. He is also a life member of the McCaul Street Synagogue. Mr. Cohen is a member of the Federation of Jewish Philanthropies, and of many charitable and welfare institutions. He is a Mason and belongs to the I.O.F.; I.O.O.F.; I.O.B.B.; and is a member of the Albany and Primrose Clubs. He was married to Miss Lena Jacobs, daughter of the late Morris Jacobs, who died in 1904, and has one son, Arthur Cohen.

ALDERMAN LOUIS RUBENSTEIN, MONTREAL

LOUIS RUBENSTEIN, Alderman of the City of Montreal, and the outstanding leader of amateur athletics in the Dominion of Canada, was born in Montreal, September 23rd, 1861, the son of the late M. Rubenstein. He was educated at the public and high schools of Montreal, and as a young man joined his brothers in the firm of Rubenstein Brothers, silver, gold and nickel platers and manufacturers. From his early days Mr. Rubenstein has been keenly interested and actively connected with all amateur sports. In 1885, he won the Figure Skating Championship of Canada and the United States, and on February 11th, 1890, at St. Petersburg, Russia, he won the Amateur Figure Skating Championship of the world. He has frequently skated before notabilities at the Government House, Ottawa. Mr. Rubenstein has also been successful at other branches of sport, and he is an enthusiastic curler. He was a director and afterwards President of the Montreal Amateur Athletic Association; President of the Amateur Skating Association; President and Life Governor, Province of Quebec branch, Royal Life Saving Society; Vice-President, Canadian Bowling League. In 1899 he was elected President of the Canadian Wheelman's Association, and in 1911 he was elected Honorary President. He was Treasurer, Vice-President, and President, 1907-1909, International Skating Union of America. Mr. Rubenstein is regarded as the "father" of bowling in Canada. He frequently acts as judge at amateur athletic meetings in Canada and the United States. Mr. Rubenstein is active in all communal undertakings and has at all times been keenly interested in municipal affairs. He is a member of most of the charitable and welfare organizations in Montreal and was responsible for the erection of the Rubenstein baths, for the public use. In April 1914, he was elected member of the Montreal City Council and has been returned at every election since, frequently officiating as acting Mayor. For years he has been regarded as the outstanding member of the Council. He is a life-long member of the Spanish and Portuguese Synagogue, and is a member of the Montreal Reform Club.

THE JEW IN THE LEGAL LIFE OF CANADA

IT is only natural that the Jews as a race should show an inclination to take up the study of Law, as the first laws ever given to man were entrusted to their keeping. The laws of Moses are the basis of all others since, and a study of the Talmud is a very good preparation for the study of the laws of the country.

The first Jews to arrive and settle in Canada were those who were in the English armies, and the merchants and traders who followed in their wake, so among the first generation there were none who took up the practice of law exclusively. But one of those first settlers, Uriah Judah, later on was appointed prothonotary at Three Rivers, a position today given only as a recognition of legal ability.

Ezekiel Hart, born in Three Rivers on May 15th, 1770, took up the study of law, and became an eminent member of the profession. He took much interest in public affairs and was elected member of the Lower Canada Assembly in 1807, 1808, and 1809, but was not allowed to take his seat, he refusing to take the oath of office "on the faith of a Christian". One of his sons, Samuel Becancour Hart, who was also a member of the legal profession, was mainly responsible for the complete enfranchisement of the Jews, in 1831.

Henry and Thomas Judah, nephews of Uriah Judah, both took up the practice of law and were highly respected members of the profession, both in Three Rivers, where they lived, and in Montreal where they frequently practised. Thomas Judah later settled in Montreal, where some of his descendants are still living.

Three of Ezekiel Hart's sons, Samuel Becancour, Aaron Ezekiel, and Adolphus Mordecai Hart were all in the legal profession and attained a very high standing. Samuel practised in Three Rivers, Aaron in Quebec, and Adolphus in Montreal. Aaron Philip Hart also practised in Montreal and became one of the leading members of the profession in that city. Aaron Moses Hart and Ezekiel Moses Hart were both well-known advocates in Three Rivers, the latter being at one time appointed Registrar of that town, a position which he held until his death.

Several instances may be given of the important standing that these members of the legal profession occupied. On July 17th, 1838, Aaron Philip Hart was the examiner at the examinations held for admissions to the practice of Advocates. On November 3rd, 1837, he and Henry Judah were counsel for the defence in the celebrated case of Girod vs Pinet, and in the same year we read of Thomas Judah presiding at the dinner of the Bar of Montreal.

Eleazer David was admitted to practise as an Advocate in May, 1830, and he was a leading member of his profession in Montreal for many years. In June, 1837, Mr. David was retained as Counsel by five seamen who were charged with desertion by the master of the ship "Chieftain." The charge against them was dismissed, the court being of the opinion, after hearing several witnesses, that owing to violence used towards them as well as the want of sufficient food, that they were justified in leaving the ship. A Mr. Edmonstone of the firm of Miller, Edmonstone & Co. to whom the ship in question had been consigned, published statements in the Montreal press making certain allegations against Mr. David. Mr. David demanded an apology, which was refused. He then challenged Mr. Edmonstone to a duel, which challenge was also refused. Mr. David then published a full statement of the entire case in the daily papers, summing it up with the following statement: "Notre Dame St., 29th June, 1837. From this statement of Dr. Johnston's and the explanation that I have given above it will be perceived that Wm. Edmonstone of the firm of Miller, Edmonstone & Co. has by his unwarrantable mention of my name and base insinuations, proved himself to be a vile, low slanderer; and moreover by his subsequent refusal either to retract his aspersions or afford me satisfaction established himself a dastardly coward and unworthy of any further notice. Signed E. D. David." From this it will be seen that they had their own methods of expressing an opinion in those days. Eleazer David for many years was clerk of the Court at Montreal.

GERSHOM JOSEPH, Q.C.
First Jewish Queen's Counsel in Canada

Many of these men went to England for their education, but others received it at home, and thus in the records of Montreal College, in 1834, Samuel David graduated in that year and then entered upon his duties in the office of the Solicitor-General. After two years there, he "concluded arrangements with Driscoll to attend lectures with him until his time was up, one hour per day—to pay £25, £12.10 in six months, and the balance when his time was up". He was admitted to practise as Advocate in 1837. In 1844, Samuel David was appointed clerk of the Court at St. John's, Que., a position he filled until his death in 1852. In 1837, Gershom Joseph was attending college at Toronto, from which he graduated. He later became one of the leading members of his profession in Lower Canada, and was the first member of his faith to be appointed Queen's Counsel.

In 1852, Henry Joseph Meyers was a well-known Notary Public in Montreal, and in 1869 Lewis Alexander Hart after a brilliant career at McGill University, was admitted to the practice of Notary Public. He practised his profession in Montreal for over half a century, and attained a very high standing in it. In 1880, he was appointed Lecturer in the Faculty of Law, on the Theory and Practice of Notarial Deeds and Proceedings, at

McGill University, which marked the installation of a new course, and he remained a member of the Faculty many years. Samuel Shultz, of Victoria, B.C., received his legal training at Osgoode Hall Law School, Toronto, and at European universities. In 1914, he was appointed Judge of the County Court at Vancouver, B.C., and won universal esteem through his knowledge of law. Judge Shultz died only a few years ago.

Maxwell Goldstein, of Montreal, is the oldest Jewish, as well as one of the most distinguished members of the Bar. He graduated from McGill University in 1884, and was appointed King's Counsel in 1903. He has on more than one occasion been offered a seat on the Bench. Samuel William Jacobs graduated from McGill University in 1894, and has won the respect of the entire country, both as a brilliant member of his profession, and as a member of the House of Commons. He was appointed King's Counsel in 1906. He has acted as counsel for different foreign governments in Canada, and has represented the Attorney-General of Quebec abroad. Mr. Jacobs was Senior Counsel for plaintiff in the Quebec Anti-semitic libel case, 1913. He appeared for the Attorney-General of New York to secure the return of Harry K. Thaw to Matteawan Asylum, in 1913. He was one of a committee of Jewish citizens which successfully opposed the efforts of Queen's University to have itself declared by Parliament a National University, while insisting on remaining "distinctively Christian." Much important legislation respecting the Jews of Canada owes its origin to Mr. Jacobs. He is author of "Railway Law of Canada", and joint editor of "Jacobs' and Garneau's Code of Civil Procedure". In 1918, he introduced in the House a Bankruptcy Bill, which was subsequently adopted by the Government and enacted into legislation as a Government measure at the following session. He introduced measures (also accepted by the Union Government and later passed into law), which declare that no member of the House of Commons can sit for more than one electoral division, and that when a seat in Parliament becomes vacant, an election to fill such seat must be held within six months. Gabriel Levy of Hamilton, Ont., is one of the leaders of the Ontario Bar. After graduating from Osgoode Hall Law School, he attended European universities, and has since followed the practice of his profession in Hamilton. Mr. Levy was appointed King's Counsel in 1921, being the only member of his faith up to the present time in Ontario to be so honoured. Peter Bercovitch, of Montreal, is another member of the Bar who has achieved a very high standing, both as a member of his profession and as one of the representatives of Montreal City in the Quebec Legislature. He is regarded as one of the most capable members of the House. He was appointed King's Counsel in 1911. He has been prominent in introducing legislation for the amelioration of the poor and only in the present session was responsible for the passing of the "Exemption from Seizure" bill. He took the leading part in opposing proposed legislation which would have abrogated the agreement of 1903 regarding the granting of equal rights to Jews in Protestant schools. He also introduced the bill to validate Jewish marriages and to authorize Rabbis to keep registers of civil status. Samuel King, of Toronto, occupies a very high standing at the Bar of that City where he is the oldest Jewish member. He was admitted to the Bar in 1891.

In late years there has been a great inclination amongst the Jewish youth to take up the legal profession, and the graduating classes of most seats of learning contain a large percentage of them. In the west as well as in the older settled parts of the country, there are many who are making a leading name for themselves. Max Steinkopf, of Winnipeg was the first Jew to graduate in the prairie provinces into the legal profession, and he has been followed by many others. Max J. Finkelstein, also of Winnipeg, is one of the leading members of the Manitoba Bar. He was the counsel in the famous Fedorenko case against the Russian Government. Marcus Hyman, a graduate of Oxford, England, and a member of the Bar of Gray's Inn, was for some time lecturer in the Faculty of Law at Manitoba University. He is practising in Winnipeg. Harry A. Friedman was the first Jewish lawyer in Alberta, and has built up for himself a very high standing at the Alberta Bar. The late E. R. Levinson was for a time Crown Prosecutor in Winnipeg, as was also S. Hart Green, who also sat in the Manitoba Legislature. Max Grossman, of Vancouver, occupies a leading position at the British Columbia Bar, and is also very active in public life.

EZEKIEL MOSES HART
Registrar, Three Rivers, Lower Canada

Among the younger members of the profession in Toronto who have attained prominence, both in their profession and in the public life of the community, may be mentioned Louis M. Singer, Joseph Singer, and Abraham Cohen. Although young men, they have achieved a prominence worthy of the record made by members of their faith in Canada. In Montreal, among the younger members of the profession who have already become prominent may be mentioned Henry Weinfield, Nathan Gordon, who was City Prosecutor, Marcus M. Sperber, K.C., and Bram C. de Sola. Henry Weinfield is one of the leading Counsel for the Home Bank Depositors' Association. He also was Counsel for the Jewish Orphans' Home, Montreal, in the celebrated Berlin case. And in Montreal, as elsewhere, there is a rising generation of young Jewish lawyers, who, to judge from the records that they have made at the different seats of learning and from their success to date, will worthily fill the places made in the legal profession by elder members of their faith in Canada.

THE LATE LEWIS ALEXANDER HART, M.A., B.C.L.

LEWIS ALEXANDER HART, M.A., B.C.L., N.P., was born at Three Rivers, Que., on the 16th July, 1847, and died at Montreal on the 25th November, 1923. He was the youngest son of Alexander Thomas Hart, a leading citizen of Three Rivers and Seignior of the Fief Courval, and of Miriam (Judah) Hart. He received his early education at Three Rivers and at the Montreal Collegiate Institute, and entered McGill College when only fifteen years of age. In his first session at McGill, Mr. Hart took the prize for an English essay, and obtained first class standing in Hebrew and English literature. He graduated as B.A. in 1866, and as B.C.L. and M.A. in 1869, being first in his class in Roman Law; and shortly before the completion of his twenty-second year, was admitted to the practice of the Notarial profession. In 1880 Mr. Hart was appointed lecturer at McGill University upon the theory and practice of notarial deeds and proceedings, being the first notary ever appointed a professor in the McGill Law Faculty. Mr. Hart married in 1878, Fanny Elizabeth, daughter of Henry and Emma (Joseph) Benjamin of Montreal, and had four sons; Alan J., Claude B., Arthur D., and Philip B., and four daughters; Mrs. Michael A. Michaels, Mrs. Albert Freedman, and the Misses Gladys J. and Dorothy M. Hart. Mr. Hart practised his profession as notary in Montreal for more than a half century. He was known and respected by all classes, and held in the highest esteem by his colleagues. His knowledge of the law was thorough, and his opinion was frequently sought by leading members of the legal, as well as of the notarial profession. Mr. Hart was a writer of note upon civil, legal, educational and religious subjects, and was the author of "A Jewish Reply to Christian Evangelists." He was one of the charter members of the Young Men's Hebrew Benevolent Society, and was later President of the Baron de Hirsch Institute; and he was a life-long member, and at different times held various offices, including that of President, in the Spanish and Portuguese Synagogue of Montreal. Mr. Hart was a mason and held office in Royal Albert Lodge, A.F. & A.M., Montreal.

THE LATE JUSTICE S. SHULTZ

THE LATE JUSTICE SAMUEL SHULTZ, the first Jewish member of the Judiciary of Canada, was born at Victoria, B.C. in 1865. His parents were Mr. and Mrs. Herman Shultz of Victoria, and he was a grandson of the late Mr. J. P. Davies, one of the pioneer Jewish residents of British Columbia. He was educated in the public schools of Victoria; at the University of Toronto; and at Osgoode Hall Law School, Toronto. After completing his education, he travelled for a number of years, and on his return to British Columbia, at first devoted himself to Journalism. He was a frequent and valued contributor to the press and periodicals. Mr. Shultz was a very talented musician and composer, among his compositions being the military march, "Charge at Dawn", which he composed in honor of the men who fell at Paardeburg, in the South African War. In 1909-1910, he was elected and served as Alderman for North Vancouver. He was called to the Bar of British Columbia and practised Law at different times in Nelson, Victoria and Vancouver, and in 1914, he was appointed Judge of the County Court at Vancouver. Judge Shultz won universal esteem on account of his fairness and thorough knowledge of Law. He took an active interest in communal undertakings, and was a liberal supporter of all worthy causes, devoting much time to philanthropic undertakings. He was very much interested in the Zionist Movement, and was delegate at the Convention held in Winnipeg. His kindness and charity won him innumerable friends, and his sterling reputation will long remain to the credit of the Jews in British Columbia. He took a prominent part in all public questions, particularly those affecting his native province. Judge Shultz was married in 1904 to Maude, daughter of J. C. Squarebriggs of Prince Edward Island, and on his death he was survived by his widow and three sons. He was active in the Masonic Order, and was a member of the Connaught Lodge, A.F. & A.M. His mother was the first Jewish woman to be married in British Columbia, and was also the first woman to be buried in the Jewish cemetery at Victoria.

MAXWELL GOLDSTEIN K.C., MONTREAL

MAXWELL GOLDSTEIN, K.C., one of Montreal's most public-spirited citizens, and senior member of the law firm of Goldstein and Engel, Montreal, was born in Quebec City, on May 13th, 1863, the son of the late Adolphe and Rebecca (Stein) Goldstein. He was educated at the National and High Schools, Quebec, from which he matriculated to McGill University, Montreal. He graduated from McGill as Gold Medalist in 1882, with the degree of B.C.L. He studied law with the late W. H. Kerr, K.C., C. B. Carter, K.C., and R. D. McGibbon, K.C., and upon being called to the Bar in 1884 (when he attained his majority), became a member of the legal firm of Kerr, Carter and Goldstein. He was appointed King's Counsel in 1903. Mr. Goldstein has been one of the leaders of the Reform Movement since its inception in Canada and is one of the founders of the Temple Emanu-El, Montreal. He has been connected with it in an executive position ever since its formation, being president from 1907 to 1923, and at present holding the position of Honorary President. He is Honorary President of the Federation of Jewish Philanthropies, Montreal; Member of the Committee of Sixteen; Member of the Managing Committee, Victorian Order of Nurses; President, Jewish Court of Arbitration; Governor of both Montreal General and Western Hospitals, Councillor, Bar of Montreal, 1922-13; Chairman, Committee on Laws, Grand Council, Royal Arcanum, Quebec. He was the first President of the Hebrew Naturalization Association, and in 1909 was elected a director of the Montreal Citizens' Association. He was instrumental with others, in having the law of Quebec altered so as to secure equal rights in the schools for Jewish children. Mr. Goldstein is a member of the Canadian Bar Association; McGill Graduates' Society; Art Association of Montreal; Menorah Graduates' Society; the Montreal Club; Montefiore Club; Canadian Club; Fairview Country Club; and Y.M.H.A. On June 15th, 1892, Mr. Goldstein was married to Miss Rosalie Stern, daughter of Charles Stern of Toronto, and he has one son, Charles Adolphe, and one daughter, Amy Jeannette (Mrs. Franklin B. Fuld).

S. W. JACOBS, K.C., M.P., MONTREAL

SAMUEL WILLIAM JACOBS, born at Lancaster, Ont., May 6th, 1871, the son of the late William and Hannah (Aronson) Jacobs; educated at the High School, and McGill University (B.C.L. 1893, first rank honors); Laval University (L.L.M 1894, cum laude); called to the Bar in 1894, and created K.C. in 1906. On April 23rd, 1917, he was married to Amy, daughter of the late Michael Stein, of Baltimore, Md. He has one son and three daughters. Mr. Jacobs has figured in many important cases before the Courts in matters affecting Jewish citizens and their rights under the Civil Law. He was instrumental in the passing of various acts by the Legislature, whereby certain disabilities against Jews were removed; also in obtaining amendments in the constitutional law of Quebec respecting the status of Jews in relation to the School Law, Marriage License Act, etc. He was counsel for the Government of Roumania in the Costachescu extradition case, and has appeared in other extradition cases. In 1909, he was appointed by the Attorney-General, as Special Commissioner to visit Ireland to obtain evidence regarding the prisoner's sanity in the Dillon murder case. He was a senior Counsel for plaintiff in the Quebec anti-Semitic Libel Case, 1913, and appeared for the Attorney-General of New York, in Sherbrooke, to secure the return of Harry K. Thaw to Matteawan asylum, in 1913. He was president of the Baron de Hirsch Institute, 1912-14; Treasurer, Bar of Montreal, 1916-17; Council, Canadian Bar Association; Life Governor, Montreal General Hospital; Mt. Sinai Sanatorium; Y.M.H.A.; and Hebrew Free Loan Society; Vice-President, Jewish Publication Society of America; Director, Montreal Life Assurance Co. of Canada and Laurentian Insurance Company; Vice-President, General Asbestos Co. Ltd. Mr. Jacobs is the author of "Railway Law of Canada"; and the joint editor, "Jacobs' & Garneau's Code of Civil Procedure." He was first elected to House of Commons at the general elections, 1917; and was re-elected at the general elections in 1921, when all four of his opponents lost their deposits.

G. H. LEVY, K.C., HAMILTON

GABRIEL HERMAN LEVY, K.C., one of the most prominent members of the legal profession in Ontario, and the first and only Jewish barrister in that province to receive the appointment of King's Counsel, was born in Hamilton, Ont., on August 12th, 1874. His parents were the late Herman and Camilla Levy, pioneer residents of Hamilton, and in their lifetime the most prominent Jewish citizens there. Gabriel Levy was educated at the Central School, Hamilton; Hamilton Collegiate Institute; the University of Toronto; and the University of Bonn, Germany. On his return to Canada he entered the Ontario Law School, Osgoode Hall, Toronto, from which he graduated in 1894, and on being called to the Bar, commenced the practice of his profession in the City of Hamilton, where he is a member of the law firm of Gibson, Levy, Scott and Inch. In 1921, Mr. Levy received the appointment of King's Counsel from the Ontario Government. Mr. Levy is married to Blanche Ruth, daughter of Adolph and Yetta Shire, of Chicago, and they have two sons; Gabriel Shire and John Gibson, and one daughter; Miss Marion Louise Levy. Mr. Levy was formerly president of the Hughson Street Synagogue, a congregation that his father and uncle, Mr. Edmund Scheuer, were largely instrumental in organizing. This was the first Reform Jewish Congregation in Canada, established in 1882, and on resigning from office, he was succeeded by his brother, Mr. Adolph Levy. His family has always been prominent in communal and philanthropic undertakings, and his activities are not confined to any one creed. Mr. Levy occupies an outstanding position in the social life of Hamilton, and is regarded as one of the most progressive residents of that city. He is a member of the Hamilton Club; Hamilton Golf and Country Club; Buffalo Club; Caledon Trout Club; Yamahoon Club; and the University Club, Toronto. Mr. Levy is a member of the Supreme Council of the Ancient and Accepted Scottish Rite for the Dominion of Canada, being the only Jew in Canada to hold this honor. He is an enthusiastic sportsman, and is particularly interested in fishing and golf.

PETER BERCOVITCH, K.C., M.P.P., MONTREAL

PETER BERCOVITCH, son of Hyman and the late Feigel (Goldberg) Bercovitch, was born in Montreal, September 17th, 1879. He was educated in the Montreal public schools, by private tuition, and at McGill and Laval Universities. In 1900 he graduated from McGill with the degree of B. C. L. and in 1906, he received the degree of LL.M. from the Laval University. Entering the practice of law, in 1911 he was appointed King's Council by the Quebec Government, being the youngest barrister in Canada to be honored with that title. Early in his career he interested himself in politics and allied himself with the Liberal party. In 1918, he was elected to the Provincial Legislature from the St. Louis Division, Montreal, having the distinction of being the first Jew to sit in the Legislature of Quebec. He gave his constituency such satisfaction, that in 1919 he was re-elected by acclamation and in 1923, Peter Bercovitch's record in the house and his personal popularity enabled him to keep his seat, as the only Liberal from the Island of Montreal. His legal knowledge has made him indispensable to the government in the shaping of legislation. The Liquor Bill is one of pieces of legislation that he took a prominent part in framing. Bills for the amelioration of the poor have always concerned him and the Rent Bill was introduced by him. His championship of Jewish educational rights in the 1923 session was largely responsible for the defeat of the pernicious Bill designed to abrogate the Agreement of 1903 and to rob the Jews of Quebec of equal rights in the schools. He is also responsible for the bill to validate Jewish marriages and to authorize Rabbis to keep registers of civil status. Mr. Bercovitch was the first president of the Jewish Immigrant Aid Society and is a member of the executive board of Temple Emanu-El. He is senior partner of the firm of Bercovitch and Calder, a firm enjoying an outstanding position at the Montreal Bar. He is the President of the Laurentian Insurance Company. He married Florence, daughter of Simon Levine, of San Francisco, Cal., and has one son, Henry George, and two daughters, Ruth and Elise Bercovitch.

M. J. FINKELSTEIN, WINNIPEG

M. J. FINKELSTEIN, senior member of the legal firm of Finkelstein, Finkelstein, White, Berg and Layton, arrived in Winnipeg with his parents Mr. and Mrs. J. Finkelstein, when a child. He was educated in the public schools of Winnipeg and passed the entrance examination into the Collegiate Institute in 1897, when he received the highest marks in Manitoba. In 1900, Mr. Finkelstein matriculated to the University of Manitoba winning several scholarships. In 1904, he graduated from the University with honors, and entered the law firm of Hough and Campbell, where he read law until he was called to the Bar. Since he was admitted to the Bar, Mr. Finkelstein has practised his profession in Winnipeg, where he is regarded as one of the most brilliant members of the Manitoba Bar. In the famous case of the Czar of Russia against Fedorenko, Mr. Finkelstein acted for the defendant whose release he secured after a legal battle lasting four months. He has also been counsel in many other important cases. Mr. Finklestein is also interested in different financial and commercial institutions and is a director of the Laurentian Insurance Company, Montreal. He has ever since his youth, taken a foremost position in the communal life of Winnipeg, and practically every Jewish organization of young men formed between 1897 and 1907, had him as its founder. He is a past President of the Winnipeg Lodge, I.O.B.B.; past Vice-President of the Zionist Organization of Canada; and he was elected Vice-President of the Canadian Jewish Congress, held in Montreal in 1919. He is a past President of the Zionist Council of Western Canada and has taken an active part in the Winnipeg Orphanage, Talmud Torahs and Old Folks' Home. He has always taken a keen interest in political affairs and he has been very active in all matters pertaining to Jewish immigration. He has on different occasions been offered a nomination to both the Provincial Legislature and the Federal Parliament, and his influence has been of much value to the members elected from Winnipeg. In 1923, Mr. Finkelstein was married to Rose, daughter of Mr. and Mrs. S. A. Ripstein of Winnipeg.

H. WEINFIELD, B.A., B.C.L., MONTREAL

Photo by Notman

HENRY WEINFIELD, B.A., B.C.L., one of the leaders of the younger members of the Montreal Bar, and senior member of the law firm of Weinfield, Sperber, Levine & Shavmar, was born in Galicia, Austria, March 8th, 1880, the son of the late Israel and Esther (Zwibel) Weinfield. He arrived in Canada in 1887 with his parents, and settled in Montreal, where he has since resided. He was educated at the Montreal public and high schools, and at McGill University, from which he graduated with the degree of B.A. in 1900, and B.C.L. in 1903. On December 18th, 1907, he was married to Pauline, daughter of the late Connel Levine and has one son, Mortimer, and two daughters, the Misses Vera and Rose Weinfield. Shortly after graduation, Mr. Weinfield was called to the Bar and he has since followed the practice of Law in Montreal and enjoys a large and enviable clientele. He has acted as Solicitor in many important cases and at the present time is a Counsel for the Home Bank Depositors' Association. He was also Counsel for the Orphans' Home of Montreal in the celebrated Berlin Case in the Superior Court. He is a frequent contributor to the Press and has done considerable writing on various subjects. Mr. Weinfield has always taken a deep and active interest in welfare work and philanthropic undertakings in Montreal, and he is a member of the Federation of Jewish Philanthropies. His legal services have always been at the disposal of all worthy institutions, and he is honorary solicitor for many charitable organizations. He is a good example of the Jewish citizen who takes an active interest in all public questions, whether they be for the local or general good of the community, and his own affairs come second to the public need. He is greatly interested in Municipal, Provincial and Federal politics, and is a member of the Conservative Association of Montreal. Mr. Weinfield is also a member of the Montefiore Club; St. George's Lodge, No. 10, A.F. & A.M.; and of the Independent Order B'nai B'rith. He is a member of the Shaar Hashomayim Synagogue. Mr. Winfield is one of the original directors of the Laurentian Insurance Company.

LOUIS M. SINGER, TORONTO

LOUIS M. SINGER, Barrister, and ex-Alderman of the City of Toronto, was born in Austria, May 1st, 1885, the son of Samuel Singer. He arrived in Canada with his parents in 1886, settling in Toronto, where he has since resided. He received his education at the public and high schools of Toronto and at the Ontario Law School, Osgoode Hall, Toronto, from which he graduated in 1908, as Gold Medallist. He was called to the Bar in the same year and has since practised his profession, specializing in Commercial, Corporation, and Bankruptcy practice. Always keenly interested in public affairs, in 1914 he was elected Alderman of the City of Toronto, being the second Jew to occupy a seat in the Toronto City Council. During his term as Alderman (during the war), an attempt was made to put through the Council a memorial to the Federal Government, advocating the disenfranchisement of all citizens of foreign birth. Although sprung as a complete surprise on Alderman Singer, his speech in opposition to the memorial was so impressive that it was reproduced verbatim in all the daily papers with eulogistic references. He held office for four years and on resigning in 1917, he was the subject of much favorable comment in the Press, which stated that the Council had lost its most able and outstanding member. In an Editorial, the Toronto Daily Star says;—"Alderman Singer has qualities of a legislator and an administrator—a student and a worker, does not trade upon racial or religious prejudice. He tries to show that the interests of his own people are identical with the interests of Toronto and Canada." Mr. Singer was formerly President of the Beth Medrosh Hagodel Synagogue, and at the present time is a member of the Holy Blossom Synagogue. He is Past Master of the Mount Sinai Lodge, A.F. & A.M.; Past First Principal of the Mount Sinai Chapter, R.A.M.; President of the Toronto Lodge, I.O.B.B.; and Secretary-Treasurer of the Primrose Club. On July 6th, 1911, Mr. Singer was married to Dr. Bessie T. Pullan, daughter of Morris Pullan of Toronto, and he has two sons, Burrell M. and Ralph M., and one daughter, Miss Queenie S. Singer.

ISAAC KERT, B.A., B.C.L., Notary, was born in Montreal, November 30, 1890, the son of Levi Kert. He was educated at the Dufferin School, Montreal High School and McGill University, winning matriculation scholarship at High School and first class honors in Economics and Political Science in the Arts Course at McGill. He also won the Elizabeth Torrance Gold Medal for leading his class, and the Macdonald Travelling Scholarship to Paris. In his graduation year he was President of all faculties. Mr. Kert is Honorary Notary for the Shaar Hashomayim Congregation; Hebrew Free Loan Association; Montreal Hebrew Maternity Hospital; etc. He is a Justice of the Peace and a commissioner of the Superior Court. He is keenly interested in Athletics and was Captain of the Senior Y.M.C.A. Basket Ball Team from 1915-1923. He is a director of the Y.M.H.A., and of the Montreal Hebrew Orphans' Home. He is a member of the Federation of Jewish Philanthropies, and of the Montefiore Club, Montreal. On April 30th, 1919, Mr. Kert was married to Sara, daughter of Abraham L. Gittleson, and has one daughter, Doris Maxine Kert.

A. C. M. DE SOLA, M.A., B.C.L., MONTREAL

ISAAC KERT, B.A., B.C.L., MONTREAL

ABRAHAM CHARLES MELDOLA DE SOLA, Barrister, and member of the law firm of Bercovitch and Calder, was born in Montreal, September 11th, 1890, the son of the late Rev. Meldola de Sola, Rabbi of the Spanish and Portuguese Synagogue, and the grandson of the late Rev. Dr. Abraham de Sola. He was educated at the Montreal High School; McGill University (B.A. 1910, with first class honors in Economics and Political Science); B.A. St. John's College, Oxford 1912, with honors in Jurisprudence; B.C.L. McGill 1914; M.A. (Oxon) 1921. He was admitted to the bar of the Province of Quebec, in 1914. Mr. de Sola was engaged in journalism before commencing the practice of law, being connected with the Montreal Star. He was also foreign editor of the Canadian Times. He received a commission as lieutenant in the 22nd Battery, C.F.A. in 1916; was transferred to the 71st Battery, C.F.A., C.E.F. in 1918; and went overseas as lieutenant with the 2nd Canadian Tank Battalion, Canadian Expeditionary Force. On May 15th, 1924, Mr. de Sola was married in London, England, to Cathleen, daughter of the late Edward Quain of Montreal.

HARRY A. FRIEDMAN, EDMONTON

HARRY A. FRIEDMAN, Barrister, was born at Buffalo, N.Y., on August 16th, 1890. As a young boy, he accompanied his parents when they moved to St. Catharines, Ontario, and he was educated in the public and high schools of that city, and at Osgoode Hall Law School, Toronto, from which he graduated in 1913. In 1916, Mr. Friedman was married to Frances, daughter of Mr. and Mrs. Barney Lepofsky of Toronto, and they have one daughter, Miss Miriam Friedman. Upon graduating from Osgoode Hall, Mr. Friedman took up his residence in Edmonton, Alberta, and he was called to the bar of the Province of Alberta in the same year, being the first Jewish barrister in that province. He has since followed the practice of his profession in Edmonton, where he has attained a very high standing at the bar as the senior member of the law firm of Friedman and Lieberman. Mr. Friedman has, ever since his arrival in Edmonton, taken a leading part in the communal activities of that city. Early becoming one of the chief aids of Mr. Wm. Diamond, the patriarchal leader of the Jewish community of Edmonton, he has been identified with all philanthropic and educational matters that have arisen. He is an active member of the Edmonton Hebrew Association and the Edmonton Talmud Torah, and the high standing of these two organizations is largely due to his labors on their behalf. He is a past President of Edmonton Lodge, No. 732, Independent Order B'nai B'rith, and is a member of the Canadian Club; Edmonton Golf and Country Club; Board of Trade; and Saskatchewan Lodge, No. 92, A.F. & A.M. An ardent Zionist, he was for some years a member of the Council of the Zionist Organization of Canada. He took an active part in the relief campaigns in aid of the Jewish war sufferers, and in general relief drives, his activities being non-sectarian. Mr. Friedman has been ably assisted in his communal undertakings by his wife, who is a member of the Council of the Western Division of the Zionist Organization of Canada, and who has been President of the Edmonton Council of Jewish Women since its inception in 1920.

S. HART GREEN, B.C.L., EX. M.P.P., WINNIPEG

S. HART GREEN, B.C.L. and former member of the Manitoba Legislature, was born in Saint John, N.B., October 23rd, 1885. He is the son of the late Mr. Louis Green of that City, and grandson of Nathan Green and Solomon Henry Hart, two of the Jewish pioneers there, and received his education at Saint John in the public and high schools. He then went to Montreal where he made an initial step in commercial circles in the cigar manufacturing business. Feeling that a professional career would prove more congenial, he became an articled law student with the law firm of MacRae and Sinclair at Saint John, and was called to the Bar of New Brunswick in 1906. The West with its broadening opportunities attracted him and in January 1907, he arrived in Winnipeg, becoming associated with the law firm of Campbell, Pitblado and Company until called to the Manitoba Bar in that year. He then formed a partnership with E. R. Chapman and is today the senior member of the law firm of Green and Mathers. Mr. Green has always taken a keen interest in public questions and has the distinction of being the first Jew to occupy a seat in the Manitoba Legislature, being elected member for North Winnipeg in 1910, and had the further distinction of being the youngest member of the Legislature at that time. From 1916 to 1921, Mr. Green was Crown Prosecutor of the Assize Court at Winnipeg. He occupies a very high standing at the Manitoba Bar, and is regarded as one of the most representative citizens of Winnipeg, taking a very prominent part in the communal life of that city, and he has been actively associated with all the philanthropic institutions of Western Canada. He was president of the Winnipeg Lodge, I.O.B.B., is Master of Mount Sinai Masonic Lodge, and a member of numerous other fraternal organizations. For years he has been President of the United Hebrew Relief of Winnipeg, is President of the Hebrew Immigrant Aid Society, and a member of the Shaarey Zedek Synagogue. On the 27th August, 1912, Mr. Green, was married to Miss Aimee Lyone, daughter of Mr. and Mrs. Martin Lyone of Winnipeg, and has four children.

MARCUS SPERBER, K.C., MONTREAL
Photo by Notman

MARCUS MEYER SPERBER, B.C.L., K.C., was born February 15th, 1886, the son of David Sperber, J.P. and Peppie (Rosenbaum) Sperber. He was educated at the Public and High School, Montreal, and at McGill University, from which he graduated in 1906, when he was awarded the MacDonald Travelling Scholarship. He takes a keen interest in communal work and is the Vice-President of the Baron de Hirsch Institute. He is a Trustee of the Federation of Jewish Philanthropies and of the Spanish and Portuguese Synagogue. He was one of the founders and first President of the Y.M.H.A. of Montreal, and is a Director of the United Talmud Torahs. He is honorary solicitor of the Baron de Hirsch Institute, Immigrant Aid Society, B'nai Jacob Synagogue, etc., etc. Mr. Sperber is an enthusiastic supporter of the Zionist Movement and in 1923 went to Palestine where he remained for some time studying conditions. He is a member of the Jewish Educational Committee formed to protect the rights and status of Jewish children in the schools of Montreal and he is also interested in the advancement of Hebrew education of Jewish children. In 1912, Mr. Sperber was President of the Hebrew Independent Citizens' League. He was chairman of the East End Division of the War Sufferers' Relief Committee and was a member of the Speakers' Committee of the Victory Loan Campaigns. Mr. Sperber has always been interested in military matters and was an officer in the first Prince of Wales Fusiliers, in the 64th Regiment, and in the 206th battalion, C.E.F. In 1912 he was an Independent Liberal candidate in St. Louis Division and he is a Vice-President of the North End Liberal Club. Mr. Sperber is Vice-President, Mt. Royal Lodge, I.O.B.B.; Past Deputy for the Province of Quebec, I.O.B.B.; Canadian Representative of District Grand Lodge, I.O.B.B.; member of General Committee and Anti-Defamation Committee; and President, I.O.B.B. lodges in Canada. He is a member of the Montefiore, Montreal Reform, and Press clubs. On June 11th, 1924, he was married to Miss Lisa Blanche Jacobs, daughter of the late Rabbi Solomon Jacobs of Toronto.

MAX STEINKOPF, B.A., WINNIPEG

MAX STEINKOPF was born at Praagh, Austria, March 2nd, 1881, the son of Herman and Justine (Schoenfeld) Steinkopf. He came to Canada in 1889, and received his education at the public schools of Morden, Man., and at the University of Manitoba. He read law in the offices of the Hon. Justice Haggart and Hon. Sir Hugh John Macdonald, in 1902-5, and was called to the Manitoba Bar in 1905, being the first Jewish barrister in the Prairie Provinces. He has since practised his profession in Winnipeg. Mr. Steinkopf is Vice-Pres., Alma Mater Society, Manitoba College; member, Greater Winnipeg District Council of the Boy Scout Movement; Canadian Chairman of the Anti-Defamation League of the I.O.B.B.; Canadian Vice-Chairman, Jewish European Orphans' Committee; Member, Advisory Board, Winnipeg Children's Hospital; Member, Board of Trustees, Winnipeg General Hospital; and Treasurer, Archaeological Institute of America. He is a member of the Winnipeg Cenotaph Committee (1924); Member, Finance Committee, Federated Budget (1924); President, Zionist Council, Winnipeg; Member, Court of Honour of the Boy Scouts of Manitoba; Past-Chairman, Building Committee of Winnipeg Public School Board; President, Winnipeg Hebrew Free School 1912 to 1922; Treas., University of Manitoba Alumni; and member, Executive Committee, League of Nations' Society, Winnipeg Branch. His business interests are many, and he is President, Canada National Securities Co., Ltd.; President, City Dairy Co., Ltd.; President, Purity Ice Cream Co. Ltd.; President, City Creamery Co. Ltd., Regina, Sask.; Sec.-Treas., Archibald-Martin Motors Ltd.; and President, Bonded Investments Ltd. Mr. Steinkopf was married in 1907 to Miss Hedwig Meyer, and he has one son, Maitland Bernard Strauss, and three daughters, Audrey Eleanor, Helen Theresa, and Maxine. He is a member of the Executive of the Canadian Club, and also a member of the Adanac, Assiniboine, and Fort Garry Motor Clubs. He is a prominent member of the Masonic Order, Ancient Order of United Workmen, and Independent Order B'nai B'rith, Winnipeg Lodge.

EX-CONTROLLER JOSEPH SINGER, TORONTO
Photo by Milne

JOSEPH SINGER, Barrister, and ex-Controller of the City of Toronto, was born in Toronto on March 23rd., 1890, the son of Samuel and Rosie Singer. He received his education in the Toronto public schools, Jarvis Street Collegiate Institute, and at the Ontario Law School, Osgoode Hall, from which he graduated in 1911 as Gold Medallist, and was the first winner of the Van Koughnet Scholarship. He was called to the Bar in the same year and has since successfully followed the practice of law. Mr. Singer became interested in public affairs at an early age, and in 1920 was elected Alderman of the City of Toronto, and was re-elected in 1921 and 1922, heading the Aldermanic vote. In 1923 he was elected to the Board of Control, being the first Jew who was ever nominated for this appointment, and he was recognized as being the outstanding member of the Board, and the leader in all reform movements. Whilst a member of the Council, Alderman Singer was the instigator of the investigation which resulted in the cleaning up of the police department. He also headed the campaign in 1922 and 1923 against the agreement sponsored by Sir Adam Beck affecting the Toronto waterfront, which agreement was defeated by the electors on January 1st., 1923. Controller Singer is held in the highest esteem by the whole community and on resigning as Controller, was requested to allow himself to be nominated for Mayor of the City of Toronto, but he declined this honour. In 1923 he was the Liberal Candidate for south-east Toronto, in the Provincial elections. In 1925, he was again elected to the City Council. He is a trustee of the Holy Blossom Synagogue, Federation of Jewish Philanthropies, and of Toronto Lodge, I.O.B.B. and many other institutions. He is a member of Sunnyside Lodge, No. 449, I.O.O.F., Primrose Club, and of the Ontario Jockey Club, Toronto. Mr. Singer is a member of the Executive of the Toronto Men's Liberal Association. In 1915, he was married to Gussie, daughter of Alex Sundel of New York City, and has one son, Vernon Milton, and one daughter, Doris Beverley Singer.

M. M. GROSSMAN, VANCOUVER

MAX MALIT GROSSMAN, Barrister, and one of the prominent younger members of the British Columbia Bar, was born in Toronto, August 19th, 1892, the son of Abraham and Minnie Grossman, now of Los Angeles, Cal. He was educated in the Vancouver schools, and at McGill University, Montreal, and studied law with the late Joseph Martin, K.C., ex-Premier of British Columbia, and C. W. Craig, K.C. He was admitted to the Bar of British Columbia in 1917, and has since followed the practice of his profession in Vancouver, being a member of the law firm of Grossman and Holland. Mr. Grossman is married to Dorothy, daughter of Jacob Goldstein of Montreal, and he has one son, Edgar Hyman Grossman, and one daughter, Miss Janice Carol Grossman. He is a member of the Canadian Club; Terminal City Club; Vancouver Board of Trade; Automobile Club of British Columbia; Burquitlam Golf Club; Canadian Bar Association; Vancouver Lodge, No. 68, A.F. & A.M.; and Scottish Rite. Mr. Grossman is one of the leaders of the Jewish community of Vancouver, and has been actively associated with every undertaking in the city and province. He was President, 1915, 1918, and 1924 of the Samuel Lodge, No. 668, I.O.B.B. From 1916 to 1924, he was District Deputy, and in 1924 was appointed member of the Executive Committee for District Grand Lodge, No. 4, I.O.B.B. He is a past President of the Hebrew Aid Society, Vancouver; Ex-Chairman of the Building Committee of the Congregation Shaarey Zedeck and Talmud Torah; was the first President of the Vancouver Hebrew School; and is Honorary life President of the Congregation Shaarey Zedeck and of the Vancouver Hebrew School. He is Honorary life member of the Samuel Lodge, I.O.B.B., and was Chairman of the Immigration Committee, Samuel Lodge. Mr. Grossman was on the Speakers' Committee of all the Victory Loan and War Relief Campaigns, and was the Chairman of the local Jewish War Relief Committee. His aid is regarded as indispensable to any undertaking pertaining to the advancement or improvement of conditions in his community.

E. F. SINGER, B.A., LL.B., TORONTO

EPHRAIM FREDERICK SINGER, Barrister, was born in Toronto, July 19th, 1889, the son of the late Jacob and Annie (Fogler) Singer. He was educated at Lansdowne public school; Harbord Collegiate Institute; and University of Toronto, from which he graduated (B.A. 1909). He then entered Osgoode Hall Law School, graduating in 1912, in which year he also obtained the degree of LL.B. from the University of Toronto. In the same year he was called to the Bar of the Province of Ontario, and has since practised his profession in Toronto where he is a member of the law firm of A. & E. F. Singer. On June 7th, 1917, Mr. Singer was married to Zelma Claire, daughter of Henry Guttman, of New York City, and he has one son, Harvey, and two daughters, the Misses Vivian and Roslyn Singer. Mr. Singer has always been keenly interested in communal matters and is a member of all local philanthropic organizations, in many of which he holds, or has held, executive office. Since 1915, he has been Secretary of the Holy Blossom Congregation, and for seven years he has been Superintendent of the congregational Sabbath school. Since 1922, he has been President of the Mount Sinai Hospital, and his labor on behalf of this institution is largely responsible for the splendid position it occupies amongst the public institutions of Toronto. He is on the executive, and in charge of the literary work of the Young Men's Hebrew Association, and is on the executive of the Jewish Boys' Club. He is a former President of the Big Brother Movement, Jewish branch. He is much interested in fraternal work and is a charter member of Palestine Lodge, A.F. & A.M., and is a member of St. Alban's Lodge, A.F. & A.M., and Mt. Sinai Chapter, R.A.M. He is a past Wor. M. of Palestine Lodge. Mr. Singer takes an active interest in public questions, and is interested in anything tending to the betterment of the community. In 1924, he was unanimously elected Vice-President of Ward Four Conservative Association. He is a member of the Independent Order of Foresters; Independent Order of Oddfellows; Independent Order B'nai B'rith; and Primrose Club, Toronto.

L. W. JACOBS, K.C., MONTREAL

Photo by Notman

LYON WILLIAM JACOBS, K.C., Barrister, and formerly Alderman of the City of Montreal, was born in Montreal, September 13, 1887, the son of William A. Jacobs. He was educated at the Aberdeen School; Montreal High School; McGill University, B.C.L., (1910); and Laval University, Montreal, from which he graduated in 1911, with the degree of LL.M. He is married to Sarah, daughter of B. Florin, and he has one son Alvin Bernard, and three daughters, Sybil, Pearl and Dorothy Jacobs. Mr. Jacobs, since graduating from Law School, has followed the practice of his profession in Montreal. He was appointed King's Counsel in 1923. He was President of the Law Commission of the City of Montreal, 1921-1924. From 1918-1924, Mr. Jacobs represented St. Louis Ward in the Montreal City Council, and he acted as pro-Mayor at different times, in 1918 and 1919. He was Honorary Vice-President of the Baron de Hirsch Book Club, 1921-1924; Honorary Vice-President, Hebrew Consumptive Aid Association, 1921-1924; Honorary President, Malbish Arumim Association, 1922-1924; President, "Mishpot Hasholim" Jewish Court of Arbitration, 1924-1925; Vice-President, Jewish Community Council; Honorary Counsel, Mount Sinai Sanatorium; Honorary Solicitor, Hebrew Sick Benefit Association; Honorary Solicitor, Independent Hebrew Sick Benefit Association. In 1919, Mr. Jacobs was appointed a Commissioner of the Superior Court, and in 1920 a Marriage License Commissioner. He was the leader of a protest parade of thirty thousand Jews to protest against the Polish Pogroms. Mr. Jacobs was the "father" of the municipal golf links of Montreal, which he fought for in the City Council for four years before having it put through, his idea being to make golf a game for the poor as well as the rich man. He is a member of the Liberal Speakers' Association. Mr. Jacobs is a life governor of the Notre Dame Hospital, and is a member of the Montefiore Club; Montreal Reform Club; Maimonides' Club; Masonic Order; and Knights of Pythias. He is a life member of the National Amateur Athletic Association.

Milne Studio

A. COHEN, TORONTO

ABRAHAM COHEN, Barrister and Solicitor, was born at Hartlepool, England, on October 18th, 1888, the son of Saul and Leah (Simon) Cohen. He received his education at the Hanson Higher Grade School, Bradford (Yorkshire), Jewish School, Manchester, and at Osgoode Hall Law School, Toronto, from which he graduated with honours, in 1911. He accompanied his parents to Canada in 1898, settling with them some years later in Toronto, where he has since resided. He was called to the Bar of the Province of Ontario in 1911, and follows the practice of his profession in Toronto, where he has attained a very high standing, and where he is the senior member of the firm of Cohen & Cohen. On December 17th, 1917, Mr. Cohen was married to Melba, daughter of Mr. and Mrs. Benjamin Chon, of Chicago, formerly of Toronto, and he has one son, William Ira, and one daughter, Miss Myrah Adele Cohen. Mr. Cohen is one of the most active communal workers in Toronto, and is the real "father" of the Federation of the Jewish Philanthropies of that city. It is in this connection that he is prominently before the public. He devoted much study to existing forms of Federation in other cities in Canada and the United States, and it was due entirely to his vision and faith in Federation that the first organization committee was formed, in 1917, and he has been the honorary secretary of the Federation continuously since its formation. He is a former secretary of the Goel Tzedec Congregation, University Avenue, and was the principal of the religious school in connection with that congregation. He is a charter member, and a past president of Toronto Lodge, Independent Order B'nai B'rith. Mr. Cohen is honorary secretary of the Toronto Hebrew Free Loan Association, and is past president, Young Judaea of Toronto. He was the secretary of the Zionist Committee of Toronto, Limited, and was a member of the Zionist Council of Canada. Mr. Cohen is a member of Palestine Lodge, A.F. & A.M., Sunnyside Lodge, I.O.O.F., B'nai Zion Society, Oakwood Bowling Club, Canada Club, and the Primrose Club.

M. HYMAN, M.A., LL.B., WINNIPEG

MARCUS HYMAN, M.A. (Oxon), LL.B. (Man.), Barrister, was born in Russia, on July 3rd, 1883, the son of Rabbi Aaron Hyman of London, England. He received his education at the London Board School; Central Foundation School; Worcester College, Oxford; Gray's Inn, London, and graduated with the degrees of M.A. (Oxford), and LL.B. (Man.). In 1914, he was married to Miss Erna Ziembinska, and he has one son, Ernest Roy Hyman. Mr. Hyman was a brilliant scholar, and during the course of his educational career, was the winner of many scholarships, among them being, the Junior L.C.C. Scholarship, 1895; Hickson Starling Exhibitioner, 1896; Intermediate L.C.C. Scholarship, 1898; Senior L.C.C. Scholarship, 1902; Senior Anthony Dreath Exhibitioner, 1902; Mathematical Exhibitioner, Worcester College, Oxford, 1902; Honors, Law School, 1906; Holt Scholar, Gray's Inn, 1905. After leaving Law School, for two years, in 1908 and 1909, Mr. Hyman was engaged as tutor to the son of His Highness, the Gaekwar of Baroda, and as private secretary to the Gaekwar. Returning to London in 1910, he was called to the Bar of Gray's Inn, London, and practised his profession as Barrister until he came to Canada in 1913. In that year, he was called to the Bar of Manitoba, and he has since practised his profession in Winnipeg. In 1915, he was appointed lecturer at the Manitoba Law School, on International Law, History of English Law, and Jurisprudence. Mr. Hyman has always been keenly interested in public affairs, and in 1923-1924, he was elected the Labour Representative for North Winnipeg, on the Public School Board. Mr. Hyman has always taken an active part in the philanthropic and welfare undertakings in his community, and he is a member of all the various charitable institutions. From 1916 to 1922, he was President of the Western Canada Jewish Fund for the relief of war sufferers, which during that period raised over half a million dollars for Jewish sufferers in the war area. Mr. Hyman is a member of the Law firm of Hyman and Hestrin.

E. R. SUGARMAN, VANCOUVER

EPHRAIM R. SUGARMAN, Barrister and Solicitor, was born at Alexandria, Ont., June 3rd, 1890, the son of Mr. and Mrs. Caspar Sugarman of Toronto. He was educated at the Kitchener and Toronto public schools; Edmonton High School; University of Toronto; and Osgoode Hall Law School, Toronto, from which he graduated in 1913. Mr. Sugarman is a member of the Bars of Ontario, Alberta and British Columbia, and he has practised his profession at different times in Toronto, Edmonton and Vancouver. In 1921, in Vancouver, he organized the Concordia Club, and was its first President. This is a club organized to bring the younger business and professional men of the community in closer personal touch with each other. He organized the Junior Menorah Society of Vancouver, of which he is the Honorary President, for the purpose of keeping the younger element of the community together and giving them advanced study on Jewish History and affairs. In 1922, he was instrumental in organizing the Jewish Sunday School of Vancouver, of which he is Superintendent. He was also instrumental in organizing the Vancouver Jewish Community Chest, which has just completed its first successful drive for a central fund for local needs, and is identified with all the various institutions of a similar nature in Vancouver. Mr. Sugarman is married to Annie Dorothea, daughter of Mr. and Mrs. Max Wodlinger of Winnipeg, Man., and he has two sons, Lester Caven, and Selwyn Wilbur Sugarman. Mrs. Sugarman is also very actively interested in all communal work and philanthropic undertakings in the community, and is President of the Vancouver Branch of the Council of Jewish Women, which she was instrumental in organizing some years ago. She is also associated with all the other Jewish activities of Vancouver. She is an ardent Zionist and staunch supporter of the Hadassah. Mr. Sugarman is a member of the I.O.B.B., and Shaarey Zedec Synagogue. Both in Toronto and Edmonton, Mr. Sugarman took an active part in Jewish undertakings, and he has extended his communal work very much since his arrival in Vancouver.

NATHAN PHILLIPS, TORONTO

NATHAN PHILLIPS, Barrister, and Alderman of the City of Toronto, was born at Brockville, Ontario, November 7th, 1892, the son of Jacob J. and Mary (Rosenbloom) Phillips, for over forty years residents of Cornwall, Ontario. He received his early education at Cornwall Model School and matriculated from Cornwall High School at the age of 15 years, entering the law offices of Robert Smith, K.C., now Hon. Mr. Justice Smith of the Supreme Court of Ontario, as a student-at-law. Two years later he attended the Ontario Law School, Osgoode Hall, Toronto, graduating in 1913 but was obliged to wait almost a year before being called to the Bar, not being then 21 years of age. Although yet a young man Mr. Phillips is taking an active part in public life and communal and welfare work. He founded and was Vice-President of the Toronto Hebrew Free Loan Association, and is a Director of both the Young Men's and Young Women's Hebrew Association, and of the Canadian Progress Club. He is a member of the Federation of Jewish Philanthropies and the Primrose, Canadian, Empire, and Liberal Conservative Business Men's Clubs, Toronto, and was President (1922) of the Toronto Lodge, I.O.B.B., and was Canadian Representative on General Committee, District Grand Lodge No. 1, Independent Order of B'nai B'rith 1923-4. He is a member of Mount Sinai Lodge No. 522 A.F. and A.M., G.R.C.; Palestine Lodge No. 559, G.R.C.; and Mount Sinai Chapter No. 212 G.R.C.; Sunnyside Lodge No. 449, I.O.O.F.; and Court McCaul, Independent Order of Foresters. In January, 1924, he was elected to the Toronto City Council as Alderman for Ward 4, being the fourth Jew to hold office as Alderman in Toronto. In 1925, he was re-elected to the Council, heading the Aldermanic vote in his ward. Mr. Phillips was married in 1917, to Esther, daughter of Jacob and the late Amelia (Mohr) Lyons and has two sons, Lewis Sigmund Farrand and Howard Arnold, and one daughter, Madeline Ruth Phillips. He is a member of the Holy Blossom Synagogue, Toronto, and is an active Conservative in politics.

M. I. LIEBERMAN, EDMONTON

MOSES ISAAC LIEBERMAN was born in Toronto, Ont., June 16th, 1891, the son of Mr. Abraham H. Lieberman, of that city. He was educated at the Kingston Collegiate Institute; Technical High School, Toronto; Faculty of Applied Science, University of Toronto, from which he graduated in 1911 as Mining Engineer. As a result of post-graduate work, he received the degree of B.A.Sc. in 1912. After practising Mining Engineering for some time in Cobalt and in Western Canada, Mr. Lieberman took up the study of law in Edmonton, and in 1917, he was called to the Bar of Alberta. He at once entered the practice of the legal profession in Edmonton, where he is a member of the firm of Friedman and Lieberman, who occupy a very high standing at the Alberta Bar. On January 1st, 1918, Mr. Lieberman was married to Emily, daughter of H. N. Sereth of Seattle, Wash., formerly of Calgary, Alta., and he has one son, Samuel Sereth, and one daughter Ethel Brauna. Mr. Lieberman is one of the leaders of the Jewish community of Edmonton, and he is associated with all the Jewish undertakings in that city. He devotes much time to communal and philanthropic work, and has held office in most of the local institutions. He has always taken a keen interest in athletics, and for some years has been Manager of the Edmonton Rugby Football Team, which under his management, on different occasions, won the Championship of Western Canada. On two occasions Mr. Lieberman conducted the team to Toronto in search of the Dominion title. He is a member of the executive of the city playground committee, having charge of the supplying of proper playgrounds for the younger athletes of the city. He takes an active interest in all public questions affecting the betterment of the community, and is as highly regarded by his Christian as by his Jewish friends. Mr. Lieberman is a member of the Canadian Club; Edmonton Golf and Country Club; Board of Trade; Edmonton Lodge, No. 732, I.O.B.B.; Saskatchewan Lodge, No. 92, A.F. & A.M.; and Benevolent and Protective Order of Elks, No. 387.

BENJAMIN GOLDFIELD, OTTAWA

Photo by Castonguay

BENJAMIN GOLDFIELD, Barrister, was born in Elizabethgrad, the Province of Kerson, Russia, on October 4th, 1892, the son of Myer Goldfield. In 1899, he came to Canada with his parents, settling in Ottawa, where he has since resided. He was educated at the George Street Public School, Ottawa, and the Ottawa Collegiate Institute. He then went to Toronto where he attended Osgoode Hall, from which he graduated with honors, and where, in his second year, he received a scholarship. After being called to the Bar, he returned to Ottawa and opened an office there, where he has since followed the practice of law. Mr. Goldfield was the second Jewish barrister in Ottawa, Ont. He has built up for himself a large legal practice in his city, and is recognized as one of the leaders among the younger lawyers. He has always taken a keen and active interest in all philanthropic and communal work undertaken by the Jews in his community. During the War he gave up much of his time and energy to the local war relief activities, and he was made the Honorary Secretary of the Ottawa Jewish War Sufferers' Relief Committee. He can be especially identified with the Canadian Jewish Immigration Society, and is the present Honorary Secretary of the Ottawa branch. His efforts on behalf of Jewish immigrants may be specially mentioned. He devotes much of his time to, and takes a deep interest in the religious and secular education of Jewish children, and he was one of the founders of the Hebrew Sunday School of Ottawa, of which he has been the principal for several years. He is also one of the founders of the Ottawa Talmud Torah. Mr. Goldfield is an ardent Zionist believing in "Palestine as a Homeland for the Jews," and he has been a member of the Zionist National Council since 1921. He is President of the Ottawa Lodge, Independent Order B'nai B'rith; and member, Ottawa Hebrew Benefit Society; Machezike Hadath; The Ottawa Talmud Torah Board; and the Canadian Club. He is a member of the Adath Jeshurun Synagogue. Mr. Goldfield was married in 1922, to Lillian Libbie Rapp, daughter of Mr. and Mrs. Morris Rapp of Montreal.

NATHANIAL WILLIAM JACOBS, B.C.L., Barrister, was born in Montreal, Que., July 12th, 1895, the son of William A. and Fanny (Gittleson) Jacobs. He was educated at the Aberdeen School, Montreal High School and McGill University, graduating in 1916. He has since successfully practised his profession in Montreal. Mr. Jacobs devotes much of his spare time to writing and is a contributor to many periodicals. At one time he was associate editor of "The Canadian Jewish Leader". Some of his works are:— "The Past and Future of Zion", which served as valuable propaganda for the Zionist Cause, and "Knowledge the Hope-Ignorance the Curse", the text of which is to encourage the speaking of Jewish as a language. Mr. Jacobs is President, Baron de Hirsch Book Club, and past President of District No. 4, Local Council, Zionist Organization. He is a Director of the Library Club, the Lyceum Club, and Peretz School, and is an Honorary Solicitor of the Hebrew Consumptive Aid Association and Malbish Arumim Society. He is a member, Knights of Pythias; The Maccabees (A Sir Knight); Royal Antediluvian Order of Buffaloes; and Independent Hebrew Sick Benefit Association.

JOSEPH COHEN, MONTREAL

Notman

N. W. JACOBS, B.C.L., MONTREAL

JOSEPH COHEN, Barrister, was born in Russia, August 12, 1891, the son of Rev. Myer & Riva (Benyus) Cohen. He was educated at Dufferin School; Montreal High School; McGill University; and later took a post-graduate course at Laval University, graduating in 1912. After graduation Mr. Cohen practised his profession in Montreal, specializing in Criminal Law. In 1923, he was a Liberal Candidate in the St. Lawrence Division, for the Provincial House. Mr. Cohen has always taken an active interest in communal work. He is a member of the Federation of Jewish Philanthropies, Montreal, and of the United Talmud Torahs. He is a member of the Montreal Reform Club; Montreal Press Club; Montefiore Club; Canadian Club; Y.M.H.A.; Corinthian Lodge, A.F. & A.M.; Syracuse Lodge; the Knights of Pythias and the Benevolent Order of Elks. Mr. Cohen was married on May 25th, 1913, to Miss Ada Belle, daughter of the late Bernard and Rachel (Lecker) Gross. They have one son, Hesse Saul, and two daughters, Sybil and Anna Lee Cohen. Mr. Cohen is a member of the Shaar Hashomayim, New Adath Jeshuran and Austro-Hungarian synagogues.

P. MEYEROVITCH, MONTREAL

PHILIP MEYEROVITCH, Barrister, was born in Pomerla, Roumania, March 15th, 1899, the son of Julius Meyerovitch. He was educated at the Aberdeen School, Montreal High School, and McGill University, from which he graduated (B.C.L. 1921). In his second year at Law School, Mr. Meyerovitch won the Alexander Morris Scholarship. Mr. Meyerovitch is the Secretary of the Hebrew Orphans' Home; and is a member of the Y.M.H.A.; I.O.B.B.; and a former member of the Literary Society of McGill University.

H. COHEN, B.A., B.C.L., MONTREAL

HARRY COHEN, Barrister, was born in Sherbrooke, Que., September 12th, 1899, the son of Benjamin Cohen, of that city. He was educated at the Sherbrooke Public Schools; Sherbrooke High School; and at the University of Bishop's College, graduating with the B.A. degree, in 1919. He then entered McGill University, from which he graduated in 1922, with the degree of B.C.L. Mr. Cohen has since followed the practice of his profession in Montreal, where he is a member of the law firm of Bercovitch, Calder and Cohen.

M. BERNFELD, B.A., B.C.L., MONTREAL

MAX BERNFELD, Barrister, was born in Montreal, November 11th, 1893, the son of Charles Bernfeld. He was educated at the Mount Royal School; Montreal High School; and McGill University, and graduated (B.A. 1914), (B.C.L. 1917), with first class honors. On December 18th, 1923, he was married to Sylvia, daughter of Julius Benewick. Mr. Bernfeld is a member of the Montefiore and Montreal Reform Clubs, and St. George's Lodge, A.F. and A.M. He is a past President, I.O.B.B. (1923), and has been Honorary Secretary of the Baron de Hirsch Institue for three years, and is chairman of the School Committee.

L. PHILLIPS, MONTREAL

LAZARUS PHILLIPS, Barrister, and member of the firm of Jacobs & Philips, was born October 10th, 1895, in Montreal, the son of Fischel Phillips. He was educated at the Aberdeen School, Montreal High School, and McGill University, from which he graduated with honors in 1918. On March 6th, 1923, he was married to Rosalie Idelson, of Johannesburg, S. Africa. During the War, Mr. Phillips entered the Laval Commissioned Officers Training Corps, and in 1918-9 he was on the Headquarters Staff, Canadian Expeditionary Force in Siberia. He is a member, Montefiore and Montreal Reform Clubs; and National Council, Zionist Federation.

C. M. HERLICK, LL.B., TORONTO

J. D. PEARLSTEIN, B.A., TORONTO

CARL M. HERLICK, Barrister, was born in Austria, on January 9th, 1891, the son of Jacob Herlick. He attended the public schools in New York City, Harbord Collegiate Institute, Toronto, and the St. Lawrence University, New York, graduating (LL.B. 1910). He then entered Osgoode Hall, from which he graduated in 1915. Mr. Herlick is a member of the Y.M.C.A.; Canadian Hebrew Benevolent Society; and Secretary of the Sunday Students' Group of Toronto. He is also a member of the Arbeiter Ring, and Solicitor for this society in Canada.

JACOB D. PEARLSTEIN, Barrister, the son of David Pearlstein, was born in Montreal, Que., on October 1st, 1894. He was educated at the public school and high school in Hamilton, and at the University of Toronto, graduating in 1916, with the degree of B.A. He then entered Osgoode Hall Law School, from which he graduated in 1919. He is a member of the firm of Finkle and Pearlstein. Mr. Pearlstein takes an active interest in all Jewish Movements, and can be especially identified with the I.O.B.B., Toronto Lodge. He is a frequent contributor to the Press.

Milne Studio
A. SINGER, TORONTO

Milne Studio
H. M. FINKLE, TORONTO

ABRAHAM SINGER, Barrister, was born in Toronto, December 29th, 1891, the son of Samuel and Rose Singer. He was educated at the Jarvis Street Collegiate Institute, and Osgoode Hall, Toronto, from which he graduated in 1914. He is married to Bertha, daughter of Mrs. G. Marrus, and has one daughter. Mr. Singer was instrumental in organizing the Jewish branch of the Big Brotherhood Movement in Toronto, and for some years acted as President. He is a member of the Mt. Sinai Lodge, A.F. & A.M., and Sunnyside Lodge, Independent Order of Oddfellows.

HENRY MORTIMER FINKLE, Barrister, the son of Moses Finklestein, was born in Toronto, Ont., on August 14, 1893. He was educated in the public schools, Jarvis Street Collegiate Institute, and University of Toronto, graduating in 1914. He then entered Osgoode Hall Law School, from which he graduated in 1917. In 1917-1920 Mr. Finkle was attached to the Department of Militia and Defence, under Judge Advocate General. Mr. Finkle has always taken an active interest in amateur athletics. He is Secretary of the Toronto Lodge, I.O.B.B., and is a member of the McCaul Street Syngogue.

J. H. GREENBERG, TORONTO

JACOB HENRY GREENBERG, Barrister, was born in Roumania, March 17th, 1896, the son of Sluva Greenberg. He was educated in Toronto and graduated from Osgoode Hall in 1920. Mr. Greenberg won the scholarship in his second year at Law School, and was called to the Bar with honors. He is a member of the firm of Mercer, Bradford & Company, which law firm he entered in 1911 as office boy. He is a member of Mt. Sinai Lodge, A.F. & A.M.; charter member, Toronto Lodge, I.O.B.B.; and is a well-known local amateur sportsman.

MAX AIKEN, TORONTO

MAX AIKEN, Barrister, was born in London, England, April 23rd, 1899, the son of Maurice and Sarah Aiken. He came to Canada in 1904 settling in Montreal and in 1907 came to Toronto, where he has since resided. He received his education in the public schools, Toronto, Parkdale Collegiate Institute, and Osgoode Hall, from which he graduated in 1922. He has since followed the practice of Law in Toronto. Mr. Aiken is a member of the Humber Valley Golf Club; I.O.B.B.; and I.O.F.

Milne Studio
B. LUXENBERG, TORONTO

BENJAMIN LUXENBERG, Barrister, was born in Brooklyn, N.Y., September 24th, 1897, the son of Morris B. & Anna (Stein) Luxenberg. He was educated at the high school, Brooklyn, Harbord Collegiate Institute and Osgoode Hall, Toronto, graduating in 1918 with silver medal and honours. He studied law in the office of Sir Alan Aylesworth. Mr. Luxenberg was one of the organizers of the I.O.B.B., Toronto, and Herzl Club. He was Honorary Secretary of the Big Brother Movement, and is an officer in Mt. Sinai Lodge and Chapter.

Milne Studio
J. M. GORDON, B.A., TORONTO

JOSEPH MURRAY GORDON, Barrister, was born in Toronto, November 26th, 1895, the son of the late Harris and Dora Gordon. He was educated at the public schools, Harbord Collegiate Institute, and at the University of Toronto, from which he graduated in 1916 with the B.A. degree. He was called to the bar on graduating from Osgoode Hall in 1919, when he was awarded the Van Koughnet Scholarship. Mr. Gordon is a member of the Board of Education of the City of Toronto, being elected in 1925.

BENJAMIN FOX, OTTAWA

S. FACTOR, TORONTO

BENJAMIN FOX, Barrister and member of the City of Ottawa Public School Board, was born in Budapest, Hungary, February 26, 1897, the son of Joseph and Rose (Bleich) Fox. He attended the public school and Collegiate Institute, Orillia, and in 1916 entered University of Toronto. In 1918, however, he went overseas, serving with the Canadian Tank Corps. He entered Osgoode Hall on his return, graduating in 1922. He then went to Ottawa where he has since followed the practice of Law. He is a member of the I.O.B.B.; Y.M.H.A.; Ottawa Reform Ass'n; and Secretary, Ottawa Talmud Torah Board.

SAMUEL FACTOR, Barrister, was born in Russia on October 26th, 1891, the son of the late Morris Factor. He was educated in the public schools, Jarvis Street Collegiate Institute, and Osgoode Hall Law School, Toronto, from which he graduated in 1915, with honors, scholarship and silver medal. In 1923, Mr. Factor was elected member of the Board of Education for the City of Toronto, and re-elected to this position in 1924. He is a member of the Mt. Sinai Lodge, A.F. & A.M., and I.O.B.B., Toronto Lodge. He is a member of the McCaul Street Synagogue. He is married to Ida, daughter of Mr. and Mrs. David Lavine, and has one son, Martin Factor.

F. A. SILVERMAN, B.A., TORONTO

J. J. GLASS, B.A., TORONTO

FRANK ARTHUR SILVERMAN, Barrister, was born at Sudbury, Ont., December 1st, 1897. He was educated at the High School, Kenora, at the University of Toronto, from which he graduated in 1920, and at Osgoode Hall graduating with honors, (1923). He is a member of Mt. Sinai Lodge, A.F. & A.M., I.O.B.B., and Sigma Alpha Mu Fraternity. He served overseas with the first Canadian Tank Battalion. In 1920, he was married to Dorothy, daughter of Harris Andrews of Toronto, and has one son, Harold Philip.

JOHN JUDAH GLASS, Barrister, was born October 31st, 1895, the son of Morris and Pearl (Cheyfetz) Glass. He received his education at the public and high schools, at the University of Toronto, (B.A., 1917), and at the Law School Osgoode Hall, Toronto. He was called to the bar in 1919 and practises his profession in Toronto. He served during the war with the 58th Bn. C.E.F. Mr. Glass is a member of the I.O.F.; I.O.B.B.; and Canadian Club. He is a Director of the Y.M. & Y.W.H.A.

H. PAPERNICK, TORONTO

M. L. KEYFETZ, TORONTO

HENRY PAPERNICK, Barrister, was born at Toronto, August 8th, 1897, the son of David Papernick of that city. He was educated in the public and high schools of Toronto, Central Technical School and Osgoode Hall, from which he graduated in 1920, with honors. He was called to the Bar the same year. He saw service during the latter part of the war. Mr. Papernick is a member of the Masonic Order, I.O.B.B., and the Habonim of Toronto. On January 25, 1922, he was married to Rose Wallitzer of New York, and has one son.

MURRAY LUCKE KEYFETZ, Barrister, was born in Toronto, October 22nd, 1900, the son of Mark and Leah Keyfetz, and grandson of the late Nathan Keyfetz of Toronto. He was educated at the public school, Harbord Collegiate Institute, and at Osgoode Hall, Toronto, from which he graduated in 1923. Mr. Keyfetz is a member of the I.O.B.B.; I.O.F.; Habonim Lodge; and Herzl Zion Club. He is a Past President of the Young People's League of the University Avenue Synagogue.

D. S. DENBERG, TORONTO

Milne Studio

L. N. SUKLOFF, TORONTO

DAN S. DENBERG, Barrister, son of Solomon Denberg, was born on November 24, 1894 in Rovno, Russia, where he received his public and high school training. He went to Winnipeg in 1914, entering the Manitoba University in 1915. After graduating from Arts Faculty with the B.A. degree, he entered Law School, from which he graduated (LL.B. 1920). In 1922 he opened a Law office in Toronto. Mr. Denberg has contributed to various newspapers and magazines and can be particularly identified with the Zionist Movement.

LOUIS NORMAN SUKLOFF, Barrister, was born in Wilna, Russia, on August 12th, 1897, the son of Norman and the late Dora Sukloff. He came to Canada in 1904, settling in Woodville, Ont., where he attended the public school and later went to the Peterborough Collegiate Institute. He then came to Toronto and entered Osgoode Hall, from which he graduated in 1921, with honors. Mr. Sukloff is a member of the Young Men's Liberal Club; Mt. Sinai Lodge, A.F. & A.M.; R.A.M.; and I.O.B.B.

S. LEPOFSKY, OTTAWA

SAMUEL LEPOFSKY, Barrister, was born in Toronto, April 2nd, 1896, the son of Benjamin Lepofsky of that city. He received his education at the Brighton Public and High Schools, McMaster University, and Osgoode Hall Law School, from which he graduated in May 1922. He was admitted to the Bar in October of that year, and went to Ottawa where he has since followed his profession. He is a member of the Ottawa Hebrew Benefit Society, and I.O.B.B., Ottawa Lodge. Mr. Lepofsky is a member of the Adath Jeshurun Synagogue.

P. PHILLIPS, HAMILTON

PINCUS PHILLIPS, Barrister, was born at Fall River, Mass., December 17th, 1896, the son of Phillip Phillips. He was educated in Toronto, graduating with honors from Osgoode Hall, in 1918. He is married to Esther Agnes, daughter of Eli Levey, and has one son. Mr. Phillips practises his profession in Hamilton where he is senior partner of the law firm of Phillips and Kamins. He is an active communal worker and Zionist, and is a member of the I.O.B.B., and various local fraternal societies.

MAXWELL SCHOTT, B.A., L.L.B., WINDSOR.

MAXWELL SCHOTT, the first Jewish Barrister in Windsor, Ontario, was born in London, Ontario, May 22nd, 1895, the son of Isaac Schott. He was educated at the public school, London; the St. Thomas, Ontario, Collegiate; and at the University of Toronto, graduating (B.A. 1918). He then entered Osgoode Hall Law School, from which he graduated in 1921, with the degree of LL.B. After graduation, he went to Windsor, where he has since followed the practice of law. Mr. Schott is a member of the Primrose Club, Sigma Alpha Mu Fraternity, and Masonic Order.

A. A. KAMINS, HAMILTON

ARTHUR ABRAHAM KAMINS, Barrister, was born at Odessa, Russia, February 28th, 1896, the son of the late Isaac Kamins. He was educated in Toronto, and graduated with honors from Osgoode Hall, in 1920, and has since practised his profession in Hamilton. He is married to Thelma, daughter of Leon Bercowitz, Hamilton. Mr. Kamins was active in Toronto communal undertakings before taking up his residence in Hamilton, and was formerly editor of "Young Zionist." He is a member of the Toronto Zionist Council, and of the local Jewish societies.

S. L. GOLDSTINE, WINNIPEG

SIDNEY LYON GOLDSTINE, Barrister, was born in Winnipeg, June 5th, 1891. He was educated at the Winnipeg public schools; Manitoba College; and Osgoode Hall, Toronto, graduating in 1913. He went overseas as Captain in the 152nd Battalion. On his return to Canada, he was appointed Staff Captain and D.A.A.G., M.D. 10. On December 6th, 1921, he was married to Esther, daughter of Solomon Levitan, and has one daughter. Mr. Goldstine is a member of the Canadian Club; Ionic Lodge, A.F. & A.M.; Prince Rupert Chapter, R.A.M.; and Mt. Sinai Lodge, A.F. & A.M.

CAPT. WM. V. TOBIAS, M.C., WINNIPEG

WILLIAM VERNER TOBIAS, Barrister, was born at Morden, Man., March 10th, 1892, the son of the late David and Elizabeth Tobias. He was educated at the public schools; Central Collegiate; and University of Manitoba. He enlisted in 1915 as a private, and served in France, earning a commission and being awarded the Military Cross, which he received from His Majesty the King. He is prominent in all sports and in Jewish communal institutions. Mr. Tobias is a member of the Y.M.H.A.; Habonim; and I.O.B.B., Winnipeg Lodge.

I. D. RUSEN, WINNIPEG

ISRAEL D. RUSEN, Barrister, was born in Russia, January 5th, 1895, the son of David and Fanny Rusen. He was educated at St. John's College, and Manitoba University. For some time he was employed as Secretary to the Commissioner of Immigration, and served during the War. He is President of the Young Zionists, and was on the executive of the Talmud Torah, the Zionist Council and Jewish War Relief Committee. Mr. Rusen is a member of the Montefiore Club; Deer Lodge Golf Club; Habonim; and Independent Order, B'nai B'rith.

J. A. CHERNIACK, B.A., LL.B., WINNIPEG

JOSEPH A. CHERNIACK, Barrister, was born in Chislavich, Russia, October 5, 1885, the son of Baruch Cherniack. He was educated in the Yeshivas of Russia; St. John's College; and University of Manitoba, graduating (B.A. 1915), (LL.B. 1918). He is married to Fannie, daughter of Mendel Goldin. Mr. Cherniack was nominated for School Trustee in North Winnipeg in 1922. He is organizer and President of the Peretz School; member, Hebrew Immigrant Aid; Jewish National Workers' Alliance; and Independent Labor Party.

C. E. FINKELSTEIN, WINNIPEG

CHARLES E. FINKELSTEIN, Barrister, was born at Shumsk, Russia, September 9th, 1889, the son of Joseph and Miriam (Lieberman) Finkelstein. He was educated at the Winnipeg public schools and Manitoba College, from which he graduated in 1913. He was called to the Bar on the 26th of November, 1913, and has since practised his profession in Winnipeg. During the war, Mr. Finkelstein was appointed legal representative to the Canada Food Board for the Western Canadian Division. He is a member of the I.O.B.B.; Knights of Pythias; and I.O.O.F.

MORRIS SOSKIN, VANCOUVER

MORRIS SOSKIN, Barrister, was born in Mogelov, Russia, November 22nd, 1889. He went to London, England, in 1893, and it was there he received his education. He came to Canada in 1907, and after a short period in Montreal, settled in Vancouver, where he studied law, and graduated in 1920. He was married to Miss Hyams of Montreal. Mr. Soskin is interested in communal affairs, welfare work and Zionism. He is President of the Concordia Club, and member of the Board of Trade; Moose Lodge; and Governor, Junior Order of Moose.

N. W. SHAFFER, LL.B., SASKATOON

NAT W. SHAFFER, Barrister, was born at Vama, Bukowina, Roumania, January 25th, 1895, the son of Wolf Shaffer. He came to Canada in 1911, first settling in Regina and Prince Albert. He received his education at the Nutana Collegiate and University of Saskatchewan, from which he graduated (LL.B., 1921). Mr. Shaffer has since practised his profession in Saskatoon. He is married to a daughter of Aaron Volansky. Mr. Shaffer is President of the Zionist Organization of Saskatoon, and is a member of Progress Lodge, No. 92, A.F. & A.M., and of the Chevra Kedisha.

N. C. LEVIN, LL.B., VANCOUVER

NORMAN CECIL LEVIN, Barrister, was born in Winnipeg, August 13th, 1894, the son of John Levin. He was educated in Winnipeg and graduated from the University of Manitoba, in 1913, where he was Secretary of the University Students' Union. He was admitted to the Manitoba Bar in 1920, the same year receiving the LL.B. degree. In 1923, he was admitted to the British Columbia Bar, where he has since practised his profession. He is very active in all communal undertakings and holds office in most of the Vancouver Jewish institutions.

D. B. KLIMAN, REGINA

A. GARDNER, B.A., LL.L., MONTREAL

ADOLPH GARDNER, Barrister, was born in Quebec City, December 5th, 1895, the son of Nathan Gardner. He was educated at the Quebec High School; McGill University (B.A. 1916); and Laval University (LL.L. 1919). He studied law in the office of Mr. Maxwell Goldstein, K.C. Mr. Gardner was for some years associated with the Editorial Department of the Quebec Telegraph. He is a member of the Zeta Beta Tau Fraternity, and Montreal Reform Club. On December 16th, 1924, Mr. Gardner was married to Jessie, daughter of M. J. Glickman of Westmount, Que.

DAVID BERTRAND KLIMAN, Barrister, was born in Winnipeg, April 17th, 1895, of Russian Jewish parents. He was educated at the Winnipeg public schools, and attended the Manitoba Law School, from which he graduated in 1916, in which year he was admitted to the Manitoba Bar. He practised law in Winnipeg for two years, and in 1918 removed to Regina, Sask. He was called to the Bar of Saskatchewan in the same year, and has since followed his profession in Regina. In 1917, Mr. Kliman was married to Bertha Dubinsky of Winnipeg, and he has one son. Mr. Kliman has taken an active part in all Jewish affairs in both Winnipeg and Regina. He is a past President of the Louis D. Brandeis Lodge, No. 833, I.O.B.B., and is District Deputy of the Grand Lodge, I.O.B.B., for Saskatchewan. He is a past President of the Zionist Societies in Regina, and is senior Trustee of the Regina Hebrew School. At the opening ceremony of this institution, when the Lieut.-Governor, Chief Justice, and other dignitaries were present Mr. Kliman occupied the chair and he is held in the highest esteem by all sections of the community.

S. EISEN, B.A., TORONTO

SOLOMON EISEN, Barrister, was born in Galicia, Austria, February 15th, 1898, the son of the late Abraham Eisen. He received his education at the Harbord Street Collegiate Institute; University of Toronto (B.A. 1918); and Osgoode Hall Law School, graduating in 1921. In 1918, he was President of the Menorah Society, and in 1919 was elected a delegate to the Canadian Jewish Congress. He is a member of Mt. Sinai Lodge, A.F. & A.M.; Palestine Lodge, A.F. & A.M.; I.O.O.F.; I.O.F.; I.O.B.B.; Royal Canadian Institute; Liberal-Conservative Club; and Humber Valley Golf Club. On June 14th, 1922, he was married to Rebecca, daughter of Elias Dunkelman of Toronto.

CANADIAN JEWS IN THE MEDICAL AND DENTAL PROFESSIONS
Applied Science, Pharmacy, Etc.

IT will be of particular interest to the young graduate and medical or dental student to learn that the first graduating class in medicine, at McGill University, Montreal, in 1835, had among its members a member of the Jewish faith, Frank N. Hart. He, however, did not practise for any considerable time in Canada but moved to the States and took up his residence in St. Louis, where he had a very distinguished career. There had been a few Jewish doctors in Canada prior to this graduating of Dr. Hart, but they were connected with the army as surgeons.

In 1833, Aaron Hart David (born in Montreal October 9th, 1812) after studying in Montreal, went to Edinburgh, Scotland, and received his degree of Doctor of Medicine from the Royal College of Physicians and Surgeons. He returned to Montreal the same year and entered into the practice of his profession in Montreal and he became one of the leading physicians of that city. He was a prominent member of the Medical Society and was one of the earliest members of the Natural History Society, in which he held office. He later removed to Three Rivers, where he practised, but again returned to Montreal and resumed his practice there. Dr. David was the author of numerous medical works and was appointed Dean of the Faculty of Medicine at the University of Bishop's College, Montreal, an appointment that he held until his death. Dr. David also held the presidency of the Province of Quebec Board of Health.

David Alexander Hart graduated as M.D., C.M. from the University of Bishop's College in 1874, and was the valedictorian of his class in his graduating year. He practised for many years at Upper Bedford in the Eastern Townships, before moving to Montreal. Dr. Hart was in command of the Service Company of the Prince of Wales' Fusiliers during the Fenian Raids, and for many years has held the rank of Surgeon-Major in the Militia. He is the oldest living Jewish doctor in Canada.

DR. A. H. DAVID

In 1878, Hiram N. Vineberg graduated from McGill University with the degree of M.D., C.M., after a brilliant college career, being Primary prizeman and Holmes gold medallist. He later moved to New York where he became instructor in the Post-Graduate School of Medicine and New York Polyclinic Hospital. He also was visiting gynaecologist, St. Mark's Hospital, and attending gynaecologist, Mount Sinai Hospital, and Home for Chronic Invalids. For some time Dr. Vineberg lived in New Zealand and the Sandwich Islands. He has written much for the medical press, and is one of the founders and was president of the McGill Graduates' Society of New York.

In recent years, there has been an increased tendency amongst the Jewish youth to take up the practice of medicine, and numbers of them have graduated and are holding very high positions in the profession, both locally and in other countries. Jewish students have occupied and are today occupying the highest standing in the universities, and are going in, to a very large extent, for post-graduate work, so much so, that it is not possible to pick out individual cases. Jewish women are also showing much interest in the study of medicine, the first one to graduate as a physician being Dr. Bessie T. Pullan, of Toronto (Mrs. L. M. Singer).

Numbers of Jewish doctors saw service during the Great War, and their duties were carried out in many different fields. They were amongst the medical officers attached to fighting units, hospitals in France and other sectors, and on trans-Atlantic conducting duty, as well as in hospitals in England and Canada. Jewish nurses also saw service during the war in various sections, as well as in France.

The first Jew in Canada to graduate as a surgeon dentist was Edward Elkan, of Montreal, who graduated from the Faculty of Dentistry, University of Bishop's College, in 1904. In 1905, Dr. Jacob Rubin graduated from the same university, it being the only university at that time in the Province of Quebec to grant the dental degree. Dr. Sydney Stern, however, was the first Jew to practise as a dentist in Canada, he having graduated from an American college. Since then Jewish dentists in increasing numbers have taken up the practice of the profession, and in many cases they have achieved a prominence worthy of special mention.

Amongst the older dentists in Toronto may be mentioned Drs. Kates, Schwartz, and Pivnick, who graduated in 1912-13-14. In 1924, there were thirty Jewish dentists practising in Ontario and fifty in Quebec. There are also many scattered throughout the other provinces of Canada, and in most cases they occupy a high standing in their communities.

Dr. Jacob Rubin of Montreal was a Governor of the College of Dental Surgeons of the Province of Quebec in 1922, 1923 and 1924. He was also instrumental in the organization of the Mount Royal Dental Society, a Jewish institution, which was formed for the purpose of studying advanced dentistry, and which was found necessary owing to prejudices against some of the Jewish dentists in the existing societies. The Mount Royal Dental Society has a membership of over fifty dentists, and has more than proved the necessity of its existence. At its meetings it has been addressed by some of the foremost members of the profession in America.

During the War, several members of the dental profession enlisted and gave their services to the country, serving in various capacities.

In science, arts, pharmacy and other professions, the Jewish young men of Canada have shown an increased desire to enter the field, and the proportion of Jews attending the universities shows a much larger percentage than their proportion of the population of the country warrants. They have shown also in their studies that they are not behind any others in their standing, and they are frequent winners of scholarships and medals.

Sigismund Mohr, of Quebec, was the first Jewish Electrical Engineer in Canada, and he may be regarded as the father of anything electrical in this country. He was a graduate of a German university. Samuel W. Cohen, of Montreal has built up a reputation as a mining engineer that is recognized throughout America, and also in Europe. Others have also won fame in their professions, and have contributed to the development of the natural resources of Canada, and it will not be many years before there will be Canadian Jewish scientists with world-wide reputations.

DR. D. A. HART, MONTREAL

DAVID ALEXANDER HART, Physician and Surgeon, is the oldest representative of the oldest Jewish family in Canada. He is a great-grandson of Aaron Hart, who settled in Three Rivers in 1760. He was born in Three Rivers, Quebec, the 22nd of June, 1844 the son of the late Alexander Thomas and Miriam (Judah) Hart. He received his education at Lawlor's School, Three Rivers; The Montreal Collegiate Institute; McGill University; and University of Bishop's College, Montreal, from which he graduated in 1874, with the degree of C.M., M.D. He was married to the late Sarah Matilda, eldest daughter of the late Dr. Aaron Hart David, L.R.C.P.S. (Edinburgh), and Catherine (Joseph) David. Dr. Hart has six sons, G. Alex, Vivian S., Roslyn E., Sydney D., Reginald J., and Cecil M. Hart. He is a member of the University Club of Montreal, and of the Montreal Medico-Chirurgical Society. Dr. Hart was the second Jewish doctor to graduate in Canada. For many years he practised his profession in Bedford, Quebec, later moving to Montreal, where he has since resided. He was the first physician attached to the Baron de Hirsch Institute in Montreal, and started the first Jewish Dispensary in that city, in connection with the Baron de Hirsch Institute. He also was Chairman of the Board of Physicians of the Baron de Hirsch Institute. He was formerly Captain of the 1st Prince of Wales Rifles, and later in the 60th Missisquoi Battalion, and was also Surgeon-Major of this Battalion. He saw active service during the Fenian Raids in 1870. He was Secretary of Royal Albert Lodge, A.F. & A.M., Montreal, and was instrumental in organizing Bedford Lodge, A.F. & A.M., and Bedford Chapter, R.A.M. Dr. Hart was the first President of the first Zionist Society in Canada, and he has always taken a great interest in this Movement. He has been a life-long member of the Spanish and Portuguese Congregation (Shearith Israel), Montreal, and has the distinction of being the oldest living member of this congregation. With his late brothers he was Seigneur of the Fief and Seigneurie de Courval, in the County of Yamaska, Quebec.

DR. A. I. WILLINSKY, TORONTO

ALTHOUGH a young man, Dr. Abraham Isaac Willinsky, B.A., M.B., L.M. (Rotunda), F.A.C.S., has achieved a prominence not usually attained by a man of his years, and he holds an enviable position in the medical world of Canada. He was born in Omaha, Nebraska, U.S.A., March 29th, 1885, the son of M.L. Willinsky, and was educated at the Jarvis Collegiate Institute, Toronto, and at the University of Toronto, which he entered in 1902. He graduated in Biological and Physical Science in 1906 with first class honors, and in Medicine in 1908, with honors ranking for the George Brown Memorial Scholarship in Medical Science. Continuing his studies, in the summer of 1908, he went to Dublin, Ireland, spending six months as House Physician at the Rotunda Hospital, and in the following year took the post-graduate course in Internal Medicine in Vienna, Austria, studying under the celebrated professors, Von Noorden, Strumpell, Weichselbaum, and others. He then visited the clinics in Paris, Berlin, and London, and on returning to Toronto in the fall of 1910, commenced the practice of Medicine. After successfully practising for some years, in June, 1915, he gave up his practice and went to New York for post-graduate study in surgery, and served an internship of 22 months in surgery at the New York Polyclinic Hospital. In June, 1917, he returned to Toronto and commenced the practice of surgery. In January, 1918, he was appointed Genito-Urinary Surgeon to the Western Hospital. In 1920, he was made Director of the Venereal Clinic of the same hospital. Dr. Willinsky is regarded as one of the leading members of his profession in Toronto, and enjoys a very large practice. He is prominent in welfare work and devotes much time to communal activity, being a member of most of Toronto's charitable institutions. He is a member of the Academy of Medicine, Canadian and Ontario Medical Associations, and North American Radiological Society. He belongs to the Pi Lambda Phi Fraternity, and to the Masonic Order. He was married on July 1st, 1911 to Sadie, daughter of J. Dobensky of Belleville, Ontario, and has three children.

Rembrandt Studio

DR. SIMON S. SPERBER, MONTREAL

DR. SIMON S. SPERBER, L.R.C.P.S., (Edinburgh), was born in Austria in 1882, the son of David Sperber, J. P. and Peppie (Rosenbaum) Sperber. He came to Canada with his parents when a young boy, and received his education in the public and high schools of Montreal; University of Bishop's College, Montreal; and at the Royal College of Physicians and Surgeons, Edinburgh, Scotland, from which he graduated in 1904 with the degree of L.R.C.P.S. Dr. Sperber was the second Canadian Jewish doctor to graduate from Edinburgh; the first being the late Dr. A. H. David, who graduated from this college in 1834, and who was later President of the Province of Quebec Board of Health. After graduation, he was appointed Clinical Assistant of the Royal Infirmary, Edinburgh, later, in 1905, receiving the appointment as Superintendent of Victoria Memorial Hospital, Manchester, England, which is the oldest Jewish hospital in England. He took a post-graduate course for a year in Paris, and then continued his studies at the University of Brussels, Belgium, where he obtained the degree of M.D., coming first in his class. He then returned to Montreal, where he commenced the practice of Medicine, which he has since successfully followed. For five years he held the appointment as Assistant Demonstrator in Bacteriology in McGill University, and he is to-day one of the oldest practising Jewish physicians in Montreal. Dr. Sperber has been keenly interested in communal work, and he was one of the founders of the Herzl Dispensary, and of the Hebrew Maternity Hospital, both of which institutions he has been connected with since their inception. He has always been a member of the Federation of Jewish Philanthropies, Montreal. It was his appeal to Mayor Martin of Montreal, that was responsible for the granting of a tag day for the benefit of Jewish hospitals. He is connected with most of the charitable organizations in Montreal. Dr. Sperber is a member of the Corinthian Lodge, A.F. & A.M.; and of the Independent Order B'nai B'rith. He is a member of the Reform Congregation, Temple Emanu-El, Montreal.

DR. D. M. BALTZAN, SASKATOON

DAVID MORTIMER BALTZAN, M.D., C.M., Physician and Surgeon, was born in Roumania, May 10th, 1897, the son of Moses and Yetta (Bondar) Baltzan. He came to Canada in 1903, with his parents, his father being one of the first Jewish settlers in Saskatchewan, who had homesteaded at Lipton in 1903, in the colony established there by the late Baron de Hirsch. Dr. Baltzan received his education at the public school in the Jewish colony at Lipton, and at the Saskatoon Collegiate Institute. He then entered McGill University, Montreal, Faculty of Medicine, from which he graduated in 1920, with the degrees of M.D., C.M. He has since followed the practice of his profession in Saskatoon, where he specializes in Internal Medicine. Dr. Baltzan is the first of the younger members of the colony to enter professional life, and he has set a standard that is a credit to the community. He occupies a very high standing in the life of his community, and is a member of the staff of both the Saskatoon City Hospital, and St. Paul's Hospital, Saskatoon. He holds the position as lecturer to the nurses of the City Hospital, and at St. John's Ambulance. Dr. Baltzan takes a keen and active interest in Jewish questions and is associated in all communal and welfare undertakings in the city of Saskatoon, where he is regarded as a leader of the Jewish community. He is a member of the Saskatoon Academy of Medicine, and is Honorary life member of St. John's Ambulance Association. He is also a member and officer of the Independent Order B'nai B'rith, Saskatoon Lodge. Dr. Baltzan is an enthusiastic Zionist and spends much of his time and energy for this cause. He devotes all the time not taken up by his practice to welfare work and his interests are not confined to any one creed, but any cause for the improvement and betterment of the community as a whole has his hearty support. He endeavours to create a better understanding between Jew and non-Jew, based on mutual respect, and his efforts in this are highly successful.

DR. L. J. SOLWAY, B.A., M.B., M.R.C.P., TORONTO

DR. LEON JUDAH SOLWAY, B.A., M.B., M.R.C.P., physician, was born in Teterin, Gov. of Mohiliev, Russia, on April 10th, 1885, the son of Mr. and Mrs. Matthew Solway of that city. He received his early education in the schools of his native city and came to Canada in 1898, but remained here only a few months. He then went to New York and entered the Rabbi Isaac Elchanan Seminary which he attended from 1898-1902. On returning to Toronto he attended University College and later the Faculty of Medicine, University of Toronto, from which he graduated with the degrees of B.A. in 1907, and M.B. in 1909. After graduation he went to New York City and spent some time studying in the hospitals there, but came back to Toronto and started practising Medicine in 1911. Dr. Solway has built up for himself a large practice, and is held in high esteem in the Medical world of Canada. After successfully practising in Toronto for several years, he again returned to the States for post-graduate work and studied first in Boston in 1915, at the John Hopkins Hospital, Baltimore in 1917, and in the Hospitals of New York in 1919. Continuing his post-graduate work, in 1921-22 he went to London and was admitted as a member of the Royal College of Physicians of London, attaining the degree of M.R.C.P. He was Assistant in Medicine in the out-patient department of the Toronto General Hospital for about five years, from 1914-1919, and also Assistant in Medicine at the Faculty of Medicine, University of Toronto, 1917-18. Dr. Solway is a member of the Academy of Medicine, Canadian and Ontario Medical Association, and the Canadian Radiological Association. He is also a member of the Independent Order B'nai Brith, Mount Sinai Lodge, B'nai Zion and the Primrose Club, and is a supporter of the various charitable organizations of Toronto. He attends the Holy Blossom Synagogue. On November 28th, 1911, Dr. Solway was married to Libby, daughter of Mrs. Jacob Levi Genesove, and has one son, A. Jacob Levi, and two daughters, Helen and Merle Solway.

DR. A. B. ILLIEVITZ, MONTREAL

DR. A. BERNARD ILLIEVITZ, M.D., C.M., Demonstrator in Biological Chemistry at McGill University, was born in the town of Reni, Bessarabia, March 9th, 1890, the son of the late Manis and Freda (Siguidin) Illievitz. He received his early education in the public school of his native town, which he left at the age of sixteen (in 1906) arriving in Montreal in that year. He continued his studies in Montreal, later attending McGill University, from which he graduated in 1914 (Medicine). He then went abroad for further study, and did post-graduate work both in Medicine and Chemistry. Although a young man, Dr. Illievitz has built up for himself a large practice in the City of Montreal. During the early days of the war Dr. Illievitz qualified as a Captain, and he held a commission as such in the Canadian Army Medical Corps, Canadian Expeditionary Force, and was attached to hospitals and units in the camps at Rhyl, Witley, Shorncliffe and Epsom. In 1917 he was attached to the Military Hospitals Commission, and also to the Grey Nuns' Military Hospital. Dr. Illievitz was formerly House Physician and Surgeon at the Murray Bay Convalescent Home; at the Montreal General Hospital; and at the Mount Sinai Sanatorium, St. Agathe, Que. He was assistant in Surgery at the Montreal General Hospital, and assistant Physician at the Montreal Baby and Foundling Hospital. Dr. Illievitz is on the staff of the Herzl Dispensary, and is a member of the Medical Board of the Mount Sinai Sanatorium. He received the appointment as Demonstrator in Biological Chemistry, Faculty of Medicine, McGill University, in 1922. Dr. Illievitz is a member of the Montreal Medico-Chirurgical Society, and of the Canadian Medical Association. He takes an interest in welfare and communal affairs, and is a supporter of the various charitable movements. He belongs to the Independent Order B'nai B'rith and to the Menorah Society. Dr. Illievitz is a member of the Spanish and Portuguese Synagogue, Montreal. On 16th June, 1921, he was married to Blanche Micheline, daughter of the late David Levi and Pauline (Saxe) Levi, of Montreal.

DR. L. J. BRESLIN, B.A., M.B., L.C.S.O., TORONTO

DOCTOR LOUIS JUDAH BRESLIN, B.A., L.C.S.O., Physician, was born in Russia, on July 13th, 1891, the son of Solomon and Annie Breslin. He accompanied his mother to Canada in 1893, where his father had previously taken up his residence, and he received his education in the public schools of Toronto, and at the University of Toronto, from which he graduated in 1910 with the degree of B.A. Taking up the study of Medicine, in 1912 he received the degree of M.B., L.C.S.O. Dr. Breslin was the first Jewish Medallist in medicine at the Toronto University. He commenced the practice of medicine in 1914, and from then until 1920, he was physician in the out-patient department of the Toronto General Hospital. During this period, he went to the United States and did post-graduate work at the John Hopkins Hospital, Baltimore, in Philadelphia, and at the Bellevue Hospital and Mt. Sinai Hospital, New York, where he studied Internal Medicine. In 1914, Dr. Breslin was married to Miss Reba Nathanson, who died on October 22nd, 1918, leaving one son, Winston Ira Breslin. Dr. Breslin held the appointment as Jewish Coroner of Ontario, for seven years, from 1914 to 1921, succeeding the late Dr. Singer in this position. He is keenly interested in welfare work, especially amongst the Jewish poor, and devotes much time to charitable endeavor. He is an attending physician at the Mt. Sinai Hospital, Toronto, and is also in charge of the Pathological Department of this institution, and is a member of the Social Relief Committee of the Federation of Jewish Philanthropies, and local medical representative of the Los Angeles Consumptive Sanitarium. Dr. Breslin is a member of the Academy of Medicine, Toronto, and is an active supporter of the various Zionist organizations. He is a member of the Mt. Sinai Chapter, Royal Arch Masons; Independent Order B'nai B'rith; Independent Order of Oddfellows; and of the Primrose Club, Toronto. He is a member of both the Bond Street and McCaul Street Synagogues. On January 18th, 1923, Dr. Breslin was married to Miss Rae Cohen, daughter of Max and Fannie Cohen of Toronto.

DR. H. DOVER, OTTAWA

DR. HARRY DOVER, physician and surgeon, was born in Ottawa, Ont., on April 9, 1890, the son of Mr. and Mrs. John Dover of that city. He was educated at the Ottawa public schools, and Ottawa Collegiate Institute, from which he graduated in 1907 with a gold medal and where he received several diplomas. He entered into business as a general merchant in the Ottawa Valley district and met with considerable success. During this time he was also a fur trader and acted as postmaster for that part of the country. In 1909 he went to Montreal and entered the Faculty of Medicine, McGill University. During his course at the University, Dr. Dover was awarded the Sutherland Gold Medal in 1912, for all branches of chemical science, and the Joseph Hils prize for therapeutics in 1913. After graduating in 1914, he spent several years at post-graduate work in Ottawa and New York hospitals. During the war he was attached to the Canadian Army Medical Corps with the rank of Captain, and for two years was neuro-psychiatrist to the Cobourg Military Hospital. Since 1920, Dr. Dover has been practising medicine in Ottawa, and he has held the post of specialist in neuro-psychiatry for the Department of Soldiers' Civil Re-establishment at Ottawa. He is also an associate member of the surgical staff of the Protestant General Hospital, Ottawa. Dr. Dover is an enthusiastic amateur athlete, and is a member of both the Ottawa Tennis and Bowling Clubs. He has always taken a keen interest in the welfare undertakings of the Jews of his community, and is a supporter of the various charitable institutions. He is a charter member and first president of the Ottawa Lodge, I.O.B.B.; and is a member, Rideau Lodge, No. 595, A.F. & A.M.; Ottawa Valley McGill Graduates' Society; The Women's Hospital Society, New York; and the Canadian Club. He attends the King Edward Avenue Synagogue. On February 24th, 1923, Dr. Dover was married to a daughter of Mr. and Mrs. Jacob Lecker of Montreal, and has one daughter, Mina Daintry Dover.

DR. A. BRODEY, TORONTO

ABRAHAM BRODEY, M.A., M.B., Physician and Surgeon, was born in New York, June 15th, 1890, the son of Isaac and Annie (Draimin) Brodey. He moved to Toronto with his parents in 1893, where he has since resided. He received his education at the public schools of Toronto; Jarvis Street Collegiate Institute; and University of Toronto (B.A. 1910), (M.A. 1911) and (M.B. 1913). In his graduating year in Medicine, Dr. Brodey received the silver medal. In 1909, he spent some time in study in England and France. He was Fellow in physiology, U. of T., 1910-1911, and spent one year in research work under the celebrated Professor T. G. Brodie, on the glomerular function of the kidney. He was demonstrator at the University of Toronto, in applied chemistry, under Professor A. B. McCallum. From 1913 to 1916, Dr. Brodey did post-graduate work in the Mount Sinai Hospital, New York. For a year and a half he studied the etiology of typhus fever, under Drs. Libman and Plotz. On his return to Toronto in 1916, Dr. Brodey was appointed acting Professor of pharmacology and materia medica at the University of Toronto, during the absence of Professor B. Henderson, from 1916 to 1919. In 1919, he received the appointment as demonstrator in practical physiology at the Royal College of Dental Surgeons, Toronto, and from 1916 to 1921, he was pathologist at Grace Hospital, Toronto. Doctor Brodey takes a keen interest in communal affairs and is a member of most of the Jewish charitable institutions of Toronto. He is attending physician at the Mount Sinai Hospital, Toronto. On November 24th, 1915, Dr. Brodey was married to Blanche, daughter of Abraham Levy of Toronto, and he has three sons, Arthur, Donald and Warren Brodey. He is a member of the Academy of Medicine of Toronto; Independent Order B'nai B'rith; and is Wor. M. (1924-5) Palestine Lodge, A.F. & A.M.; and a member of St. John's and St. Andrew's Chapters, R.A.M. Dr. Brodey is a member of the Primrose and Empire clubs.

DR. E. WERSHOF, EDMONTON

DR. E. WERSHOF, Physician and Surgeon, was born in Kovno, Russia in 1894, the son of A. Wershof. He was educated at the public schools of Manitoba and at the Manitoba University, Faculty of Medicine, from which he graduated in 1917. He also did post-graduate work for some time in London, Eng. After graduating, Dr. Wershof joined the Canadian Army Medical Corps as Lieutenant, and went overseas in the fall of 1917. He received his Captaincy in 1918, and during the war served in the Canadian hospitals at Witley Camp and Buxton, England, and at Kimmel Park, North Wales. He also was appointed to a trans-Atlantic conducting staff as a medical officer, where he was in charge of the physical condition of the troops that were going overseas, and those who were returning, invalided home. This was particularly dangerous work, as on each of these voyages the transports were obliged to pass through the submarine zone, and several of the troopships were torpedoed. Dr. Wershof was demobilized in England, and spent a year there doing post-graduate work. On his return to Edmonton, he commenced the practice of his profession, and some years later returned to England, but ultimately went back to Edmonton, where he has since resided, and where he is regarded as one of the leading members of the Jewish community, and one of the most public-spirited residents of that city. Dr. Wershof occupies a very high standing in his profession, and much of the success achieved by the Jews of Edmonton in their various philanthropic activities and undertakings, is due to the co-operation and assistance furnished by him. He takes a keen and active interest in all Jewish communal work, and is President of the Edmonton Lodge of the Independent Order B'nai B'rith. He is a member of the National Council of Canadian Zionists, is Vice-President of the local B'nai Zion Society, and a member of the Edmonton Hebrew Association. He is also associated with all other communal undertakings, and is a member of the various charitable institutions. Dr. Wershof is a member of the Independent Order of Oddfellows.

DR. J. N. NATHANSON, OTTAWA

DR. JOSEPH NORMAN NATHANSON, physician and surgeon, the son of Benjamin and Fannie (Bach) Nathanson, was born in New York on April 24th, 1895. He came to Canada as a child with his parents, and received his early education at the Ottawa public schools and in the Ottawa Collegiate Institute. He then went to Montreal and entered the McGill University, from which he graduated in 1919. In 1918 he won the Joseph Hils prize for the highest standing in therapeutics, and he obtained honors in his final year at the University. He then took post-graduate work in the Protestant General Hospital, Ottawa, where he was house surgeon, and later at the New York Lying-In Hospital. He was resident obstetrician at the Bellevue Hospital, New York. Dr. Nathanson was the only Jewish physician holding office in connection with the Convention of the Canadian Medical Association held in 1924, when he was secretary of the section on pathology and bacteriology, and also secretary of the committee on exhibits. He was intimately connected with the organization of the first prenatal clinic at the Ottawa Maternity Hospital, where he now serves as one of the attending physicians, in connection with this clinic. He is a member of the staff at the Protestant General Hospital, Ottawa. Dr. Nathanson has delivered several papers on technical matters in Ottawa and other cities, before various medical societies. He is a frequent contributor to medical papers and journals on obstetrics and on other allied subjects. He is a member of the Ottawa Medico Chirurgical Society and of the Zeta Beta Tau Fraternity. Dr. Nathanson has always taken a keen and active interest in welfare and philanthropic work in the Jewish community of Ottawa. He has been associated with the Keren Hayesod since 1921, and devotes much time to other charitable endeavors. He is a member of the Board of Trustees of the King Edward Avenue Synagogue, Ottawa, and is a former director of the local Y. M. H. A. Tennis is his chief recreation, and his hobby is sociological studies. He was married to Harriet Dover, daughter of John Dover of Ottawa, in 1921.

Castonguay
DR. J. RUBENSTEIN, OTTAWA

DR. JACOB RUBENSTEIN, Dentist, was born at Ottawa, Ont., on April 1st, 1899, the son of Isaac and Lena (Cook) Rubenstein. He received his education at the public schools and Collegiate Institute of Sault Ste. Marie, and at the Royal College of Dental Surgeons, Toronto, from which he graduated in May, 1920, with the degrees of L.D.S. and D.D.S. After graduating, Dr. Rubenstein was attached to the Red Cross Society in Saskatchewan for three years. He has since followed the practice of his profession in Ottawa. Dr. Rubenstein is a member of the Masonic Order.

DR. WM. HARRIS, TORONTO

DR. WILLIAM HARRIS was born at Grand Rapids, Mich., February 2nd, 1895, the son of Samuel and Sarah (Ruben) Harris. He was educated at the public schools and University of Toronto, from which he graduated (B.A. 1915) (M.B. 1918). He served overseas as captain in the C.A.M.C. and was attached to No. 12 Canadian General Hospital, Bramshot, England. He is a member of Mt. Sinai Lodge, A.F. & A.M. and I.O.B.B. On Feb. 24, 1918, he was married to Tillie, daughter of Dr. John Shayne and he has two sons, Frederick and Lawrence Harris.

DR. M. FINKELSTEIN, WINNIPEG

DR. MANLY FINKELSTEIN, physician, was born in Winnipeg, August 5th, 1899. He is the son of Moses and Sarah (Rosen) Finkelstein of that city. He was educated in the public schools, high school and University of Manitoba, graduating in 1922, when he was awarded the Hudson Bay Fellowship. In 1923 he was appointed City Bacteriologist, which position he still occupies. He is a frequent contributor to medical journals, particularly on the subject of Dio-Deanel Drainage. Dr. Finkelstein takes an active interest in the Y.M.H.A., and is Vice-President of the I.O.B.B., Winnipeg Lodge.

Milne Studio
DR. (BESSIE T. PULLAN) SINGER, TORONTO

DR. (MRS. L. M.) SINGER, is the daughter of Morris E. Pullan of Toronto. She graduated from the Ontario Medical College for Women, and University of Toronto in 1909, and was the first Jewish woman to graduate in medicine in Canada. In 1908-9, she was President of the Women's Medico-Literary Society. Dr. Pullan was house surgeon in the Jewish Maternity Hospital, Philadelphia, and in the Ventnor Hospital, Atlantic City. She also did post-graduate clinical work at the Hospital for Sick Children, Toronto. On July 6th, 1911, Dr. Pullan was married to L. M. Singer, Toronto.

DR. J. RUBIN, MONTREAL

Portrait by Jacoby

DR. JACOB RUBIN, Surgeon Dentist, was born in the province of Kovno, Russia in 1883. He came to Canada with his parents in 1889 and settled in Montreal, where he was educated in the Anne Street School, and Montreal High School. In 1901 he entered Bishop's College (Faculty of Dentistry) and in 1905 he graduated with the degrees of L.D.S. and D.D.S., being one of the first two Jews to graduate in Dentistry in the Dominion of Canada. At that time the only dental degrees given in the Province of Quebec were obtained at this University. He has since practised his profession in Montreal. In 1922 Dr. Rubin had the honor of being elected a governor of the College of Dental Surgeons of the Province of Quebec, and he was re-elected to this position both in 1923 and 1924. In 1911 he was instrumental in organizing the Mount Royal Dental Society, a Jewish organization for the purpose of studying advanced dentistry. This Society has a membership of about fifty Jewish dentists. Dr. Rubin served as a Lieutenant in the Canadian Army Dental Corps during the war, 1914-1918. He has always taken a keen and active interest in all welfare and communal affairs, and in 1909 was elected on the Board of the Baron de Hirsch Institute, Montreal. He held many executive positions in the constituent societies of the Federation of Jewish Philanthropies, and in the capacity of honorary dentist, is connected with many charitable organizations. Dr. Rubin was formerly well known in amateur athletics. He is a life member of the Montreal Amateur Athletic Association with whom he formerly played football, lacrosse and hockey. He was president of the Quebec Rugby Football Union in 1909, and was secretary of the Montreal Football Club in 1909-1911. He is a member of the Montefiore Club and of the Masonic Order. In 1901, Dr. Rubin was married to Rose Blumenthal, daughter of ex-alderman and Mrs. A. Blumenthal of Montreal, and he has two sons and one daughter. Dr. Rubin has been a life-long member of the Shaar Hashomayim Synagogue.

DR. MAURICE PIVNICK, B.A.Sc., TORONTO

DOCTOR MAURICE PIVNICK, Dentist, was born at Minsk, Russia, in 1888, the son of Noah and Anna Pivnick. He studied in the Yeshiva in Minsk, and came to Canada to join his parents in 1902, settling in Toronto, where he received his education at the public schools and at the Jarvis Street Collegiate Institute, from which he graduated to the University of Toronto. In 1908 he graduated from the Faculty of Applied Science, University of Toronto, with the degree of B.A.Sc., and in 1909 as Electrical Engineer. In order to put himself through University, he taught at night school, worked on a fruit farm at Winona, and also worked with the Canada Foundry Company, Toronto. He was employed as a draftsman for the General Electric Co. of Schenectady, N.Y., and also in Pittsburg. He worked in the coal mines in Monongah and Fairmont, West Virginia. In 1913 Dr. Pivnick graduated in Dentistry from the Royal College of Dental Surgeons, Toronto, and was Historian of the class of 1913. He has since practised his profession in Toronto. In 1918 he took a post-graduate course in Dentistry at Columbia University, New York City. Dr. Pivnick takes a prominent part in communal activities and was elected a delegate to the Canadian Jewish Congress in 1919. In 1917-18 he was a trustee of the Federation of Jewish Philanthropies. He is a member of the Building Committee, Toronto Hebrew Free School; governor, Board of Trustees, University Avenue Synagogue; director, Hebrew Free Loan Association; member, Sunday School Committee, Goel Tzedek Synagogue, and other institutions. He is a member of the Engineering Alumni, University of Toronto; Academy of Dentistry; Judean Literary Club; B'nai Zion Association; Mount Sinai Lodge, A.F. & A.M.; Independent Order B'nai B'rith; Primrose Club, and other societies, and is the editor of the Educational Board of the Jewish Dental Society of Toronto. He is a supporter of the Labor party. In June 1913, Dr. Pivnick was married to Esther, daughter of Nathan Keyfetz, and he has one son, Nathan, and two daughters, Misses Helen and Lucille Pivnick.

DR. HARRY A. LANDSBERG, TORONTO

DR. B. D. GARFIELD, TORONTO

DR. HARRY A. LANDSBERG, Dentist, the son of Abraham and the late Rebecca Landsberg, was born in Toronto on December 26, 1900. He was educated at the public, high schools and at The Royal College of Dental Surgeons, graduating (1922) with the degrees of L.D.S. and D.D.S. He is a member of the Toronto Jewish Dental Association; Canadian Travel Club; and the Alpha Omega Fraternity. On June 22, 1924 Dr. Landsberg was married to Emma, eldest daughter of Mr. and Mrs. S. Jolofsky, of Toronto.

DR. BENJAMIN DAVID GARFIELD, Dentist, was born in Kruglae, Russia, on August 26th, 1900, the son of Esther and the late Louis Garfield. He came to Toronto in 1904 and was educated at the public, high schools and The Royal College of Dental Sugeons, Toronto, graduating (1922) with the degrees of L.D.S. and D.D.S. He is a member of the Toronto Jewish Dental Association; I.O.F.; Canadian Travel Club; and the Alpha Omega Fraternity. Dr. Garfield is a member of the Tzemach Tzedec Congregation.

DR. S. I. MOSS, TORONTO

DR. J. J. LAVINE, TORONTO

DR. SAMUEL ISADORE MOSS, Dentist, the son of Wolfe and Jennie Moss, was born the 25th of May, 1896, in Odessa, Russia. He was educated at the public schools, Toronto (he was the first Jewish pupil in Wellesley School); University of Toronto (Royal College of Dental Surgeons), from which he graduated in 1920, with the degrees of L.D.S. and D.D.S. He has since practised his profession in Toronto. He is married to Edythe Rose Smookler of Toronto, and has one daughter, Shirley Barbara. He is a member of the Independent Order B'nai B'rith, Pride of Israel and I.O.F. Dr. Moss is a member of the McCaul Street Synagogue.

DR. JULIUS JUDAH LAVINE, Dentist, was born in Russia, July 5th, 1892. He was educated in Toronto, and after serving his apprenticeship to the late Dr. Marin at the N. Y. College of Dentistry, took the course at the Royal College of Dental Surgeons, Toronto, from which he graduated in 1919. In 1922, he took a course in the post-graduate school of Dr. Chayes, New York. Dr. Lavine is active in communal, Zionist and literary matters, and is a member of Mt. Sinai Lodge and Chapter, Federation of Jewish Philanthropies and Alpha Omega Fraternity. In 1922, he was married to Belle, daughter of Charles Sher, and has one daughter.

DR. B. L. HYAMS, MONTREAL

DR. BERNARD L. HYAMS, Orthodontist, was born in Montreal, August 4th, 1899, the son of Mayer Hyams. He received his education at the Mt. Royal School; Montreal High School; and McGill University, graduating in 1921, with the prize in his final year, obtaining the degrees of L.D.S. and D.D.S. Dr. Hyams then went to New York City, where he did post-graduate work at the Dewey School of Orthodontia. He returned to Montreal in 1921 and took up his practice, specialising exclusively in Orthodontia. Dr. Hyams is the only Jewish doctor in Canada to carry on this particular branch of his profession. He is Treasurer of the Mt. Royal Dental Society, and is a member of the American Society of Orthodontists. He is also a member of the Dewey Alumni Society; Art Association of Montreal; Photographic Circle of Montreal; St. George's Lodge, No. 10, A.F. & A.M.; and Shaar Hashomayim Congregation. Apart from his profession, Dr. Hyams is an artist, and is particularly interested in sculpture. He is a consultant on the Dental Board of the Montreal Hebrew Orphans' Home.

DR. S. I. PERLMAN, TORONTO

DR. H. H. PEARSON, MONTREAL

DR. SAMUEL IRVING PERLMAN, Dentist, was born in Toronto, Ont., June 2nd, 1890, the son of Joseph Perlman. He was educated at the Public Schools; Toronto Technical School; and at the Royal College of Dental Surgeons, from which he graduated in 1917, with the degrees L.D.S., D.D.S. On December 2nd, 1919, he was married to Sara, daughter of M. H. Keyfetz of Toronto, and has one daughter. Dr. Perlman is a member of the Y.M.H.A.; I.O.B.B.; Mt. Sinai Lodge, A.F. & A.M.; Mt. Sinai Chapter, R.A.M.; and Alpha Omega Dental Fraternity.

DR. HYMAN HERBERT PEARSON, Dentist, was born in Montreal, March 10, 1894, the son of Harris Pearson. He was educated at the Montreal Public and Technical High Schools; Shortell's Academy and McGill University, graduating (L.D.S., D.D.S., 1917). He is married to Marie, daughter of Louis Goldberg and has one daughter. Dr. Pearson is a member of the Mt. Royal Dental Society; Allied Dental Council of U.S.; and National Dental Association. He is also a member of the Montreal Reform Club; Y.M.H.A.; and is one of the originators of the Dental Department, Herzl Dispensary.

THE LATE SIGISMUND MOHR

THE LATE MR. SIGISMUND MOHR was born in Breslau, Germany, October 21st, 1827, the son of the late Herman Mohr of that city. He was educated at the College of Breslau, from which he graduated in 1849, as Electrical Engineer. In 1856, he was married to Blume, daughter of the late Phillip Levi of New York. Mrs. Mohr still resides in New York. They had two sons, Eugene Phillip, and Henry Ralph, and five daughters, Phillipine, Amelia, Lenorah, Fanny and Clara. Mr. Mohr came to Canada in 1871, and resided in Quebec City until his death, which took place on December 15th, 1893. He was the "father" of Hydro Electric in Canada, and everything electrical in Quebec. He promoted and installed the City and District Telegraph Company, and operated at a City Fair, the first set of telephones in Quebec, which were sent to him by Professor Bell, and he gave to Quebec City its first telephone service. He later formed a company, known as the Quebec and Levis Electric Company, giving Quebec and its vicinity, the finest electric light system in the world, at that time. To do this, he utilized the water power of Montmorency Falls, situated at a distance of twelve miles from the city, requiring a circuit of twenty-four miles to carry the electrical energy to the city. This was the first attempt made to utilize water power at a distance to generate electric light current, or for other electrical purposes. After proving that business places and private homes could be successfully lighted by electricity, the City of Quebec gave Mr. Mohr the contract for lighting the City, and on the completion of his work, the Mayor, the City Council and many prominent citizens, assembled on Dufferin Terrace to witness the inauguration of the service. Mr. Mohr was the first member of the Jewish faith in Canada to practise as an Electrical Engineer. Sigmund E. Lyons and Harry Lyons of Toronto, are grandsons of Mr. Mohr's, and Mrs. Nathan Phillips, Mrs. Israel Singer, and Mrs. Kenneth Joseph of Toronto, are granddaughters.

MARTIN WOLFF, MONTREAL

MARTIN WOLFF, Civil Engineer, was born December 16th 1881, the son of Julius and Sarah (Andrade) Wolff. He was educated at Clifton College, Bristol, England, where he was a member of the Rev. J. Polack's Jewish House, later taking the Civil and Mechanical engineering course at the City and Guilds of London Central Technical College. During the South African War he served with the Electrical Engineers, R.E., in Cape Colony, Orange Free State, and the Transvaal, his work consisting of search-light installation and operation, bridge repairs, field telegraphs, etc. He received the Queen's medal with five bars. In 1905-06 he attended the Camborne School of Mines, Cornwall, England, studying mineralogy and geology, and making underground surveys in the tin mines. In 1906, Mr. Wolff came to Canada and became engaged in survey work with the Canadian Northern Railway, later on during the same year joining the National Transcontinental Railway, first on the survey line from Quebec to New Brunswick, and later having charge of a section under construction. On the outbreak of war in 1914, he attended the Officers' Training Corps in Quebec and qualified as a lieutenant in infantry, later being attached to the Department of Militia and Defence Quebec District, on secret service. From 1916 to 1917, he was attached to the Imperial Ministry of Munitions, shell inspection branch, Quebec, where the shells manufactured all over Canada were tested. In the fall of 1917, Mr. Wolff was sent to the Yellow Head Pass to assist in the lifting of the rails of the Grand Trunk Pacific Railway, which at that point paralleled the Canadian Northern tracks for 200 miles, and which were sent to France for use in the war area. On the completion of this work he joined the staff of the Department of Railways and Canals, later being appointed Assistant Engineer in the Bureau of Economics, Canadian National Railways. In 1909, Mr. Wolff was married to Irene Rachel, daughter of Montefiore Joseph of Quebec, and he has six daughters, the Misses Sarah, Annette, Rachel, Rosetta, Fanny, and Esther Wolff.

SAMUEL W. COHEN, E. M., MONTREAL

SAMUEL WILLIAM COHEN, Consulting Mining Engineer, was born at St. Paul, Minn., U. S. A., May 26th, 1882, the son of David L. and Anna B. (Goldstone) Cohen. He was educated at the St. Paul Central High School, and at the University of Minnesota, from which he graduated with the degree of Engineer of Mines. He had the distinction of being unanimously elected President of the School of Mines Society, University of Minnesota, which society embraced the whole student body of the School of Mines, and he had the further distinction of being the first Jew to graduate from the School of Mines, University of Minnesota. After graduation, Mr. Cohen worked in Montana, Idaho, Colorado, and other western states. In 1906, he came to Canada, where he was one of the pioneers in the silver fields of Cobalt. As superintendent of the Kerr Lake Mining Co., he developed that property in its early stages and in 1907, took over the management of the Crown Reserve Mine, and was for ten years the general manager of that company. He developed that property to the unique distinction of probably the richest silver mine ever known in the world. He was general manager, Porcupine Crown Mines Ltd.; vice-president and general manager, Bluestone Mining and Smelting Co.; vice-president and chief engineer, Jacobs Asbestos Mining Co.; general manager, Crœsus Gold Mines Ltd.; chief engineer, Federal Asbestos Co., Ltd.; Dominion Reduction Co., Ltd., and many other mining companies in Canada and the United States; president and general manager, General Asbestos Co., Ltd. Mr. Cohen has had many dangerous experiences in various parts of the world. He is a member of the Canadian Institute of Mining and Metallurgy, and of the American Institute of Mining Engineers, life governor of the Western Hospital, and a member of the Canada Club (Montreal), and Engineers' (Toronto) Club. He is married to Irma Livingston, daughter of David Livingston, of San Francisco, Cal., U.S.A., and has one son and one daughter. In 1924, Mr. Cohen was appointed by the Quebec Government to the commission, to study the question of Jewish education.

THE LATE ABRAHAM PINTO JOSEPH

H. S. KAPLAN, TORONTO

THE LATE ABRAHAM PINTO JOSEPH, eldest son of Montefiore and Annette (Pinto) Joseph, was born at Quebec, July 31st, 1883. He graduated from McGill University in Electrical Engineering, and followed his profession in Pittsburgh, until his death in 1922. Mr. Joseph was a prominent Zionist and active in all communal work. He represented Pittsburgh Zionists at several National Conferences. On his death, a number of his friends and admirers raised a fund for a memorial in Palestine, to perpetuate his name. In 1909, he married Hortense Ury, of Schenectady, and is survived by two sons, Horace and Edward.

HAROLD SOLOMON KAPLAN, Architect, was born in Bucharest, Roumania, September 10th, 1895, the son of Frank Kaplan. He was educated in the public schools, and at Toronto Technical School, from which he graduated in 1915. After serving ten years with prominent Toronto and Philadelphia architects, he entered into partnership with Mr. A. Sprachman, forming the firm of Kaplan and Sprachman. He is married to Dorothy, daughter of Mr. and Mrs. A. M. Spain. He is a member of Mount Sinai Lodge, A.F. and A.M.; Sunnyside Lodge, I.O.O.F.; I.O.B.B.; and the Y.M.H.A.

A. SPRACHMAN, TORONTO

K. DE SOLA JOSEPH, TORONTO

ABRAHAM SPRACHMAN, Architect, was born in Hanczarow, Galicia, July 12th, 1894, the son of Hyman Sprachman. He was educated in the public schools, Toronto; Technical School; and High School of Commerce, from which he graduated in 1917. He was married, on June 14th, 1921, to Mina, daughter of the late Mendel Sprachman. He was formerly Secretary of the Primrose Club, and is a member of Sunnyside Lodge, I.O.O.F.; I.O.B.B.; and Herzl Zion Club. Mr. Sprachman is one of the first members of the Y.M. and Y.W.H.A. He is a member of the firm of Kaplan and Sprachman.

KENNETH DE SOLA JOSEPH was born at Quebec, October 6th, 1892, the youngest son of Montefiore and the late Annette (Pinto) Joseph. He graduated with honors in engineering from McGill University in 1913, obtaining the British Association medal and prize. He was on the C.P.R. operating staff until 1918, being their youngest Assistant Superintendent. During the war, Mr. Joseph, after failing to get overseas, donated a machine gun, in lieu of his services. In 1917, he was married to Pauline Evelyn, daughter of Jacob H. and the late Amelia (Mohr) Lyons of Toronto, and has two children, Montefiore Lyons and Enid Beryl.

THE SOCIAL LIFE OF THE JEWS IN CANADA

No section of the population of Canada held a higher social position than the pioneer members of the Jewish community. They brought with them to this country education, culture, pride in their traditions, and steadfast observance of their faith. In most cases they brought considerable wealth and they gave to the young country more than they received. Never forgetting that they were Sephardim, they were proud of their blue blood, as they moved about in the powdered wigs and lace frills of the time. They were accepted as social equals by the French nobility remaining in the country, as well as by the commanding officers of the British armies. Thus it was not strange that when the Duke of Kent, the father of Queen Victoria visited Canada in 1795, and spent some time in Three Rivers, he was the guest of Aaron Hart, who entertained for him in sumptuous style.

It was some years later that Cardinal Bourbon, a Prince of the Royal House of France, as well as the first dignitary of his rank to visit this country was also the guest, whilst in Three Rivers, of a son of Aaron Hart. It was indeed an honour that the home of a Jew should be selected as his residence while he was in that catholic town. This will be enlightening to the Jew of today, as from old diaries we read that these early Jewish settlers would not attend such social functions as parties that were held on a Friday night, nor the races or other entertainments that were held on Saturday. It was undoubtedly this strict observance of their religion that had much to do with the respect in which they were held. It was the officers of the congregation that established the laws under which they lived (subject of course to the laws of the country) and when, in the minutes of the Shearith Israel Congregation we read that the members were fined for non-attendance at the Sabbath services, unless they had lawful excuse for their absence, there seems to be no doubt but that they were respected for their religious observances.

Not only these pioneer settlers, but their descendants for several generations, were held in this same respect, and we find proof of this in the fact that in almost every instance the young Jewish man was invited by the Governor of the time to take up a commission in His Majesty's Militia. Those were not the days when the officer rose from the ranks—they were selected from the best class of citizens. Consequently we find that in the Rebellion in 1837 and even as late as during the Fenian Raids, most of the Jewish men of military age were serving as officers and members of the militia.

During the first hundred years of the British rule in Canada, we read of Jews being among those who regularly attended the Governors' Levées. In the early days of the nineteenth century one reads of them attending the banquets of the St. George's Society, the St. Andrew's Society, and the St. Patrick's Society. In 1800, they were members of the Curling Club in Montreal, and the Beaver Club, where the chief officials of the Hudson's Bay Company and the North-West Company were wont to assemble. They were members of the Whist Club, which met at the homes of the different members, and when such gatherings took place at a Jewish home, the names of some of those present are names that are today outstanding in Canadian history. And we have failed to find an occasion when the Whist Club met on a Friday night when the Jewish members would be unable to be present.

We find in old records that they were members of the Hunt Club, as well as regular participants in the military hunts. It is interesting to note that on July 27th, 1836, the King's Plate was raced for the first time in Lower Canada, at Three Rivers. There were five horses in the race, which was won by a mare belonging to Aaron Philip Hart, a well-known Jewish advocate of Montreal. Another Jew, Moses E. David, had a horse in this race. Records also show that at other horse races members of the small Jewish community often acted as stewards and clerks of the course, and in all other social activities they took a prominent part.

During the early and mid-Victorian period, when the British troops were stationed in Montreal and Quebec, the centre of social activity was around many of the Jewish homes, and on June 24th, 1834, we read of a musical soirée at Mrs. Henry Joseph's house where some two hundred were present, including the Governor-General and Lady Aylmer. Beautifully situated on the slopes of Mount Royal, the home of Jesse Joseph was also a centre of the social life of Montreal for over half a century. And when Benjamin Hart died in Montreal in 1848, every store in the city was closed during his funeral, and the officers of the garrison attended in a body, wearing military mourning. Such was the standing of the Jews, socially, in the old days.

Up to this time (1850), practically all the members of the Jewish community had come from England. They spoke nothing but English and French and were imbued with a fine spirit of loyalty towards anything British. It was at this period that the first considerable influx of German Jews took place, followed in a short time by a number of Russian and Polish Jews. They arrived in many cases with considerable wealth and soon became settled to conditions here. They were the first who arrived who spoke Yiddish and at the start did not mingle with their neighbors as did their predecessors but established a social status amongst themselves. Thus when the first large immigration of Russian and Polish Jews took place in the early eighties, due to the pogroms, on the arrival of the refugees in this country they were met by their co-religionists who could speak to them in a common tongue—Yiddish. They maintained the use of Yiddish among themselves and spoke English to their English-speaking neighbors, but socially they remained apart. It was therefore only natural that they should establish gatherings where there were none present but members of their own faith, and from these first gatherings, where literary and other subjects were discussed, sprang the first Jewish social clubs. It was in 1880 that the Montefiore Literary and Dramatic Club was first started in Montreal (now the Montefiore Club) and the members held entertainments and raised funds for charitable and communal purposes. The different hospitals all benefitted from this source, as well as the building fund of the German and Polish Congregation. And in a few years many other Jewish clubs came into existence, both in Toronto and Montreal. There are no finer or better equipped club-houses today in Canada than the Montefiore Club in Montreal, or the Primrose Club in Toronto, and much of the Jewish life in these two cities is centered around these institutions.

The Jewish population continued to increase very rapidly, practically all from Eastern European immigration, and the scope of the existing social clubs was enlarged to meet with changing conditions. Numerous societies of all descriptions were formed, all with the purpose of bringing the Jewish people together in social ways. Fraternal organizations, athletic clubs, auxiliaries to the synagogues and other societies, where the social life of the members and their friends would be improved were established, and philanthropic work was not neglected.

In athletics the members of the Jewish communities have always taken a prominent part and it is only proper to mention here that Henry Joseph of Montreal was one of the members of the first Canadian lacrosse team to visit England, where they played before Her Majesty, Queen Victoria. In 1890, Louis Rubenstein, now the well-known Montreal alderman, won the figure skating championship of the world at St. Petersberg, Russia.

With the construction of the transcontinental railway the western country was opened up, and the Jewish immigrants flocked there in large numbers. Wherever they settled together in sufficient numbers they organized clubs, societies and branches of fraternal institutions. In every phase of Jewish life these societies played their part, and brought the community together. Invariably all these societies were for Jewish members only and they kept very much to themselves. The use of Yiddish was maintained to a large extent, particularly in the homes, and instead of being, as in the old days an integral part of the community, they have become a distinct part. Even in Masonic affairs this same situation applies, but to a lesser extent. Jews have always, particularly in Canada, been members of the craft, and they have held office in different lodges at all times. As members of these lodges they met the other members on equal footing, irrespective of creed, and in this manner a certain understanding and sympathy with each other was bound to take place.

It is indeed a matter of pride to read that on December 18th, 1838, an emergency meeting of St. Paul's Lodge, Montreal, was called to initiate as members Theodore Hart and Jacob Joseph, who were about to leave for active service, as officers of the militia.

In late years a number of lodges have been formed where the membership is composed almost entirely of members of the Jewish persuasion, and it does not seem possible that in such cases an equal undertsanding with members of other faiths can be reached. To know one another and respect one another it is necessary that people should associate together. It will be said, and justly said, that there have been objections made to Jews joining certain organizations and clubs, simply on the grounds that they were Jews—that because they were of the same faith as the founder of the dominant religion, they were ineligible to associate on terms of equality with followers of that religion. That this is a fact cannot be denied and it can only be overcome by educating the followers of other religions to realize, as their ancestors in Canada did many years ago, that the Jew is the most desirable type of citizen this country possesses—that they are loyal—that they obey the laws of the country—that they develop the resources of the country—and that in their home life they maintain a moral standard that others would do well to imitate. The Jew must set the lesson and show, as their fathers did, that they strictly observe their religion—the religion that has held them together for thousands of years and for which they have suffered banishment, torture, and death. They must show that they respect themselves in order to create respect. There is a lesson in this article for the Jews as well as others and it is to be hoped that it will be beneficial. The Jews have their faults, many of them, but in philanthropy, in social service, and in business integrity they can give a lesson to all others. The record contained in this book is one that every Canadian should take pride in, because it is a record of achievement performed by loyal Canadians.

THE B'NAI B'RITH IN CANADA
By Nathan Phillips, Alderman, City of Toronto.

ALTHOUGH the Independent Order of B'nai B'rith was founded in the City of New York on October 14th, 1843, it was not until after the lapse of thirty-two years that it spread its benign influence to, and established itself in the Dominion of Canada. The history of B'nai B'rith in Canada has kept pace with the development of Canadian Jewry, until today it is fair to say that the B'nai B'rith lodges established throughout the length and breadth of our fair domain stand for the best in the Jewish communal life of the communities in which they exist; and in a very great sense interpret Jewish thought and ideals to the non-Jewish world. Wherever today you find Jewish rights being assailed or the many headed monster of anti-Semitism showing its spleen, there you will find B'nai B'rith with all its vigour demanding justice and defending the fair name of the Jew.

One of the early features of B'nai B'rith was an insurance benefit to its members, in which the members of the first Canadian lodges participated. The insurance idea, however, has long been abandoned and the order is now a purely Jewish world wide service organization. No better definition can be given of the aims and objects of the order than is contained in the preamble to the Constitution which is as follows:—

"The Independent Order of B'nai B'rith has taken upon itself the mission of uniting Israelites in the work of promoting their highest interests and those of humanity; of developing and elevating the mental and moral character of the people of our faith; of inculcating the purest principles of philanthropy, honor and patriotism; of supporting science and art; alleviating the wants of the poor and needy; visiting and attending the sick; coming to the rescue of victims of persecution; providing for, protecting and assisting the widow and orphan on the broadest principles of humanity."

The preamble is not a mere empty conglomeration of words. Canadian lodges are carrying out the aims and objects with the true B'nai B'rith spirit and there is no branch or service in which you will not find B'nai B'rith assuming a leading role.

The history of B'nai B'rith in Canada may be divided into two branches, the early Canadian Lodges and those of recent birth.

The Early Canadian Lodges

Little data is available concerning the early Canadian lodges. The first Canadian lodge was established in Toronto on June 13th, 1875, under the jurisdiction of District Grand Lodge No. 1 and was known as Canada Lodge No. 246. Notwithstanding that the Jewish community in Toronto at that time was very small there were twenty-two charter members. Their names were: Sim Solomon, Max B. Solomon, Mark Marks, J. Alexander, Lipman Wolters, Levi Blankenstein, Lawrence Cohen, Chas. Stern, H. Stol, J. Cohen, I. Anhalt, Louis Harfeld, Alex Miller, Joseph L. Levy, David Bernhard, A. Bonestin, Louis Blumburgh, M. Morris, Isaac Mintz, Chas. Cohen, L. Hart, I. Lipman. Of these members Magistrate Jacob Cohen of Toronto, a past president of the lodge, is the sole survivor. The lodge carried on for nineteen years and ceased activities officially on June 24, 1894.

The second Canadian lodge was established in Montreal on June 5th, 1881, under the same jurisdiction and was known as Montreal Lodge No. 327. The following thirty names appear as charter members;—E. Lichtenheim, S. Abrahams, S. L. Bernstein, Marcus Brown, P. Cohen, P. Goldstein, Aaron S. Jacoby, Marks Kutner, M. B. Lauterman, A. Moses, H. Rutenberg, F. Schutz, D. A. Ansell, L. Aronson, Jacob Berman, Jacob Cohen, Louis Fus, I. S. Goldenstein, J. Kaufman, M. Lightstone, B. Levy, Morris Rut, Jacob Rosenthal, M. Steinberg, M. Samuels, J. Steinberg, A. Silverstone, H. Steinberg, J. Silverstone, Lyon Silverman. This lodge operated for twenty-two years and surrendered its charter in 1903.

The third Canadian lodge known as Victoria Lodge No. 365 was established in Victoria, B.C., on September 7th, 1886, under the jurisdiction of District Grand Lodge No. 4, but disbanded after being in existence a short time.

Lodges at the Present Time

There are at the present time twelve B'nai B'rith lodges established in Canada in the following cities: Montreal, Toronto, Ottawa, Hamilton, London, and Windsor, under the jurisdiction of District Grand Lodge No. 1, having its headquarters in New York; Winnipeg, Calgary, Edmonton and Saskatoon, under the jurisdiction of District Grand Lodge No. 6, having its headquarters in Chicago; and Vancouver and Victoria, under the jurisdiction of District Grand Lodge No. 4, having its headquarters in San Francisco. The number of B'nai B'rith lodges in Canada must of necessity be always limited to the number of Jewish communities and until there are a sufficient number of lodges in Canada to form the nucleus of a Canadian District Grand Lodge, Canadian lodges must remain under the jurisdiction of the District Grand Lodges of the United States. While there are really no boundaries or dividing lines in B'nai B'rith work and the various District Grand Lodges of the United States have always treated our Canadian lodges with the utmost consideration, there exists today the hope that we will in Canada some day have a District Grand Lodge.

Toronto Lodge No. 836, Toronto

On the 10th day of March, 1919, after the lapse of a quarter of a century from the time Canada Lodge, the first Canadian lodge established in Canada ceased its activities, Toronto again embraced the spirit of B'nai B'rith, and Toronto Lodge No. 836, which today boasts a membership of five hundred, was instituted in a very impressive manner by Brothers Charles Hartman, Joseph H. Ullman, Charles Shapiro and Rabbi Joseph Silverman of District Grand Lodge No. 1, with the following charter members:—Joseph Abramson, J. J. Allen, Jule Allen, J. Bernstein, Edward Blankensee, Max Bloch, Meyer Brenner, Dr. A. Brodey, Isadore Brodey, Abraham Cohen, Arthur Cohen, Mark Cohen, Leo Danson, Frank Davis, Jacob Davis, Archibald Draimin, Charles Draimin, Murray Draimin, Julius Eisman, J. Epstein, Meyer Fischer, Chas. Fremes, Simon Fremes, Nathaniel Friedlander, Bernard Goldstein, Milton M. Goldstein, H. H. Greenberg, B. M. Greene, L. I. Greisman, Jules Heim, Julius Hershman, J. D. Isaacs, Dr. A. Isaacson, Ralph Jacobs, Sidney Kahn, L. Kert, Phil Kauffman, Hyman King, Frederick J. Levenston, Abraham Levy, Lester Levy, M. L. Levy, B. Luxenberg, H. Mendoza, H. Nusbaum, Asher Pritzker Chas. M. Pritzker, Nathan Phillips, Samuel Phillips, Benj. Raz, Ralph Raphael, Louis F. Sapera, Dr. B.

Schaffer, Edmund Scheuer, Reuben Schutz, Lawrence Simonsky, Murray Simonsky, A. Singer, Israel Singer, Joseph Singer, Louis M. Singer, M. J. Singer, S. Steinberg, Theo. Weil, Wolfe Wilder, Jos. Wolfe, Julius Hirshman and Jess Kaplan.

The following have served as presidents since the inception of the lodge, Meyer Fischer (1919-20), Abraham Cohen (1921), Nathan Phillips (1922), Mortimer L. Levy (1923), Louis M. Singer (1924), and Saul Kaufman (1925).

One of the first accomplishments of the lodge was the dedication of a cot in the Toronto Hospital for Sick Children at a cost of $2,000. In 1921, a summer camp for under privileged boys was established and the same has been carried on annually ever since under the auspices of the lodge, the number of boys accommodated last year being over five hundred. In 1922, the lodge established the Toronto Hebrew Free Loan Association (now the Toronto G'milath Chasodim Association) with a capital of $4,000 in addition to making a donation of $3,500 to the Federation of Jewish Philanthropies, while in 1923 the lodge donated a library to the Boys' Club on Simcoe Street. An outstanding event in the lodge was the holding of Canada Night in the fall of the year 1924, at which the ritual was exemplified for the first time in Canada, before a gathering of Canada's non-Jewish citizens. Among the guests present were His Honour the Lieutenant-Governor of the Province of Ontario, Hon. Henry Cockshutt; The Right Honourable Arthur Meighen, former Prime Minister of Canada and at present leader of the Opposition; Chief Justice Sir William Mulock of the Supreme Court of Ontario; Hon. Mr. Justice Riddell; Hon. Mr. Justice Lennox; Father Minehan, and R. H. Greer, K.C. In addition to the above specific accomplishments, the lodge has at all times actively assisted the various local Jewish institutions in their undertakings. Notwithstanding the serious side of the lodge's work, its social activities are not neglected and take the form of dances, smokers and luncheons at which prominent speakers deliver addresses. Meyer Fischer was the first member of a Canadian lodge to be elected on the General Committee of District Grand Lodge No. 1, with the office of Chairman of Canadian Activities. He was succeeded by the writer who held office for the year 1923-1924.

Mount Royal Lodge No. 729, Montreal

Mount Royal Lodge instituted on the 9th day of February, 1913, is a successor to Montreal Lodge, the second lodge established in Canada, as hereinbefore stated. Owing to local conditions and the outbreak of the war, the lodge became inactive and was again reorganized in 1920.

Since that date the lodge has established itself on a firm basis. Comprising a membership of about 250, it embraces in its ranks leading representatives of professional and commercial life, and has been a forum for current Jewish thought and activity. Social service work varying from actual philanthropic endeavour to fields of religious education and Big Brother work have occupied the attention of the lodge.

For four consecutive years the lodge has maintained a summer camp for under privileged boys and to date has looked after over 500 boys. Conducted under the most favourable auspices, marked by a distinct Jewish atmosphere, the camp has won most favourable commendation and is listed by the Montreal Association of Big Brothers (non-sectarian) as the model camp of Montreal and vicinity.

During the past five years under the leadership of Marcus M. Sperber, K.C., (member of General Committee, District Grand Lodge No. 1, and Chairman of Canadian Activities for 1924-25), Simon Kirsch, Ph.D., Max Bernfeld, Horace R. Cohen and Lewis Faber, the lodge has introduced and developed the study of problems of national and civic importance, and many well known and prominent persons in national life have lectured to the members. Social features take the form of formal and informal dances, get-together meetings, smokers, and celebrations of religious festivals.

Ottawa Lodge No. 885, Ottawa

On the 19th day of February, 1921, Ottawa Lodge was impressively dedicated and today has a membership of over one hundred members. So enthusiastically has the spirit of B'nai B'rith seized the Jewish community in Ottawa, that a Ladies' Auxiliary has been formed, the first of its kind in Canada. The lodge has established a Free Loan Association. It contributes annually towards the support of an orphan in Turkey. Big Brother work occupies an important place in the lodge's activities. Credit is due to Dr. H. Dover, J. J. Marks and Benj. Goldfield (who have held the office of president) for the great progress made by the lodge.

Viceroy Reading Lodge No. 886, Hamilton

Viceroy Reading Lodge No. 886 was instituted with great splendour and enthusiasm at the Royal Connaught Hotel, Hamilton on the 20th day of February, 1921. Under the leadership of David Sweet, M. Levy, C. Levinson and Joseph A. Sweet respectively, the lodge has made remarkable progress. With a membership of about fifty it has founded a Free Loan Association with a capital of $2,000. It supports a war orphan at the cost of $100 a year in addition to making an annual grant of $50 to the local Sanatorium. Every worthy communal undertaking receives the support of the lodge.

Windsor Lodge No. 1011, Windsor
London Lodge No. 1012, London

Windsor Lodge and London Lodge have just been added to the fraternal chain of B'nai B'rith lodges in Canada, Windsor Lodge having been instituted with a membership of thirty-four members on March 15th, 1925, while London Lodge was instituted on the following day with a membership of forty. From the enthusiastic manner in which the respective Jewish communities participated in the institution of these lodges, a very bright future is predicted for them. Mr. J. A. Glanz is the president of Windsor Lodge and Mr. I. Goldstick is the president of London Lodge.

Winnipeg Lodge No. 650, Winnipeg

Winnipeg Lodge No. 650 which is just entering the sixteenth year of its existence, has had a very active and creditable career. In the spring of 1909, Mr. Max Steinkopf, realizing the need for the spirit of B'nai B'rith in Winnipeg, summoned a small band of its leading Jews for the purpose of discussing the formation of a lodge. A charter was applied for and granted and on June 27th, the following members were initiated into the Order by Bro. Ed. Sonnenschein and the late Rabbi S. N. Deinard: L. Abramovich, A. H. Aaronovitch, D. Barish, A. Black, A. H. Bloomfield, R. Druckman, M. Finkelstein, M. J. Finkelstein, M. Gardner, S. Hart Green, M. Greenblat, H. Landsberg, Rev. J. K. Levin, B. Levinson, E. R. Levinson, Dr. O. Margolese, A. W. Myers, I. Presner, P. Presner, J. L. Rill, D. Ripstein, I. Ripstein, J. Ripstein M. Ripstein, R. S. Robinson, I. Rosen, J. Rosenthal, Chas. Schachter, F. Schor, B. Shragge, H. Steinkopf, M. Steinkopf, J. Udow, M. Udow, H. L. Weidman and H. E. Wilder.

The following have held the office of President:— M. Steinkopf, A. J. Bloomfield, S. Hart Green, A. H. Aaronovitch, I. Ripstein, D. Beckerman, L. Rice, M. J. Finkelstein, E. R. Levinson, A. J. Abramovich, M. Haid,

N. J. Weidman, S. L. Goldstine, Rabbi H. J. Samuel and James Shaen.

Among the earlier activities of the lodge was the establishment of a Free Loan Fund, which operated on a considerable scale for several years until circumstances rendered the same no longer necessary. The B'nai B'rith Free Employment Bureau was established and maintained until all employment bureaus were taken over by the Provincial Government. A great service was rendered the community in its early days by the purchase of a hearse at the cost of $1,200. In 1912 the lodge took the first step towards the establishment of a Jewish orphanage.

The lodge has been most energetic in protecting the good name of the Jew. Its Publicity and Defence Committee has done effective work in counteracting attacks on the Jew in the press, and preventing objectionable portrayals on the stage and film. Early in 1919, the lodge petitioned the Rt. Hon. Sir Robert Borden, Canada's delegate to the Peace Conference, on the question of the rights of the European Jews, and secured his personal and sympathetic activity in this matter.

Big Brother work has a regular place among the activities of the lodge. Winnipeg Lodge conceived the idea of establishing branch lodges. These lodges operate without a charter, and their members are members of Winnipeg Lodge and are recorded on the books of the Grand Lodge as such. Winnipeg Lodge has three branches at present in existence, at Leader, Sask. (started November, 1921) membership, forty; at Yorkton, Sask. (started April, 1922), membership, forty; and at Estevan, Sask. (started May, 1922), membership, thirty.

Edmonton Lodge No. 732, Edmonton

Founded twelve years ago on the 9th of March, 1913, Edmonton Lodge No. 732 has a record of which it might well feel proud. With a membership of only seventy-five it has exerted tremendous influence in obtaining justice and fair play for the Jewish community in which it exists. The work of its anti-defamation committee has been very effective with the result that those in the community who moved public thought and opinion have been careful not to publish anything of an offensive nature.

The lodge has been largely instrumental in keeping religious teaching out of the public schools. Several unsuccessful attempts have been made to introduce religious instruction in the public schools.

The Talmud Torah is a product of the lodge which contributes $300 annually towards its upkeep. From a class of only fifteen children this institution of learning has grown to a class of sixty. The following have served as presidents of the lodge;—Paul Levy, J. S. Berkman, A. H. Goldberg, Chas. Horwitz, B. M. Goldman, H. A. Friedman, M. I. Lieberman, Julius Erlanger, J. N. Sternberg, S. Waldman, J. H. Chmelnitsky, J. D. Dower, A. A. Dower, M. B. Cohen and Dr. E. Wershof.

Calgary Lodge No. 816, Calgary

Calgary Lodge was instituted on the 17th day of June, 1917. With the exception of having taken over the work of the Immigration Aid Society, the activities of the lodge have been of a general nature and have not been confined to any specific undertakings. The lodge has a membership of about ninety. The following have served as presidents since its inception, B. Ginsberg, Marcel Marcus, A. S. Horwitz, M. A. Wener, and Charles Greenfield.

Lake City Lodge No. 696, Fort William

Lake City Lodge No. 696 was instituted at Fort William on March 9th, 1913. After operating for several years it ceased its activities on account of the small number of Jews in the community.

Saskatoon Lodge No. 739, Saskatoon

Saskatoon Lodge No. 739 was instituted on June 27th, 1919, and notwithstanding that the Jewish community in Saskatoon is small the lodge is functioning in a very creditable manner.

Louis D. Brandeis Lodge No. 833, Regina

Louis D. Brandeis Lodge was instituted on the 4th day of August, 1913, but after being in existence for ten years it ceased to exist. The re-organization of the lodge is, however, being considered. The lodge took a leading part in building the new Regina Hebrew School at a cost of approximately $45,000. It also established a loan fund of $3,000 to assist the poor in the community.

Samuel Lodge No. 668, Vancouver

Instituted fifteen years ago on the 24th day of July, 1910, Samuel Lodge has played an important part in the Jewish communal life of Vancouver and almost every Jewish organization in the city owes its existence to the enthusiasm of its one hundred and fifty members. The plans for the formation of the Hebrew School, the building of the new Synagogue and the re-organization of the Hebrew Aid Society were all formulated within the lodge and carried out by committees of the lodge. During the war, the lodge took a prominent part in the various Victory Loan drives.

Possibly the most important work undertaken by Samuel Lodge has been the handling of immigrants arriving at the port of Vancouver. With only volunteer help the lodge has handled over three thousand immigrants.

For the first time in the history of Canadian B'nai B'rith, District Grand Lodge No. 4 held its convention at Vancouver in 1924. A great deal of credit for the present high standing of the lodge is due to Max M. Grossman, J. B. Jaffe, A. H. Fleischman, A. G. Hirschberg and A. C. Cohen, who have served as presidents.

Victoria Lodge No. 758, Victoria

Victoria Lodge instituted on July 19th, 1914, is the successor to the third oldest B'nai B'rith lodge established in Canada. With a membership of only fifteen in a Jewish community of twenty families, the lodge is looking after the interests of the community in a very creditable manner. The following have served as presidents of the lodge;—Dr. S. H. Hartman, I. Warshock, I. M. Nodek, J. B. Jaffe, J. Datz, J. Rose, L. J. Levy, H. Burns and H. A. Mallik.

United Efforts by Canadian Lodges

While, as hereinbefore stated, all Canadian Lodges are under the jurisdiction of Grand Lodges having their headquarters in the United States, the Canadian Lodges recognize that they have Canadian problems which can be dealt with more advantageously by themselves than by District Grand Lodges in another country.

The spread of the Order in Western Canada prompted Winnipeg Lodge to form a Sister Lodge's Committee to keep in touch with other lodges. Common interests and common problems required constant communication between the lodges.

In November, 1920, a Canadian Anti-Defamation Committee was formed. The committee was as follows;—Chairman, Max Steinkopf; Treasurer, S. L. Goldstine; Secretary, Rabbi H. J. Samuel; together with one local representative appointed by each lodge.

This action did not at first meet with the approval of the Constitution Grand Lodge, but at its meeting in Washington, in May, 1921, which was attended by Rabbi Samuel, the Executive Committee of the Order changed its attitude, and the Canadian Anti-Defamation Committee was sanctioned and given full authority to function. This committee very soon justified its existence. It began to operate when the Ford agitation was showing an influence in Canada. The Ford agitation was, however, only part of the problem. English papers having a large circulation in Canada contained a great amount of anti-Jewish propaganda connected with the Morning Post charges of "World Revolution" and the publication of the forged "Protocols of Nulus." As an antidote the committee supplied the Western Canadian press with articles refuting this nonsense. Five hundred copies of the Chief Rabbi's "Book of Jewish Thoughts" and one hundred copies of Lucien Wolf's "The Myth of the Jewish Menace" were distributed amongst university professors, school principals, high school teachers, government and municipal officials, the clergy, the judiciary and other public men.

A second conference of Canadian Lodges was held in Winnipeg in January, 1922, and was attended by delegates from the Toronto and Hamilton lodges of District Grand Lodge No. 1, the Vancouver and Victoria Lodges of District Grand Lodge No. 4, and all the lodges of District Grand Lodge No. 6. For two days the thirty delegates of the said lodges discussed the problems of Canadian Jewry. This Conference confirmed the Canadian Anti-Defamation Committee and created a provisional council of Canadian lodges.

A Committee on Canadian Affairs was appointed at the Convention of District Grand Lodge No. 6, held at Duluth in July, 1923, and the establishment of a Canadian Council for District Grand Lodge No. 6 was approved. The Convention also created the office of Director of Canadian Affairs, the person so appointed to be a member of the General Committee and to have supervision over the activities of the Canadian Lodges of the District.

At the Convention of District Grand Lodge No. 1, at New York in 1924, the following paragraph appeared in the writer's report as Chairman of Canadian Activities:

"I would, however, like to point out that Canadian Lodges have problems separate and distinct from the lodges of the United States, and at a conference just held it was unanimously resolved that a deliberative body be formed, to be known as "A Conference of Canadian Lodges in District Grand Lodge No. 1" to be composed of representatives of the various Canadian Lodges in the District, for the purpose of deliberating upon questions which particularly affect Canadian Lodges, and making recommendations to the District Grand Lodge. I feel sure that the formation of such a body for the purpose aforesaid will go a long way to strengthen the position of B'nai B'rith in Canada."

Since the convention, "A Conference of Canadian Lodges of District Grand Lodge No. 1" has been formed. All the lodges in the District are represented in the conference, which is governed by a constitution of its own. The Chairman of Canadian Activities on the General Committee from time to time is Chairman of the Conference. Thus there is always a link uniting the Canadian Lodges to the General Committee of the District Grand Lodge. The first meeting of the Conference was held at Montreal on the eighth day of February, 1925. The following officers were elected:— Chairman, Marcus Sperber, K.C., Montreal; Secretary, Isidor Markus, Toronto; Treasurer, Nathan Phillips, Toronto; Vice-Presidents, L. M. Singer, Toronto, H. R. Cohen, Montreal, Dr. H. Dover, Ottawa and M. Levy, Hamilton.

The spirit of B'nai B'rith in Canada has been planted in fertile soil. The seed sown has taken root, and the fruits of the efforts put forth are plainly discernible in the communities in which lodges exist. The future of B'nai B'rith in Canada is assured.

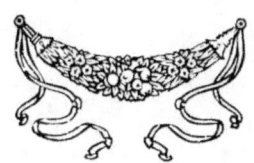

A. BROOKSTONE, J.P., TORONTO

ARTHUR BROOKSTONE was born in Toronto, May 17th, 1872, the son of the late Sinai and Louisa (Fogler) Brookstone. He was educated in the public schools of Toronto, and then entered the jewellery trade, in 1910 starting the business in which he is still actively engaged. In 1917, he was appointed Justice of Peace for the City of Toronto. Mr. Brookstone is one of the outstanding Jewish members of the Masonic Order in Toronto. In May, 1900, he joined Alpha Lodge, No. 334, and September, 1900, Antiquity Chapter, No. 91. There being considerable objection to accepting Jews in the existing lodges, Mr. Brookstone saw the necessity for a Lodge of Jewish persuasion, and with the assistance of three Past Masters of Alpha Lodge, in 1913 was instrumental in the founding of a Lodge for members of the Jewish faith only. It was named Mount Sinai Lodge in honor of the name of Mr. Brookstone's father, and also owing to the fact that his life had shortly before been saved by an operation performed at the Mount Sinai Hospital of New York. In 1916, the Mount Sinai Lodge had a membership of over four hundred, and Mr. Brookstone was instrumental in founding a Royal Arch Chapter on the same lines, which was called by the same name. At the time he was Worshipful Master of the Lodge, and in 1920, he was made Principal of the Chapter. Mr. Brookstone helped to resurrect the Royal and Select Masters which had been dormant in Canada for twenty-five years, and he is now Grand Treasurer for Canada of the Grand Council of the R. & S. M. with the title of Rt. Ill. Comp. He also represents Florida in the Grand Council for Canada in the R. & S. M. He was instrumental in suggesting the formation of Palestine Lodge, A.F. & A.M., and it was he who suggested the name that was adopted. On retiring from the various ruling chairs, he was presented with magnificent jewels. Mr. Brookstone is a life member of Mount Sinai Lodge; Mount Sinai Chapter; and King Solomon's Chapter, No. 22. He was Regent of the Beaver Council, Royal Arcanum, and for twenty-five years he has been a member of the Order of Foresters. He is a lifelong member of the Holy Blossom Synagogue.

HISTORICAL SKETCH OF MOUNT SINAI LODGE A.F. & A.M., NO. 522, G.R.C.

MOUNT Sinai Lodge owes its inception to Bro. A. Brookstone, a well known member of Alpha Lodge, in which he was initiated as long ago as May, 1900. It had long been his desire to see the formation of such a Lodge, and he eventually succeeded in interesting several of his brethren of Alpha Lodge in the movement. R. W. Bro. Harry Scully, a popular P.M. of Alpha and a recent D.D.G.M. of District 11, was among the first to offer active assistance, and R. W. Bro. Geo. Tait, also a P.D.D.G.M. of District 11, another P.M. of Alpha, and W. Bro. W. Porteous, also expressed their willingness to join in the proposal, so that it may fairly be said that Alpha Lodge was the parent of Mount Sinai Lodge.

Bro. J. D. Bland, an old friend of Bro. Brookstone, and a life member of Wilson Lodge, also agreed to assist, and on his introduction W. Bro. C. E. Garrard (an English Mason) P. Prov. Gd. Reg. of Essex, England, offered his services as Secretary.

A meeting of those interested was then held at Bro. Brookstone's office on October 27th, 1913, at which W. Bro. Garrard was appointed Secretary (pro tem.), and instructed to prepare the necessary petition to the G.M. for a Dispensation.

The necessary number of signatures were readily obtained, among them being W. Bros. J. D. Bailey, Ashlar Lodge, and S. E. Hall (also of Alpha), Bro. A. L. Tinker, Wilson Lodge, and Bro. S. Nankin, of Jasper Lodge, Edmonton, Alta.

Application in accordance with the Constitution was then made to the Lodges in the District for their consent to the grant of the Dispensation, and it is worthy of mention that the reply of one Lodge only prevented a unanimous consent of all those appealed to, several of the Lodges passing resolutions of very kind welcome to the proposition.

These preliminaries having been completed, and R. W. Bro. Scully, R. W. Bro. G. Tait and W. Bro. Porteous having been respectively nominated as the first Master and Wardens, the petition was duly forwarded to R. W. Bro. J. Stephens, then D.D.G.M.

The Gd. Master having granted the Dispensation, a special meeting was held on Saturday, March 14th, 1914, at the Freemasons' Hall, College Street, to receive it and for the formal opening of the Lodge. R. W. Bro. Stephens, D.D.G.M., occupied the chair and performed the ceremony of inauguration, assisted by W. Bro. Charlton, Dir. of Ceremonies, and other distinguished brethren. The Dispensation was read by W. Bro. W. Birrell, Dist. Sec., and afterwards delivered to R. W. Bro. H. C. Scully, who named his officers as follows, viz:—R. W. Bro. G. Tait, S.W.; W. Bro. W. Porteous, J.W.; W. Bro. C. E. Garrard, Secy.; Bro. A. Brookstone, S.D.; Bro. J. D. Bland, J.D.; Bro. A. L. Tinker, S.S.; Bro. S. Nankin, I.G.; Bro. Jas. Davis, Tyler.

It may be a matter of interest to mention that the name of the Lodge was suggested by Bro. Brookstone, not alone from its scriptural connection, but as a remembrance of benefits received in Mount Sinai Hospital at New York.

The Lodge having been thus established it was at once seen that a real necessity for it had existed, and applications for membership came quickly—15 being handed in to the Secretary before the close of the inauguration meeting.

The first regular meeting of the Lodge was held on the site of the proposed new Masonic Hall on Spadina Road, and was honored by the presence of the M. W. the G. M., W. D. McPherson, Esq., K.C., M.P.P.; R. W. Bro. J. Stephens, D.D.G.M., and several other distinguished brethren.

During the short period remaining before the summer recess 17 candidates were initiated, and at the meeting of Grand Lodge held at Niagara in the July following, the Warrant of Constitution of Mount Sinai Lodge No. 522 on the Grand Roll of Canada was formally granted. The consecration and constitution of the Lodge took place on October 16th, 1914, the new D.D. G.M., R. W. Bro. G. H. Smith, being the Consecrating Officer, assisted by the following Grand Officers, viz;— W. Bro. Rev. W. J. Armitage, P.G. Chap.; R. W. Bro. C. E. Edmunds, Gd. D. of C.; R. W. Bro. E. M. Carleton, Gd. Sec'y., etc., etc.

R. W. Bro. Harry C. Scully was again appointed W.M., and invested his officers as above mentioned, with the addition of Bro. A. I. Willinsky, Chap.; Bro. M. G. de Y. Greenberg, Treas.; W. Bro. J. D. Bailey, D. of C.; Bro. E. R. Sugarman, J.S.; Bro. Isadore Feldman, I.G.; Bro. M. S. Stein, Org.

At the regular meeting held on the 12th day of January, 1915, after notice of motion in that behalf had been given, the following members were unanimously elected Honorary Members of the Lodge in appreciation of their efforts in its formation, viz;—R. W. Bro. H. C. Scully, W.M.; R. W. Bro. G. Tait, S.W.; W. Bro. W. Porteous, J.W.; W. Bro. C. E. Garrard, Secy.; Bro. A. Brookstone, S.D.; Bro. J. D. Bland, J.D.; Bro. A. L. Tinker, J.S., and S. Nankin, I.G.

During the first year, 27 candidates were initiated, and the Lodge at the present time numbers over 400 members.

From the time of its institution the Lodge has received great assistance from W. Bros. T. Barber, T. J. Bennett and W. Moull, in addition to the names already mentioned, and on January 8th, 1918, W. Bros. Barber, Bennett and Moull were elected Honorary Members of the Lodge as some slight recognition of their valuable services. Similar compliments were also paid to the Rev. J. Bennett Anderson and the late Rabbi Solomon Jacobs.

The following have been presiding officers of the Lodge since its inception;—Wor. Bros., Arthur Brookstone, 1916; J. D. Bland, 1917; A. L. Tinker, 1918-19; S. Stein, 1920; J. J. de Young Greenberg, 1921; J. B. Danson, 1922; L. M. Singer, 1923; S. M. Hansher, 1924.

The officers for 1925 are as follows;—W. Bro. Isidor Finberg, W.M.; W. Bro. S. M. Hansher, I.P.M.; Bro. A. Singer, S.W.; Bro. S. Factor, J.W.; W. Bro. J. B. Danson, Chaplain; Bro. H. R. Fox, Treasurer; W. Bro. C. E. Garrard, Secretary; Bro. M. G. Cohen, Asst. Secretary; W. Bro. L. M. Singer, D. of C.; Bro. A. Clavir, S.D.; Bro. N. Phillips, J.D.; Bro. B. Seigler, I.G.; Bro. B. Luxenberg, S.S.; Bro. M. Cooper, J.S.; Bro. M. Stein, Organist; and Bro. J. Davies, Tyler.

HISTORICAL SKETCH OF PALESTINE LODGE A.F. & A.M., NO. 559, G.R.C.

AT a meeting held on September 10th, 1919, at the residence of Brother Morris Phillips, 686 Bloor Street West, Toronto, it was decided that the interests of the Craft in general would be advanced by the formation of another Masonic Lodge, and as a result, the preliminary steps in the formation of Palestine Lodge were undertaken. Petitions were sent to the various Lodges of the jurisdiction for their consent. The petition bore the following names;—W. Bro. Edward J. Repath, Harmony Lodge, No. 438, G.R.C.; R. W. Bro. George Tait, St. Andrew's Lodge, No. 16, G.R.C.; Bro. Ed. Fellman, Mt. Sinai Lodge, No. 522, G.R.C.; Bro. Nathan Blumbergh, Harmony Lodge, No. 438, G.R.C.; Bro. M. Joel Singer, St. John's Lodge, No. 75, G.R.C.; Bro. Rabbi Jacobs, Mt. Sinai Lodge, No. 522, G.R.C.; Bro. Laurie Blumbergh, High Park Lodge, No. 531, G.R.C.; Bro. Morris Phillips, Mt. Sinai Lodge, No. 522, G.R.C.; Bro. E. Frederick Singer, St. Albans Lodge, No. 514, G.R.C.; Bro. William N. Winkler, Mt. Sinai Lodge, No. 522, G.R.C.; Bro. Harry Turofsky, Mt. Sinai Lodge, No. 522, G.R.C.; and Bro. Harry Melvin, Tuscan Lodge, No. 541, G.R.C.

This sanction having been obtained, the petition was duly presented to Right Worshipful Brother Ernest W. E. Saunders, the District Deputy Grand Master, Toronto District, No. 11b, and a favorable report being presented from him to the Most Worshipful the Grand Master, Frederick W. Harcourt, a dispensation was granted, authorizing the formation of Palestine Lodge.

The Institution Ceremonies were held on January 28th, 1920, under the direction of Rt. Wor. Bro. Ernest W. E. Saunders, the D.D.G.M., assisted by Rt. Wor. Bro. Tim Barber, G.S.W.; R. Wor. Bro. J. Tanner, G.J.W.; Rt. Wor. Bro. Geo. Purchase, Grand Chaplain; V. Wor. Bro. C. H. C. Wright, and other Grand Lodge Officers. The proceedings were attended by fully three hundred members of the Craft. The dispensation being announced, Wor. Bro. Edward J. Repath was called to the East to assume the gavel and directed to preside over the Lodge as the First Worshipful Master.

From this date, splendid progress was made, petitions for initiation being presented from many men of high character and standing in the community, and when the Worshipful Master presented the petition for a warrant to the Grand Lodge in annual session at Niagara Falls, Ontario, on July 21st, 1920, the Charter was immediately granted, and the organization was duly entered on the Grand Register of Canada as Palestine Lodge, No. 559.

The Brethren were of the opinion that very distinguished ceremonies should mark the Consecration of this Lodge. This took place at the Regular Meeting, held on October 27th, 1920, under the personal direction of the Most Worshipful the Grand Master, Fred W. Harcourt, who was assisted by forty-four other Grand Lodge Officers. The ceremonies were given with full musical ritual, and were attended by one of the largest and most representative gatherings ever held under Masonic auspices in the City of Toronto.

During the course of the evening, Bro. Arthur Cohen presented to the Lodge, various necessary paraphernalia, gifts from the brethren as follows;—

Volume of Sacred Law and Square, and Compasses by Bro. Abraham Cohen. Three Gavels by Bros. Nathan Blumbergh, Laurie Blumbergh and Milton Blumbergh. Set of Wands by Bro. Gordon T. Williams. Set of Working Tools by Bros. M. Joel Singer, E. Fred. Singer, Abe Singer, Israel Singer and Isador Singer. Altar Cloth by Bros. Abraham Rosenthal and William Rosenthal. Director of Ceremonies' Baton by Bro. Louis Soren. Candidates Suits by Bro. A. Lipson.

On behalf of the Lodge, Bro. Charles Draimin presented to a representative of the Toronto General Hospital Trust, who was present, a cheque for two thousand dollars, to perpetually endow a cot in that institution to be known as the "Palestine Lodge Cot."

The following brethren, M. W. Bro. Fred. W. Harcourt, R. W. Bro. W. N. Ponton, R. W. Bro. Ernest W. E. Saunders and Bro. the Hon. William Renwick Riddell, having been elected Honorary Members with full privileges at a previous meeting were then presented with Honorary Membership certificates.

The proceedings at the "Fourth Degree" were marked by an elaborate banquet and programme of entertainment, and distinguished by the presence of many ladies, who were invited by the members of the Lodge.

Thus Palestine Lodge was launched upon its career under splendid auspices and with excellent promise of success.

The officers of the Lodge for 1925 are;—Wor. Bros. Dr. Abraham Brodey, W.M.; E. Frederick Singer, I.P.M.; William Gittes, S.W.; Abraham Singer, J.W.; Rabbi B. R. Brickner, Chaplain; Harry Rosenthal, Treasurer; Harry Melvin, Secretary; Louis Greisman, Asst. Secretary; M. J. Singer, D. of C.; Egmont L. Frankel, S.D.; Laurie Blumbergh, J.D.; Carl M. Frankel; I.G.; Abraham Cohen, S.S.; Murray Draimin, J.S., Dr. Bernard Schaffer, Organist; C. Godkin, Tyler.

MOUNT SINAI CHAPTER, ROYAL ARCH MASONS, NO. 212, G.R.C.

MOUNT Sinai Chapter owes its origin to Mount Sinai Lodge, A.F. & A.M. Ex. Comp. Brookstone, the second Master of that Lodge, having enlisted the sympathies of Rt. Ex. Comp. E. J. Repath, a well-known figure in Capitular Masonry in Toronto, and with the aid of a number of his Craft brethren obtained numerous signatures to a petition to the Most Ex. First Principal, A. S. Gorell. Among the other signatories were V. Ex. Comp. Porteous, Ex. Comp. C. H. B. Johnson, Ex. Comp. A. L. Tinker and Comp. Bland, all of King Solomon's Chapter; Comp. W. Moull, St. Patrick's Chapter; Ex. Comp. W. Riddell, Antiquity Chapter; all of whom became officers of the Chapter on its institution. The petition being favorably received by the then Grand Superintendent, R. Ex. Comp. G. L. Gardiner, and recommended by him, the Grand Z. also approved and granted the Dispensation, and on February 19th, 1918, the new Chapter was formally instituted by Rt. Ex. Comp. Gardiner, assisted by the Grand Scribe E., R. Ex. Comp. H. T. Smith; Rt. Ex. Comp. R. J. Reade and V. Ex. Comp. H. Hardy, and immediately got to work. Thirty four applications for membership, all from members of Mount Sinai Lodge, were handed in at the Institution meeting and ballotted for at the first Regular Convocation. Rt. Ex. Comp. E. J. Repath was appointed 1st Principal, Comp. A. Brookstone, 2nd Principal, and Comp. J. D. Bland, 3rd Principal; Comp. C. E. Garrard, Scribe E.; Ex. Comp. C. H. B. Johnson, Scribe N., and Comp. W. Moull, P. Soj. A large number of Royal Arch Masons from the city and outside Chapters attended to start the new Chapter on its way and the outlook for a successful Chapter was very bright.

Nor has this promise been in any way disappointing as up to the time of writing this sketch a goodly number of the best members of Mount Sinai Lodge have sought and obtained further light in this Chapter. At the postponed Convocation of Grand Chapter held at Toronto in May, 1919, the warrant for the Chapter was issued and on October 21st, 1919, the ceremony of Consecration and Dedication was performed by the newly-elected Grand Z., W. N. Ponton, Esq., K.C., assisted by the greater number of his Grand Chapter officers and in the presence of a majority of the Ruling 1st Principals and leading R. A. Masons of the city.

The first elections of the Warranted Chapter took place December 2, 1919, Ex. Comp. Brookstone being elected 1st Principal and Comps. W. Moull and L. M. Singer 2nd and 3rd Principals, and the first Installation was held on January 6th, 1920, conducted by Rt. Ex. Comp. G. L. Gardiner, P.G.S., assisted by Rt. Ex. Comp. H. T. Smith, G.S.E.; Rt. Ex. Comp. R. J. Reade, P.G.S.; V. Ex. Comp. H. Hardy, these being the same officials who officiated at the institution, when the following officers were installed and invested, viz.; Ex. Comp. Arthur Brookstone, Z.; R. Ex. Comp. E. J. Repath, I.P.Z.; Ex. Comp. Wm. Moull, H.; Ex. Comp. Louis M. Singer, J.; Comp. C. E. Garrard, Scribe E.; Comp. Ed. Bernstein, Scribe H.; R. Ex. Comp. A. L. Tinker, Treasurer; Comp. Isidor Finberg, P.S.; Comp. Maurice Phillips, S.S.; Comp. Michael Berwitz, J.S.; Ex. Comp. John D. Bland, Chaplain; V. Ex. Comp. Wm. Porteous, D. of C.; Comp. Abe Cohen, M. of 4th Veil; Comp. A. W. Lipson, M. of 3rd Veil; Comp. Harty Tait, M. of 2nd Veil; Comp. Louis Prager, M. of 1st Veil; Comp. Abe. Singer, Standard Bearer; Comp. Abraham Singer, Sword Bearer; Comp. Isaac Soskin, Steward; Comp. Isidore Bernstein, Steward; Comp. Mark Hands, Steward; Comp. Murray Wilson, Steward; Ex. Comp. W. Dalton, Janitor.

The present officers are;—Ex. Comps. Mark G. Cohen, Z.; Edward P. Bernstein, I.P.Z.; A.M. Clavir, H.; H. R. Fox, J.; B. Silverberg, S.E.; F Schipper, S.N.; A. Brookstone, Treasurer; V. Ex. Comp. I. Finberg, D. of C.; Comps. B. Seigler, P.S.; M. Cooper, S.S.; B. Luxenburg, J.S.; H. Alexander, M. 4th V.; M. Rosenthal, M. 3rd V.; A. Fox, M. 2nd V.; S. Eisen, M. 1st V.; M. Wilkes, Stand. Bearer; Mort. L. Levy, Sword Bearer; Mark Levy, Steward; Ben Kassel, Steward; C. H. Godkin, Janitor.

JEWISH INTERESTS IN MASONRY IN THE EARLY DAYS OF BRITISH COLUMBIA

JEWS have always taken a keen interest in Masonry from the time of its inauguration in British Columbia.

Among the charter members of Victoria Lodge was Kady Gambitz who established the first dry goods business in Victoria. Of the twenty-one members of Victoria Lodge in its first year, six were Jews, among them being included Lumby Franklin, who later became Worshipful Master and who was the third Mayor of Victoria City, and Gustav Sutro and Lewis Wolff, tobacconists, Moses Sperberg and Samuel Goldstone, merchants, and John Malownowsky, also a charter member of the lodge. Seilim Franklin, another charter member, was keenly interested in public affairs and entered politics, being elected a member of the Provincial Legislature.

The first occasion in which the Masons of Victoria held a public ceremony, was the occasion of the laying of the corner-stone of the Synagogue at the corner of Pandora and Blanchard Streets, on June 2nd, 1863. In the corner-stone of the Synagogue is a vellum scroll in a sealed bottle, which reads:-

"The corner-stone of this edifice was laid in due form on the second day of June A. L. 5863, A.D. 1863, by a Provincial Grand Lodge of the Province of British Columbia, consisting of Victoria Lodge, No. 1085, held under the United Grand Lodge of England, of which Thomas Dundas, Earl of Zetland, is Grand Master; and Vancouver Lodge, No. 421, held under the Grand Lodge of Scotland, of which the Duke of Atholl is Grand Master. The names of the officers and members of each lodge will be found in a copy of the bye-laws." (N.B. These were also deposited in the stone.)

It was a gala event. The band of H.M.S. Topaz came from Esquimalt. The congregation was also met by the Germania Sing Verein, at their rooms on Yates Street, and the procession then marched to the Star and Garter Hotel, where the Hebrew and French Benevolent Societies and St. Andrew's Society joined, and the parade went on to the corner of Yates and Langley Streets where the two Masonic Lodges met, and about seventy strong, joined the procession to the site, where the Masonic fraternity was ranged on northeast, other societies on the southern side, and a large platform was built for the ladies.

THE YOUNG MEN'S HEBREW ASSOCIATION, MONTREAL

AFTER several unsuccessful attempts had been made to organize a Young Men's Hebrew Association in Montreal, the day at last arrived when definite steps were taken that led to the formation of the present Y.M.H.A.

On April 8th, 1908, a group of young men met under the auspices of the Disraeli Conservative Political Club in the old Standard Hall at the corner of St. Lawrence and St. Catherine Streets. During the progress of this meeting a suggestion was made from the floor to organize a Y.M.H.A. The majority of those present approved of this suggestion and with this purpose in view it was decided to call a meeting for the following week at the Baron de Hirsch Institute. This was actually the initial meeting at which the Y.M.H.A. was formally organized. An election of officers was held, and Mr. Marcus Sperber was elected president.

In a comparatively short time the membership grew to 60, and meetings were held every Sunday. At this period, however, no definite activities or inducements were offered to the members so that their numbers steadily decreased until only ten enthusiasts were left. These ten members decided that if the organization was to continue drastic steps would have to be taken to further its interests with the community, otherwise it was felt that their labours would have been in vain and the idea of a Y.M.H.A. would come to an untimely end.

On January 1st 1910, a house was rented at 54 Ontario Street West at a rental of $25 per month. There being only $15 in the treasury these ten men formed themselves into a board of directors and assessed themselves $2.50 each, bringing their bank balance up to $40. These ten directors constitute the founders of the organization that has steadily continued in growth from that period and has reached the status that it now enjoys. The names of these directors are;—Messrs. M. Soskin, W. Singer, C. Schnaer, S. Rawson, S. Goldfield, L. Golland, N. W. Goldstein, M. Singer, D. Spector, and M. Goldberg. The first month's rent was paid, together with a commission of $5 to the agent. A deposit of $9 was given for furniture, which was bought on the instalment plan. With $1 left the Association started on its activities. Nothing daunted by the lack of funds this handful of enthusiasts started a series of activities that consisted of literary work, boxing, wrestling and gymnastics. At this stage some of the prominent citizens of the community became interested and a meeting was arranged at which the sum of $350 was raised. The donations were started by ex-alderman James Robinson, a non-Jew, with $100, who who thus became the first life member. The Y.M.H.A. of Montreal undoubtedly owes a debt of gratitude to this public-spirited man who has since departed this life, and whose initiative and broadmindedness acted as an example to others, and who thus helped to stimulate the interest in an organization that was an absolute necessity in the community. The members now commenced to increase rapidly, and on the 10th of March, 1910, the Association was incorporated by charter under the Provincial law. The following is a list of the charter members;—Messrs. W. Singer, N. W. Goldstein, Solomon Goldfield, Simon Rawson, Morris Goldberg, Lazarus Golland, Charles Schnaer, Daniel Spector, W. W. Sweedler, H. Gold, Morris Soskin, Abraham Albert, and Max Singer.

On May 1st, 1910, a move was made to more convenient quarters at 52 Ontario Street West. Additional activities were undertaken, and Mr. Charles Lambert volunteered his services which were gratefully accepted and he was appointed honorary physical director. He also conceived the idea of a Y.M.H.A. orchestra. This he organized and it is still in existence, having met with continued success. Financial troubles again loomed on the horizon and the directors had to finance the organization from their own pockets. Finally through the efforts of Mr. Bernard Rose who had early been an interested and active member, sufficient funds were obtained from several Jewish citizens to tide the organization over its difficulties. The following year the Association moved to larger premises on St. Charles Borromee Street, now known as Clarke St. The rental here was $35 per month. Once more the financial status became critical, the general trend was towards discouragement and in consequence the membership began to dwindle and continued to decline until finally the organization was constituted of practically the ten directors and a few junior members. It seemed as if the years spent in hard work were to be all in vain.

At this juncture the interest of a prominent citizen, Mr. Jacob Goldstein, was attracted, and in January, 1912, he was elected president. Due to his intense activity the financial troubles were eliminated; old members returned, new ones were enrolled and the organization was once more in full swing. Mr. Goldstein's entrance into the institution marks the most successful epoch in its history and it is entirely due to him that the organization began to advance rapidly and constitute itself a power in the community. The time now arrived to look for more spacious quarters, and on May 1st, 1912, the opportunity presented itself of obtaining the building previously occupied by the St. Patrick's Amateur Athletic Association at 492 St. Urbain Street. The building consisted of three stories and a basement, and adjoining this was a gymnasium. In the fall of the same year a membership campaign was held which resulted in the addition of 1260 names to the roll. However, as there was not sufficient accommodation for this number, unfortunately most of the new members dropped off. Another factor that caused the loss of many members about this time was the condemning of the gymnasium in 1913. Since the gymnasium activities were a prominent feature of the organization this was indeed a heavy blow. To offset this a paid secretary was engaged to devote his time to reorganizing and creating other activities. The basketball team coached by Mr. Lambert managed to secure the use of the Shamrock A.A.A. gymnasium and continued their work so successfully in spite of their handicaps that they succeeded in capturing the championship of the Shamrock League. The orchestra, which had begun to attract considerable attention, progressed favourably under the leadership of J. J. Gagnier. Mr. Sol Kellert became its patron and his valuable interest in the Association was thus established. Mr. Kellert has ever since maintained his interest in the Y.M.H.A. and is indeed a power of support to the institution. The question of revenue to continue the work of the Association again occupied the attention of the board of directors, and as the membership fees did not produce sufficient income various other revenue producing activities were decided upon, such as the annual dance and dramatic play. These have become permanent features of the Y.M.H.A. work.

The membership began to grow rapidly, so that the building was found to be inadequate, and on May 1st, 1916, another move was made. The new quarters were at 283 Sherbrooke Street West. They were similar in style to the old building but much larger. There was still no gymnasium however, but classes were held once a week at the Montreal High School, and by the kind permission of the Shamrock A.A.A. basketball was practised at their gymnasium.

January 1st, 1917, marked the entrance into the Association of Alderman Louis Rubenstein, probably the most prominent sportsman in Canada. Mr. Rubenstein became president of the Association and proved a stepping stone to the success of the institution. His previous experience in similar organizations was of great benefit and under his leadership, combined with the interest of Messrs. Kellert and Goldstein the Association was established on a firm basis.

The younger active members realized the necessity of a gymnasium and clamoured for a bigger building with a gymnasium and a swimming pool. In consequence in September 1918, a campaign was held to obtain funds for a new building and about $20,000 was raised. This sum was not sufficient for the requirements and was laid aside to be used at a more opportune moment. The occasion arose when the Shamrock A.A.A. decided to dispose of their building at 697 St. Urbain Street. This was exactly suitable for the Y.M.H.A. as it was being used by a similar organization for a similar purpose, and the sum of money involved was within the reach of the Association. The purchase was made with the funds on hand and the small additional sum necessary was raised by a mortgage on the building. On April 1st, 1920, the Association moved into this building, establishing themselves in their own home and now possessing their own gymnasium. The latter proved to be a great incentive and a large number of new members was enrolled.

Mr. Charles Lambert was officially engaged as superintendent and physical director and also continued his work as manager of the orchestra. Business and professional men's classes were organized, thus bringing into the Association for the first time a new type of member which has since turned out to be of the greatest value to the Association. With the increased facilities the activities of the Association increased in scope and now included literary work, dramatic societies, gymnasium, orchestra and choral work; chess and checkers, billiards, etc. Religion was not neglected and services which had been commenced in previous premises were now carried out regularly.

In March, 1921, the Association received the sum of $1,000 which had been left by the bequest of the late Mr. Lazarus Cohen, president of the Shaar Hashomayim Congregation, who was a noted Hebrew scholar and a power in the community. This gracious bequest was used to pay off a portion of the steadily decreasing mortgage.

For several years the basketball teams of the Association had been forging ahead and had won an enviable reputation for themselves in the various leagues in which they were entered. In April 1923, they crowned themselves with glory when their first team in the Intermediate Section won the city championship. They were then invited to play the senior champions for the honour of representing Montreal in the inter-city games. They surprised their most ardent supporters by winning this signal honour. The success of this team turned the eyes of the members more forcibly to the gymnasium, which was an old wooden structure, and in a rather dilapidated condition. Mr. M. Levitt, the captain of the team, suggested that a new gymnasium be built and this suggestion was favourably received by the Board, who appointed Mr. Levitt as chairman of a committee to raise the necessary funds. About $7,000 was quickly obtained and in October 1923, the new gymnasium of brick and steel, constructed at a cost of about $11,000 was ready for use; the additional amount of money being obtained by a mortgage on the building.

The new gymnasium resulted in another increase in membership which now stands at about one thousand. The members are now looking forward to the time, which they hope is not far distant, when a modern structure embracing all the activities of the Y.M.H.A. in its fullest sense will be erected and be a model institution in our midst.

The Association is a member of the Young Men's Hebrew and Kindred Associations merged with the Jewish Welfare Board, New York, and has benefitted from the regular visits of their field secretary.

Following is a list of the present Board of Directors: Hon. Presidents, Sir M. B. Davis and Mr. J. Goldstein; President, Alderman Louis Rubenstein; Vice-President, Mr. Frank Bender; Treasurer, Mr. Harry Gordon; Hon. Secretary, Mr. Moe Levitt. Directors: Messrs. Louis Cohen, Philip Meyerovitch, Morris Goldberg, Norman Friedman, Leon Levin, Jos. Steinhouse. Hon. Directors: Messrs. Sol. Kellert, Sam Robinson.

YOUNG WOMEN'S HEBREW ASSOCIATION, MONTREAL

ONE of the most praiseworthy Jewish philanthropic institutions in Montreal is the Young Women's Hebrew Association. It was organized in the Spring of 1913 as THE FRIENDLY LEAGUE OF JEWISH WOMEN, for the purpose of bringing into the lives of self-supporting young women opportunities for moral, mental, physical and social improvement, and also to befriend young girls and women whenever necessary. It had its origin at a meeting of ladies held in the Baron de Hirsch Institute, upon the invitation of Mrs. J. Goldstein. The need of organised effort in behalf of young girls and women was discussed and it was unanimously decided that the ladies should especially interest themselves in those young girls and women whose incomes yield them but a bare living, and who in consequence are denied opportunities for self improvement and wholesome amusement. An organization was then formed and the drafting of the Constitution and By-Laws was left to the newly appointed Chairman, Mrs. Clarence I. de Sola. At a subsequent largely attended meeting, the Constitution and By-Laws were adopted and the following officers were elected:—President, Mrs. Clarence I. de Sola; First Vice-President, Mrs. J. Goldstein; Second Vice-President, Mrs. David Levi; Third Vice-President, Mrs. Jacob A. Jacobs; Recording Secretary, Miss Minnie Bernstein; Corresponding Secretary, Mrs. A. E. Morris; Financial Secretary, Miss Kirschberg; Treasurer, Mrs. Nathan Gordon; Directors, Mesdames Charles L. Friedman, I. S. Goldenstein, Alfred Michaels, J. Manolson, H. Vineberg, E. Berliner, A. Lesser, Archie Jacobs, J. S. Leo, John Michaels, I. Cohen, S. Hart, H. Wener, B. Groner, David Tannembaum, J. Kellert, M. Rabinovitch, D. H. Bernstein and Paul Ogulnik.

The first act of the Friendly League was the formation of The Welcome Club, and it was unanimously agreed to employ a Superintendent, Miss Ray Fleisig (later Mrs. Wechsler) a former teacher and social worker of London, England. Simultaneously a small group of earnest, enthusiastic young men and women voluntarily offered to give an evening or two of each week for the benefit of the Club and its members. Thus from the very birth of the Welcome Club opportunity for improvement along social, mental, moral and physical lines, was given to young girls and women, and at the same time a successful attempt was made to bridge the chasm that frequently exists between the daughters of poor parents of immigrants and their more fortunate sisters, those whose lives are sheltered from hardship and temptation. A healthy, steady growth followed both in Welcome Club members and in helpers and teachers who voluntarily contributed from one to two evenings a week for the benefit of the girls. Nor was the social side of the Club neglected, for it was realised that this side must be emphasised in order to make the attractions within the Club greater than any outside. With this object in view wholesome pleasures were provided for the toiler, who, upon her return from her work in the evening to a crowded or uninviting home, would be tempted to turn to the first pleasure offered. Dances, lectures, concerts, tobogganing parties all combined with the more serious classes in typewriting, English, French, hygiene, sewing, etc., to make the Club attractive to all its members, and the membership steadily grew.

Before many months the increase in the members necessitated the division of the Club into two sections—Senior and Junior—and these have been maintained to the present day. After several months had elapsed and when it was felt that the girls had grasped the ideals of the Welcome Club, a gathering of the Senior members was held, and they were told that from that time the Club was really their own; they were to elect their own officers, and conduct all activities in their own way, but always under the supervision of the Friendly League as an advisory board. An important phase of the League's work was the care of immigrant girls; through the Baron de Hirsch Institute the League was kept in touch with the Union for the Protection of Jewish Girls in England and the United States, and whenever any unprotected Jewish girl left for Canada the League was immediately notified so that she might be met on arrival and looked after. If she were going to continue her journey further than Montreal sister Societies were notified, but if she had elected to remain in the metropolis she was immediately taken under the wing of the Friendly League. She could become a member of the Welcome Club if she so desired, and could attend any of the classes held under the auspices of the League. Certain rooms in the Baron de Hirsch Institute were placed at the disposal of the League, and they were given the use of the kitchen, where cooking lessons could be taken by those of the girls wanting to perfect themselves in this very necessary branch of a girl's education. This good work continued for many years, the classes being changed from time to time to suit the needs and desires of the girls; for instance at one time some members wanted to learn basketry, and a basketry club was accordingly formed, at another time hammered brasswork appealed to a certain number, and this subject was put on the list of classes, and so forth, the ladies of the League feeling that it was only right to meet the wishes of the girls and give them what they wanted, and thus make the League stand for something real in the lives of the members. The classes in the necessary fundamentals, such as dressmaking, millinery, English for the foreign girls and the social evenings have continued uninterruptedly throughout the entire existence of the organization. From the earliest years a summer camp was run every year in the Laurentians, and at this camp many a poor working girl had a well needed rest and summer holiday, which she could have had in no other way. The camp programme, carried out under careful supervision, including swimming, tennis, hikes, sing-songs around the camp fire in the evenings, and a well ordered regular life, could not fail to set up the most tired city worker, and fit her after two weeks' stay there to once more take her place among the wage-earners fighting the battle of life. The first camp was at St. Margarets, on a piece of land procured through the generosity of Sir Mortimer Davis, but this was later sold and a new camp opened at Lac Brule near St. Agathe.

In 1917, when the Federation of Jewish Philanthropies was formed the Friendly League was one of the constituent societies under the Educational section, it being realised that this organization was doing a great and noble work in the preventative sphere, stepping in at that stage of girls' lives when difficulties are most prone to threaten, and when many problems seek solution. By a programme of activities healthful to both mind and body the League through the Welcome Club pointed the way to higher ideals, and helped the girls to find their happiness on sane and normal lines.

A number of Jewish girls who, wanting to join the Welcome Club, but finding the Baron de Hirsch Institute too far to reach of an evening, in October 1919, formed a group of clubs in Papineau under the wing of the parent organization, and a most successful little branch is working at that centre. The central provided them with volunteer leaders and they also rent for them club rooms, and in later years a part time paid supervisor was engaged to superintend the girls' activities.

In 1919, the first Jewish troop of Girl Guides in Montreal (6th Montreal) was formed from girls of the Welcome Club, with a membership of 50 in the first season. In 1919, the Welcome Club had outgrown its name, a large number of smaller clubs had been formed under its auspices and still the membership and interest grew, and new activities were continually being undertaken. At this time the Y.W.H.A. an organization which had been formed some nine years before, chiefly for the purpose of providing housing accommodation for Jewish business girls who had no homes of their own in the city, but which had discontinued activities in July 1918 owing to the small number of girls in residence, and the consequent high cost of administration, approached the Friendly League with a view to amalgamation. Negotiations were under way for some time, and finally by the end of the year were completed, and the season of 1920-21 recorded the beginning of the amalgamated Welcome Club and Y.W.H.A. under the name of YOUNG WOMEN'S HEBREW ASSOCIATION, with the officers and board of the late Friendly League as the Advisory Board. For some time there had been a good deal of dissatisfaction with the quarters of the Association, it being felt that better work could be done if the girls had their own house where they would feel perfectly at home in the knowledge that all was exclusively their own, after a great amount of time and energy had been spent in finding a suitable house, one was eventually found at 717 Clark Street, and here in 1924 the Y.W.H.A. opened their own Home and it has been found that the movement was well worth while, for the Association has grown steadily in number and interest, until there is now a membership of 550, most of whom are affiliated with one or more of the clubs or classes. The Papineau Neighbourhood House has a membership of 96.

The 1924 Board consists of the following ladies:— Mrs. C. I. de Sola, Hon. President; Mrs. A. E. Morris, Hon. President; Mrs. David Levi, President; Mrs. J. Elkin, First Vice-Presient; Mrs. A. Z. Cohen, Second Vice-President; Mrs. Phillip Levi, Third Vice-President; Mrs. A. J. Alexandor, Secretary. Finance Committee:— Mesdames David Levi, E. M. Berliner, A. Lesser; Education Committee:—Mesdames A. E. Morris, A. Z. Cohen, A. J. Alexander; Recreation Committee:— Mesdames J. A. Jacobs, Sydney Levitt, S. M. Ogulnik; Employment Committee:—Mesdames J. D. Kuppenheimer, S. M. Ogulnik and Miss Mary Vineberg. Directors:—Mrs. Alan J. Hart, Mrs. Vivian Hart, Miss E. Hirsch, Miss Hattie Kellert, Mrs. J. Kellert, Mrs. A. J. Jacobs, Mrs. J. Lewinsohn Mrs. M. Margolick, Mrs. John Michaels, Mrs. Paul Ogulnik.

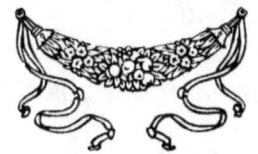

JOSEPH HARRIS, TORONTO

JOSEPH HARRIS, one of the most active welfare workers in Toronto, was born at Syracuse, N.Y., on September 22, 1870, the son of the late Ettlestone and Tobia Harris. He moved to Canada with his parents in 1876 and received his education in the public schools of that city. For a number of years he was employed with the wholesale firm of A. Bradshaw & Son, Toronto, and twenty years ago, he started the clothing business which he still conducts under his own name. Mr. Harris has always been keenly interested in communal affairs and has been particularly identified with any movements for the training of the Jewish young. To take hold of the Jewish boy and girl, when young, especially the poorer class and new arrivals in this country, and to give them the social and athletic opportunities that others are entitled to, is Mr Harris' idea. His life-long ambition has been to see a Jewish association in Toronto with all the privileges and avantages that the Y.M.C.A. and Y.W.C.A. offered to the Christian youth, and with this idea in view, some thirty years ago, he was instrumental in organizing the Young Men's Hebrew Association in Toronto. This institution was reorganized some years ago and is today known as the Young Men's and Young Women's Hebrew Association, and it appears likely that Mr. Harris' dream will shortly be realized. During the entire existence of this association, Mr. Harris has been the President. He also is an active member of the Jewish Boys' Club and takes a great interest in the boys' summer camps. He is a trustee of the Federation of Jewish Philanthropies, Toronto; and is a member of the Jewish Old Folks' Home; The Talmud Torah; and the Zionist organization. Mr. Harris was the first candidate to be initiated into the Mt. Sinai Lodge, A.F. & A.M., and he is a member of the Independent Order B'nai B'rith. He is a member of both the Holy Blossom Toronto Hebrew Congregation and Goel Tzedec (University Avenue) Synagogue, and of the Primrose Club, Toronto.

YOUNG MEN'S AND YOUNG WOMEN'S HEBREW ASSOCIATION OF TORONTO

WHATEVER merit or demerit other similar institutions may possess, they profess to be institutions managed and maintained by non-Jews, and being such they are no place for Jews. However, in the absence of anything better, there may have been some excuse, some ground, for Jewish boys to attend them, and for a time there was a very great rush to swell the ranks of Jewish members of such institutions. But the inevitable occurred as soon as their numbers reached conspicuous proportions, they became undesirable and the Y.M.H.A. idea was revived and an organization formed after many struggles and tribulations.

In the course of twenty-five years many and varied attempts were made to organize a Hebrew "Y" in Toronto, but unfortunately all were vain, struggling into existence and passing out quietly, leaving no mark. A meeting called by some Jewish business men of this city at the Strand Theatre, to consider the establishment of a "Y", also met with failure. People once more settled back in snug content, stifling their awakened consciences with the thought that Toronto was not yet ripe for such a movement. On being again aroused by a strong call from those who had faith in the possibilities of Toronto Jewry, and who believed it but wanted organization, twenty-five young men's and women's clubs answered the call and meeting at the Zionist Institute on November 27th, 1919, became the nucleus of the organization known as the Y.W.H.A. The Executive Board was built of two representatives from each of such clubs, and was presided over by Mrs. I. H. Siegel, its organizer. In this way the newly formed organization gained the support of over two thousand people, who were enthusiastic and untiring in their efforts to make the movement a success.

The work was shortly afterwards enriched by the interest of Mr. and Mrs. H. Rosenthal and of Mr. J. Harris. Temporary quarters were established at 9 Brunswick Avenue, in a residence owned by the Talmud Torah. The first home of the Y.M. & Y.W.H.A. was furnished by the donations of the affiliated clubs, and and became the centre of such activities as Friday night talks, Sunday debates, a dramatic circle, the organization of athletics, and the publication of a monthly bulletin.

Deeming it necessary to gain public recognition, an advisory board with the following personnel was called into being:—

Messrs J. Harris, E. F. Singer, A. Lipson (Deceased), J. Danson, B. Sutin, H. Rosenthal, S. Fador, J. J. DeYoung Greenberg, J. Perkins, M. Besivitz, Mesdames I. H. Siegel and H. Rosenthal.

Those clubs associated were:—

Herzl Zion, Hebrew Literary and Athletic Clubs (Sr. and Jr.), Orion Club, Felix Club, Hebrew Students, Disraeli Fraternity, Nordau Zion, D'Arcy Athletic, Imperial Legioners, Young Men's Hebrew, Judean Athletic, Independent Order of Foresters, Judah Girls, Brandeis' Girls, Kappa Delta, Alpha Kappa, Victory Girls, Herzl Girls, Boot and Shoe Society, Blossom Girls, Toronto Independent Benevolent Jubilate Club, Phœnix Social, Cheskercovah Society, Memoph Circle.

Mr. Harris and Mr. Rosenthal became very active in looking about for more adequate quarters, and for a time everyone was encouraged by the possibility of obtaining the Royal Templars' Building, Dovercourt and Queen. While negotiations were pending, several extremely successful debates were held in its halls, and these added considerable strength to the new movement, giving it the substantial recognition that helped in making it the permanent institution it now is. Many prominent people called to these meetings, proclaimed that the sight was a revelation to them, for, coming close to the young people for possibly the first time, proved not only the need, but the great future in store for such an undertaking. At this time a membership campaign was launched and proved a great success. From then on it did not seem so impossible for a "Y" to be added to our many existent organizations, and when, on the call of Mr. Harris and Mr. Joseph Singer, a plan of re-organization was worked out, the splendid response it received is evident when one pays a visit to the present quarters at 7 Brunswick Avenue, which, although only rented, meant a step forward. Through funds raised by the directors, the place has been renovated to include the conveniences they now have, which reflect great credit on these broad-visioned men. The desire is to extend the work to give the Jewish youth the accommodation they received at the Y. M. C. A., but this will require the united efforts and co-operation of every public-spirited Jewish man, woman, boy and girl. If so much was accomplished in but three years, the next five can see established a well equipped "Y" building in Toronto. The fact that it is urgently needed cannot be denied. At present, small though the quarters are, they form a veritable hive of activities under the directorship of the popular Executive-Secretary, Charles Oelbaum, successor to Miss Adelaide Cohen. The athletic work is a credit to the young people, and the literary evenings and debates prove most elevating and beneficial. The Saturday evening socials help to accommodate under a Jewish roof the youths who must dance and enjoy themselves.

The main object and ideal of this institution is a permanent building of its own, where all the facilities of first-class gym, with a swimming pool will be available, as well as quarters for literary and other activities. "One thousand members and a new bulding," is the motto.

A great deal of money was expended in fitting up the present quarters, in making them suitable even for a temporary gym; and, although confronted with what appeared insurmountable difficulties, this institution has been successful in fitting up a gym with apparatus, shower room, spacious locker room, billiard parlor, ladies' rest room, as well as an auditorium where lectures and debates are held every Sunday.

It is not what the directors of this institution would like to offer to the Toronto Jewry, but it is more than what was hoped to have in such a short existence. The greatest problem which the "Y" directors had to contend with has been the financing of this institution. To balance the "Y" budget is no easy task, especially when the opportunities offered to prospective members are not as enticing as they might be. The darkest period, however, is past, and the light is to be seen a short distance ahead. The membership of the "Y" has increased many-fold during the last year, and the business men, in particular, accepted the difficult situations as they presented themselves, with optimism and fortitude. There was a splendid broad-mindedness displayed towards all irksome, although inevitable deficiencies.

1. During the short existence of the "Y" it has enrolled 1100 members, consisting of 200 business men, 360 seniors and the balance intermediates and juniors.

2. It counts in its ranks most of the foremost Jewish athletes and embraces every branch of sport.

3. It organizes and maintains a debating league which debates every other Sunday, such debates being of

the highest order, both from the standpoint of public speaking and discussion of important live problems.

4. A Sabbath school is maintained and there is an average attendance of three hundred children.

5. It has developed championship teams in baseball, basketball and rugby, the first Jewish soccer team of this city and a host of house teams in various forms of physical activities.

6. It runs a weekly Saturday night dance maintained under the most favorable conditions and very efficient supervision.

7. It conducts semi-monthly public lectures, alternating with the Sunday debates.

8. It conducts physical classes for every grade of membership separately and under very competent and efficient instructors.

9. Five boxing tournaments were conducted on its premises, where about a hundred medals and several shields and other prizes in all were distributed.

10. The aim and object of the Y.M.H.A. of Toronto is to provide a community centre for the Jewish youth, where it will obtain recreation under proper supervision; where a healthy Jewish *esprit de corps* may be developed under suitable environment and opportunities. A healthy self-reliant and self-respecting Jewish generation will add credit to our community, to our city, and to our country.

The present officers are:—

Edmund Scheuer, Hon. President; Elly Marks, Hon. Vice-President.

Officers and Executive Committee:—Jos. Harris, President; Jos. Singer, 1st Vice-President; S. Lorie, 2nd Vice-President; Chas. Draimin, 3rd Vice-President; M. S. Till, Treasurer; Mrs. I. H. Siegel, Mrs. M. S. Till, Mrs. H. R. Wolfe, Miss Rose Manilla, Miss M. Lieberman, A. Berger, H. Clavir, B. Cross, H. Englander, B. Forer, Wm. Gittes, J. J. Glass, Harold Levy, Mort L. Levy, H. Papernick, J. Perkins, N. Phillips, R. J. Sapera, Harry Pullan, H. M. Smith, Jos. Swartz, Sam Yolles, Chas. Oelbaum, Executive Secretary.

Y.W.H.A. SENIOR BASKET-BALL TEAM
Champions, Toronto Ladies' Basket-ball League 1922-23-24. Champions, City, Ontario, and Big Four League.
Challengers for Dominion Title, 1925.

HARRY ROSENTHAL, TORONTO

HARRY ROSENTHAL, one of the most active communal workers in the City of Toronto, was born in New York on May 23rd, 1884, the son of the late Joseph Rosenthal. He moved to Toronto when a child with his parents, and was educated in the public and high schools in that city. For many years he has been in business in Toronto as a manufacturer's agent. Mr. Rosenthal was married on June 12th, 1917, to Mae, daughter of David Arnstein of New York, and he has one son, Joel Rosenthal. Although a contributor to and supporter of all Jewish institutions in Toronto, Mr. Rosenthal has taken a particularly active part in boys' work, and he is one of the originators of the Young Men's and Young Women's Hebrew Association of Toronto, and has taken a leading part during the entire existence of this association. Mrs. Rosenthal has also been one of the most active supporters of the "Y" since its inception, and has at all times been an outstanding figure amongst the welfare workers in Toronto. Mr. Rosenthal has also been a very active member of the B'nai B'rith, of which he is a Trustee. He was Chairman of the Jewish Boys' Camp (1923) organized by the B'nai B'rith Lodge, and he was Chairman (1924) of the Immigration Committee of the Lodge. He is much interested in fraternal matters and is Treasurer of Palestine Lodge, A.F. & A.M., and is a member of Sunnyside Lodge, I.O.O.F. He is also a contributing member to the Federation of Jewish Philanthropies; Old Folks' Home; Jewish Children's Home; and other local institutions. Mr. Rosenthal has been quite prominent in athletic activities and was the "discoverer" of the famous Indian runner, Thomas Longboat, who won the championship of the world in long distance running. He was also the manager of Ted Woods and Alfred Shrubb, both world famous long distance runners. Mr. Rosenthal has been a life-long member and at present is a Trustee of the Goel Tzedec Synagogue, Toronto.

HISTORY AND DEVELOPMENT OF THE BIG BROTHER MOVEMENT, TORONTO
(JEWISH BRANCH)

THE history of the Big Brother Movement Toronto, Jewish Branch, is a very unique one. It was organized in 1914, following the organization of the general movement.

In 1912, when the first Juvenile Court started in dingy rooms on the top floor of the City Hall, a great number of juvenile delinquents were appearing in court daily. It was at this critical time that the Big Brother idea came into being.

A young lad 12 years of age appeared on the charge of vagrancy. He had left his home in Hamilton and had "hiked" to Toronto. While the case was in progress a well known business man, who was a witness, became interested in this young lad, and asked the Judge if he would give the boy a chance by placing him on probation. The Judge granted this request and the man and boy, arm in arm, left the court rooms very happily. This experiment proved very successful. The boy under careful guidance and supervision and with the help of the "Big Brother", became re-established in society.

This "unknown" man became interested and started, with the assistance of a few other business men, a movement. The object of this movement was to act as a "Big Brother" to the poor unfortunate slum boy, and with careful guidance, supervision, and advice, put him back on his feet.

This movement daily grew larger, and very soon it was recognized in the courts, and the probation system was adopted. It was not until some four years later that the movement was divided into three divisions, namely; the Protestant, the Catholic and the Jewish.

The Jewish branch started under the presidency of Mr. M. M. Brodey, with some excellent young men who were enthusiastic in their work, but in the course of time their interest diminished. Later the work was resumed under the direction of Mr. E. M. Blankansee, until his departure for England. The presidency was then filled by that ardent boy worker and B'nai B'rith man, Mr. Ralph Raphael. Notwithstanding, delinquency among the Jewish boys rose in undue proportion to the population. The situation was becoming more serious daily. As time crept on it became obvious from experiments that the old idea of individual work with the boy was not so satisfactory. In order to save the boy, something more feasible had to be done. The idea of individual work had to be continued, however, because there were always some boys who required individual attention.

In 1921, Mr. M. M. Cohen, a retired business man, and a member of the Toronto Boy Life Council, who had been active in Big Brother work, came to the conclusion that the boy could best be saved through his gang, under the supervision of a trained and inspired leader. The natural instincts of the boy must be recognized as they are necessary to his wholesome development, but must be directed along lines that make the best in manhood. Mr. Cohen succeeded in surrounding himself with a number of excellent young men, among whom were M. E. Williams, Dave Brodey, Nat Gollom, Sam Rosenbaum, Ben Miller, Louis James, N. W. Bronstein, Harry Kasky, Martin Cohn, Monte Beder, Leon Weil, Ben Kasky, Julian Weil, and James Montagnes. These men underwent a course of training in Psychology of the Adolescent, and best methods of boy nurture, by recognized authorities on boy work, such as Mr. Taylor-Statten, General Secretary of the National Boy Work Board, and Dr. P. Heyward, at present General Secretary of the Junior Branch of the International Religious Educational Council in Chicago.

The club known as the Jewish Boys in Training (J. B. I. T.) was organized. Small clubs working on what is known as the four-fold programme; namely, intellectual, devotional, social and physical work were formed. Boys from 9 to 11 years of age are known as "Wanderers" and from 12 to 15 years as "Men of David". These boys wear the insignia of their groups, open their meetings, and invest their new members with an intensely Jewish ritual, have special instructions in Safety-first, Care of Body, First Aid, Observation Work, Athletic Work, Parliamentary Procedure, Bible Study, Debating and Oratorical Work, etc.

In 1922 Miss J. Bronstein (now Mrs. Efrein of Baltimore, Md.) was appointed secretary for the Big Brother work. She enlisted the sympathy and co-operation of the leaders of the Jewish Boys in Training, of which M. E. Williams was then presiding officer. From that time the delinquency among Jewish boys, notwithstanding the increase in population, steadily diminished.

In 1922—January to August—164 boys appeared in Court, 84 repeaters.

In 1923—January to August—98 boys appeared in Court, 32 repeaters.

In 1924—January to August—48 boys appeared in Court, 15 repeaters.

Within two years delinquency was reduced 70% and repeating brought down 82%.

In 1923, Mrs. Efrein was transferred to Case-Work, and Mr. M. E. Williams was appointed Executive Secretary of the Big Brother Work and afterwards Executive Director of the Jewish Boys' Club. From that time on the Jewish Boys in Training, (who are all members of the Jewish Boys' Club) and the Big Brother Movement became practically one. Mr. Williams having the confidence of the leaders received their full and hearty co-operation, and it is to the zeal of these young men under his leadership, working along the fourfold lines set forth, that is to be attributed the remarkable reduction in delinquency.

Up to 1923 the groups of the J.B.I.T. met in the Public Schools, but in that year as a mark of appreciation of the excellent work that was being done, and in order to get better facilities for further development, the Federation of Jewish Philanthropies presented them with the handsome Club House at 218 Simcoe Street. At the instigation of Rabbi B. R. Brickner a committee under the sponsorship of Mr. N. L. Nathanson, succeeded in raising sufficient money to renovate and remodel the building.

There are at present associated with the Club House, 225 boys between 12 and 15 years of age, known as "Men of David", under 12 Mentors, and 200 boys between 8 and 11 years of age, termed "Wanderers" under 10 Mentors. Besides this they have 5 Mentors taking care of five groups of 100 boys at the Branch Club at 336 Annette Street.

These boys meet from once to twice a week. They are organized with their officers and taught to conduct their meetings in a parliamentary way, developing their powers of self-expression through debates and essays. They adopt the badge and crest system along the lines of the Canadian Standard Efficiency Tests, whereby special recognition is given in the form of a badge for a certain standard of merit in any one of the various activities of the organization. They have a stamp collecting club of 20 boys, a radio club of 15, a printing club of 15, and a music club is now under way.

The latest feature is the "Toy Craft Shoppe," where 35 boys are busy making wooden mechanical toys which are durable and artistic. The aim is to develop the manual dexterity in the boy, who at the same time derives a certain amount of fun and pleasure. Again it is aimed to develop the thrift idea, of saving and spending money wisely. For this reason the boys are paid for the work they do. A bank account is started for each boy where he deposits all money earned. The boy watches his bank book figures grow and becomes intensely interested. The result is that he is encouraged to save. Again the experience gained in the shop, in handling tools and painting-brushes will be of important use in his later life.

Altogether there are over 750 boys who use the Club House weekly, and derive benefits thereof, or from the organization.

At present the organization has acquired the branch at the Junction, already referred to, and also a paid assistant director.

Athletics in all its branches, under the capable leadership of Mr. I. Lyons, who has given his time unselfishly, encourage the physical development of the boys. Inter-club leagues of baseball, volley ball and basketball are organized. They compete with other communal centres in both intellectual and athletic activities and have distinguished themselves in 1923, by winning first and second prizes in the Y.M.C.A. community boys' contest in Oratory; junior championship in the Y.M.C.A. Basket Ball League, bantam championship in the Boys Tel'y Soft Ball league, and championship in the Y.M.C.A. senior basket ball, and Boys Tel'y Baseball league; and third in the Y.M.C.A. 105 lb. class. The boys are taught to play the game and play it fair.

The Pantages A.B.C. class under the auspices and at the expense of Mr. N. L. Nathanson is composed of boys acquiring a certain percentage of marks in "Attendance," "Behaviour", and "Cleanliness," who are treated to the Pantages theatre and later to supper. Last June over 200 boys qualified.

The Club House has seven meeting rooms, two game rooms, a billiard room, and a spacious back yard which provides recreation six nights a week and all day Sunday to over 750 boys a week. A beautiful library of over 1000 volumes, both for circulation and reading, the gift of the B'nai B'rith, is filled every night. The shower baths are utilized by scores of boys daily, not only contributing to their cleanliness, but affording them much joy.

Loyalty to the "gang", respect and love for parents, and playing of life's game in a sportsman-like manner, are the cardinal ideals of the club.

The work of the Big Brother Movement is presided over by Mr. Ralph Raphael, while the Jewish Boys' Club has at its head, Mr. Harold Levi. The Leaders, known as Mentors, are organized into a club where boy problems and discussions are held in order that the work with the boys be intelligently conducted. Mr. Lionel Singer is President of this club.

With the excellent co-operation of the combined forces of the Big Brother Movement and the Jewish Boys' Club, and the Mentors of the J.B.I.T., it is expected to still further materially reduce the number of Jewish boys appearing in court. The watchword of the J.B.I.T. is "Prevention Is Better Than Cure."

CONCORDIA CLUB, VANCOUVER

THE CONCORDIA CLUB, VANCOUVER, was established in September, 1920, by a few business and professional men of the city, headed by Mr. E. R. Sugarman, for the purpose of providing a medium of better social intercourse among the young Jewish men, and to create an atmosphere of good fellowship and understanding amongst its members.

By reason of the fact that it is composed of the younger men of the community, it has, since its inception been ready to help in any worthy cause, and public spirit has always been the key-note of its activities. The club has also been active in furthering social, athletic and recreative activities in the community.

To encourage the idea of good-fellowship, the membership has deliberately been limited to thirty.

Mr. E. R. Sugarman was the first President, and the present officers consist of;—President, Morris Soskin; Vice-President, Harry Rosenbaum; Secretary, Phil Sorsky; Treasurer, William Steiner.

The club holds regular weekly luncheons throughout the year, at which are heard well-known speakers, both from within and without the community. It takes an active part in all drives, etc. for the benefit of any good cause.

BARON DE HIRSCH BOOK CLUB, MONTREAL

THE Baron de Hirsch Book Club was founded in 1914, for the purpose of developing amongst its members, general culture and literature, particularly Jewish culture and science. It has its own library, which conists of over three thousand volumes, and the headquarters are at the Baron de Hirsch Institute. Miss Rebecca Ratner is the librarian. The Club holds special literary evenings for the members and the public in general. Their objects are to invite and provide a public platform for noteworthy speakers and others prominent in worldly circles, and to place at the disposal of members good books of all kinds. This enables the members to enjoy the privileges of a circulating library and permits them to take books to their homes. The Club receives the co-operation of prominent members of the St. James Literary Society and other literary organizations. The present officers are:—President, Nat. W. Jacobs, B.C.L.; Hon. President, Robert H. Blumenthal; and sponsors. A. J. Livinson, M.A.; Geo. F. Wright, Ed. "Montreal Star;" John Gardiner, Ed. "Montreal Standard;" Howard S. Ross. K.C.; Mrs. Harry Bloomfield; Lyon W. Jacobs, K.C.; John Sullivan, K.C.

M. ALBERT, MONTREAL

Jacoby Studio

MOSES ALBERT, an outstanding figure in Masonic circles in the Province of Quebec, was born at Morrisburg, Ontario, November 4th, 1877, the son of the late Harry Albert, who was one of the founders and a President of the University Avenue Synagogue, Toronto. Mr. Albert was educated at Jarvis Collegiate Institute and University of Toronto, and at the Montreal College of Pharmacy. He was apprenticed to the late Hugh Miller, J.P., Toronto, subsequently taking the O.A. examination in the State of Pennsylvania and finally graduating from the Montreal College of Pharmacy. Mr. Albert holds certificate No. 6 and passed the final examinations of the Pharmaceutical Association of the Province of Quebec, at the head of the class of 1899, and he is the pioneer Jewish druggist of Canada. He was a member of the Board of the Pharmaceutical Association of the Province of Quebec at the time of its affiliation with McGill University. He is the proprietor of two drug stores in Montreal. Mr. Albert has held office in the Hebrew Free Loan Association, Montreal since its formation, at the death of Mr. Fineberg assuming the Presidency. He is now Treasurer of this Association. He is a director of the Hebrew Orphans' Home and one of the divisional heads of the Business Men's Council. He is a trustee of the Montefiore Club and was one of the first Secretaries of the Zionist Federation. Mr. Albert is a Past Chief Ranger, Court Cornwall and York and Past District Chief Ranger, A.O.F.; Past Chancellor and Past District Deputy C.C., Ivanhoe Lodge, K. of P.; Past Master, St. George's Lodge, No. 10., A.F. & A.M.; life member and Past Grand Steward of the Grand Lodge of Quebec, A.F. & A.M.; Past Z. of Mount Horeb Chapter, No. 6, Grand Chapter of Quebec, R.A.M.; Past Grand Principal Sojourner of the Grand Chapter of Quebec, R.A.M.; Past officer of Victoria Council, No. 13, Eryplic Rite of Free Masonry; and a member of the Masonic Board of Relief. On June 12th, 1913, Mr. Albert was married to Lottie, daughter of Isaac Hershberg of Rochester, N.Y., and he has two daughters, the Misses Marjorie and Beatrice Albert.

MONTEFIORE CLUB, MONTREAL

THE MONTEFIORE CLUB stands out as one of the most noteworthy of Montreal's organizations, and during the entire range of its career the community has taken a pride in it, which, far from being too chauvinistic, has always been considered justified and fully deserved.

It was formed in September, 1880, by a number of Jewish young men, all residents of the city, for the purpose of fostering literary and social intercourse among its members, and for the encouragement of amateur dramatic pursuits. The revered name of the great and famous philanthropist, Sir Moses Montefiore, was adopted as the name of the organization, and it accordingly began its existence as the Montefiore Social and Dramatic Club. In its earlier days, under the guidance and instruction of Neal Warner, a great deal of the time of its members was devoted to amateur theatricals, and many of the city's charitable institutions benefitted materially by the performances given in their behalf. Among these the Montreal General Hospital, Western Hospital for Women, Montreal Press Association, Quebec Fire Fund and the Building Fund of the Shaar Hashomayim Synagogue, were all beneficiaries of the Club's charitable efforts. As the members advanced in years, however, and business duties became more weighty, this part of the Club's work was entirely lost sight of, or rather abandoned, and even the name was changed to the Montefiore Club.

In 1889 the Club received its first charter from the Quebec Legislature, and at the fall session of the local House in 1905 it was renewed and extended to meet its present requirements. This was necessitated by a determination of the members to erect, as a fitting celebration of the Club's attainment of the twenty-fifth anniversary of its existence, a suitable home, which should meet all the requirements of the Club's various activities, and the new Club house is the result. It is safe to say that no handsomer or more commodious club quarters exist in Montreal than the new Montefiore Club on Guy Street, and the completion of the building in such an ornate and magnificent manner, is a credit to the arduous efforts and labors of the members' committee which had the matter in hand, viz.; Messrs. M. and B. Goldstein, E. Blout, A. Z. Cohen, M. J. Hirsch, Michael Hirsch, I. and C. L. Friedman, A. E. Myers, B. Aronson, J. Michaels. The following is a description of the new Club building;

The front of the building, which stands back some twenty or thirty feet from the sidewalk, has a frontage of fifty feet, and is fifty feet from sidewalk to cornice. The exterior, which is of light buff brick, with sandstone facing, is dignified and well proportioned, and readily suggests the character of the building.

It has been treated in this simple manner intentionally, the largest portion of the expenditure having been left for the interior, which in point of excellence, completeness and good taste surpasses any clubhouse of its size in Montreal at the present time. All the rooms are spacious, lofty and well-ventilated, a special system of forced draught ventilation drawing off the vitiated air from each room in the building.

The entrance vestibule is floored and walled in solid marble; the ceiling is vaulted and frescoed. The Club crest is specially designed, leaded glass being here introduced. The main hall is the gem of the apartments. On entering it one feels completely at his ease. The whole interior is furnished in the Dutch style, with heavily beamed ceilings, great fireplaces, which reach to the ceiling, polished floors, and leaded windows. It is twenty feet square, is panelled eight feet high, and has a lofty mantel. Opening off this are the lounging room, cafe, writing room, cloak rooms and broad staircase leading to the first floor. The lounging room and the cafe are further examples of good taste and judgment in selection of their decoration. The walls are panelled in a plain, heavily woven fabric, which forms an excellent background for pictures. The furniture, electric fixtures, which are of pewter, and Donegal rugs, are especially designed to suit these rooms. The effect has been studied as a whole and there are no discordant or startling notes of color which one so often finds in the average room.

Special study has been given to the electric lighting and a subdued, mellow light pervades the rooms at night, with the lights placed exactly where they are needed for reading, writing, etc. The cafe is lit by electrical candelabra placed on each table. The first floor is occupied by a large sitting room, fifty by twenty-two feet, and is used for entertainments and functions of a social nature. The room contains a large fireplace and broad windows which overlook the street, and is furnished in keeping with the other rooms. The billiard room, which is twenty-five by thirty feet, occupies the remaining part of the floor, and is thoroughly equipped with everything requisite for such a room. The top floor is given over to game rooms of all sorts, and are all marked by an air of individuality in their decorative treatment, manifest in their rugs, draperies and wall designs.

A portion of the basement is given over to bowling alleys, and space for other alleys has been provided, to be utilized as necessary. The remainder of the basement is occupied by the kitchen, butler's pantry, store rooms, and all the conveniences required by the chef and his staff, together with janitor's quarters, etc.

The service department has access to all floors in the building through service staircase and dumb waiter, communication being private and complete in itself.

One feature which the Club has kept continually in view has been the literary work, which has so grown in importance that it is today one of the strongest attractions offered to the members. Then, too, its social record has been one of signal success. It has enabled the community to come together with such good results that too much importance can not be attributed to this beneficial work. Some of the most noted and best social functions ever held in that community were under the auspices of the Club, and the standard of entertainment set has not only been the highest, but has been emulated by all.

The Montefiore Club has stood for everything elevating and useful in the community, and at its helm there have been and still are men of ability and intelligence, who know best how to lead the institution onward in its useful path of good work.

The following gentlemen have been presidents of the Club:—

Messrs. E. Blout, L. Cohen, B. Goldstein, J. Goldstein, M. Goldstein, K.C., Michael Hirsch, A. Michaels, and J. Michaels.

The present officers of the Club are:—

Mr. Michael Hirsch	President
Mr. Edgar M. Berliner	Vice-President
Mr. B. Gardner	Hon. Treasurer
Mr. David Kirsch	Hon. Secretary
Messrs. M. Albert, E. V. Gilbert, Alan J. Hart, A. H. Jassby and A. Lesser	Council
Mr. Maxwell Goldstein, K.C.	Hon. Counsel
J. Charles Langston	Secretary

THE MONTEFIORE CLUB, WINNIPEG

THE Montefiore Club of Winnipeg is an institution of which the Jews of Manitoba can justly be proud.

Founded in 1911 for the purpose of affording a meeting place for the young business men, it soon became a very popular club and has taken an active part in all affairs of the city.

Although a social club, the Montefiore has done so much work for other institutions that it could be called a community centre of a very high order. There has not been any undertaking in the city during the past ten years in which it has not taken part. During the campaign for funds for the purpose of building the Jewish Orphanage, a team of Montefiores collected the largest sum of money and were given a trophy. The Talmud Torah has never appealed to them in vain. The Sunday School children look forward to the picnics at the Montefiore camp grounds. The files of the Club are loaded with letters of thanks from the various local charities in acknowledgment of wonderful work done.

In the Great War, thirty members out of a total membership of sixty-five enlisted for active service, many of the boys distinguishing themselves in the field.

In the field of sport the Montefiore Club has always taken a leading part. It was this club that called the first meeting to organize an inter-club bowling league, which is still in a flourishing condition. They also organized a Hebrew Amateur Athletic Association, mainly devoted to baseball and football, and won three cups put up by the league. They are first in the field of tennis, with their own court, and run the only known Jewish golf tournament in the world, under the leadership of the club's professional, Monty Stall, and offer unlimited inducements to the young sports of the city.

The following cups are held by the Club for annual competition:

The Kimmel Cup for billiards.
The Steineal Cup for debates.
The Copp Cup for checkers.
The Stall-Lenoff Cup for snowshoers.
The Welsh Cup for golf.
The Harris Cup for bowling.
The Bronfman Cup for football.

The members are always eager to keep up the good name of the Jew before their fellow-citizens, never overlooking an opportunity to create a favorable impression. When the Chief Rabbi of England visited the city he placed a beautiful wreath, fashioned in the shape of the Shield of David, on the Cenotaph, in memory of the Jews killed in the war. This wreath was the gift of the returned soldiers of the Montefiore Club.

THE PRIMROSE CLUB, TORONTO

THE Primrose Club was built nearly five years ago at 41 Willcocks Street, Toronto, and is ideally situated on a well shaded street in close proximity to the business as well as the residential section of Toronto.

It stands on a plot of ground 60 x 130 feet, and its entire colonial exterior denotes the use for which it was built.

There are two entrances to the building, a main and a ladies' entrance. The main entrance, which is located in the centre of the building, leads into a marble panelled vestibule which in turn leads to the main hall. To the right of the main hall is the spacious and luxuriously furnished lounge, the walls of which are panelled in oak, the ceiling heavily beamed, a huge fireplace together with numerous oriental rugs, inviting chesterfields and golden-coloured plush drapes which are in harmony with the lighting effect make it one of the most comfortable and cosy rooms of any club in the city.

Leading from the lounge is the ballroom, which can accommodate four hundred people. This room is treated in the simple and dignified Adam style. At one end of the room is a graceful little balcony which is used for the orchestra. The lighting of the room is obtained from three beautiful suspended crystal chandeliers, and crystal wall brackets.

From the main hallway and also adjoining the ballroom is the dining room which is panelled in oak and seats eighty people comfortably.

The ladies' room which is on the left of the main hall directly opposite the lounge, is prettily done in wicker and chintz. The decorations in this room are carried out in gray and rose.

Adjoining the dining room is the fully equipped kitchen, modern in every respect.

The banquet hall is located on the first floor, also the library and card rooms for those who wish to indulge in such pastimes.

The basement contains a fully equipped billiard room, cloak room and up to date washrooms.

In designing the building special attention was paid to the comfort and entertainment of the ladies who were entitled to full membership privileges and who frequently avail themselves of these privileges.

The accommodation of the Club has been used for the initiation and promotion of most of the important communal activities of Toronto and its establishment on that ground alone has been more than justified.

The Club consists of a joint stock company and is governed by a board of nine directors. The officers and directors of the company for the year 1925 are as follows: President, Joseph Singer; Vice-President, Elly Marks; Secretary-Treasurer, Louis M. Singer; Directors, Max Singer, Norman Helpert, M. H. Epstein, Morris Greisman, Charles Draimin, Jack Perkins.

The first President of the Club was Mr. Max Singer, who retained that office continually until 1924 when his absence from the city made it impossible for him to continue. The success of the Club is largely due to his diligent and persistent efforts during his years of office.

THE HEBREW FRIENDS' LODGE, WINNIPEG

THE Hebrew Friends' Lodge of Winnipeg was organized January the 1st, 1917, during the World War. It was organized largely through the instrumentality of Mr. W. Rabinovitch, an idealist who from childhood had dreamed of a lodge that would consist of members with the spirit of true brotherhood.

The first meeting was held in a private home and there this idea was told to but a few people. Mr. Rabinovitch explained to those present that the City of Winnipeg had many lodges, sick benefit societies, loan societies, etc., but that the brotherly feeling was not as it should be, and he therefore appealed to them to organize a lodge that would be an exception and that would teach the doctrine of true brotherhood.

For the first three years the organization grew very slowly. It was not a question of getting a large membership, but rather of selecting the best obtainable members. "Quality not quantity" was the maxim. The Hebrew Friends' Lodge was built on a solid rock on which three words were engraved, namely, CONCORD, BENEVOLENCE and FIDELITY.

The first Council Commander of this Lodge was the organizer, Mr. W. Rabinovitch, and although he was not a great speaker, he was successful in interesting many people who are now members of the Lodge, to the work he was doing. The second Council Commander was Mr. L. Rotenberg, who also greatly assisted in the progress of the Lodge.

The present Council Commander is Mr. M. Waisman, who with his enthusiasm and hard work has brought the Hebrew Friends' Lodge to such a standard that it is now as highly respected as any fraternal organization in Winnipeg.

From this parent Lodge a number of similar organizations have sprung up both in Canada and the United States, but Winnipeg can boast of being the pioneer of this movement.

At the present time the membership of the Winnipeg Lodge consists of sixty, the constitution calling for only seventy-five members. The Lodge has a temple of its own, where all meetings and social entertainments are held. The work that the Lodge has done for its members speaks for itself. Real harmony and true brotherhood exist among its members, and among the members are counted many of the most prominent men and women of the Jewish community of Winnipeg.

GRAND ORDER OF ISRAEL, HAMILTON

THE Grand Order of Israel Benefit Society, Hamilton, Ontario, was organized in 1907, by Mr. Isaac Lewis and Mr. Hyman Cohen, past officers of the Grand Order of Israel of London, England. The first meeting was held on August 17th, 1907, and many of those present were enrolled as charter members. It was organized as a branch of the Grand Order of Israel of the United Kingdom, with the first rituals, constitution and charter from the Head Office. The Canadian Government authorities intervened however, and would not recognize the English charter, and the society was compelled to obtain a charter in Canada. On October 22nd, 1908, they obtained a charter from the Ontario Department of Insurance, and thus withdrew from the jurisdiction of the English Order.

The first executive officers were;—Noble Master, I. Lewis; Vice-Master, S. Hoffman; Secretary, H. Sherrin; Treasurer, S. Frank; and Trustees, H. Cohen, M. Goldberg and M. Yeretsky. The following are some of the present members who were charter members; I. Lewis, H. Cohen, S. Hoffman, M. Yeretsky, M. Goldberg, S. Frank and S. Dulborg.

The benefits of the Society include, free doctor and medicine for members and family, with all minor operations and surgical attention, compensation for inability to work, special aid to members in distress, Shivah Benefit and Funeral Benefit.

The Ladies' Auxiliary was organized by the officers of the Society on the occasion of the 15th annual banquet, which was held on November 12th, 1922, with the following objects; to unite the bonds of sisterhood among the wives of the members; to increase sociability among the members; and to provide help during sickness and maternity. The first officers of the Auxiliary were;—Noble Mistress, Sister H. Kenter; Vice-Mistress, Sister J. Klappholz; Secretary, Sister B. Caller; Treasurer, Sister M. Goldberg Jr.; and Trustees, Sisters J. Freedman, M. Goldberg Sr. and B. Cohan; Marshalls, Sisters B. Raphael and H. Wanger; and Guardian, Sister P. Wright.

The dues of the Society are small and it is at the present time in a flourishing condition. Benefits amounting to $350.00 are paid out per annum.

The Executive Board is at the present time working to organize branches of this Society throughout Canada. The cemetery of the Society is situated at Waterdown.

The present officers are;—Noble Master, M. Littner; Vice-Master, S. Lipschultz; Financial and Recording Secty., J. Freedman; Treasurer, P. Wolfe; Trustees, I. Lewis, L. Miller, S. Barrs; Marshalls, S. Bloom, J. Caplan, M. Raphael, L. Silver; Guardian, J. Klappholz; and Physician, Dr. J. I. Morris.

The officers of the Ladies' Auxiliary are;—Noble Mistress, Sister J. Mandel; Vice-Mistress, Sister A. Stein; Secretary, J. Caplan; Treasurer, Sister M. Levitt; Trustees, Sisters S. Goldin, N. Latner, D. Milgrove; Marshalls, Sisters I. Berkowitz, H. Cohen; and Guardian, Sister H. Berger.

REUBEN BRAININ

REUBEN BRAININ, Author and Journalist, was born in Russia, in 1862. He was educated in Moscow, and at the Universities of Vienna and Berlin. He is married to Marie, daughter of Isaac Amsterdam, and has one daughter, Mrs. Schuller, and two sons, Moses and Joseph Brainin. From his early youth, Reuben Brainin participated in the revival of the Hebrew language and Jewish national movements, and amongst his circle of friends were many who afterwards became great leaders of the Zionist Movement. Although to a large extent a Hebrew author, he has also written a great deal in Yiddish, writing for the European and American Yiddish press, in which he has published many short stories, literary reviews, etc. In 1909, some of his Yiddish writings were published in book form in Warsaw. As a Zionist, Reuben Brainin contributed his great share to the development of modern Zionism, and participated in many of the worlds' Zionistic Congresses. About fifteen years ago, he went to New York, where for a short time he edited a Hebrew magazine, and he then removed to Montreal, where he became Editor-in-chief of the "Jewish Daily Eagle." His stay in Canada was very fruitful, and he contributed greatly to Canada's Jewish journalism, and to the spread of Hebrew culture. During the Great War, he helped to organize the relief work for the Jewish war sufferers. He participated actively in the development of the Zionist Movement in Canada, and was a strong advocate for the Canadian Jewish Congress. To his many works, published in late years, a notable addition was the publishing in Hebrew of the biography of his intimate friend, the late Dr. Herzl, under the title of "The Life of Herzl." After spending some years in Montreal, Mr. Brainin returned to New York where he is editing the Hebrew monthly "Hatoren," and where he is active in many Hebrew cultural affairs. He occupies a foremost place as a contributor to Hebrew literature. On the anniversary of his sixtieth birthday, a group of his admirers organized a publication committee, which intends to publish his Hebrew works in thirty volumes.

THE JEWISH PRESS IN CANADA
By A. Rhinewine

THE Jews of Canada, until recent years but few in numbers, have always contributed to the general Canadian Press, and many of the participants have also achieved great success as editors. Thus a Jew from Alsace, M. Helbronner, edited for many years, the Montreal French Daily "La Press", and Jacob G. Ascher, a Canadian born Jew, edited the "Montreal Daily Star".

It was with the increase of Jewish immigration into the country however, that the foundation was laid for a Jewish Press, both in English and in the common tongue of the Jew—Yiddish.

As early as 1891, G. Zelikovitch, now with the New York "Tageblatt" made an attempt to found a small Yiddish publication, but only four numbers were issued, and not until 1897 was another attempt made in Montreal with the English bi-weekly "The Jewish Times", the first number of which was published on December 10th, 1897. In its first editorial, the publication accounted for its founding in the following words;—"The Jewish population of Montreal now numbers 7,000 souls and for the whole Dominion probably exceeds 15,000. It has therefore been thought that a community so large and having many interests in common, should possess an organ of their own, for the dissemination of Jewish news, interchange of ideas, and the advocacy as well as the defence of Jewish rights as free citizens of a free country."

"At the present juncture of affairs, it is doubly important that the Jews of Canada should have a reliable vehicle for the expression of their sentiments. The anti-semitic movement in Europe is not without an echo in this country. It is to be found daily in those newspapers, which take their old world inspiration largely from those organs of opinion which are inimical to the Jewish people."

"The Jewish Times Publishing Company" were the publishers, and Captain Carol Ryan, an experienced journalist, a non-Jew, but having a thorough acquaintance with Jewish affairs, was appointed as editor of the bi-weekly. Captain Ryan had been for many years on the staff of the Montreal "Witness". He was an eminent author and poet, many of his poems and essays being on Jewish subjects, and until his death, in 1910, he was closely connected with "The Jewish Times". "The Jewish Times", during its many years of existence, sought to record all important occurrences in Canadian Jewish life, and its files therefore give an excellent account of that period.

In 1908, also in Montreal, "The Canadian Jewish Tribune", with Hyman P. Nervich as its editor, was started, but of this only several numbers were published. The two publications were then amalgamated, and in January, 1909, "The Jewish Times" began to appear weekly with the word "Canadian" added to its name, and was published under that name until April 1914, when in changing ownership it also changed its name to that of the "Canadian Jewish Chronicle". The latter is still being published in Montreal.

In 1905, 1907 and 1912, attempts were made for the founding of Yiddish weeklies, but their existence was of short duration; the only successful attempt being with "Der Kanader Adler". In the month of July, 1907, a publishing company was organized to publish a weekly under that name, but soon the publishers were convinced that a weekly could neither cover its expenses nor satisfy its readers. They changed it therefore into a semi-weekly, but neither did this solve the problem. The publishers then decided to convert it into a daily, and since then its management also acquired, in 1914, the above mentioned Anglo-Jewish publication, now known as the "Canadian Jewish Chronicle".

Besides trials for a labour press, attempts were also made in Montreal to found a number of publications of various kinds, literary and humorous, both in Yiddish and in English, but their existence was of very short duration. Reuben Brainin, one of the editors of the "Adler" also tried in 1915 to publish another Yiddish daily "Der Weg", but it only existed for about a year.

The beginning of the Jewish press in Toronto occurred about the year 1906, when the "Toronto Jewish Weekly", containing reading material in Yiddish and in English was published for a short period. In 1907, a further attempt was made with the "Toronter Yiddishe Presse", but the existence of both was of very short duration, and not until 1912, was a successful attempt made on the 29th of November, 1912, when "Der Yiddisher Journal" appeared as a weekly, being changed a year later into a daily. This and the "Canadian Jewish Adler" are the only two Jewish daily publications now existing in Canada.

Since 1922, Toronto has also had an Anglo Jewish weekly, "The Canadian Jewish Review", with Rabbi B. R. Brickner as contributing editor.

THE LATE JACOB G. ASCHER

The year 1906 marks the beginning of a Canadian Jewish press in the western metropolis, when a Jewish publication "Der Wiederklang" made its appearance. Of this, however, only several issues were published. A further attempt to establish a Jewish publication was made in 1910, with "Der Kourier", which existed for over a year, when it sold its plant and the name was changed by the new owner to "Der Kanader Yid". For a short time it was continued as a weekly, and then as a semi-weekly, until 1914 when it became a daily, but the number of Jews in the West, a territory which it chiefly covered, was not large enough to support a daily. It therefore ceased publication and not until 1917 was it renewed, under the name of "Dos Yiddishe Wort", first as a weekly and again later as a semi-weekly, and which is now being published by "The Israelite Press", of Winnipeg.

Many more attempts to establish publications as well as an attempt to found an Anglo-Yiddish Organ (The Jewish Guardian) were made in Winnipeg, but they did not exist for any length of time.

"The Folks' Zeitung", and "Dos Folk", two labor weeklies in Montreal appearing in 1911 and in 1917, and the "Arbeiter Zeitung", a labor weekly in Toronto, which was published for about six months in 1918, were the only labor publications which appeared for a period longer than any of the other attempts, that had previously been made.

A. RHINEWINE, TORONTO

A. RHINEWINE, Editor of The Toronto Daily Hebrew Journal, was born in Poland in 1887. He was raised in a very strict orthodox Jewish environment, and was given a broad secular and Jewish education with the intention of preparing him for the Rabbinate. With this purpose, his parents sent him at an early age to study at the famous Yeshiva of Kovno, known as "Keneseth Israel", but the new surroundings and acquaintances had quite a different influence, and there he joined at an early age, the Jewish labor movement, affiliating himself with the Social Zionist Labour Party. After the Russian Revolution in 1905, in order to avoid arrest, he left for England, where he continued his studies for a short period in London. In 1907, Mr. Rhinewine arrived in Toronto, where he has since resided. In Toronto he continued his university studies and took up literary work. In 1912, when the Toronto Daily Hebrew Journal was founded, he joined the staff as City Editor, and three years later in 1915, he was appointed Editor, a position which he still holds. Mr. Rhinewine continues to take an active interest in the Labor Movement and in the Peretz Schule. He takes a keen interest in all public questions, particularly those affecting the Jewish community, or those relating to organized labor. In communal matters Mr. Rhinewine has been of much assistance to the various charitable institutions, and his aid is eagerly sought in all undertakings of a philanthropic nature. He has continued to devote himself largely to a literary career, and has contributed to many Jewish and English publications and magazines. He published in book form a novel "In a Canadian City", and among his other works are included "Palestine in Yiddish Literature and Life", "Canada—its History and Development", and "The History of the Jew in Canada", in two volumes. A drama of Jewish life in four acts "The Assimilator", was written by Mr. Rhinewine and is now on the repertoire of the Jewish stage.

H. WOLOFSKY, MONTREAL

H. WOLOFSKY, Author and Journalist, was born in Poland on Sept. 15th, 1876, the son of Felix Wolofsky. He was educated in the Yeshivas in Poland and at private schools, and was married in Poland to Sarah, daughter of Pincus Bercovitz. He has five sons, Phillip, Daniel, Max, Moses, and Saul, and two daughters, the Misses Sophie and Miriam Wolofsky. Mr. Wolofsky came to Canada as a young man, and has made himself a power for good in the Jewish life of this country. Settling in Montreal, where he has since continued to reside, he occupies a prominent position in the community, and his advice and assistance is sought in all undertakings affecting the Jewish people. He is an active supporter of all the charitable and welfare organizations in Montreal, and he took a very prominent part in Jewish War Relief Work, and was a member of the Central War Relief Committee. Mr. Wolofsky is one of the most active members of the Zionist Organization, and is a member of the Executive for Canada. He is an active propagandist for the establishment of separate schools for the teaching of the Jewish young, and is a strong exponent for the maintenance of the Yiddish language, and his editorials and views on these subjects are well known. He took a leading part in the Canadian Jewish Congress held in Montreal in 1919. He has always taken a great interest in Jewish immigration, and has done an immense amount of work in assisting the new arrivals, and in instructing them in the duties of citizenship. Mr. Wolofsky is the Editor and publisher of the Jewish Daily Eagle, Montreal, which he established in 1907, and he is also the publisher of the Canadian Jewish Chronicle, which he was instrumental in establishing in 1912. In 1920, he printed an American edition of the Talmud, in 18 large volumes, similar to the Vilna edition. In 1923, he published a book of some 400 pages "Europe and Palestine after War." This contains an immense amount of information regarding Palestine, and is invaluable propaganda for the Zionist movement.

THE JEWISH LABOUR MOVEMENT IN CANADA
By A. Rhinewine

Trade-Unions and Political Organizations—Fraternal Insurance Societies—Cultural Work—The Jewish Labour Press—Jewish Secular Schools.

THE Jewish Labour Movement is everywhere an organic part of the general movement; a member of the labour family as a whole, and the movement in Canada is not an exception to this rule. The Jewish worker lives and struggles under the same economic and political conditions as does labor in general, and it differs only in its more progressive character.

Small was the number of the Jewish workers in the first periods of Jewish immigration, and their number began to increase only with the great stream of Jewish immigrants from Eastern Europe, when at the end of the nineteenth century, the ranks of Jewish labour were already so large, that an attempt was made to organize them into labour unions.

Jewish labour has made great contributions to Canadian industry, especially to the clothing industry. The manufacturing of men's and women's garments employs a great number of Jewish workers, of whom by far the largest majority are members of the International Ladies' Garment Workers' Union and the Amalgamated Clothing Workers of America.

Jewish labour is also to be found in the fur industry, cap and hat manufacturing industries, and the building trade, where they are members of the respective unions.

The *Workmen's Circle* and the *Jewish National Workers' Alliance* are two fraternal organizations, providing their members with life-insurance and various benefits functioning on a co-operative basis, and doing cultural work among their members.

The *Poale Zion* and the Jewish socialistic organizations are educating Jewish labour politically, working hand in hand with Canadian labour on the political field.

The Jewish Labour Movement has made several attempts to have its own labour organs in the Yiddish language. From time to time such experiments were made at Montreal, Toronto and Winnipeg, but they could not exist for any length of time on account of the lack of funds.

Thus there appeared in Montreal in 1911 for a short while the "Maccabean" with Zionist-Socialistic tendencies, edited by S. Schneyer. In 1912, another attempt was made, the "Volkszeitung", edited by L. Chazanovitch, but the lack of finances made its continued existence impossible. The "Arbeiter Zeitung", "Das Volk", and a monthly, "Arbeit" were other attempts in Montreal to found a labour press.

In 1915, the Cloakmakers' Union of Toronto made an effort to publish an unperiodical bulletin, "The Cloakmakers' Bulletin" but only very few issues appeared. "Die Neie Zeit" a monthly, and "Die Arbeiter Zeitung" a weekly, were other labour publications which existed in Toronto for a short period.

"Die Volkszeitung", "Die Yiddishe Arbeiter Zeitung", "Die Zeit", "Die Neie Zeit", were names of labour publications appearing in Winnipeg from time to time.

PERETZ INSTITUTE, WINNIPEG

In 1911, a Jewish labour organization, which was then known as the "Socialist Territorialists" made also an experiment in Jewish education. As most of the Jewish education given in the Talmud Torahs and other schools was of a religious character, they decided to establish a secular school excluding all religious subjects from its programme. The J. L. Peretz School was then founded, teaching the children Yiddish, Hebrew, Jewish history and folk songs. Several similar schools were organized in the cities of Montreal and Winnipeg.

Toronto has at present three such schools, Montreal six, Winnipeg three, and several are to be found also in other cities, and about fifteen hundred children attend these schools after the regular public school hours.

In some of these schools classes for adults are also held, and all subjects are taught without any religious bias, the branches of the Workmen's Circle and the Jewish National Workers' Alliance supplying in the most cases the funds for this educational work.

It is also interesting to note that early in the nineties when the Jewish tailors were organized in branch-unions of the United Garment Workers of America, it was on their initiative that the Government began to investigate the sweating system, existing then in some of the shops, and as a result of this, Labor Laws were enacted in the later years. Thus the Jewish Labour Movement gave the first impetus to the enactment of Labor Laws in Canada.

JEWISH COLONIZATION IN CANADA

By S. Belkin

DURING the last twenty-five years of the past century, Jewish immigrants from Central and Eastern Europe began to arrive in Canada in appreciable numbers. The Jewish community in Montreal realized the necessity of helping the new arrivals to become established in the country of their adoption, and in 1863 the Young Men's Hebrew Benevolent Society was formed to help the local poor and arriving immigrants. The members of the Society felt that it would be preferable for the new arrivals to be settled on farms instead of taking up trade in the cities.

At a meeting of the Young Men's Hebrew Benevolent Society which was held on January 25th, 1874, Mr. Mona Lesser spoke of "the general movement in progress, in which all the national and charitable societies in the city were to take part, to form a colonization society," and urged the Young Men's Hebrew Benevolent Society to co-operate in the matter.

In 1882, the great wave of Jewish pogroms in Russia brought a large number of Russo-Jewish refugees to London, Hamburg and other northern Atlantic ports. Of these, large groups were sent to Canada through various Jewish philanthropic agencies. Sir Alexander T. Galt, Canadian High Commissioner in London at the time took an active interest in the fate of the Jewish refugees. The Russo-Jewish Committee in London considered it advisable to form colonies for the refugees in America—one of these colonies to be organized in the Canadian North West. The Committee, which acted previously under the name of The Mansion House Fund for the Relief of Russo-Jewish Refugees, obtained in 1882, through Sir Alexander's agent, Mr. W. A. Thomson, a tract of land in the North West Territories and made the first attempt to organize a Jewish colony in Canada. The settlement nicknamed "New Jerusalem" was situated in Range 2, Townships 11 and 12 west of the 2nd Meridian (land surveyor's meridian)* about twenty-five miles from Moosemin.

The Young Men's Hebrew Benevolent Society assisted the prospective colonists in every possible way. Mr. L. Weinstein of Winnipeg took an active interest in the immigrants upon their arrival in that city. Lacking proper supervision and advice, having little farming experience and no knowledge of conditions in the Canadian North West, the colonists struggled for several years against recurring crop failures, but without much success.

In the appendix of the Privy Council Order Number 622 dated Ottawa, April 4th, 1887, which granted a lien to The Mansion House Fund for $10,521.44 on the homesteads advanced to Jewish settlers, we find the following list of some of the first Jewish settlers in Western Canada:

NAME OF SETTLER	DESCRIPTION OF LAND			
	Section	Township	Range	West
Berel Wiedman	10	12	2	2nd
Wolf Lerner	20	11	2	2nd
Abraham Werman	30	11	2	2nd
Joseph Barsky	32	11	2	2nd
Hirsh Dulkan	34	11	2	2nd
Chajem Wolk	30	11	2	2nd
Kieve Barsky	32	11	2	2nd
Moses Dulkan	34	11	2	2nd
Menasha Zawalkow	28	12	2	2nd
Simon Lechtzier	4	12	2	2nd
Herz Galgeran	16	12	2	2nd
Samuel Milstein	18	12	2	2nd
Solomon Naroflansky	18	12	2	2nd
Abraham Weitzman	20	12	2	2nd
Wolf Moskowitz	24	12	2	2nd
Chajem Abraham Grobman	30	12	2	2nd
David Galgeran	16	12	2	2nd
Juda Leib Waksengiesser	30	12	2	2nd
Shmaje Petezky	32	12	2	2nd
Moses Obrashimoff	6	12	2	2nd
Abraham Lechtzier	4	12	2	2nd
Joseph Joselowitz	2	12	2	2nd
Leib David Joselowitz	2	12	2	2nd
Mordechai Weidman	10	12	2	2nd
Kadish Lavin	12	12	2	2nd
Berel Selitzky	12	12	2	2nd
Naphtali Katz	28	12	2	2nd

*The second land surveyor's meridian conforms with the 102nd geographical meridian.

In January, 1885, in commemoration of the centenary of Sir Moses Montefiore, the Montefiore Agricultural Aid Association was formed in Montreal. The purposes of this Association were to settle Jewish immigrants in communities so they would not remain isolated, and to assist them in their undertakings. The president of the Association was Mr. Mark Samuel, of Toronto, and the secretary was Mr. Lewis A. Hart, of Montreal. But beyond making a study of the various methods of settlement, little of a practical nature was accomplished by the Association, and it soon disbanded.

As the years passed, the influx of Jewish immigrants into Canada continued. The Young Men's Hebrew Benevolent Society being in need of funds endeavoured to obtain them from abroad. At the meeting of the Society which took place on April 13th, 1890, Mr. L. Aronson, referring to the grant of $120,000 by the Baron de Hirsch to benevolent societies in the United States suggested that the Society make an effort to obtain a portion of these funds. He was supported by Mr. Julius Sherman, the Vice-President. The Board of Directors, presided over by Mr. Harris Vineberg, immediately took up the matter with the Baron de Hirsch. The influence of Mr. Moise Schwob, Vice-Consul for France in Montreal, helped the Board in its endeavour to obtain assistance, and in August of 1890 a donation of $20,000 was received from the Baron. This gave fresh impetus to the Society; the scope of its work was enlarged and more concentrated attention was given by it to the matter of Jewish colonization.

A Colonization Committee headed by Mr. D. A. Ansell was formed to study the matter. Canadian Government officials were approached as to suitable land for the settlement of Jewish immigrants and they gave the Society every possible encouragement. Very characteristic is the letter addressed to the Society on January 15th, 1891 by the Dominion Immigration Agent at Regina, Mr. John J. Stemshorn. In his letter, Mr. Stemshorn informed the Society that there were a large number of homesteads within a radius of ten miles from Regina, and offered his services.

On October 7th, 1891, a letter was addressed to the Baron de Hirsch in which it was stated "That the Institution (The Baron de Hirsch Institute—founded with the monies received from the Baron) is unable to receive during the coming year or to take any cognizance of the new arrivals without some definite and decided system of

SCENE AT LIPTON, SASK.

colonization being organized for the immigrants from Europe." Letters were also sent to Jewish philanthropic organizations on the other side and to Mr. Hugh Sutherland, Secretary to Sir Charles Tupper, Canadian High Commissioner in London at the time, asking him to urge Jewish leaders in England to renew their efforts in matters of Jewish colonization.

In September 1891, Baron de Hirsch created the Jewish Colonization Association which became of great consequence to Jewish colonization efforts in Canada and elsewhere.

On November 1st, 1891, the twenty-eighth annual meeting of the Young Men's Hebrew Benevolent Society took place, at which Mr. Harris Vineberg was elected President for the third time, Mr. D. S. Friedman, Treasurer and Mr. Lyon Cohen, Secretary. The Colonization Committee was re-elected and consisted of:— Chairman, Mr. D. A. Ansell and Messrs. S. Davis, Moise Schwob, L. Davis, Maxwell Goldstein, Harris Vineberg, Lyon Cohen and D. S. Friedman. Shortly afterwards, an important letter was received from the Jewish Colonization Association in Paris dated November 3rd, 1891, signed by Dr. Sigmund Sonnenfeld, General Manager of the Jewish Colonization Association. This letter acknowledged receipt of the communication of October 7th, 1891, mentioned above, addressed to the Baron de Hirsch. Dr. Sonnenfeld outlined the system of colonization employed by the Jewish Colonization Association in South America and requested information as to the cost of establishing a family of ten persons, so that the European Committees would know the total amount required for the colonization plans submitted by the Young Men's Hebrew Benevolent Society.

On November 16th, 1891, the Trustees of The Mansion House Fund for the Relief of Russo-Jewish Refugees offered to transfer the land which they had acquired near Moosemin to the Young Men's Hebrew Benevolent Society. Mr. N. G. Joseph, Honorary Secretary of the Russo-Jewish Committee stated "That the Trustees would not incur any new liability or outlay in respect of the land, but would simply transfer their interest in it for the benefit of Russo-Jewish refugees whom you might recommend as able to make their way without our assistance."

The Colonization Committee of the Young Men's Hebrew Benevolent Society immediately started to work and on December 13th, 1891, submitted a report that they had held "several lengthy meetings and had given most earnest attention to the problem sent to them for deliberation and in obtaining information from colonization agents and from every practical and experienced person." The Committee set forth the amount of Five Hundred Dollars ($500) as the minimum required to establish a family and recommended that the new colony shall not exceed one hundred families "averaging ten persons each." This amount included the cost of the necessary implements, cattle, seed, material for the building of a home and also the cost of maintenance of the colonists during the first year of their settlement on the land.

On January 10th, 1892, a delegation was sent by the Society to Ottawa and was received by the Prime Minister, the Minister of Agriculture, and the Minister of the Interior. The Government promised to grant land to Jewish settlers in a district selected by the Society, the homesteads to comprise one block.

Meanwhile, immigrants continued to arrive in large numbers. A group of sixty Russo-refugee families, numbering in all about four hundred people, arrived in Montreal from Hamburg with the intention of settling as colonists in Canada. The Young Men's Hebrew Benevolent Society sent urgent cables for relief to the Anglo-Jewish Association, L'Alliance Israelite, and the Baron de Hirsch. The immigrants, seeing that there was some delay in acknowledgment by Dr. Sonnenfeld of the report submitted by the Colonization Committee of the Young Men's Hebrew Benevolent Society, organized themselves and selected two delegates—Messrs. T. Herschovitch and A. Leibovitch, and sent them abroad. The delegates carried with them a list of seventy-four families anxious to settle on the land and went to Paris, via London, where they saw Baron de Hirsch and presented a petition to him asking that he advance these families sufficient means to establish a colony in Canada. The report of the Colonization Committee of the Young Men's Hebrew Benevolent Society which was examined in the meanwhile by Baron de Hirsch, L'Alliance Israelite, and the Russo-Jewish Committee, made a favourable impression. Baron de Hirsch was greatly moved by the appeal of the delegates and in a letter from the Jewish Colonization Association dated January 27th, 1892, Dr. Sonnenfeld advised the Young Men's Hebrew Benevolent Society that "the sum of Thirty Thousand Dollars ($30,000), sufficient to instal sixty families, could be procured in Paris." Dr. Sonnenfeld pointed out that the monies could be advanced only in the form of loans and that the Committee should examine the families to see if they be suitable for colonization purposes as otherwise it might be preferable to have them established differently. Upon receipt of this letter, the Committee reported that the seventy-four immigrant families were fit for agriculture. Mr. Ansell, Chairman of the Colonization Committee, went to Europe where he negotiated with the Russo-Jewish Committee, Jewish

HARVESTING IN MONTEFIORE, ALBERTA

Colonization Association, and L'Alliance Israelite representatives and endeavoured to obtain a definite decision on the project to establish a Jewish colony in Canada.

Early in March, 1892, a cable was finally received from Dr. Sonnenfeld, reading as follows:

"L'Alliance and the Baron de Hirsch will place at your disposal for the installation of colonists near Moosemin one hundred thousand francs."

The Colonization Committee engaged the services of Messrs. I. Roth and Charles McDiarmid who went to the North West and investigated the Moosemin property. They also examined the lands at Red Deer, Prince Albert, and Regina, suggested by the Department of Agriculture. As the buildings erected on the Moosemin land had been destroyed and the land being about twenty-five miles distant from the railroad, it was thought to be of questionable value for the purpose of establishing a new colony. These officials of the Society recommended townships fourteen and fifteen, in ranges seventeen and eighteen, west of the second meridian in the neighbourhood of Regina. The Colonization Committee, however, desired on the advice of Mr. Ascher Pierce, to take up land in the vicinity of Oxbow where his father, Mr. Jacob Pierce, his sons, and a group of Jewish farmers were pioneer settlers. Mr. McDiarmid visited the district and finally selected township thirty-three, range five, and advised the Committee in Montreal in his letter dated April 25th, 1892, accordingly. The Commissioner of Dominion Lands at Winnipeg, Mr. H. H. Smith, was requested to hold the land and to make no entries for homesteads until the arrival of the settlers from Montreal.

The Government then granted to the Young Men's Hebrew Benevolent Society this tract of land—each quarter section to be occupied by a Jewish settler. The candidates were again carefully examined and forty-seven families were sent forward to Winnipeg in the spring of 1892. The contract for the loans that were to be advanced to the farmers was drawn by Mr. Maxwell Goldstein, the Honorary Solicitor of the Society. It devolved upon Messrs. Harris Vineberg, D. S. Friedman, and Lyon Cohen, the Executive Officers of the Society, to sign the first contracts with these settlers. The settlers reached Oxbow early in May and then proceeded to the site selected for the colony.

In addition to the above-mentioned townships, sections were also taken up in township two, range five and township three, ranges four and six. The colony was named Hirsch in honour of Baron de Hirsch and comprised during the first season about one hundred and fifty souls. The railway line was extended through the colony

NARCISSE (LEVEN), MANITOBA

and the station was also named Hirsch. A shochet was engaged and a building was erected to be used as a synagogue. A school was built for the secular education of the children and a teacher was engaged. In July, 1892, two of the Trustees of the Society—Messrs D. S. Friedman and Moses Vineberg paid a visit to the Colony.

During the years 1893 and 1894 about Forty Thousand Dollars ($40,000) were received from Paris for colonization purposes.

The new Chairman of the Colonization Committee, Mr. Lazarus Cohen, visited the Colony in the winter of 1893. Mr. Cohen took a sympathetic interest in the colonists and helped them with his sage advice. In the minutes of the meeting of November 9th, 1893, we find that Mr. Moses Vineberg, in order to facilitate Mr. Cohen's trip to the Colony even "promised to lend the Chairman a fur coat to use during his visit to Hirsch." In 1894, Mr. Isaac Mendels, Vice-President of the Baron de Hirsch Institute, also visited the Colony.

Mr. Lazarus Cohen continued to serve as Chairman of the Colonization Committee from 1893 to 1896 devoting much energy and zeal to this work. Mr. Isaac Mendels acted as Chairman of the Committee in 1897 and 1898. Mr. Ansell was again Chairman in 1899.

During the first two years the colonists at Hirsch met with many hardships, the greatest of all being the successive crop failures. In the third year, the crop was a partial failure and a number of farms were abandoned. Some of the colonists held on and as the years passed new settlers came to the colony. In 1896, five Jewish farmers who had settled at Red Deer, Alberta, were transferred to Hirsch. In 1897, the Jewish Colonization Association sent Professor H. L. Sabsovich, Superintendent of the Baron de Hirsch Woodbine Agricultural School at Woodbine, New Jersey, as a special commissioner to study the situation in the Colony. According to the minutes of the Young Men's Hebrew Benevolent Society, his report was most favourable. During this year, the crop was good—the wheat graded No. 1 and sold at seventy-three and seventy-four cents a bushel. In the minutes of the Society, it was also recorded that "many settlers were returning to the farms and that cattle raising had improved." During the same year, the Jewish Colonization Association ordered the Society to buy a threshing machine for the colony. In 1898 the Jewish Colonization Association sent Mr. Shalit, the Secretary in Paris, to inspect the colony and a second school was opened in Hirsch to meet the growing needs of education. In 1899 another representative of the Jewish Colonization Association, Mr. Walter Cohen of London, visited the settlement.

As the years went on, a group of Jewish

HARVESTING AT SONNENFELD, SASK.

farmers concentrated around Wapella, thus forming a new colony.

In 1900, the Jewish Colonization Association decided to separate the work of colonization from the general immigrant aid and relief work. The latter was carried on by the Young Men's Hebrew Benevolent Society, whereas the colonization work was transferred by the parent body to the Jewish Agricultural and Industrial Aid Society in New York.

In 1901, a Jewish colony was formed to the north of Qu'Appelle by refugees who came from Roumania during the anti-Semitic outbreaks in that country. A number of these immigrants were forwarded under the auspices of the Jewish Colonization Association from Roumania to Montreal. The Young Men's Hebrew Benevolent Society, which at the time was also called the Baron de Hirsch Institute, sent these immigrants to the Yorkton-Melville district and large groups of Jewish homesteaders established themselves north of Qu'Appelle. Later a railway line crossed the district. The colony, which was originally called Qu'Appelle was later named Lipton. The group of farmers situated further west constituted the Cupar Colony.

In 1903 another Jewish colony was formed north of Winnipeg by Jewish immigrants led by Mr. Bender. In addition to the homesteads granted to the immigrants, the Government placed at the disposal of the Bender group one hundred and sixty acres of land which were divided into twenty lots. Each house in the settlement is built on an eight acre lot. The colony which was first called Bender Hamlet, was later changed to Narcisse Leven Colony, in honour of the late President of the Jewish Colonization Association.

During the years 1900 to 1907, the Jewish Agricultural and Industrial Aid Society disbursed for the Jewish Colonization Association one hundred and forty-three (143) loans to various colonists in Canada. In 1902, the Jewish Colonization Association and the Jewish Board of Guardians in London delegated Mr. A. N. Simon of Hanover and Mr. N. J. W. Cohen of London to visit Canada. They inspected the Hirsch Colony and also studied the immigration work of the Young Men's Hebrew Benevolent Society. In 1906, Mr. O. E. D'Avigdor Goldsmid of London, representative of the Russo-Jewish Committee of London, and acting unofficially as representative of the Jewish Colonization Association, paid a visit to Canada and inspected the Hirsch Colony. In the same year, a number of other Jewish farming settlements sprung up in Western Canada. The Colonies of Trochu and Rumsey were formed northeast of Calgary and the large colony of Edenbridge was formed north of Melfort. During this year, a new colony was also founded by the graduates of the Jewish Colonization Association Slobodka-Lesna School in Galicia. The Jewish Colonization Association sent a number of these immigrants to the Hirsch Colony where they worked for a couple of years. After becoming acquainted with Canadian methods of agriculture and saving a little money from their work with other farmers, they took up homesteads about sixty to seventy miles west of Hirsch and formed the New Herman settlement south of Tribune Station, which was later renamed—Sonnenfeld Colony in honour of the first General Manager of the Jewish Colonization Association.

The Jewish Colonization Association in Paris had long desired to have the management of their immigration work in Canada separate from the charitable work of the Young Men's Hebrew Benevolent Society, and the Baron de Hirsch Institute and had intimated as far back as 1898 that their part of the work in Canada "should be carried on by a special committee to act in direct communication with Paris and to be entirely independent of the Young Men's Hebrew Benevolent Society." In the discussions which took place during Mr. D'Avigdor Goldsmid's visit in 1906, the matter was threshed out and acting upon Mr. Goldsmid's report, the Jewish Colonization Association decided to form a Canadian Committee. In a letter dated November 5th, 1906, to the Baron de Hirsch Institute, the Jewish Colonization Association stated as follows:

"Our Administrative Council is of the opinion that the time has come to re-organize on a new basis arrangement concerning immigration—reception of immigrants on landing, dispersion to points in the interior, general and technical education, etc. Our Council considers it advisable therefore to create a special committee of six for the purpose—three of the members be nominated by you and approved by us, the other three being chosen by our Association from among such persons as we may think likely to help substantially in the common work."

S. BELKIN
Secretary, Canadian Committee,
Jewish Colonization Association

On December 10th, 1906, the Baron de Hirsch Institute, acting in accordance with this request, nominated Messrs. Harris Vineberg, D. A. Ansell and Bernard Goldstein as representatives of that institution, which step was approved by the Association in Paris. The Council of the Jewish Colonization Association in Paris named Messrs. M. B. Davis, (later Sir Mortimer B. Davis), Lyon Cohen and S. W. Jacobs direct to act on the Committee.

In 1907, Mr. D'Avigdor Goldsmid returned as official representative of the Jewish Colonization Association to Canada and asked the members of the Committee to "take over from the Jewish Agricultural and Industrial Aid Society of New York the business heretofore carried on by that Society on behalf of the Jewish Colonization Association consisting of loans and assistance of a like nature made from time to time to Jewish colonists in the Canadian Northwest. The work will consist of collecting interest on loans and receiving payment of principal and the general management of the loan department of the Jewish Colonization Association work in the Northwest."

The Jewish Colonization Association in Paris sent a letter to the new Committee dated February 22nd, 1907 (No. 174), in which it clearly defined the duties of the Committee:

1. To disperse immigrants in places and towns in the Dominion and prevent congestion in Montreal.
2. To control and report on the settlements of Hirsch and Qu'Appelle (Lipton) and to assist Jewish farmers generally.
3. To keep the books in connection with the loans granted by the Jewish Colonization Association.

The Canadian Committee of the Jewish Colonization Association held its first meeting on July 3rd, 1907, at which Mr. Mortimer B. Davis was elected Chairman; Mr. Lyon Cohen, Treasurer; and Mr. S. W. Jacobs, Secretary. The Committee prepared a lengthy program of work which it forwarded to the Central Administration in Paris and performed its work in behalf of the Jewish Colonization Association as a semi-autonomous body. The composition of the Committee underwent the following changes: In 1908, Mr. Jacob A. Jacobs was named as a member replacing Mr. D. A. Ansell who resigned. In April 1910, Rev. Dr. H. Abramowitz was asked by the Administrative Council in Paris to act as a Member of the Committee which proposal was accepted by him. The last meeting of the Committee attended by Mr. M. B. Davis was in 1913. Since then, Mr. Lyon Cohen assumed the active leadership of the Committee. In June, 1923, Mr. Lyon Cohen was elected Chairman and Mr. B. Goldstein, Treasurer. The personnel of the present administrative staff is as follows: S. Belkin, Executive Secretary; M. C. Ellman, Colony Administrator, and L. Rosenberg, Assistant to Mr. Ellman. Of the Jewish Colonization Association past officials special mention must be made of Messrs. H. Horsfall and Louis Lewis.

The years 1907 to 1914 brought a large influx of Jewish immigrants to Canada. Following the first Russian revolution and pogrom waves of 1905, thousands of Jewish immigrants arrived at the shores of Canada and credit is due to the keen foresight of the Jewish Colonization Association in having created a Canadian Committee, thus being in a position to enlarge its activities. The actual reception and maintenance of immigrants continued under the auspices of the Baron de Hirsch Institute, the funds being supplied by the Jewish Colonization Association through the Canadian Committee. The Canadian Committee also represented the Russo-Jewish Committee, and the Jewish Board of Guardians, in matters of immigration and administration of the funds supplied by these two organizations at the time for Canadian immigration work, which funds had hitherto been administered by Messrs. D. S. Friedman and A. M. Vineberg.

During the Great War there was no immigration but with its termination large numbers of immigrants began to arrive. The Jewish Immigrant Aid Society, which was formed in August, 1920, took over the immigration work which was hitherto done by the Baron de Hirsch Institute. Large funds were supplied to this organization by the Jewish Colonization Association.

One of the greatest acts ever accomplished by the Jewish Colonization Association and its Canadian Committee was the rescuing of about thirty-three hundred Russo-Jewish refugees who were stranded in Roumania. A special permit was obtained from the Government in October, 1923, through the good agencies of Messrs. Lyon Cohen and S. W. Jacobs, K.C., M.P., to admit these unfortunate immigrants to Canada. The Jewish Colonization Association supplied the money required for the ocean transportation and entirely defrayed the cost of railway fares of the immigrants in Canada in connection with their distribution throughout the country. The Jewish Colonization Association has expended, through its Canadian Committee, large sums for this branch of its work.

The main attention of the Canadian Committee, however, was given to its colonization work. A number of new colonies were formed during its existence. During the years 1907 to 1911, the colonies of Pine Ridge and Bird's Hill were founded in the vicinity of Winnipeg. The Jewish colonies of Macaza and Ste. Sophie in the Province of Quebec which were founded in 1904 have developed. In 1910, the Eyre settlement was formed north of Alsask, Saskatchewan. In 1911, a colony was formed near Sibbald Station in Alberta and named in honour of the Montefiore family. In the same year, a Jewish colony sprung up at Camper, about one hundred miles north of Winnipeg which colony was afterwards named New Hirsch. A Jewish farming settlement was founded in May 1911, near Rosetown, Saskatchewan.

In 1907, Dr. Sonnenfeld visited Canada and inspected the colonies at Hirsch and Lipton. In 1908, the Committee invited Rev. Dr. Herman Abramowitz, Rabbi of the Shaar Hashomayim Synagogue, Montreal, to visit the Hirsch and Lipton Colonies and a Hebrew School system was introduced under his direction throughout the Colonies thus helping the farmers to give Hebrew instruction to their children. In 1913, Dr. Abramowitz and Mr. S. W. Jacobs K.C., M.P., visited the Central Administration in Paris and discussed various matters appertaining to the work. In 1924, the Chairman, Mr. Lyon Cohen, visited Paris where he attended a meeting of the Administrative Council of the Association. In 1921 and 1923, Mr. Edouard Oungre, Associate Manager of the Jewish Colonization Association, spent several months in Canada and thoroughly studied the situation in each colony. Due to his visits, a closer co-operation and effective contact was established between the parent body and its Canadian organization.

SONS AND DAUGHTERS, EDENBRIDGE COLONY, SASK.

The Committee helped the farmers by advancing loans to them—the funds being supplied by the Jewish Colonization Association. Between the years 1908 to December 31st, 1923, the Committee advanced 1,822 loans, the total of which runs into an enormous figure. The interest rate charged by the Association is only five percent and the repayments are spread over a number of years. Real estate mortgages represent the bulk of securities taken, but some loans have been granted on secondary security. It must also be mentioned that the Association has assisted the farmers to erect their communal buildings and has subsidized the religious education of their children.

In 1920, a more or less complete survey of Jewish farming was made by the administration in Canada. According to the survey, there were about seven hundred independent Jewish farmers in Canada of whom three hundred and ninety-one were indebted to the Association. The number of Jewish souls on farms was estimated at no less than three thousand five hundred. The acreage owned by Jewish farmers was approximately 150,000 acres; real estate value was estimated at $4,500,000; livestock $1,000,000; machinery $500,000; value of yearly crop produced $1,000,000. The gross assets reached the appreciable figure of $6,500,000; liabilities about $1,500,000; and the net equity $5,000,000.

In addition to the organized settlements already mentioned, there are groups of Jewish farmers at the following points: MANITOBA—Ste. Anne, Gimli, Lorette, Transcona, Rosenfeld; SASKATCHEWAN—Maxwellton, Theodore, Limerick, Kamsack, White Bear, Watrous and Dumfernline; ALBERTA—Compeer, Empress and near Edmonton; QUEBEC—St. Lin, New Glasgow, Ste. Agathe, Joliette, Ste. Julie and near Montreal; ONTARIO—Cedar Valley, Pontypool, Timmins and near Ottawa, Toronto and Hamilton. There are also individual Jewish farmers to be found at various points in Canada of whom we have no records. In addition, a large majority of Jewish storekeepers and cattle dealers located in Western Canadian rural communities are also engaged in farming, in most cases on an extensive scale.

In enumerating the names of those who have shown zeal and devotion towards the ideal of Jewish farming in Canada, and in giving due praise to the great work of the Jewish Colonization Association in Canada, we regret that we are unable to give the names of all those who have actively done pioneer work on the virgin land of the Canadian West. The story of their lives is one of great struggle against adverse conditions. The Jewish farmers although not large in number, have proven to be of good mettle and have contributed to the opening of this vast country. In 1907, the district where the Edenbridge Colony is now situated was a wilderness covered with woods and marshes. In 1923, just sixteen years later, this colony had more than four thousand acres under crop. Thousands of tons of stones have been removed from fields in Hirsch, Sonnenfeld and elsewhere. The majority of Jewish farmers have remained on the land and have become deeply rooted in Canadian soil. They have proven to the world that Jews can be and are good farmers.

With the adjustment of after war conditions and with the improvement of the world market, Jewish farming in Canada should receive a new impetus which may have far-reaching effects.

In conclusion, we would quote from a letter received by the Winnipeg office of the Jewish Colonization Association, from a farmer in Edenbridge. It is very characteristic of the idealistic Jew, who has striven for a life of independence and creative work:

"I sit upon my plow and my eye is enchanted with the sight of the brown earth being turned upwards furrow by furrow. If the field is a long one and one starts with a straight furrow, it takes on the appearance of a Tallith, with broad blue stripes at the edges and when the sun's rays strike the eye and the breeze blows the squadrons of little flies past one, it seems as if the black strips of ploughed land twist and turn. It is a picture which I am not able to place upon paper. Later, when one has to run after the harrows, no matter how hard it is, the work draws like a magnet. The field behind takes on another appearance. From a piece of coarse common cloth it becomes like linen, and another stroke of the harrows makes it into velvet, silk or a piece of smoothly polished furniture. It serves as an enchantment which prevents the feet from feeling tired."

"Then comes the drill and the eye is strained to see that the horses on the ploughed side should follow the wheel mark and draws you until the stomach gives the signal to raise your eyes and see the sun in the south."

"How beautiful are the fields afterwards when they become green. This draws you and draws you and makes you willing to root out forests, turn over fields, even drink the sweat that pours from your forehead and yet be satisfied."

"And who can describe the rhythm of the binder, especially when you have enough feed for the horses and the horses feel their oats and the machine is in good repair. You sit upon the binder and you become one with the machine, and the joyfulness of the horses passes through the binder to you and you become a part of them. Should the field be good and the straw straight you cannot distinguish between the iron of the machine, the blood and bone of the horse and the man. They form one happy piece of machinery."

Men with such a spirit cannot but succeed and reap the fruits of their labour.

THE FEDERATED JEWISH FARMERS OF ONTARIO

"BACK-TO-THE-LAND is a new clarion call resounding in the ears of the modern Jew.

Back-to-the-land was heard and heeded by the Chalutzim who are now rebuilding Palestine.

Back-to-the-land has been heeded in large numbers by our co-religionists in the United States of America, and in many other countries the world over.

Back-to-the-land has also reached the ears and hearts of our Canadian Jewry.

Be it known that a group of Jewish farmers have recently organized themselves under the name of United Jewish Farmers of Ontario, with experience and plans that will be of benefit to every Jew in the Dominion."

The foregoing was the introduction of hundreds of letters that went out in the early spring of 1925, sent by a small group of men who were wont to meet in Mr. Levine's office at 475 Queen Street West, Toronto.

The Jewish farmers like farming for itself. They feel how much outdoor life strengthens their bodies and how much healthier they become than their city brethren. They have also found that at the same time farming offers them a good livelihood, and last but not least, it is the basic industry of this country—the most productive occupation from the point of view of the whole community. The Jewish farmers had found and still find associations with their Christian neighbors to be very congenial. They have come to feel how much of a real home this country has become to them, as their memories go back to the time when they first came as immigrants to Canada. Mr. Morris Saxe conceived the idea of a Jewish farmers' organization which would enable more Jews to settle on the land, and he stuck to this idea until he brought it into being.

The movement started with a notice in the *Canadian Jewish Review* inviting the public to a meeting at the Holy Blossom Synagogue, Toronto, to be held on Sunday afternoon, March 29th, 1925. Mr. Saxe invited all of the Jewish farmers in Ontario, whom he was able to locate, numbering about eighty, but only half of whom were present. Rabbi Brickner was in the chair and explained, in an impressive manner, the purpose and necessity of such a movement. Upon Mr. Saxe's motion, the farmers present organized themselves into the United Jewish Farmers of Ontario, electing Rabbi Brickner, honorary president, Mr. Saxe, president, and an executive of twelve members.

The same evening a mass meeting was held which was full of fervor, despite the small attendance. Rabbi Brickner again addressed the meeting. Professor Dean of the Agricultural College, Guelph, Mr. J. J. Morrison of the United Farmers of Ontario, and Mayor LeRoy Dale of Georgetown welcomed the members of the new organization and discussed farming conditions in general.

Non-farmers who were in sympathy with the movement were enrolled as associate members. Four of them were elected members of the executive, in order to help spread the movement in Toronto. A provincial charter was applied for and granted after the name had been changed to Federated Jewish Farmers of Ontario. The following programme of activities was decided upon;—

(1) Attendance to special necessities of Jewish farmers as Shochets, teachers and the strengthening of social contact.
(2) Placing of Jewish applicants for work on the land.
(3) Spreading of the agricultural idea among the Jewish population.
(4) The establishment of a training farm for Jewish immigrants.
(5) Preparatory work for settling Jewish families, either scattered or in colonies, on the land.

A special committee in charge of the estimating work visited the Agricultural College in Guelph and received valuable information from the president and members of the staff as to which of the projects could first be put into practice, and how.

After a few weeks of investigation, the committee took an option on the old Eaton farm near Georgetown, comprising about four hundred acres, and recommended its purchase as a training farm for newcomers.

On May 3rd, 1925, a public meeting was held in Hamilton under the auspices of Mr. David Sweet with Mr. M. Saxe, Mr. A. Rhinewine and Rabbi Freund as the principal speakers.

On May 17th, 1925, at the annual meeting of the Jewish Immigrant Aid Society of Canada, held in Montreal, Rabbi Brickner pointed out the necessity for the whole Jewish community to direct its attention towards agricultural settlement and to give active support to the Ontario farming movement in their efforts to establish a training farm. This met with the greatest sympathy, and the following resolution, moved by the delegates, was carried, practically giving this movement a charter among the provincial and local institutions.

"Whereas the fact that Canada has a Jewish farming population of about 5,000 souls is widely unknown, and

Whereas farming offers to newcomers to this country a healthful vocation which will establish them firmly and successfully as Jewish Canadians and will bring credit to the Jewish community as a whole, and

Whereas as farming, when taken up by trained and suitable men and started carefully, can be made a better paying success than many of the city occupations which hitherto too many of the newcomers used to flock to.
RESOLVED,

That the annual meeting of the Jewish Immigrant Aid Society of Canada welcomes the movement of the Federated Jewish Farmers of Ontario, which tends to strengthen morally and materially the Jewish farmers of Ontario, and

That it declares as most desirable the spreading of this organization among the Jewish farmers of the other provinces, and

That a plan of this organization of establishing a training farm for the purpose of training Jews for agricultural work deserves our consideration and full support, and

That it is recommended to all provincial local boards of the Jewish Immigrant Aid Society of Canada to delegate members into the farmers' committees of their localities, and

That it hopes sincerely that the Jewish Colonization Association, which has done such great work for Jewish agricultural colonization in this country, will take an interest in the work of the Federated Jewish Farmers of Ontario."

On May 24th, 1925, a second public meeting was held in Toronto at the McCaul Street Synagogue, which was attended by about four hundred people. Mr. M. Saxe, Rabbi J. Gordon and Rabbi L. Graubart were the speakers. The first donations were collected and a new membership was enrolled. Toronto Jewry was awakened, as, in the previous week, Montreal Jewry had been.

HISTORY OF THE JEWISH IMMIGRANT AID SOCIETY OF CANADA

By S. B. Haltrecht, B.A.

ALL important events in history appear unconsciously and come about at certain specific moments when they are most needed. The end of the World War was marked by universal chaos and indecision on the part of the various civilized nations throughout the world, particularly by those situated in Central and Eastern Europe. Reaction and chauvinism reigned supreme. The strong did their utmost to oppress the weak; whether from the point of view of nationality, or for other unreasonable causes. Under such circumstances it was only natural to expect a flood of restless groups wanting to migrate to any place under the sun where peace and safety would be their reward. Millions knew not in the morning where they would sleep at night, nor in the evening whether they would wake up alive the next morning

The main question for these unfortunates was **EMIGRATION.** The problem was where to emigrate. Many of them had stopped believing that there was such a thing as hospitality and friendship in this world. Black clouds covered the horizon, and it looked as if the sun of hope had stopped shining for ever. When the World War terminated, it seemed therefore quite natural that although all people suffered enormously, the Jewish people suffered most. The question of emigration from Europe then became a vital one: it affected the Jews to a larger degree than other nationalities.

In Canada, the Jews from coast to coast organized into what was called the CANADIAN JEWISH CONGRESS for the purpose of showing a united front in matters pertaining to Jewish problems. The details and the workings of this "Congress" are not within the scope of the present article, but after it had accomplished the immediate task for which it was organized, it erected a monument in Canadian Jewish History by which it will always be remembered. By this monument I mean the organization of the Jewish Immigrant Aid Society of Canada.

The leaders of the Canadian Jewish Congress realized that one of the greatest problems to face Canadian Jewry for years to come was the question of IMMIGRATION. They considered it a matter of fortunate accident that Jews happened to come to this country some years before, and therefore felt a moral responsibility to do their bit towards their brothers and sisters on the other side.

The first meeting to deal with the immigration question was called by Mr. Lyon Cohen, President of the Canadian Jewish Congress, and was held on the evening of June 23rd, 1920, at the Zionist Headquarters, Montreal, with Mr. H. M. Caiserman, General Secretary of the "Congress" as Secretary. In addition to the representatives of the Canadian Jewish Congress, there were also representatives from the Canadian Committee of the Jewish Colonization Association, Hebrew Ladies' Immigrant Protective Association, The Associated War Relief Societies, the Roumanian Verband and the Ukranian Verband.

A second meeting took place on June 30, 1920, at which there were representatives from the Canadian Jewish Congress, the Roumanian, Ukranian and Polish Verbands. The delegates from the Roumanian and Ukranian Verbands pledged their organizations to contribute $500 each towards the work of the new Society. At this meeting the foundation stone of the Jewish Immigrant Aid Society of Canada was laid, and the following resolutions were adopted:

1. That the Society be named the Jewish Immigrant Aid Society of Canada with headquarters in Montreal, and branches to be organized throughout the length and breadth of the Dominion, wherever possible.
2. That a Committee be immediately sent to the Port of Quebec to study the immigration question from its source and to engage an intelligent man to meet the steamers and to render the Jewish immigrants every necessary assistance.
3. That the declared purpose of the newly formed organization will be to meet the immigrants at the ports and at the stations in the various cities and towns, to give them the required advice and protection, as well as the legal and other assistance that they may require.
4. That a temporary executive be elected from those present to conduct the work until such a time when a public meeting be arranged and a permanent Board of Directors secured.

Mr. Lyon Cohen was offered the Presidency but as he was Chairman of the Canadian Committee of the J.C.A., felt he could best serve the cause by not accepting office in the new Society.

The following were then elected as the first executive of the Jewish Immigrant Aid Society of Canada; Mr. Louis Fitch, Vice-President of the Canadian Jewish Congress, President; Mr. H. M. Caiserman, General Secretary of the Canadian Jewish Congress, General Secretary; Rabbi Hirsch Cohen, Treasurer; and Messrs. B. Goldstein and L. Lewis ex officio representing the J.C.A.

The General Secretary threw himself into this work with all his heart and soul. He sent letters to all the branches of the Canadian Jewish Congress informing them of the urgency. Toronto and Winnipeg responded at once. Immigrants began coming into the country and required material assistance as well as administrative advice. At the executive meeting on August 11, 1920, it was decided to ask the J.C.A. to provide for inland transportation and shelter, while the Immigrant Aid Society would look after the other requirements. The J.C.A. responded most sympathetically.

The work which was expected of the Society was growing from day to day. From its inception it was evident that an executive consisting of volunteers could not be expected to be taxed with work which required the attention of specialists. With that end in view, the Canadian Committee of the J.C.A., who had many years of experience, suggested the appointment of a man for the purpose of organizing and consolidating the work of the Society both in Montreal as well as at the ports. On August 16th, 1920, Mr. S. B. Haltrecht, a young university graduate, who had made a special study of the Canadian immigration problem, was requested to accept the appointment just described with authority to take full charge of the administration. Mr. Haltrecht set to the task of establishing the work on a systematic basis.

There is a certain amount of romance attached to the early history of almost every great movement or institution. When the Society was first established it had no home, no headquarters, no centre where to meet or to perform its required work of daily routine. The Secretary and General Manager had his first office in a corner of the Baron de Hirsch Institute. The Zionist Headquarters offered one of its rooms as a private office for the Manager while the Canadian Jewish Congress which shared with the Mizrachi a joint office on the top floor of the Molson's Bank Building, offered the services of their stenographer for an hour or two a day. The Federation of Jewish Philanthropies, as well as the Canadian Committee of the Jewish Colonization Association, were also ready to help.

This state of affairs could however not continue, so we moved into the joint office of the Congress and the Mizrachi, and within a short time with the arrival of immigrants, the top floor was filled with baggage and people, until neither the Congress nor the Mizrachi were able to do anything for their own organizations. One fine morning the Manager of the Molson's Bank Building walked into our office with one of his sturdy assistants and told us politely but very sternly that we must move at once. An empty store was found at 900 St. Lawrence Boulevard, which became the headquarters. In the fall of 1920 Jewish immigration into Canada assumed considerable proportions. With the arrival of a great number of new immigrants, restrictions were rigidly enforced, with the result that many immigrants arriving at our shores found themselves detained and in danger of deportation to the countries from which they had made every effort to flee. Those detained had relatives in every part of the American continent who worried the officials of the Society. Appeals had to be made on their behalf. To deport them was equivalent to sending them to certain death. It is very difficult to realize the magnitude of the work as well as the multiplicity of details that the Society performed in those days.

More than a hundred telegrams a day went out from the office to all parts of the North American Continent consoling relatives of detained ones, telling them that they were not being neglected. Telegrams arrived at our office from every corner of the continent asking for information and pleading for assistance. Long distance telephone calls were received from morning to evening, from Toronto, Ottawa, Milwaukee, Indianapolis, Chicago, New York, Boston, Philadelphia and elsewhere.

S. B. HALTRECHT, B.A.

Conditions became more unbearable from day to day. It was evident that this Society in order to meet the situation and to be equal to the task for which it was established, must enlarge and extend. The Society required proper national headquarters where offices adequate for the work could be established, and where a sheltering home and a meeting place could also find space. The building situated at 725 Notre Dame Street, West, was purchased by the Board of Directors. The net purchase price of the building was thirteen thousand dollars, while it required another seven thousand dollars to cover the carpentry and plumbing expenses, as well as the outfitting of the kitchen and dormitories. Mr. Louis Cohen, the Chairman of the House Committee at the time, deserves a great deal of credit for the close attention he gave to the establishment of the Notre Dame Street Headquarters.

On the ground floor there was a kitchen, dining room, baggage room, and bath room with shower baths. On the first floor, a flat of administrative offices with a dispensary containing all first aid material and a board room to serve for the directors' meetings. The upper two flats were used for dormitories.

The general meeting took place on Sunday afternoon, November 14th, 1920. Reports showed that Montreal contributed nearly eleven thousand dollars, while the other parts of Canada about four thousand dollars. This was quite inadequate and had it not been for the assistance of the J.C.A., the work could not have been carried on.

The Quebec representatives at the meeting pointed out that nearly three hundred were detained at that port, who required immediate attention, and that additional immigrants were expected to arrive in the course of the following few days, and that if something were not done immediately, the reputation of Canadian Jewry would suffer. Some of the detained were there for months and the deportation of the first fourteen Jewish immigrants to Europe had created a panic. The representatives were placing the responsibility on the larger community of Montreal.

At the elections that followed, Mr. Peter Bercovitch, K.C., M.P.P., was elected as National President for the coming year; Mr. Joseph Cohen as Vice-President; Mr. Simon as Treasurer, and Mr. Caiserman was re-elected as General Secretary. In addition, ten active Directors were elected and the following organizations were given the privilege of having two representatives on the Board: Canadian Jewish Congress, Canadian Committee of the Jewish Colonization Association, Roumanian Verband, Ukranian Verband, Hebrew Ladies' Immigrant Protective Society, Jewish Labour Unions. Every branch in the Dominion was entitled to be represented by one Director, namely, the local President. Mr. S. W. Jacobs, K.C. M.P., was elected Honorary President.

With the coming of the fall and winter of 1920-1921, the work of the Society was extended to meet the requirements of the moment. When the Port of Quebec closed, several hundred detained were transferred to Montreal. At the same time, the Port of St. John opened and boats began to come there as well as to Halifax, bringing many immigrants, a good portion of whom were rejected for non-compliance with small technicalities of the Immigrant Act. The irony of it all was that the detained, although held for no fault of their own (they all innocently boarded the steamer and paid their regular fare, being informed that the doors of Canada were open to them) had to suffer not only the inconvenience and unpleasantness of involuntary detention, but were forced to pay for their board and room at $1.50 a day, which was later increased to $1.75 a day. The government held the steamship companies responsible for the payment of such maintenance expenses in case immigrants were deported without paying what was due. The companies demanded, in addition to the $20 which the Government required as a deposit from each detained immigrant whose case was appealed to Ottawa, an additional cash deposit or satisfactory guarantee from responsible persons that the maintenance for any length of time would be paid, otherwise they insisted on having the immigrant deported immediately the $20 originally deposited were used up.

The Jewish Immigrant Aid Society, in its extreme desire to help, took upon itself a responsibility, the magnitude of which was not forseen—to be responsible for the cost of maintenance of those appealed detained cases of Jews. It did not take many months before the bills of the steamship companies amounted to over $10,000. It was an enormous burden, almost impossible to carry. Many have criticized the Society for being too liberal. Such criticism may find some justification, but when dealing with human lives we cannot always be dictated to by logic.

The work continued to extend and before the end of 1920, the Society established a Legal Bureau in Ottawa to look after appeal cases. The Government also realized that the situation became an almost impossible one, and was willing to help in clearing it up as quickly as it was possible. They issued an order permitting the temporary entry into Canada under a cash bond of $500 for each of those detained who wanted to apply for admission to the United States. As a result, over one hundred detained Jewish immigrants were saved from being deported back to Europe.

The conditions of the detained became so unbearable, that the Society seriously considered sending a commission to Europe to open offices in various centres for the purpose of warning emigrants against migrating to Canada. Fortunately, news of these conditions spread through Europe and during the latter part of the winter of 1921, less immigrants arrived which saved the situation for the time being.

In the beginning of January the official opening of the Society's headquarters took place. Invitations were sent to organizations both in Canada and the United States. The affair was a very inspiring one. Advantage was taken of the occasion and appeals for funds were made to Canadian Jewry. A campaign for funds and membership was held in April 1921.

When the immigration question became acute, the western branches in conjunction with the Jewish farmers of Saskatchewan and Alberta called a conference which took place in Saskatoon on February 13th and 14th, 1921. The Mayor of Saskatoon as well as Professor Swanson of the Saskatoon University were present to greet the conference. A number of resolutions were adopted, amongst which was the formation of a Jewish Agricultural Association to disseminate among Jewish immigrants reliable information about the opportunities in Western Canada, as well as to organize lecture tours and special courses for farmers. The new organization was to be a part of the Jewish Immigrant Aid Society. Due to the fact that immigration during the winter of 1921 was somewhat reduced, nothing of a permanent nature resulted from the conference, but showed the potentiality of the Jewish community of Western Canada.

The annual membership meeting was held on May 29th, and the following were elected to hold office for the ensuing year;—Mr. S. W. Jacobs, K.C., M.P., Honorary President; Mr. Peter Bercovitch, K.C., M.P.P., President; Messrs. Louis Cohen and L. Coviensky, Vice-Presidents; Mr. A. Wolofsky, Treasurer; Mr. H. M. Caiserman, Honorary Secretary, (till July when he was to leave for Palestine).

The spring and summer season of 1921 saw the work of the Society more efficiently organized than during the first six months. The immigrants who arrived were well looked after. They were given shelter and protection, and positions were found for them.

From ten to twelve per cent of the arrivals were generally detained by the immigration authorities on account of some technicality, but in the majority of cases after appeal was made to the Minister, their entry was secured. The only difficulty the Society experienced was the procuring of the necessary funds to carry on their work, but the J.C.A. through its committee, realizing the importance of the existence of the Society, always came to their assistance.

In July, 1921, Mr. Edouard Oungre, one of the administrators of the head office of the J.C.A. in Paris, visited Canada for the purpose of looking over their interests in this country. He took a deep interest in the Jewish Immigrant Aid Society and visited its city and port offices. A special meeting of the executive of the Society was called to meet Mr. Oungre. Mr. Lyon Cohen, the Chairman of the Canadian Committee of the J.C.A., in introducing Mr. Oungre, outlined the great work which the J.C.A. was doing throughout the world. He stated that it was fortunate that half a century ago there lived a great philanthropist whose name was Baron de Hirsch, and that this good man had founded with his own funds, the Jewish Colonization Association to assist in establishing Jews upon land. The Association also gave assistance to persecuted Jews to emigrate to countries where they could enjoy freedom and equality. The Jewish Colonization Association, he said, would help the Society in the good work it was doing, providing that they could obtain a certain amount of assistance from Canadian Jewry, and provided the Society awakened Canadian Jewry to its responsibilities towards new arrivals. Mr. Cohen lauded Mr. Oungre's zeal and indefatigable energy in behalf of the Association and the work which it performed. Mr. Oungre expressed his complete accord with the sentiments uttered by the Chairman of the Canadian Committee, and reiterated the statement that the Association was prepared to assist in the good work they were doing. He expressed the opinion that the function of the Society should rather be in the nature of advice and protection than relief work.

An Order-in-Council was passed at Ottawa on July 26th, 1921, and was put into force in the beginning of September of that year, leaving about five weeks' time for spreading the information throughout Europe. This lapse of time was not sufficient to warn intending immigrants of their danger. The result was that from the two boats which arrived at the Port of Quebec on September 3rd and 4th, namely, from the "Megantic" and "Corsican" 253 Jewish passengers were rejected, fully 50% of the arrivals. The S.S. "Canada" which arrived in Quebec on September 18th with 269 passengers had 170 rejections. The S.S. "Saxonia" which reached the port of Halifax in October with a Jewish passenger list of 156 had every one of them rejected and ordered deported.

The unfortunate immigrants, who, after running away from war torn and pogrom stricken Eastern Europe, after breaking up their homes and gathering sufficient money to bring them to Canada in order to qualify their entry, on arrival on Canadian soil—the country on which they had placed all their hopes—found themselves rejected and ordered deported back to countries from which they made every effort to flee in order to save their lives. Their cries of despair ascended to the heavens. The following is a sample of the appeals received from those detained at the ports:

> "Brothers! Remember the issue. It is a question of life and death for men, women and children, who in coming to this country hoped to establish for themselves a quiet and restful home. If we are sent back we have nothing

left to do but to throw ourselves into the ocean. Remember that Petlura, Deniken, Balachovitch and others have already thrown into the sea enough of our brothers, sisters, mothers, fathers and little children. Do not be a party to such tragedy, for on you lies the duty to help us."

It looked as if the bright sun which these poor unfortunate immigrants had once upon a time seen on the western horizon had forever stopped shining. The Society was determined to do everything in its power not to permit our unhappy brethren to be deported back to the hell from which they had barely escaped with their lives.

If an intelligent and resourceful lot of immigrants were to be barred from entry into Canada, then there must be some other country where these people would be received. On no condition must they be sent back to Europe. After considerable trouble, Mr. and Mrs. A. J. Frieman of Ottawa, in conjunction with our Ottawa bureau, succeeded in making arrangements with the Cuban Consul General that all Jewish immigrants detained at the Eastern Canadian ports should be admitted into Cuba. The Canadian Government agreed to stay deportation. Thus a great relief came. Negotiations also commenced with different steamship companies for the transfer of the immigrants to Cuba, and Mrs. Frieman was preparing to conduct them to that country personally.

While these preparations were being made, the Department of Immigration ordered the re-examination of the immigrants once more, and those that complied with the regulations were admitted under special permits. The following is taken from a letter signed by forty-seven immigrants who were detained, and was addressed to Mr. Zwerling and Mr. Katz, Chairman and Treasurer respectively of the Halifax branch of the Society:

Halifax, N.S.—

"On the great historical day when a large number of immigrants were released from jail and saved from the horrible fate which awaited them, namely, deportation."

"To our dear friends, Messrs. Zwerling and Katz of the Halifax Branch of the Jewish Immigrant Aid Society of Canada."

"On this day of our release, we the undersigned, take the opportunity to express to you the warmest thanks from the depths of our souls."

"No words or phrases can describe the feeling of the freed man towards his liberator. Our Jewish history is almost fully covered with blood and tears, and anywhere the Jew has trespassed, a mysterious power would lead that country to prosperity and the Jew to desolation. The only piece of earth on this globe, that is— thank Heaven—not yet acquainted with the horrible events that happened to other lands of our goluth, is that of Canada and the United States, and when the doors of Canada were about to be closed upon us and we were to be deported back to Europe, with nothing to greet us there but suffering, the only ray of hope which gleamed on us was extinguished and a Jewish community of old and young men, women and children were about to be crushed."

"Therefore, our kind liberators, we would ask you to accept the only means with which we can thank you, that is our blessings from the depths of our hearts which we hope will reach the gates of Heaven and be sanctioned by the Almighty."

With the election of the new Government, little if any change of policy on the immigration question took place. In fact, as time went on the doors of Canada were still more tightly shut against all immigration from Europe except from the British Isles. But the administration of the Immigration Department underwent a change for the better. When hundreds of innocent immigrants found themselves on reaching our shores detained and in dread of deportation, we appealed to the Government not to permit the sailing of emigrants from Europe to Canada unless they complied with all the regulations. We asked that the evil be checked at its source and that no emigrant should be encouraged, advised or given any hope whatsoever to break up his home before he was reasonably certain he was entitled to admission into Canada.

The Government was quick to remedy this evil and sent agents to the various European centres such as Antwerp, Danzig, Warsaw and Riga for the purpose of examining would-be immigrants. This resulted in a positive and definite check to immigration. Opinions were expressed time and again that a more liberal policy of immigration should be adopted by the Canadian Government in order to allow the entry of a larger number of desirable immigrants. The restrictions enacted by the United States against immigration gave the Canadian Government a wonderful opportunity to get the best European material for this country. Our Winnipeg branch called a special mass meeting in that city for Sunday, December 18th, 1921, to which the Hon. E. J. McMurray was invited as the guest speaker, and at which resolutions were adopted favouring a more liberal immigration policy.

The Society applied for a Federal Charter which in due course it received under the name of "Jewish Immigrant Aid Society of Canada" with headquarters in Montreal, and with full powers to organize branches from coast to coast.

With the slackening of immigration, however, the Society was again handicapped by lack of interest. Our Toronto branch for a while closed its doors. In order to secure funds to help the organization, the Winnipeg branch arranged during the spring of 1922, a novel undertaking, namely, an Old Country Fair known as "YARID". As a result of it they secured a sum of nearly $10,000.

A National Immigration Conference of the Society was called at the Chateau Laurier in Ottawa on July 5, 1922. There were in attendance fourteen duly accredited representatives from the Montreal headquarters, nine from the Toronto branch, eight from Ottawa, three from Winnipeg, two from Hamilton, and one from Saskatoon. The Conference was divided into two sessions, the first of which opened at 10.30 A.M. Addresses were delivered by Mr. S. W. Jacobs, K.C., M.P., and Mr. Lyon Cohen of Montreal, while Mr. S. B. Haltrecht delivered the General Manager's and Treasurer's reports. Mr. B. Sheps of Winnipeg submitted the report on behalf of the western branches, and Rabbi Julius L. Siegel of Toronto on behalf of the Toronto branch. The following resolutions were adopted:

1. That a committee of seven be appointed to study and prepare a constitution and by-laws.
2. That a drive for membership and funds throughout the Dominion take place about the 15th of September, 1922.
3. That Naturalization Aid Bureaus and Free Legal Aid Committees be formed.
4. That another National Conference be called within a year.

During the summer of 1922, an experiment was made of sending out Jewish harvesters to the West. In view of the reduced harvesters' fare in August, the Society in Montreal endeavoured to send to the West as many of the newcomers as were anxious to go harvesting or who wished to settle there. Brief announcements were made in the local Jewish Eagle and soon we had swarms of applicants all eager to leave the congested city atmosphere for the open air of the Western Prairie Provinces. They all had to pay their own fare, but were informed that the machinery of the Society was at their disposal for information and advice, but that they could expect no other material assistance. 146 responded within the space of a week, determined to go to the West. Arrangements were made with the C.P.R. to send to our Head Office two of their ticket agents on Thursday, August 10th, (the day before the train of harvesters left for the West) and the tickets were sold in our own building. The following morning, Friday, August 11th, this group of sturdy young men left Windsor Station for Winnipeg. After leaving Winnipeg, it was impossible to keep track of them, but from various reports, we are safe in saying that at least half of them remained in the West for good.

The annual meeting of the Society took place on Sunday afternoon, December 3rd, 1922. The officers elected for the coming year were Mr. Louis Fitch, President; Messrs. Louis Cohen and Lionel Coviensky, Vice-Presidents; Mr. A. Wolofsky, Treasurer; and Mr. Benjamin Robinson, Honorary Secretary. Mr. S. W. Jacobs, K.C., M.P., was re-elected Honorary President.

The next few months were chiefly occupied with the reduction of staff to a minimum to meet the situation. The immigration regulations had become extremely stringent, practically prohibiting the entry into the country of Jewish people from Eastern Europe. Only wives destined to their husbands, and minor children to their parents were admitted; excepting only farmers, farm labourers and domestics, provided they had reasonable assurance of employment awaiting them.

Under such conditions while the detailed work of the office was, as a result of individual requirements for permits, considerably increased, the public at large began to look upon the organization with indifference. Public interest waned and very little funds were received from the community for the upkeep of the Society. The headquarters, in accordance with the decision at the annual meeting, were closed and small offices were rented in the centre of the city at the corner of St. Lawrence Boulevard and Sherbrooke Street.

In this contracted way the work of the Society was carried on throughout the summer of 1923, until an event happened, which for actual rescue work stands out in the annals of our history. A number of Jewish refugees who had escaped from the pogroms in the Ukraine had found a temporary refuge in Roumania, but the Roumanian Government had given them notice that they must either leave Roumanian territory voluntarily or they would be deported back to the country from which they had come. This appeared to them to mean certain death. The doors of practically every country were closed to them and their distress was indescribable. The Jewish Colonization Association of Paris, which had interested itself in their temporary support, cast about for some spot on God's earth to which to send them. Canada was looked upon as a possible haven of refuge and the officers of the Jewish Colonization Association cabled to their Canadian Committee to intervene with the Canadian Government on behalf of the refugees. Mr. Lyon Cohen, Chairman of the Canadian Committee of the Jewish Colonization Association, and Mr. S. W. Jacobs, K.C., member of the Federal Parliament and Secretary of the Committee, immediately proceeded to Ottawa and laid the case before the Government. The Minister of Immigration, the Honourable Mr. Robb, moved by their appeals, granted a concession for the entry of 5000 of the refugees at the rate of 100 a week, on the understanding that the Jewish Colonization Association would be responsible that none of them would become public charges.

This noble act on the part of our Government which was so unselfishly performed for no other than humanitarian reasons, will forever be deeply engraved in the hearts of the Jewish people, not only of this country but of the world at large. At a time when almost every other country refused to lend a sympathetic ear to our oppressed people, the Canadian Government showed its magnanimity by receiving the refugees.

We have already experienced that when Jewish immigration was reduced to small numbers, many clamoured for the discontinuance of the Society. It was good fortune that the skeleton of the organization remained. Had it not been for the existence of the Jewish Immigrant Aid Society of Canada, the refugees could not have been so successfully and efficiently handled. The work of receiving these people, their distribution throughout the country, the placing of them, and the care taken of them until they were finally absorbed, was of such magnitude, that only those closely in touch with the Society can appreciate it. It was important that the arriving refugees should be distributed throughout the Dominion in as many localities as possible.

The Society established connections with over fifty small communities throughout the country. The whole community rose as one man to support it. The headquarters at Notre Dame Street were re-opened in order to accommodate the newcomers. Toronto reorganized with an efficient Committee, headed by Rabbi Barnett R. Brickner assisted by Mr. Samuel B. Kaufman to handle the situation there. Winnipeg redoubled its efforts and Mr. S. Hart Green took the lead with the assistance of Mr. M. A. Gray as Secretary. The branches in Ottawa, Hamilton, Windsor, London, Fort William, Regina, Saskatoon, Calgary, Edmonton, Vancouver and other places were thoroughly reorganized and a score of new branches were established.

Communications were sent to every town and village in the Dominion where Jews were known to reside, advising them of the expected arrival of the refugees. Every effort was made to assign to each locality the type of immigrant which was most adaptable for that section.

Early in January, Mr. Lyon Cohen called an emergency conference in Toronto, to mobilize the Canadian Jewish communities to the task of assistance. At this conference, it was felt that, as the doors of the United States were closed for immigration, American Jewry should be called upon to assist the undertaking. A delegation headed by Mr. Cohen was appointed to proceed to New York to lay the situation before the representative American Jewish institutions, and through Mr. Bernard G. Richards and Mr. Joseph Barondess, succeeded in arranging a conference, at which the American Jewish Congress, the Ukranian Verband and the H.I.A.S. were represented. Mr. Cohen also appealed to the Joint Distribution Committee. As a result of this, and subsequent conferences in which Mr. Cohen was assisted by Rabbi Brickner and Mr. A. H. Jassby, the H.I.A.S. contributed $15,000.

At the conference which was held in Toronto, it was resolved that 40% of the arriving refugees were to be retained in Montreal and the East, 30% were to be forwarded to Ontario, and 30% to Western Canada.

The most representative members of the community took the lead in the work and received the support of every section. In Montreal, a number of conferences were called by Mr. Lionel Coviensky, the President of the Society. Campaigns for funds and donations in kind were waged everywhere. At the annual meeting which took place in May, 1924, Mr. A. Levin, Treasurer of the Zionist Federation of Canada was elected President, and Mr. Joseph Levinson, Sr., President of the Federation of Jewish Philanthropies of Montreal, became the Treasurer of the Society. Messrs. Louis Cohen and H. Barsky were elected as the Vice-Presidents, and Mr. Benjamin Robinson, B.A., B.C.L., was re-elected as Honorary Secretary. Messrs. S. W. Jacobs, Lyon Cohen and Peter Bercovitch were elected as Honorary Presidents.

The Society was now firmly established everywhere. It was prepared to handle the most difficult situation. Although economic conditions in this country were far from satisfactory, and our people were heavily burdened, nevertheless the movement was supported freely. Butchers supplied meat free of charge; bakers supplied bread at their own expense; manufacturers, wholesalers, retailers and private individuals by the hundreds gave the Society clothing, underwear and furniture for the arriving refugees. The amount spent by Canadian Jewry on this undertaking will never be estimated. The records of the Society only show the actual cash that went through its books, but it does not reveal the amounts spent by all the small communities throughout the country, by various organizations, and different individuals; nor does it show the donations in kind worth many tens of thousands of dollars.

The Jewish Emergency Committee for the relief of Jewish refugees with its headquarters in New York, also came to the assistance of the Society in its hour of need with further substantial sums, while the Jewish Colonization Association of Paris financed the inland transportation of the arriving refugees from the port of entry to their assigned destination.

The first lot of one hundred refugees arrived on December 1st, 1923, while the last reached our shores by the end of November 1924, so that the movement lasted exactly one year. During the year over 3,400 refugees came into Canada. Nearly 2,000 less came than were expected. The Department of Immigration and Colonization claimed that their permit was strictly for Russian Jewish refugees stranded in Roumania, and since they were informed that there were no more refugees of that type left in that country, the permit was cancelled.

Messrs. Cohen and Jacobs realizing the great boon to our people of the quota allotment and feeling the responsibility to try and revive it, requested of the Government that the unfilled quota be allowed to apply to near relatives of Canadian residents who were besieging them for admission into Canada. After considerable negotiations, this permission was granted recently, and at the time of writing detailed arrangements for carrying out the project were just being completed.

The history of the Jewish Immigrant Aid Society of Canada as traced here during its short five years' existence performed work of great significance to the pogrom sufferers. In looking back on its accomplishments under unfavourable conditions, one can but admire its courage and perseverance. With sympathetic co-operation and proper assistance from the community, the Jewish Immigrant Aid Society of Canada can be expected not only to fill the simple purpose of affording temporary relief to immigrants, but to encourage the further rescue by immigration of our benighted people from lands like Russia, Poland and Roumania from the blight of persecution which threatens to annihilate them.

POPULATION OF THE JEWS IN CANADA

THE first census of the Dominion was taken in 1871, and similar censuses have followed in every tenth year thereafter, namely, in 1881, 1891, 1901, 1911, and 1921. The figures given herewith have been taken from the Sixth Census of Canada, Vol. I, Parts II and III.

In 1921, there were 126,196 persons in Canada of Hebrew origin, or 1.44 of the total population. In 1911 there were 75,681 persons of Hebrew origin, or 1.05 of the population. In 1901 there were but 16,131 persons in Canada of Hebrew origin, or .30 of the entire population.

By Provinces they were distributed as follows:—
In 1921—Prince Edward Island 21, Nova Scotia, 2,161, New Brunswick 1,243, Quebec 47,977, Ontario 47,798, Manitoba 16,669, Saskatchewan 5,380, Alberta 3,242, British Columbia 1,696, Yukon 8, North West Territories 1.

In 1911—Prince Edward Island 38, Nova Scotia 1,360, New Brunswick 1,021, Quebec 30,684, Ontario 27,015, Manitoba 10,741, Saskatchewan 2,066, Alberta 1,486, British Columbia 1,265, Yukon 41.

In 1901—Prince Edward Island 17, Nova Scotia 449, New Brunswick 395, Quebec 7,607, Ontario 5,337, Manitoba 1,514, Saskatchewan 198, Alberta 17, British Columbia 543, Yukon 54.

By Provinces, male and female, 1921, they were as follows:—Canada M. 64,029, F. 62,167; Prince Edward Island M. 11, F. 10; Nova Scotia M. 1,123, F. 1,038; New Brunswick M. 636, F. 607; Quebec M. 24,310, F. 23,367; Ontario M. 23,905, F. 23,893; Manitoba M. 8,449, F. 8,220; Saskatchewan M. 2,930, F. 2,450; Alberta M. 1,750, F. 1,492; British Columbia M. 909, F. 787; Yukon M. 5, F. 3; Northwest Territories M. 1.

By Provinces, Canadian born, 1921—Canada 50,892; Prince Edward Island 11; Nova Scotia 1,109; New Brunswick 588; Quebec 20,143; Ontario 18,448; Manitoba 6,579; Saskatchewan 2,191; Alberta 1,209; British Columbia 609.

By Provinces, male and female, Canadian born, 1921—Canada M. 25,256, F. 25,636; Prince Edward Island M. 4, F. 7; Nova Scotia M. 553, F. 556; New Brunswick M. 285, F. 303; Quebec M. 10,142, F. 10,006; Ontario M. 8,871, F. 9,577; Manitoba M. 3,327, F. 3,252; Saskatchewan M. 1,146, F. 1,045; Alberta M. 626, F. 583; British Columbia M. 302, F. 307.

In 1921, resident of Canada, born in the United States—Total 4,851; P.E.I. 1; N.S. 104; N.B. 66; Que. 1,493; Ont. 2,125; Man. 413; Sask. 177; Alta. 242; B.C. 228; Y.T. 2.

By sexes they were as follows:—Total M. 2,332, F. 2,519; P.E.I. M. 0, F. 1; N.S. M. 58, F. 46; N.B. M. 26, F. 40; Que. M. 689, F. 804; Ont. M. 1,002, F. 1,123; Man. M. 210, F. 203; Sask. M. 94, F. 83; Alta. M. 128, F. 114; B.C. M. 123, F. 105; Y.T. M. 2.

The following was the Jewish population of cities and towns of 5,000 and over, in 1921.

City	Pop.	City	Pop.	City	Pop.
Montreal	42,667	Lachine	531	Pembroke	31
Toronto	34,377	Brandon	221	St. Johns	21
Winnipeg	14,390	Port Arthur	80	River du Loup	13
Vancouver	1,248	Sarnia	57	Grand'Mere	15
Hamilton	2,548	Niagara Falls	87	Lindsay	11
Ottawa	2,796	New Westminister	24	Truro	8
Quebec	371	Chatham	56	Prince Albert	109
Calgary	1,233	Outremont	1,195	Cornwall	89
London	696	Galt	67	Yarmouth	183
Edmonton	805	St. Boniface	94	Walkerville	10
Halifax	578	Charlottetown	16	Midland	51
St. John	844	Belleville	61	Barrie	31
Victoria	148	Owen Sound	72	Smith's Falls	41
Windsor	979	Oshawa	89	Granby	26
Regina	860	Lethbridge	107	Portage la Prairie	81
Brantford	241	St. Hyacinthe	16	Cap de la Madelaine	7
Saskatoon	599	North Bay	66	North Sydney	8
Verdun, Que.	148	Shawinigan Falls	22	Prince Rupert	14
Hull	37	Brockville	46	Trenton	13
Sherbrooke	265	Amherst	18	Collingwood	39
Sydney	396	Woodstock	21	Ford City	98
Three Rivers	38	Medicine Hat	76	Springhill	11
Kitchener	298	Valleyfield	12	New Waterford	50
Kingston	303	Joliette	59	La Tuque	33
S. Ste. Marie	115	Nanaimo	14	Campbellton	28
Peterboro	136	New Glasgow	65	Hawkesbury	52
Fort William	288	Chicoutimi	14	St. Jerome	17
St. Catharines	224	Orillia	66	Preston	26
Moose Jaw	119	Welland	15	Kenora	64
Guelph	87	Sudbury	126	Cobourg	15
Westmount	999	Sydney Mines	21	Eastview, Ont.	46
Moncton	73	Sorel	42	Nelson	7
Glace Bay	441	Fredericton	62	Magog	2
Stratford	46	Dartmouth	10	Yorkton	167
St. Thomas	74	Thedford Mines	15	Ingersoll	3

THE JEW IN THE MILITARY LIFE OF CANADA

THE Jews of Canada have every reason to take pride in the record made by members of their faith in the different wars in which this country has been engaged, and have shown that their loyalty to the British Crown is equal to that of any other section of the population. It is with the spirit of their teachings that this must be so—that to be good Jews they must first be good Canadians. The first Jew to settle in Canada was an officer in the English army that conquered Canada, and in this same army were some of the other early Jewish settlers. But even before this, there was the Franks family. Jacob Franks (who came to America in 1707 and who died in New York in 1769, where he was buried in the cemetery of the Spanish & Portuguese Jews) and his sons David and Moses, were appointed the chief agents of the British Crown for the furnishing of supplies for the British Armies in Canada and the American Colonies during the French and Indian wars, from 1755 to 1760. The official papers and correspondence of Generals Monckton, Amherst and Gage, contain numerous references to the splendid services rendered by these three members of the Franks family at that time, and mention in terms of special commendation their highly efficient organization of this branch of the military service.

Commissary Officer Aaron Hart enlisted with General Amherst in New York, in 1760, and accompanied him as a member of his staff when he entered Montreal, after the capture of that city. Emanuel de Cordova, Hananiel Garcia, and Isaac Miranda were also officers in the army of conquest. These officers all served on the Loyalist side in the American Revolutionary war, as did also David Franks (mentioned above) and Jacob Franks and Abraham Franks. David Franks was one of the wealthiest residents of Philadelphia before the war, but his whole fortune was lost by confiscation on account of his loyalty to England. He was ordered to leave the United States and to give a security of £200,000 that he would not return until after the war. He had been offered large grants on the Ohio as a recognition of his services, and owned large tracts in Pennsylvania, Virginia, Indiana, and Illinois previous to the war of the Revolution. He founded the town of Frankstown, Ohio, named after him. Aaron Hart was appointed by General Haldimand his Commissary General, and Ezekiel Solomons was an officer in this campaign. Samuel Jacobs of Chambly was also connected with the army, and he at one time had the contract to provision the troops. Levy Solomons, who took a prominent part in attempting to heal the difficulties between the English and the colonists, was, at the time Montreal was captured by General Montgomery, ordered to establish hospitals for the care of his troops.

Others of the Franks family who espoused the cause of the American colonists, were David Salesby Franks, son of Abraham Franks, and his cousin, Isaac Franks. The latter became the confidential aide-de-camp to General George Washington. They both had very distinguished military careers.

CAPT. ALEXANDER THOMAS HART

Most of the Jewish residents of Canada during these years held commissions in the militia, and we read that on July 9, 1812, among the military officers attending the Governor's Levee were Meyer Michaels, Benjamin Franks, Benjamin Solomons, Samuel David, David David, Henry Joseph, Jacob Graves, Alexander Hart, Benjamin Hart and Jacob Franks.

During the War of 1812-14, four of the sons of Aaron Hart, Moses, Ezekiel, Benjamin and Alexander, held commissions in the Canadian militia and saw service. In 1812, at the time when Sir George Provost was desirous of arming 100 men to form a garrison at Fort William Henry, the commander-in-chief and the paymaster stated that one thousand pounds at the very least would be required and that it was impossible to carry his wishes into effect without this sum to pay the recruits their bounty and daily pay, and that not one dollar could be raised in either Quebec or Three Rivers.

In this emergency, Benjamin Hart stepped forward and offered the Governor the amount, which offer was accepted. In November of the same year Benjamin Hart was ordered by Colonel Battersby to proceed to Three Rivers with orders to the entire militia to hold themselves in readiness to march against the enemy. Samuel, David and Moses David, three brothers, Henry Joseph and Jacob Franks were also all officers who saw service in this war, and all acquitted themselves with distinction. Samuel David was Lieut.-Col. of the Long Point Regiment of the militia, and had a long and notable military record. We read of him being presiding member of a general court martial in 1813, to try a Major Dunlop. Ezekiel and Benjamin Hart were also Colonels of Militia. Moses Judah Hays, Meyer Levy and Meyer Michaels, although merchants having an extensive trade, all volunteered their services and received commissions, and served throughout the war.

After peace was declared and the incorporated militia was disbanded, the members of the Jewish community still maintained their interests in it and their names were frequently mentioned as taking turns in giving instructions to the provincial militia. The younger members of the community followed in the footsteps of their elders and assumed their interests in the militia. Thus in the Montreal Gazette, on May 23rd, 1835, Samuel David and Moses David were gazetted as Ensigns of Militia, Eleazer David as Lieutenant and Adjutant of Cavalry, and Isaac Valentine as Captain of Militia, and on October 24th, 1836, the David brothers were in charge of the cavalry patrol which was detailed to assist the police in putting down incendiarism in Montreal. On November 14th, 1836, which was the date of the first paid military watch to be established in Montreal, Eleazer David was detailed as Captain. On August 4th, 1837, Capt. Eleazer David was the officer in charge of the cavalry that escorted the sheriff when he made the various proclamations in Montreal announcing the accession to the throne of Queen Victoria.

In the Rebellion of 1837-8, the Jews again showed

that they appreciated the treatment received by the British Crown, and again they rallied to the Loyalist side in this unfortunate affair. Eleazer, Samuel and Dr. Aaron H. David, all sons of Samuel David, and Moses E. David, son of Major Moses David, were officers in the militia. Eleazer David was promoted to Major for gallantry at the Battle of St. Charles, where his brother also took part in the fighting. Samuel David was several times entrusted with the carrying of despatches, at one time making the trip to Toronto by horse, carrying despatches from Sir John Colborne to Sir F. B. Head, an account of which is preserved in his diary. Jacob Henry, Jesse and Abraham Joseph, sons of Henry Joseph, were all officers, the two former being in the Montreal militia, and serving on the Richelieu, where they both on occasions carried despatches between General Wetherall and the Governor, Sir John Colborne; and the latter being at Quebec, where he was Major in the Quebec Light Infantry. Isaac Valentine was stationed at Three Rivers. Bocco Hays and Hoffstetter were at Cedars on the St. Lawrence. Aaron Moses, and Alexander Thomas, sons of Moses Hart; Samuel Becancour and Aaron Ezekiel, sons of Ezekiel Hart; Aaron Philip, Theodore, and Arthur Wellington, sons of Benjamin Hart; Alexander, son of Alexander Hart, and Henry and Thomas Judah were also all officers on the Loyalist side. Col. David of Chambly was in command of the militia in that district. Again they showed themselves appreciative of the privileges they enjoyed in this country, and Aaron Philip Hart raised a company of militia at his own expense, which he commanded. On March 4th, 1838, he was entrusted with the carrying of despatches by Sir John Colborne, to the British Ambassador at New York. In Upper Canada the Benjamin Brothers, Samuel and Goodman, of Toronto, had the contract to supply great-coats to the soldiers. It was during the winter and as there were no railways in those day and no manufacturing was done in Toronto, they had to make the trip to Montreal by sleigh and await the manufacture of the garments and take them back to Toronto by sleigh. During the Campaign of 1838, Major Eleazer David was appointed Acting Quarter-Master General. Samuel David was attached to Sir John Colborne's Staff. He later was, for a long time, stationed in command of the detachment of cavalry at Odelltown, in the Eastern townships, but he finally resigned his commission and retired to private life.

CAPT. DAVID A. HART

At the outbreak of the Rebellion, Benjamin Hart, who was on the Commission of the Peace as a magistrate, took the first deposition as to the treasonable intent of the rebels, and on the 6th November, 1837, when the rebels made their first attack on the dwellings of the Loyalists, he took the leader prisoner, and then signed the requisition to the commandant of the garrison, calling out the troops. There is no question that but for his firmness there would have been much destruction of property in Montreal. On the nights of the 6th, 7th, 8th, and 9th of the same month he remained on duty at the main guardhouse, in the capacity of magistrate in charge, and for almost three months he was at the office of the Clerk of the Peace, taking almost every deposition, and issuing upwards of one hundred warrants at the request of the Attorney-General. At this period the opinion prevailed that no official protection would be afforded the magistrates in the event of suits being brought for false arrest, and for this reason many of the English magistrates withdrew from acting. Solicitor-General Day was requested by the merchants of Montreal to wait on Colonel Hart to ask that he would not be intimidated, as the merchants would indemnify him against all loss. Even the secret service agents of the government gave their reports to Colonel Hart, who transmitted them to the proper authorities. Most of the confessions made by the prisoners were taken by him. On the morning of the second revolt, Nov. 4th, 1838, it was Colonel Hart who was requested by General Clitherton, in the name of Sir John Colborne, to cause to be arrested every man that he (Hart) suspected as a leader of the rebels. This order he obeyed by arresting that day upwards of twenty of the leaders. In May of that year Lieut.-Col. Barnard, of the Guards, and Major Dickison, of Sir John Colborne's Staff, were attacked by the rebels. Both were felled and would have been murdered, but that Col. Hart ran to their assistance and saved them, at the risk of his own life. He also risked his life in many other instances, in order to protect the Loyalist troops.

Although the Jewish population of Canada at that time was less than two hundred souls, it will be seen that they occupied no small part in the public affairs of the day and were foremost in action when it came to the question of the defence of their country. It is a fact that in most cases the Jewish citizens were invited by the Governor to accept commissions in the army, as they were recognized as being the type desirable for such appointments. The loyalty of a Jew was never questioned.

During the Fenian Raids in 1870, Capt. David A. Hart was in command of the 1st Prince of Wales' Rifles, on active service, and took part in the important events. His brother, Lewis A. (sons of Alexander T. Hart) was on duty at Laprairie. Reuben Hart and other members of this family also were on duty at this time, as were also members of the Joseph family. Major R. Sullivan David, a son of Dr. A. H. David, and Henry Benjamin were also officers of the militia on active service at this period.

Members of the Miller family of Toronto held commissions during the Riel Rebellion, and were on active service. Max Goldstine, one of the pioneers of Western Canada Jewry, was a trooper in the same campaign. In the South African War, although the total number of Canadians who saw service was not large, again the Jews were represented; Hyman Lightstone of Montreal being one who gave distinguished service.

It is not possible to give absolutely accurate details as to the number of Jews who fought in the Canadian army during the Great War, as the Militia Department, when recording nationalities of the members of the Canadian Expeditionary Force, did not place Jews in a category by themselves. A Jew who was born in England is recorded as being of English birth, and the same applies to Jews born in any other country, that is, they were designated as citizens of the country in which they were born. Consequently, the only figures available with regard to Jews are the number who, on enlistment,

COL. H. H. LIGHTSTONE, D.S.O., M.C.

stated that they belonged to the Jewish faith. This number is recorded as being 2574. The Militia Department states that it is impossible to select from the many thousands of documents, those who gave their religion as of the Jewish persuasion.

In addition to the above figure, there were numbers of Canadian Jewish citizens who served in the Imperial army, in the American army, and in the Jewish Legion, which raised for service in Palestine some five hundred Canadian Jews who, after a preliminary training at Windsor, N.S., left for active service. In all, it is conservatively estimated that considerably over three thousand five hundred Jews from Canada served in allied armies.

The 1911 census gives the Jewish population of Canada as 74,564, but this includes the total Jewish population at that date, irrespective of whether they were naturalized citizens or retained their foreign citizenship. In fact in 1921 the Dominion census gives the population of Jewish born Canadians as only 50,892. In view of the fact also that the 1901 census gives the total Jewish population as only 16,401, it can safely be assumed that in 1914, at the outbreak of war, the Jewish born population of military age did not exceed 25,000, males and females. Taking these figures as a basis, the Jews showed that they were as patriotic as any other denomination in the country, as this would show, allowing for the usual percentage of females, that over 25% of the number of Canadian born Jews saw active service in the Canadian army.

Another point to be stressed, is that the rapidly increasing Jewish population of Canada came largely from Russia and Poland (which at that time was part of Russia) and had fled to this country to escape religious persecution in their old home. In spite of the fact that over 600,000 Jews were enrolled in all branches of the Czarist armies, the families of these men were cruelly expelled from their homes, or were robbed or persecuted mercilessly. At that time it will be remembered that Russia was allied with us, and these newer arrivals, and also their relatives who had been here for some time, and who had also come to escape the most rigorous persecution, could hardly be blamed for not wanting to fight for Russia. It cannot be wondered that the kith and kin of these unfortunates hesitated to shed their blood for a cause, which when successful, would strengthen the Russian autocracy. Later events showed that there was much ground for this hesitancy as it was undoubtedly the treachery of Russia that prolonged the war, many, many months. Nevertheless, they rallied to the flag and followed the teachings of their leaders, and results speak for themselves. The following instance will illustrate the foregoing. The Rev. Marcus Berner, leader of the Jewish community of Hirsch, Saskatchewan, himself escaped from Russian persecution and settled in Canada some years ago. Of his five sons, three were members of the Canadian Expeditionary Force. Out of a total membership of 65 in the Montefiore Club, Winnipeg, 30 enlisted for active service.

LIEUT. ALEX SOLOMON
Killed in action

Every branch of the service had its Jewish members, and in all they showed up well and won the commendation of their superiors. An interesting story may be told here of Albert Freedman, who enlisted as a private in the 5th C. M. R. Bn. in Montreal, and who went overseas as orderly room sergeant in the 2nd Brigade, C.M.R. He was with the Brigade staff on the S.S. Hesperian. A rumor had reached the Brigadier that there were spies on the boat, and two men were arrested and put in confinement. Attempts to discover whether they really were spies were made in vain and Freedman was asked to allow himself to be arrested and also confined, and to see if the prisoners could speak German, as he was thoroughly familiar with that tongue. He was successful in his undertaking, and as a result the two men were removed from the transport by a destroyer and a confederate at Quebec was also arrested. As the ship was carrying a big load of munitions as well as troops, this was regarded as a very important arrest, and Freedman was thanked by the Brigadier and ship's commander.

EDWARD YOUNGHEART

He later was, after a long period in France, attached to the Intelligence Branch of the 2nd British Army, and in 1916 was granted his commission. He was then attached to the trans-Atlantic Conducting Services as paymaster, and when the pay procedure was changed during demobilization, of all the paymasters in the Canadian forces, Capt. Freedman, the only Jewish one, was selected to work out the new plan, which he did on the S.S. Empress of Asia, when that troopship made the trip through the Panama Canal, carrying home British Columbia troops. He was highly commended for his work and until the completion of demobilization was kept in England, as the representative of the Paymaster General, Ottawa, instructing the other paymasters in the procedure.

Another Canadian officer to distinguish himself was Capt. Hyman Lightstone, one of four brothers who saw service. Capt. Lightstone, who was a veteran of the South African War, was in the medical services. He was decorated with the Military Cross, and the Distinguished Service Order, and was several times mentioned in despatches. He was also decorated by the French Government for his exceptionally fine work in stamping out an epidemic of typhoid in a French division. Capt. Lightstone was the medical officer on Gen. Rawlinson's staff at Versailles when the latter was appointed to the Supreme War Council. He was promoted to the rank of Colonel and at present occupies the position of Inspector-General of Military Hospitals in Great Britain.

It is not the intention here to pick out individual cases of merit displayed by members of the Canadian forces, but rather to give a general record of the great work done by all. Suffice to say that the Jewish members of the C.E.F. in whatever field they served in, did so with credit to the record previously established by members of their faith in Canada. Those who were not qualified to serve also did their duty, and the leading Rabbis throughout Canada were all doing their share as chaplains to the Jewish troops. Other older members of the community served with credit on the civil boards established by the passing of the Military Service Act, and by work with the Patriotic Fund and the Red Cross.

Jewish women were not backward in their activities, and several chapters of the Daughters of the Empire were established, where comforts and supplies were sent to the troops, and where care was taken of the dependants who were in need of assistance. It is only just to mention in this connection the almost unbelievable work done by the late Mrs. Montefiore Joseph of Quebec. Although there were at all times a large number of men stationed at Valcartier Camp, Mrs. Joseph had a standing invitation for any Jewish soldier to visit her home at any time, and particularly during the Holy Days, when numbers of them attended services in her house. She was never missing when troops were leaving Quebec, with gifts for the men, irrespective of religion, and there are very many who will remember her kindness and cheer.

The Third Battalion C.E.F. (Queen's Own Rifles of Toronto) had a special Jewish section that was maintained throughout the battalion's existence, and which for a long time was commanded by Sergt. J. J. Samuels. This section was very often assigned to the post of honour in any advance made by the regiment, and the Jewish men always carried their objective with credit and glory. The percentage of Jewish casualties was quite heavy, which in itself is indicative of the courage, eagerness and bravery of the men. Records of actual Jewish casualties are impossible to secure, for the reasons stated before, but numbers of the flower of young Jewish manhood fell on the field of battle.

Almost every unit had its Jewish members, and in 1916, at the request of the then Minister of Militia, General Sir Sam Hughes, a Jewish Reinforcement Company was raised in Montreal. This task was entrusted to Isidore Freedman, who had taken the necessary courses of instruction and had been granted a commission. Captain Freedman was assisted in the organization of the unit by Lieuts. Alex Solomon (who was later killed in action), Herbert Vineberg (who later joined the Air Force and was awarded the Distinguished Flying Cross), Albert Freedman (mentioned elsewhere), Charles Lesser (who served on the Western Front for a long time), and others. The financial assistance required for this undertaking was supplied by the leading Jews of Montreal. Over four hundred men were enlisted and after a course of training the Company went overseas in 1917. From England they were sent to various Montreal units as reinforcements, and the members acquitted themselves in the same manner as the rest of their coreligionists who were on service.

Although the majority of those who were in the service were in France and Flanders, the Canadian Jews were represented at Gallipoli, Mesopotamia, Saloniki, in Africa, in Palestine and Egypt, and with the Siberian Expeditionary Force. They were also numbered with the British Forces on the Italian Front, and several Jewish young men from Toronto served with the Anzacs. There were a number of British, French and Belgian reservists among them, and these went back and joined their own regiments. Among the latter may be mentioned Capt. William Sebag Montefiore of Montreal. He had previously been in the British Army as an officer in the Fifth Lancers, but had retired. Rejoining his regiment at the earliest possible moment after the declaration of war, he served on the Western Front, was promoted to Captain, and later appointed to the 14th Corps Headquarters Staff with the British Forces in Egypt. He was in command of a squadron of cavalry when the British Forces invaded Palestine. He personally captured seven of the German Staff Officers at the point of his revolver, was mentioned in despatches in both 1916 and 1917, and was decorated with the Military Cross. John Alfred Benjamin, a son of a former president of the Holy Blossom Synagogue, Toronto, was another who enlisted in the Imperial army. He made the supreme sacrifice, being killed in action in France in 1916. William Cowan is another example of the calibre of the Jewish soldier. Qualifying as a sergeant at the outbreak of war, through sheer pluck and ability he rose to the rank of captain and adjutant of the Fort Garry Horse, and was awarded the Military Cross. Captain Cowan was wounded on five different occasions. He was for a long time a prisoner of the Bolsheviks and is only now recovering from the privations he underwent.

CAPT. ALBERT FREEDMAN

In the Canadian Army Medical Corps, Jewish doctors saw service on all fronts, as well as on the trans-Atlantic Conducting Service, and Jewish dentists were likewise to be found in the Dental Corps. In all cases they won the praise of their superior officers and their share of honors and awards. Jewish young ladies were not backward in offering their services as nurses, and several qualified and were sent overseas. Miss Esther Rubenstein was for over two years attached to the Harper Hospital Unit, in France, and Miss Rosetta Joseph was attached to hospitals in England.

Among those who were too old to volunteer their services for the army yet wished to do his share may be mentioned Mr. Montefiore Joseph, of Quebec, one of the best known residents of that city, and a former president of the Quebec Board of Trade. For a considerable time he gave his services in a Government munition plant, as inspector, serving without any recompense. Among the Jewish firms who were given contracts for the manufacturing of munitions was L. Cohen & Son, of Montreal, who handled one of the largest contracts for the manufacture of shrapnel, placed in Canada.

Maurice Alexander of Montreal, who had been an officer in the Canadian Grenadier Guards, was on the General Staff throughout the War, and in August 1916 was appointed Judge Advocate General of the Canadian Corps. In January 1917 he was mentioned in despatches by Lord Derby. In February 1917 he was attached to the Imperial War Office (General Intelligence Staff.) On January 26th, 1917, Lieut.-Col. Alexander was created a Companion of the most Distinguished Order of St. Michael and St. George.

When peace was declared, and demobilization finally completed, the Jewish soldiers returned to their former pursuits, and lost very little time in re-establishing themselves in the civilian ranks of the country. There have been among them very few cases indeed of men who have become a drag on the community; in fact, no record can be found of this description. They have in large numbers joined the veterans' societies, and in Montreal and Toronto have established Jewish veteran organizations, where the spirit of the sacrifices they have made will be maintained and given to the younger generation.

In recent years there have been a number who have taken a keen interest in the militia, among whom may be mentioned Frank D. Benjamin of Toronto, who was with with the Queen's Own, Lt.-Col. M. Lauterman, of Montreal, and the late Edward Youngheart. At various times in the last two decades there have been Jewish cadet corps, notably the Baron de Hirsch Cadets and the Zion Cadets of Montreal, and the Zion Cadets of Toronto. In every community where the Jewish population is large enough, there are at the present time, Jewish troops of Boy Scouts. Max Steinkopf of Winnipeg, and Charles Benjamin of Calgary, have both held high offices in this movement. Albert Belasco, of Montreal, also deserves great credit for the work he has accomplished in organizing the first Jewish Boy Scout troop in Canada.

A military record that is probably unequalled in Canada, is that of the Hart family. For five generations, starting with the conquest of Canada in 1760, members of this, the first Jewish family to settle in Canada, have taken part in every war in which Canada has been engaged. Two were killed in action during the Great War, serving with the Canadian Forces. Even though some branches of this family have moved to the United States, they have kept up the record, and among the great-great-grandsons of Commissary Aaron Hart who fought in the Great War, in the American forces, may be mentioned Colonel Noble B. Judah, of Chicago, who saw service with the 149th U.S. Field Artillery, and who received the Croix de Guerre from the French Government, and the Distinguished Service Medal from the United States Government, and A. Wellington Hart, who was on active service in France for a long period. Another, ex-Congressman Archibald C. Hart, served during the Spanish-American War.

MISS ESTHER RUBENSTEIN, R.N.

MISS ROSETTA JOSEPH, V.A.D.

LIEUT. ALEX LYONE
Killed in action

SGT. J. GORBACK, M.M.
Killed in action

LIEUT. MEYER T. COHEN, M.C.
Killed in action

BOMBARDIER EDGAR H. GOLDSTEIN
Killed in action

CAPT. JOHN A. BENJAMIN
Killed in action

LIEUT. MARVIN WORKMAN
Killed in action

Sergt. J. Gorback, M.M. of Toronto, enlisted with the 60th Battalion, and was transferred to the 87th Battalion, Canadian Expeditionary Force. He was awarded the Military Medal and was killed in action on Sept. 27th, 1918, after thirty-eight months' active service.

Lieut. Meyer T. Cohen, M.C., son of M. M. Cohen, of Toronto, received his commission in April, 1915, in the 77th Wentworth Reg't. In 1916, he sailed for England and two months later was ordered to France, attached to the 42nd Canadian Royal Highlanders, (Black Watch). In a raid on the enemy trenches in October, 1917, he captured three of the enemy as prisoners, making a further raid and capturing three more. This was at a period when the allied forces were most anxious to obtain prisoners for the purpose of getting information about them, and the feat was accomplished without casualties. For this daring act he was awarded the Military Cross. On Nov. 3rd., 1917, Lieut. Cohen was ordered to storm a strong enemy position at Paschendale. At the head of his men he reached his objective. No reinforcements were available, and with his few men he held the position until all were killed. A special panel, commemorating the bravery of Lieut. Cohen has been inserted in the memorial window erected in the church of St. Andrews and St. Paul, at Montreal, in honor of the officers and men of the 42nd Royal Highlanders who fell during the war. The special panel represents King David, when as a youth he fought in the ranks of the armies of the Lord of Hosts, the God of the armies of Israel.

Lieut. Marvin J. Workman, son of Chas. A. Workman, of Montreal, enlisted with a Montreal unit, and made the supreme sacrifice, being killed in action shortly after his arrival at the Front.

Lieut. Alex. Lyone, of Winnipeg, son of Martin Lyone, enlisted in the 27th Winnipeg Battalion as a private. After considerable service at the Front he received his commission in the Northumberland Fusiliers, and was killed in action during the Battle of the Somme.

Bombardier Edgar H. Goldstein, son of Jacob Goldstein of Montrel, enlisted in Montreal in March, 1916, and went overseas with a draft of the 66th Battery, C.F.A. His first stripes, given up voluntarily when he left for France, he regained on the Somme Front when attached to a Howitzer Battery of the 2nd Division, Canadian Field Artillery. He refused a medal, offered him for distinguished service, saying that he was no braver than others and that all had done their best, and was recommended for a lieutenancy. He was killed at the Battle of Loos, August 15th, 1917, at the age of twenty years, on the very day of his departure for England to take up his commission, after ten months' continuous service at the Front, including action at Courcelette, the Somme, Albert, Arras, Vimy Ridge and Lens, and was buried in the British cemetery at Maroc, Bully-Grenay.

Captain John Alfred Benjamin, son of the late A. D. Benjamin of Toronto, was an officer in the Duke of Wellington's West Riding Regiment. He was killed in action at Contalmaison, France, on June, 16th, 1916.

JEWISH REINFORCEMENT DRAFT COMPANY, MONTREAL

IN 1916, Captain Isidore Freedman was requested by the late General Sir Sam Hughes, Minister of Militia, to raise a Jewish battalion for overseas' service. Captain Freedman declined this honor, but undertook to raise a Jewish Company, in which undertaking he was assisted by the leading members of the Jewish community of Montreal, and by Lieuts. Alex Solomon (killed in action), Herbert Vineberg, Charles Lesser, Albert Freedman, and Sol Rubin. Several hundred men were recruited, and, after a thorough course of training under the forementioned officers in Montreal, the Company sailed for overseas in 1917. On their arrival in England, the members were despatched as reinforcements to various Montreal battalions, where they saw service. Numbers were killed and wounded, and all conducted themselves in a most praiseworthy manner, several receiving promotions, commissions, and honors. The Jewish citizens of Canada have every reason to take pride in the record of the Jewish Reinforcement Draft Company.

These five Montreal Officers had this photograph taken in Brighton, England, in the Fall of 1918, where they met when on leave to observe Yom Kippur.

Top Row, Left to Right.

LIEUT. NATHAN B. COHEN, C.E.
14th Royal Montreal Regiment, C. E. F., District-Commandant, in Army of Occupation, Germany.

LIEUT. HERBERT A. VINEBERG
Royal Air Force. Special Instructor Aerial Navigation, Market-Drayton, was awarded the D. F. C.

Bottom Row, Left to Right.

CAPT. JOSEPH LEAVITT.
Canadian Army Medical Corps. Medical Officer 18th Battalion, C. E. F. Medical Commissioner for Jewish War Orphans' Committee in Ukrania.

CAPT. HORACE R. COHEN
Quartermaster, 163rd Battalion, C. E. F., (Canada and Bermuda). Quartermaster, 10th Reserve Battalion, Overseas Military Forces of Canada.

CAPT. LEO LIVINGSTONE
Quartermaster, 5th Pioneer Battalion, C. E. F., also Quartermaster in the Canadian Forestry Corps, in Scotland.

CAPTAIN WILLIAM SEBAG-MONTEFIORE, M.C., MONTREAL

CAPTAIN WILLIAM SEBAG-MONTEFIORE is the son of the late Arthur and Harriette Sebag-Montefiore of East Cliff Lodge, Ramsgate, Kent, England. He was born the 26th of August, 1885, and was educated at Clifton College, Bristol, England. In 1903 he joined the 3rd Battalion Welch Regiment (English Militia) as 2nd lieutenant, and obtained a regular commission in the 5th Royal Irish Lancers in December, 1904. In January, 1912, he resigned and came to Canada, joining the firm of Solomon & Spielman. Mr. Solomon being killed in the war, the firm was reorganized as Spielman Agencies in 1919. At the outbreak of the Great War he returned to England and rejoined his regiment, proceeding to France in April, 1915, and serving with his regiment until April, 1916, when he was appointed Staff Captain of the XIV Corps, Heavy Artillery. He served in this capacity during 1916 and 1917, receiving the Military Cross for bravery and being twice mentioned in despatches. In the fall of 1917 he returned to England and was sent out to Palestine, and served on that front with various yeomanry regiments until the end of the war, when he returned to Canada. Captain Sebag-Montefiore is President of the Spanish and Portuguese Synagogue (Shearith Israel) Montreal, and takes a great interest in all matters affecting the Jewish population of Montreal. He comes by his communal activity naturally, as he is a grandson of the late Sir Joseph Sebag-Montefiore and a grandnephew of the late Sir Moses Montefiore, the great Jewish philanthropist and statesman. He is a member of the Montefiore Club, and Royal Montreal Golf Club, Montreal, and the Cavalry Club, London, England, and of St. Paul's Lodge, 374 E. R., A. F. and A. M. In 1914 Captain Sebag-Montefiore was married to Sybil Matilda Joseph, who died during his service overseas, and in 1920 he married Marguerite Maud Joseph, both being daughters of Horace and Celine (Joseph) Joseph, of Montreal. He has one son Robert Horace, and two daughters, Daphne Celine and Nancy Sebag. Capt. Montefiore is a Director of the Laurentian Insurance Co.

INTERCOLLEGIATE MENORAH ASSOCIATION
FOR THE STUDY AND ADVANCEMENT OF
JEWISH CULTURE AND IDEALS

IN CANADA there are four Menorah Societies affiliated with the Intercollegiate Menorah Association. They are at the following universities: McGill University, University of Toronto, University of Manitoba and University of British Columbia.

The purpose of these Societies is the study and discussion of all aspects of Jewish life, past and present, approached from a non-partisan unbiased point of view. This purpose is carried out by holding regular forums addressed by either local or out-of-town speakers, or by the students themselves; by the formation of study groups led by Rabbis or other persons competent to lead study work; by the presentation of plays, concerts, debates, symposia, etc.

Among the speakers to address the McGill University Menorah during the past year were Dr. Schmarya Levin of the World Zionist Organization, Mr. Henry Weinfield, barrister, of Montreal, Mr. Louis Fitch, also a barrister, of Montreal, and Mr. Maurice Samuel of the Zionist Organization of America. The meetings conducted by the students consisted of a debate between the Freshman and Sophomore members of the Menorah Society on the question, "Resolved, that Jews should develop a distinct cultural life in America as well as in Palestine", and a symposium on the subject "The Chosen People". A study group was conducted by a graduate member of the McGill Menorah on "The Origin of the Jews".

An Inter-Menorah debate was held between the Societies of the University of Toronto and McGill University at Montreal on February 21, 1925. The subject was: "Resolved, that the Jews of the Diaspora, while continuing to lend material aid toward the up-building of the Jewish Homeland, should leave its political, social and religious structure to be determined by the Jews of Palestine alone."

At the University of Toronto regular meetings were also held, with one meeting a month, an open one, to which all interested townspeople were invited. Dr. Schmarya Levin and Mr. Henry Hurwitz, Chancellor of the Intercollegiate Menorah Association addressed this group.

The Menorah Society of the University of Manitoba, besides holding regular meetings addressed by Rabbi Morton Goldberg, Professor J. H. Heinzelman of the German Department of the University and Professor Guthrie Perry, also of the faculty, and other meetings addressed by the students, succeeded in conducting four study groups on the following subjects: "The Story of the Bible," "The Jew in Literature", "The History of Zionism", and "Discussion of Articles in The Menorah Journal".

In addition, this Society presented their third annual play, "If You Were A Jew" by Sholom Aleichem, translated for the first time from the Yiddish by a member of the Society, Mr. N. B. Zimmerman.

The Society at the University of British Columbia was only recently organized, having affiliated with the Intercollegiate Menorah Association in January 1925. A number of interesting meetings have already been held and the interest and enthusiasm displayed by the students there augur well for the future success of this Menorah Society.

One of the ways in which the Intercollegiate Menorah Association assists the Societies is by furnishing them with syllabi, bibliographies, and pamphlets. Among the syllabi supplied within the past year were: "The Jew in the Modern World", "Jewish Factors in Western Civilization", and "An Outline of Jewish History"; and the pamphlets were "Escaping Judaism" by Professor Harry A. Wolfson of Harvard, and "The Hebrew Contribution to the Americanism of the Future" by Professor Hartley Burr Alexander of Nebraska. Menorah members are also entitled to the regular receipt of The Menorah Journal, the bi-monthly magazine published by the Intercollegiate Menorah Association.

THE JEWISH WAR ORPHANS COMMITTEE OF CANADA

THE story of the Jewish War Orphans Committee is entitled to be described as one of the romances of Canadian Jewish life. Conceived in time of grave emergency, raised swiftly to full maturity of service, and carrying out a relief and rescue work that was as unique as it was humanitarian and practical, the Committee surely have the right to pride themselves upon having carved a deep and lasting niche in the annals of Jewish accomplishment.

It was in the summer of 1920 that the pitiable condition of the Jewish child population of Ukrainia first came to the attention of Canadian Jewry in a direct and authoritative way. Professor Elie Heifetz came to America from Europe in July of that year with a story of suffering and tragedy that would have seemed unbelievable had it not been fully substantiated. There were more than 137,000 Jewish orphans in the Ukraine, he reported, children of tender ages practically living wild and semi-barbarous lives, without homes or means of obtaining regular sustenance beyond their own puny resources, which were mainly the garbage lots of Ukrainian towns and villages, and when this source failed to provide for them, they were trying to assuage the pangs of hunger by eating such edible wild roots and herbs as were left in a territory that had been sadly ravaged by war and post-war excesses. It was felt that aid for these orphans was an imperative duty of the Jews of the American continent, who had known nothing of such terrible privation.

Professor Heifetz was first in touch with the People's Relief Committee of New York. While seeking relief supplies for Ukrainia, he had uppermost in mind the complete rescue of many of the orphans by their emigration to this side. The United States immigration laws militated against the accomplishment of such an undertaking as far as that country was concerned, and Professor Heifetz came to Canada, and through Jewish relief organizations and workers in Montreal, including the People's Relief Committee, Federation of Ukrainian Jews and Central Relief Committee, he found that the scheme might be successfully carried out in Canada.

At a meeting held in Montreal on July 11th, Lyon Cohen, president of the Canadian Jewish Congress was chairman, and a committee was formed to lay plans for the work here. It was realized at the outset that the task would be a big one and would require the interest and support of all Canadian Jewry if it were to be conducted efficiently. The question of forming a Dominion-wide organization came up, and it was resolved to invite Mrs. A. J. Freiman of Ottawa, a woman much respected and beloved by her people, who had been a dominant figure in both Jewish and non-Jewish social and relief work, during the years of the Great War, and the years that followed the signing of peace, to become the head of the orphans activity.

On July 14th, 1920, Mrs. Freiman received a telegram which read as follows:

"Myself and Prof. Heifetz of Ukrainia, and Mrs. Joseph Selick of Toronto, coming to see you to-morrow morning on important mission about Ukrainian orphans. I am sure our journey will be a success".

The message was signed by H. Hershman of the People's Relief Committee, Montreal, and he, with Prof. Heifetz and Mrs. Selick, a leading social worker of Toronto, went to Ottawa on July 15th, where they placed all the facts in their possession regarding the Ukrainian orphans before Mrs. Freiman. If there was anything calculated to stir up the fullest sympathy of Mrs. Freiman, it was a story of children in distress, particularly orphans, and she promptly pledged herself to the pressing cause. She wasted no time getting matters started and arranged a conference with Mr. F. C. Blair, then secretary of the Department of Immigration and Colonization, which was attended by herself, Prof. Heifetz, and Mr. Hershman. The situation was fully explained to Mr. Blair and permission asked for the admission of 1,000 orphans from Ukrainia, to be adopted by Canadian Jewish families. Consideration was promised by the departmental authorities who evinced every desire to co-operate with Mrs. Freiman and her co-workers. The Department felt, however, that the mass immigration of 1,000 children might be too big a problem to handle, and so on July 24th, Mr. Blair wrote to Mrs. Freiman advising that the government would consent to the admission of 200 orphans, as an initial experiment, intimating that further numbers might be allowed to enter Canada if the settlement of the first 200 were made in a manner satisfactory to the Department of Immigration. It was stipulated that complete arrangements for the reception and adoption of the children in Canada had to be made in advance of their coming, and also that a proper organization be formed to carry on the work, to all of these conditions there being immediate agreement by Mrs. Freiman and her colleagues.

On August 8th, 1920, a meeting took place in Ottawa, at which Louis Zucker, president of the People's Relief Committee, Mrs. Freiman and Prof. Heifetz, went further into the plans for the work. They decided that the most propitious time to appeal for Canadian Jewry's support would be during Rosh Hashonah. On August 9, there was a conference in Montreal, at which delegates representing more than 100 organizations were present. This conference formally named Mrs. Freiman as Dominion President of the Ukrainian Orphans Committee, and Prof. Heifetz as director. A committee to look after the appeal in Montreal was appointed to comprise Lyon Cohen, Rabbi H. Cohen, Leon Meltzer, S. D. Cohen, Louis Zucker, Lionel Coviensky, and Harry Barsky.

A stirring message was sent by Mrs. Freiman to all the rabbis and presidents of congregations throughout the Dominion, just prior to the High Holidays, in which she asked them to speak to their people on Rosh Hashonah, of the plight of the Jewish orphans in Ukrainia. The response was both immediate and liberal, and truly representative of the spontaneous charitableness of Canadian Jewry. In the meantime, meetings had been held with leaders of other communities. Prof. Heifetz addressed large gatherings in Winnipeg, on Aug. 17th and 24th, and in Saskatoon, on Aug. 29th, at a conference of delegates from western Canadian cities and towns, called together by the Western Canada Jewish War Relief Organization. At this conference, it was decided to carry on the work in the west, through that organization. Mr. A. J. Freiman and Prof. Heifetz both spoke at a meeting of Toronto business men on Sept. 19th, and on Sept. 30th, Mrs. Freiman addressed two large meetings in Montreal, one of them a mass meeting of the local Jewish public held in Prince Arthur Hall, at which great enthusiasm for the undertaking was displayed.

As the magnitude of the work to be done necessitated the fullest interest and support of Jews in all parts of Canada, it was felt that a representative Dominion-wide conference was essential to perfect the organization that had been tentatively formed, and also to ensure proper recognition of all sections and districts. On Oct. 1st, 1920, a telegram in the name of Mrs. Freiman and Prof. Heifetz was sent to leaders in the different communities from coast to coast, reading as follows:

"Cordially invite you to be guest at Dominion-wide conference of delegates of Jewish Ukrainian Orphan Relief Organization to be held in Chateau Laurier, Ottawa, Oct. 6th, 7th, 8th. Jewish hearts all over Canada have been deeply stirred by authentic accounts of suffering of these Jewish orphans and everywhere great enthusiasm prevails for our plans to rescue and bring some here for adoption in homes where they will be given the love and care they now so pitiably lack. May we not have your co-operation in this noble undertaking."

This conference, one of the most momentous gatherings of its kind held by Canadian Jewry, took place in Ottawa, as scheduled. Mrs. Freiman held a reception at her beautiful home for the delegates on the evening of Oct. 6th, and the main business sessions took place the following day, with Mrs. Freiman presiding. Mr. Harold Fisher, then mayor of Ottawa, delivered an address of welcome, in which he bestowed felicitations on those who had gathered together for so worthy a purpose. Mr. F. C. Blair, then secretary of the Department of Immigration, and now, at the time of writing, assistant deputy minister of the same department, also spoke to the delegates, explaining his department's attitude and promising all the co-operation and assistance possible.

The official register of delegates at the conference contains the names of the following:—Mr. and Mrs. A. J. Freiman, Ottawa, Ont.; Joseph Graner, Toronto. Ont.; B. Lastar, London, Ont.; M. Shnier, Melfort, Sask.; E. Herman, Toronto, Ont.; H. Isenstein, Calgary, Alta.; Mrs. Asher Pierce, Montreal; Mrs. Lisle Isaacs, St. John, N.B.; Mrs. Joseph Rosenbloom, Sherbrooke, Que.; Mrs. J. Kushner, Sherbrooke, Que.; H. Potter, Toronto, Ont.; Mrs. J. Selick, Toronto, Ont.; Harry Kitz, Halifax, N.S.; Charles Zwerling, Halifax, N.S.; H. Hershman, Montreal; Prof. Elie Heifetz, Ukrainia; Lionel Coviensky, Montreal; Rabbi S. Levin, Hamilton, Ont.; Mrs. L. Lazarovictz, Quebec, P.Q.; H. Wolofsky, Montreal; Miss Ida Seigler, Montreal; M. Budovitch, St. John, N.B.; Mrs. Moe Levy, Hamilton, Ont.; S. Guttman, Montreal; Nathan Bacal, Quebec, P.Q.; N. Gardner, Quebec, P.Q.; D. Goldenberg, Campbellton, N.B.; Sam Berger, Ottawa; Lyon Cohen, Montreal; D. S. Friedman, Montreal; A. H. Coplan, Ottawa; J. A. Cherniack, Winnipeg; Benjamin Goldfield, Ottawa; Louis Epstein, Ottawa; Max Mains, Winnipeg; Max Steinkopf, Winnipeg; Mrs. C. J. Gross, Montreal; Rabbi Julius Berger, Hamilton, Ont.; Louis Zucker, Montreal; S. W. Jacobs, K.C., M.P., Montreal; and Solomon Lowenstein, Charles Zunser, and Reuben Brainin of New York City, the first two mentioned representing the orphans branch of the Joint Distribution Committee of America, the latter being a noted journalist.

Plans for the work, as outlined by Mrs. Freiman and Prof. Heifetz to the conference, were enthusiastically endorsed by the delegates. It was decided to name the organization, the Canadian Jewish European Orphans Committee, the title being afterwards changed to Jewish War Orphans Committee of Canada. An appeal to all Jews for funds with which to carry on the work was also agreed on, the dates of the campaign being fixed at December 26th, 27th and 28th, which would permit time for thorough organization of all districts. Mrs. Freiman announced her intention of making a tour of the entire Dominion, to deliver addresses on the urgency of the work, and to assist in the forming of local committees. The conference chose the following officers and committees:—Mrs. A. J. Freiman, Ottawa, Ont., Dominion President; A. J. Freiman, Ottawa, Ont., executive chairman; Max Steinkopf, Winnipeg, Man., first vice-chairman; Sam Kronick, Toronto, second vice-chairman; Lionel Coviensky, Montreal, third vice-chairman; D. S. Friedman, Montreal, Dominion treasurer; Max Mains, Winnipeg, Man., Dominion secretary. Executive committee, Mrs. C. J. Gross, Mrs. Asher Pierce, A. Levin, Louis Zucker, Montreal, Que.; J. H. Holzman (since deceased), and A. H. Coplan, Ottawa; Mrs. J. Selick and H. Potter, Toronto; Mrs. L. Lazarovictz, Quebec; Max Mitchell, Winnipeg, Man. Advisory committee, Lyon Cohen, Horace R. Cohen, S. W. Jacobs, K.C., M.P., H. Wolofsky, S. D. Cohen, Miss Ida Seigler, representing Montreal; M. Goldstick, Joseph Graner, M. Gelber, Toronto; J. M. Franklin, Halifax, N.S.; M. I. Lieberman, Edmonton, Alta.; J. B. Jaffe, Vancouver; Mrs. Moe Levy, Hamilton, Ont.; B. Lastar, London, Ont.; Mrs. J. Kushner, Sherbrooke, Que.; M. Shnier, Melfort, Sask.; D. Goldenberg, Campbellton, N.B.; M. Budovitch, St. John, N.B.

During their stay in Ottawa, the delegates were also entertained by A. H. Coplan and the Hadassah Chapter.

Mrs. Arthur Meighen, wife of Rt. Hon. Arthur Meighen, who was then prime minister of Canada, graciously consented to accept the office of honorary president of the committee, and Lady Davis, Montreal, Lady Borden, Ottawa, and Mrs. Mark Workman, Montreal, became honorary vice-presidents. Her Excellency the Duchess of Devonshire, wife of Canada's Governor-General at that time, had been informed of the projected work of the organization by Mrs. Freiman, and her private secretary, Miss Elsie Saunders, had written Mrs. Freiman, as follows:

Bear Point,
Burbidge, P.Q.
25th Aug. 1920.

"Dear Mrs. Freiman:—

I have placed your letter of Aug. 17th before the Duchess of Devonshire.

Her Excellency was much interested to hear of the formation of the Jewish Ukrainian Orphans Organization of Canada.

Her Excellency feels that under your leadership the scheme will be carefully worked out and will prove a very successful one.

I shall be glad to hear how your organization progresses and shall be happy to lay before Her Excellency, any reports on the adoption of the first 200 orphans in Canadian families."

Following the conference at Ottawa, offices were opened in that city for the organizing work, and Mr. Sam Berger, was appointed secretary to the executive. Under the personal supervision of Mrs. Freiman, an extensive publicity campaign was planned, and considerable quantities of literature dealing with the orphan situation in Ukrainia were sent out to all parts of Canada. In November, 1920, Mrs. Freiman, accompanied by Miss Ida Seigler, Montreal, a member of the advisory committee for that city, set out on a tour of the leading cities from Halifax to Vancouver. Both ladies did not spare themselves, for they were fired with ardour for the success of the undertaking. Mrs. Freiman delivered scores of addresses, met delegations in every community visited, and assisted in the organization of numerous local committees. Jewish communal leaders everywhere responded in a fine way to the appeal so movingly and convincingly made by Mrs. Freiman, and very soon, wherever Jews were gathered together, the all-absorbing topic was of the work for the orphans. At the meetings which were addressed by Mrs. Freiman, applications were taken from Jewish families who were willing to prepare their homes to receive orphans when they would be brought to Canada. These applications were turned over to the local committees for investigation and report so that the orphans should be assigned only to those homes offering the right sort of care and advantages for the future. Applications were also made by individuals and societies who wished to contribute $120 annually for the maintenance of orphans in their own countries. Groups of women in each community started to sew garments for the little ones. The hearts of mothers filled with pity at the thought of thousands of boys and girls, just like their own, wandering in the streets of Ukrainian towns and villages, ragged, hungry and footsore.

When Mrs. Freiman returned from her tour, the entire Dominion had been well prepared for the campaign. Already a large sum of money was in hand, representing the free-will offerings at the synagogue services on Yom Kippur. Prominent men and women had been secured as heads of local committees. Everywhere there was great enthusiasm for the unique work of relief, for it had been learned that no other country had attempted the actual bringing of orphans from Ukrainia to homes selected and waiting for them, such as was to be done by Canada.

Very valuable assistance was also rendered by Mrs. Anna Selick of Toronto, who was appointed secretary for the Province of Ontario, and visited many cities and towns doing organizing work. The Hadassah chapters, B'nai B'rith lodges, local councils of Jewish Women, Hebrew ladies' auxiliaries, and synagogue ladies' auxiliaries, all co-operated heartily in the work. The campaign on December 26th, 27th and 28th, was participated in by thousands of workers, and the sum of $96,000 was raised to finance the work. In addition, tremendous quantities of children's clothing were contributed, over 43 huge cases being afterwards sent abroad. The City of Winnipeg raised $5,000 cash for the purpose of buying clothing and other supplies. Special attention had been given to interesting the boys and girls of Canada, in their less fortunate brothers and sisters of Ukrainia, and many were the sacrifices made so that outfits of clothing and shoes could be provided by the offerings from the children's penny banks. The result of the campaign was indeed a striking and inspiring illustration of the seemingly interminable charitableness of Canadian Jewry, young and old, for it must be borne in mind, that there had been many previous appeals for other relief objects, and hundreds of families were sacrificing, also, in order to send aid to needy relatives in Europe. Non-Jews, as well as Jews, supported the cause, for through the very generous publicity given by the press generally, the sad plight of helpless children had touched Christian hearts, too. Charity, after all, knows no race nor creed. An instance of this is, that in Yarmouth, Nova Scotia, Mr. J. M. Walker, the mayor was treasurer of the campaign committee, and Mr. K. Kilty, another Christian, was an active member of the committee.

The Province of Ontario, which has the largest Jewish population, subscribed $32,700 of the grand total; other provinces contributing as follows: Quebec, $18,142; Manitoba, $15,500; Alberta, $11,450; Nova Scotia, $7,250; Saskatchewan, $4,600; New Brunswick, $3,450; and British Columbia, $3,000. The sum raised was afterwards supplemented by an appropriation of $50,000 for the special orphans work, made by the Associated Jewish War Relief Societies, Inc., but it was later found unnecessary to use this money.

It had been hoped by the executive committee to despatch the unit to Ukrainia to select and bring the orphans to Canada, on November 24th, 1920, but delays occurred in connection with the provision of travelling documents for Prof. Heifetz, who had been appointed director. Finally, after several weeks of inaction, it became evident that Prof. Heifetz, who was a subject of Soviet Russia, could not obtain the documents that were indispensable to enable him to pass unhindered through different European countries, and to ensure that he would be in a position to seek the co-operation of the governments of these countries. For this, and other reasons, the executive committee at a meeting in Montreal on December 21st, 1920, appointed Mr. Gregory Sanders of Montreal, as director of the unit, vice Prof. Heifetz, the latter being amply compensated for the time he had given to the work. The rest of the personnel of the unit was named to be as follows:—Mr. Harry Hershman, Montreal, assistant director; Dr. Joseph Leavitt, Montreal, medical director; and Mr. William Farrar, Hamilton, Ont., director of transportation. Both Mr. Sanders and Mr. Hershman were highly respected members of the Montreal community, and had been active in social work. Mr. Hershman had the added qualification of having personally visited the destitute regions of Poland and Ukrainia that same year. Dr. Leavitt's appointment was particularly pleasing for he had gained an enviable record in service during the war. Special mention should be made of Mr. Farrar, who is a non-Jew, and a former alderman of the City of Hamilton. He is a much beloved figure among Hamilton Jewry. For many years he has taken an active interest in Jewish affairs, and has shown himself to be a great friend of the race. He even attends the synagogue very frequently, especially on the Holy Days. When the Committee learned that Mr. Farrar would like nothing better than to serve as a member of the unit, his appointment was unanimously made, for he was reputed as a business man and organizer, with special knowledge of transportation problems. It was characteristic of Mr. Farrar that after his connection with the unit ended, he reimbursed the Committee for all the money spent on his transportation and maintenance while with the unit.

In view of the practical experience of the Joint Distribution Committee of America, in caring for the stricken population of Eastern Europe, a delegation comprising Mr. and Mrs. Freiman and Mr. Gregory Sanders went to New York in December and conferred with representatives of that Committee, as a result of which an agreement was made which provided that the facilities of the Joint Distribution Committee in Europe, including personnel, records, offices, warehouses, automobiles, etc., would be placed at the disposal of the European unit of the Canadian Orphans Committee. This agreement, which was signed on February 2nd, 1921, also dealt with co-operation between the two organizations in regard to the financial adoption of orphans through provision for their maintenance in Europe, and for the re-union of orphans with relatives, in cases where the latter resided in Canada. The Canadian Orphans Committee agreed to, and did deposit $10,000 with the Joint Distribution Committee, as a guarantee for the payment of any costs which that Committee would incur through the operations of the unit in Europe. Mr. Freiman was elected as Canadian member of the Joint Distribution Committee on December 30th, 1920, and in the following February, Mr. Freiman with D. S. Friedman and Lyon Cohen of Montreal, accepted, on the invitation of Solomon Lowenstein, places on the war orphans committee of the Joint Distribution Committee, of which Mr. Lowenstein was the chairman. These appointments assured the close co-operation for the work ahead, which it was realized was most essential. Had the Canadian committee been forced to provide for their own equipment in Ukrainia, it would have cost many thousands of dollars.

In accordance with the wishes of some of those who

had contributed funds, it was intended to try and carry on relief work among the orphans in that part of Ukrainia which was under Soviet rule, as well as in Ukrainia in Poland. The information which was gathered by the delegation which went to New York showed that it would not be practical to enter Soviet territory, and it was therefore determined to concentrate on efforts in Polish Ukrainia, where the situation was perhaps more acute. As a matter of fact, however, many of the orphans rescued were from towns and villages in Soviet Ukrainia, from which they had fled in terror of their lives following pogroms against the Jewish inhabitants. A conference was held in Montreal on Feb. 2nd, 1921, to discuss this necessary change in plans, following which, arrangements were rushed for the departure of the unit to Europe. Unfortunately, the wife of Mr. Gregory Sanders became seriously ill at this time, and he was obliged to resign the position of director. Mr. Hershman was raised from the position of assistant director to fill the vacancy, and it was decided that no assistant director would be appointed in Mr. Hershman's place. The Department of External Affairs of Canada very kindly co-operated with the Committee by issuing special documents in both the English and French languages, in which the co-operation of British representatives abroad was requested. As all three members of the unit were British citizens, all the necessary passports and visas were speedily procured.

The interest of Canadian Jewry in their unique undertaking was quickened when the unit sailed for Europe by the White Star liner *Cedric* on Feb. 5th, 1921. Applications for the children began to come in in increasing numbers to the Dominion headquarters at Ottawa, where the executive secretarial work had been taken over by Mr. G. Garrow-Greene, private secretary to Mr. and Mrs. Freiman, who had succeeded the original incumbent of the office, Mr. Sam Berger. A total of 228 approved applications were soon on hand, this number representing only a small proportion of the applications actually made, most of which had to be rejected because of the decision of the Committee to give preference to homes where the children would have the greatest advantages, and also due to the fact that only 200 children were to be brought to Canada, and it was considered desirable that the children should be divided up among as many communities as possible. Applications recorded included 84 from Toronto; Montreal, 56; Ottawa, 25; Winnipeg, 14; St. John, N.B. 9; Windsor, Ont., 5; Hamilton, Ont., 5; Sydney, N.S., 4; Saskatoon, Sask., 3; Halifax, N.S., 2; Bateman, Sask., 2; and Pembroke, Ont., Farnham, Que., Vancouver, B.C., Quebec, Que., Yarmouth, N.S., Stratford, Ont., Timmins, Ont., Chatham, Ont., 1 each. These applications were sorted out according to sexes and ages to facilitate the work of selection by the unit in Europe.

Scores of appeals came from families in all parts of the country, who wished the unit to enquire for child relatives in Europe of whom nothing had been heard for several years. The committee promised these families that every effort would be made to locate the missing children, and instructions were sent abroad for the guidance of the unit. Eleven of the children specifically enquired about were found and brought to Canada with the other children, at their relatives' expense. Many others who could not be brought, were placed in touch with their relatives in Canada.

The Committee was incorporated under the War Charities Act, 1917, with a federal charter, on Feb. 28, 1921, under the name "Jewish War Orphans Committee of Canada," the applicants for incorporation comprising Mr. and Mrs. A. J. Freiman, J. J. Marks, A. H. Coplan, J. Holzman and Benjamin Goldfield, all of Ottawa.

In the meantime, the unit had arrived in England and its members were busy making enquiries and securing visas in London. On reaching Paris, the members of the unit received a great reception from the Jewish community there. At a reception held in their honour, M. Sliosberg, noted Franco-Jewish advocate, Nahum Sokolov, chairman of the world executive of the Zionist Organization, and Dr. J. Bogen of the Joint Distribution Committee of America, delivered addresses in which they paid generous compliments to Canadian Jewry for having embarked on a unique humanitarian undertaking. En route to Warsaw, the unit stopped at Vienna where they interviewed the British and Polish ambassadors. The latter furnished letters which facilitated the speedy continuation of the journey to Warsaw which was reached on March 12th. Here, it was welcome news for the unit to learn that the Canadian dollar was worth 900 marks, which ensured more economical carrying on of the work than had been expected. Some considerable time was spent preparing in advance for the movement of the children to be selected, the unit holding conferences with the Polish ministry of foreign affairs, in regard to passports, and with the Polish ministry of transportation, in connection with assuring an adequate supply of railroad cars. Permits had to be obtained from the police officials to remain in Poland for the time necessary.

Although they had been prepared for very tragic conditions, the members of the unit were shocked to discover the indescribable plight of the war and pogrom sufferers in the small cities and villages of Polish Ukrainia. Writing from Warsaw, on March 17, 1921, Mr. Farrar said "The Jews in Ukrainia have been in Hell. Young girls come here with the most heartrending stories. I am made sad from morning until night."

After completing the preliminary work in Warsaw, the unit proceeded on its way, reaching Rovno, which had been selected as the base for activity, on April 3rd. It was the glorious hopeful season of spring, but alas, such a spring in Poland. How the thoughts of each member of the unit must have turned toward Canada, where the springs come year after year under happy circumstances. Spring meant nothing of what it had in Canada, to these Canadians in Poland. True, here and there, the trees were green with budding foliage, and the ground had splotches of grass, but there was so much of desolation that the signs of spring became insignificant. Trees everywhere gaunt and charred, met their gaze, trees that seemed to speak of war and pillage, and upheaval; and most indelibly impressive of all, was a population which faced the picture of utter hopelessness and misery. Women clutching their skirts, their eyes darting hither and thither filled with the fear that experience had taught them to have. And the children! What horrible mute stories the faces of the little ones told. They did not need to speak. Children of perhaps four or five with features of aged persons, eyes sunken, cheeks nothing but skin and bone, bodies almost mere skeletons. Surely, thought these missionaries of humanitarianism, this was the saddest spot on earth.

There was no lack of children for the unit to examine. Thousands had been registered by the representatives of the Joint Distribution Committee, and the fortunate ones accommodated in the three homes that had been established in Rovno. But there were also many others living in sheds and in the open, for space in the homes was limited. Did they want to go to Canada? The excitement, and the anxiety to be chosen which prevailed amongst the children of Rovno, stirred pangs of pity in the hearts of each member of the unit, for sad though it was to decide that way, very few, if any of the children first examined were fit to pass the physical and mental tests. With the valuable co-operation of the agents of the Joint Distribution Committee, the unit set to work. The memory of the week that followed their arrival in Rovno will probably never be erased from their minds. Over 1,000 children were examined by Dr. Leavitt and he found only 46 whom he thought might be of the standard required. The pale thin faces of the little ones, the eyes which mirrored years of intense suffering, almost unnerved the doctor. Over 8,000 children had to be examined eventually before the number brought to Canada was selected. Three children who came before the doctor were all that remained of a happy family of fifteen members. All the others had been killed or had died of diseases brought on by wounds and hunger. One of the three was a cripple, and so the Jewish community of Rovno refused to allow the other two to be taken, as it was felt that they would likely be the sole means of support of the crippled child in later years. In a letter which he wrote to Mr. Freiman from Rovno on April 7th, Mr. Hershman said, "We examined children from the Felstin district, and out of 80, found only 15 to comply with our regulations. Most of the others are in a very poor physical state, some of them maimed and crippled from the effects of pogroms they were in." In this letter, Mr. Hershman expressed the belief that it would take from two to three months longer to pick out the required number of children. And then, in a later letter, he wrote:

"Children born in the Ukraine from 3 to 6 years ago, could not survive, especially if they had become orphans at the ages of 1 or 2 years. Those who survived are the fortunate ones whose parents were spared, and only superhuman sacrifices on the part of the parents saved them."

A cable was received from Mr. Hershman, by Mr. Freiman, dated April 10th, advising that the unit had 50 children selected from the Zwihil, Chudnow, Zhitomar, and Felstin districts. On April 21st, he cabled that this number had been increased to 60 children, between the ages of 4 and 12 years.

The people in Canada were getting anxious for the children to be brought to Canada, and so on April 25th, headquarters at Ottawa cabled the unit to send the first party, as soon as possible. The unit was meeting with tremendous difficulties. First, there were no suitable houses in Rovno in which they could place the children after they had been selected. There had been delay in the arrival of the cases of clothing, and the greatest difficulty of all, was the absolute lack of official records relating to the births of the children. This, of course, was vitally essential.

The unit was greatly assisted in regard to the accommodation problem by Mrs. Anita Muller of the Soziale Hilfsgemeinschaft Anita Muller of Vienna. Mrs. Muller was well known throughout Central and Eastern Europe through the practical social work she carried on from her homes in the Austrian capital. She loaned the unit the services of her secretary, Miss Salomea Andermann, and the latter's familiarity with Polish customs and language, besides her training in just such work as was being carried on, was of immense help. It was through the influence of Mrs. Muller that a letter was written by the Polish Ambassador at Vienna, to Polish officials, generally bespeaking their interest and co-operation in the Canadian orphans undertaking. The plans of the unit were to select the children and send them to Antwerp, the port of embarkation, in parties of fifty, but it was impossible to find places to house them at necessary stopping points such as Lemberg and Warsaw. Mrs. Muller, the unit personnel and representatives of the Joint Distribution Committee conferred at both Rovno and Lemberg in regard to this worrisome problem. It was finally decided that the first party of children should go to a home in Vienna which Mrs. Muller agreed to provide for them.

In the selection of the children, the unit tried to keep brothers and sisters together. There was much time spent in trying to get accurate information as to the origin of the children who were considered healthy enough to be chosen. The parents of the children were dead, official records had been destroyed in pogroms, and the information on file in the offices of the Joint Distribution Committee was too meagre to be of service. Mr. Hershman had to make dozens of visits here and there, interviewing old residents who had known the parents of the orphans, and so, in this way, a sufficient record was built up, and when finished, the documents of origin were certified to by the local rabbinate. One can appreciate the quandary of the unit in this respect when it is stated that 55 of the children chosen were from the district of Novograd Wolinsk which had been burned and pogromed no fewer than 15 times, and records of vital statistics had been completely destroyed.

The work of the unit had been held up by delay in the arrival of the cases of clothing, as the children could not make the journey in the rags they wore when selected. The clothing did not reach Danzig until May 20th. Dozens of telegrams and telephone messages had to be exchanged, and personal conferences held with transportation authorities to arrange for railroad cars in which to convey the children from Rovno. As was the case in Canada, following the close of the war, there was a shortage of cars in Europe, and the different governments refused to allow any equipment to pass beyond their respective frontier lines. The people of Canada were during all this time, chafing a little under the protracted delay in the consummation of the undertaking, it being naturally hard for them to understand why it was taking so long to collect the children.

Appreciating the need for expediting the work, Mr. Freiman cabled the unit on May 20th, 1921, instructing them that as conditions in Canada necessitated quick conclusion of the work, the number of children to be brought to Canada should be reduced to 150, instead of the original number of 200. One of the reasons which forced this decision on the part of the Committee was that most of the children found eligible for emigration were older than as desired by the families making application for them here. Mr. Hershman had reported that there were very few children under 6 years of age left alive in Ukrainia, and the records at headquarters in Ottawa indicated that 70 per cent of the applications were for children under that age. As news came from the unit, bulletins were sent out to all the local committees and to those who had applied for children, informing them of the situation as reported by the unit, and the biggest proportion of the families who had signified their willingness to adopt orphans, was found ready to take children a little older than they had originally stipulated. A further cable was sent to the unit, instructing them to endeavour to finish their work by June 15th.

At length, nearly ten weeks after the unit had arrived in Rovno, the first party of orphans was ready for departure. They left on June 14th. The children had to be taken in auto busses ten miles out from the town to a junction point named Zdolbunow, because the cars were on a railroad line that did not touch Rovno. In a description of the leaving of the children, written to Ottawa, Mr. Hershman stated, "To the greatest joy of the children and the grief of the population, the children departed." There were 51 little boys and girls in the first party, and they reached Vienna two days later, June 16, where they were comfortably housed, under the supervision of Mrs. Anita Muller and Mr. Wm. Farrar. While they were in Vienna, Mr. Farrar taught the children some of the simple words of the English language, and described to them in an interesting way Canada, Canadians and Canadian customs, all of which, needless to say, increased the eagerness of the children to come here. Mrs. Muller and Mr. Farrar went to Antwerp to prepare the way for the arrival there of the entire party of orphans. They were most warmly received by the leaders of the Antwerp Jewish community. Several meetings were held at which both Mrs. Muller and Mr. Farrar delivered addresses, and scores of families offered to take one or two children into their homes during the time they would be in Antwerp waiting for the ship to sail for Canada. While the first party of orphans were in Vienna, they were visited by Mr and Mrs. A. Levin of Montreal, who were then on their way to visit Palestine. As Mr. Levin was one of the members of the executive committee, he was naturally much interested in the children, and he wrote back to Canada, highly praising them. Mrs. J. Kushner of Sherbrooke, Que., member of the advisory committee, was also a visitor to Vienna at about the same time, and she was able to render valued assistance to Mrs. Anita Muller in making the little ones comfortable during their stay there. She was also with members of the unit at Warsaw and Antwerp.

In view of the reduction of the quota from 200 to 150 orphans, it was decided to concentrate them all at Antwerp, until the date of sailing. While the first party of 51 children were at Vienna, Mr. Hershman and Dr. Leavitt were speeding up the selection of the remainder. Finally, after the elapse of another month, all obstacles had been surmounted. Passports and visas had been secured. A cable was despatched to Canada advising headquarters to purchase steamship transportation, which was done through the Canadian Pacific Ocean Services. The main body of children in care of Mr. Hershman and Dr. Leavitt left Rovno on July 22nd, this time the railroad cars having been placed in Rovno station. Simultaneously, the other children started from Vienna for Antwerp. A Sabbath intervening during the railroad journey was spent in Dresden, Germany, and Antwerp was reached on August 6th, just three days before the date of departure of the *S.S. Scandinavian*, which was to take the first party.

When word was received in Canada of the readiness of the children for the sea voyage, Mrs. A. J. Freiman, Dominion President of the Committee, who had been largely responsible for the carrying out of the momentous scheme, prepared to leave for Europe to take charge of the orphans and return with them to Canada. She sailed for Southampton on July 17th, with Mrs. Asher Pierce of Montreal, a member of the executive committee. Their arrival at Antwerp was a great event for the children, who were all delighted to meet the lady they had heard so much about.

The members of the unit were helped in many ways by the Societe Philanthropique pour la Protection des Emigrants of Antwerp. Through Mr. Shul Singer, of that organization, all the details incidental to departure, were quickly settled, and when it developed that owing to a slight outbreak of skin affection a number of the children would have to remain behind until a later date, this organization eased the minds of the Canadian relief workers by arranging for their accommodation and care until they were well enough to make the journey across the Atlantic. Co-operation was also extended the unit by the Canadian immigration officials, through the then director for Europe, Col. J. Obed Smith of London. Included in the first party of children were four who were being sent to Canada by the Societe Philanthropique pour la Protection des Emigrants of Antwerp, and two Polish boys who were escorted in behalf of the Canadian immigration officials, coming to join their father in Ottawa, who was a veteran of the great war.

The first party of children, numbering in all 108, including the 6 escorted children, left Antwerp on August 9, 1921. One can imagine the hearts of the little ones beating more rapidly as their thoughts centered on the land of promise to which they were at last on their way.

Each child had an outfit of clothing and shoes, and fastened to each little jacket and blouse was a tag on which the identity of the child in question, had been inscribed. The steamship officials had made special preparations to ensure a comfortable and pleasant voyage. A kitchen for the cooking of kosher foods was one very much appreciated feature. On the voyage across, Mrs. Freiman and Mrs. Pierce worked with the members of the unit in classifying the children according to sexes and ages, so as to avoid delay in the assignment of the children when Quebec, the port of debarkation, would be reached. Four special nurses had been engaged in Europe to travel with the children and attend to their wants, arrangements having been made for the admission of these adults when Canada was reached. The officers of the steamship did everything possible for the little ones in their care, and as for the passengers, they quickly made 'pets' of the orphans, and showered them with attention and presents. The little ones were having a taste of the human kindness which awaited them in Canada.

The *Scandinavian* arrived at Quebec on August 20th, at night. What excitement prevailed! The children spent the last few hours on the boat scurrying around, gathering up their little keepsakes, now and then rushing to the sides of the boat to gaze with marvelling eyes at the twinkling lights of the St. Lawrence shore. The landing of the children in the early hours of August 21st, was a great event in the history of the Jewish community of Quebec. Great preparations had been made to welcome the children. A newspaper despatch describing the debarkation, read in part as follows:

"Over a hundred little Jewish orphans from the Ukraine, bereft of parents, relatives and homes by the cruel fortunes of war and by the barbarous pogroms on defenceless people which are one fruit of the still seething political conditions of Central Europe, landed from the ocean liner *Scandinavian*, when she docked here Saturday morning. When they trod the soil of old Quebec and saw the comforting Union Jack, flying in the breeze from the citadel, they sang 'God Save the King' . . . "

The party was met by those who had been leaders in the work of the Jewish War Orphans Committee, including:—A. J. Freiman, Ottawa; D. S. Friedman, Montreal; Horace R. Cohen, Montreal; Lionel Coviensky, Miss Hattie Silverman, Montreal; G. G. Greene, Ottawa; Asher Pierce, Montreal; Dr. C. J. Gross, Montreal, (since deceased); Mrs. P. Kaufmann, Mrs. M. Kamarner, Mrs. Anna Selick, Toronto; Max Budovitch, St. John, N.B.; and Mrs. M. Levy, Hamilton, Ont.

The children were speedily passed through the immigration examinations, and then formed up into a procession, each child carrying a tiny Union Jack, and knapsacks on their backs. In this way, they marched through the principal streets of Quebec, to the community hall, where a fine repast had been prepared for them by a committee under the convenership of Mrs. L. Lazarovicz. Miss Rachel Smilovitz read an address of welcome to Mrs. Freiman, in English, and Mrs. Lazarovitcz, an address in Yiddish. Speeches were delivered by Mr. Freiman, Mrs. Freiman, Mr. Farrar, Mr. D. S. Friedman and Mr. Hershman. The children will probably never forget that first meal on Canadian soil. There was a huge quantity of deliciously cooked chicken, vegetables, and a supply of fruit that was too much for even a hundred hungry boys and girls. When the children had been adequately cared for, the executive committee conferred at the Chateau Frontenac, and allotted the children according to the local requirements, being careful to keep brothers and sisters together for adoption in the same communities. The children were rested during the day and left Quebec on the evening of August 21st, destined as follows: 55 to Toronto, for that city, and various western Ontario points; 21 to Montreal and Ottawa; 12 to Winnipeg, and 16 to St. John, N.B.

It was both a joyful and sad hour for the little orphans when the time came to break the happy union which had been maintained during the weeks that had elapsed since they had been accepted by the unit at Rovno. Tears were freely shed. There were loving embraces, murmured endearments, and promises to write, and then the children destined to proceed in separate directions were gently separated and taken to the station, where they were made comfortable in their berths for the night. The railroad arrangements were made by the C.N.R., and everything possible had been done for the comfort of the little travellers on the journey to their future homes. Mrs. Freiman accompanied the children to Montreal and Ottawa; Mr. Hershman took the children to Toronto; Mr. M. Budovitch escorted the children to St. John for the Maritime Provinces, and Miss Hattie Silverman took the children to Winnipeg.

The orphans who had been left behind at Antwerp came at later dates, 24 arriving on Sept. 3rd, 16 on Sept. 24th, 1 on Dec. 6th, and 1 on Jan. 24th, 1922. The Societe Philanthropique pour la Protection des Emigrants looked after them while they were in the Belgian port, and provided necessary medical attention. On reaching Quebec, the little ones were welcomed by the community in the same warm, practical way that the first party had been received.

At Montreal, Toronto, Ottawa, St. John and Winnipeg, there were notable demonstrations when the children arrived. Able committees looked after the assignment of the children, who were all placed in good homes, several of them with very wealthy families. Since they were first assigned, there have been a number of changes, made at the discretion of the local supervisory committee, with the approval of the central executive committee. Some families found, after a few months, that they could not keep the children they had adopted, due to illness or change of circumstances.

Of the number of 146 brought to Canada, 34 were eventually united with relatives who had been living in Canada for some time previous. When it was ascertained that there were near relatives of the children living in Canada, and that these relatives desired to have the children join them, careful enquiry was made by the Committee as to the standing of the families, whether the advantages offered were as good as the children were enjoying with their foster-parents, the main considerations, however, being in regard to the desire of the children themselves to go to their relatives, and the willingness of the foster-parents to relinquish them. There were cases in which the Committee did not deem it in the interest of the children concerned to turn them over to relatives. At the time of writing, there are 103 children living with foster-parents, and they have been a credit to themselves, the Committee and the families that have undertaken to bring them up. Adopted children are living in Beloil, Que., Halifax, N.S., Farnham, Que., Hamilton, Ont., Montreal, Que., New Waterford, N.S., Pembroke, Ont., Quebec, St. John, N.B., Ottawa, Sydney, N.S., Toronto, Winnipeg, and Woodstock, N.B. In four cases, there are two children adopted by one family. In addition, 9 children, for whom, owing to ages and individual characteristics suitable homes could not be found, are being cared for at the expense of the Committee in Montreal, Toronto and Winnipeg. Five of them are learning trades and going to night schools, the others are attending the day schools, preparatory to taking up some vocation, under the supervision of the Committee. It is sad to record that one child died in Toronto on July 9, 1923, from an organic disease, although everything possible was done to save his life. In view of the terrible hardships suffered by the children before they came to Canada, the fact that only one child died is regarded as a favorable commentary on the homes they were placed in and the care given the selection of such homes by the Committee.

For about two years after the children were settled in Canada, Mr. Hershman occupied the position of field superintendent, and made occasional trips of inspection to the children in their homes. He resigned from this post on Aug. 6, 1923. Four of the children not adopted who were being cared for in the Hebrew Orphan Home, Montreal, had a thrilling experience when the Home's country branch at Shawbridge, Que., where they were spending the summer was burned to the ground on August 16, 1922. Fortunately they were rescued.

The orphans became rapidly accustomed to Canadian life, and quite a large number of them showed unusual intelligence and quickness. A glance through reports received by the Committee brought to light the following interesting examples of the progress of the children at school. (It must be remembered that they started out handicapped by lack of knowledge of the English language). One child promoted in first term from 4th to 9th reader; another child promoted from 4th to 5th grade in less than a term; a child was promoted over the next three classes, and still another child was passed over two classes. There is the case of a boy passing with an average of 99 marks, after the first year. A girl went up to the 3rd grade after her first term, another girl went from one grade to two grades higher. A boy after $2\frac{1}{2}$ years in Canada, ranked first in the 6th year at public school with a percentage of 92.7.

The foregoing deals with purely general education, and many of the children have shown talent in the arts of singing and of music. Records at headquarters contain references to 19 boys and girls who are already excellent pianists, and the foster-parents are doing everything in their power to develop this talent in their adopted children. Four children are really expert violinists, and eight others have promising voices. One little chap has shown singular ability in mastering musical instruments and plays the piano, saxophone and xylophone with a finish that marks him for greater things in the future. He has already appeared in public. His foster-father is training him for a professional career.

Following the conclusion of the work of settling the orphans in Canada, there was a number of events worthy of record. On June 3, 1923, Mr. Wm. Farrar was honored by the Committee by a dinner to show appreciation for his services as a member of the overseas unit, held in the Royal Connaught Hotel, Hamilton, Ont. Mr. Farrar was presented with a beautiful loving cup, suitably inscribed, as a memento of his work, and of the occasion. This cup was bought by members of the Committee and friends of Mr. Farrar.

In October of the same year, the regrettable death of Dr. C. J. Gross, occurred in Montreal. Dr. Gross had actively served on the Committee from the commencement of the work in 1920, and had done a great deal to ensure the successful carrying out of the undertaking. His loss was a cause of deepest sorrow to all his colleagues and to a wide circle of friends. His widow, Mrs. C. J. Gross, was also a member of the Committee, and like her late husband, was both energetic and enthusiastic for the cause of the orphans.

In November, Dr. Jos. Leavitt was appointed a member of the Montreal Advisory Committee, as medical officer to supervise the health of the orphans unplaced.

Following a visit to Canada of a delegation headed by Dr. Leo Motzkin of the Jewish World Relief Conference, Paris, the Committee met to consider the advisability of voting part of the moneys left on hand for the work of the Conference in succouring the orphans of the Ukraine. The meeting was held on Feb. 8, 1924, and the sum of $12,000 was voted, this amounting when remitted to 255,861 francs. With this money, the Conference opened a kitchen in Elizavetgrad, Russia, where 500 children were fed daily. The kitchen was located in the heart of the Jewish quarter, where resided 'the poorest of the poor'.

On Feb. 10, 1925, the Toronto committee held a banquet in honor of Mr. and Mrs. Freiman, at which there were many leading members of the local community, and speeches were delivered which extolled the humanitarian work which both Mr. and Mrs. Freiman had directed to a successful conclusion.

The work of the Jewish War Orphans Committee has been worth while in every way. Nearly 150 children were brought to Canada. They were undoubtedly saved from a hopeless situation from which it is quite probable that they would have eventually been victims. They are all giving promise of becoming good citizens, and are also being brought up to manhood and womanhood in an environment which will enable them to live the true Jewish life. Cold statistics cannot be used to measure the value of the Committee's contribution toward the welfare of humanity.

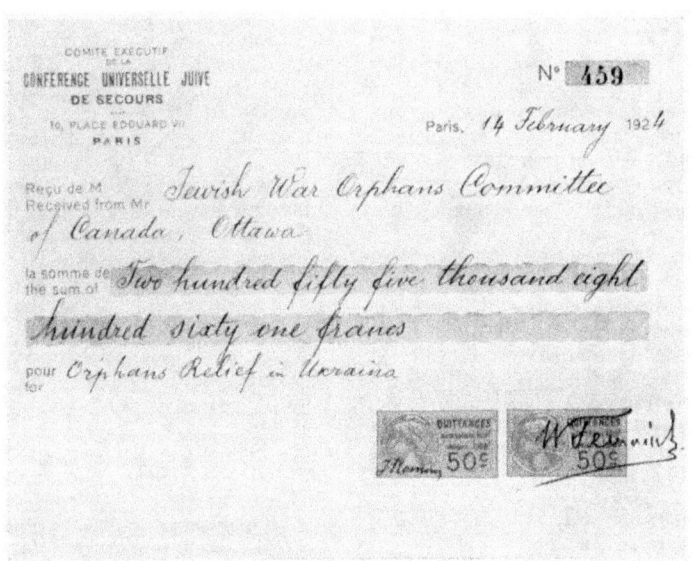

The equivalent of $12,000.00 given by the Jewish War Orphans Committee to establish a kitchen for the needy orphans in Elizavetgrad, Russia

MRS. L. M. SCHWARTZ, TORONTO

MRS. L. M. (ELIZABETH) SCHWARTZ, the daughter of the late Pincus Winerip, renowned as a Talmudist, and Frances Winerip, was born in Russian Poland on May 1st, 1887. She accompanied her parents, as a child, when they took up their residence in Boston, Mass., where she received her education at the public and high schools. On February 1st, 1905, she was married in Toronto to Louis M. Schwartz, son of Samuel Schwartz, a pioneer resident of that city, and one of the first members of the Goel Tzedec synagogue. Mr. and Mrs. Schwartz have one son, Alfred, and four daughters, the Misses Freda, Frances, Shalomath Hadassah, and Mae Schwartz. Mrs. Schwartz has been an active communal worker in Toronto for many years, her first work being the formation of the Hebrew Polish Ladies' Aid Society, of which she was vice-president. She was a member of the old Co-operative Board of Charities, and as a member of the Board took an active part in the formation of the Federation of Jewish Philanthropies of Toronto. She has been a very active member of the Hebrew Ladies' Maternity Aid Society, and has held office as secretary and first vice-president of this organization. Mrs. Schwartz organized the Hebrew Beaches Auxiliary, and she has been the president of this organization since its inception. She was one of the first members of the Ladies' Auxiliary of the Goel Tzedec Congregation, of which she has been treasurer for the past three years. She took a prominent part in war relief work, and was one of the leaders of the first Jewish tag day for this purpose. As one of the first members of Hadassah in Canada, she has taken much interest in Zionist work, and is a member of the Dominion Executive of the Hadassah Organization, treasurer of the Toronto Council, and president of Central Chapter, the "mother" Chapter of Canada. She is also a member of the Zionist Council of Canada, and of the Keren Hayesod Committee. Mrs. Schwartz is a vice-president of the United Synagogue League, and she organized the Home and School Club of the Kew Beach School, of which she was secretary for three years.

THE LATE MARKUS MARKUS

THE LATE MARKUS MARKUS was born on April 30th, 1862, in Frankfort-on-Maine, Germany, and died December 9th, 1920, in Montreal, Que. He received his education in Germany and came to Canada in 1888. Mr. Markus was married in New York City on December 5th, 1886, to Fanny Kahn, also of Frankfort-on-Maine, and he was survived by his widow, three sons, Arthur A. Markus, Richard J. Markus and Ernest M. Markus, and one daughter, Miss Hortense Markus. Mr. Markus always took an active interest in communal affairs and was first life governor and a director of the Baron de Hirsch Institute at the time of the erection of the building on Bleury Street; trustee of the Spanish and Portuguese Synagogue; trustee of the Shaar Hashomayim Synagogue; member of the Building and Finance Committee for the erection of the new edifice for the Congregation Shaar Hashomayim, (Cor. Kensington Ave. and Cote St. Antoine Road;) first vice-president of the Young People's Society of the Shaar Hashomayim Synagogue, at the time of its organization; trustee and chairman of the Board of Education of the Montreal Hebrew Orphans' Home; vice-president and trustee of the Talmud Torahs of Montreal; president of the Hebrew Maternity Hospital of Montreal, and founder of the Ladies' Auxiliary of the Hebrew Maternity Hospital. Mr. Markus was chairman at the time of his death, of the Million Dollar Campaign for the relief of Jewish war sufferers; governor of the Young Men's Hebrew Association; life governor of the Western Hospital; member of the Executive of the Federation of Jewish Philanthropies. He was one of the founders of the Zionist Movement in Canada and first vice-president of the Zionist Organization; president, Agudath Zion Society; treasurer and founder of Court McGill No. 494, and first and only Jewish District Deputy High Chief Ranger for the Province of Quebec, C.O.F.; member of St. George's Lodge, No. 440, A.F. & A.M.; Montreal Board of Trade; and of the Montefiore Club, Montreal. In 1888 he founded the firm of M. Markus & Sons, Limited and the Standard Umbrella Mfg. Company.

A. M. VINEBERG, MONTREAL

Jacoby

ABRAM MOSES VINEBERG, financier and philanthropist, was born in Montreal, on May 7th, 1876, the son of the late Moses Aaron and Fanny (Freedman) Vineberg. He received his education in the Montreal High School, and at the age of fourteen entered into the wholesale fur business established by his father under the name of M. Vineberg & Co. Abram Vineberg was largely responsible for the tremendous growth of this business, and upon the retirement of this firm in 1915, he became interested in real estate and finance with the Moses Vineberg Investment Corporation, of which he is the present head. On April 16th, 1902, Mr. Vineberg was married to Anna, daughter of Joseph Berman of Cleveland, Ohio, and he has two sons, Arthur Martin and Stanley Alvin, and one daughter, Miss Evelyn Fanny Vineberg. Mr. Vineberg has for many years taken a foremost part in communal undertakings in Montreal, and he has been particularly identified with the Federation of Jewish Philanthropies and its constituent bodies. For many years he held office on the Board of the Baron de Hirsch Institute, and was one of the most active founders of the Federation. He was one of the incorporators of this organization, and was chairman of the Executive Committee in 1918. In 1917 and 1918 Mr. Vineberg held the office of president of the Montreal Hebrew Orphans' Home, and it was during his term of office that the splendid new building on Claremont Avenue was purchased. No man has taken a keener and more active interest in the welfare of the orphans than has Mr. Vineberg, and in 1925 he again assumed the chairmanship in order to rectify the many faults that had arisen in the management. His conscientiousness, energy and business ability have again placed this institution among the finest of its kind in Canada. A life-long member of the Shaar Hashomayim Congregation, Mr. Vineberg has for many years held office in this institution, and at the present time he is the Honorary Secretary. For almost twenty-five years he has been a member of the Cemetery Committee of the synagogue.

JEWISH WAR RELIEF ACTIVITIES IN CANADA

By S. K. B.

UPON the outbreak of the World War, a commercial depression set in throughout Canada and the financial position of the Jewish organizations of Montreal became very serious. Communal leaders in this city met on November 23rd, 1914, under the chairmanship of Mr. S. W. Jacobs, K.C., to devise ways and means to cope with the situation. This resulted in a Jewish Relief Campaign Committee being formed under the leadership of Mr. Lyon Cohen, representing all groups in the community, with Mr. D. S. Friedman as Treasurer.

A drive for funds was launched early in 1915, and a total of $24,010.17 was raised, of which $2778.60 was obtained from other cities in Canada, the larger outside donations coming from Ottawa, Hamilton, Halifax, Victoria, Sydney, Sherbrooke and Quebec.

The purpose of the campaign was not only to help the charitable organizations in the City of Montreal, but also to render relief to Jewish war sufferers on the other side, which cause soon became a great problem. Of the money received, $1,061.50 was sent to Palestine and $5,931.85 to the War Victims Committee in London (of which Lord Rothschild was President) for Jewish war sufferers in allied countries. Thus, the first effort by united Jewry in Canada was made to help our poor people on the other side.

The beginning of the second year of the war marked a renewal of the activities in the various sections of the community for Jewish war relief. Following the example of American Jewry, three distinct committees were formed in Montreal:

(1) The Canadian Jewish Alliance, later known as the People's Relief Committee of Montreal—representing labour organizations, fraternal societies, etc.

(2) The Central Relief Committee representing various synagogues and orthodox organizations.

(3) The Canadian Jewish Committee representing the older settlers in the community. Relief work was also done by the Roumanian Verband, Polish Verband and Ukrainian Verband, the latter being known also as the Canadian Alliance of Ukrainian Jews. A conference on war victims was held in Toronto in the latter part of 1915 and a branch of the Canadian Alliance of Ukrainian Jews was formed in 1919. An organization known as the Western Canada Relief Alliance was started at the end of 1915. We shall describe briefly the activities of these organizations:

The Canadian Jewish Alliance

The Canadian Jewish Alliance came into existence in the spring of 1915 due to conferences of various labour and fraternal organizations called by Branch 8 of the Jewish National Workers Alliance. Mr. Reuben Brainin was appointed President; L. Zuker, Vice-President; Yehuda Kaufman, Secretary; George Rabinovitch, Treasurer; and J. Figler, Financial Secretary. The aims of the Canadian Jewish Alliance were mostly political, the principal plank in their platform being the calling of a Canadian Jewish Congress.

In August of the same year, the Canadian Jewish Alliance decided to start collecting funds for Jewish war sufferers, and a special department was created of which Mr. S. Belkin was appointed Manager. Black painted boxes were distributed in Jewish homes which were visited periodically by volunteers to collect the money dropped therein. Collections were also made amongst workers in factories, synagogues, etc. It is interesting to note that on Sunday, September 12th, 1915, when the first round up was made, seventy-eight volunteers visited two thousand, one hundred and fifty-four homes and collected from one thousand, five hundred and forty-one boxes—two hundred and forty-two dollars and forty-one cents ($242.41). This amount comprised 5,700 single cents, which serves as an indication of the participation in the campaign by the poorer people.

Up to December 21st, 1916, the Canadian Jewish Alliance sent to the People's Relief Committee in New York, $12,100. The Relief Committee of the Canadian Jewish Alliance later became a branch of the People's Relief Committee of New York.

As the War went on, collections were continued by the Relief Committee. The Trade Union Organizations in the city also took an active part in this work. According to the statement issued by Messrs. C. H. Hershman, Leon Meltzer, B. Richikoff, I. Rachlenko and N. Frankel, the People's Relief Committee in conjunction with the Canadian Jewish Alliance collected up to February 16th, 1919, an approximate sum of $50,000.

Central Relief Committee

The Central Relief Committee was organized in the fall of 1915 by a conference of various synagogues. Mr. N. Sloves was elected Chairman; Mr. Menasche Lavut, Treasurer; and Mr. S. Guttman, Secretary. Among other members acting on the Central Relief Committee were Rabbi H. Cohen, Mr. S. Rosen and Alderman Lyon W. Jacobs. The Central Relief Committee was affiliated with the organization of the same name in the United States to which they forwarded all monies collected by them. They did not confine themselves to only one method of collection. A system of certificates was adopted and these certificates were distributed in the Jewish homes. Volunteers visited the homes and attached stamps to the certificates for the amounts collected each time. Appeals were made in synagogues from time to time and collections were taken up at Jewish weddings, brith-milah ceremonies, etc. According to a statement issued by Mr. S. Guttman, the Secretary, the sum of $57,000 was raised by this organization. This amount includes $5,000 collected by the Central Relief Committee from the smaller communities in Canada.

Canadian Jewish Committee

The Canadian Jewish Committee commenced to function on October 19th, 1915. Sir Mortimer B. Davis, Messrs. Mark Workman and Moses A. Vineberg were elected Honorary Presidents; Mr. Lyon Cohen, President; Rev. Dr. H. Abramowitz and Isaac Friedman, Vice-Presidents; D. S. Friedman, Treasurer; and A. Z. Cohen, Honorary Secretary. Amongst the more prominent members on the several committees were the following:—

Messrs. S. W. Jacobs, K.C., M.P., Maxwell Goldstein, K.C., Peter Bercovitch, K.C., M.P.P., Nathan Gordon, K.C., Michael Hirsch, A. M. Vineberg, Jacob Kellert, Jos. Levinson, H. M. Levine, A. Rudolph, Samuel Wener, A. Lesser, A. Pierce, J. A. Jacobs and H. Wolofsky.

The Committee, which was composed of the wealthier element in the community with such men as Mr. Lyon Cohen and Mr. David S. Friedman as executive officers, who threw themselves untiringly into the work, could not help but raise a considerable sum of money for the war sufferers' relief. From the date of its inception to January 25th, 1919, the Committee raised in Montreal $164,182.25. $4,084.68 was raised from the smaller communities in the Province of Quebec. Ontario collected $49,003.71, of which amount Hamilton raised $19,540.43 and Ottawa $19,246. Vancouver and Victoria, B.C., raised $20,418.45. Nova Scotia raised $15,379.40, of which Sydney collected $6,370.81, Glace Bay $4,213.50 and Halifax $2,914.00. Alberta raised $8,402.29, of which Edmonton contributed $6,200, Calgary $1,623.19. Saskatchewan raised $5,795.50 of which Regina contributed $4,770.45. New Brunswick raised $3,538 of which St. John collected $3,236.45. Smaller amounts were also received from Newfoundland and a few places in Manitoba. The total amount raised by the Canadian Jewish Committee up to January 27th, 1919, was $271,118.18.

Most of the funds collected by this organization were transmitted to the War Victims' Committee of London, England. However, as the years went on, the Canadian Jewish Committee came into touch with the Joint Distribution Committee in New York to which the former commenced to send large sums of money.

Early in 1919, the dissenting relief committees began to realize the advisability of unity by Canadian Jewry in order to increase collections for war relief. This uniting of the relief organizations introduced a new chapter in Jewish war relief work in Canada. We shall deal with this separately at the conclusion of this article.

Roumanian Verband

This organization, which was in existence before the war, was revived by appeals from the other side. It raised considerable sums of money from membership dues, donations, affairs, etc., for the relief of suffering Jews in Roumania. It was particularly interested in the fate of Jewish orphans in Roumania. Among the most active workers were Messrs. M. Silverman, J. Finkelstein, Joseph Shubert and H. M. Caiserman. The funds collected by the Verband were either transmitted direct to Roumania or sent to the Roumanian Verband in the United States.

Russian-Polish Society

The Russian-Polish Society was formed by Canadian residents of Polish origin. It collected some money for the relief of "landslite" in Poland.

Canadian Alliance of Ukrainian Jews

Because of the extreme suffering of the Jewish population in Ukrainia, the Ukrainian Jews in Canada were greatly stirred and formed an organization of their own for relief work. It was believed that taking advantage of the sentiments aroused in the Ukrainian Jewish community here, they would be able to raise large sums for their countrymen by forming a special organization.

The Ukrainian Verband did not devote itself to the collection of money only, but also organized campaigns for clothing, soap, candles, medicines, etc. During the period of September 14th, 1919, to November 23rd, 1921, they raised in cash $20,467.53, of which $3,000 was collected by the Toronto Branch of the Ukrainian Verband and $619.82 by other branches in Canada. The value of clothing and other supplies collected by the Ukrainian Verband is estimated at $190,000.

The cost of organizing the campaigns and expenses for various affairs such as benefit balls, mass meetings, etc., amounted to $4,170.23 and administrative expenses to only $2,165.57.

The clothing and other supplies collected by the Ukrainian Verband were forwarded to Ukrainia in 1920, and the cost of transportation which amounted to nearly $20,000 was defrayed by the Associated War Relief Societies of Canada. Mr. Lyon Cohen, the President, took a deep interest in the shipment of these articles.

The first shipment of 500 cases of clothing and several cases of medicines (medicines were purchased for the sum of $25,000 voted by the Western Canada Relief Alliance) were sent under the auspices of a special delegation to Russia. The delegation consisted of Mr. S. Belkin of Montreal and Mr. H. Salzman of Winnipeg. Mr. Belkin succeeded in penetrating the war-stricken areas in the Ukraine and visited many of the pogromstricken cities bringing back a report on the terrible conditions which existed in the Ukraine at the time. Mr. Belkin also brought information as to the whereabouts of 60,000 refugees who were compelled to abandon the small towns and to seek refuge in the larger centres. Being the first relief worker to enter Soviet Ukraine, Mr. Belkin obtained the first list of people killed in the pogroms, as well as the first photographs depicting the great calamity which had befallen the victims.

When the American Relief Administration instituted a delivery of food supplies in Russia, the Ukrainian Verband shipped food parcels in behalf of individuals valued at about $46,350. They also shipped parcels of clothing at an appraised value of $4,319.95.

The officers of the Ukrainian Verband comprised the following:

S. Belkin, President; W. Baranovsky, Acting Chairman; Sam Polisuk, Financial Secretary; W. Wolf, Treasurer; R. Dashevsky, Trustee; and Messrs. Jacob Abel, R. Blachman, A. Parness, H. Barsky and Louis Holzman, Directors.

Toronto Conference on War Victims

The Toronto Conference was organized through the initiative of the Toronto Organization of the Poale Zion at the end of 1915. The first Conference was attended by representatives of one hundred organizations and synagogues. Soon the Committee was incorporated by an Ontario Charter. Mr. A. M. Goldstick was elected President, Mr. H. Vineberg, Treasurer; and Mr. L. Rosenberg, Secretary. The Committee had a number of volunteer collectors who made weekly rounds of Jewish homes. In addition, three campaigns for clothing took place and the supplies received were valued at tens of thousands of dollars. The Committee sent its money to the People's Relief and to the Central Relief Committees in New York. The total amount collected was about $150,000.

The Toronto Conference received a permit for a tag day which was the only tag day held in the Province of Ontario. This method of collection brought in $15,000. The clothing collected by the Toronto Conference was sent to Russia through the People's Relief Committee of New York. One large shipment of clothing was also made to Jews in Poland.

Toronto Branch of the Ukrainian Verband

This organization worked in conjunction with the Toronto Conference for War Victims. They organized a special campaign for clothing and collected a fund of $3,000 which was sent to the Head Office of the Ukrainian Verband in Montreal.

Western Canada Relief Alliance

All the Jewish organizations in Winnipeg and other cities in Western Canada united under the above name for the purpose of raising funds for war relief. Two delegates of each organization in Western Canada were appointed to the Council of the Western Canada Relief Alliance. An Executive Committee of twenty was in charge of the work. Representatives of the Committee visited every city, town and hamlet in Western Canada making propaganda for the cause. An approximate amount of $390,000 in cash was raised by this organization. It also collected clothing, tools and supplies valued at $100,000. Most of the funds were collected by a special collection brigade of two hundred young boys and girls who made periodical visits to Jewish homes.

Mr. Marcus Hyman of Winnipeg was the President; Messrs. Almazov, M. A. Gray and Max Mains acted as Secretaries during the time of its existence.

Up to 1918, the Western Canada Relief Alliance forwarded its money direct to Poland, Roumania, Palestine and the Balkan States. After that date, it sent money to the Joint Distribution Committee, the People's Relief Committee, World Relief Committee and the Idgescom in Moscow. A large amount of clothing and also $25,000 in cash for the purchase of medicines were sent, as above stated, directly to Russia with the delegation of the Ukrainian Verband.

The Winnipeg Branch of the Ukrainian Verband was a constituent Society of the Western Canada Relief Alliance.

Palestine Helping Hand Fund

This campaign for war relief in Palestine was inaugurated, organized and carried out early in 1919 under the Chairmanship of Mrs. A. J. Freiman of Ottawa. $159,297.21 was raised in cash and $20,000 was raised in clothing. The Zionist Organization in Canada through the Hadassah branches gave Mrs. Freiman splendid co-operation. It must be mentioned that there were appreciable contributions in cash collected from non-Jews also.

The clothing was sent with the assistance of the Canadian Red Cross to London free of charge. The Women's Zionist Organization took care of the supplies in London and reshipped them to Palestine for distribution. The money was sent to Dr. Chaim Weitzman, President of the World Zionist Organization. A large part of the money was used for the Passover needs of the populace in Palestine. The balance was handed over to the American Medical Unit of Hadassah and was used for other purposes along the same lines as the Palestine Restoration Fund.

Canadian Jewish War Orphans Committee

A movement for the relief of Ukrainian refugees was inaugurated by the Canadian Alliance of Ukrainian Jews when Professor A. Cheifetz arrived in Canada early in 1920. Soon a number of prominent communal workers became interested in the work. After a series of conferences were held, a National Committee for War Orphans was formed with the object of bringing over to Canada a number of Ukrainian orphans and also to establish and maintain orphan homes in the Ukraine. Mrs. A. J. Freiman was appointed National President, and Mr. A. J. Freiman, Chairman of the Executive Committee. The following accepted office as Directors:

Messrs. Lyon Cohen, D. S. Friedman, *Dr. C. J. Gross, Lionel Coviensky, H. Wolofsky, L. Zucker, H. Hershman, Nathan Sloves and others.

The Committee collected more than $100,000 throughout the Dominion. Mr. H. Hershman, Dr. J. Leavitt and Mr. Wm. Farrell of Hamilton, Ont., were designated as delegates to Europe to select 150 refugees and bring them to Canada. The delegates returned in the fall of 1921 with 150 children. Great enthusiasm was shown by the Jewish community and the children were placed in various homes. In most cases they were adopted and are being well looked after. The following is an account of the children adopted in the various cities of Canada:—

Montreal	50
Toronto	50
St. John, N.B.	8
Ottawa	4
Sydney	4
Winnipeg	2
Halifax	2
Quebec	2
Woodstock	2
Hamilton	2
Bateman, Sask.	1
New Waterford	1
	128

Of the rest, twelve children were sent to the United States to join their relatives and ten children were placed in private homes at the expense of the Committee. Out of the money collected by the Committee, about $20,000 was used for the transportation of the children from Europe and for the expenses of the delegation. The Committee also sent some money to the World Relief Conference and continued to spend money on the children placed in private homes. The Committee still has a balance on hand.

Associated Jewish War Relief Societies of Canada

The idea of centralizing the relief work in Canada gained ground as the war continued. It was felt that a campaign by united Jewry would result in an increase of subscriptions and thereby help the cause greatly. When Canadian Jewry began to organize for the first Canadian Jewish Congress, a united front to aid our poor and suffering brethren in Europe financially and politically was decided upon.

On February 16th, 1919, the first meeting of representatives of the Canadian Jewish Committee, Central Relief Committee and the People's Relief Committee was held in the Baron de Hirsch Institute under the chairmanship of Mr. Lyon Cohen. The Canadian Jewish Committee was represented by Mr. Cohen, Rev. Dr. H. Abramowitz, Rabbi S. Schwartz, Al. Lesser, H. Wolofsky and Miss Hattie Silverman. The Central Relief Committee was represented by N. Sloves, M. Lavut, Rabbi H. Cohen, Alderman Lyon W. Jacobs, S. Guttman, M. Rapp and S. Rosen. The People's Relief Committee was represented by B. Richikoff, H. Hershman, Leon Meltzer and L. Zuker. The Jewish community of Toronto was represented by Rabbi H. M. Levy. Miss Birdie Phillips represented Cornwall. Mrs. L. Echenberg, D.R. Waxler, M. Mosel and M. Miller represented Sherbrooke. There were also present, Messrs. S. W. Jacobs, K.C. M.P., Rabbi I. Rosenberg, Dr. P. Malamud, H. M. Caiserman and Mr. Stanley Bero of New York, representing the Central Relief Committee of the United States.

In addressing the meeting, Mr. Lyon Cohen touchingly dwelt on the relief work for the war sufferers as being the highest form of humanitarianism. He said: "What has brought us together here this afternoon is the greatest catastrophe the world has ever known. Europe is smirched in blood. Those who have been to the scene of battle say that the privation and misery are beyond description. Other nations have suffered much, but none have suffered in any measure comparable to the Jewish people. They have been particularly subjected to indescribable tortures. Apart from those who died on the field of battle, hundreds of thousands have been the victims of pogroms in Poland and Ukrainia. It is necessary for us to raise a substantial amount to meet the cry of despair which comes to us from across the seas. Our relief work has been weakened by division in our ranks.

---
*Deceased

Better results and greater benefits would be obtained through united effort. Let us therefore all unite and work together with heart and soul for our sore-stricken brethren."

The Chairman's words found a wide echo not only amongst those present at the meeting, but throughout the Dominion. The Conference organized the Associated Jewish War Relief Societies of Canada. Mr. Lyon Cohen, who was already President of the Canadian Jewish Congress, was elected President of the new Association to assume the leadership in this great work of rescue. Sir Mortimer B. Davis and Mr. Mark Workman were elected Honorary Presidents; Messrs. Nathan Sloves, A. J. Freiman, Ottawa; M. Goldstick, Toronto; and Marcus Hyman, Winnipeg, were elected Vice-Presidents; Messrs. D. S. Friedman and M. Lavut were named as Joint Treasurers; Mr. Samuel Guttman and Miss Hattie Silverman acted as Secretaries.

Other members of the Committee were:—

Montreal—Rabbi Hirsch Cohen, Rev. Dr. H. Abramowitz, Edgar Berliner, *M. Markus, Maxwell Goldstein, K.C., H. Wolofsky, J. B. Miller, Lionel Coviensky, J. Levinson, Sr., L. Zuker and H. Hershman, etc.; Toronto—Rabbi Jacob Gordon, Leo Frankel, Edmund Scheuer, Elias Pullan, etc.; Winnipeg—Max Steinkopf, K.C., H. Hestrin, J. A. Chmelnitsky, J. A. Cherniak, Max Mains, etc.; Vancouver—Max M. Grossman, etc.

After a series of conferences, the Associated Jewish War Relief Societies launched a campaign for one million dollars throughout the country. A special Campaign Committee was appointed in Montreal with *Mr. M. Markus as Chairman. A Committee was appointed in Toronto under the chairmanship of Mr. Leo Frankel— Edmund Scheuer was elected Treasurer and A. Cohen, Secretary.

The Associated Jewish War Relief Societies in Canada succeeded in collecting large sums of money. The campaign in Montreal brought in $143,218.60. The People's Relief Committee transferred to the Associated Jewish War Relief Societies $25,700; The Central Relief Committee transferred $61,921.19; The Canadian Jewish Relief Committee $1,077.88. The campaign in Ottawa brought in $23,752.77; Vancouver collected $3,625.17; Victoria $13,878.; Edmonton $19,000; Regina $6,263.41. In all, the central treasury in Montreal received from January 27th, 1919, (the day the Central Organization commenced its financial operations) to June 5th, 1925, the sum of $363,194.50. The Ontario division of the Associated Jewish War Relief Societies collected $184,100.01 in the City of Toronto during the campaign in April, 1920, and also collected $65,599.46 from other cities in Ontario, the largest amount coming from Hamilton, where $20,000 was collected. Windsor contributed $8,760, Brantford $6,700, and Sudbury $4,000. The Western Canada Relief Alliance also made an effort to raise a large amount which is included in the total sum raised by this Committee as given above and the objective of the Associated Jewish War Relief Societies to raise $1,000,000 was nearly reached.

The Associated Jewish War Relief Societies of Canada sent most of its money to the Joint Distribution Committee in New York. However, various grants were made from time to time to other organizations. The Canadian Alliance of Ukrainian Jews received the sum of $15,926.85 to pay for the transportation of their clothing and other supplies to Europe. The Associated Jewish War Relief Societies also sent money to the Jewish World Relief Committee in Paris. It has helped Chalutzim. It contributed to the campaign launched by Chief Rabbi Kook of Palestine for the Yeshivas. It aided Jewish schools in Poland, etc., etc. From the money collected in Toronto $87,377.94 has been used for the purchase of supplies in Canada which were sent under the auspices of the Joint Distribution Committee to Europe.

Conclusion

War relief work in Canada was the great test of our communal strength and devotion to our people. It proved that Jews in this country were ready to give all they could to help their war-stricken brethren of Europe.

From the foregoing, it may be estimated that about $1,825,000 was raised in cash throughout the country by the Associated Jewish War Relief Societies and other Committees, and that not less than $500,000 was raised in clothing and other supplies by the various relief organizations.

Canadian Jewry, by this great contribution to Jewish war relief, has written one of the most glorious pages in its history. The deeds of those who gave of their time and energy to this great work will be remembered by future generations, and the blessings of our unfortunate brothers and sisters in war and pogrom-stricken Europe will rest upon them.

---

*Deceased

JEANETTE ENZER, MONTREAL

MISS REGINA SEIDEN, MONTREAL

MISS JEANETTE ENZER, Pianist, daughter of Joseph Enzer, was born in Montreal. She removed to Fort William with her parents, where she was the pianist and leader for the Child Orchestra, the only one in Canada. In 1915, she returned to Montreal and attended McGill University. Miss Enzer has devoted most of her time to the study of music, under the capable tuition of Mr. Alfred Laliberte, and has for some years been giving lessons in piano music. She is Treasurer of the Music and Dramatic Club in Montreal.

MISS REGINA SEIDEN was born at Rigaud, Que., and received her education at Montreal. Her parents were the late Wolf and Jente (Rosenbaum) Seiden. After a brilliant career at the Art School, where she was the winner of every competition she entered, and and also of several scholarships, she studied in France and Italy. Miss Seiden shows great versatility in her work, but specializes in portrait painting. At the age of twenty, she sold a painting to the National Art Gallery, Ottawa.

HARRY ADASKIN, TORONTO

MILTON BLACKSTONE, TORONTO

HARRY ADASKIN, Violinist and teacher at the Toronto Conservatory of Music, was born at Riga, Russia, on October 6th, 1901, the son of Samuel and Bessie (Perstnova) Adaskin. The greater part of his musical education he received in Toronto, later taking an artist's course in Chicago. In 1915 he was the winner of a very valuable violin, which he received from the Toronto Conservatory of Music, and which though offered every year, has been awarded only twice in twelve years. In 1923 he was awarded the Catherine Hambourg memorial gold medal, by the Hambourg Conservatory of Music. Mr. Adaskin is a member of the Hart House String Quartette, and of the Arts and Letters Club, Toronto.

MILTON BLACKSTONE, Violinist, was born in New York City, November 27th, 1894. He inherits his musical tendencies from his grandfather, a noted Cantor of Grodno, Russia. In 1912, he came to Toronto at the invitation of the Toronto Symphony Orchestra, and adopted Canada as his permanent domicile. He is a member of the Hart House String Quartette, and is a member of the Faculty of the Toronto Conservatory of Music. Mr. Blackstone also conducts the Junior Orchestra of that institution. Besides his regular duties as lecturer and pedagogue, he finds time for musical composition, and among many other works which he has written, is the opera "October" which will have its premiere in Canada next winter.

THE JEW IN THE CULTURAL ARTS

By Milton Blackstone, Professor of Music, Toronto Conservatory, University of Toronto

NO nation can achieve its self-assertiveness, unless its contribution to the Arts are so pronounced as to command the attention of the other nations of the world. Finance is to a nation what the skeleton is to a human body; but it is the Arts, which supply the flesh and blood, that round out into beautiful forms, the character, strength and dignity of a people.

Proof of this dates back to the 7th century, when we hear of the Jew, at that time the money-lender of the world, being barred from every social privilege, even to being forced to wear the terrible "Judenhüte." On the other hand, we read of other Jews of the same period, even in the very same cities, who were the recipients of the most marked attentions and highest honors from their rulers; not for their financial success, but for their achievements as Physicians, Orators, Musicians and Painters.

So it is even today! A host of Jewish celebrities are constantly adding lustre, beauty, and form to our glorious nation, rounding it into an homogeneous unit, which is commanding, more than ever before, the respect and admiration of the entire universe. The contribution of the Jewish race to the Arts is a matter of common knowledge. Some of the immortal names were borne by Jews—Spinoza in philosophy, Sarah Bernhardt in drama, Mendelssohn and Meyerbeer in music, to mention but a few. The Jews' appreciation of the beautiful and his desire to create it, his passion for knowledge and resolve to widen its bounds, are as characteristic as his burning patriotism and religious fervour. Once he becomes enthusiastic in an intellectual or aesthetic cult, he pursues it with all the zeal of his being.

The Jews of Canada have ample cause to be proud of the contributions made by fellow members of their faith to the Arts. Even in the early days of their settlement in the Dominion, when they numbered but a few score families in all, they strengthened the cultural and intellectual life of the community. As their numbers have increased, so have their achievements grown, and Canada owes much to their efforts.

As far back as 1858, Abraham de Sola, Rabbi of the Spanish and Portuguese Congregation in Montreal, was honored with the degree of Doctor of Laws by McGill University, in recognition of his outstanding reputation as a scholar. Internationally famous, he was the author of many books, among which were "The Cosmography of Peritsol," "Scripture Zoology," "The Mosaic Cosmogony," "Shabethai Tzevi," "History of the Jews of Poland," and "The Jews of France." An address, which he delivered on the "Study of Natural Science" before H.R.H. Prince Arthur, (now Duke of Connaught), called forth a personal letter of commendation from the late Queen Victoria. Dr. de Sola was Professor of Hebrew and Oriental Languages at McGill University, an appointment which he held from 1848 until his death in 1882.

Dr. Aaron H. David, for many years President of the Natural History Society of Montreal, wrote several valuable works on the study of Medicine and other subjects.

Lewis Alexander Hart was the author of "Some Questions Answered," and "A Jewish Reply to Christian Evangelists," both valuable works on the proselytizing attempts of missionaries to the Jews. He attained eminence in the legal profession, and in 1880 was appointed professor in the Faculty of Law at McGill University.

Gerald E. Hart is recognized as a leading writer on Canadian History, among his writings being "The Fall of New France," "The Quebec Act of 1774," and "Notes of 1837." For some years he has been engaged on a work dealing with the early days of the American Republic.

Isadore G. Ascher, of Montreal, won considerable fame as a poet, his "Voices from the Hearth," being highly commended by Longfellow.

Among others who have made their impressions on the Art World are Reuben Brainin, Hyman Edelstein, Abraham Rhinewine, Benjamin G. Sack, Ray Levinsky (now Mrs. Joshua Smith), and Henry Borsook, whose plays have already been produced at that great centre of artistic endeavor, Hart House Theatre, University of Toronto.

Abraham Nordheimer, of Toronto, may well be called the "father" of music in Canada, for it was he who established the first music room, or hall, in connection with his piano business; and was instrumental in bringing to this country many great artists, whose tours he arranged. He originally came to Canada as musical instructor to the family of the then Governor-General, Sir Charles Bagot. Shortly after his arrival he organized the first Musical Society in Upper Canada, which he himself conducted.

Among the brightest stars that illuminated the horizon of Canadian Artdom, one places Madame Pauline Donalda (Lightstone) of Montreal, considered the greatest Canadian prima donna since the heyday of Albani.

The Hart House String Quartet, whose perfection is recognized by the musical world, and whose engagements will take them on extensive tours through the United States, Canada and England within the next fifteen months, includes Harry Adaskin and Milton Blackstone, two outstanding Jewish artists, whose achievements are bringing much credit to Canadian Art.

Saul Brant, Professor of the Violin Department of the McGill University, is another outstanding figure in our musical world. A pupil of the great Leopold Auer and Eugene Ysaye, he brings to Canada a knowledge, which so many young students think, erroneously, that they can obtain only in Europe.

Others whose reputations extend more than locally are Madame Povlaska (Levi), Sophie Meyers, Miss Ballon, Jeanette Enzer, Jacques Sterin, Louise de Sola, Freddy Kahn, Albert Jaffey, Max Meller, Albert Kotzer, Florence Singer, and Éva Gebirtig. It is interesting that the Royal College of Music, London, England, awarded the Dominion Scholarship to a young man from Winnipeg, Ben Loban. This is indeed an achievement for Jewish Art, as students from the entire Dominion competed.

Not a few Jews in Canada have achieved distinction in landscape and portraiture painting, notably among whom may be mentioned Joshua B. Smith, R.B.A. and Miss M. Kallmeyer. Mr. Smith, since his arrival in Canada, has been commissioned to paint some of the most distinguished and influential people. It was in recognition of his great art, that he was invited, a few years ago, to paint the portrait of Canada's most beautiful child, to be placed in the celebrated "Doll's House," which was presented to Her Majesty, Queen Mary. Among others who have achieved success in their artistic pursuits are Regina Seiden of Montreal, Matilda Samuel of Toronto, and N. Soboloff, M. Kayler, and Jacob Dainoff, whose reputation as a sculptor is rapidly growing.

Looking back at this wonderful review of cultural achievements, dating from the 19th century, and remembering how few Jews there were in the Dominion, Canadian Jewry may well feel proud of the place their brethren have taken in the development of the Canadian Arts.

GERALD E. HART

GERALD EPHRAIM HART, Author, Journalist and Numismatist, was born in Montreal on March 26th, 1849, the youngest son of the late Adolphus M. Hart, in his lifetime a well-known advocate of Montreal, and a great-grandson of Aaron Hart, the first Jew to settle in Canada. Gerald Hart was educated in Montreal, New York and Three Rivers, P.Q. He entered the insurance field as a young man and advanced until he became General Manager of the Phoenix Fire Insurance Company, Montreal, which position he held for some years. He was the author of numerous works on history, among the best-known being "The Fall of New France", "Notes of 1837", and "The Quebec Act, 1774". He also published an insurance hand book (1899), and at the present time is engaged in the compilation of a book which will contain the correction of wrong statements made in the histories of all countries concerning America in its early days, a work on which he has spent over a quarter of a century, Mr. Hart is recognized as one of the outstanding historians of Canada, and his works are recognized as standard in all important libraries. He has been a frequent contributor to the Press on subjects on which he is an authority, and has always taken a keen interest in all questions affecting the Jewish community of Canada, being a staunch upholder of the rights and privileges granted them—largely through the instrumentality of members of his own family. Mr. Hart has formed several valuable collections of coins, one of which was sold to the Dominion Government, and another collection he sold in New York in 1888 for over $4,000. He also formed valuable collections of paper money and autographs. He is one of the earliest members of the Numismatic and Antiquarian Society of Montreal, of which he was a Vice-President and founder, and was President of the Society of Historical Studies for many years. Mr. Hart has resided in New York for a number of years, and at present he is living in France.

MADAME PAULINE DONALDA

PAULINE LIGHTSTONE (Madame Donalda), one of the greatest operatic singers that Canada has produced, was born in Montreal, on March 5th, 1884, the daughter of Michael Lightstone. She was educated at the public and senior schools of Montreal and at Royal Victoria College, where she took a complete musical course, studying under Miss Lichtenstein, and where she was awarded a scholarship. Her unusual musical ability was brought to the attention of the Right Honourable Lord Strathcona and Mount Royal, then High Commissioner of Canada in London, through whose patronage she was enabled to proceed to Paris, France, where she continued her studies under Professor Duvernoy, at the Paris Conservatory, making her debut as a grand opera singer, in Massenet's "Manon" at Nice, on December 30th, 1904. In May, 1905, she sang before Their Majesties at Covent Garden, London, and at the Monnaise Opera House at Brussels. As a compliment to both the Royal Victoria College and to Lord Strathcona (formerly Sir Donald Smith), Miss Lightstone adopted the stage name of Madame Donalda. In 1906, which was the first season that Hammerstein opened the Manhattan Opera House in New York, Madame Donalda sang there during the entire season. In November of that year she sang in her native city, and was presented with an address from the mayor and council. She has made several tours through Europe, singing in both concerts and grand opera, and on many occasions performing before royalty. Madame Donalda was on a concert tour of Canada in 1914, and when the war broke out she remained in Montreal and took an active part in relief work, raising large sums of money for different causes through her concerts. She sang for patriotic purposes only, and the hall or theatre was always sold out when it was known that she was to sing. As a young girl, Miss Lightstone took a great interest in communal work, and for some years she was a voluntary teacher at the Baron de Hirsch Institute, Montreal. She also did social service work, particularly on behalf of Jewish immigrants.

H. EDELSTEIN, OTTAWA

HYMAN EDELSTEIN, Journalist, Author and Poet, was born in Dublin, Ireland, September 9th, 1889, the son of Abraham Maurice and Jeanette (Moissell) Edelstein of Russia. He received his education in the High School, Dublin, and Trinity College, University of Dublin, where he obtained the following honors; First in-all-Ireland, Classical Exhibitioner, 1905; First Classical Exhibitioner, Prizeman Irish Intermediate Examinations, 1906-1908; Classical Sizar, Erasmus Smith Exhibitioner, Entrance Prizeman Greek and Latin Prose Composition, and Hebrew, Trinity College, Dublin University, 1908. While at the University, Mr. Edelstein organized the University Zionist Society. Mr. Edelstein left Trinity College in 1912 and came to Canada, where he first settled in Ottawa, but later moved to Montreal. He was Editor, "Canadian Jewish Times", Montreal, 1913-14; Editor, "Canadian Jewish Chronicle", Montreal, 1914-17; Publisher and Editor, "Jewish Weekly", Montreal, 1917-18. Mr. Edelstein is the author of "Canadian Lyrics and Other Poems", the first edition of which was published in Toronto in 1916, and a second edition in Montreal in 1921. In 1924, he published a volume of verse entitled "Latter Rose". He received flattering mention in the Presidential address delivered to the Royal Society of Canada, on "Canadian Poets of the Great War". His poems, etc. have frequently been recited by the Hadassah, Young Judaean and Zionist societies. He is the author of "From Judaean Vineyards", 1914, and his poems have appeared, first written when a boy of fourteen, in the Dublin "Evening Mail"; in the London "Weekly Budget"; Canadian and United States Jewish periodicals; Montreal "Gazette", "Star", "Canadian Bookman", etc. In August, 1915, he was married to Elsie, daughter of Samuel Hornstein, and has two sons, Herzl and Raphael Edelstein. In 1923, he again took up his residence in Ottawa. Mr. Edelstein is a member of the Canadian Authors' Association, and Jewish National Workers' Alliance of America, Ottawa branch. Mr. Edelstein is an accomplished musician and an enthusiastic chess player.

DR. A. A. ROBACK

DR. A. A. ROBACK, Psychologist, Author, and one of the most brilliant graduates from McGill University, Montreal, was born on June 19th, 1890, the son of Isaac and Libby (Rahver) Roback. He received his education at the Montreal Public Schools and McGill University, from which he graduated in 1912, obtaining the Prince of Wales Gold Medal for Philosophy. He proceeded to Harvard, where he obtained his Master's degree in the following year, and the Doctor of Philosophy degree in 1917. Since that time he has been a Travelling Fellow at Princeton University; Instructor in Psychology at Harvard from 1919 to 1923; Professor at Northeastern University and University of Pittsburgh; Special Lecturer at Simmons College, Boston, and Clark University, Amherst, Mass.; and Special Summer School Lecturer at New Hampshire College. Dr. Roback is the author of many important publications on certain phases of psychology in which he has conducted special research and has made many important original contributions to science. Among the more important of his publications may be mentioned: "Psychology", "Behaviorism and Psychology", "The Psychology of Confession", "The Interferences of Will Impulses", besides a vast number of articles, pamphlets, etc. He is also the author of a collection of essays on Jewish subjects of a cultural nature, some of which have been reprinted in Anglo-Jewish weeklies from coast to coast in America, and even in Australia and Africa. Dr. Roback attracted world-wide attention some time ago with the elaboration of certain mental tests, known as the "Roback Mentality Tests for Superior Adults", which have been adopted in many schools and colleges, and have recently been used by one of the defence alienists in the famous Leopold-Loeb murder case of Chicago. He is a Fellow of the National Research Council; member of the American Psychological Association; the American Philosophical Association; Eugenics Research Association; American Academy of Social and Political Science; the American Association for the Advancement of Science; and the Jewish Publication Society of America.

A CHRONOLOGICAL TABLE OF EVENTS
OF INTEREST TO CANADIAN JEWRY

1724
Aug. 16th—Aaron Hart born in London, England.

1731
Jan. 29th—David Gradis made a citizen of Bordeaux, France.

1752
April 17th—Ship *"Benjamin"* owned by Gradis, sailed with provisions for the colonists in Canada.

1759
Aug. 21st—Royal Letters Patent granted to Abraham Gradis.

1760
June 10th—Aaron Hart made a Free Mason in New York.
Sept. 8th—Aaron Hart—the first Jew to settle in Canada, entered Montreal as Staff Officer with General Amherst.

1761 to 1763
—Samuel Judah, Lazarus David, Uriel Moresco, Abraham Franks, Levy Solomons, Ezekiel Solomons, Manuel Gomez, Simon Levy, Meyer Michaels, Fernandez de Fonseca, Hananiel Garcia, Jacob de Maurera, Andrew Hays, Isaac Judah, Uriah Judah, Joseph Bindona, and Emanuel de Cordova settled in Montreal, Three Rivers, and Quebec.

1764
Dec. 8th—David David born at Montreal.
—Second Post Office in Canada opened in Aaron Hart's house at Three Rivers.

1766
Oct. 22nd—Samuel David born at Montreal.

1768
Jan. 14th—Aaron Hart married to Dorothea Judah in London, Eng.
—Congregation "Shearith Israel" formed at Montreal.
Nov. 26th—Moses Hart born at Three Rivers.

1770
May 15th—Ezekiel Hart born at Three Rivers.

1775
—Ground purchased for cemetery in Montreal.
—David Salesby Franks elected Parnas of Congregation.
—Several Jewish signatures on petition asking for a House of Assembly for Quebec.
—David S. Franks arrested in Montreal charged with seditious utterances.
—Henry Joseph born in England.
—Aaron Hart and other Jews, Loyalist officers.
—Levy Solomons ordered by General Montgomery to establish hospitals for the American troops.

1776
Oct. 12th—Lazarus David died in Montreal—the first Jew to be buried in Canada.

1777
—The first synagogue erected in Canada, at Montreal.
—Jacob Kuhn appointed Court Cryer in Montreal.

1778
Feb. 13th—Rev. Jacob Cohen, of London, Eng., elected Minister of Montreal Congregation.
Sept. —Levy Solomons elected Parnas, and Uriah Judah, Gabay of the Congregation. Isaac Judah, Meyer Michaels and Andrew Hays fined for refusing to accept office.

1779
Aug. 10th—Benjamin Hart born at Three Rivers.

1780
July 17th—Abraham Gradis died at Bordeaux, France.
Oct. 2nd—David Franks arrested in Philadelphia, charged with giving aid to the British.

1783
Oct. 14th—Jewish Loyalists granted lands in the Eastern Townships.

1784
May 6th—Decision given by Appeal Court in action taken by Rev. J. Cohen vs Congregation "Shearith Israel".

1789
Mar. 23rd—Samuel Judah died at New York.

1791
—Duke of Kent entertained at home of Aaron Hart.

1792
May 18th—Levy Solomons died at Montreal.

1800
—Aaron Hart donated land in Three Rivers for Jewish cemetery.
Dec. 28th—Aaron Hart died and was buried at Three Rivers.

1801
Jan. 21st—Meyer Michaels arrived in Montreal from the Mississippi.
Mar. 7th—Accounts received of the *"Ewretta"* arriving in England.
April 15th—Meyer Michaels left for the "western country".
Sept. 7th—Yom Kippur. Accounts received in Montreal of the capture of Egypt.

1802
April 7th—Samuel David elected curator of Davidson Estate.

1803

July 20th—Water-works pipes first laid in Montreal.
Aug. 7th—Samuel David accompanied other officers to Lachine to review Militia.
Sept. 5th—Meyer Michaels and others arrived in Montreal from Mackinac.
Sept. 28th—Henry Joseph married to Rachel Solomons.
Dec. 8th—Jews of Montreal subscribed to building of English church.

1804

July 26th—Moses David arrived in Montreal from Detroit in 7 days.

1805

—Jacob Franks erected first saw and grist mill in Canada.
Mar. 30th—David and Samuel David present at dinner given by the Merchants' Association of Montreal to members who voted against the tax on commerce.

1806

Jan. 24th—Jewish residents of Montreal among those who dined at "Hamiltons" to celebrate the news of Nelson's victory at Trafalgar.
Feb. 28th—Benjamin Lyons died at Montreal.

1807

Jan. 29th—Ezekiel Hart elected to Assembly of Lower Canada.
Feb. 20th—Ezekiel Hart expelled from Assembly as a Jew.
July 3rd—Wm. Hyman of Gaspe born in Russia.
Sept. 24th—Solicitor-General of England declared Jews eligible to sit in Legislature.

1808

May 10th—Ezekiel Hart elected the second time.

1809

May 5th—Ezekiel Hart expelled the second time.
May 15th—Bill introduced to declare Jews ineligible to sit in the Assembly.
May 15th—Assembly dissolved by the Governor, Sir James Craig, so that Bill could not be passed.
Aug. 22nd—Sir James Craig acted as god-father to son of Ezekiel Hart.
Oct. 8th—Ezekiel Hart offered nomination for third time.
Oct. 22nd—Steamboat owned by Moses Hart made its first trip from Montreal.

1810

Mar. 5th—Citizens of Montreal signed address of thanks to the Governor for his firmness in dissolving the Assembly.

1811

Oct. 27th—Rabbi Lyons and Mr. Seixas of the "Shearith Israel" congregation, New York, pay pastoral visit to Montreal and Three Rivers, performing needed rites.

1812

July 9th—Samuel David, Meyer Michaels, Benjamin Franks, Benjamin Solomons, David David, Alexander Hart, Henry Joseph, Benjamin Hart and Jacob Franks were among the officers who attended the Governor's Levee.
Oct. 9th—Aaron Hart David born at Montreal.
Nov. —Benjamin Hart advanced the Governor-General the amount necessary to garrison the forts on the St. Lawrence.
—Many Jewish officers on service with Canadian troops.
—Benjamin Hart advanced necessary money to pay recruits.

1813

Mar. 9th—Isaac Judah died.
Nov. 1st—Appeal made for Patriotic Fund for relief of sufferers in Upper Canada.
Dec. 10th—Samuel David appointed member of General Court Martial.

1814

Apl. 11th—Adolphus Hart born at Three Rivers.
June 8th—Jacob Henry Joseph born at Berthier.
Sept. 26th—Moses David died at Sandwich, Upper Canada.
Dec. 19th—Jews of Montreal present at dinner given to Sir James Yeo and General Drummond.

1815

Nov. 14th—Abraham Joseph born at Berthier.
Nov. 25th—Abraham Joseph Sr., died at Berthier.

1816

May 11th—Benjamin Levy married to Miss Elkah Seixas of New York.

1817

Jan. 14th—Samuel David appointed member of the Grand Jury.
Feb. 14th—Subscription taken up for poor of Montreal; 1500 on list in need of wood and provisions.
July 16th—Jesse Joseph born at Berthier.
—Reference made to Jews in Toronto.

1818

Feb. 27th—Henry Joseph, M. J. Hays and David David charter members of the Bank of Montreal. David David was elected a Director.

1820

Aug. 30th—Isaac Valentine of Three Rivers married to Miss Phoebe Hays.

1822

Apl. 11th—David David elected president of the "Committee of Trade".
May 12th—Dr. de la Motta of New York made pastoral visit to Canada.
Sept. 24th—Yom Kippur—services held at home of Benjamin Hart.
Dec. 3rd—Every doctor in Montreal assembled at David David's to watch operation performed on him by Dr. Nelson.

1823

Apl. 1st—Samuel David gazetted Lieut.-Colonel in Long Point Division of Militia.
June 11th—Levy Solomons died in New York.

1824

Jan. 3rd—Samuel David died in Montreal.

1825

Sept. 18th—Dr. Abraham de Sola born in London.
—Hart Logan & Company appointed agents in Montreal of the Canada Company.

1826
—Nathan Green born at Amsterdam.

1827
Aug. 17th—Mrs. Aaron Hart died at Three Rivers.
—Heirs of Aaron Hart donate cemetery in Three Rivers to Jews of the Province.
—Lewis Samuel born at Hull, England.

1828
Dec. 4th—Jews of Montreal petition Legislature to be incorporated as a religious body.

1829
—Aaron Rosenthal born in Germany.
—Moses Bilsky born in Russia.

1830
—Eleazer David admitted to practise as advocate.

1831
Jan. 3rd—Jews petitioned Legislature of Lower Canada that they be granted full civil rights.
Jan. 5th—Mrs. Samuel David died in Montreal.
Feb. 7th—Samuel Becancour Hart petitioned Legislature to allow his appointment as magistrate, taking an oath in a manner acceptable to a Jew.
—Religious census shows 107 Jews in Lower Canada.

1832
Jan. 1st—David Oppenheimer born in Bavaria.
Apl. 12th—Bill passed giving full civil rights to Jews in Lower Canada.
June 21st—Henry Joseph died at Berthier.
—Abraham Joseph settled in Quebec.
—Cholera outbreak in Lower Canada.

1833
Jan. 30th—Jacob Hirsch born in Germany.
—Toronto directory shows L. Joseph, Arthur Wellington Hart, William Myers, P. J. Samuel and S. Sylvester as residents of that town.
—Levey Brothers and Henry Benjamin settle in Quebec; Henry Benjamin opening up largest dry-goods store in that town.

1834
July 2nd—Aaron H. David passed his examinations at the Royal College of Physicians and Surgeons, Edinburgh, and returned to Montreal to practise.
Aug. 13th—Mrs. Seixas Nathan died in New York.
Aug. 30th—Moses Hart candidate in Three Rivers for Assembly.
Sept. 16th—Ezekiel Hart died in Three Rivers.
—Adolph Goldstein born in Russian Poland.
—Samuel and Goodman Benjamin established wholesale dry-goods business in Toronto.

1835
Mar. 11th—A. Judah died at Three Rivers.
May 23rd—Eleazer David gazetted as Lieut. and Adjutant of Cavalry, Isaac Valentine as Captain of Militia, and Moses and Samuel David as Ensigns of Militia.
May 25th—F. Hart received the degree of M.D. from McGill College.
May 31st—Cornerstone of new synagogue sold to M. E. David for fifty pounds.
June 1st—Cornerstone of new synagogue in Montreal laid.
July 30th—E. D. David in charge of cavalry escort to Lord Aylmer.
Sept. 17th—Alexander Hart died in Montreal, buried in Three Rivers.
Sept. 25th—Miss Fanny David elected an officer in the Ladies' Benevolent Society, Montreal.

1836
Jan. 28th—Samuel David took part in benefit performance at Theatre Royal, Montreal, for General Hospital.
Feb. 7th—Mrs. J. Levey died in New York.
Feb. 10th—Capt. E. David one of stewards at Bachelors' Ball, Montreal.
May 10th—Moses Hart's steamer "Toronto" arrived at Montreal from sea.
June 23rd—Thomas Judah delegate from Three Rivers to Constitutional Society.
July 21st—Champlain and St. Lawrence Railway opened at Laprairie.
July 27th—A. P. Hart's mare won the King's Plate at Three Rivers Races—first time raced in Canada.
Oct. 12th—Dr. A. H. David married in Montreal to Miss Catherine Joseph, by Isaac Valentine.
Oct. 24th—Eleazer and Samuel David in charge of cavalry patrol in Montreal, to put down incendiarism.
Nov. 14th—Capt. E. David in charge of first paid military watch in Montreal.

1837
Jan. 4th—Montreal Whist Club met at Dr. David's.
Apl. 16th—Herman Valentine an U.E.L. died in New York.
May 1st—Jacob Levey died in New York.
July 17th—Aaron Philip Hart examiner at Bar Examinations at Montreal.
Aug. 4th—Capt. E. David in charge of cavalry at proclamation of Queen Victoria, in Montreal.
Aug. 5th—Benjamin Hart and Moses Judah Hays gazetted as magistrates for the District of Montreal.
Aug. 20th—Capt. David elected secretary of the Racing Association.
Sept. 8th—Mr. Bernstein appointed Hebrew teacher in Montreal.
Nov. 6th—Jacob Hoffstetter, a loyalist Jewish officer, severely beaten by the radicals.
—Capt. David instructed by magistrates to order out cavalry.
Dec. 1st—Eleazer David promoted Major by Sir John Colborne for gallantry at Battle of St. Charles.
Dec. 13th—Major David in command of cavalry escorting Sir John Colborne to St. Martine.
Dec. 16th—M. Samuel David carried despatches to Sir John Colborne.
—Jacob Joseph carried despatches from Sir John Colborne to General Wetherall.
—Benjamin Brothers, Toronto, given contract to supply greatcoats to the troops.
—Charles King born at Prague.

1838

Jan. 13th—Samuel David carried despatches from Sir John Colborne to Sir F. B. Head at Toronto.
Jan. 17th—Abraham Hart died at Three Rivers.
Jan. 27th—Major David appointed acting Quartermaster-General.
Feb. 20th—Large Ball at David's—all the military present.
Feb. 27th—Lieut. S. David in charge of escort at swearing in of Sir John Colborne, as Governor-General.
Mar. 4th—Col. A. P. Hart carried despatches to the British Ambassador at New York.
Mar. 5th—Samuel David appointed Adjutant, Mount Royal Cavalry.
Aug. 25th—New Spanish and Portuguese Synagogue dedicated—Myer Levy officiated.
Aug. 31st—Sale of seats for new Montreal synagogue.
Nov. 11th—Samuel David attached to Sir John Colborne's staff.
Nov. 18th—Emergency meeting of St. Paul's Lodge, A.F. & A.M. to initiate Jacob Joseph and Theodore Hart.
—Judah G. Joseph and Henry A. Joseph settled in Toronto.

1840

Apl. 17th—General and Lady Clitherton attended services at the Shearith Israel Synagogue, Montreal.
May 4th—Dr. A. H. David removed to Three Rivers.
Sept. 25th—Mrs. M. J. Hays died in Montreal.
Nov. 18th—Jacob Franks died in Montreal.
Dec. 11th—Capt. A. T. Hart married at New York to Miriam Judah.
—Rev. David Piza elected Rabbi of Montreal Congregation.

1841

Feb. 10th—Union of Upper and Lower Canada.
Mar. 4th—Mrs. S. Joseph died in New York.
Dec. 3rd—Moise Schwob born in Alsace.

1842

Feb. 10th—Dinner and presentation given to Samuel David by officers and N.C.O's of Mount Royal Cavalry.
June 3rd—Steamer "Benjamin Hart" arrived at Montreal from Liverpool.
June 18th—Dr. F. Hart died.

1843

Sept. 19th—Ezekiel Hart died at Three Rivers.
—Wm. Hyman settled at Gaspe, Que.

1844

June 22nd—Dr. David A. Hart born at Three Rivers.
July 12th—Harris Kellert born in Russia.
—Lazarus Cohen born in Poland.
—Religious census shows 154 Jewish souls in Lower Canada.
—First Jewish book published in Canada.

1845

Oct. 28th—Mrs. Camilla (Herman) Levy born in Germany.

1846

Jan. 2nd—Lyon Silverman born at Benton Harbor, Mich.

Sept. 12th—Congregation of German and Polish Jews formed in Montreal.
—Common schools established in Lower Canada.

1847

Jan. 13th—Samuel David resigned as Senior Grand Warden in the Grand Lodge of Lower Canada, A.F. & A.M.
Jan. 22nd—Dr. Abraham de Sola appointed Rabbi of Shearith Israel Congregation, Montreal.
Mar. 9th—M. S. David re-elected Secretary of the Turf Club.
July 16th—Lewis Alexander Hart born at Three Rivers.
Sept. 18th—Magistrate Jacob Cohen born in Austria.
Sept. 23rd—Dr. A. H. David attended meeting of College of Physicians at Quebec.
Oct. 5th—First telegraphic connection between Montreal and Quebec.
Oct. 13th—M. J. Hays gave the principal speech at the Cattle Show, Montreal.
Oct. 30th—Edmund Scheuer born at Berncastel, on the Moselle.
—Moses J. Hays operated theatre in Montreal.

1848

Mar. 3rd—Jacob Joseph married to Miss Moses at Philadelphia.
Mar. 9th—Dr. A. H. David attended meeting of Medical Profession at Quebec.
July 17th—Beniah Gibb returned to Montreal from a trip to Palestine.
Sept. 12th—Every store and office in Montreal closed during funeral of Benjamin Hart.
Oct. 26th—Dr. de Sola gave lecture on "Persecution of the Jews of Persia", at Montreal.
Nov. 13th—Samuel David installed as 1st Principal, St. George's Chapter, R.A.M.
Nov. 30th—Frederick Judah passed his examinations as Advocate in Montreal.
—Dr. de Sola appointed Lecturer in oriental languages at McGill College.
—Hebrew Philanthropic Society organized in Montreal.
—A. D. Benjamin born in Australia.

1849

Mar. 5th—Samuel Benjamin elected Alderman of City of Montreal.
Mar. 26th—Gerald E. Hart born at Montreal.
July 20th—Samuel David appointed Clerk of the Circuit Court at St. John's, Que.
Sept. 1st—Ground purchased for Jewish cemetery in Toronto.
Sept. 2nd—Samuel Benjamin elected President of Shearith Israel Congregation, Montreal.
—Dr. A. H. David appointed attending physician at Montreal General Hospital.

1850

Dec. 25th—Jacob Cohen of Montreal born in Poland.
Dec. 27th—Samuel David installed the officers in Dorchester Lodge, St. John's.

1852

Apl. 26th—Capt. Alexander Thomas Hart died at Three Rivers.
May 12th—J. G. Joseph died in Toronto.
Oct. 15th—Moses Hart died at Three Rivers.
Nov. 18th—Observed as day of mourning—funeral of the Duke of Wellington.

1853
May 22nd—Rev. Meldola de Sola born at Montreal.
June 9th—Several killed in religious riots in Montreal.

1854
—Mark and Lewis Samuel became residents of Toronto.

1855
—Harris Vineberg born in Lithuania.

1856
Sept. 7th—Toronto Hebrew Congregation organized.

1857
—Noah Friedman settled at North Lancaster, Ont.
—Moses Bilsky settled at Ottawa.
—Jacob Hirsch arrived in Montreal.
—Levy Brothers, Hamilton, established wholesale jewellery business.
—M. and L. Samuel, Toronto, established wholesale hardware business.

1858
Aug. 15th—Clarence I. de Sola born at Montreal.
—Nathan Green, Solomon Hart and Henry Levy settled in St. John, N.B.
—Jewish community started in Victoria, B.C.
—Wm. Hyman elected Mayor of Cape Rosier, Quebec.
—Dr. Abraham de Sola given degree of LL.D. by McGill College.
—Henry Jacobs and Michael Michaels started first cigar factory in Canada, at Dundas.

1859
Jan. 11th—Samuel Becancour Hart died at Three Rivers.

1860
May 22nd—German and Polish Synagogue, Montreal, consecrated.
—Oppenheimer Brothers started business in Yale, B.C.
—Abraham Nordheimer died in Germany.

1861
Sept. 23rd—Louis Rubenstein born in Montreal.
Dec. 11th—Jacob Goldstein born at Quebec.
—Rabbi Solomon Jacobs born in England.
—Samuel Davis started first cigar factory in Montreal.

1862
—Rabbi Hirsch Cohen born in Poland.
—Reuben Brainin born in Russia.
—Lewis Samuel elected President, Holy Blossom Congregation, Toronto.

1863
Jan. 1st—Wm. Diamond born in Poland.
Mar. 15th—David S. Friedman born at North Lancaster, Ont.
May 13th—Maxwell Goldstein born at Quebec.
June 3rd—Cornerstone of Congregation Emanuel, Victoria, laid.
July 23rd—Young Men's Hebrew Benevolent Society, Montreal, organized—L. Levey elected President.
—Anshe Sholom Congregation, Hamilton, incorporated by Parliament of Canada.
—Charles King established tannery at Whitby.

1864
Jan. 1st—Leo Frankel born in Germany.
Feb. 7th—Michael Hirsch born at Richmond, Que.
Aug. 4th—Mark Workman born at Buffalo, N.Y.

1865
Feb. 3rd—David Sweet born in Russia.
July 3rd—Elias Pullan born in Lithuania.
—Henry Nathan elected Grand Master of the Grand Lodge A.F. & A.M., of British Columbia.
—Judge Samuel Shultz born at Victoria, B.C.

1866
Feb. 6th—Sir Mortimer B. Davis born at Montreal.
—David A. Ansell settled in Montreal.
—Frank D. Benjamin born in London, Eng.
—Charles L. Levey elected President, Young Men's Hebrew Benevolent Society, Montreal.

1869
—J. L. Samuel elected President, Young Men's Hebrew Benevolent Society, Montreal.
—Lewis A. Hart admitted to practise as Notary Public.

1870
—Henry Nathan elected to British Columbia Legislature.
—Jacob G. Ascher elected President, Young Men's Hebrew Benevolent Society, Montreal.
—David A. Hart in command of service company of Prince of Wales' Rifles during Fenian Raids.
—Dr. A. H. David appointed Dean of the Faculty of Medicine, University of Bishop's College.

1871
May 6th—Samuel W. Jacobs, K.C., M.P., born at Lancaster, Ont.
Nov. 16th—Young Men's Hebrew Benevolent Society, Montreal, incorporated.
Nov. —Henry Nathan elected to Dominion Parliament from Victoria, by acclamation.
—Edmund Scheuer settled in Hamilton.
—Sigismund Mohr settled in Quebec.

1872
Oct. 8th—Rabbi I. I. Kahanovitch born in Poland.
Dec. 21st—Rabbi Joseph Corcos born at Mogador, Morocco.
—Dr. Abraham de Sola opened the United States' Congress with prayer.
—Edward Moss died in London, Eng.
—Edmund Scheuer established the first Jewish Sabbath School in Ontario, at Hamilton.
—Seilim Franklin elected to British Columbia Legislature.
—Lumby Franklin elected Mayor of Victoria.

1873
—Edmund Scheuer elected President of Anshe Sholom Congregation, Hamilton.

1874
Nov. 12th—Jacob A. Jacobs born at Montreal.
—David A. Hart received degree of M.D., C.M., from University of Bishop's College.

1875

June 13th—First B'nai B'rith Lodge established in Canada at Toronto.
—Lyon Silverman elected President, Young Men's Hebrew Benevolent Society, Montreal.
—S. I. Rittenberg appointed cantor of German and Polish Congregation, Montreal.
—Richmond Street Synagogue, Toronto, erected.

1876

—Hyman Miller settled at Fort Garry.

1877

Feb. —Ladies' Hebrew Benevolent Society organized in Montreal.
May —Rev. Nathan Robinson appointed Chazan, B'nai Sholom Congregation, Toronto.
Sept. —Rabbi Jacob Gordon born in Russia.
—Max Goldstine settled in Qu'appelle, N.W.T.

1878

—Ladies' Montefiore Benevolent Society, Toronto, organized.
—Deborah Ladies' Aid Society organized in Hamilton.
—J. P. Davies, Victoria, candidate to Federal Parliament.
—Dr. Hiram Vineberg graduated from McGill College.

1879

Feb. 23rd—Rabbi M. J. Merritt born at Omaha, Neb.
Apl. 11th—Adolphus Hart died in Montreal.
Sept. 17th—Peter Bercovitch, K.C., M.P.P., born in Montreal.
—Reuben Goldstein settled in Winnipeg.
—Aaron Rosenthal settled in Ottawa.

1880

June 6th—Archibald J. Freiman born in Lithuania.
July 7th—Lewis A. Hart appointed Lecturer in Faculty of Law, McGill University.
Sept. —Montefiore Club organized in Montreal.
—Rabbi H. Abramowitz born in Russia.

1881

June 5th—B'nai B'rith Lodge established in Montreal.
—Noah Friedman elected President, Young Men's Hebrew Benevolent Society.
—Noah Friedman died in Montreal.

1882

May 26th—S. W. Cohen born at St. Paul, Minn.
May —Number of Jewish immigrants settled in Winnipeg.
Aug. 24th—First Reform Congregation started in Montreal.
Oct. 13th—Rabbi H. J. Samuel born at Glasgow, Scotland.
Dec. 8th—Nathan Gordon born at New Orleans, La.
Dec. 8th—Wm. Hyman died in Montreal.
—Rev. Dr. Abraham de Sola died in Montreal.
—Rev. Meldola de Sola appointed Rabbi of Shearith Israel Congregation, Montreal, first Canadian-born Jewish minister.
—Large influx of Russian Jews into Canada.
—Henry Jacobs elected President, Young Men's Hebrew Benevolent Society, Montreal.
—Hughson Street Synagogue, Hamilton, erected.
—Miller-Morse Company established in Winnipeg.
—First Jewish marriage performed in the Maritime Provinces.
—N. Steiner elected Alderman, City of Toronto.

1883

Oct. 21st—Goel Tzedec Congregation, Toronto, organized.
—B. Kortosk elected President, Young Men's Hebrew Benevolent Society, Montreal.

1884

May 1st—Fred Landsberg became resident of Victoria, B.C.
—Jesse Joseph elected President, Montreal Street Railway Company.
—Louis Robinson elected President, Young Men's Hebrew Benevolent Society, Montreal.

1885

Feb. 8th—Montefiore Agricultural Aid Society formed in Montreal.
Mar. 29th—Dr. A. I. Willinsky born at Omaha, Neb.
June 6th—Mrs. A. J. Freiman born at Mattawa, Ont.
Oct. 23rd—S. Hart Green born at St. John, N.B.
—Adolph Goldstein elected President, Young Men's Hebrew Benevolent Society, Montreal.
—Miss Caroline Hart appointed to take charge of Kindergarten work at Toronto Normal School.

1886

Sept. 7th—B'nai B'rith Lodge established in Victoria, B.C.
Sept. 15th—McGill College Avenue Synagogue, Montreal, consecrated.
—Moses Vineberg elected President, Young Men's Hebrew Benevolent Society, Montreal.
—David Oppenheimer elected Mayor of Vancouver.
—Congregation Temple Emanuel, Vancouver, incorporated.
—A. D. Benjamin elected President, Holy Blossom Congregation, Toronto.

1887

Mar. 1st—N. L. Nathanson born at Minneapolis, Minn.
Apl. —Lewis Samuel died.
Dec. 6th—Beth Jacob Congregation, Hamilton, chartered.
—McCaul Street Synagogue, Toronto, formed.
—Jesse Joseph elected President, Montreal Gas Company.
—Unsuccessful attempt made in Montreal to organize a Zionist Society.

1888

—Harris Vineberg elected President, Young Men's Hebrew Benevolent Society, Montreal.
—Austrian Synagogue, Toronto, organized.
—Charles King elected Warden of County of Ontario.
—Congregation formed in London, Ont.
—D. A. Ansell appointed Consul-General for Mexico in Montreal.

1890

Feb. 11th—Louis Rubenstein won figure-skating championship of the world at St. Petersburg, Russia.
—Spanish and Portuguese Synagogue, Stanley Street, Montreal, dedicated.
—Baron de Hirsch gave $20,000 for relief work in Canada.
—Benjamin Zimmerman appointed Justice of the Peace, Winnipeg.
—Act passed by Quebec Legislature placing Jewish congregations on equal basis with Christian.

1891

Sept. 14th—Rabbi B. R. Brickner born at New York.

1892

Sept. 16th—Synagogue of Temple Emanu-El, Montreal, dedicated.
—Lewis A. Hart elected President, Young Men's Hebrew Benevolent Society, Montreal.
—William Diamond settled in Calgary.
—Chovey Zion Society organized in Montreal.
—Young Men's Hebrew Association formed in Winnipeg.

1893

Jan. —Lazarus Cohen visited Palestine as a Zionist delegate.
May 23rd—Gershom Joseph appointed Queen's Counsel by Lord Stanley.
Dec. 15th—Sigismund Mohr died.
—D. A. Ansell elected President, Young Men's Hebrew Benevolent Society, Montreal.
—Shearith Israel Congregation, Montreal, celebrated 125th anniversary.

1895

Oct. 30th—Samuel Davis died in Montreal.
—Adath Jeshuran Congregation formed in Ottawa.
—Mortimer B. Davis elected President, American Tobacco Company of Canada.

1896

Apl. 21st—Baron de Hirsch died in Hungary.
May 17th—Union Prayer Book adopted by Temple Emanu-El Congregation, Montreal.
—Rev. Meldola de Sola officiated at laying of cornerstone of Spanish and Portuguese Synagogue, New York.

1897

July —Central Conference of American Rabbis met in Montreal.
Sept. —Bond Street Synagogue, Toronto, dedicated.
Dec. 10th—"The Jewish Times" founded in Montreal by Lyon Cohen.
Dec. 21st—Mrs. Samuel Davis died in Montreal.
—Council of Jewish Women, Toronto, organized.
—Rev. Meldola de Sola officiated at dedication of Spanish and Portuguese Synagogue, New York.

1898

Mar. 13th—Agudath Zion Society, Montreal, organized.
—Talmud Torah opened in Montreal.
—Ottawa Ladies' Hebrew Benevolent Society organized.

1899

Jan. 11th—Synagogue consecrated at St. John, N.B.
Apl. 1st—Baroness de Hirsch died in Paris.
Apl. 27th—Rev. Marcus Berner established Jewish colony at Yorkton, N.W.T.
—Toronto Ladies' Hebrew Aid Society organized.
—Henry Street Synagogue, Toronto, formed.

1900

Dec. 23rd—First Canadian Zionist Convention held at Montreal.
—Ottawa Men's Hebrew Benevolent Society organized.
—Daughters of Israel, St. John, organized.
—Daughters of Zion organized in Toronto.
—Montefiore Joseph elected President, Quebec Board of Trade.
—A. D. Benjamin died.

1901

Dec. 18th—Second Zionist Convention held at Montreal; C. I. de Sola elected President.
—Rabbi S. Jacobs accepted call to Holy Blossom Synagogue, Toronto.
—F. D. Benjamin elected President, Holy Blossom Congregation, Toronto.
—Jewish cemetery at Three Rivers desecrated.
—Dominion census shows 16,131 Jews in Canada.

1902

May 28th—Baron de Hirsch Institute, Montreal, opened by Lord Minto.
Aug. —Abraham Kirschberg died in Montreal.
—Edmund Scheuer appointed Justice of the Peace for Toronto.
—Case of Pinsler vs Protestant Board of School Commissioners.
—Nathan Green died at St. John, N.B.

1903

Feb. 1st—Third Zionist Convention held at Montreal.
—Jewish community established at Regina.
—Rabbi H. Abramowitz accepted call to Shaar Hashomayim Congregation, Montreal.
—Maxwell Goldstein appointed King's Counsel.

1904

Feb. 24th—Jesse Joseph died at Montreal.
July 3rd—Theodore Herzl died.
Dec. 30th—Madame Donalda made her debut at Nice, France.
—Rabbi J. Gordon accepted call to University Avenue Synagogue, Toronto.
—Dr. Edward Elkan first Jew in Canada to graduate in Dentistry.
—Clarence I. de Sola appointed Belgian Consul in Montreal.

1905

June 4th—Fourth Zionist Convention held at Montreal.
—Moses Finkelstein elected Alderman of Winnipeg.
—Dr. S. Sperber appointed superintendent of Victoria Memorial Hospital, Manchester, England.
—Orthodox Congregation organized at Vancouver.
—Winnipeg Talmud Torah organized.

—Max Steinkopf admitted to Manitoba Bar—first Jewish lawyer in Prairie Provinces.

1906

July 1st—Fifth Zionist Convention held at Toronto.
Aug. 12th—Edmonton Hebrew Association organized.
Aug. —Sultan of Turkey withdrew all restrictions against Jewish immigration to Palestine.
—Rabbi Nathan Gordon accepted call to Temple Emanu-El, Montreal.
—University Avenue Synagogue, Toronto, erected.
—Samuel W. Jacobs appointed King's Counsel.
—Congregation formed in Calgary.

1907

Feb. 28th—Jacob Henry Joseph died in Montreal.
May 7th—Cornerstone laid of Shaar Shomayim Synagogue, Winnipeg.
June 30th—Sixth Zionist Convention held at Ottawa.
Oct. 16th—Maxwell Goldstein elected President, Temple Emanu-El, Montreal.
—Simcoe Street Talmud Torah, Toronto, opened.
—Rabbi Kahanovitch appointed Chief Rabbi of Winnipeg.

1908

Feb. 29th—Lyon Silverman died in Montreal.
Apl. 8th—Young Men's Hebrew Association, Montreal, organized.
Sept. 5th—Seventh Zionist Convention held at Montreal.
Dec. 28th—Frank Sylvester died at Victoria, B.C.
—Mortimer B. Davis elected President, Baron de Hirsch Institute.
—Simon Leiser elected President, Victoria Board of Trade.
—Rabbi Nathan Gordon appointed Professor of oriental languages at McGill University.
—William Diamond elected President, Edmonton Hebrew Association.
—Hebrew Ladies' Maternity Aid Society organized in Toronto.

1909

June 10th—Dr. Bessie Pullan received degree of M. B. from University of Toronto—first Jewess to graduate in medicine in Canada.
June 27th—I.O.B.B. organized in Winnipeg.
Sept. 15th—Jewish Children's Home, Toronto, organized.
Oct. 1st—Aaron Rosenthal died in Ottawa.
Nov. 20th—Tenth Zionist Convention held at Montreal.
—Lyon Cohen elected President, Baron de Hirsch Institute, Montreal.
—Reading room and library opened in Baron de Hirsch Institute, Montreal.
—Samuel Shultz elected Alderman of Vancouver.
—Expropriation of Jewish cemetery at Three Rivers; bodies removed to Montreal.

1910

Feb. 23rd—Eleventh Zionist Convention held at Toronto.
July 24th—I.O.B.B. Lodge, No. 608 established at Vancouver.
—S. Hart Green elected member of Manitoba Legislature.
—Synagogue erected in Kingston.
—Capt. Carrol Ryan died in Montreal.
—First Young Judaea Club organized in Montreal.

1911

May 28th—Hebrew Free Loan Association, Montreal, incorporated.
Sept. 17th—Temple Emanu-El Synagogue, Westmount, dedicated.
—Peter Bercovitch appointed King's Counsel.
—Mount Royal Dental Society organized.
—Dominion census shows 75,681 Jews in Canada.

1912

June 29th—Twelfth Zionist Convention held at Ottawa.
Nov. 29th—Toronto Hebrew Journal founded.
—Edmonton Talmud Torah opened.
—Calgary Talmud Torah organized.
—Jewish Orphanage opened in Winnipeg.
—Samuel Gintzburger elected Councillor of West Vancouver.
—United Hebrew Association, Hamilton, organized.
—Sigmund Samuel elected Councillor, Toronto Board of Trade.
—Abraham Blumenthal elected Alderman of Montreal.
—Synagogue built at Saskatoon.

1913

Jan. 2nd—Winnipeg Free Loan Society organized.
Feb. 9th—I.O.B.B. Lodge, No. 729 established at Montreal.
Mar. 9th—I.O.B.B. Lodge, No. 732 established at Edmonton.
Mar. 9th—I.O.B.B. Lodge, No. 696 established at Fort William.
June 29th—Mount Sinai Sanatorium opened at St. Agathe.
Oct. 27th—Mount Sinai Lodge, A.F. & A.M., Toronto, organized.
Dec. 25th—Thirteenth Zionist Convention held at Montreal.
—D. A. Ansell died at Montreal.
—Mortimer B. Davis elected President, Baron de Hirsch Institute, Montreal.
—Zeta Beta Tau Fraternity introduced to McGill University.
—Samuel Gintzburger appointed Consul for Switzerland in British Columbia.
—Mortimer B. Davis endowed Chair at Laval University.
—Anti-Semitic case at Quebec.
—Young Women's Hebrew Association, Montreal, organized.
—Synagogue built at Regina.
—H. A. Friedman admitted to Bar of Alberta, first Jewish barrister in Province.

1914

Jan. 13th—Committee appointed to study formation of United Charities in Montreal.
Mar. —Rabbi H. J. Samuel accepted call to Shaarey Zedek Congregation, Winnipeg.
June —Folk's Shule opened in Montreal.
July 19th—I.O.B.B. Lodge, No. 758 established at Victoria.
Aug. 1st—Hebrew National Association, Toronto, organized.
Oct. 12th—Mr. and Mrs. Adolph Goldstein celebrated diamond wedding anniversary in Montreal.
Nov. 29th—Lazarus Cohen died in Montreal.

—S. W. Jacobs elected President, Baron de Hirsch Institute, Montreal.
—Herzl Dispensary opened at Montreal.
—Hebrew Maternity Hospital, Montreal, opened.
—Toronto Jewish Old Folks' Home organized.
—Lord Reading Chapter, I.O.D.E., organized at Quebec.
—Louis Rubenstein elected Alderman of Montreal.
—L. M. Singer elected Alderman of Toronto.
—Samuel Shultz appointed County Court Judge at Vancouver.
—Dr. L. J. Breslin appointed Jewish coroner at Toronto.

1915

Jan. —Vancouver Hebrew Free Loan Association organized.
Feb. 22nd—Charles King died at Toronto.
Nov. 14th—First Canadian Jewish Conference held at Montreal.
Nov. 15th—Fourteenth Zionist Convention held at Montreal.
—Saskatoon Talmud Torah opened
—A. Rhinewine appointed editor of Toronto Hebrew Journal.

1916

Jan. 14th—Mrs. Camilla Levy died at Hamilton.
Mar. 16th—Montreal Federation of Jewish Philanthropies incorporated by Provincial Legislature.
Mar. 19th—Jacob Hirsch died in Montreal.
Oct. 28th—Federation of Jewish Philanthropies formed in Toronto.
Dec. 13th—Grace Aguilar Chapter, I.O.D.E., organized in Montreal.
—Mrs. Martin Wolff elected Regent, Quebec Municipal Chapter, I.O.D.E.
—Mark Workman elected President, Dominion Steel Corporation.
—Jewish Reinforcement Company raised in Montreal for active service.
—S. W. Jacobs, K.C., elected Treasurer, Bar of Montreal.
—Dr. A. Brodey appointed Professor of Pharmacology at the University of Toronto.
—Colonel M. Alexander appointed Judge Advocate General of Canadian Army Corps.

1917

Jan. 9th—Adolph Goldstein died in Montreal.
Jan. 26th—Colonel M. Alexander created a Companion of the Order of St. Michael and St. George.
Jan. —First Canadian Hadassah Chapter organized in Toronto.
Mar. 18th—Maxwell Goldstein elected President, and Mortimer B. Davis and Mark Workman Honorary Presidents, of the Federation of Jewish Philanthropies, Montreal.
May 12th—Simon Leiser died in Victoria.
June 17th—I.O.B.B. Lodge, No. 816 established at Calgary.
July 1st—Fifteenth Zionist Convention held at Winnipeg.
Nov. 5th—Balfour Declaration regarding Palestine made public.
Nov. 27th—Zigmond Fineberg died at Montreal.

—Edmund Scheuer elected President, Toronto Federation of Jewish Philanthropies.
—Sir Mortimer B. Davis knighted by His Majesty King George V.
—Young Judaea Federation organized at Winnipeg Convention.
—S. W. Jacobs, K.C., elected member of the House of Commons.
—Jewish Reinforcement Company sailed for active service.
—Jewish newspaper established in Winnipeg.

1918

Feb. 19th—Mount Sinai Chapter, Royal Arch Masons, instituted in Toronto.
Apl. 29th—Rev. Meldola de Sola died in Montreal.
July —Disraeli Chapter, I.O.D.E., organized in Ottawa.
Sept. 20th—Jacob Cohen appointed Police Magistrate in Toronto.
Sept. 25th—Council of Jewish Women, Montreal, organized.
—Vancouver Talmud Torah opened.
—Spanish and Portuguese Synagogue Montreal celebrated 150th anniversary.
—Mrs. C. I. de Sola decorated by the King of Belgium.
—Peter Bercovitch elected to Quebec Legislature.
—Lyon W. Jacobs elected Alderman of Montreal.

1919

Jan. 5th—Sixteenth Zionist Convention held in Montreal.
Mar. 10th—I.O.B.B. Lodge, No. 836 established at Toronto.
Mar. 14th—First Canadian Jewish Congress held in Montreal.
June 27th—I.O.B.B. Lodge, No. 739 established at Saskatoon.
July 1st—Leon Goldman appointed Executive Secretary, Zionist Organization of Canada.
Aug. 4th—I.O.B.B. Lodge, No. 833 established at Regina.
Sept. 10th—Palestine Lodge, A.F. & A.M. Toronto, instituted.
—A. J. Freiman elected President, Zionist Organization of Canada.
—Nathan Gordon appointed Prosecuting Attorney for the City of Montreal.
—Jewish Old Folks' Home, Winnipeg, opened.
—Sinai League organized at Ottawa.
—Clarence I. de Sola decorated by Belgian Government.
—Lyon Cohen organized and elected President, Associated Clothing Manufacturers of Canada.
—Dr. A. A. Roback appointed instructor in Psychology at Harvard University.

1920

Feb. 1st—Opening of new Jewish Orphanage at Winnipeg.
April 24th—San Remo Conference confirms the Balfour Declaration.
May 10th—Clarence I. de Sola died in Montreal.
June 30th—Immigrant Aid Society of Canada organized.
Sept. —Edmonton Council of Jewish Women organized.
Dec. —Calgary Council of Jewish Women organized.

—Rabbi M. J. Merritt accepted call to Temple Emanu-El, Montreal.
—Graduate Menorah Society organized in Montreal.
—N. S. Fineberg elected President, Montreal Hebrew Free Loan Association.
—Elias Pullan elected President, Toronto Federation of Jewish Philanthropies.
—Fund raised throughout Canada for relief of needy Jews of Europe.
—Joseph Singer elected Alderman of Toronto.
—Rabbi Solomon Jacobs died in Toronto.
—Rabbi B. R. Brickner accepted call to Holy Blossom Synagogue, Toronto.
—Chief Rabbi of England visited Canada.

1921

Jan. 29th—First Hadassah Convention held at Montreal.
Jan. 30th—Seventeenth Zionist Convention held at Montreal.
Feb. 7th—A. J. Freiman appointed by Government to sign permits for passports to Palestine.
Feb. 19th—I.O.B.B. Lodge, No. 885 established at Ottawa.
Feb. 20th—I.O.B.B. Lodge, No. 886 established at Hamilton.
May —Dr. Chaim Weizmann toured Canada in interests of the Zionist Organization.
Oct. 18th—Mrs. Montefiore Joseph died at Quebec.
Oct. —New Jewish Orphanage opened at Montreal.
Nov. 10th—Cornerstone of new Shaar Hashomayim Synagogue at Westmount laid by Lyon Cohen.
—Nathan Keyfitz died at Toronto.
—Michael Hirsch elected President of Federation of Jewish Philanthropies, Montreal.
—Gabriel Levy, Hamilton, appointed King's Counsel.
—Louis Green died at St. John, N.B.
—Dominion Census shows 126,196 Jews in Canada.
—S. W. Jacobs, K.C., re-elected to House of Commons.

1922

Jan. —Conference of Canadian Lodges, I.O.B.B., held at Winnipeg.
Mar. 6th—Bill introduced in Quebec Legislature to validate certain marriages.
June 30th—Second Hadassah Convention held at Ottawa.
July 1st—Eighteenth Zionist Convention at Ottawa.
Sept. 22nd—Shaar Hashomayim Synagogue at Westmount consecrated.
—Rabbi Joseph Corcos accepted call to Shearith Israel Congregation, Montreal.
—British Columbia Board of Education decided against introduction of religious instruction in schools.
—United Talmud Torahs of Montreal incorporated by Quebec Legislature.
—Rabbi B. R. Brickner elected President of Toronto Federation of Jewish Philanthropies.
—Mount Sinai Hospital, Toronto, organized.
—Mrs. A. Rosenthal died in Ottawa.
—Hamilton Council of Jewish Women organized.

—Maxwell Goldstein, K.C., elected Councillor, Bar of Montreal.
—Dr. J. Rubin elected a Governor of the College of Dental Surgeons for the Province of Quebec.
—Canadian Jewish Review, Toronto, founded.

1923

Jan. 4th—Moses Bilsky died in Ottawa.
June —Mrs. C. I. de Sola presented her daughter to Their Majesties, the King and Queen.
Oct. 28th—Mrs. (Rabbi) Jacobs died at Toronto.
Nov. 25th—Lewis Alexander Hart died at Montreal.
—Lyon Cohen elected President, Montreal Federation of Jewish Philanthropies.
—Toronto Hebrew Free Loan Association organized.
—Joseph Singer elected to the Board of Control of the City of Toronto.
—Samuel Factor elected to the Board of Education, Toronto.
—Benjamin Fox elected to the Board of Education, Ottawa.
—Peter Bercovitch, K.C., M.P.P., re-elected by acclamation to the Quebec Legislature.
—Marcus Hyman elected to Board of Education, Winnipeg.
—Dr. M. Finkelstein appointed City Bacteriologist, Winnipeg.

1924

Jan. 5th—Third Hadassah Convention at Toronto.
Jan. 6th—Nineteenth Zionist Convention at Toronto.
Mar. 21st—Cornerstone laid of Toronto Hebrew Free School and Community Centre.
Mar. —Vancouver Council of Jewish Women organized.
Sept. 7th—New Talmud Torah opened in Regina.
Oct. 6th—Laurentian Insurance Company organized at Montreal.
—Rabbi H. J. Samuel appointed Chaplain, Canadian Club, Winnipeg.
—Quebec Talmud Torah opened.
—Michael Hirsch, S. W. Cohen and J. Shubert appointed by Provincial Government members of Commission to report on Jewish educational problems in Montreal.
—Nathan Phillips elected Alderman of Toronto.
—Convention of District Grand Lodge, No. 4, I.O.B.B., at Vancouver.
—Rabbi M. J. Mintz accepted call to Adath Jeshuran Congregation, Ottawa.
—Act passed by Quebec Legislature legalizing certain Jewish marriages.

1925

Jan. 1st—Joseph M. Gordon elected to Board of Education, Toronto.
Mar. 5th—I.O.B.B. Lodge, No. 1011 established at Windsor, Ont.
Mar. 6th—I.O.B.B. Lodge, No. 1012 established at London, Ont.
Apl. —Harry Rotenberg elected President, Toronto Federation of Jewish Philanthropies.
May —Al. Lesser elected President, Montreal Federation of Jewish Philanthropies.
June 1st—Harris Kellert died at Montreal.

KNIGHTS
Sir Mortimer B. Davis

SEIGNEURS
St. Marguerite / Marquisat Dusable — *Aaron Hart, *Moses Hart, *Areli Blake Hart.

Becancour — *Aaron Hart, *Ezekiel Hart, *Samuel Becanour Hart, *Adolphus M. Hart.

Courval — *Moses Hart, *Alexander Thomas Hart, *Moses A. Hart, *David A. Hart, *Lewis A. Hart.

CONSULAR CORPS
*Jesse Joseph (Belgium). Moise Schwob (France.) *Abraham Joseph (Belgium).
*Clarence I. deSola (Belgium). *David A. Ansell (Mexico).
Samuel Gintzburger (Switzerland) *Samuel Nordheimer (Germany).

FOREIGN DECORATIONS
*Jesse Joseph, Knight of the Order of Leopold (Belgium).
*Clarence I. deSola, Chevalier, Order of Leopold (Belgium).
Mrs. C. I. deSola, Order of Elizabeth (Belgium); Cross of Mercy (Serbia).

MEMBERS OF PARLIAMENT
*Ezekiel Hart, Legislature of Lower Canada, 1808-9.
*Henry Nathan, Legislature of British Columbia, 1870; House of Commons, 1871-2.
*Seilim Franklin, Legislature of British Columbia, 1872.
S. Hart Green, Legislature of Manitoba, 1910.
Peter Bercovitch, K.C., Legislature of Quebec, 1916-19-23.
S. W. Jacobs, K.C., House of Commons, 1917-21.

MEMBERS OF THE JUDICIARY
*Samuel Shultz, County Court Judge, Vancouver, B.C., 1914.

KING'S COUNSEL
*Gershom Joseph, Q.C., Maxwell Goldstein, S. W. Jacobs, M.P.,
Gabriel Levy, Peter Bercovitch, M.P.P., Marcus M. Sperber,
Lyon W. Jacobs, Louis Fitch.

MAGISTRATES
*William Hyman, Gaspe, *Benjamin Zimmerman, Winnipeg, Jacob Cohen, Toronto.

MAYORS AND REEVES
*William Hyman, Cape Rosier. *L. Franklin, Victoria. *Charles King, Whitby.
*David Oppenheimer, Vancouver. B. Rothschild, Cochrane.
George Simon, Alexandria.

ALDERMEN AND COUNCILLORS
*Samuel Benjamin, Montreal, *Isaac Oppenheimer, Vancouver, *N. Steiner, Toronto,
*David Oppenheimer, Vancouver, *Abraham Joseph, Quebec, *Samuel Shultz, Vancouver,
Samuel Gintzburger, West Vancouver, Abraham Blumenthal, Montreal, Louis Rubenstein, Montreal,
Lyon W. Jacobs, K.C., Montreal, A. Skaletar, Winnipeg, D. Levine, Montreal,
M. Finkelstein, Winnipeg, Joseph Singer, Toronto, A. A. Heaps, Winnipeg,
L. M. Singer, Toronto, S. Baum, Windsor, Nathan Phillips, Toronto,
S. Rosenthal, Ottawa, S. Obendorfer, Kingston, Jacob Miller, Cornwall,
J. Shubert, Montreal, I. Cohen, Kingston, Julius Miller, Cornwall,
Nathan J. Fraid, Cornwall, M. Clavir, North Bay.

MEMBERS OF BOARDS OF EDUCATION
I. Cohen, Kingston, *Charles King, Ontario County, B. Fox, Ottawa,
S. Factor, Toronto, Marcus Hyman, Winnipeg, J. M. Gordon, Toronto,
Sam. Meyerowitz, Rockland.

*Deceased

ADDENDA

*The biographies that follow were received
too late for proper classification
in this edition.*

MRS. M. BILSKY, OTTAWA

MRS. M. BILSKY, widow of the late Moses Bilsky, one of Canada's pioneer Jews, was born in Berlin, Germany, in June, 1857, the second eldest daughter in a family of six children, of Mr. and Mrs. Abraham Reich. When she was 9 years of age, she was taken by her parents to the United States, where the family settled in Brooklyn, N.Y. When she was 17 years of age, she was married to Mr. Bilsky in Brooklyn. They went to Ottawa direct and spent the first 8 years of their married life in the Capital, moving to Montreal about 1881, where Mr. Bilsky was engaged in business. They remained in Montreal about 5 years and then returned to Ottawa, where Mrs. Bilsky has resided ever since. As one of the first families in Ottawa, the Bilskys naturally took a lead in communal work, and Mrs. Bilsky is today remembered in a grateful way by many of the old pioneer members of the community, whom she was able to help in her characteristic unostentatious way. When Mrs. Bilsky was an active charitable worker, there were no organized benevolent societies as there are today, and the burden of caring for the needy and sick fell on the shoulders of those who realised their responsibility. Mrs. Bilsky was one of these. For many years she was the kindly, ministering friend of her fellow Jews of Ottawa, loyally co-operating with her late husband in his work for the advancement of the community in a spiritual as well as in a social way. Mrs. Bilsky is the proud mother of a large and public-spirited family. There are six daughters: Mrs. A. J. Freiman, Ottawa; Mrs. A. W. Jacobs, Montreal; Mrs. A. J. Shragge, Winnipeg; Mrs. A. Bronfman, Montreal; and the Misses Eva and Tillie Bilsky, Ottawa. There are also five sons: Alex, Montreal; Sam, Jack, Dave and Nathan, Ottawa. Mrs. Bilsky is honorary president of the Ladies' Auxiliary of the Adath Jeshurun Synagogue, Ottawa; and of the Ladies' Hebrew Benevolent Society. She also takes an active interest in the activities of the Hadassah movement, of which there are two chapters in Ottawa.

THE LATE MRS. NATHAN SMITH

THE LATE MRS. NATHAN SMITH (Sarah Lossinger) was born in 1861 in Lithuania, a daughter of the renowned talmudist, Selig Lossinger. In 1884 she was married to Nathan Smith and accompanied her husband when he went to Toronto. Mrs. Smith became interested in communal undertakings in that city shortly after her arrival, and retained her interest to the time of her death, which took place March 15th, 1917. She was prominently identified with many charitable organizations, and was one of the founders of the Jewish Children's Home, and the Hebrew Ladies' Aid Society, being for many years treasurer. She was instrumental in forming the Co-operative Board of Charities and was elected its first treasurer, which office she held for a long period. Inspired by her example, her children are also active in communal work. Mrs. Smith was predeceased by her eldest son, Mr. Abraham Isaac Smith, founder of the Judaean Literary Society. Dr. I. R. Smith, a well-known surgeon of Toronto, is the chief medical officer at the Jewish Children's Home, and held a commission as Captain in the Royal Army Medical Corps during the World War. Hyman M. has taken a foremost place in communal undertakings. In 1924 he was elected Vice-President of the University Avenue Congregation, of which he has been a life-long member, and of which he is at present a member of the Board of Governors. He is a trustee of the Federation of Jewish Philanthropies, and a member of the executive of the Y.M.H.A. Another son, the late Julius M. Smith passed away in 1923. Mrs. Smith had four daughters, Mrs. A. Rapp of Montreal; Mrs. H. Pullan of Toronto; Miss Lillian Smith who is one of the organizers of the University of Toronto Menorah Society, member of the executive of the University of Toronto Women's Press Club, the Women's Canadian Club, and the Heather Chapter, I.O.D.E. She also holds high rank in the Girl Guides Organization. The youngest daughter, Miss Annie Smith, is a member of the choir of the Holy Blossom Congregation.

SAMUEL HART, MONTREAL

SAMUEL HART, one of the most prominent business men and a well-known philanthropist of Montreal, was born in that city in 1873, the son of the late Louis Hart. He received his education at private schools, and at an early age entered the industry of which he is now one of the leading factors in Canada. He was a member of the firm of Wener Bros. & Hart, and many years ago founded the firm of Samuel Hart & Company, some years later starting in Canada the Society Brand Clothes Limited. Mr. Hart's reputation as a philanthropist is well-known throughout Canada, and he is always ready to assist both financially and with his time and ability, any cause whether Jewish or Gentile, which will help those less fortunate. Mr. Hart is one of the large supporters of the Federation of Jewish Philanthropies of Montreal, and one of the founders of the Hebrew Orphans' Home, which is the pride of the Montreal community. He has also taken great interest in the organization and building of the Mount Sinai Sanatorium at St. Agathe, Que., the home for Jewish consumptives. He is an ardent supporter of and donor to the Zionist Organization, and subscribes annually to the Home for consumptives in Denver, Colorado. Mr. Hart is a life governor of the Montreal General Hospital, and of the Montreal Protestant Home for the Insane. He is a trustee of the Shaar Hashomayim Congregation, of which he has been a life-long member. He is a member of the Canadian Manufacturers' Association, Montreal Board of Trade, Canadian Club, Montefiore Club, and one of the founders of the Elmridge Golf and Country Club; a member of the Country Club, St. Lambert; a life member of Killwinning Lodge, A.F. & A.M., and of Mt. Horeb Chapter, R.A.M. Mr. Hart is the President of the firm of Samuel Hart & Co. Limited, wholesale clothing manufacturers, Vice-President of Society Brand Clothes Limited, and director of several other prominent institutions throughout the country. He was married in 1897 to Edith, daughter of the late Selig Wener, of Montreal, and has one daughter, Ruth (Mrs. Leon H. Fischel).

JOHN MICHAELS, MONTREAL

JOHN MICHAELS, one of the best known citizens of Montreal, and a member of a family whose name is synonymous with the tobacco trade in Canada, is the second son of the late Michael and Rose (Levi) Michaels, formerly of London, England. He was born in New York City, on June 26th, 1856, and received his education in the public and high schools of Montreal, to which city his parents had removed. On February 22nd, 1882, he was married to Sarah, daughter of the late Wolfe and Caroline Misell of Montreal, and has two sons, Michael A. and Alfred E., and one daughter, Rosie, wife of Douglas Mire. As a young man, Mr. Michaels became interested in the cigar factory founded by his father and Mr. Henry Jacobs, under the name of H. Jacobs & Company, (which was the first cigar factory in Canada, established in 1858 in Dundas, Ont.). This business John Michaels developed until it became the largest cigar factory in Canada, with a reputation that extended from coast to coast. He was the originator of the "Stonewall" cigar, which in its day had the largest sale of any cigar in Canada. Mr. Michaels' sons were also associated with him in the cigar business. He retired from business in 1917, and has since interested himself largely in all matters for the benefit of the community, being particularly interested in the question of Jewish education in the public schools of the Province of Quebec. A patron and recognized judge of art, Mr. Michaels is a staunch friend to young artists, to whom his advice and assistance have been of much aid. He was one of the founders and was elected the first president of the Montefiore Club, Montreal, when it was known as the Montefiore Literary Society, and he held this office on several occasions. Mr. Michaels has always been much interested in communal work, and he has been a supporter of most of the charitable institutions of Montreal, and has long been recognized as one of the public-spirited residents of that city. He is a member of the Royal Arcanum and of the Montefiore Club, Montreal.

THE LATE NATHAN GREEN

NATHAN GREEN was born in Amsterdam, Holland, on June 12th, 1828. At the age of 14, after completing his education, he left his home and settled in London, England, where he learned the trade of cigar-maker, together with Moses Gompers, father of the late Samuel W. Gompers. In 1850, Mr. Green came to New York. While there, the Civil War broke out, and he immediately offered his services. In the States, Mr. Green continued his former business, and at the age of 34, branched out into Canada where he made his permanent residence. When Mr. Green came to St. John, New Brunswick, he was the second Jew in the Maritime Provinces, and was happy to assist his coreligionists who settled there in the following years. Mr. Green was blessed with a large family, three sons, Harry of San Francisco; Sol of Chicago; and the late Louis of St. John, and three daughters, Mrs. Gustav Fischel, Montreal; Mrs. Harry Franks, Chicago; and Mrs. Emile Berger, New York. His sons proved valuable assistants in building up what was at that time the largest tobacco business in the Maritime Provinces. Mr. Green was the first Jew in St. John to join the Masons. The St. John fire in 1877 was an experience of which Mr. Green was proud to relate, as in 48 hours after this conflagration, he again established himself, making a fresh start. Mr. Green was an extensive traveller, and crossed the Atlantic Ocean 73 times. He not only was a charitable and enthusiastic communal worker for those of the Jewish faith, but gave freely of time and money to all of mankind. He was particularly interested in the County Poorhouse, which it pleased him to personally visit regularly. He organized the first Jewish cemetery in New Brunswick, which today bears his name—The Green Hart Cemetery. At the age of 60, Mr. Green retired from active business, and the business is now in the hands of the founder's grandson, Harry Green. After his retirement, Mr. Green moved to Chicago with his family and remained there until his death in 1922, at the age of 94. A few years before he died, he returned to visit St. John and was accorded a very enthusiastic civic welcome.

THE LATE MARK COHEN

THE LATE MARK COHEN was born in New York City, on January 15th, 1830. He was the son of the late Moses and Rachel Cohen. Moses Cohen was the founder of the first agricultural colony that was settled by Jews in the United States, at Warwarsing, Ulster County, N.Y., in 1837, and which was named Sholom (Peace). It was under his leadership that thirteen Jewish families went to that place, leaving New York City, where they had been living, to engage in agriculture on farms which they had purchased. Mark Cohen came to Canada in 1882 and first settled in Hamilton, Ontario, where he became an active member of the Jewish community, taking a keen interest in all its undertakings. He was one of the three members of the Anshe Sholom Congregation who took an active stand in introducing the Reform Movement to the congregation, and he was instrumental in the building of the Hughson Street Synagogue of that congregation. In 1886 Mr. Cohen took up his residence in the City of Toronto, where he also actively interested himself in all communal and philanthropic endeavors. He was instrumental in the erection of the Bond Street Synagogue of the Holy Blossom Toronto Hebrew Congregation, and in 1892 was elected President of the congregation. Closely associated with his friend, Edmund Scheuer, he was interested in all communal undertakings during his residence both in Hamilton and Toronto, and in later years, when there was a large influx of immigrants to Toronto, Mr. Cohen was always ready to lend his assistance when required. On December 4th, 1859, Mr. Cohen was married to Elizabeth Tützer, and their surviving children are, Moses Mark and Jacob of Toronto; Isaac of Baltimore, Md.; Rachel, (wife of F. L. Kahn of Toronto); and Charlotte, (wife of Dr. L. J. Isaacs of Chicago, Ill.). Mr. Cohen during his lifetime was engaged in life insurance, in which business he was very successful. He had a reputation of writing the largest policies and more insurance than any other agent in his day. His death occurred in Chicago, on October 7th, 1910, while on a visit to his daughter.

RABBI J. SCHWARTZ, TORONTO

RABBI JESSE SCHWARTZ, of the University Avenue Synagogue, Toronto, was born in New York City, on January 8th, 1892, the son of Michael and Rose Schwartz of that city. He received his education at the New York public schools; Townsend Harris High School; College of the City of New York, where he received the degree of Bachelor of Science in 1912, and where he obtained honors in history, economics and debating; and at Columbia University Law School, from which he graduated with the degree of LL.B., in 1915. After graduation, he was called to the bar of New York in the same year, and followed the practice of law in New York for about two years. In 1918, he joined the United States' army, in which he remained until after the armistice was signed. He became interested in the field of Jewish educational work, and was educational director of the Central Jewish Institute of New York City in 1919-1920. In 1921, he entered the Jewish Theological Seminary of America, where he received the Louis J. Stroock Scholarship for 1924-1925, and where he received his rabbinical degree in June, 1925. While at the Seminary, Rabbi Schwartz was president in his senior year of the student body. In June, 1925, he was called to the pulpit of the Goel Tzedec Congregation (University Avenue Synagogue), Toronto, of which he is the present spiritual head. Rabbi Schwartz has always taken a keen and active interest in all philanthropic movements and charitable undertakings in his community, but has been particularly interested in Zionist affairs, and is a member of the Zionist Organization of America. He has devoted a great deal of time and energy to this cause, taking an active part in all Keren Hayesod campaigns in New York City. He was director of the adult educational activities of the Zionist Organization, in 1920-1921. Rabbi Schwartz has also been identified with the Young Judaea Organization, and has been a leader of its various circles. On August 9th, 1925, he was married to Miss Rebecca Lattman, daughter of Mr. and Mrs. Max Lattman. A brilliant career is prophesied for Rabbi Schwartz in Canada.

RABBI FERDINAND M. ISSERMAN, TORONTO

RABBI FERDINAND M. ISSERMAN was born in Antwerp, Belgium, and went to the United States when eight years of age. He graduated from the Central High School of Newark, in 1914. In 1917 he received the degree of bachelor of Hebrew Literature from the Hebrew College, and in 1919, he received his B.A. from the University of Cincinnati. He graduated from the Hebrew Union College in 1922. At the University, Rabbi Isserman was a member of the University debating team and was on the staff of the University News. At the Hebrew Union College Rabbi Isserman was captain of the basketball team, president of the Students' Literary Society, and in his senior year was president of the student body. During the war he served at Camp Grant, Ill., and was a member of an infantry officers' training camp. After graduation Rabbi Isserman received a call to become assistant rabbi to Dr. Harry W. Ettelson at the Rodeph Shalom Synagogue, Philadelphia, entering upon his duties on July 1st, 1922, and later was given full charge. He was instrumental in establishing the high school department of the congregational school on a firm basis, and in raising a fund for a new school building. He continued his studies at both the Dropsie College and the University of Pennsylvania, and in June 1924, received the M.A. degree. Rabbi Isserman served as a member of the Kearny Community Centre Board, and organized the first confirmation class at the Jewish Foster Home. He was chairman of the Philadelphia Hebrew University Committee, vice-chairman of the Central Zionist Committee, and a member of the Board of Directors of the Keren Hayesod. He was for two years a member of the national board of the Sigma Alpha Mu Fraternity, and an associate editor of its magazine, "The Octagonian." He is a member of the Social Justice Commission of the Central Conference of American Rabbis. In 1925 he was called to the pulpit of the Holy Blossom Toronto Hebrew Congregation. On June 6th, 1923, Rabbi Isserman was married to Ruth, daughter of Dr. and Mrs. V. S. Frankenstein, of Chicago, and they have one daughter.

A. M. P. GOLDBERG, TORONTO

ABRAHAM MOSES PHILIP GOLDBERG, territorial Vice-President of the Sun Life Assurance Company, was born in Warsaw, Poland, September 25, 1873, the son of Shrago Moses and Fruma (Finkelstein) Goldberg. He arrived in New York with his parents in April 1880, and received his education in the public schools of New York City. He then took up the trade of cloak-making, which business was at that time in its infancy. He spent some years in this branch of work in New York, later on going to Toronto and Montreal. In April, 1897 he took up his residence in Toronto where he has since remained. In 1909 he retired from the garment trade, and in 1911 Mr. Goldberg entered the insurance business, and has built up for himself the reputation of underwriting more life insurance than any other agent in Ontario. He has made a life study of insurance, and is the leading representative in Western Ontario for the Sun Life Assurance Company, which is the largest Life Assurance Company in Canada. He was appointed territorial vice-president of the company. Mr. Goldberg has been a member of the Zionist Organization since its inception, and was the organizer of the B'nai Zion Society in Montreal. Although always keenly interested in communal and welfare work, he has not accepted office in any organization, but has kept in the background where he considers his efforts do the most good, and he is a liberal supporter of all charitable and educational works. Always interested in public and municipal questions, and a Conservative in politics, in 1923 Mr. Goldberg allowed himself to be nominated as a candidate for the Toronto City Council, but was defeated by a small vote in the elections. He is largely responsible for the formation of the Primrose Club, Toronto, of which he is a charter member. He also is a member of the Independent Order B'nai B'rith and the Knights of Pythias. He is unmarried. Mr. Goldberg is a member of both the University Avenue and Henry Street Synagogues.

PAUL FRUMHARZ, TORONTO

PAUL FRUMHARZ, Vice-President and founder of the United Press, Limited, was born in Makarov, Ukrania, September 24th, 1892, the son of the late Meyer and Anna Frumharz. He was educated at the High School of Commerce at Ekateranoslaw, and came to Canada with his brother when he was thirteen years of age. He settled in Toronto where he continued his education through private tuition. At the age of sixteen he began to learn the printing business, and after receiving a thorough practical knowledge of this industry, in 1914 he started for himself under the name of the United Press. For a number of years he did commercial printing in a small way, but seeing an opportunity for a large Jewish printing establishment, where quality and service would be the standard, he interested Mr. E. Palter, and in 1920 incorporated the present business under the name of the United Press Limited. In 1921, Mr. Chas. Garfunkel joined the firm. Mr. Frumharz takes charge of the practical end of the business and with his associates, he has developed it into the largest Jewish printing establishment in Canada, doing all sorts of printing, embossing, engraving, lithographing, bookbinding and publishing. In December, 1922, this firm, in competition with the largest printing establishments in Canada, secured a long term contract with the Provincial Government. The concern occupies almost thirty thousand feet of space in their own building, and gives employment to one hundred and forty skilled hands, with a weekly pay-roll of four thousand dollars. The value of the plant is over a quarter of a million dollars. Mr. Frumharz finds time, outside of his business, to interest himself in communal work, and he is one of the earliest members of the Peretz School of Toronto. He was very active in European War Relief work, in which he was greatly assisted by his wife. In 1913, Mr. Frumharz was married to Miss Minnie Greenevsky of Toronto, daughter of the late Mr. Chaim Greenevsky, and he has one son, Chaim, and one daughter, Esther.

R. A. DARWIN, MONTREAL

ROBERT A. DARWIN, Merchant and one of the leading Zionists of the City of Montreal, was born in Petrograd, Russia, on February 18th, 1880, the son of Wolf Darwin of that city. He was educated in the public and high schools of his native city. Later he went to Dorpat (Jurjev), where he entered the University, Faculty of Dentistry, from which he graduated in 1903. He was married to Freda, daughter of Mordecai and Taube Gest, and has three sons, Samuel of Ottawa, and Harry and Jacob of Montreal; and two daughters, Mrs. Maurice Tiznower of Woonsocket, R.I., and Rebecca Darwin of Montreal. Mr. Darwin came to Canada in 1907, settling in Montreal, where he has since resided. He first started as a clerk in one of the departmental stores of that city and he has continually worked himself up in business, until at the present time he is the owner of four large retail stores in Canada, three in the City of Montreal, and one in Ottawa. He is also proprietor and active head of a concern manufacturing ladies' dresses, and of a large cloak and suit factory. A great deal of Mr. Darwin's success in his business enterprises and charitable endeavors has been due to the unselfish and constant help of Mrs. Darwin. Although a man of large business interests, Mr. Darwin devotes much of his time to philanthropic work in his community, and he is a supporter of most of the charitable organizations in Montreal. He is an ardent Zionist and is President of the National Fund of the Zionist Organization of Canada; Chairman of the City and District Zionist Council of Montreal; and member of the National Executive Zionist Organization of Canada. He is one of the oldest members of the Zionist organization in Canada and has contributed much to its success. He is a life governor of the Montreal General Hospital; Baron de Hirsch Institute; and Hebrew Free Loan Association, Montreal. He is a member of the Habonim Lodge, Montreal. He is a Director of the Hebrew Maternity Hospital; member, Board of Directors, United Talmud Torahs; Retail Merchants' Association of Canada; and Montreal Board of Trade. Mr. Darwin is a member of the Shaar Hashomayim Synagogue, Montreal.

M. M. COHEN, TORONTO

MOSES MARK COHEN, the son of Mark and Elizabeth (Tützer) Cohen, was born in New York City, September 28th, 1865. He was married on June 3rd, 1890, to Annie Goslar of Philadelphia, and their children are, Mark Goslar of Toronto; Irving Charles of Baltimore; Miss Rosetta of Toronto; and Charlotte, (wife of David Brodey of Gary, Ind.) Another son, Lieut. Meyer T. Cohen made the supreme sacrifice during the Great War, being killed in action at Passchendaele. Mr. Cohen, who some years ago retired from active business, was at one time head of the firms of Cohen Brothers, Toronto, and the Montreal Optical Company of Montreal, both now incorporated into the Consolidated Optical Company. He has made a special study of business methods and efficiency, and since his retirement from business has devoted himself to social service work, being particularly interested in the welfare of the under-privileged boy. In 1921 he became associated with the Toronto Boy Life Council, with which he served as statistician, and as a result of a summary compilation by him, complete changes were made in the policy of the organization. Mr. Cohen was also a member of the National Boy Work Board. He studied under such eminent boy workers as Taylor-Statten, head of the National Boy Work Board, and Dr. Percy Heyward, the present General Secretary of the Young People's Department of the International Sunday School Association, with headquarters at Chicago. As a result of his studies, Mr. Cohen became convinced that the Big Brother Movement system of looking after the boy was built on a psychological fallacy—that the boy must be saved by recognizing his instincts as natural when he goes wrong, but only as far as his natural instincts are perverted. His system is not to work for the boy but to work with the boy, and in connection with this he founded the Jewish Boys in Training. Practical results of the work instituted by Mr. Cohen are shown in the following figures: in 1922, 13% of the juvenile delinquents appearing in courts were Jewish boys, in 1923, there were 9%, and in 1924, 4¼%.

M. E. WILLIAMS, TORONTO

J. J. MARKS, OTTAWA

MAURICE EDWARD WILLIAMS was born in Dover, England, in 1898. Although a young man, he has distinguished himself as a boy welfare worker, becoming interested in this work in 1921, at the suggestion of Mr. H. M. Cohen. In 1922, he was elected president of the club of Mentors of the Jewish Boys in Training and in 1923 was appointed Executive Secretary of the Big Brother Movement. He is at present the director of the J.B.I.T. Mr. Williams' work is largely preventative, and as a result of his activities, the delinquency amongst Jewish boys has been greatly reduced. His methods are being studied and copied by Christian branches of the boy's welfare movement.

JACOB JEREMIAH MARKS was born at Wilkaviskis, Lithuania, December, 24, 1885, the son of Isaac and Sarah Marks. He received his education in Lithuania and came to Canada in 1905, settling in Ottawa, where he established the Dominion House Furnishing Company. Mr. Marks has been Secretary and Treasurer of the Adath Jeshuran Congregation. He is a Director, Ottawa Hebrew Free School; Chairman, Ottawa Free Loan Ass'n; and past President, I.O.B.B. On June 25, 1912, he married Nellye, daughter of John Golub, and has two sons.

N. J. WEIDMAN, WINNIPEG

NEIMAN J. WEIDMAN, the son of H. L. and Fanny (Daein) Weidman, was born in Winnipeg on March 10th, 1885, one of the first Jews to be born in Western Canada. He received his education at the Winnipeg Public Schools, and at the Collegiate Institute, Winnipeg. He then entered the wholesale grocery firm of Weidman Bros. Limited, of Winnipeg, and is at the present time one of the active heads of this concern. On January 6th, 1914, he was married to Pearl, daughter of Meyer and Mary Vineberg of Winnipeg, formerly of Quebec. Mr. Weidman has at all times taken a keen and active interest in all Jewish charitable undertakings and welfare work in his community, and he was for two years, President of the Winnipeg Lodge, Independent Order B'nai Brith. He was a Director, for one year, of the Canadian Credit Men's Association, and is a Director of the Young Men's Hebrew Association of Winnipeg. Mr. Weidman was treasurer of the Shaarey Zedeck Congregation, for two years, and is a member of the Canadian Club, Zionist "Habonim" Society, and Winnipeg Board of Trade.

J. M. ISAACS, WINNIPEG

JACK M. ISAACS was born in Monmouthshire, England, September 9th, 1892, the eldest son of the late Sandel Isaacs. He is a graduate of the University of Wales and settled in Winnipeg in 1911, where he studied law, graduating with honours in 1916, being called to the Bar in the same year. He has since practised in Winnipeg, specializing in criminal law, being recognized as one of the leaders of this branch of his profession. Mr. Isaacs takes great interest in Jewish communal matters, and is the vice-president and one of the founders of the Fort Rouge Hebrew Congregation.

DR. M. SIEGEL, HAMILTON

DR. MORRIS SIEGEL was born in Poland, August 11th, 1889, the son of Louis Siegel. He was educated at the Rabbinical School of Warsaw; The Hamilton Collegiate Institute; and at the University of Toronto, (Faculty of Medicine), graduating in 1918. Dr. Siegel was the first Hebrew teacher of the Hamilton Talmud Torah, and prior to moving to Hamilton, taught at the Simcoe St. Talmud Torah, Toronto. He was married in 1919 to a daughter of the late Henry Shapiro of Welland, and he has one son. He is a member of the Zionist Organization, and of the United Hebrew Charities, Hamilton.

DR. H. DAVID ISAACS was born in Monmouthshire, England, in February, 1900, the second son of the late Sandel Isaacs. He is a graduate of the University of Wales, and on arriving in Winnipeg, in 1916, entered the study of medicine, where he had the most brilliant career of any student at the University of Manitoba. In each of his years at the University he carried off all the first scholarships, prizes, and honours, in his final year being awarded the Chown Prize for Medicine, as well as the special Gold Medal for having received the highest marks during his course. He was one of the few Jewish students who became interne at the Winnipeg General Hospital, distinguishing himself so by his ability that he was invited to remain on the staff, after completing his course. Graduating in 1922, he entered into partnership with Dr. A. Bercovitch, taking charge of the practice on the latter's moving to Montreal. Dr. Isaacs is a member of the staff of the Children's Hospital and is Demonstrator in Anatomy of the Medical Faculty of the University of Manitoba, being the second Jew to hold this appointment. He is much interested in communal matters, and is Medical Officer of the Hebrew Sick Benefit Association, the largest Jewish organization in Winnipeg.

DR. H. D. ISAACS, WINNIPEG

THE LATE J. B. RUBINOVICH

THE LATE JACOB BENJAMIN RUBINOVICH was born at Georgenburg, Lithuania, on December 25th, 1869, the son of the late Joseph Rubinovich. He received his early education in Germany, and as a young man arrived in Canada, locating in Montreal, where he resided until his death, which took place on October 23rd, 1925. On his arrival in Montreal Mr. Rubinovich took up a commercial career, and in 1902 founded the firm of Rubinovich and Haskell, wholesale importers and exporters, remaining as president of this concern until his decease. His reputation for commercial integrity, honesty, and courteousness extended from coast to coast throughout Canada and wherever he had connections, and it was these qualities that made him one of the most respected and beloved of the Jewish citizens of Montreal. His broad, tolerant religious views made him a general favorite. His charity knew no creed, but was ever freely given, and he was a liberal supporter of all charitable and welfare institutions. He took a keen interest in all matters pertaining to the betterment of conditions in his city, province and country, and was much concerned with Jewish educational problems. He was the first enrolled member of the Hebrew Free Loan Association of Montreal, of which he was also a life governor; a member of the Federation of Jewish Philanthropies of Montreal since its inception; a member of the Ionic Lodge, No. 54, A.F. & A.M., Independent Order of B'nai B'rith, and of both the Spanish and Portuguese and Shaar Hashomoyim Congregations. Mr. Rubinovich was a life governor of the Montreal General Hospital, one of the oldest Jewish members of the Montreal Board of Trade, and a member of the Canadian Club. On February 14th, 1896, he was married to Essie, daughter of the late Isadore and Leba Livingstone, a lady who devoted herself to her husband's many interests, and who proved herself to be a help-mate in every sense of the word. Mr. Rubinovich was survived by his widow, and two sons, Irwin Joseph, who served during the Great War as an officer in the Royal Air Force, and Sigmund Maurice Rubinovich.

JOHN DOVER was born in Lithuania on November 15th, 1868, the son of the late William Dover. He received his education in the public schools in Lithuania. He was married on June 15th, 1889, in New York, to Miss Gavransky, and he has five sons, Dr. Harry, Joseph, Myer, David and Jack, and two daughters, Mrs. (Dr.) J. N. Nathanson and Miss Sylvia Dover. Mr. Dover has resided in Ottawa for many years, where he is one of the leaders in all communal enterprises. He was one of the organizers and first trustee of the King Edward Ave. Synagogue. He is a Director of the Ottawa Talmud Torah, and is keenly interested in the education of the Jewish youth in Hebrew and religion. Mr. Dover is a member of Eddy Lodge, No. 41, A.F. & A.M., Hull, Que.; Court Gatineau Lodge, Independent Order of Foresters; and Admiral Lodge, No. 377, New York City, Independent Order of Oddfellows.

THE LATE J. P. DAVIES

JOHN DOVER, OTTAWA

THE LATE MR. J. P. DAVIES was born in London, England, where he received his education. He went to California in the gold rush of 1849, and arrived in Victoria in 1863. He was one of the first Jews to settle on the Pacific Coast, and took an active interest in all public questions, particularly those affecting the Jewish community. He was instrumental in the building of the Synagogue, and held office in the congregation for many years. He was in business as an auctioneer until his death, and was at all times regarded as one of the leading citizens of Victoria. Mr. Davies was a founder of the Oddfellows in Victoria, and at one time was a candidate to the Dominion House, being defeated by a few votes. Mr. Davies was the father of four sons, Joshua, Henry, David and Philip, and two daughters, Mrs. Herman Shultz and Mrs. Frank Sylvester. All his children have occupied prominent positions in the communal life of British Columbia.

THE LATE MOSES VINEBERG

THE LATE MOSES AARON VINEBERG was born in Russia, on July 26th, 1852, the son of the late Aaron Moses Vineberg. He received his education in Russia, and came to Canada in 1871, settling in Montreal, where he first opened a retail store on St. Lawrence Main Street. In 1875 he entered into the wholesale hat and fur business, under the name of M. Vineberg and Company, and he developed this industry until it became the largest firm of wholesale manufacturing furriers in Canada. He retired from the fur business in 1915, and in 1919 became President of the Moses Vineberg Investment Corporation. In 1873, Mr. Vineberg was married in Montreal, to Fanny, daughter of Myer Freedman. Mr. Vineberg died on July 5th, 1924, and is survived by two sons, Abraham Moses and Herbert Alvin, and one daughter, Sarah, wife of Jacob Kellert of Montreal. Mr. Vineberg, on his first arrival in Canada, became a member of the German and Polish Congregation, and of the Young Men's Hebrew Benevolent Society, now the Baron de Hirsch Institute of Montreal. He was particularly interested in the congregation, now the Shaar Hashomayim, of which he was one of the largest supporters and a life member, and he held the office of President from 1890 to 1892, 1894 to 1896, and 1901 to 1904. In 1886, Mr. Vineberg was elected President of the Young Men's Hebrew Benevolent Society. During his lifetime, Mr. Vineberg took a very keen and active interest in all charitable work and philanthropic undertakings in Montreal, and he was particularly identified with the Mt. Sinai Sanatorium at St. Agathe, Que., of which he was one of the founders and supporters. In July, 1892, Mr. Vineberg, in company with Mr. D. S. Friedman, both of whom were Trustees at that time of the Young Men's Hebrew Benevolent Society, visited the Hirsch colonies in the Canadian West, and assisted in helping to settle all misunderstandings and disputes that had arisen amongst the colonists.

THE LATE FISCHEL SHIP

THE LATE MR. FISCHEL SHIP was born in Poland, on January 6th, 1852, the son of the late Abraham Jacob and Pearl Leah Ship. He received his education in Poland and came to Canada in 1872, settling in Montreal, where he resided until his death, which took place on April 2nd, 1922. On the 10th of Feb., 1869, he was married to Flora, daughter of Philip Blumenthal, who was the first owner of public coaches in Oserkoff, Poland. Mrs. Fischel died on October 10th, 1919, and was survived by one son, Dr. Abraham Philip Ship, and two daughters, Leah, wife of Charles Sisenwain, and Ray, wife of S. P. Myers. On his arrival in Montreal, Mr. Ship entered into the business of a merchant tailor, the training for which he had received from his father in Poland. Always taking a keen interest in communal problems in Montreal, Mr. Ship devoted much time and energy to charitable undertakings and welfare work. After his retirement from active business, in 1900, he gave practically all his time until his death to assisting his less fortunate fellow citizens. For over twenty-five years he was a life governor of the Montreal General Hospital, and for over thirty years he was a trustee of the Shaar Hashomayim Congregation. He was vice-president of this congregation for four years, and was chairman of the House Committee. He was actively connected with the Baron de Hirsch Institute for many years and was chairman of the Building Committee at the time the building on Bleury Street was erected. He was for a long period a governor of the Baron de Hirsch Institute and was treasurer and a member of the Relief Committee and of the Cemetery Committee of this institution. He also acted for a number of years as chairman of the Cemetery Committee of the Baron de Hirsch Institute. Mr. Ship was a member of the Independent Order of Oddfellows and of the Royal Arcanum. He was one of the first Jews in Montreal to be created a Justice of the Peace, receiving his commission in 1898.

Simpson Bros.

P. WOOD, TORONTO

PHILIP WOOD, a prominent business man of the City of Toronto, and a member of the firm of Regent Tailors Limited, was born in Manchester, England, on May 27th, 1882, the son of the late Solomon and Katie Wood. He received his education in the public schools in England, after which he entered into the study of the clothing business in which line he has ever since been engaged. In 1910 he took up his residence in the United States, where he remained for three years, and in 1913 Mr. Wood came to Canada, locating in Toronto, where he was appointed one of the designers of the Tip Top Tailors. Four years later, in 1917, in partnership with his father-in-law, Mr. Bernard Davis, and his brother-in-law, Mr. Louis Caplan, he was instrumental in the organization of the firm of Regent Tailors Limited, of which he is one of the present heads. This firm has a chain of clothing stores and agencies from coast to coast throughout Canada, and from a very small beginning, it has been developed into one of the largest concerns of wholesale men's tailoring in this country. Both Mr. Wood and Mr. Caplan have been responsible, through their untiring energy and business ability, for this development, and the high standing of the firm is solely due to their efforts. They are numbered among the larger employers of skilled help in the city, and the most cordial relations exist between the members of the firm and their employees. Mr. Wood has, ever since his arrival in Toronto, always taken a deep interest in communal undertakings, and is particularly interested in all Jewish matters. Although not taking an active part or holding office in any communal institution, he is a member of practically all of the charitable and welfare organizations in his city, and is a generous supporter of all philanthropic institutions. Mr. Wood was married in Toronto to Lily, daughter of the late Bernard Davis, and he has one son, Bernard Davis, and one daughter, Miss Shirley Eleanor Wood. He is a member of Mt. Sinai Lodge, A.F. & A.M.; Independent Order of B'nai B'rith; the Zionist Organization; and of the Holy Blossom Toronto Hebrew Congregation.

CHARLES DRAIMIN, TORONTO

CHARLES DRAIMIN, recognized as one of the most public-spirited of the Jewish citizens of Toronto, and a member of the fur firm of Brodey, Draimin and Company, was born in New York City on March 2nd, 1876, the son of the late Jacob Draimin, who was one of the founders and the first president of the University Avenue Synagogue, Toronto. He received his education in the public schools of Toronto, and was married in Toronto on June 20th, 1910, to Bertha, daughter of the late Charles King, of Whitby and Toronto, also a very active communal worker, and they have two sons, Theodore King, and Philip King Draimin. In partnership with his brother-in-law, Mr. Isaac Brodey, he established the firm of Brodey, Draimin and Company, manufacturing and retail furriers, and he is still actively associated with this business. Mr. Draimin is one of the outstanding communal workers of Toronto, and a supporter of every worthy cause and institution, irrespective of creed. He takes particular interest in all Jewish charitable and welfare work, and is a member of most of the philanthropic organizations of Toronto, and is particularly enthusiastic in recreational work among the underprivileged boys and girls. He was one of the most active founders and a member of the provisional Board of Trustees of the Federation of the Jewish Philanthropies of Toronto, and has been the honorary treasurer of this organization since its inception. In 1924, Mr. Draimin was chairman of the campaign that raised pledges of over $75,000 from 1600 subscribers, for the needs of Federation. As vice-president of the Young Men's and Young Women's Hebrew Association he is brought into close touch with educational and other problems of the younger generation, and his assistance has been of inestimable value to this institution. Mr. Draimin takes a keen interest in fraternal matters and he is one of the charter members of Toronto Lodge, Independent Order B'nai B'rith. He is a member of Palestine Lodge, A.F.&A.M., and a director of the Primrose Club, Toronto. Mr. Draimin is a member of the Holy Blossom Toronto Hebrew Congregation.

H. SIDERSKI, HAMILTON

HARRIS SIDERSKI, one of the leading members of the Jewish community of Hamilton, Ontario, was born in Lithuania, on December 25th, 1864, the son of the late Julius Siderski. He received his education in Lithuania, and came to Canada in 1883, settling in Hamilton in March of that year, and he has since continuously resided in that city. He is married to a daughter of the late Zelick Coopersmith of New York. Mr. Siderski arrived in Hamilton at a time when there were only about twenty Jewish families, and he was one of the organizers and a charter member of the first orthodox congregation formed in Hamilton, now known as the Congregation Beth Jacob, of which he has served as president for two terms. At present he is a life trustee of the congregation, and he has at all times taken an active part in the affairs of this institution. He was instrumental in the organization of the United Hebrew Association, in which organization he has held various offices, at the present time being vice-president. This was one of the first institutions in Canada to take up the Federation idea—the systematic distribution of charity. He was also instrumental in organizing the Viceroy Reading Lodge, No. 886, Independent Order B'nai B'rith, of which he is a charter member, and in which he held the office of treasurer for two years, at present being a trustee. He took a prominent part in the organizing of the Hebrew Free Loan Society, of which he is treasurer. Mr. Siderski has always taken a very keen and active interest in the Zionist Movement, and he held office as treasurer in the Keren Hayesod and Zionist Society of Hamilton, and has taken a leading part in helping to collect many thousands of dollars for this cause. In 1924, Mr. and Mrs. Siderski visited Palestine where they studied conditions at first hand. They visited all the Zionistic communal institutions there. Mr. Siderski is a member of the Canadian Club; Liberal Club; Hamilton Health Association; and of the Canadian Order of Oddfellows.

ISAAC COHEN, KINGSTON, ONT.

ISAAC COHEN, one of the best known citizens of Kingston, was born in Russia on September 17th, 1873, the younger son of the late Joshua Cohen. He was educated in the Yeshivas in Russia, his parents intending to prepare him for the rabbinate. Circumstances did not permit this, and in 1890 he came to Canada, settling first in Hamilton, where he was for about two years employed as a Hebrew teacher. Taking up a commercial career, for some years he was engaged as a traveller, finally, in 1898, settling in Kingston, where he made his residence and where he laid the foundation of his present business of metal dealer. By steady application to business Mr. Cohen has developed this industry into one of the largest scrap metal firms in Canada. He also entered into the manufacture of storage batteries, and organized the Monarch Battery Company, Limited, of Kingston, of which he is the President and largest shareholder. Mr. Cohen has taken a prominent part in the communal life of Kingston, and he had the distinction of being one of the first Jews in Ontario to serve on a public Board of Education, for five years being a member of the Kingston Board. He also served for two years as a member of the City Council, where he is recognized as one of the most public-spirited of citizens. Mr. Cohen was the second Jew to serve on the Council, Mr. Simon Obendorffer having preceded him. He was largely instrumental in the erection of the synagogue in Kingston, and is the present President. His efforts on behalf of the Jewish immigrants have been particularly fruitful, and he has found positions for many of them in his employment. He is an ardent Zionist, and was a member of the Zionist Council of Canada. On March 8th, 1904, Mr. Cohen was married to Anna, daughter of the late M. Steinberg, of Hamilton, and he has two sons, Sheldon Julius and Harold Arthur, and one daughter, Miss Miriam Cohen. Mr. Cohen is a member of the Council of the Kingston Board of Trade, and of the Kiwanis Club.

ISAAC BRODEY, TORONTO

ISAAC BRODEY, President of the Goel Tzedec Congregation, Toronto, was born in Poland on October 15th, 1866, the son of the late Solomon Brodey. He received his early education in Poland, and emigrated to Canada in 1883, settling in Toronto, where he has since resided. He entered into the fur business and some years later, in conjunction with his brother-in-law, Charles Draimin, established the firm of Brodey and Draimin, with which he is still actively associated. He is also the owner of considerable property. Mr. Brodey is married to a daughter of the late Jacob Draimin of Toronto, and has four sons, Dr. Abraham, Isadore, Arthur and Murray, and one daughter, Mrs. Wise, of Chicago. Another daughter, Lilly, (Mrs. Greisman) died a few years ago. Although a liberal contributor to and an active member of most of the charitable and welfare organizations in Toronto, Mr. Brodey has been particularly identified with the Goel Tzedec Congregation on University Avenue, and during the entire existence of the congregation has been a member of the Executive. He is one of the original members of this congregation and for many years held the office of Parnas and President. At the time the present synagogue was erected, Mr. Brodey was a member of the Building Committee, and he officiated at the laying of the cornerstone on April 29th, 1906. For twenty-five years he has been president of the Chevra Kadisha of the congregation, the only other person to hold this office being his late father-in-law, Mr. Jacob Draimin. Mr. Brodey was president of the Toronto Hebrew Ladies' Aid Society for over ten years, being the last man to hold this office. He also has held office and has been connected with many other philanthropic institutions, to which he has devoted much of his time. He is a member of the Federation of the Jewish Philanthropies of Toronto; the Talmud Torah and Community Centre on Brunswick Avenue; the Jewish Children's Home; and the Jewish Old Folks' Home.

L. CAPLAN, TORONTO

Simpson Bros.

LOUIS CAPLAN, one of Toronto's leading wholesale clothiers, and a member of the firm of Regent Tailors Limited, Toronto, was born in Montreal, August 11th, 1886, the son of Simon and the late Esther (Sklar) Caplan. He received his education in the public schools of Montreal, and commenced his commercial career with the firm of H. Vineberg & Co. Limited, pioneer wholesale clothing manufacturers, where he obtained a thorough knowledge of the wholesale clothing industry. He later took up his residence in Toronto, where he has since resided. In 1917, in partnership with his father-in-law, the late Bernard Davis, and his brother-in-law, Mr. Philip Wood, he was instrumental in the organization of the Regent Tailors Limited, wholesale tailors, operating a chain of retail clothing stores and agencies in every important centre in Canada, from coast to coast, and of which concern he is still one of the active heads. From a very small beginning, this business has been developed, through the energy and ability of Mr. Caplan and his associates, into one of the largest industries of its kind in the Dominion. The firm gives employment to several hundred persons, and the members of the firm enjoy a very high standing for commercial integrity. Mr. Caplan has always taken a keen and active interest in all matters affecting the betterment of conditions in his community, where he is recognized as one of the public-spirited citizens, and, although he has not held office in any institution, is particularly interested in Jewish communal undertakings, being a member and supporter of all Jewish charitable organizations in Toronto. He is also much interested in fraternal matters, and is a member of the Mt. Sinai Lodge, A.F. & A.M.; and the Independent Order B'nai B'rith. On March 17th, 1906, he was married to Becky, daughter of Bernard Davis, and they have three sons Bertram, Sydney and Elmer Caplan. Mr. Caplan is a member of the Holy Blossom Toronto Hebrew Congregation.

MORRIS SAXE, GEORGETOWN, ONT.

MORRIS SAXE, Founder and President of the Federated Jewish Farmers of Ontario, was born in the Jewish agricultural colony at Martinovitch, Russia, on February 17th, 1882, the son of Marris and the late Pearl (Suhrkolovsky) Saxe. He received his education in Russia and a short time after the colony was dispersed by the Russian Government, came to Canada (1902). First working on a farm near Georgetown, Ontario, in 1907 he purchased his own farm, and has ever since been engaged in general farming and stock raising; at the present time having two farms with two hundred and sixty acres of land. On January 7th, 1909, Mr. Saxe was married in Brantford, Ontario, to Dora, daughter of Morris Gerzog, and he has two sons, David and Percy, and three daughters, the Misses Miriam, Pearl and Leona Saxe. Mr. Saxe is a member and supporter of most of the Toronto Jewish organizations, and is a member of the University Avenue Synagogue. Keenly interested in all matters pertaining to the Jewish immigrant, he organized the Federated Jewish Farmers of Ontario, which was incorporated by Dominion Charter, and of which organization he was elected President. The idea back of this association is to assist Jewish agricultural settlers to go on farms, in communities where possible, so they can have everything required to maintain their faith and not become assimilated. Firmly convinced that agriculture is the need of this country, Mr. Saxe has persevered in his undertaking, which now numbers among its members some hundred and fifty Jewish farmers in Ontario, and largely through his instrumentality, the Eaton farm, near Georgetown, Ont., has been acquired to form the basis of a Jewish colony. Through this organization, too, arrangements have been made with the Federal Government that materially assist in permitting Jewish agricultural immigrants to enter Canada. Through his energy and sincerity, Mr. Saxe has interested the leaders of the communities of Toronto, Hamilton and Montreal, and great assistance was furnished the movement when Rabbi B. R. Brickner became the Honorary President.

SAUL KAUFMAN, TORONTO

SAUL KAUFMAN, President, 1925, of Toronto Lodge, No. 836, Independent Order B'nai B'rith, and proprietor of the Standard China Company, of Toronto, was born in London, England, on December 25th, 1886, the son of the late Louis and Miriam (Waxman) Kaufman, of that city. He received his education at the Jews' Free School, London, and following a commercial career, in 1911 came to Canada as the representative of the well-known firm of Lazarus and Rosenfeld, China Manufacturers, of London. In 1916, he severed his connection with this firm, and started in business for himself under the name of the Standard China Company, with which concern he is still actively associated. On June 11th, 1914, Mr. Kaufman was married to Ethel V., daughter of the late Mr. and Mrs. Samuel Fuller, of Leatherhead, England, and he has two sons, Louis and Bernard, and one daughter, Miss Doris Kaufman. Mr. Kaufman has taken a keen interest in all communal undertakings in Toronto since his arrival in that city, particularly those of a Jewish nature, and relating to immigrant relief work and boy welfare work. His greatest work has been done through the auspices of the Independent Order B'nai B'rith, and it was as a slight recognition of his endeavors on its behalf, that the Toronto Lodge, in 1925, elected him as president. In his capacity as such he has been largely responsible for the great work the Toronto Lodge is accomplishing, and in all branches of its activities, including as well as those mentioned, the Free Loan Society, his assistance has been invaluable. He is a member and supporter of the Federation of the Jewish Philanthropies of Toronto, and has been active in its various campaigns for subscriptions, particularly as a member of the I.O.B.B. He also takes much interest in the boys' camp and in other I.O.B.B. activities, and is never too busy to devote himself to any philanthropic undertaking. Mr. Kaufman is an accomplished amateur elocutionist, and he has won recognition for this on several occasions, both in England and in Canada. He is a member of the Holy Blossom Congregation.

H. M. LEHRER, TORONTO

HARRISON MORRICE LEHRER, Barrister, was born in Montreal, June 25th, 1897, the son of the late Karl and Rachel Lehrer. He received his education at McGill University, Montreal, and at Osgoode Hall Law School, Toronto, graduating in May, 1921. Mr. Lehrer has always taken an active interest in Zionist affairs and is President, Order of Habonim of Toronto; and member, National Council of the Zionist Organization of Canada, and of the Executive of the Zionist Council of Toronto. In 1924, he was the Executive Secretary of the Keren Hayesod Campaign for 1924.

Simpson Bros.
A. M. GUROFSKY, B.A. TORONTO

ALEXANDER MOSES GUROFSKY, Barrister, was born in Toronto, October 31st., 1893, the son of Lewis and Elizabeth Gurofsky. He was educated at the public schools, Jarvis Street Collegiate Institute, and at the University of Toronto (B.A. 1916). He then attended Osgoode Hall, from which he graduated in 1919. He has since followed the practice of law in Toronto. On May 18th, 1919, Mr. Gurofsky was married to Pearl Hudson, who died on February 5th, 1924, and has one daughter, Bernice.

Simpson Bros.
L. A. MALDAVER, TORONTO

LEO ABRAHAM MALDAVER, Barrister, was born in Russia, April 13th, 1893, the son of Solomon and Rebecca (Saxe) Maldaver. He came to Canada with his parents when one year of age, and received his education at the Brantford Collegiate Institute, Maesterschaft School of Languages, and Osgoode Hall Law School, from which he graduated in 1918, being called to the Bar in the same year. As a young man Mr. Maldaver was one of the pioneers in the moving picture industry in Ontario and operated theatres in different towns. For some years he was interested in the wholesale woollen trade, but in 1921 resumed the practice of law, in which he has since continued. He takes a keen and active interest in all communal undertakings in Toronto and is a member of most of the Jewish charitable organizations. He has always been interested in public matters, and in 1924 was a candidate to the Toronto City Council. On January 31st, 1918, Mr. Maldaver was married to Reta, daughter of Mr. and Mrs. Hirsch Herman of Manchester, England, and they have one son, Hartley Milton Maldaver.

L. KERT, TORONTO

LAWRENCE KERT, Barrister, was born in Mattawa, Ont., February 22nd, 1896, the son of H. R. Kert. He was educated at Hillbury High School; University of Toronto; and Osgoode Hall, graduating in 1920. In 1915, Mr. Kert joined the Canadian Army as Lieutenant. He was attached to the Royal Flying Corps and served in France, being promoted Captain. In December, 1917, his plane was shot down in the German lines, and he was made a prisoner of war. Mr. Kert practises his profession in Toronto, where he is a member of the law firm of J. Singer & Company.

S. J. BIRNBAUM, TORONTO

SAMUEL JOSEPH BIRNBAUM, Barrister, was born in Austria on March 15th, 1892, the son of Louis and Sarah (Rubin) Birnbaum. He came to Toronto in 1898 and was educated at the Jarvis Street Grammar School, from which he graduated with an Edward Blake Scholarship, and at the University of Toronto, receiving the degree of Bachelor of Arts and winning the P.W. Ellis gold medal in Political Science, (Class of 1911). Mr. Birnbaum first studied for the Rabbinate, then took up Medicine, and finally entered Osgoode Hall Law School. He was called to the Bar in 1914, and for seven years was a member of the law firm of Watson, Smoke, Smith, and Sinclair, in 1921 establishing his own office. Always interested in Jewish affairs, in 1912 Mr. Birnbaum wrote a history of the Jews of Toronto, which was published in the *Canadian Jewish Times* of Montreal. He is a member of the Independent Order B'nai B'rith, the Young Men's Hebrew Association, and the Holy Blossom Synagogue.

I. FINBERG, TORONTO

ISIDOR FINBERG, Barrister, was born in Toronto, February 14th, 1892, the son of Max Finberg. He was educated at Jarvis Collegiate Institute and Osgoode Hall Law School, and was called to the Bar on May 22nd, 1914. On February 12th, 1925, he was married to Betty, daughter of the late Israel Greisman. Mr. Finberg is a trustee of the Holy Blossom Congregation, and a member of the Empire and Primrose Clubs. He is a Past Grand Pursuivant of Grand Chapter of Canada, R.A.M.; Wor. M., Mount Sinai Lodge, A.F. & A.M.; and Past First Principal of Mount Sinai Chapter, R.A.M. He is also a member of the I.O.B.B.

DR. ABRAHAM PHILIP SHIP, Radiologist, a son of the late Fischel Ship, was born in Montreal, December 25th, 1886. He was educated at the Montreal High School and at the University of Montreal, from which he graduated in 1911 with the degree of M.D. On October 4th, 1911, he was married to Leah, daughter of the late Maxwell Sessenwein of Montreal. After graduation, Dr. Ship spent one year in post-graduate work at the London Hospital, in Paris, and at the Royal Charity Hospital in Berlin. Returning to Montreal, he commenced the practice of medicine, and at the present time he is doing X-ray work exclusively. He devotes much time to communal work, and is President of the Medical Board of the Montreal Hebrew Orphans' Home; Secretary of the Medical Board of the Herzl Dispensary; member of the Medical Board of the Mt. Sinai Sanitarium; and Radiologist to the Hebrew Maternity Hospital. He was one of the organizers of the Herzl Dispensary, of which he was the Medical Superintendent during the period of 1918-1924. Dr. Ship is a member of the Montefiore Club, and of Ionic Lodge, No. 54, A.F. & A.M.

DR. J. ROSENBAUM, MONTREAL

DR. A. P. SHIP, MONTREAL

DR. JACOB ROSENBAUM was born in Austria, September 25th, 1887, the son of Mr. and Mrs. Phillip Rosenbaum. He came to Canada with his parents while very young and was educated in private schools in Montreal and at McGill University, Montreal, from which he graduated in 1912. Specializing in diseases of the eye, Dr. Rosenbaum has become recognized as one of the foremost members of his profession in that particular branch of medical work, and he is an Assistant Demonstrator in the Faculty of Medicine at McGill University. He is Associate in Opthalmology at the Royal Victoria Hospital, Montreal, and is Opthalmologist to the Herzl Dispensary, the Hebrew Orphans' Home, Hebrew Maternity Hospital, Mt. Sinai Sanitarium, and the Protestant Hospital for the Insane. Dr. Rosenbaum is a member of the Faculty Club, McGill University; Montreal Reform Club; Opthalmic Club, Montreal; Montreal Medico-Chirurgical Society; The American Academy of Opthalmology and Oto-Laryngology, and of the Montreal Chess Club. Dr. Rosenbaum is a member of the Spanish and Portuguese Synagogue. On June 25th, 1922, he was married to Miss Liebling, daughter of David Liebling, and they have one daughter, Miss Rosaline Rosenbaum.

M. CLAVIR, TORONTO

MAX CLAVIR was born in Yasse, Roumania, in 1882. He came to Canada at the age of sixteen years. First settling in Toronto, Mr. Clavir started peddling. In 1904, he opened a store in the County of Simcoe, and in 1905, was appointed Post master, under the Laurier Government. He later settled in North Bay, where for about twelve years he conducted a gent's furnishing store. For a number of years he was the only Jew living in North Bay, and he enjoyed the respect of all sects. In 1916, he was elected Alderman and was re-elected to the same office in the following year. He was Chairman of the Finance Committee, and an executive member of the Board of Trade. During the war, Mr. Clavir was on the executive of the Patriotic and Red Cross Associations. Both he and his wife have been made Honorary life members of the Queen Victoria Hospital of North Bay. In 1919, he opened up the ribbon manufacturing plant which later became known as Clavir Bros., Limited, of which he was President. In his first year in Canada, Mr. Clavir became a member of the McCaul Street Synagogue and at all times remained a member, in 1923 being Chairman of the Board of Finance, and in 1924 being President of the congregation. He was re-elected to this position in 1925. Mr. Clavir is an active Zionist and has been a member of the B'nai Zion Association for twenty-two years. He is an active member of the Talmud Torah ever since it originated, and is a member of the Federation of Jewish Philanthropies, Toronto. He is a member of the I.O.O.F.; C.M.A.; and Ontario Men's Liberal Association. In the year 1911, Mr. Clavir was nominated for the Liberal candidacy in Nipissing riding for the Federal House. In 1922, he was elected to the Executive Board of the Toronto Men's Liberal Association, and was re-elected in 1923-4-5. In 1925, he was elected Vice-President of the Liberal Association of Central West Toronto. In 1925, Mr. Clavir was elected President of the Men's Auxiliary of the Mt. Sinai Hospital, Toronto. In 1904, he married Miss Jennie Brown, and he has two sons and four daughters.

APPRECIATION

FOR information and assistance rendered us, our thanks are due to Gerald E. Hart, *Beausoliel, France;* Edward A. Benjamin, *New York;* Mrs. Louis Green, *St. John, N.B.;* George G. Greene, *Ottawa;* B. G. Sack, H. M. Caiserman, S. B. Haltrecht, S. Belkin, Leon Goldman, Maxwell Goldstein, K.C., Marcus Sperber, K.C., Martin Wolff, Mrs. Martin Wolff, and Dr. Simon Kirsch, *Montreal;* A. Rhinewine, L. M. Singer, Abraham Cohen, Mrs. I. H. Siegel, J. J. Glass, and Nathan Phillips, *Toronto;* David Sweet, *Hamilton;* I. Goldstick, M.A., *London;* M. J. Finkelstein, H. E. Wilder, and N. J. Weidman, *Winnipeg;* H. A. Friedman, and M. I. Lieberman, *Edmonton;* Dr. D. M. Baltzan, *Saskatoon;* Rev. Marcus Berner, *Hirsch;* S. A. Goldston, *Regina;* Samuel Gintzburger, M. M. Grossman, and E. R. Sugarman, *Vancouver;* and Mrs. F. Sylvester and F. Landsberg, *Victoria.*

A Note About This Edition (2010)

In order *to keep this volume to a reasonable size and price, the opening section on the "History of the Jews in Canada" (by B. G. Sack) was omitted as it is readily available elsewhere. That and several other smaller omissions are marked with gray bars on the Table of Contents pages. This edition is 466 pages long but follows the pagination of the 576-page original. A Biographical Index follows the Table of Contents.*

Now and Then Books
Toronto

Website
www.nowandthenbookstoronto.com

E-mail
info@nowandthenbookstoronto.com

Enjoy All These Titles from Now and Then Books

Toronto / Canadian Jewish History

¶ One Hundred Years in Canada: the Rubinoff–Naftolin Family Tree, by Bill Gladstone. Paperback, 8.25 x 11 in., 384 pp. 700+ photographs, maps & illustrations, plus extensive genealogical charts. $40. (2008).

¶ The Rise of the Toronto Jewish Community, by Shmuel Mayer Shapiro. A colourful account to 1950 by the former editor and publisher of the *Hebrew Journal*. Paperback, 6 x 9 in., 168 pages. $22. (2010)

¶ The Jew in Canada. Abridged facsimile edition of the classic 1926 volume edited by Arthur D. Hart. Contains all of the biographical and genealogical material of the original edition; only several historical essays have been omitted. Paperback, 8.25 x 11 in., 466 pages. (2010)

Memoirs / Life Stories

¶ I'm Not Going Back: Wartime Memoir of a Child Evacuee, by Kitty Wintrob. The author recounts the experience of being evacuated as a child from London's heavily Jewish East End to the British countryside at the start of the Second World War. For pre-teen to adult. Paperback, 6 x 9 in., 176 pp. $18. (2009)

¶ Eighteen Months: A Love Story Interrupted, by Alan L. Simons. A gripping autobiographical story about a man and a woman and the illness that could not tear them apart. Paperback, 5 x 8 in., 116 pp. $18. (2010)

www.ingramcontent.com/pod-product-compliance
Lightning Source LLC
Chambersburg PA
CBHW080418230426
43662CB00015B/2139